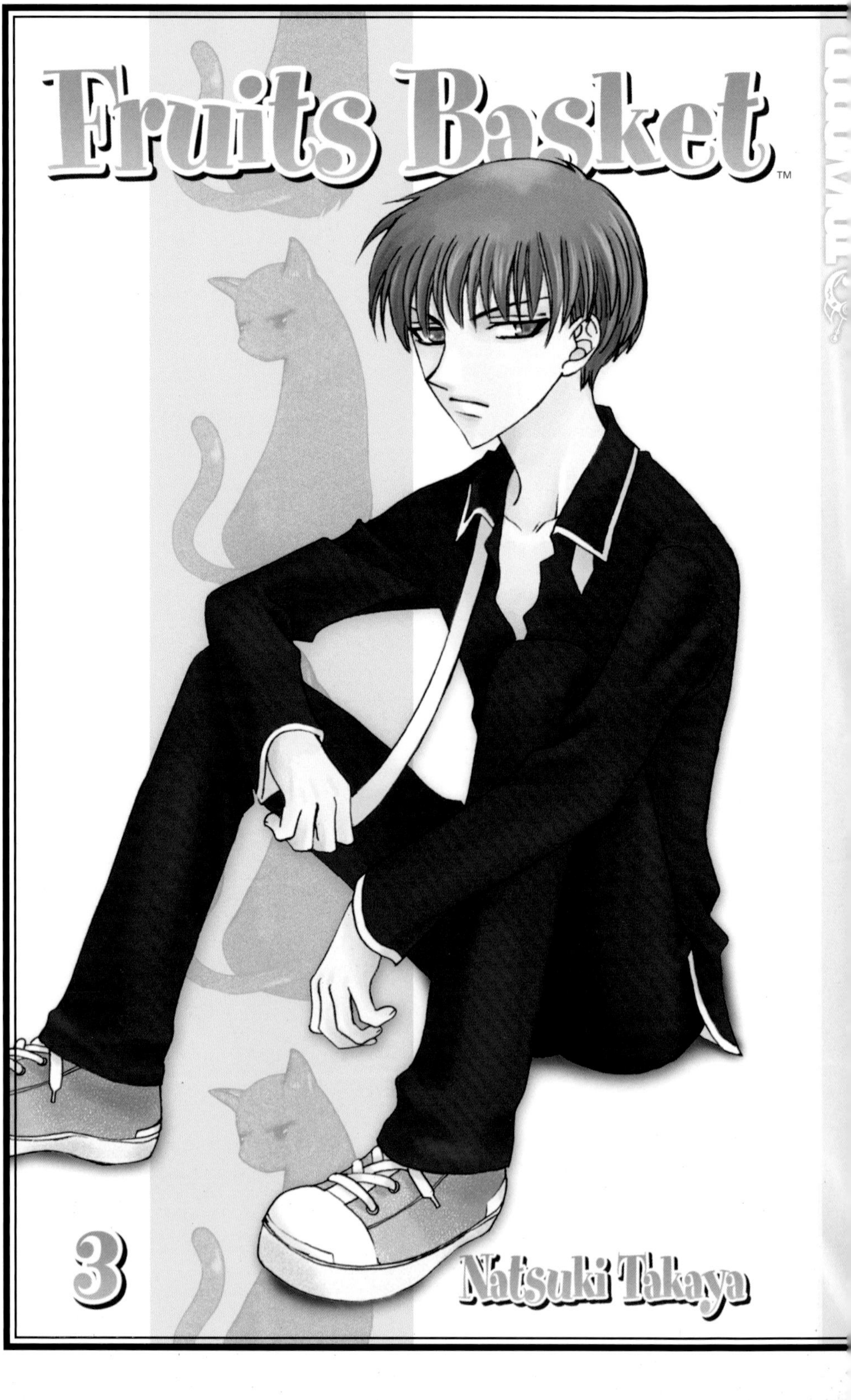

Fruits Basket™
3
Natsuki Takaya

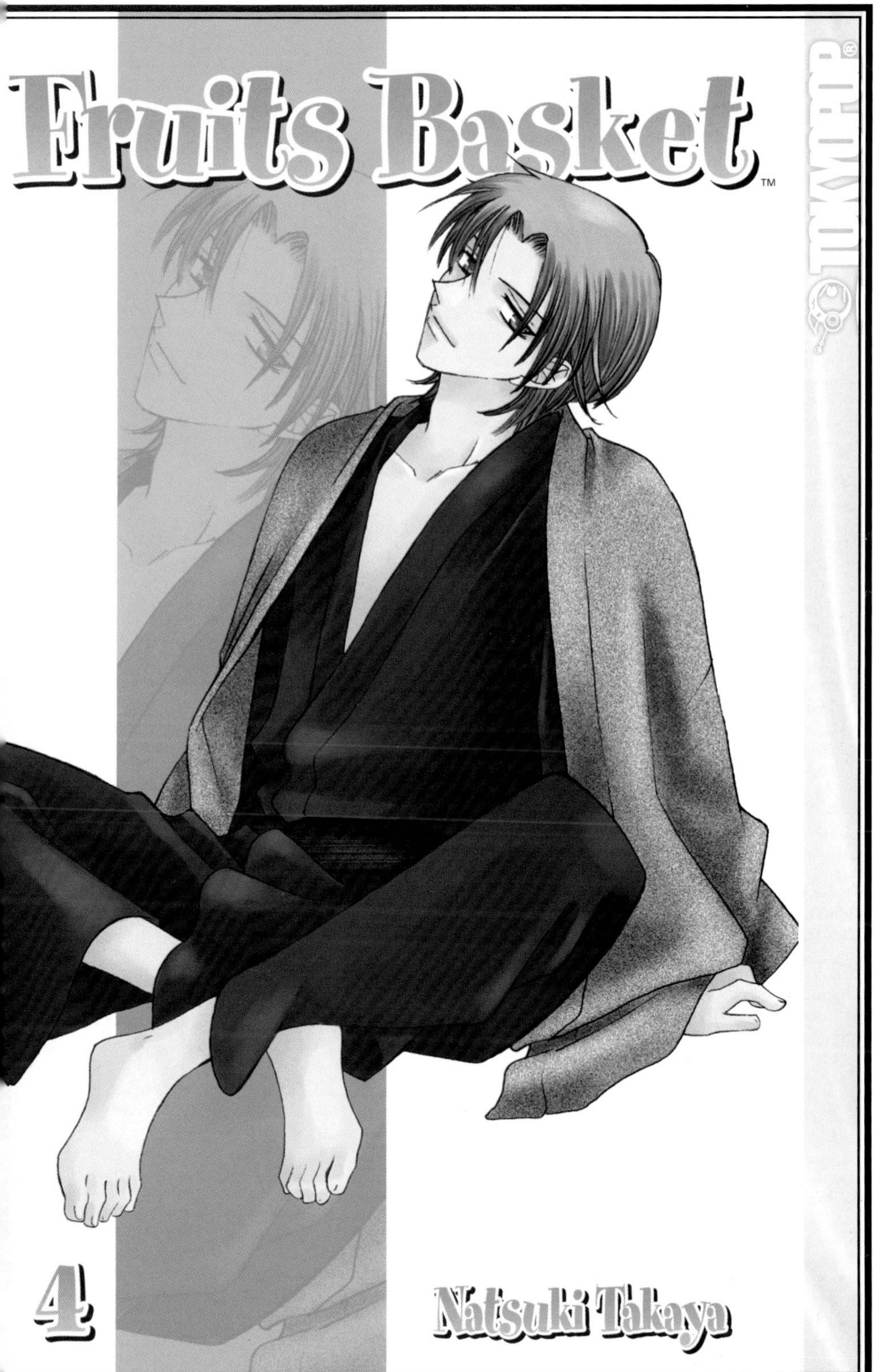
Fruits Basket™
TOKYOPOP®
4
Natsuki Takaya

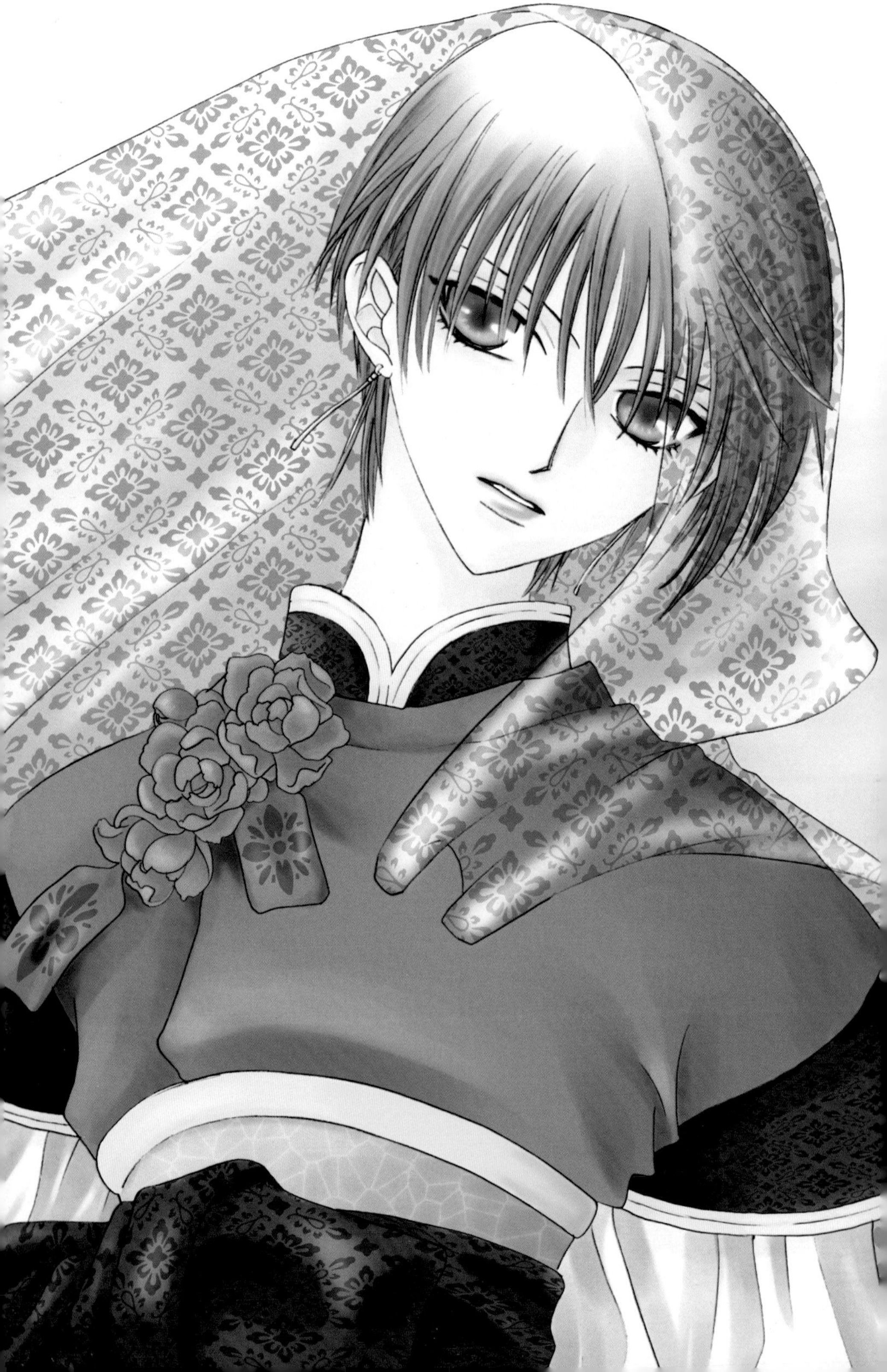

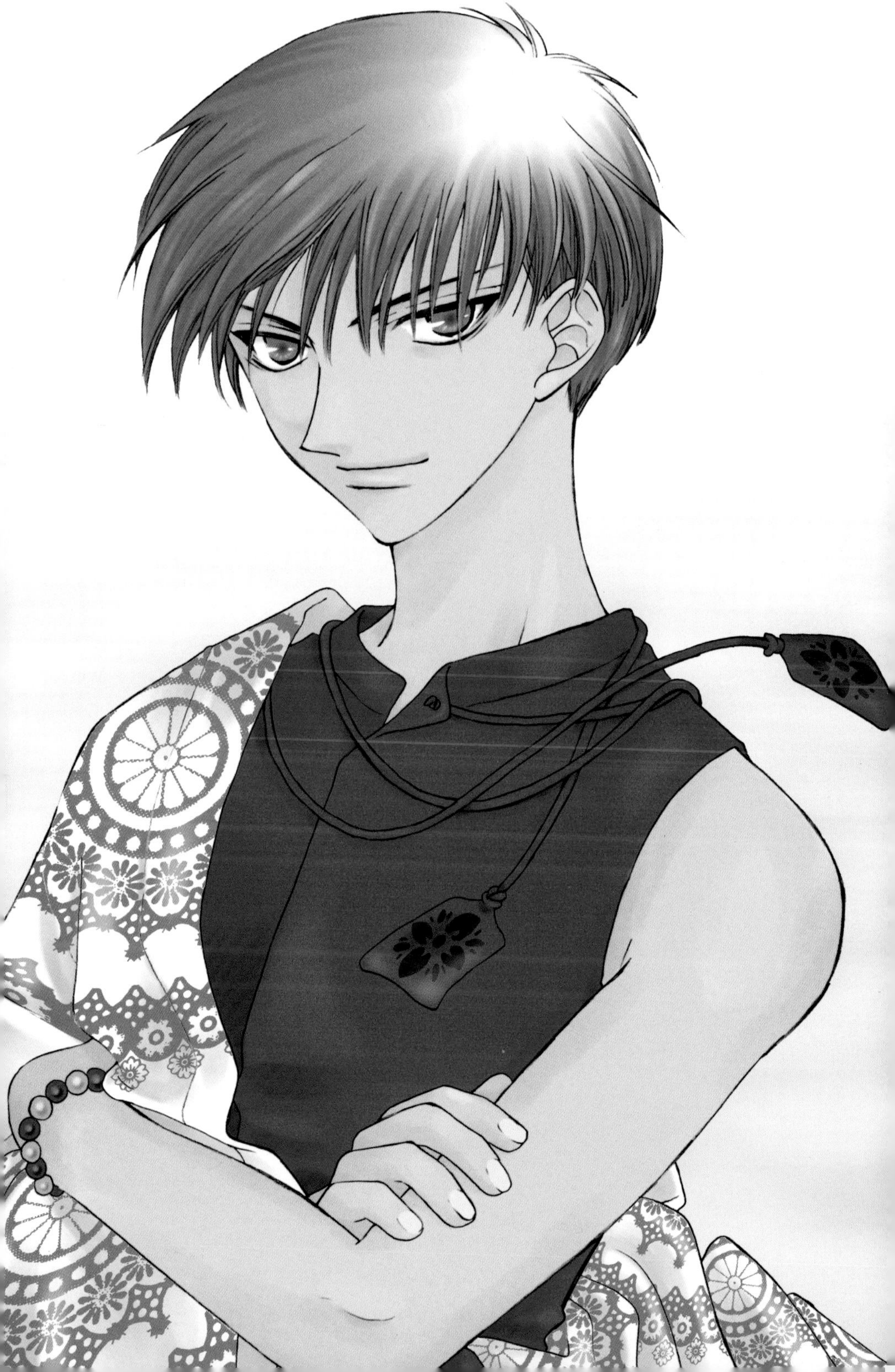

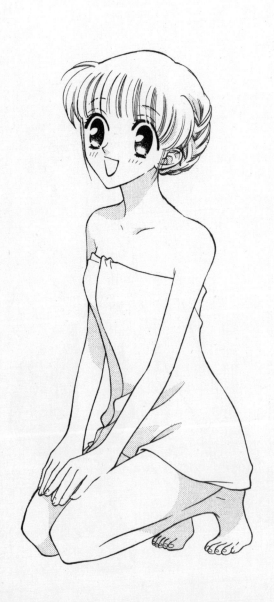

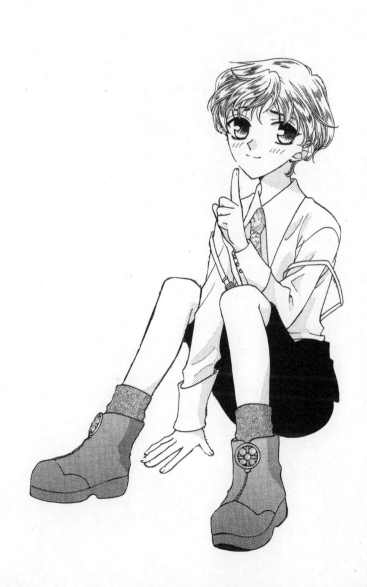

Fruits Basket

Volume 3

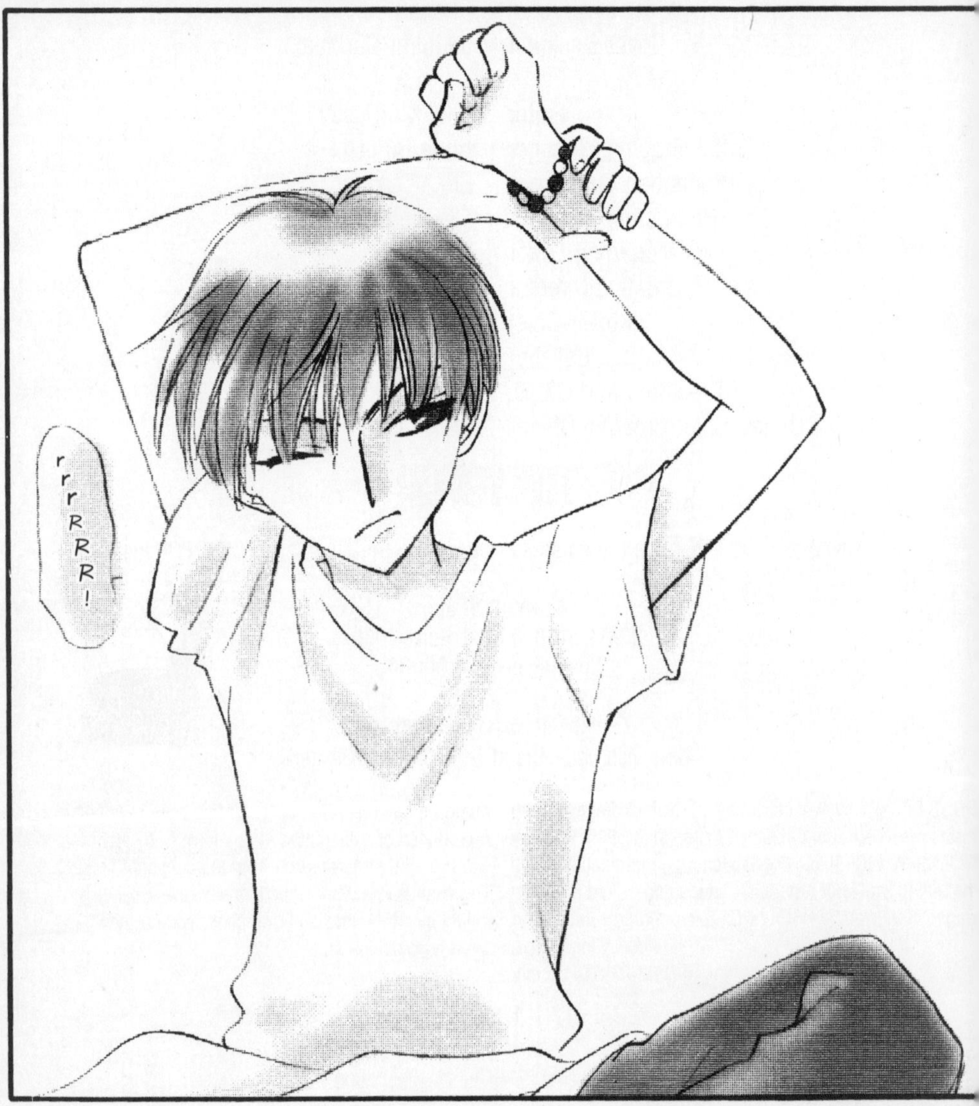
rrrRRR!

Natsuki Takaya

Fruits Basket Ultimate Edition Volume 2
Created by Natsuki Takaya

Original Series Editor - Jake Forbes
Translation - Alethea & Athena Nibley
Associate Editor - Kelly Sue DeConnick
Additional Translation - Alexis Kirsch
Contributing Writer - Adam Arnold
Copy Editor - Carol Fox

Retouch and Lettering - Deron Bennett
Production Artist - Skooter
Cover Designer - Jennifer Carbajal

Editor - Paul Morrissey
Digital Imaging Manager - Chris Buford
Pre-Production Supervisor - Erika Terriquez
Production Manager - Elisabeth Brizzi
Managing Editor - Vy Nguyen
Creative Director - Anne Marie Horne
Editor-in-Chief - Rob Tokar
Publisher - Mike Kiley
President and C.O.O. - John Parker
C.E.O. and Chief Creative Officer - Stuart Levy

A  Manga

TOKYOPOP Inc.
5900 Wilshire Blvd. Suite 2000
Los Angeles, CA 90036

E-mail: info@TOKYOPOP.com
Come visit us online at www.TOKYOPOP.com

ISBN: 978-1-4278-0729-8

First TOKYOPOP printing: February 2008
10 9 8 7 6 5 4 3 2 1
Printed in the USA

Fruits Basket

Volume 3

Table of Contents

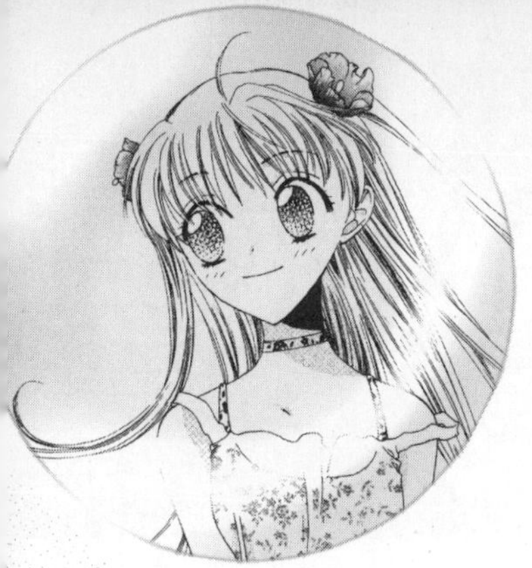

Tohru Honda

The ever-optimistic hero of our story. Recently orphaned, Tohru has taken up residence in Shigure Sohma's house, along with Yuki and Kyo. She's the only person outside of the Sohma family who knows about their Zodiac curse.

Yuki Sohma

At school he's known as Prince Charming. Polite and soft-spoken, he's the polar opposite of Kyo. Yuki is possessed by the spirit of the Rat.

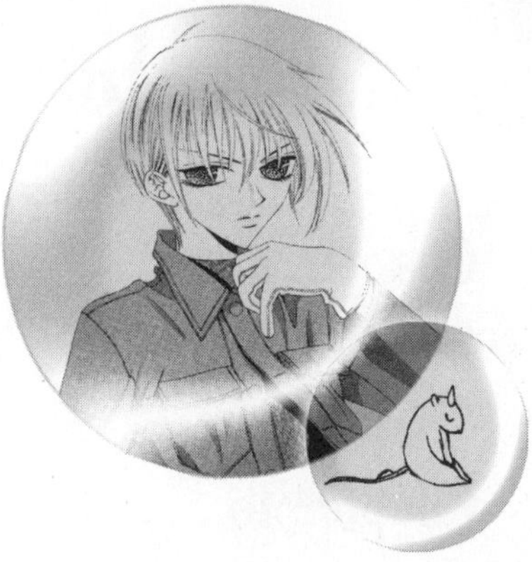

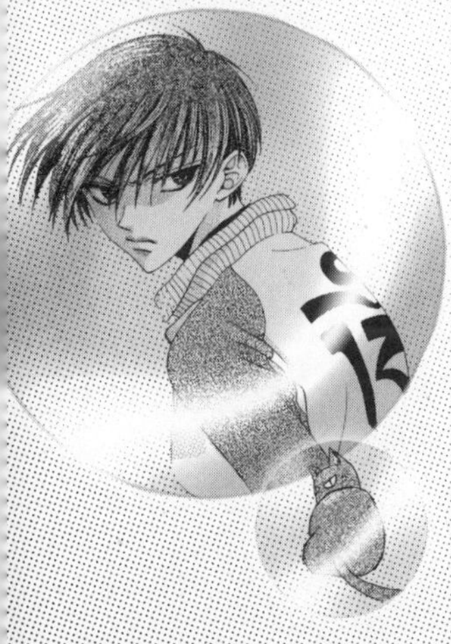

Kyo Sohma

Just as the Cat of legend (whose spirit possesses him) was left out of the Zodiac, Kyo is ostracized by the Sohma family. His greatest wish in life is to defeat Yuki in battle and win his rightful place in the Zodiac.

latori Sohma

he family doctor of the Sohma clan and one of the unishi (his symbol is the dragon, which manifests as a eahorse). When Akito wills it, he erases the memories of ose who stumble upon the family's secret. Hatori once ad to erase the memories of the woman he loved, and ver since has been firmly against letting anyone else now the secret--even Tohru.

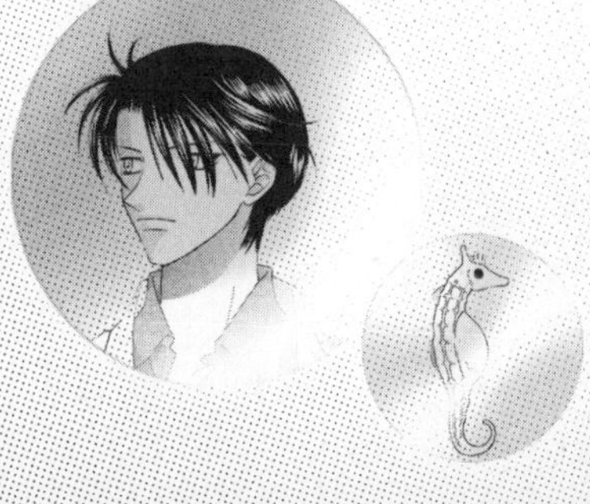

Fruits Basket Characters

Shigure Sohma

The enigmatic Shigure keeps a house outside of the Sohma estate where he lives with Yuki, Kyo and Tohru. He may act perverted at times, but he has a good heart. His Zodiac spirit is the Dog.

Kagura Sohma

Stubborn and jealous as her zodiac symbol, the boar, Kagura is determined to marry Kyo...even if she kills him in the process.

Hanajima & Arisa

The two best friends a girl could hope for. They always look out for Tohru, but they don't know about her new living arrangements...yet.

Akito Sohma

The mysterious leader of the Sohma clan, the other family members treat him with equal measures of fear and reverence. Tohru has never met him.

Momiji Sohma

Playful and carefree as the Rabbit he turns into, Momiji is the youngest member of the Sohma family that Tohru has met. He's half German and half Japanese, and switches casually between the two languages. His father owns the building where Tohru works.

STORY SO FAR...

Hello. I'm Tohru Honda, and I have come to know a terrible secret. After the death of my mother, I was living by myself in a tent when the Sohma family took me in. I soon learned that the Sohma family lives with a curse! Each family member is possessed by the vengeful spirit of an animal from the Chinese Zodiac. Whenever one of them becomes weak or is hugged by a member of the opposite sex, they change into their Zodiac animal!

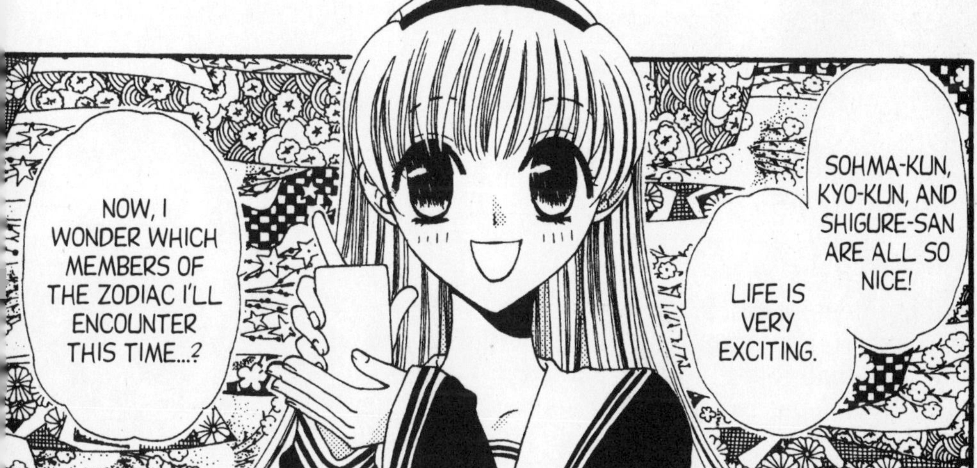
SOHMA-KUN, KYO-KUN, AND SHIGURE-SAN ARE ALL SO NICE!
LIFE IS VERY EXCITING.
NOW, I WONDER WHICH MEMBERS OF THE ZODIAC I'LL ENCOUNTER THIS TIME...?

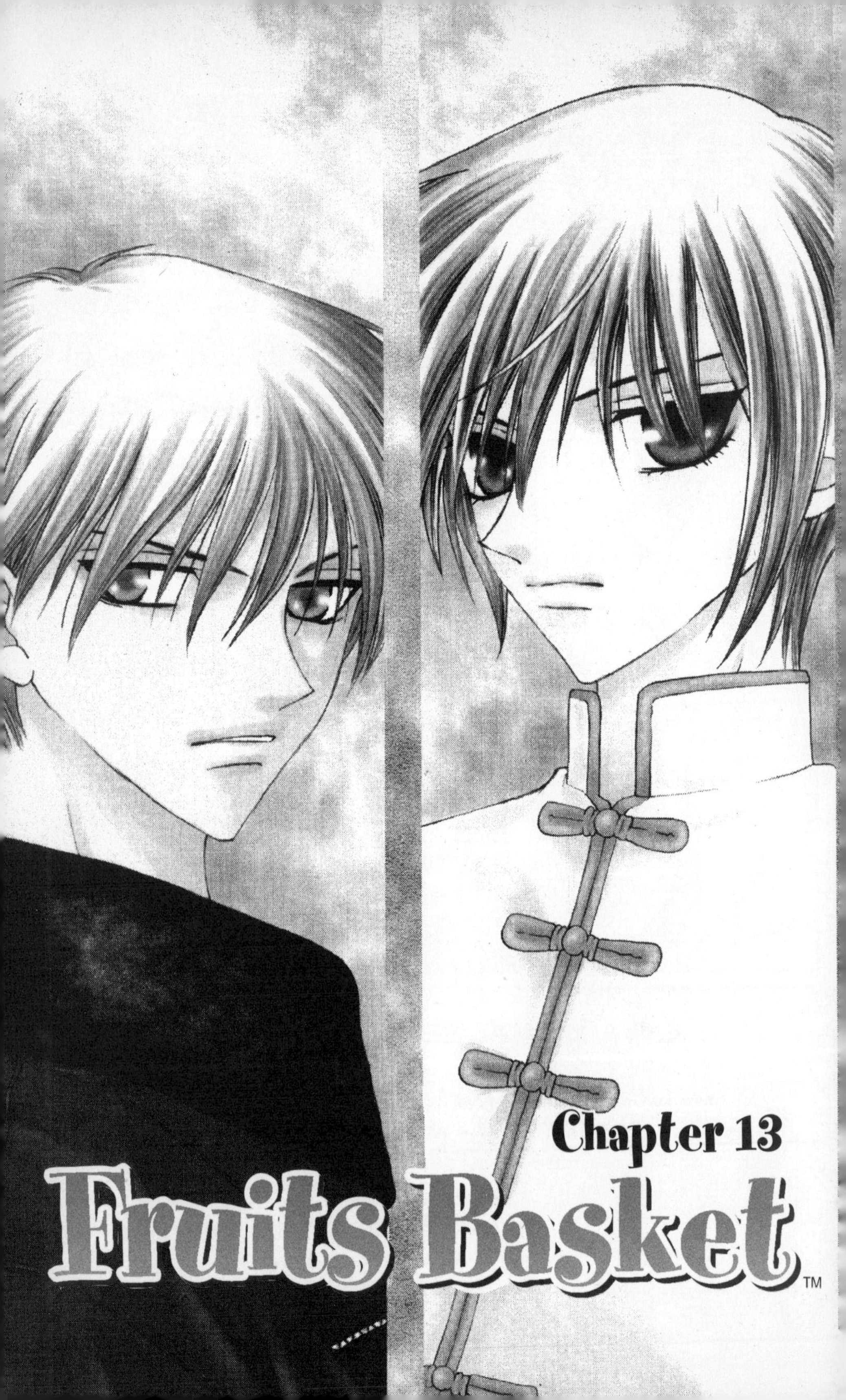
Chapter 13
Fruits Basket™

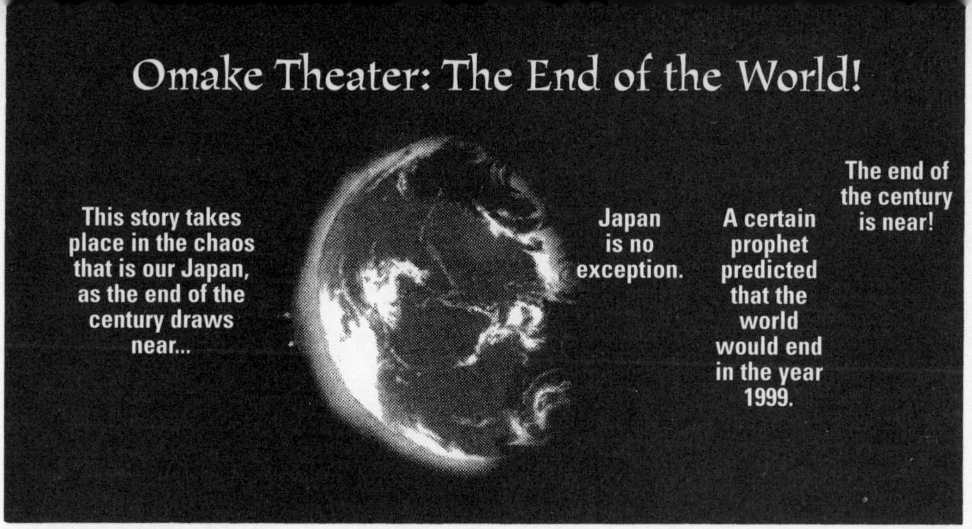
Omake Theater: The End of the World!
The end of the century is near!
A certain prophet predicted that the world would end in the year 1999.
Japan is no exception.
This story takes place in the chaos that is our Japan, as the end of the century draws near...

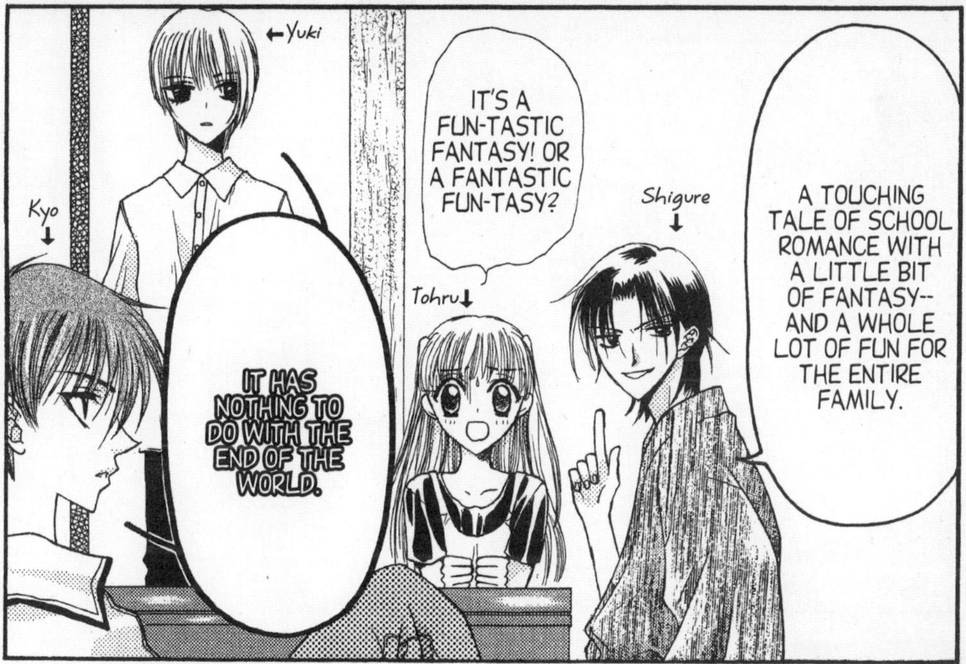
A TOUCHING TALE OF SCHOOL ROMANCE WITH A LITTLE BIT OF FANTASY-- AND A WHOLE LOT OF FUN FOR THE ENTIRE FAMILY.
Shigure ↓
IT'S A FUN-TASTIC FANTASY! OR A FANTASTIC FUN-TASY?
Tohru ↓
← Yuki
IT HAS NOTHING TO DO WITH THE END OF THE WORLD.
Kyo ↓

Pretty accurate ↑

ULTRA SPECIAL BLAH BLAH BLAH 1

You may notice Yuki and Kyo have matured a bit in this volume. They're also getting taller. (The tallest character in Furuba is Hatori, in case anyone is keeping track!)

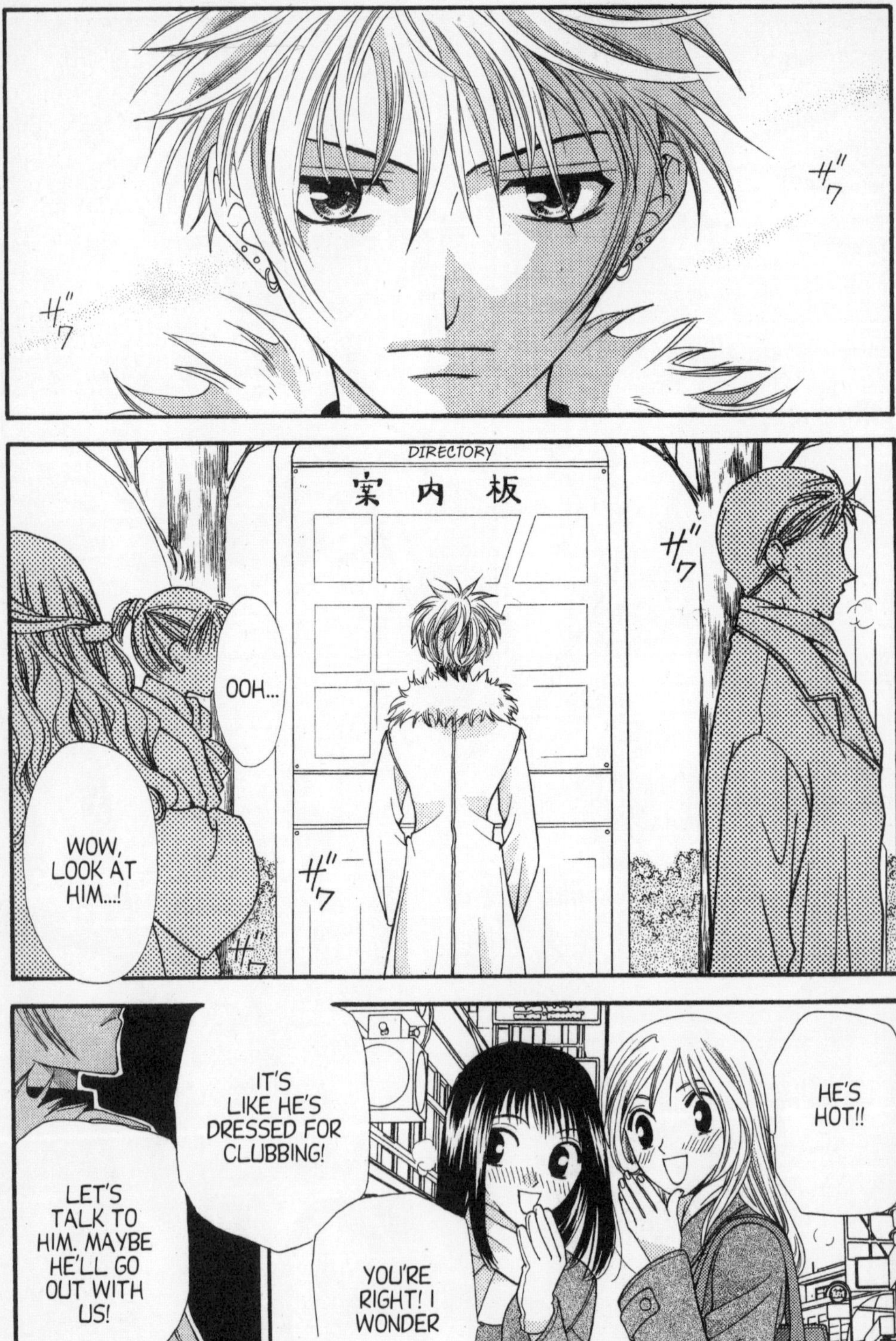
ザワ
ザワ
ザワ
DIRECTORY
案内板
OOH...
WOW, LOOK AT HIM...!
ザワ
ザワ
HE'S HOT!!
IT'S LIKE HE'S DRESSED FOR CLUBBING!
YOU'RE RIGHT! I WONDER...
Is he lost?
LET'S TALK TO HIM. MAYBE HE'LL GO OUT WITH US!

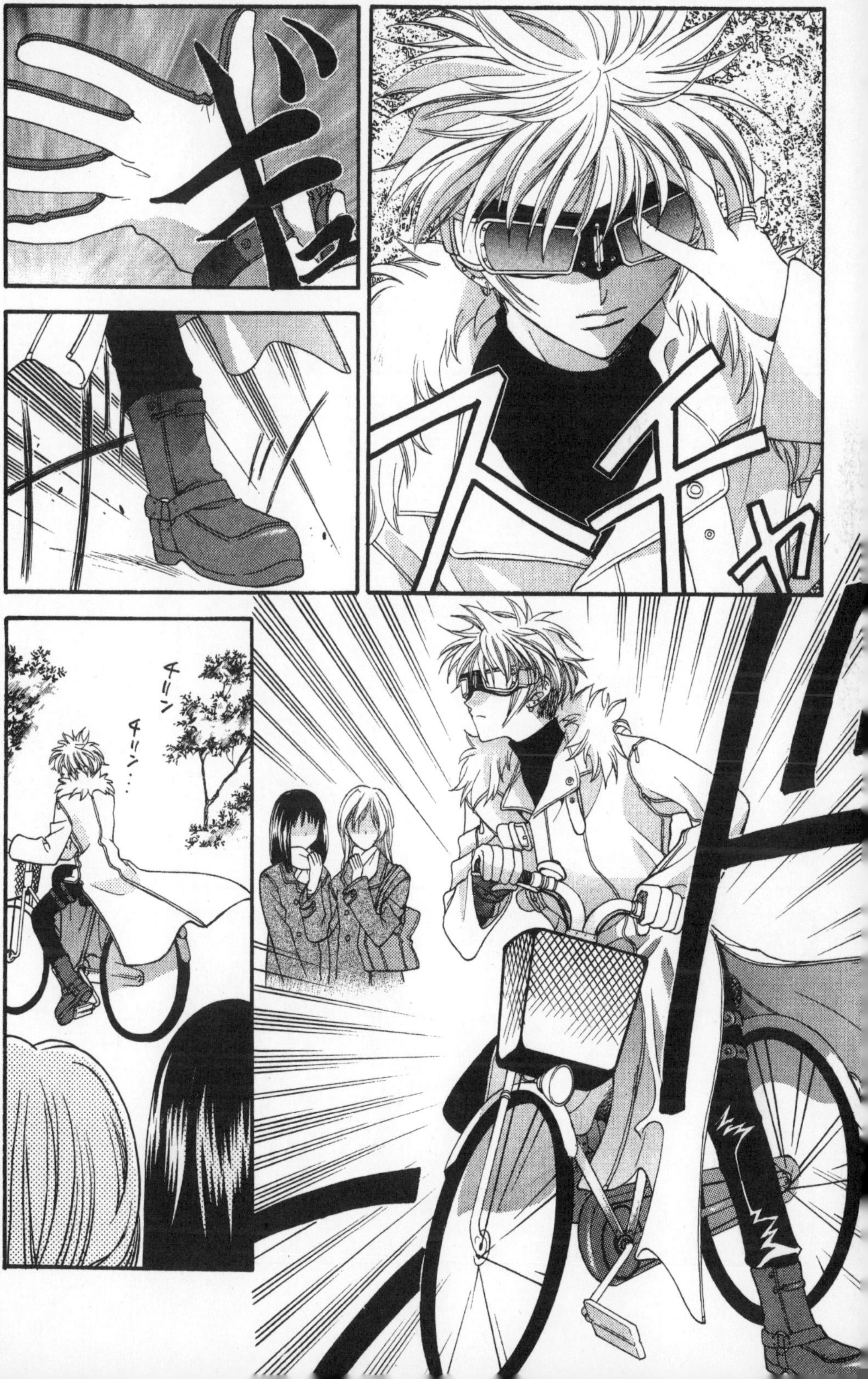
スチャ
ギュ
チリン
チリン…

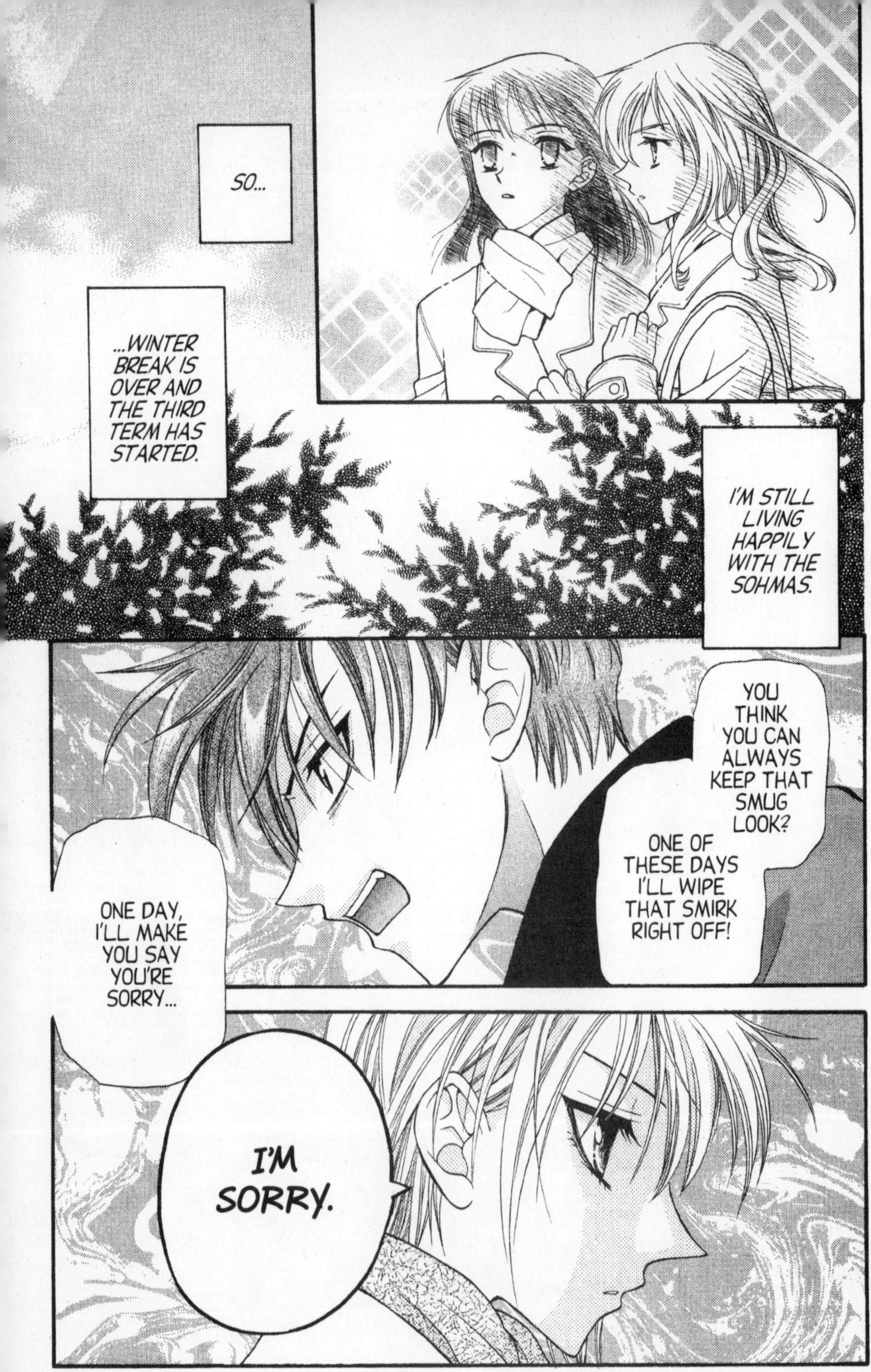
SO...
...WINTER BREAK IS OVER AND THE THIRD TERM HAS STARTED.
I'M STILL LIVING HAPPILY WITH THE SOHMAS.
YOU THINK YOU CAN ALWAYS KEEP THAT SMUG LOOK?
ONE OF THESE DAYS I'LL WIPE THAT SMIRK RIGHT OFF!
ONE DAY, I'LL MAKE YOU SAY YOU'RE SORRY...
I'M SORRY.

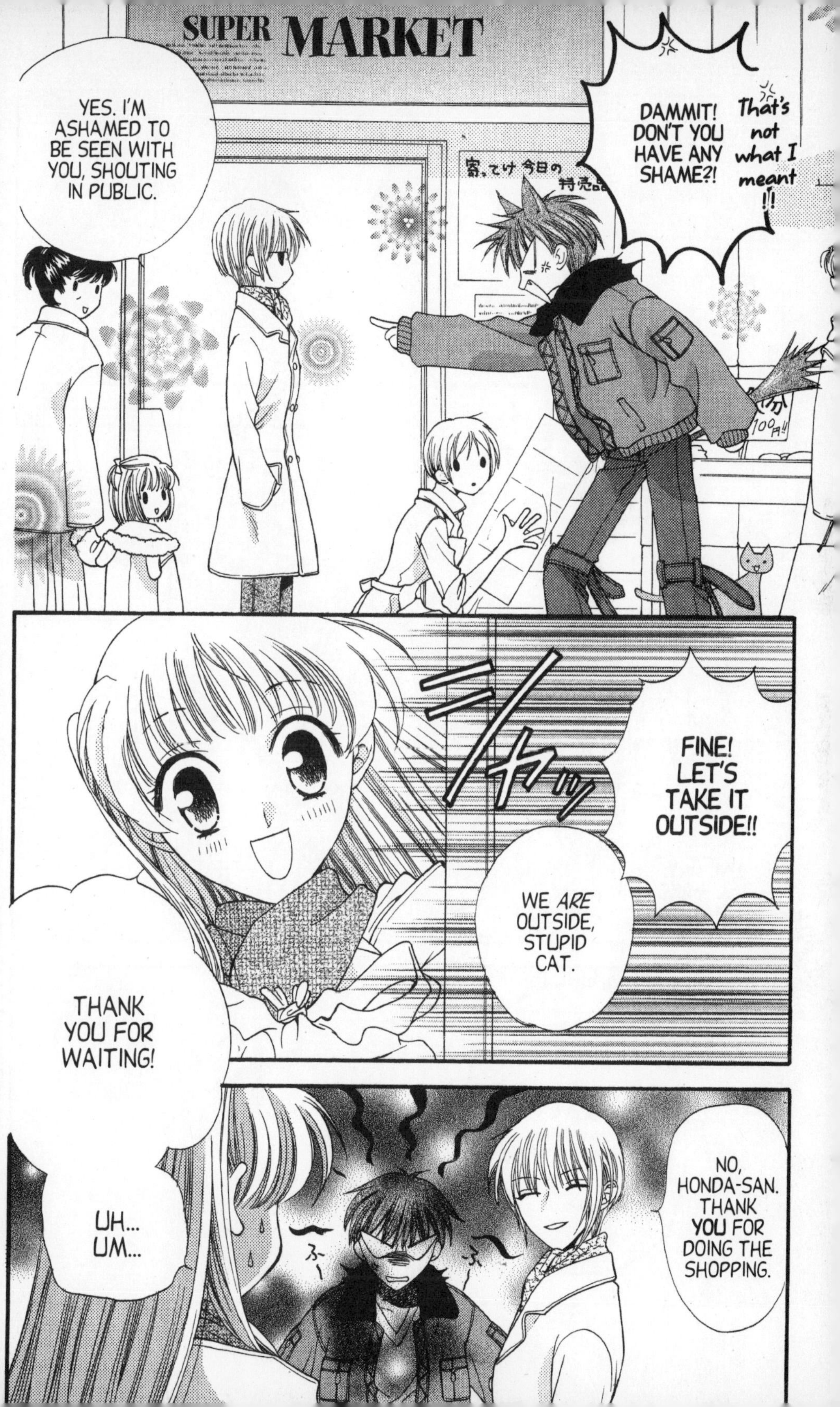
SUPER MARKET
DAMMIT! DON'T YOU HAVE ANY SHAME?!
That's not what I meant!!
YES. I'M ASHAMED TO BE SEEN WITH YOU, SHOUTING IN PUBLIC.
FINE! LET'S TAKE IT OUTSIDE!!
WE *ARE* OUTSIDE, STUPID CAT.
THANK YOU FOR WAITING!
NO, HONDA-SAN. THANK **YOU** FOR DOING THE SHOPPING.
UH... UM...

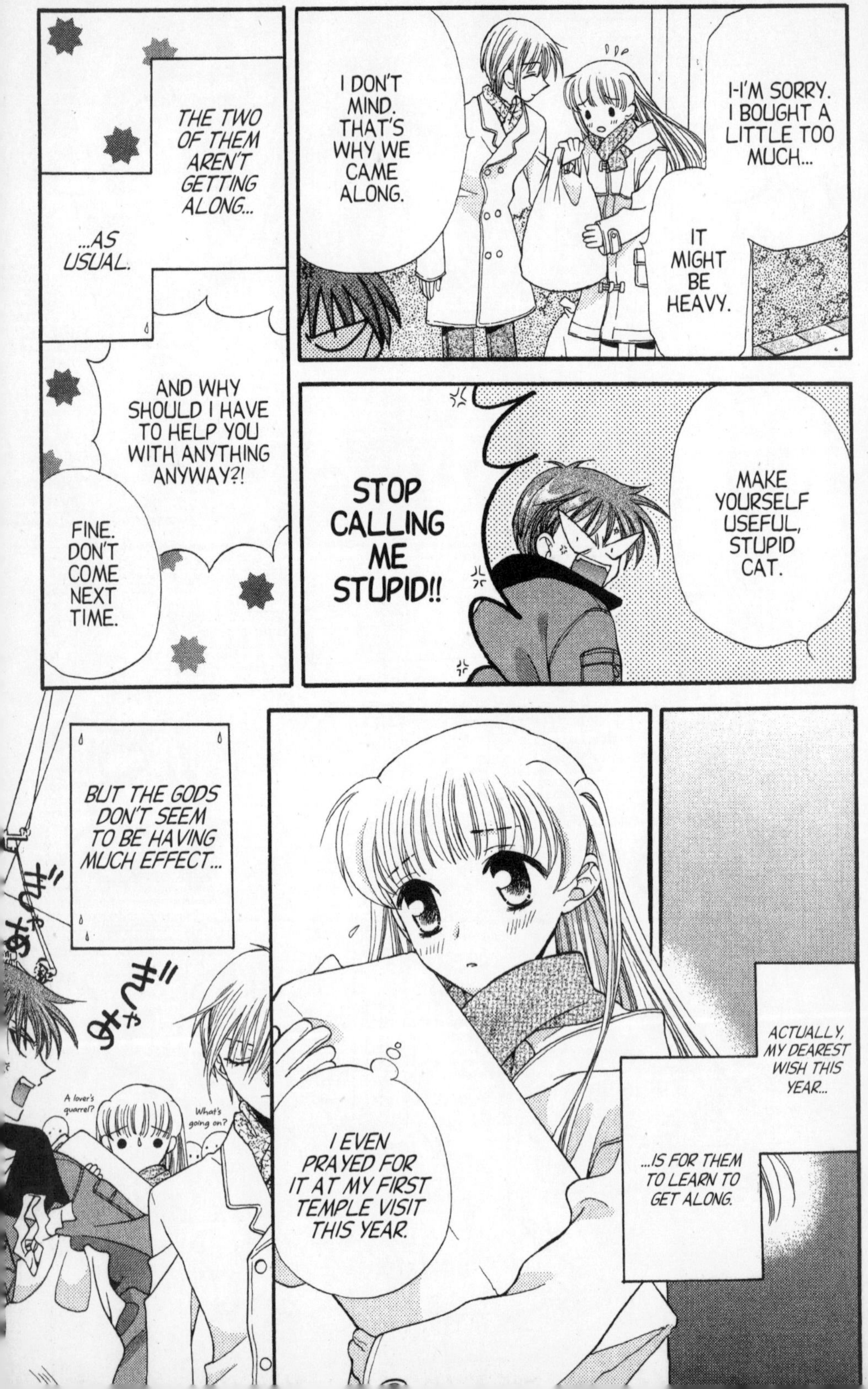
I-I'M SORRY. I BOUGHT A LITTLE TOO MUCH...
IT MIGHT BE HEAVY.
I DON'T MIND. THAT'S WHY WE CAME ALONG.
MAKE YOURSELF USEFUL, STUPID CAT.
STOP CALLING ME STUPID!!
THE TWO OF THEM AREN'T GETTING ALONG...
...AS USUAL.
AND WHY SHOULD I HAVE TO HELP YOU WITH ANYTHING ANYWAY?!
FINE. DON'T COME NEXT TIME.
ACTUALLY, MY DEAREST WISH THIS YEAR...
...IS FOR THEM TO LEARN TO GET ALONG.
I EVEN PRAYED FOR IT AT MY FIRST TEMPLE VISIT THIS YEAR.
BUT THE GODS DON'T SEEM TO BE HAVING MUCH EFFECT...
ぎゃあ
ぎゃあ
What's going on?
A lover's quarrel?

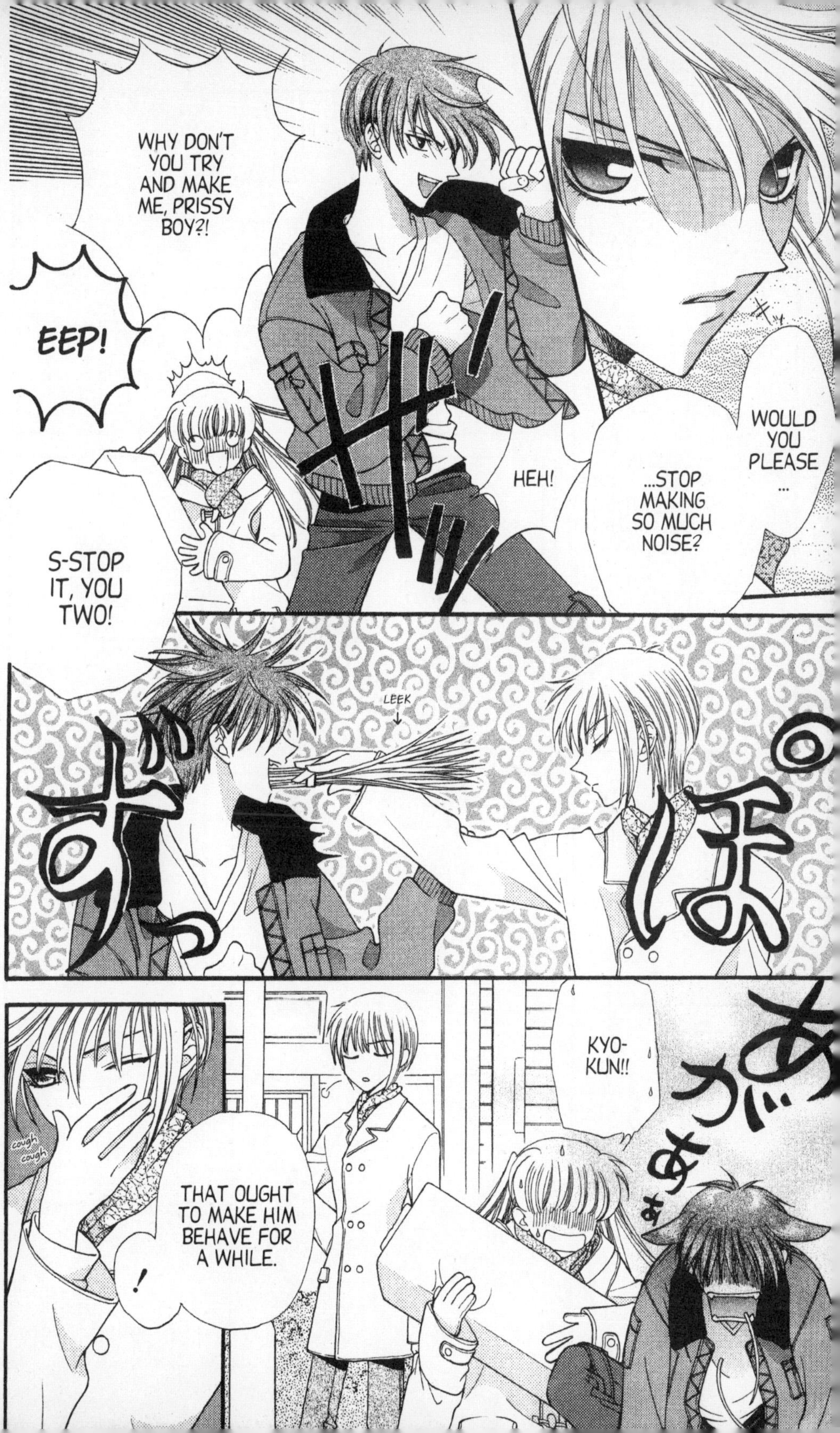
WOULD YOU PLEASE ...
...STOP MAKING SO MUCH NOISE?
HEH!
WHY DON'T YOU TRY AND MAKE ME, PRISSY BOY?!
EEP!
S-STOP IT, YOU TWO!
ぽ
LEEK
ずっ
あがぁぁ
KYO-KUN!!
THAT OUGHT TO MAKE HIM BEHAVE FOR A WHILE.
!
cough cough

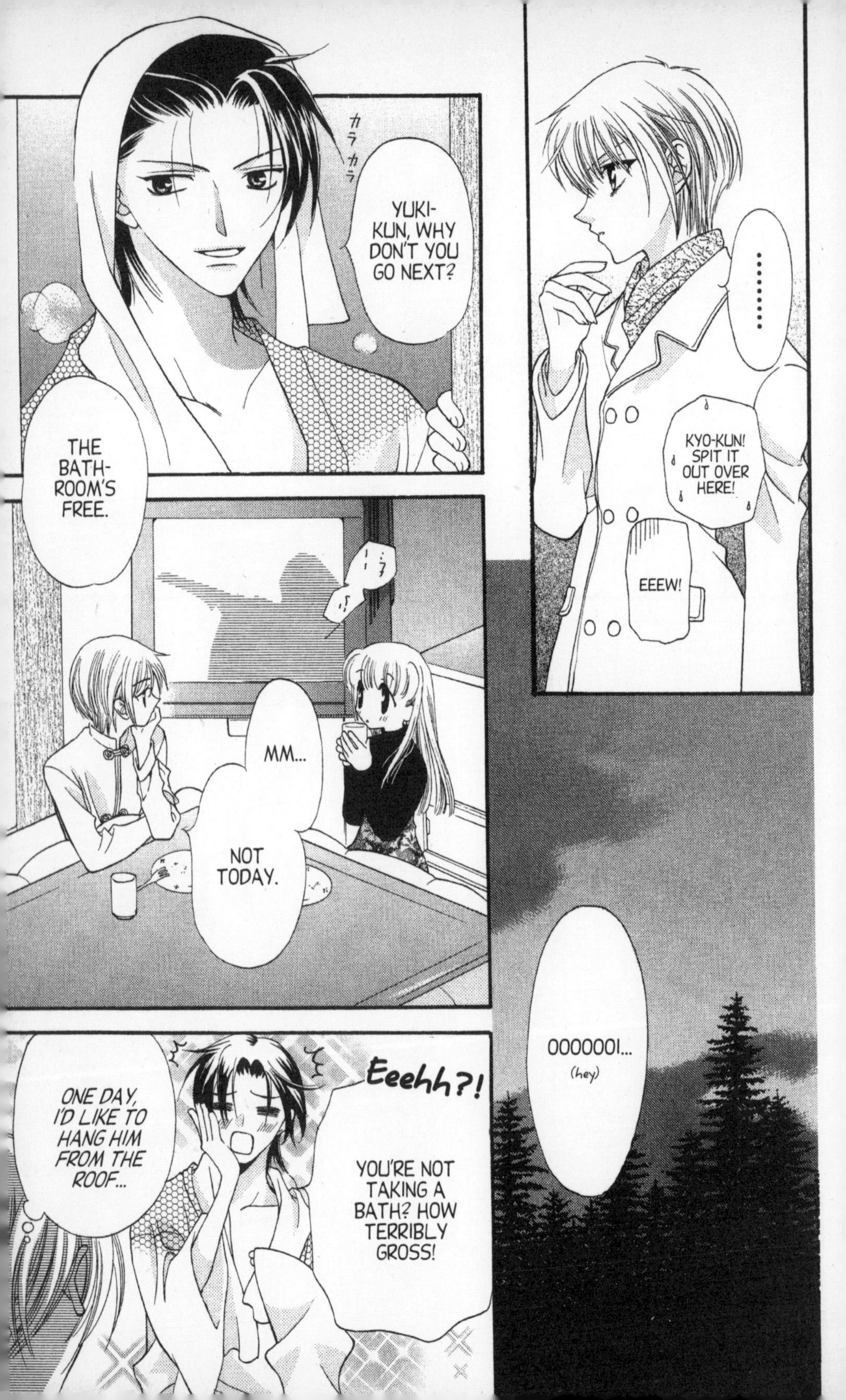

......
KYO-KUN! SPIT IT OUT OVER HERE!
EEEW!
OOOOOOI... (hey)
カラカラ
YUKI-KUN, WHY DON'T YOU GO NEXT?
THE BATH-ROOM'S FREE.
MM...
NOT TODAY.
Eeehh?!
YOU'RE NOT TAKING A BATH? HOW TERRIBLY GROSS!
ONE DAY, I'D LIKE TO HANG HIM FROM THE ROOF...

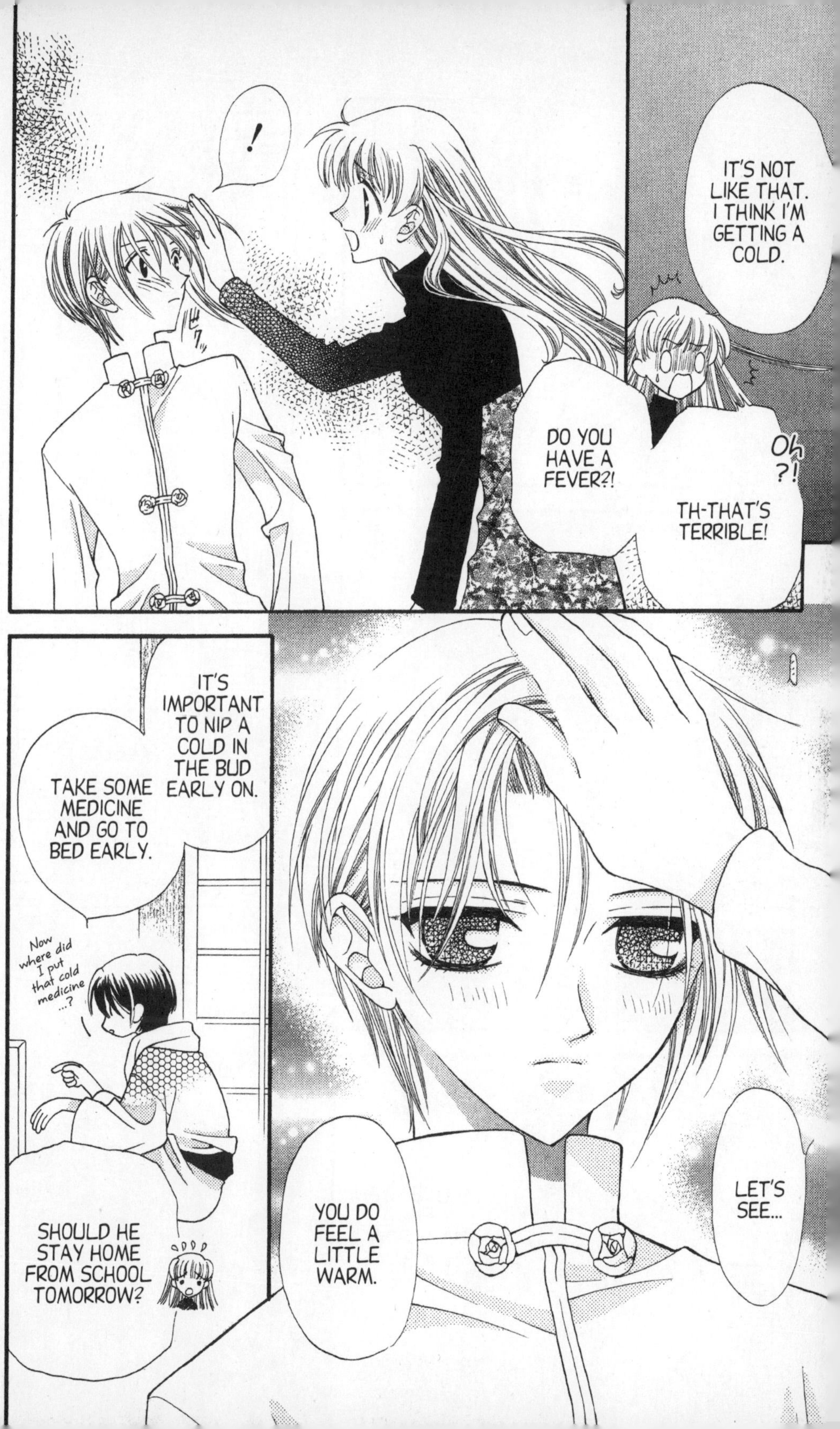
IT'S NOT LIKE THAT. I THINK I'M GETTING A COLD.
Oh ?!
TH-THAT'S TERRIBLE!
DO YOU HAVE A FEVER?!
!
...
LET'S SEE...
YOU DO FEEL A LITTLE WARM.
IT'S IMPORTANT TO NIP A COLD IN THE BUD EARLY ON.
TAKE SOME MEDICINE AND GO TO BED EARLY.
Now where did I put that cold medicine ...?
SHOULD HE STAY HOME FROM SCHOOL TOMORROW?

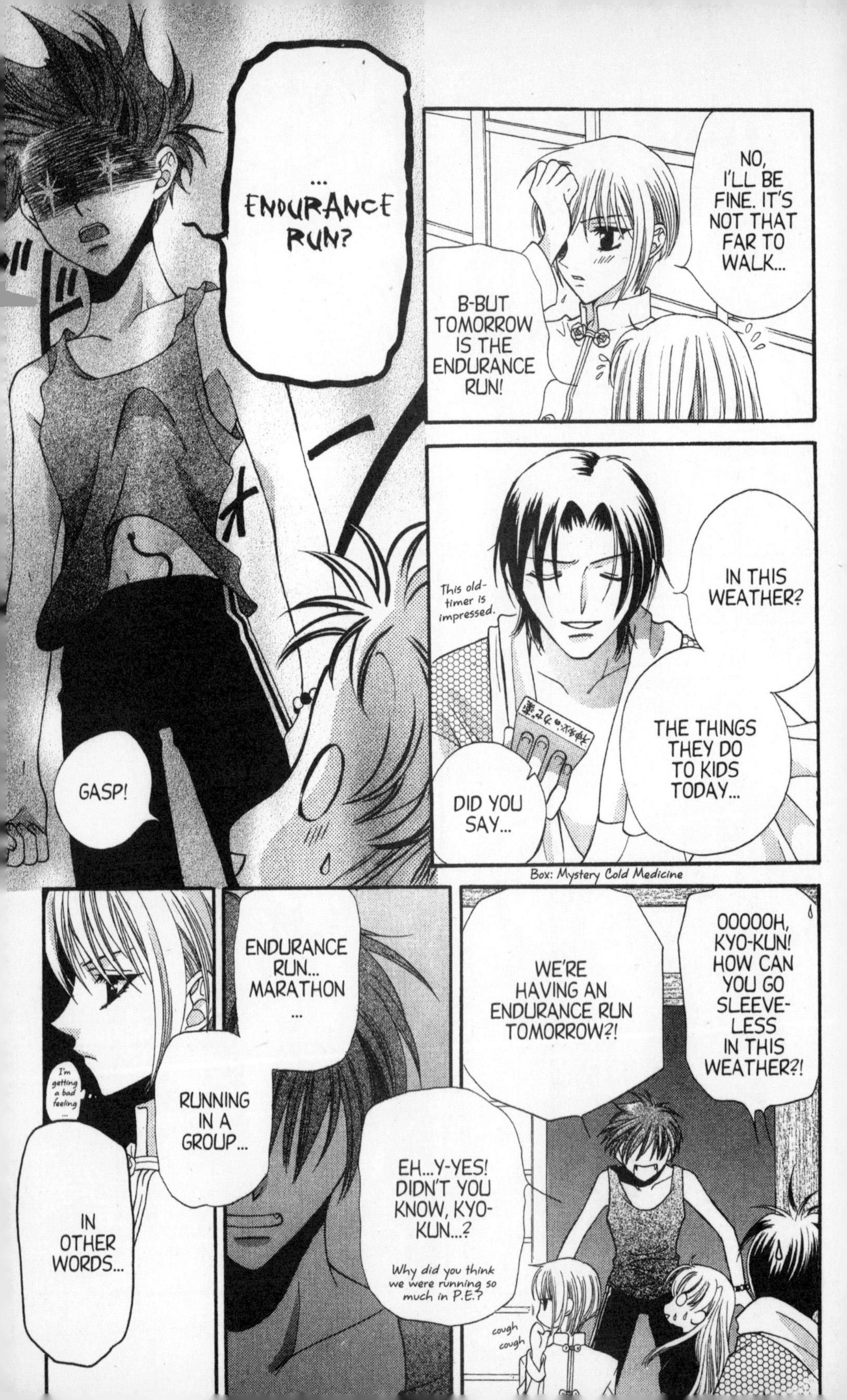
NO, I'LL BE FINE. IT'S NOT THAT FAR TO WALK...
B-BUT TOMORROW IS THE ENDURANCE RUN!
IN THIS WEATHER?
THE THINGS THEY DO TO KIDS TODAY...
This old-timer is impressed.
DID YOU SAY...
Box: Mystery Cold Medicine
... ENDURANCE RUN?
GASP!
OOOOOH, KYO-KUN! HOW CAN YOU GO SLEEVE-LESS IN THIS WEATHER?!
WE'RE HAVING AN ENDURANCE RUN TOMORROW?!
EH...Y-YES! DIDN'T YOU KNOW, KYO-KUN...?
Why did you think we were running so much in P.E.?
cough cough
ENDURANCE RUN... MARATHON ...
RUNNING IN A GROUP...
I'm getting a bad feeling...
IN OTHER WORDS...

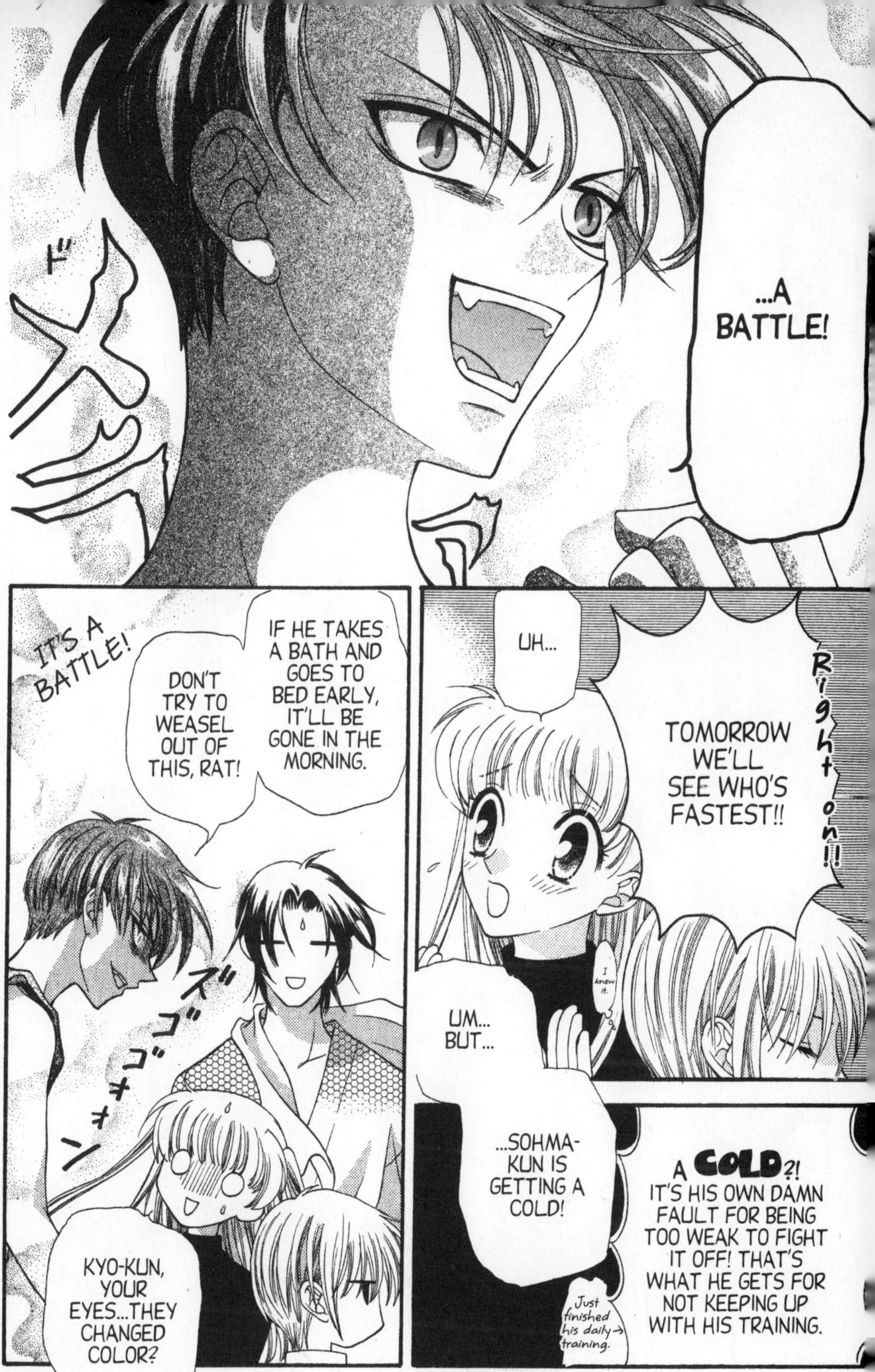
ドン
...A BATTLE!
UH...
TOMORROW WE'LL SEE WHO'S FASTEST!!
Right on!!
I knew it.
UM... BUT...
A COLD?! IT'S HIS OWN DAMN FAULT FOR BEING TOO WEAK TO FIGHT IT OFF! THAT'S WHAT HE GETS FOR NOT KEEPING UP WITH HIS TRAINING.
...SOHMA-KUN IS GETTING A COLD!
Just finished his daily training.
IF HE TAKES A BATH AND GOES TO BED EARLY, IT'LL BE GONE IN THE MORNING.
IT'S A BATTLE!
DON'T TRY TO WEASEL OUT OF THIS, RAT!
ズゴゴオオン
KYO-KUN, YOUR EYES...THEY CHANGED COLOR?

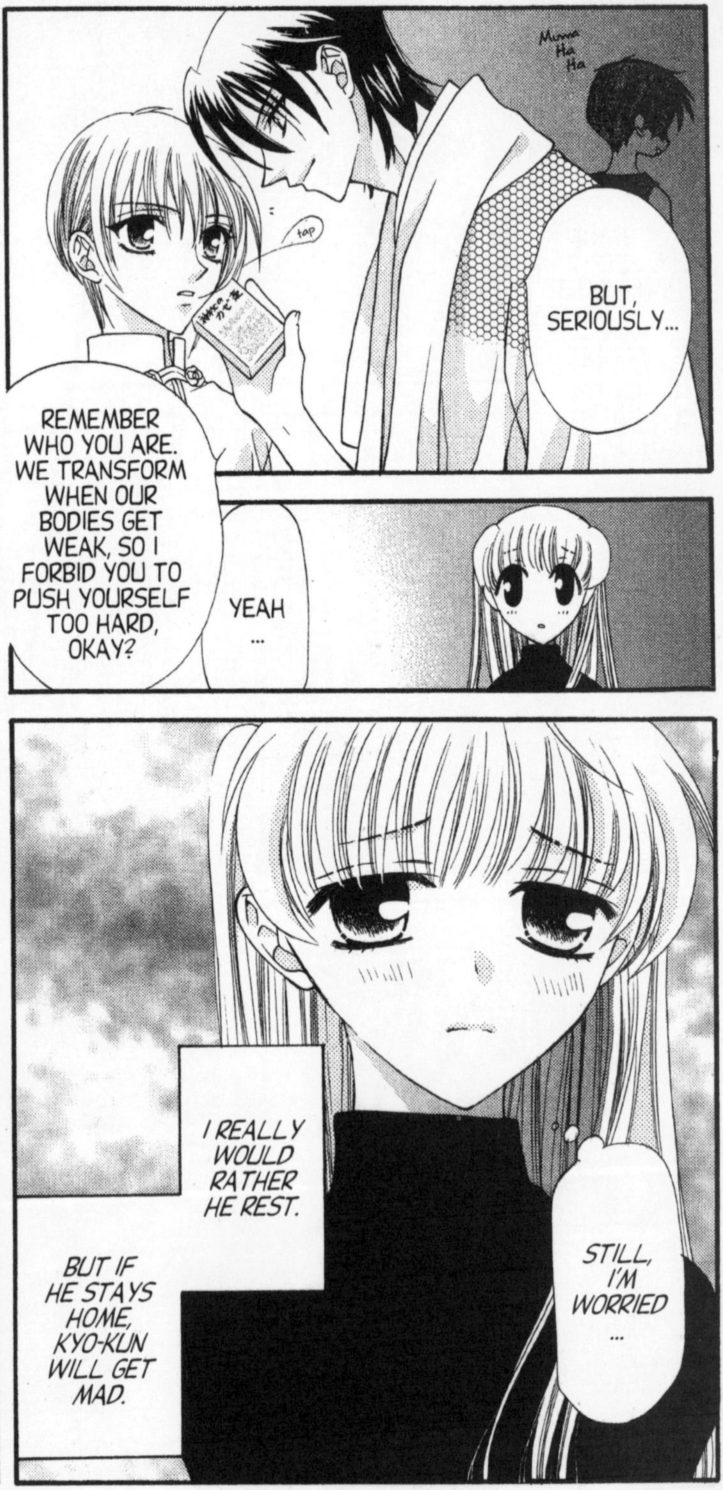
Muwa Ha Ha
tap
BUT, SERIOUSLY...
REMEMBER WHO YOU ARE. WE TRANSFORM WHEN OUR BODIES GET WEAK, SO I FORBID YOU TO PUSH YOURSELF TOO HARD, OKAY?
YEAH ...
STILL, I'M WORRIED ...
I REALLY WOULD RATHER HE REST.
BUT IF HE STAYS HOME, KYO-KUN WILL GET MAD.

Fruits Basket 3 Part 1:

Hello! Nice to meet you! I'm Natsuki Takaya. Furuba Volume 3 already! (No, really-- didn't it happen fast?) The cover features Kyon-Kyon, just like I promised. If you're wondering why Kyo doesn't wear a necktie, it's because he can't breathe with anything around his neck. He doesn't even like clothes with tight collars. (That doesn't mean he'll never wear them. It just means he prefers not to wear them.) He's a cat who doesn't like collars. (Get it?)

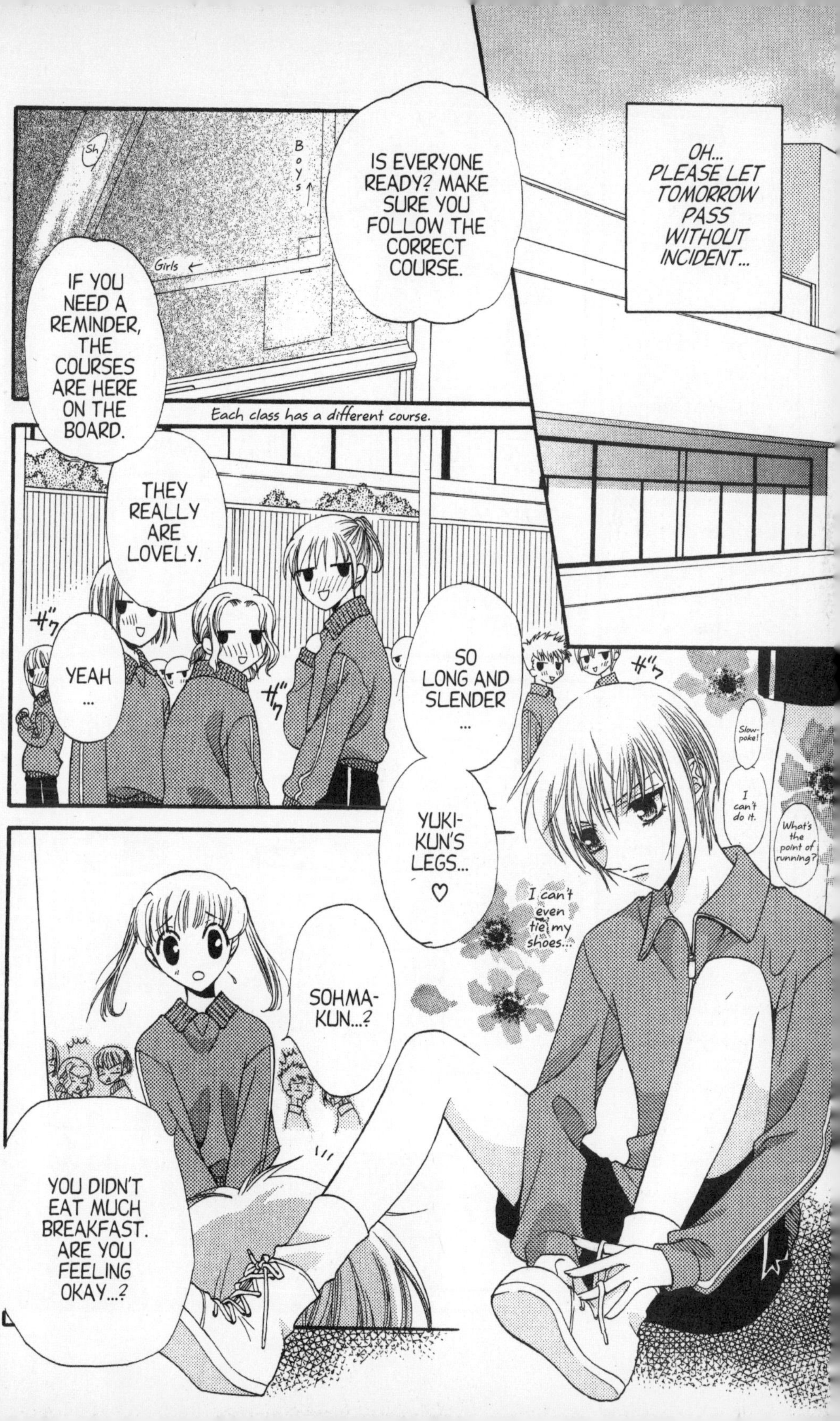
OH... PLEASE LET TOMORROW PASS WITHOUT INCIDENT...
IS EVERYONE READY? MAKE SURE YOU FOLLOW THE CORRECT COURSE.
Sh
Boys ↑
Girls ←
IF YOU NEED A REMINDER, THE COURSES ARE HERE ON THE BOARD.
Each class has a different course.
THEY REALLY ARE LOVELY.
YEAH ...
SO LONG AND SLENDER ...
YUKI-KUN'S LEGS... ♡
Slow-poke!
I can't do it.
What's the point of running?
I can't even tie my shoes...
SOHMA-KUN...?
YOU DIDN'T EAT MUCH BREAKFAST. ARE YOU FEELING OKAY...?

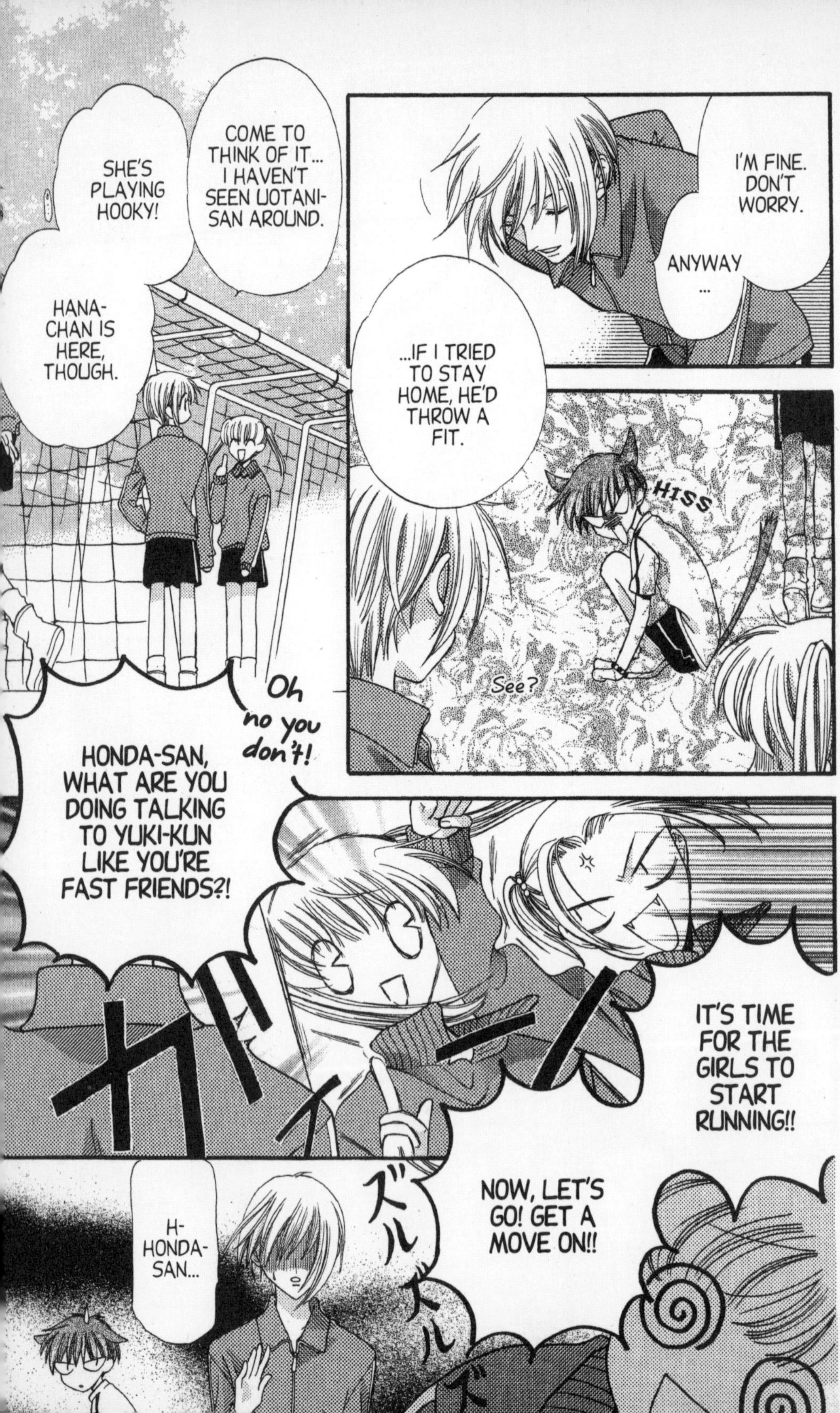
I'M FINE. DON'T WORRY.
ANYWAY ...
...IF I TRIED TO STAY HOME, HE'D THROW A FIT.
HISS
See?
COME TO THINK OF IT... I HAVEN'T SEEN UOTANI-SAN AROUND.
SHE'S PLAYING HOOKY!
HANA-CHAN IS HERE, THOUGH.
Oh no you don't!
HONDA-SAN, WHAT ARE YOU DOING TALKING TO YUKI-KUN LIKE YOU'RE FAST FRIENDS?!
IT'S TIME FOR THE GIRLS TO START RUNNING!!
NOW, LET'S GO! GET A MOVE ON!!
H-HONDA-SAN...

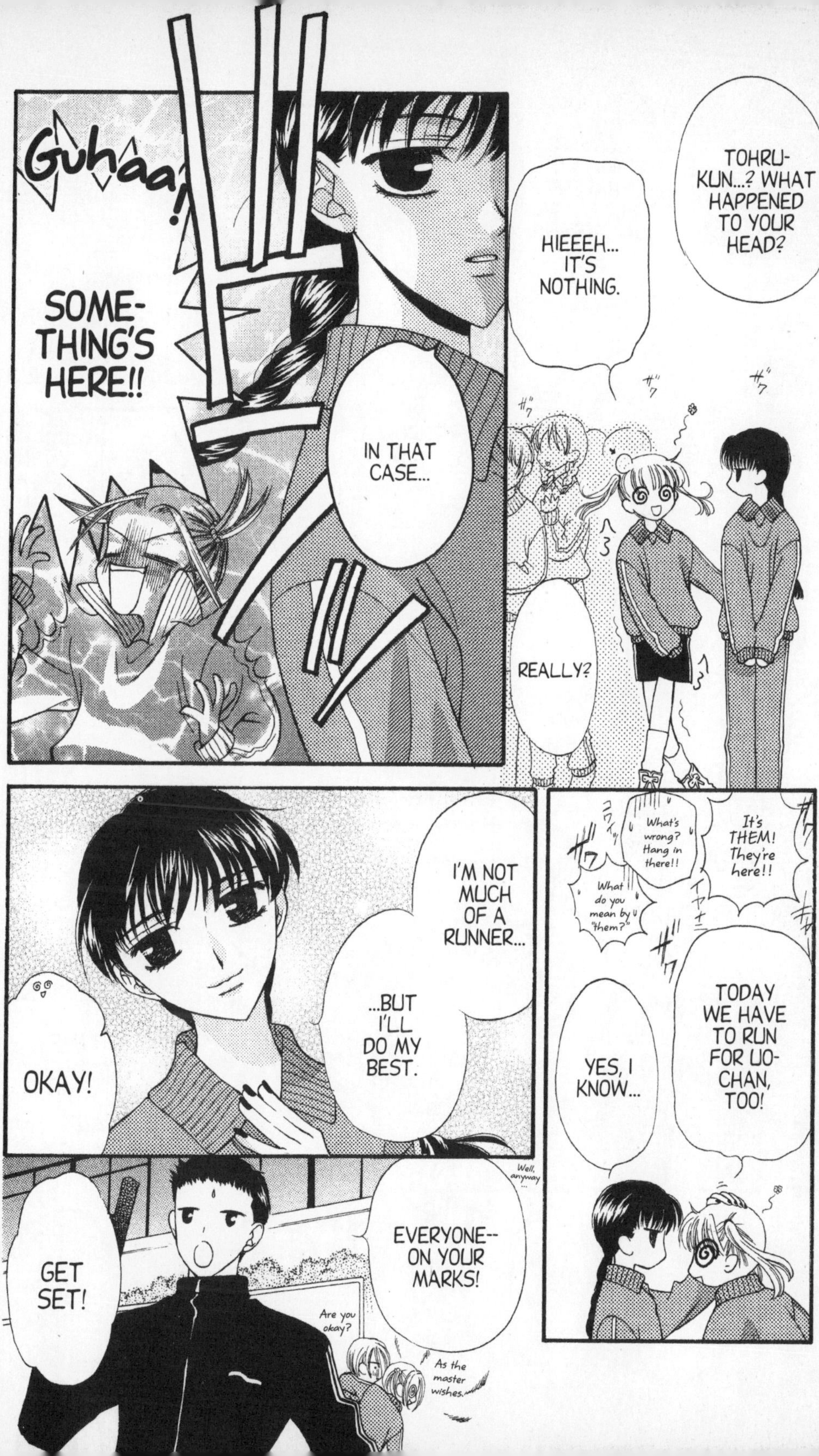
TOHRU-KUN...? WHAT HAPPENED TO YOUR HEAD?
HIEEEH... IT'S NOTHING.
REALLY?
Guhaa!
SOME-THING'S HERE!!
IN THAT CASE...
It's THEM! They're here!!
What's wrong? Hang in there!!
What do you mean by "them?"
TODAY WE HAVE TO RUN FOR UO-CHAN, TOO!
YES, I KNOW...
I'M NOT MUCH OF A RUNNER...
...BUT I'LL DO MY BEST.
OKAY!
Well, anyway...
EVERYONE-- ON YOUR MARKS!
GET SET!
Are you okay?
As the master wishes.

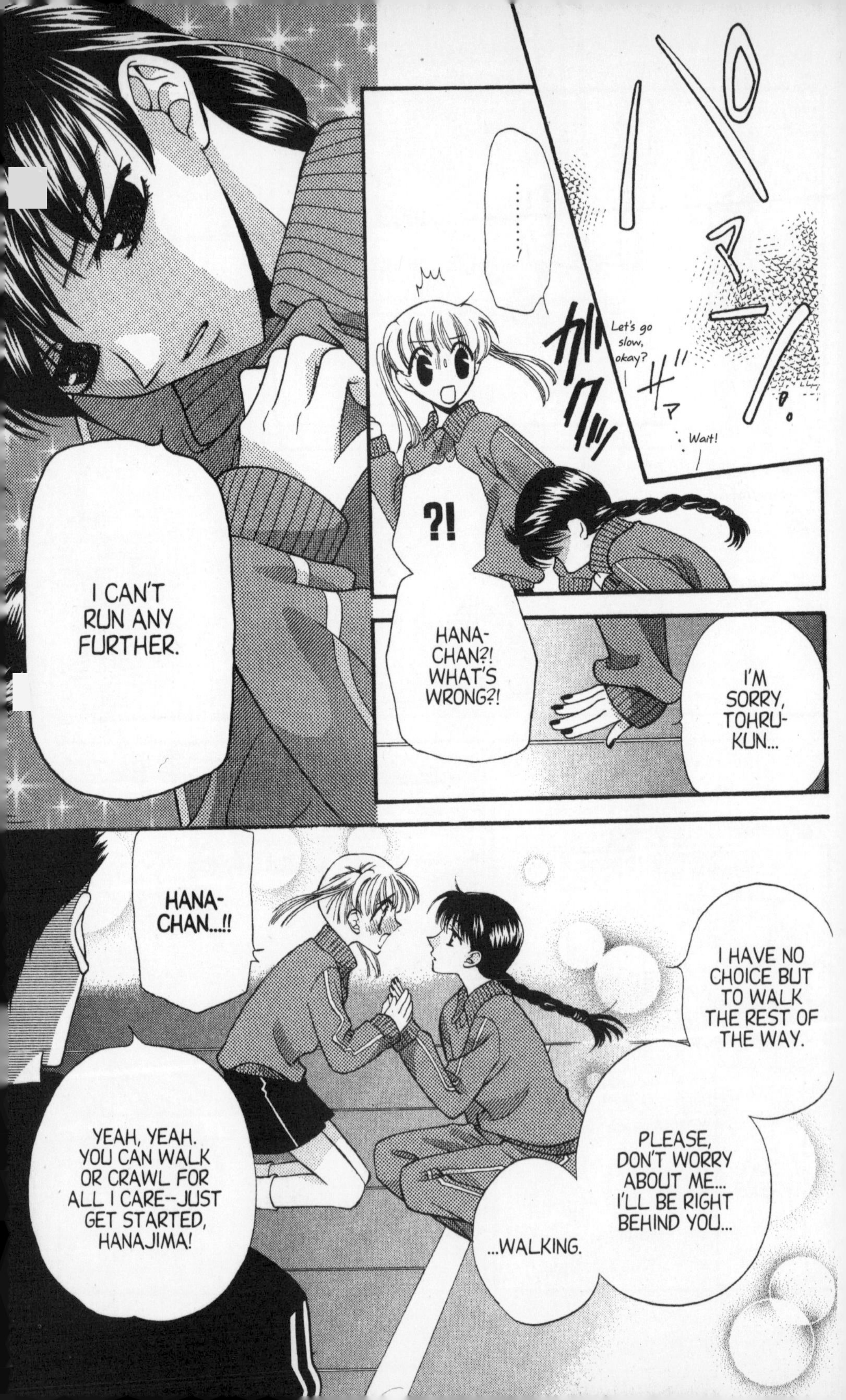
Let's go slow, okay?
Wait!
......?
?!
I'M SORRY, TOHRU-KUN...
HANA-CHAN?! WHAT'S WRONG?!
I CAN'T RUN ANY FURTHER.
I HAVE NO CHOICE BUT TO WALK THE REST OF THE WAY.
PLEASE, DON'T WORRY ABOUT ME... I'LL BE RIGHT BEHIND YOU...
...WALKING.
HANA-CHAN...!!
YEAH, YEAH. YOU CAN WALK OR CRAWL FOR ALL I CARE--JUST GET STARTED, HANAJIMA!

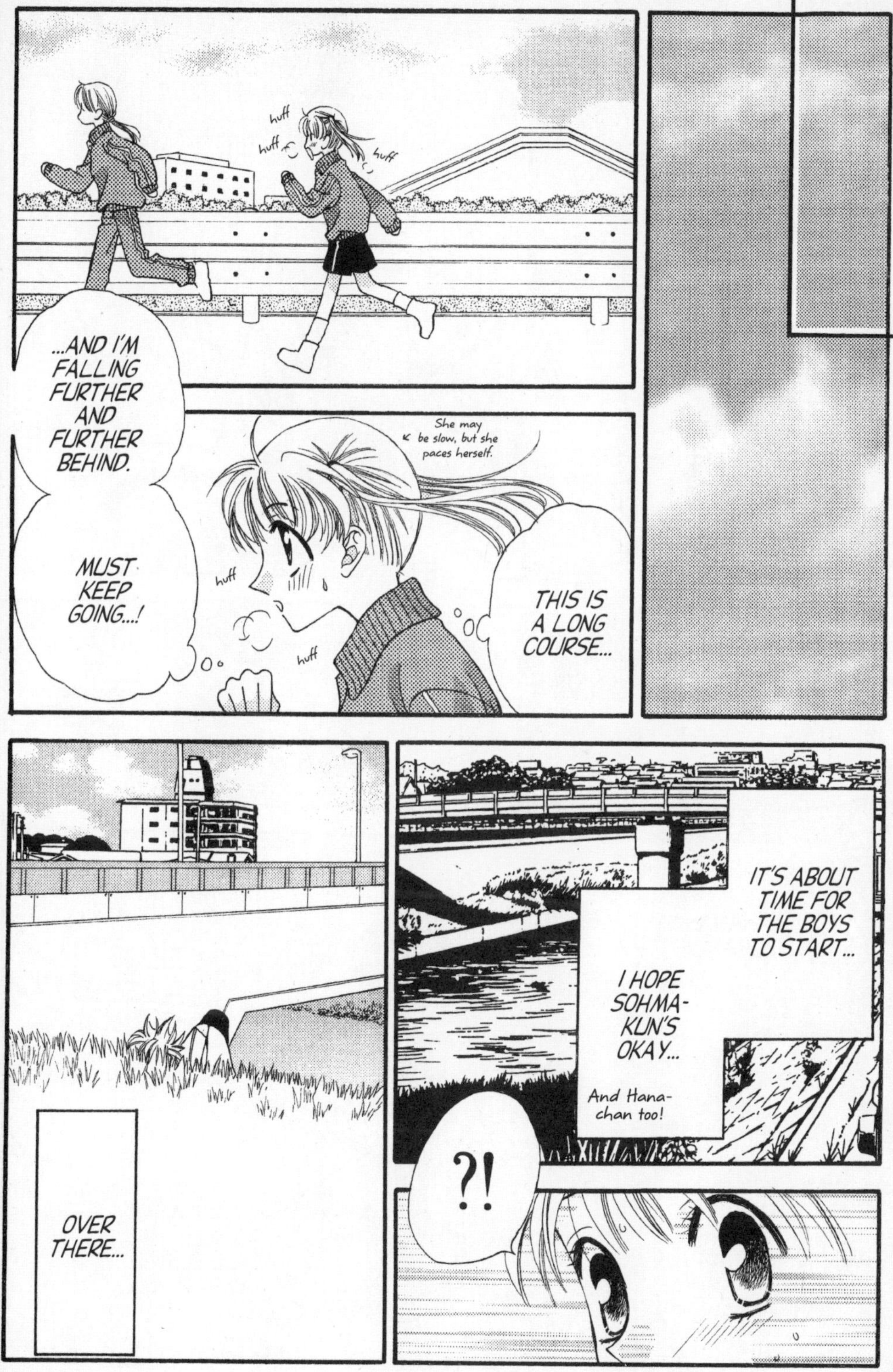
huff
huff
huff
...AND I'M FALLING FURTHER AND FURTHER BEHIND.
She may be slow, but she paces herself.
THIS IS A LONG COURSE...
huff
MUST KEEP GOING...!
huff
IT'S ABOUT TIME FOR THE BOYS TO START...
I HOPE SOHMA-KUN'S OKAY...
And Hana-chan too!
?!
OVER THERE...

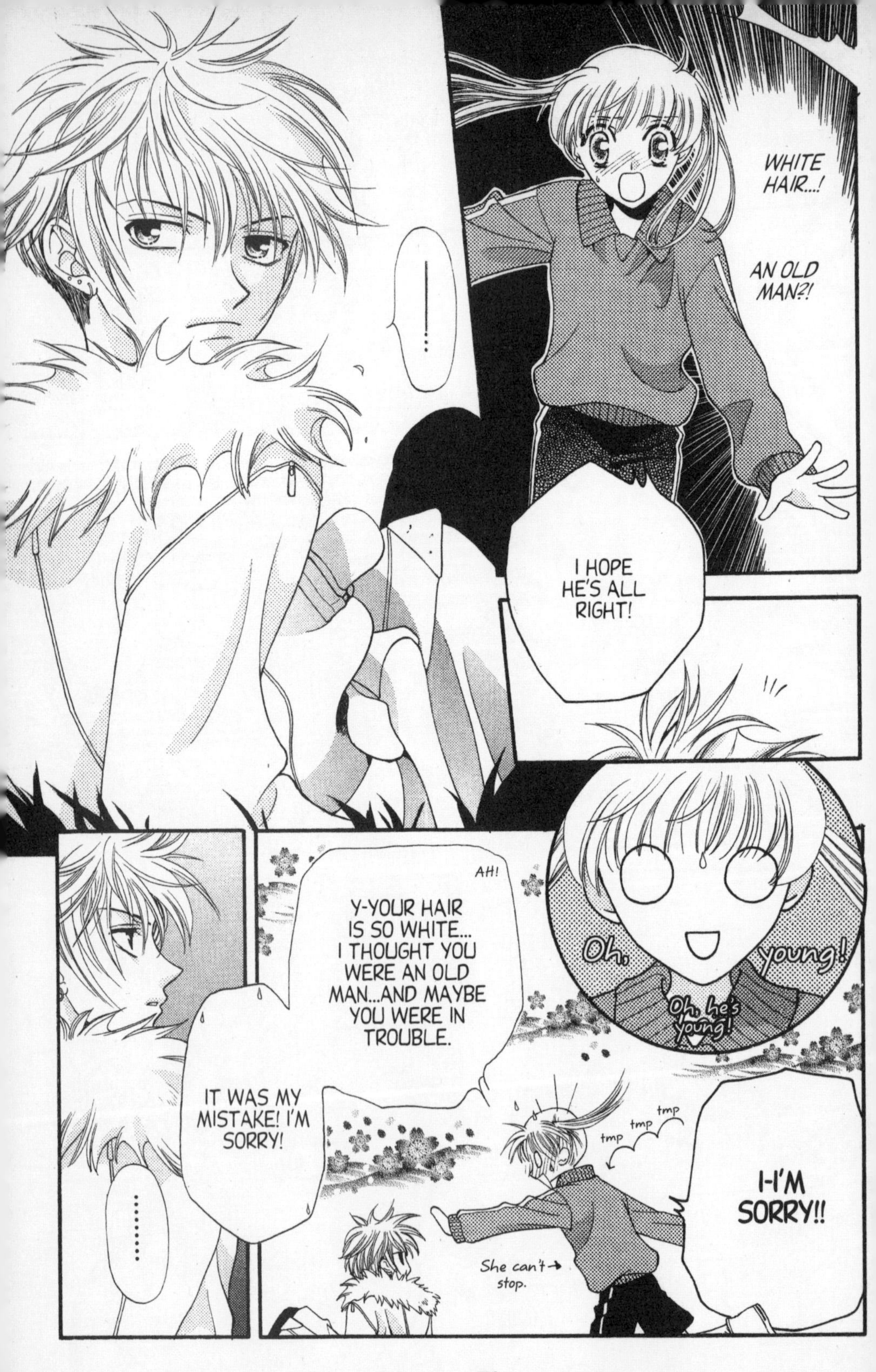
WHITE HAIR...!
AN OLD MAN?!
I HOPE HE'S ALL RIGHT!
Oh. young!
Oh, he's young!
......!
AH!
Y-YOUR HAIR IS SO WHITE... I THOUGHT YOU WERE AN OLD MAN...AND MAYBE YOU WERE IN TROUBLE.
IT WAS MY MISTAKE! I'M SORRY!
tmp tmp tmp
I-I'M SORRY!!
She can't stop.
....

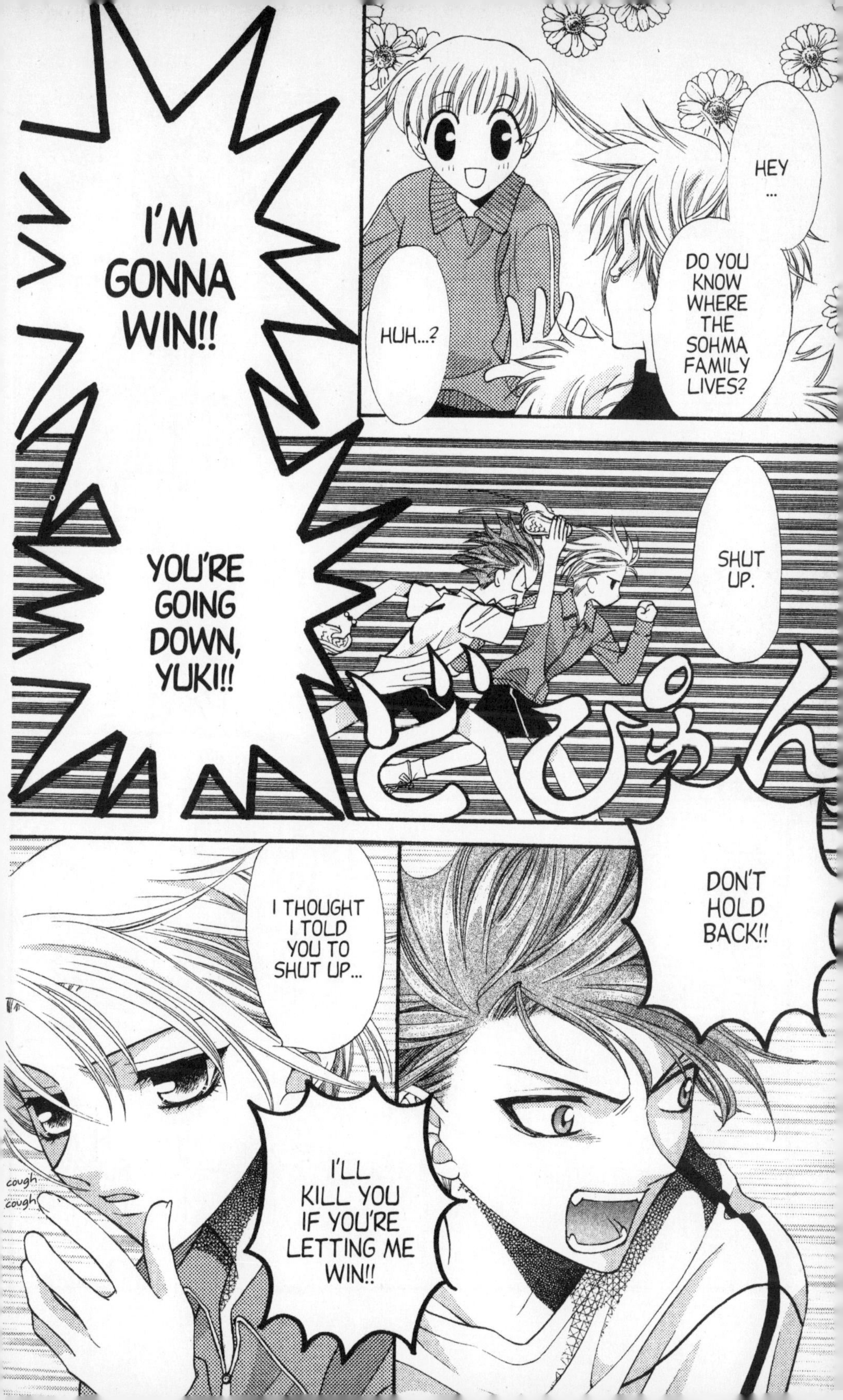
HEY ...
DO YOU KNOW WHERE THE SOHMA FAMILY LIVES?
HUH...?
I'M GONNA WIN!!
SHUT UP.
YOU'RE GOING DOWN, YUKI!!
DON'T HOLD BACK!!
I'LL KILL YOU IF YOU'RE LETTING ME WIN!!
I THOUGHT I TOLD YOU TO SHUT UP...
cough
cough

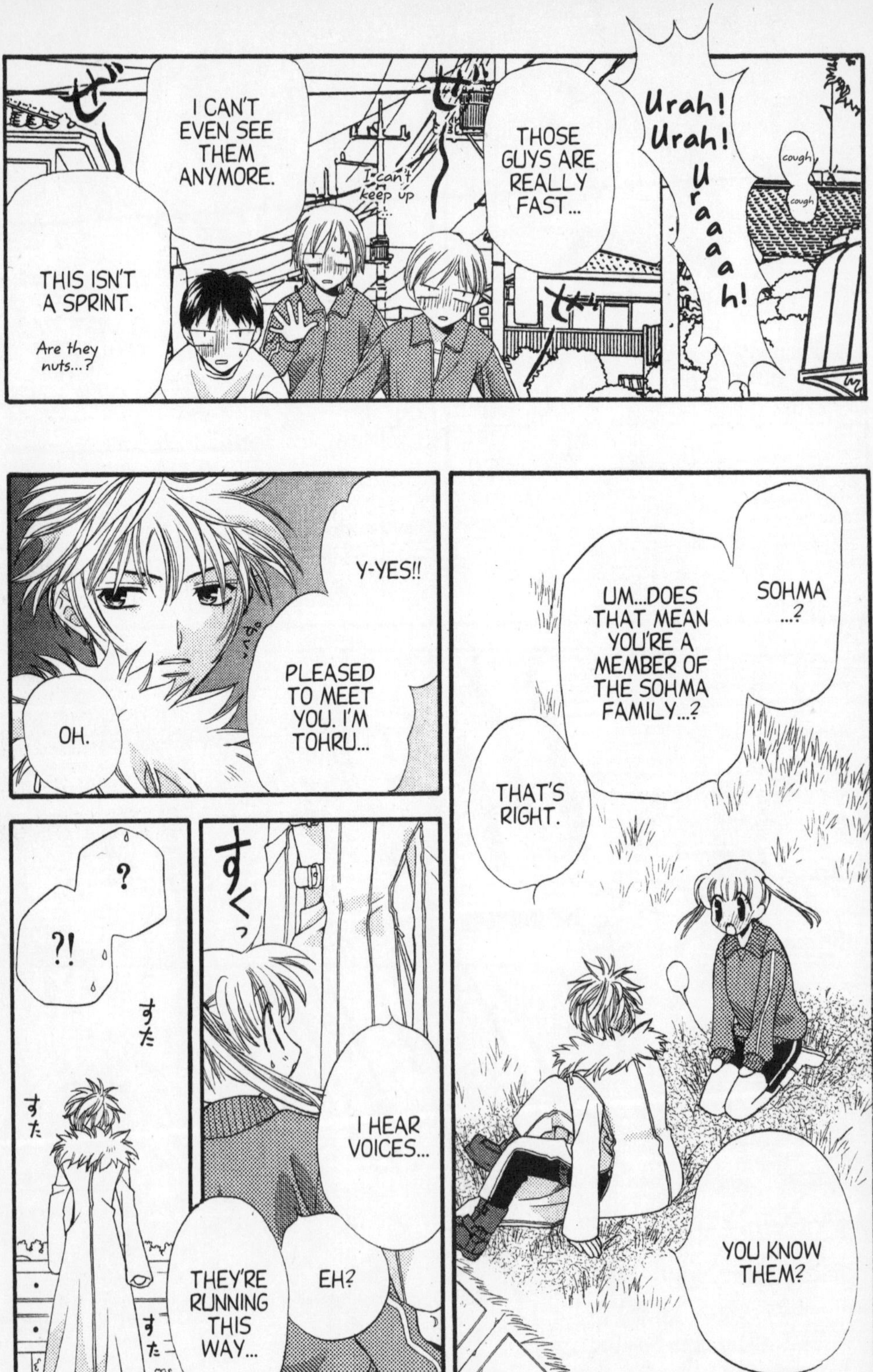
Urah! Urah! Uraaaah!
cough
cough
THOSE GUYS ARE REALLY FAST...
I can't keep up...
I CAN'T EVEN SEE THEM ANYMORE.
THIS ISN'T A SPRINT.
Are they nuts...?
SOHMA ...?
UM...DOES THAT MEAN YOU'RE A MEMBER OF THE SOHMA FAMILY...?
THAT'S RIGHT.
YOU KNOW THEM?
Y-YES!!
PLEASED TO MEET YOU. I'M TOHRU...
OH.
すくっ
I HEAR VOICES...
EH?
THEY'RE RUNNING THIS WAY...
?
?!
すた
すた
すた

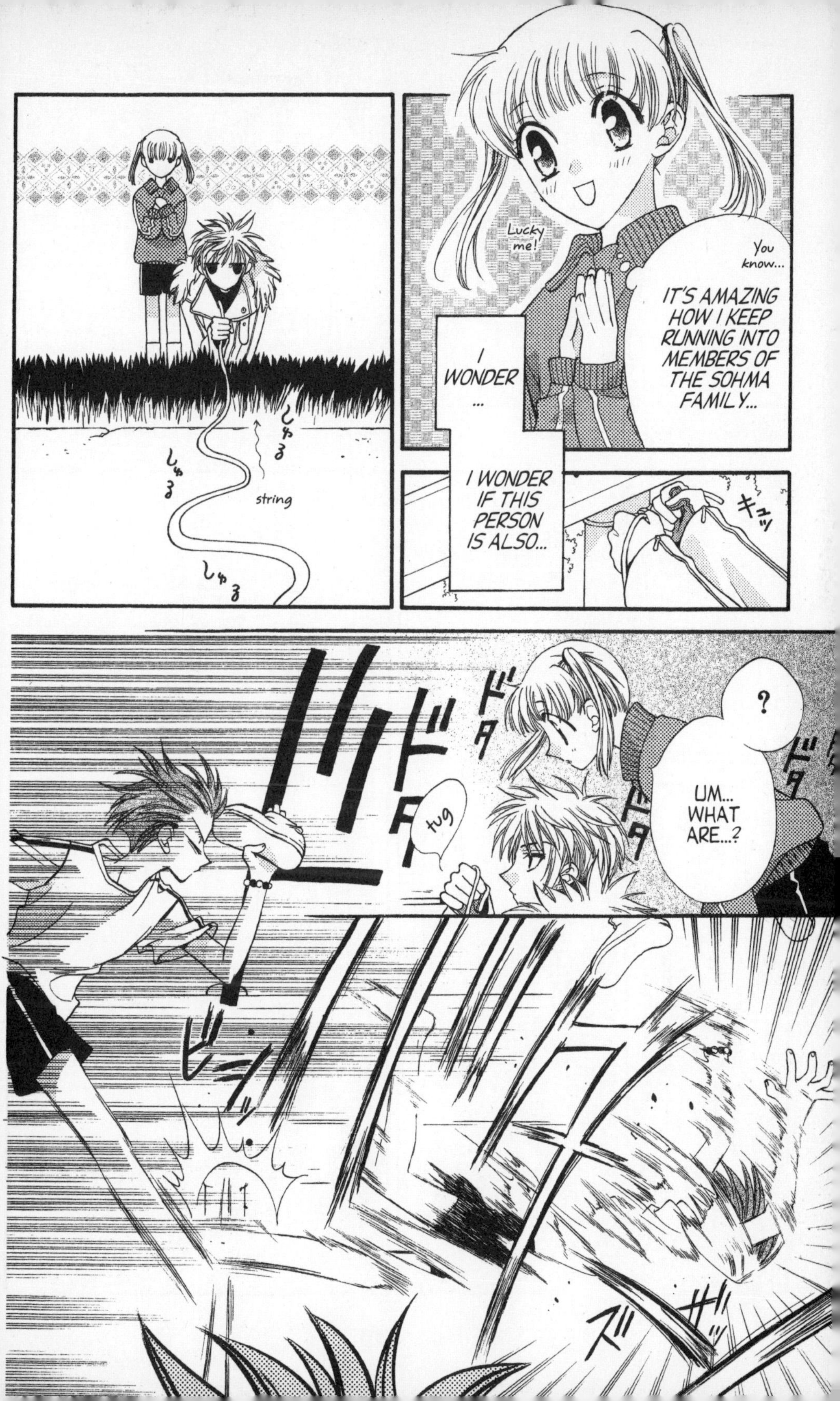
Lucky me!
You know...
IT'S AMAZING HOW I KEEP RUNNING INTO MEMBERS OF THE SOHMA FAMILY...
I WONDER ...
I WONDER IF THIS PERSON IS ALSO...
キュッ
しゅる
しゅる
string
しゅる
ドタ
ドタ
?
UM... WHAT ARE...?
tug

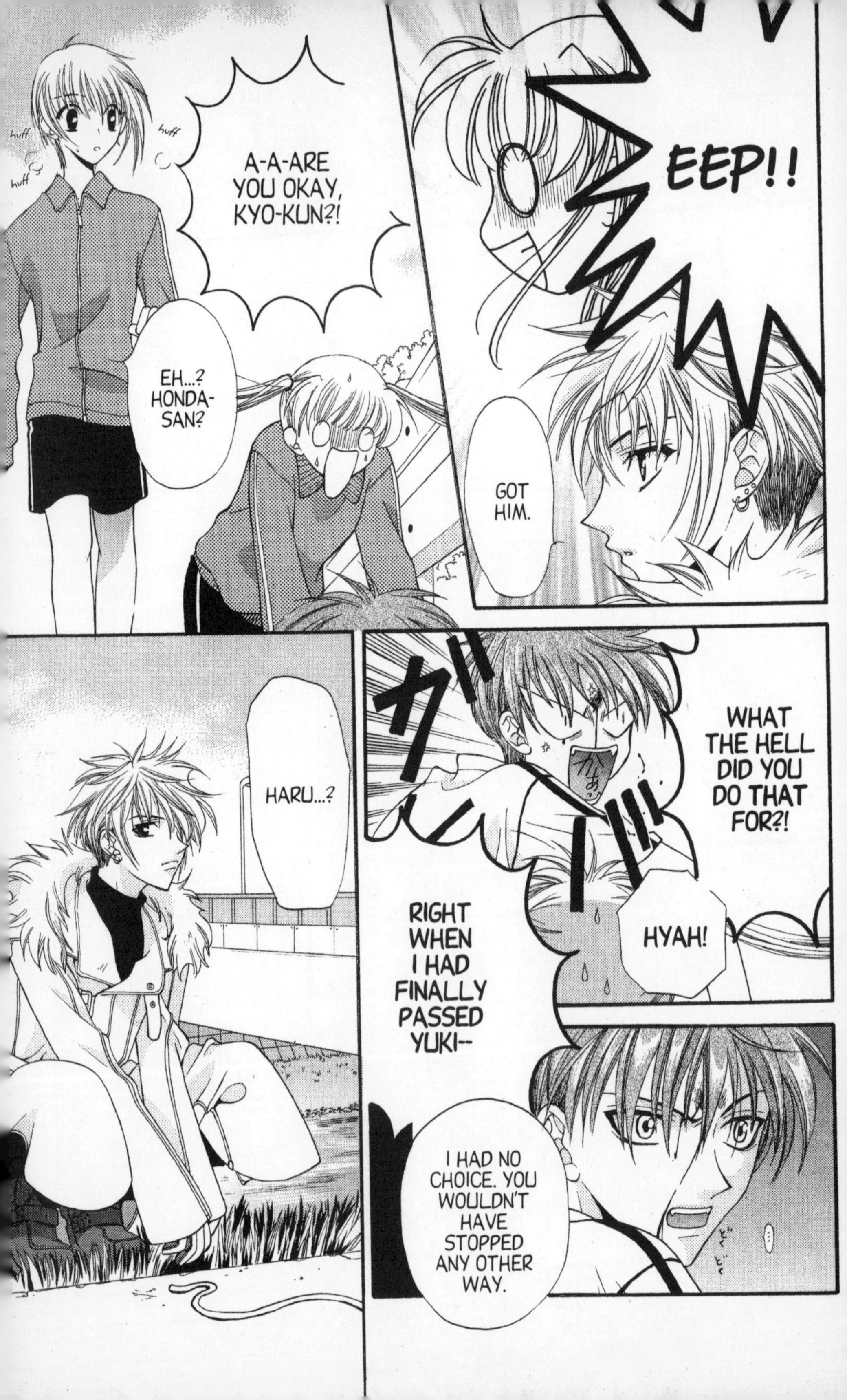
EEP!!
GOT HIM.
A-A-ARE YOU OKAY, KYO-KUN?!
huff
huff
huff
EH...? HONDA-SAN?
WHAT THE HELL DID YOU DO THAT FOR?!
HYAH!
RIGHT WHEN I HAD FINALLY PASSED YUKI--
I HAD NO CHOICE. YOU WOULDN'T HAVE STOPPED ANY OTHER WAY.
HARU...?

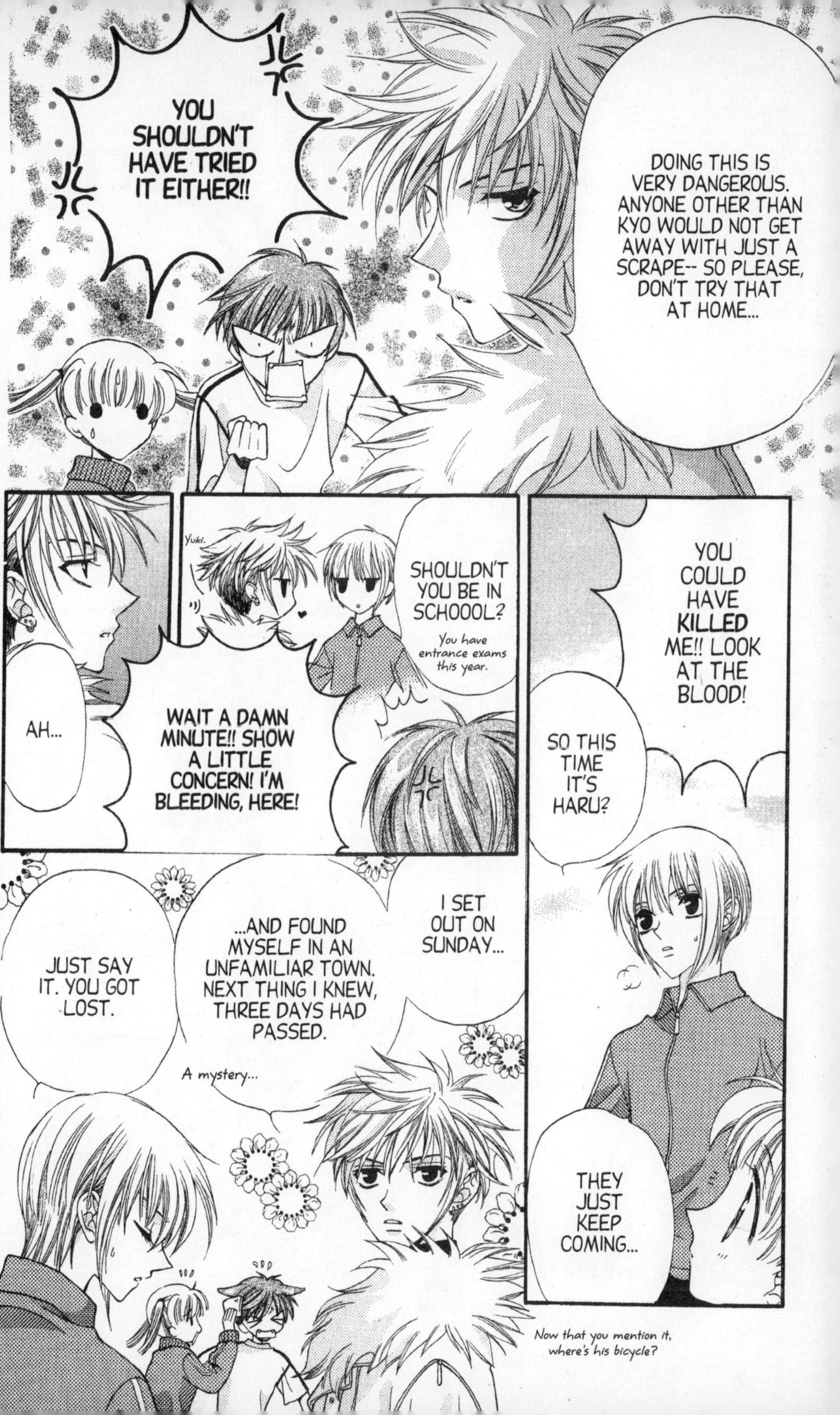
DOING THIS IS VERY DANGEROUS. ANYONE OTHER THAN KYO WOULD NOT GET AWAY WITH JUST A SCRAPE-- SO PLEASE, DON'T TRY THAT AT HOME...
YOU SHOULDN'T HAVE TRIED IT EITHER!!
YOU COULD HAVE **KILLED** ME!! LOOK AT THE BLOOD!
SO THIS TIME IT'S HARU?
THEY JUST KEEP COMING...
Yuki.
SHOULDN'T YOU BE IN SCHOOOL?
You have entrance exams this year.
WAIT A DAMN MINUTE!! SHOW A LITTLE CONCERN! I'M BLEEDING, HERE!
AH...
I SET OUT ON SUNDAY...
...AND FOUND MYSELF IN AN UNFAMILIAR TOWN. NEXT THING I KNEW, THREE DAYS HAD PASSED.
JUST SAY IT. YOU GOT LOST.
A mystery...
Now that you mention it, where's his bicycle?

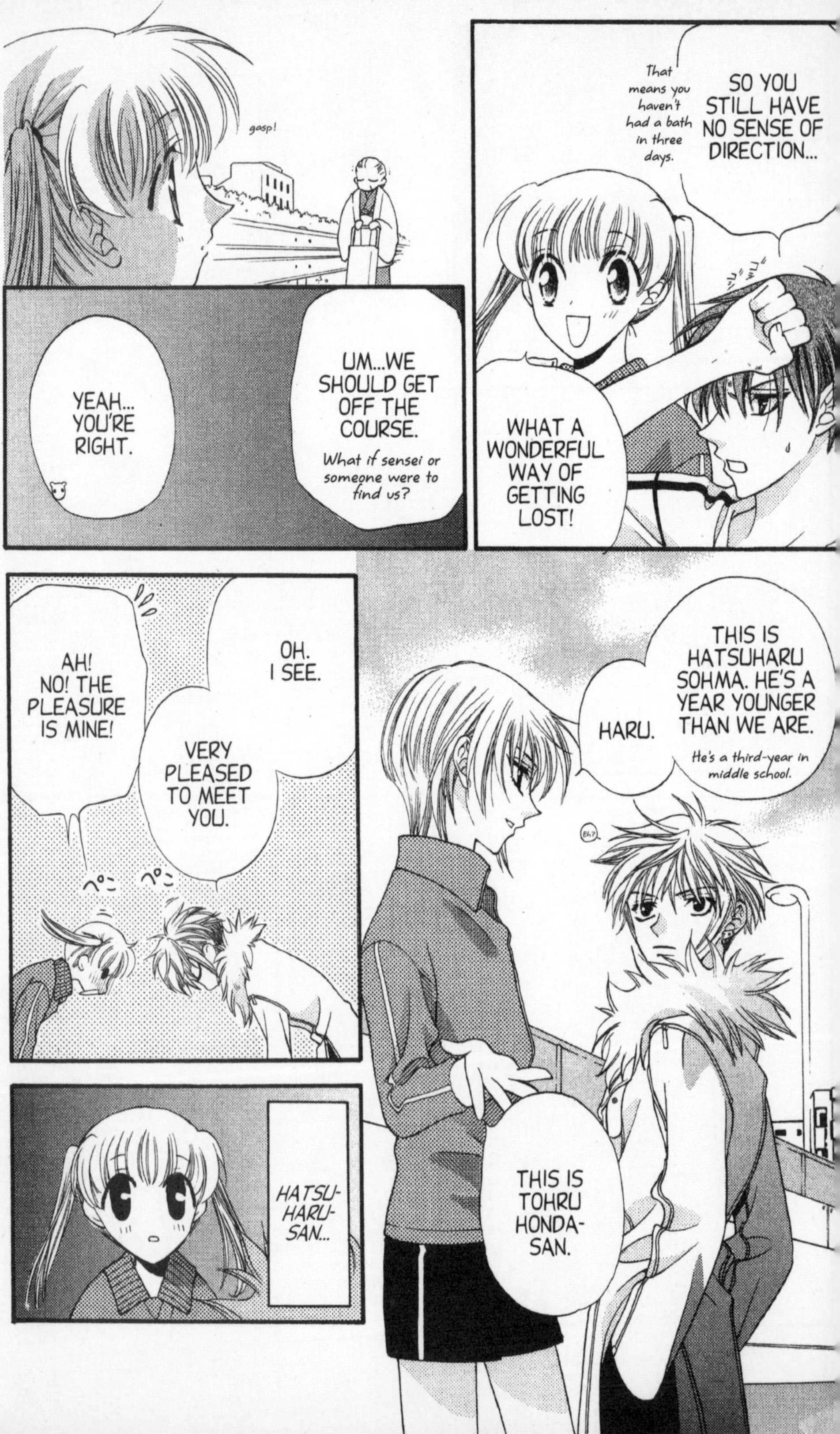
SO YOU STILL HAVE NO SENSE OF DIRECTION...
That means you haven't had a bath in three days.
WHAT A WONDERFUL WAY OF GETTING LOST!
gasp!
UM...WE SHOULD GET OFF THE COURSE.
What if sensei or someone were to find us?
YEAH... YOU'RE RIGHT.
THIS IS HATSUHARU SOHMA. HE'S A YEAR YOUNGER THAN WE ARE.
He's a third-year in middle school.
HARU.
Eh?
THIS IS TOHRU HONDA-SAN.
OH. I SEE.
VERY PLEASED TO MEET YOU.
AH! NO! THE PLEASURE IS MINE!
ぺこ
ぺこ
HATSU-HARU-SAN...

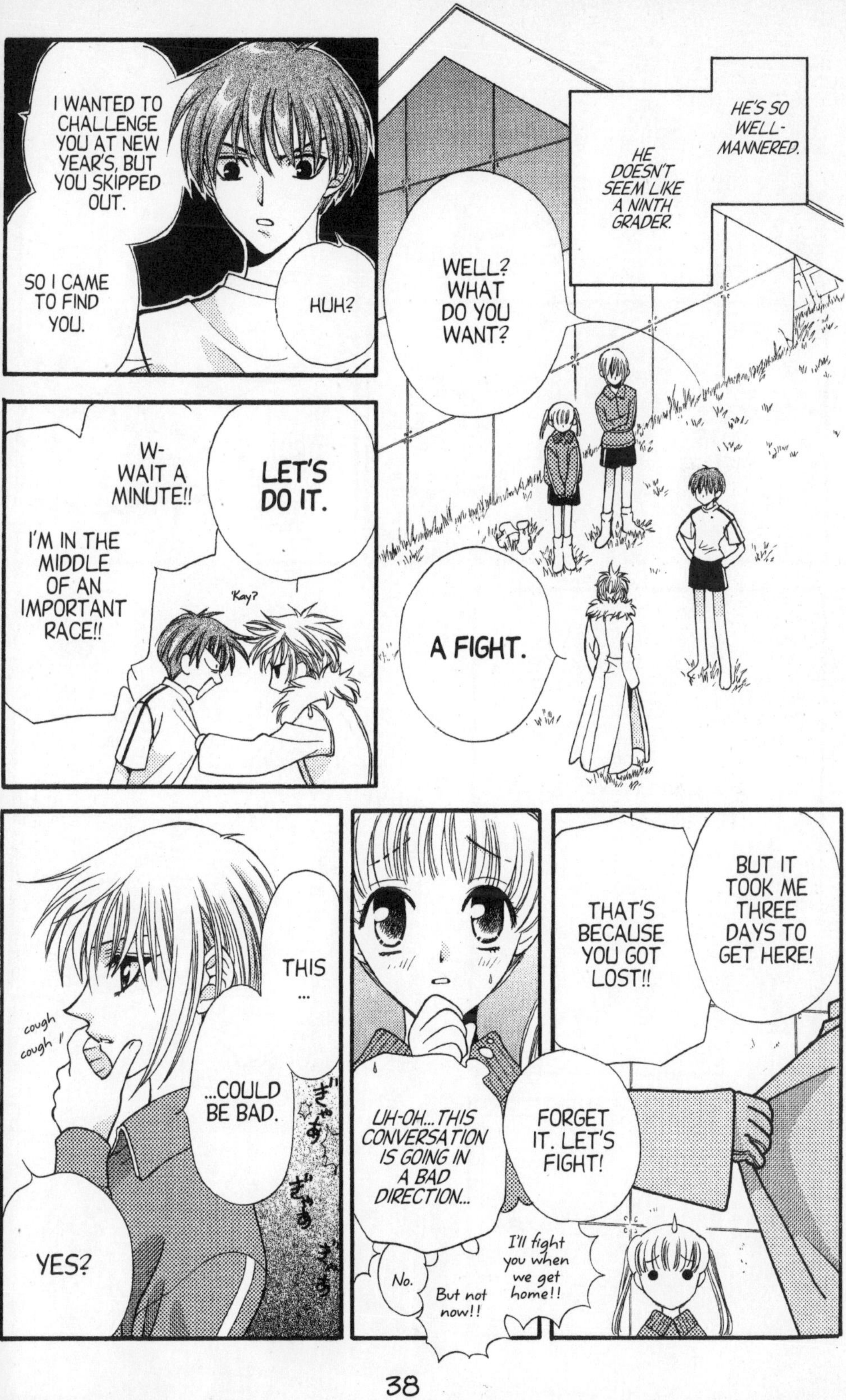
HE'S SO WELL-MANNERED.
HE DOESN'T SEEM LIKE A NINTH GRADER.
WELL? WHAT DO YOU WANT?
A FIGHT.
HUH?
I WANTED TO CHALLENGE YOU AT NEW YEAR'S, BUT YOU SKIPPED OUT.
SO I CAME TO FIND YOU.
LET'S DO IT.
W-WAIT A MINUTE!!
'Kay?
I'M IN THE MIDDLE OF AN IMPORTANT RACE!!
BUT IT TOOK ME THREE DAYS TO GET HERE!
THAT'S BECAUSE YOU GOT LOST!!
FORGET IT. LET'S FIGHT!
I'll fight you when we get home!!
UH-OH...THIS CONVERSATION IS GOING IN A BAD DIRECTION...
No.
But not now!!
THIS ...
...COULD BE BAD.
ぎゃあ ぎゃあ ぎゃあ
cough cough!!
YES?

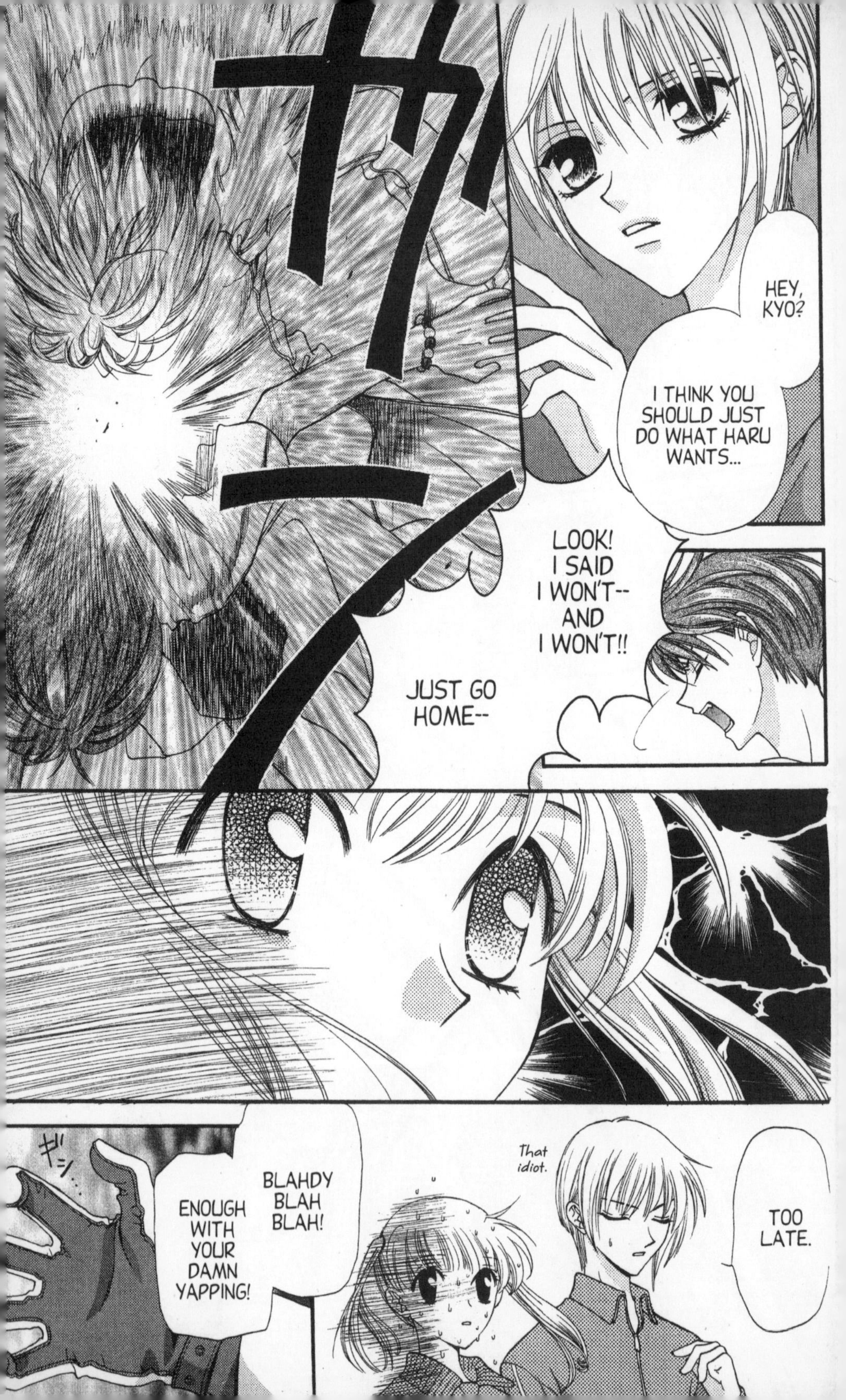
HEY, KYO?
I THINK YOU SHOULD JUST DO WHAT HARU WANTS...
LOOK! I SAID I WON'T-- AND I WON'T!!
JUST GO HOME--
TOO LATE.
That idiot.
BLAHDY BLAH BLAH!
ENOUGH WITH YOUR DAMN YAPPING!

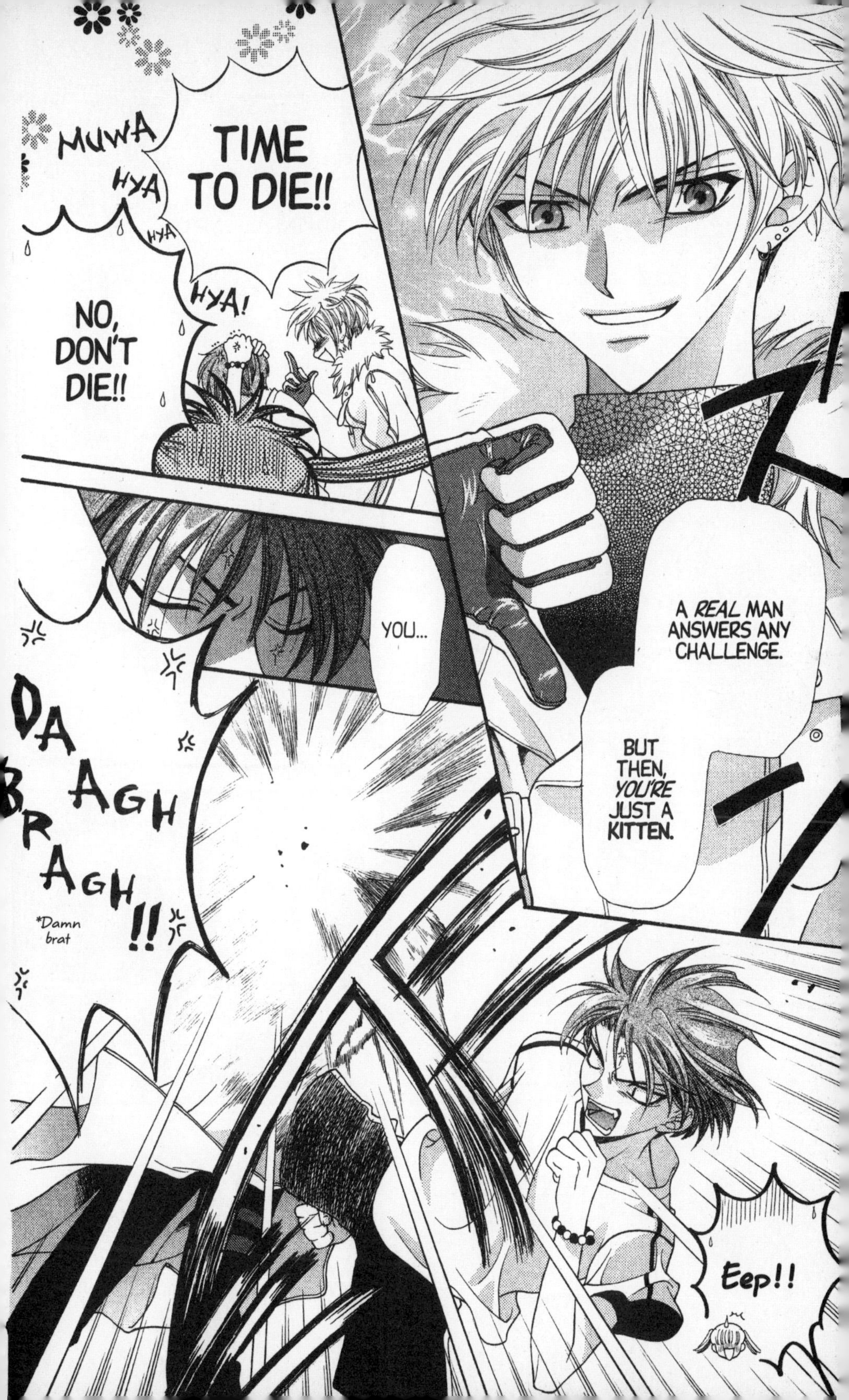
A REAL MAN ANSWERS ANY CHALLENGE.
BUT THEN, YOU'RE JUST A KITTEN.
MUWA HYA HYA HYA!
TIME TO DIE!!
NO, DON'T DIE!!
YOU...
DA AGH BRAGH!!
*Damn brat
Eep!!

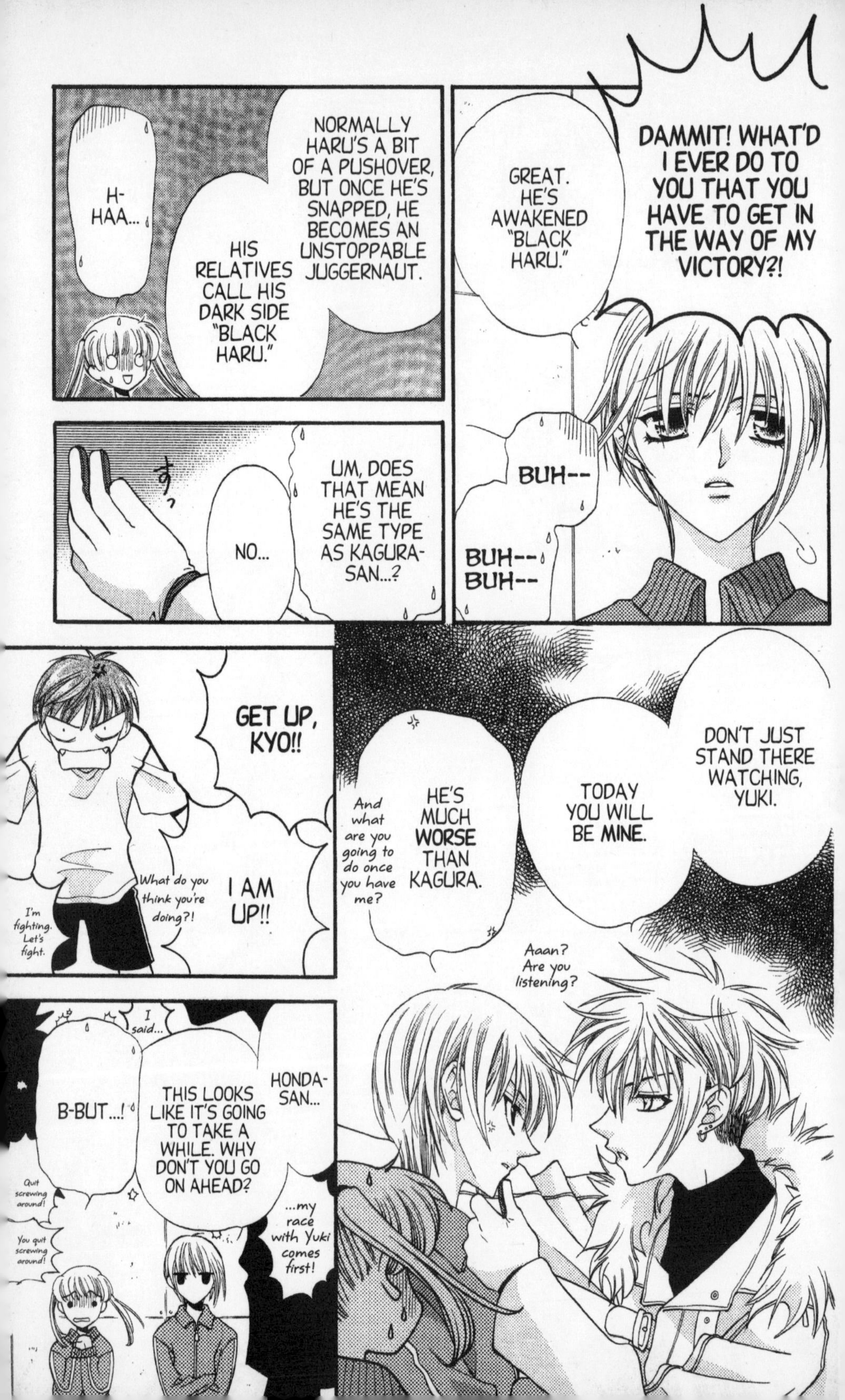
DAMMIT! WHAT'D I EVER DO TO YOU THAT YOU HAVE TO GET IN THE WAY OF MY VICTORY?!
GREAT. HE'S AWAKENED "BLACK HARU."
BUH--
BUH-- BUH--
NORMALLY HARU'S A BIT OF A PUSHOVER, BUT ONCE HE'S SNAPPED, HE BECOMES AN UNSTOPPABLE JUGGERNAUT.
HIS RELATIVES CALL HIS DARK SIDE "BLACK HARU."
H-HAA...
UM, DOES THAT MEAN HE'S THE SAME TYPE AS KAGURA-SAN...?
NO...
す
DON'T JUST STAND THERE WATCHING, YUKI.
TODAY YOU WILL BE MINE.
HE'S MUCH WORSE THAN KAGURA.
And what are you going to do once you have me?
Aaan? Are you listening?
GET UP, KYO!!
I AM UP!!
What do you think you're doing?!
I'm fighting. Let's fight.
HONDA-SAN...
THIS LOOKS LIKE IT'S GOING TO TAKE A WHILE. WHY DON'T YOU GO ON AHEAD?
I said...
...my race with Yuki comes first!
B-BUT...!
Quit screwing around!
You quit screwing around!

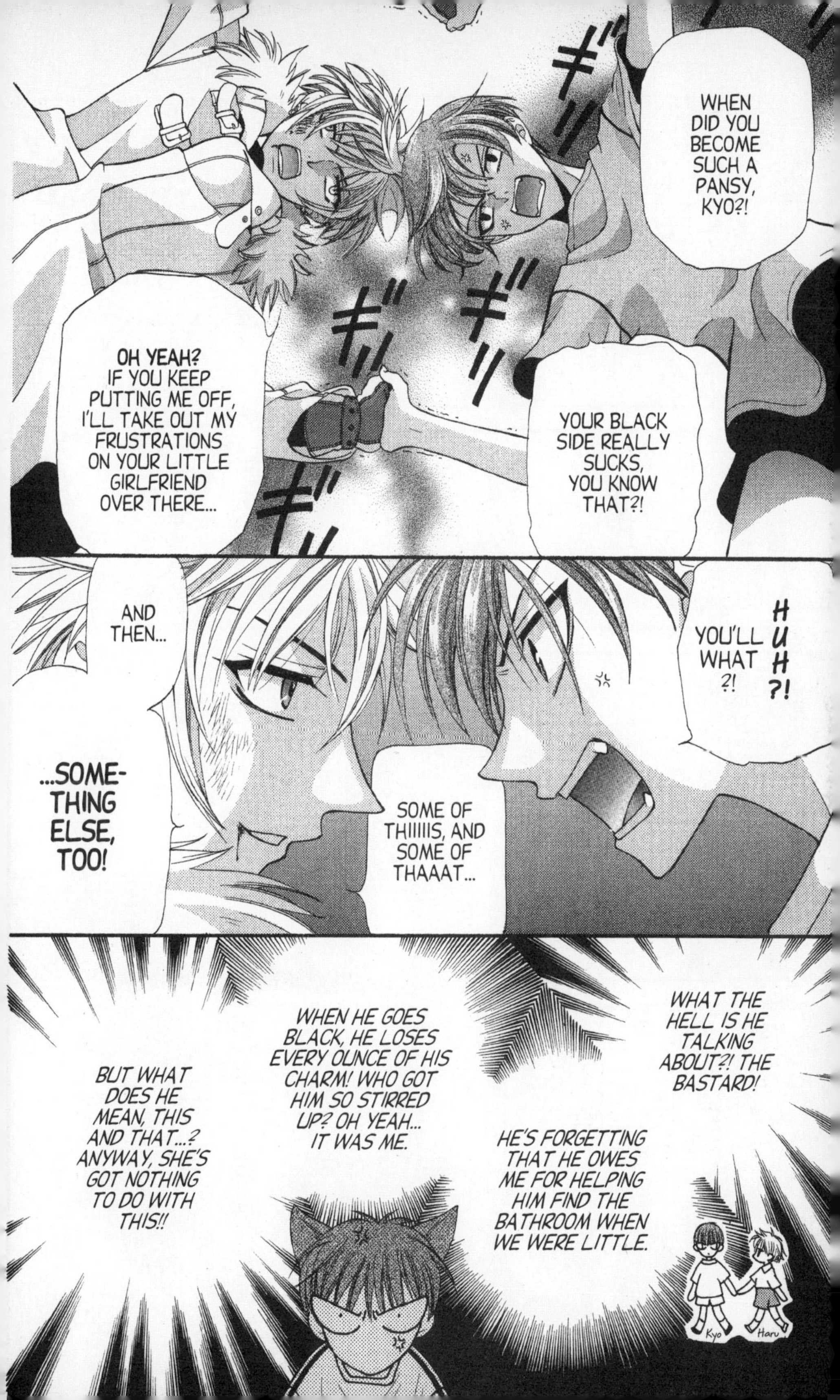
WHEN DID YOU BECOME SUCH A PANSY, KYO?!
ギリ
YOUR BLACK SIDE REALLY SUCKS, YOU KNOW THAT?!
OH YEAH? IF YOU KEEP PUTTING ME OFF, I'LL TAKE OUT MY FRUSTRATIONS ON YOUR LITTLE GIRLFRIEND OVER THERE...
HUH?!
YOU'LL WHAT?!
SOME OF THIIIIIS, AND SOME OF THAAAT...
AND THEN...
...SOME-THING ELSE, TOO!
WHAT THE HELL IS HE TALKING ABOUT?! THE BASTARD!
HE'S FORGETTING THAT HE OWES ME FOR HELPING HIM FIND THE BATHROOM WHEN WE WERE LITTLE.
Kyo
Haru
WHEN HE GOES BLACK, HE LOSES EVERY OUNCE OF HIS CHARM! WHO GOT HIM SO STIRRED UP? OH YEAH... IT WAS ME.
BUT WHAT DOES HE MEAN, THIS AND THAT...? ANYWAY, SHE'S GOT NOTHING TO DO WITH THIS!!

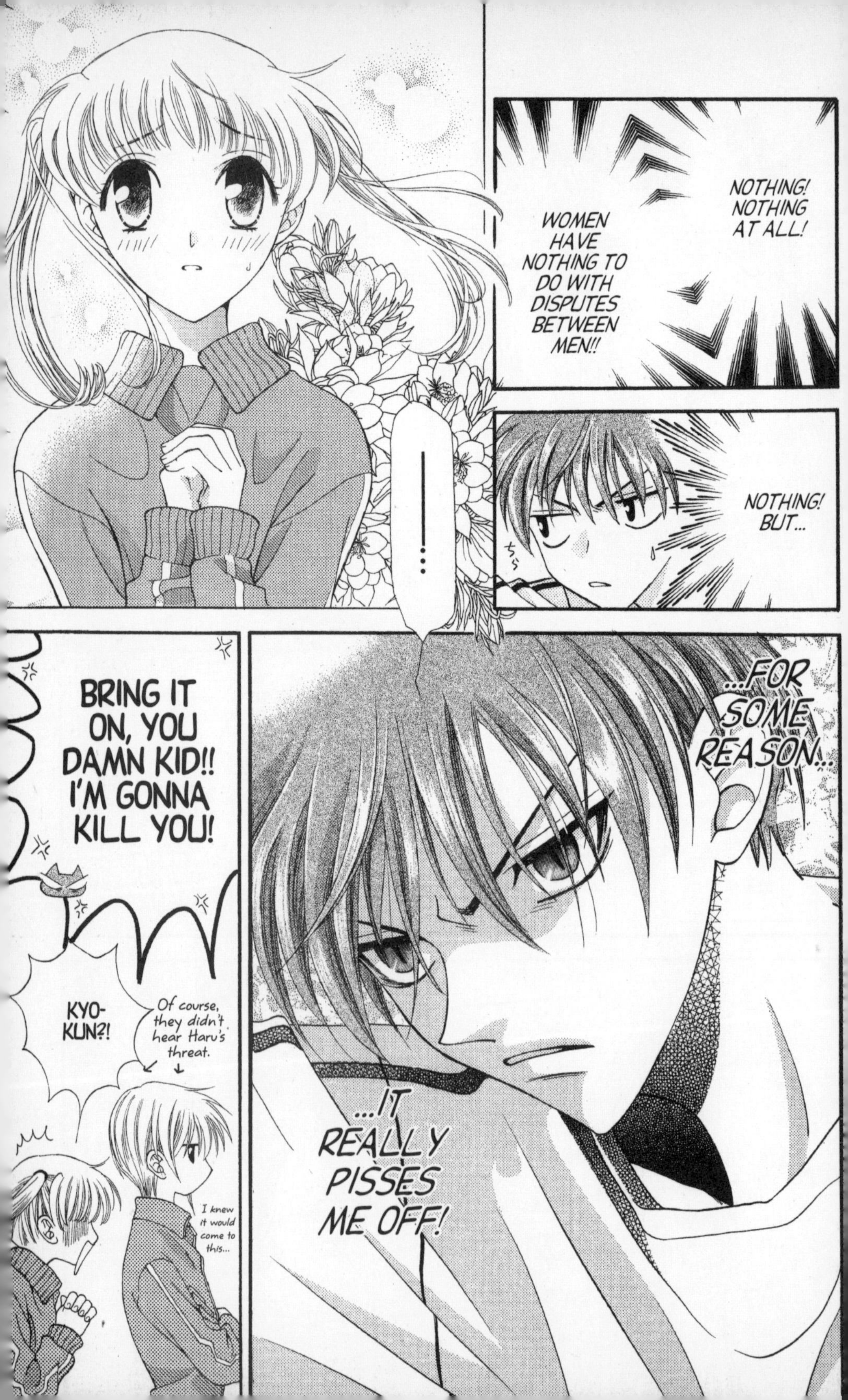
NOTHING! NOTHING AT ALL!
WOMEN HAVE NOTHING TO DO WITH DISPUTES BETWEEN MEN!!
NOTHING! BUT...
......
...FOR SOME REASON...
...IT REALLY PISSES ME OFF!
BRING IT ON, YOU DAMN KID!! I'M GONNA KILL YOU!
Of course, they didn't hear Haru's threat.
KYO-KUN?!
I knew it would come to this...

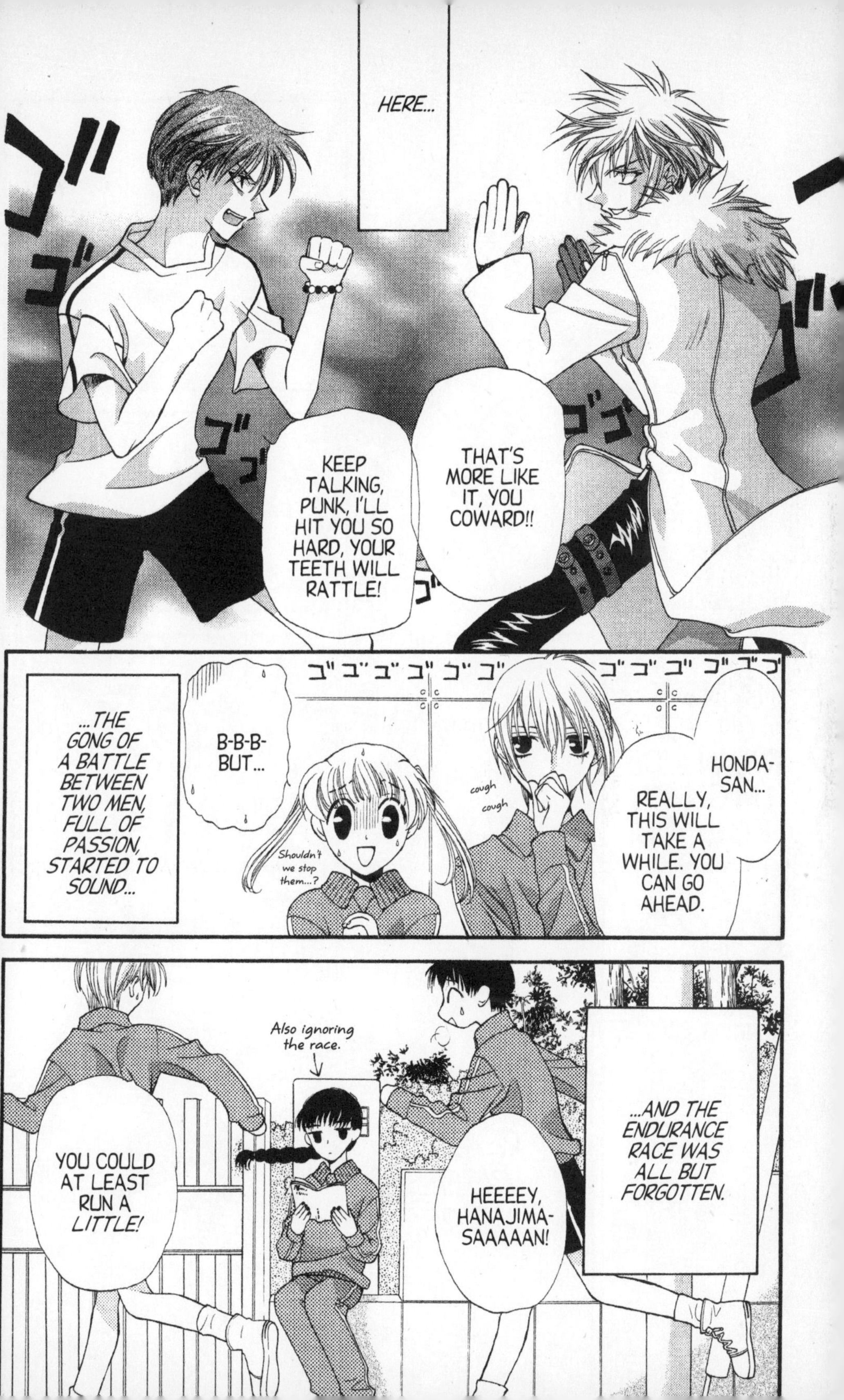
HERE...
ゴゴ
ゴゴ
THAT'S MORE LIKE IT, YOU COWARD!!
KEEP TALKING, PUNK, I'LL HIT YOU SO HARD, YOUR TEETH WILL RATTLE!
ゴゴゴゴゴ
ゴゴゴゴゴゴ
HONDA-SAN... REALLY, THIS WILL TAKE A WHILE. YOU CAN GO AHEAD.
cough cough
Shouldn't we stop them...?
B-B-B-BUT...
...THE GONG OF A BATTLE BETWEEN TWO MEN, FULL OF PASSION, STARTED TO SOUND...
...AND THE ENDURANCE RACE WAS ALL BUT FORGOTTEN.
HEEEEY, HANAJIMA-SAAAAAN!
Also ignoring the race.
YOU COULD AT LEAST RUN A LITTLE!

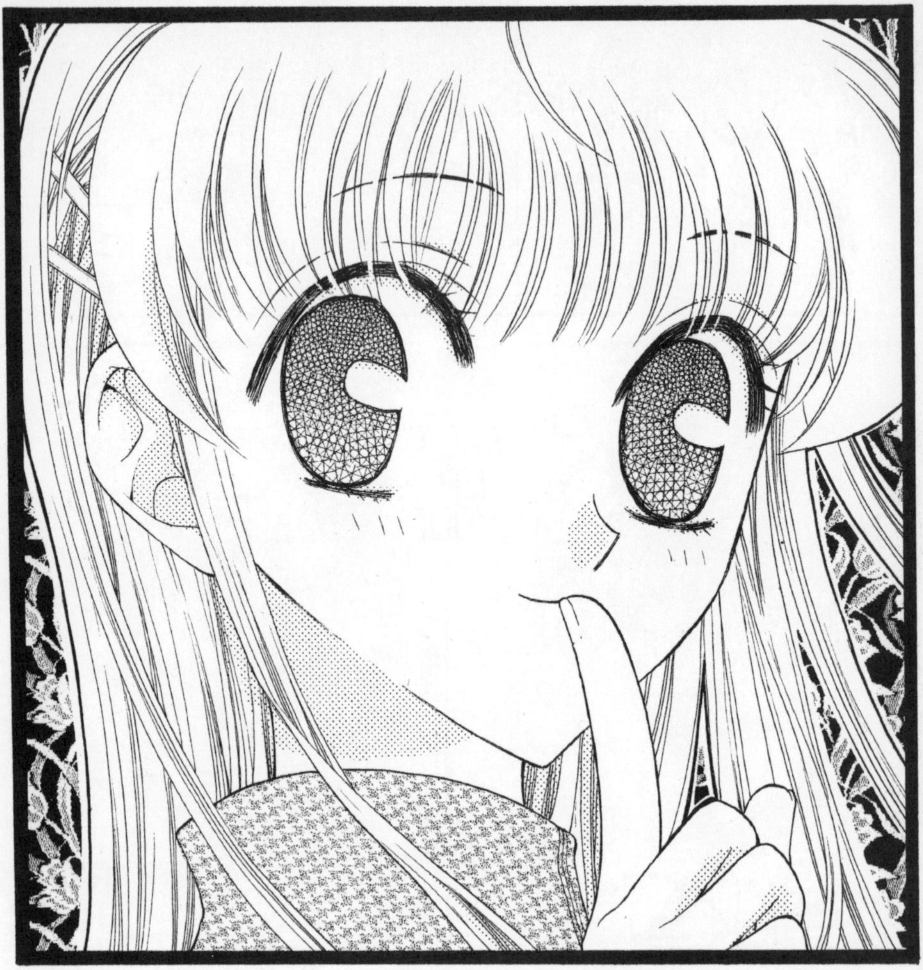

Chapter 14

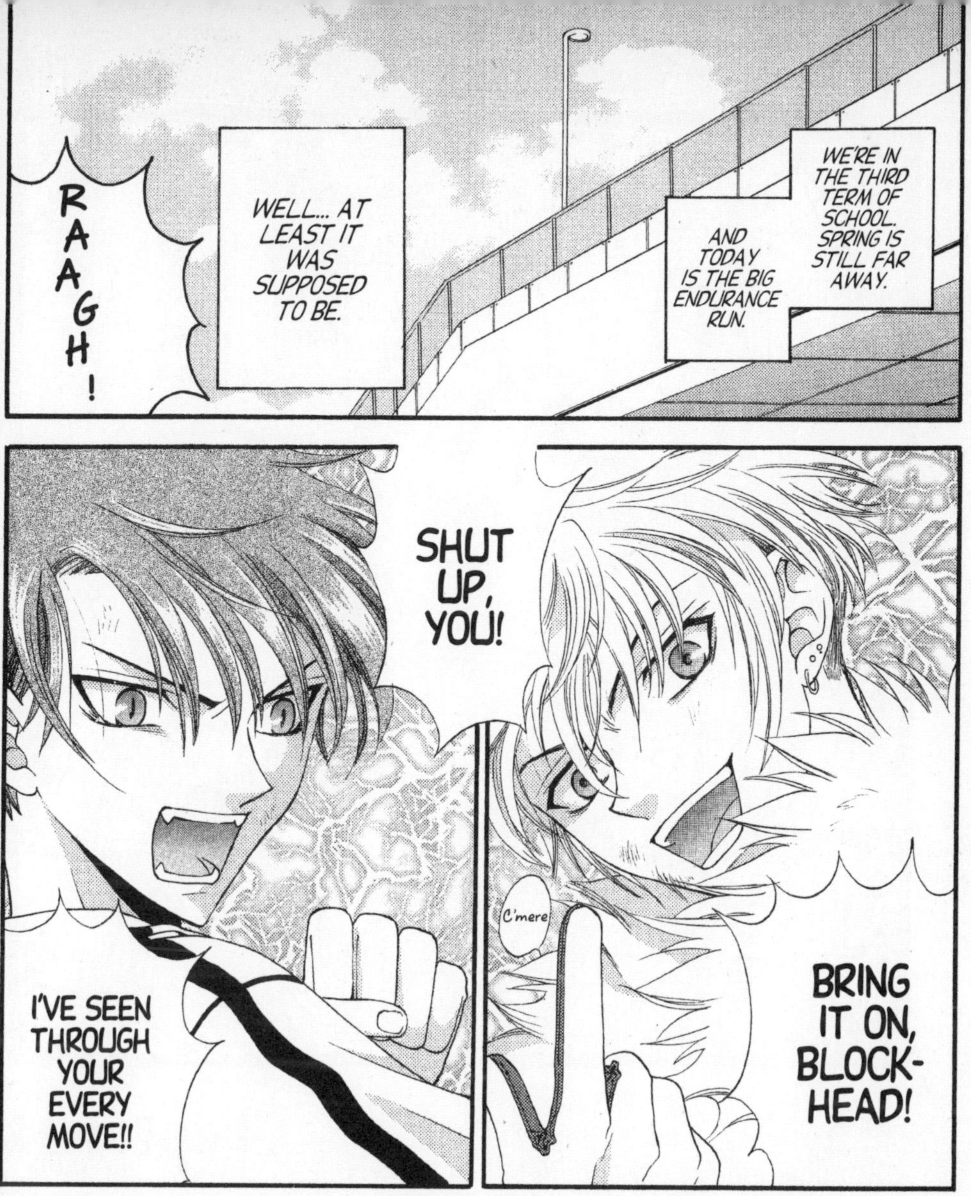
WE'RE IN THE THIRD TERM OF SCHOOL. SPRING IS STILL FAR AWAY.
AND TODAY IS THE BIG ENDURANCE RUN.
WELL... AT LEAST IT WAS SUPPOSED TO BE.
RAAGH!
SHUT UP, YOU!
C'mere
BRING IT ON, BLOCK-HEAD!
I'VE SEEN THROUGH YOUR EVERY MOVE!!

ULTRA SPECIAL BLAH BLAH BLAH 2

There were a lot of typos in this issue first time around...I got a lot of letters saying, "This line of dialogue is weird!" Of course it's weird--it's a typo! Oh well. We're human, we make mistakes. Let's be more tolerant. As it happens, I'm really bad at catching typos. (But I think I caught them all this time!)

*These words come from Takaya-sensei, but they apply to the editor as well!

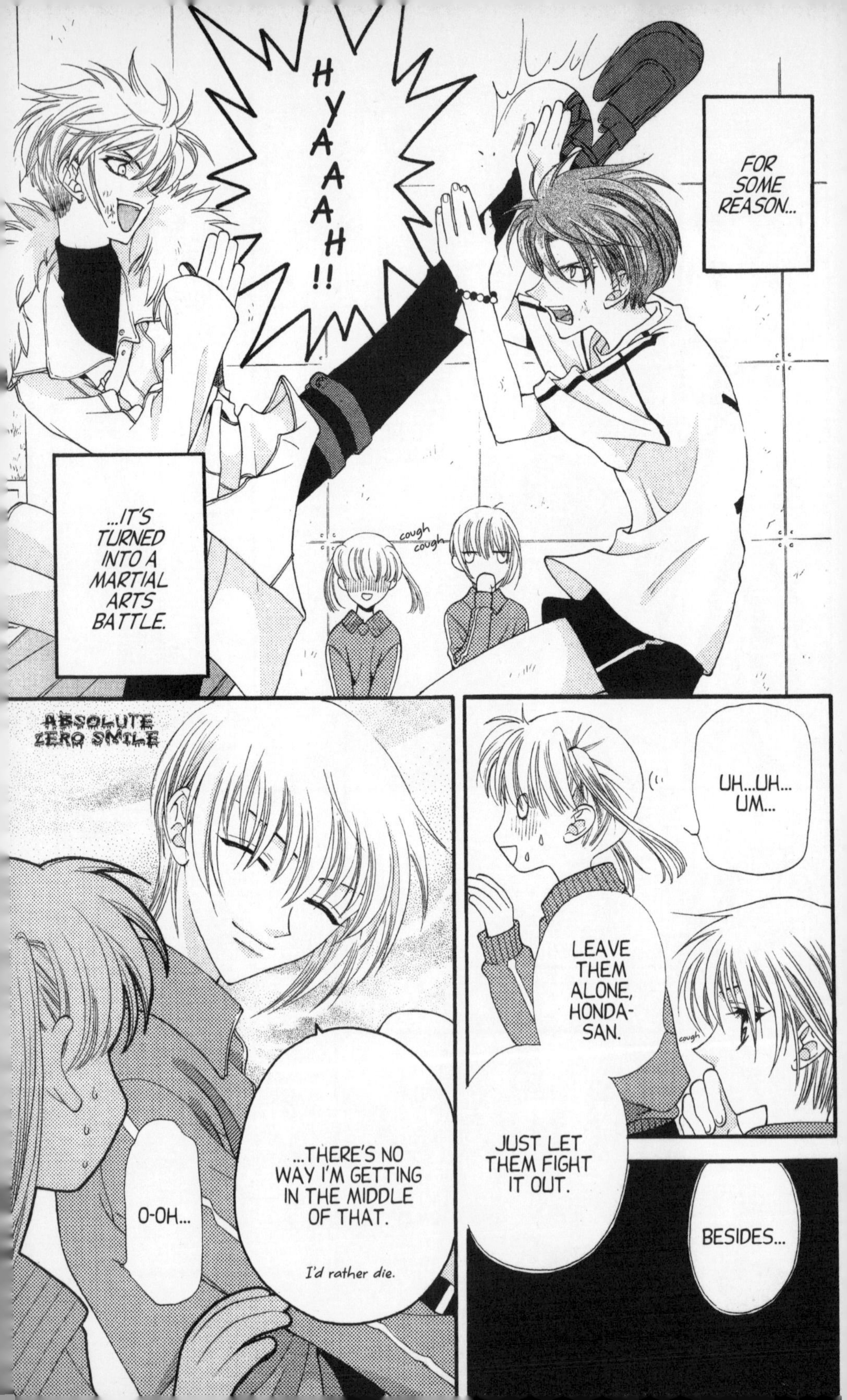
FOR SOME REASON...
HYAAAH!!
...IT'S TURNED INTO A MARTIAL ARTS BATTLE.
cough cough
UH...UH... UM...
LEAVE THEM ALONE, HONDA-SAN.
cough
JUST LET THEM FIGHT IT OUT.
BESIDES...
ABSOLUTE ZERO SMILE
...THERE'S NO WAY I'M GETTING IN THE MIDDLE OF THAT.
I'd rather die.
O-OH...

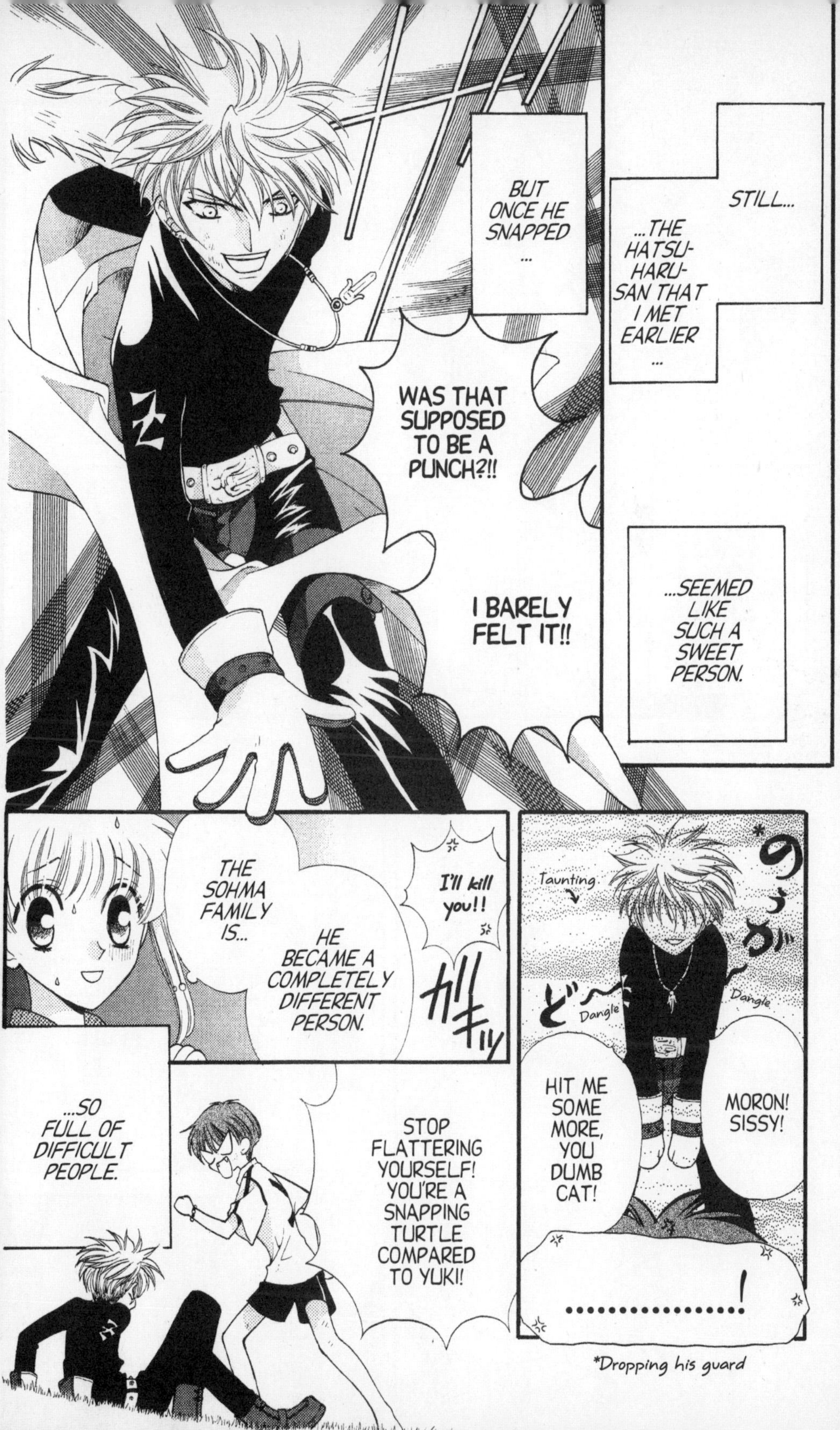
STILL...
...THE HATSUHARU-SAN THAT I MET EARLIER ...
BUT ONCE HE SNAPPED ...
WAS THAT SUPPOSED TO BE A PUNCH?!!
...SEEMED LIKE SUCH A SWEET PERSON.
I BARELY FELT IT!!
Taunting
Dangle
ど～
Dangle
MORON! SISSY!
HIT ME SOME MORE, YOU DUMB CAT!
...............!
*Dropping his guard
I'll kill you!!
ガキッ
HE BECAME A COMPLETELY DIFFERENT PERSON.
THE SOHMA FAMILY IS...
STOP FLATTERING YOURSELF! YOU'RE A SNAPPING TURTLE COMPARED TO YUKI!
...SO FULL OF DIFFICULT PEOPLE.

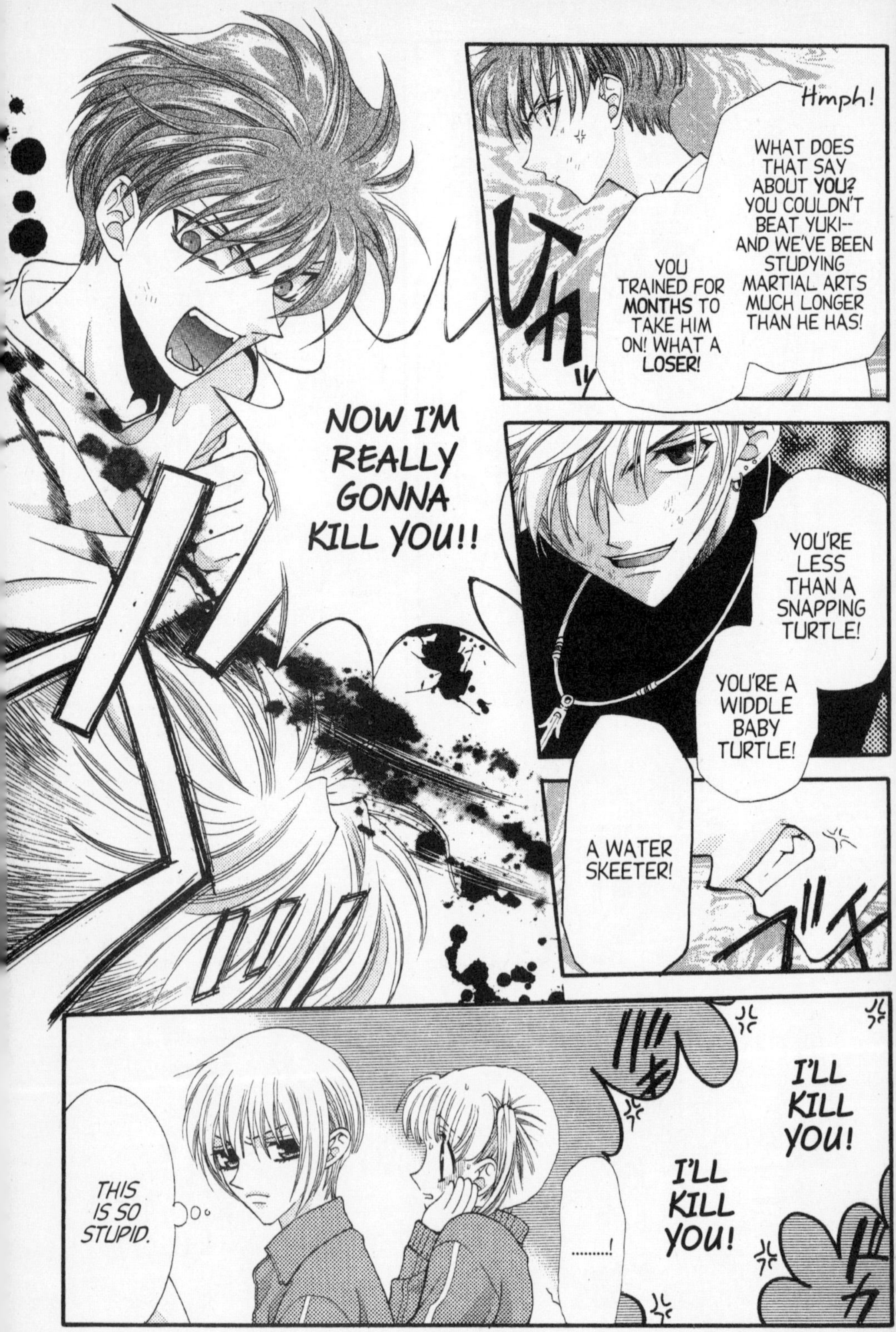
Hmph!
WHAT DOES THAT SAY ABOUT **YOU**? YOU COULDN'T BEAT YUKI-- AND WE'VE BEEN STUDYING MARTIAL ARTS MUCH LONGER THAN HE HAS!
YOU TRAINED FOR **MONTHS** TO TAKE HIM ON! WHAT A **LOSER**!
YOU'RE LESS THAN A SNAPPING TURTLE!
YOU'RE A WIDDLE BABY TURTLE!
A WATER SKEETER!
NOW I'M REALLY GONNA KILL YOU!!
I'LL KILL YOU!
I'LL KILL YOU!
..........!
THIS IS SO STUPID.

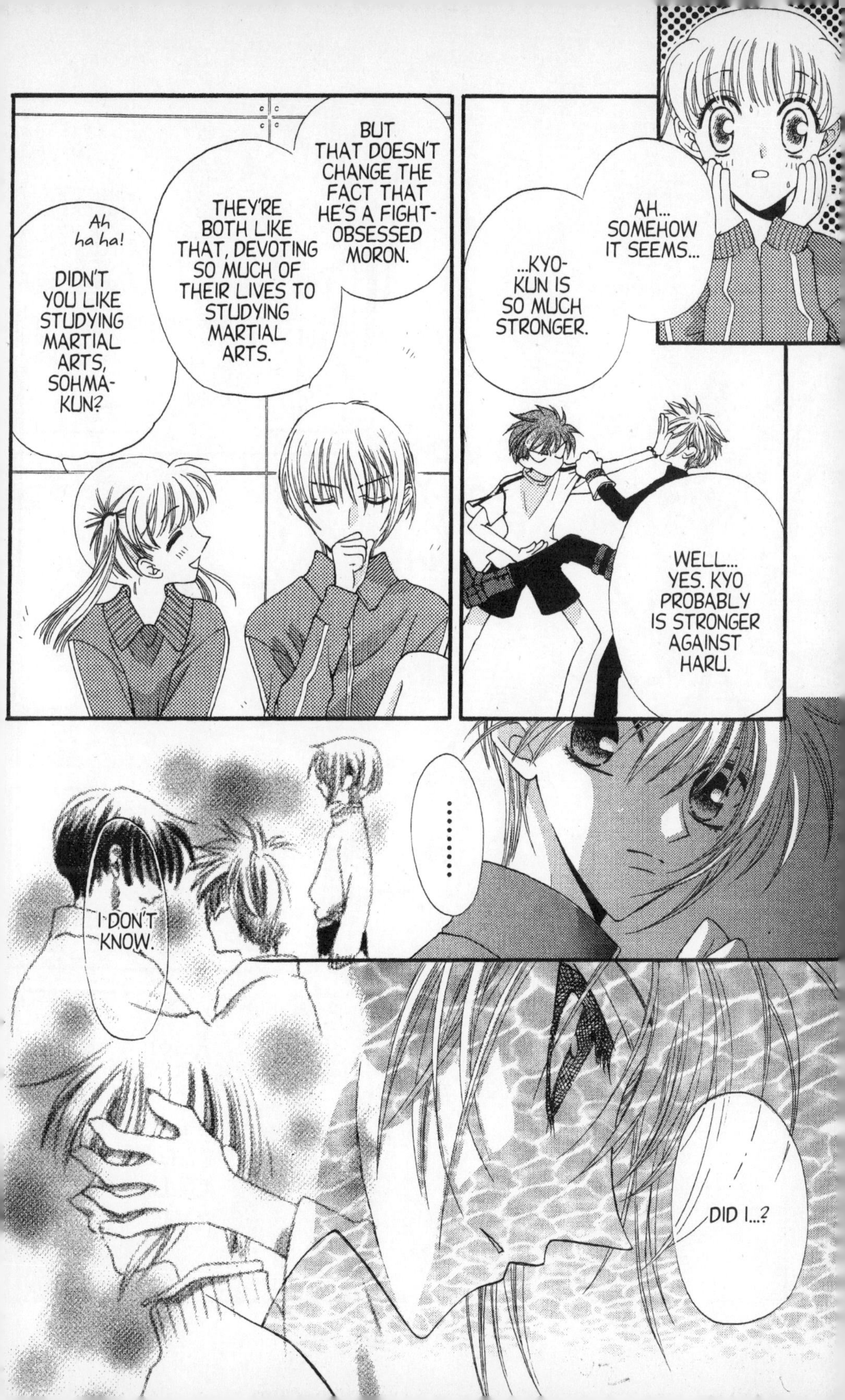

AH... SOMEHOW IT SEEMS...
...KYO-KUN IS SO MUCH STRONGER.
WELL... YES. KYO PROBABLY IS STRONGER AGAINST HARU.
THEY'RE BOTH LIKE THAT, DEVOTING SO MUCH OF THEIR LIVES TO STUDYING MARTIAL ARTS.
BUT THAT DOESN'T CHANGE THE FACT THAT HE'S A FIGHT-OBSESSED MORON.
Ah ha ha!
DIDN'T YOU LIKE STUDYING MARTIAL ARTS, SOHMA-KUN?
....
I DON'T KNOW.
DID I...?

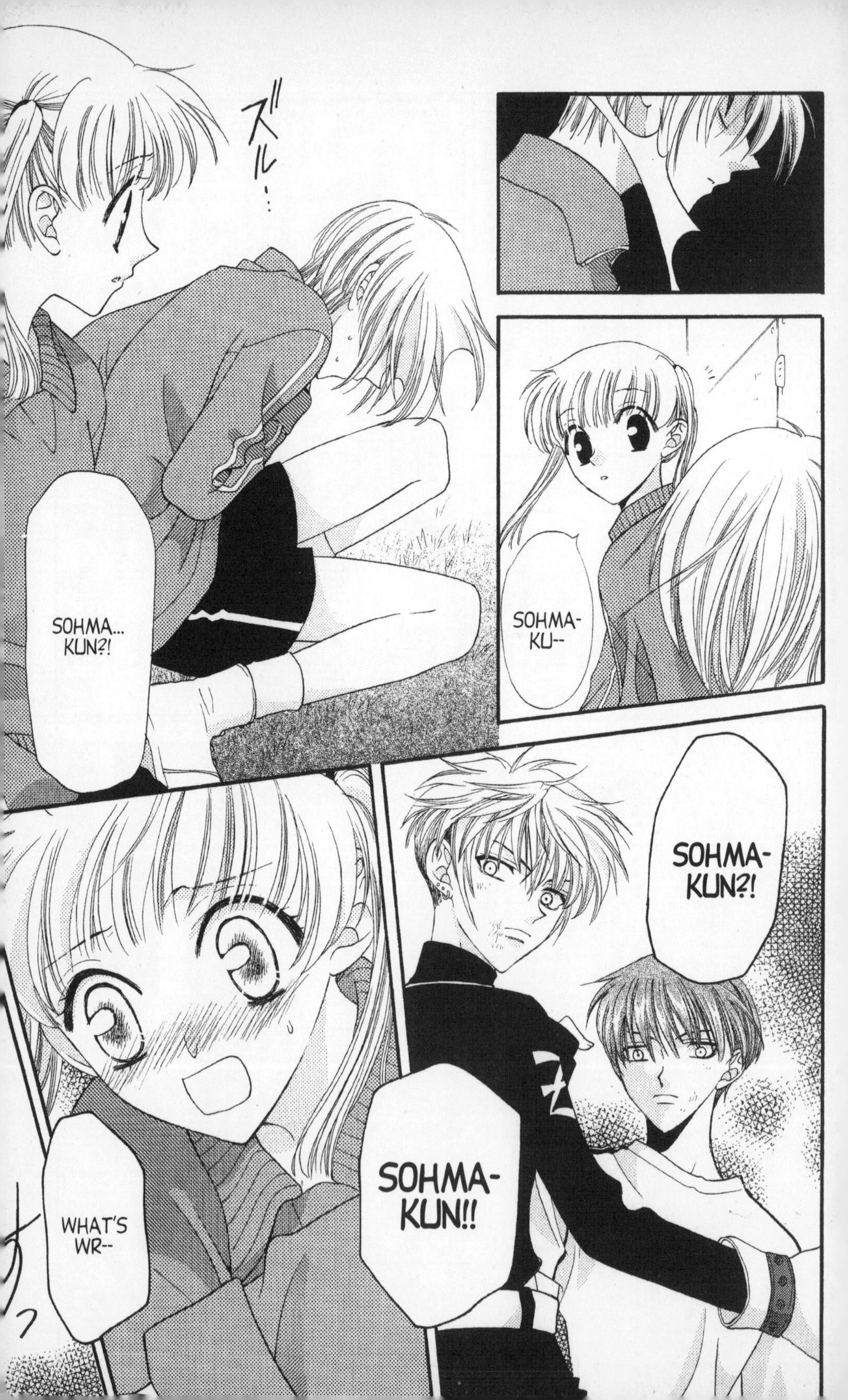
SOHMA-
KU--
ズル‥
SOHMA...
KUN?!
SOHMA-
KUN?!
SOHMA-
KUN!!
WHAT'S
WR--
すっ

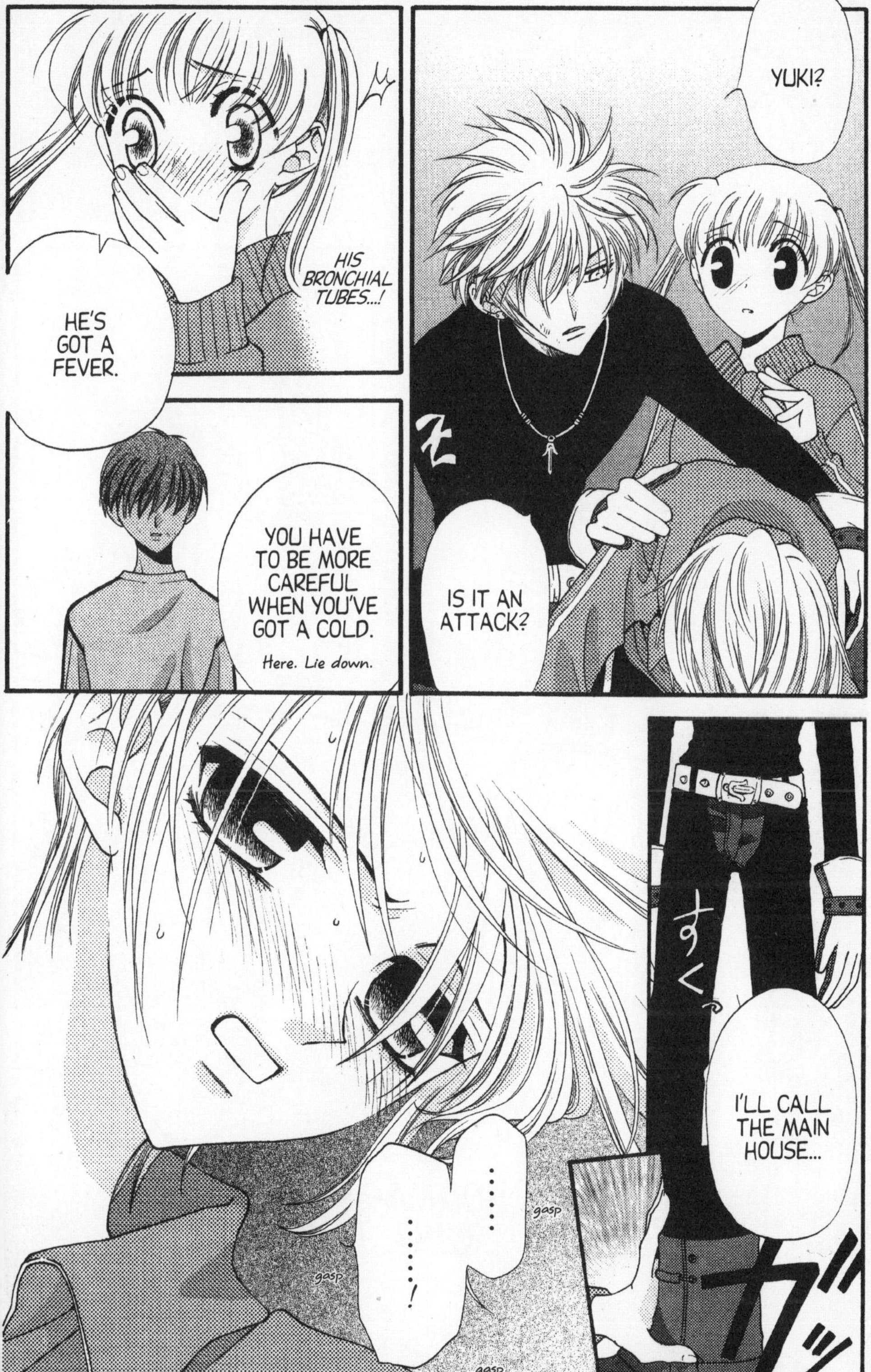
YUKI?
IS IT AN ATTACK?
HIS BRONCHIAL TUBES...!
HE'S GOT A FEVER.
YOU HAVE TO BE MORE CAREFUL WHEN YOU'VE GOT A COLD.
Here. Lie down.
すく
I'LL CALL THE MAIN HOUSE...
ガッ
......
......!
gasp
gasp
gasp

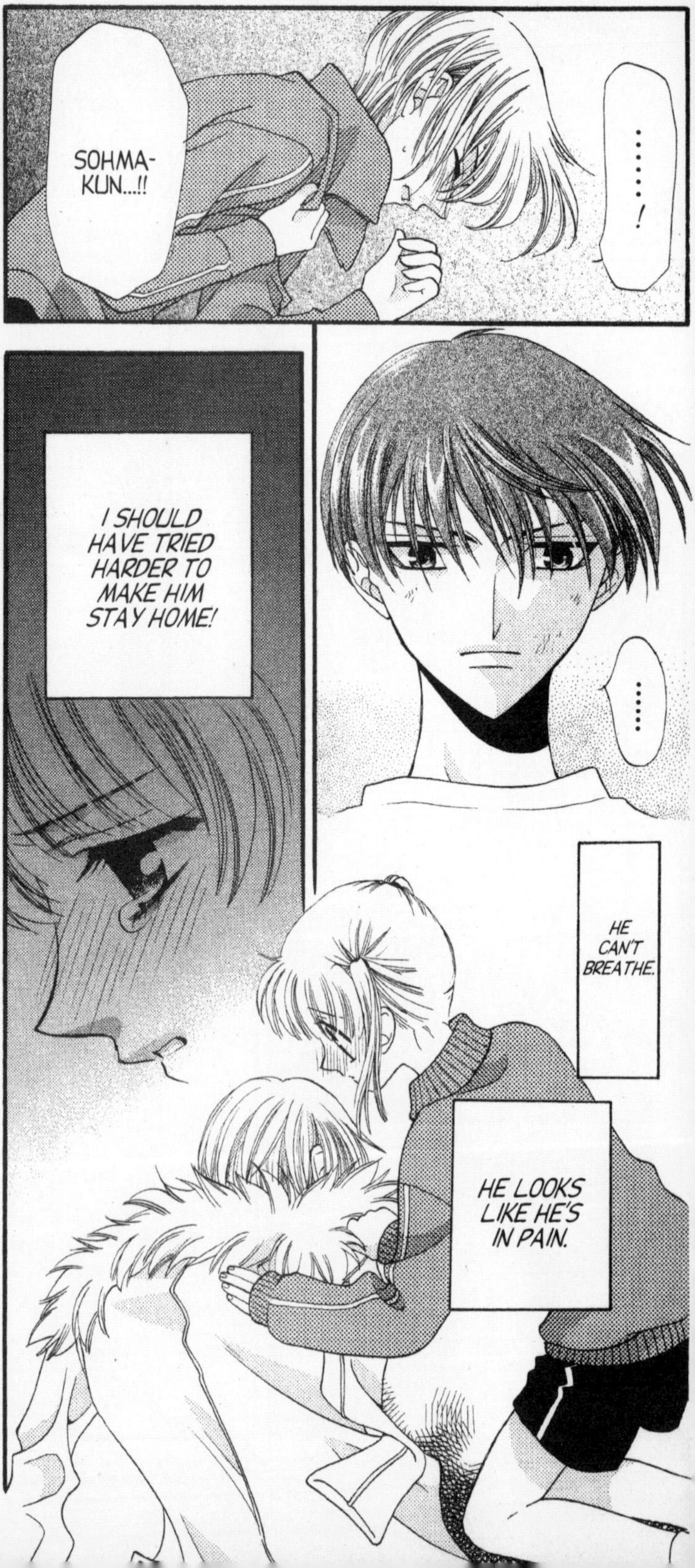
......!
SOHMA-KUN...!!
......
HE CAN'T BREATHE.
HE LOOKS LIKE HE'S IN PAIN.
I SHOULD HAVE TRIED HARDER TO MAKE HIM STAY HOME!

Fruits Basket 3 Part 2:

I got to meet my idol, Banri♪ Hidaka-sensei! Isn't that great? Aren't you jealous?! Eh heh heeehh...♪ (Someday someone's gonna smack you.) There was a thing, and we were both invited, and I met her there. (I met other authors there, too, but I didn't get permission to write about them, so I can't tell you who they were.) Well, anyway-- I haven't met many other Hana-Yume authors, so it was very exciting! Maybe I haven't met them because I don't go anywhere...like New Year's parties... (This year I had the flu and thought it would be bad to go to a party and give it to everyone else.) Hidaka-sensei was very much like the manga she writes.

To be continued...

*Hidaka-sensei is the manga ka of SEKAI DE ICHIBAN DAIKIRAI.

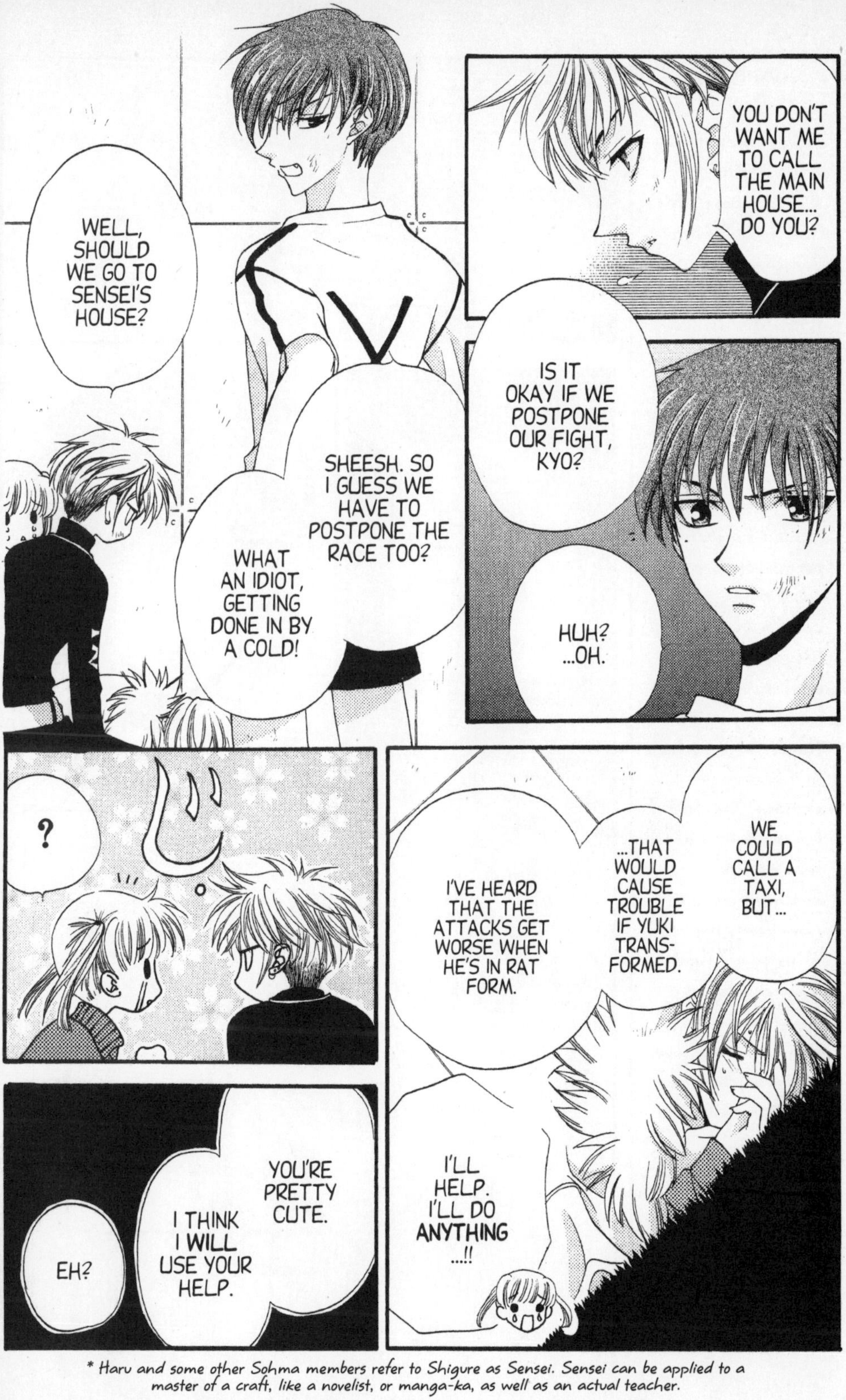
YOU DON'T WANT ME TO CALL THE MAIN HOUSE... DO YOU?
IS IT OKAY IF WE POSTPONE OUR FIGHT, KYO?
HUH? ...OH.
WELL, SHOULD WE GO TO SENSEI'S HOUSE?
SHEESH. SO I GUESS WE HAVE TO POSTPONE THE RACE TOO?
WHAT AN IDIOT, GETTING DONE IN BY A COLD!
WE COULD CALL A TAXI, BUT...
...THAT WOULD CAUSE TROUBLE IF YUKI TRANS-FORMED.
I'VE HEARD THAT THE ATTACKS GET WORSE WHEN HE'S IN RAT FORM.
I'LL HELP. I'LL DO **ANYTHING** ...!!
?
YOU'RE PRETTY CUTE.
I THINK I **WILL** USE YOUR HELP.
EH?

* Haru and some other Sohma members refer to Shigure as Sensei. Sensei can be applied to a master of a craft, like a novelist, or manga-ka, as well as an actual teacher.

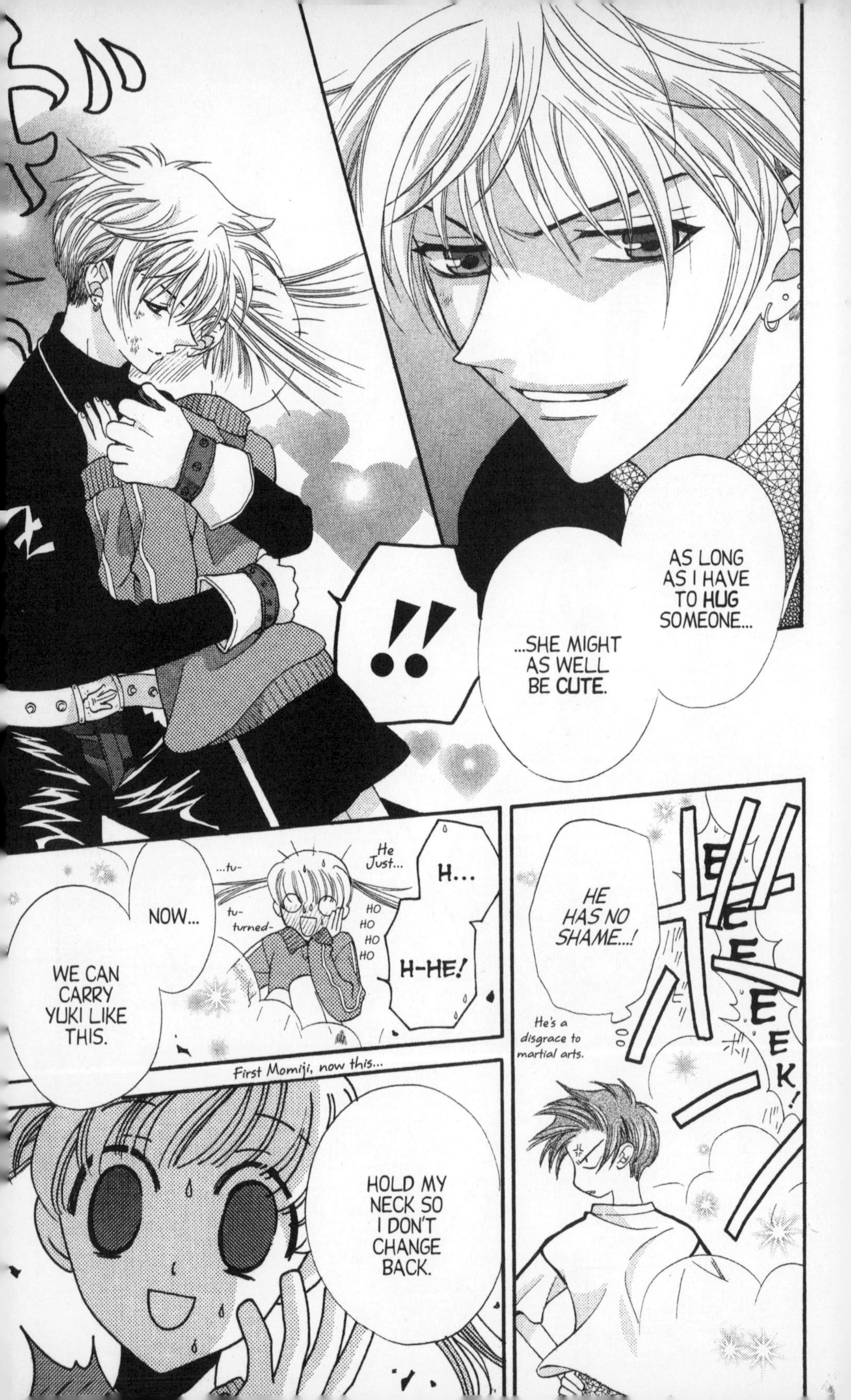
AS LONG AS I HAVE TO HUG SOMEONE...
...SHE MIGHT AS WELL BE CUTE.
!!
EEEEEK!
HE HAS NO SHAME...!
He's a disgrace to martial arts.
H...
H-HE!
He Just...
...tu-
tu-turned-
HO HO HO HO
NOW...
WE CAN CARRY YUKI LIKE THIS.
HOLD MY NECK SO I DON'T CHANGE BACK.
First Momiji, now this...

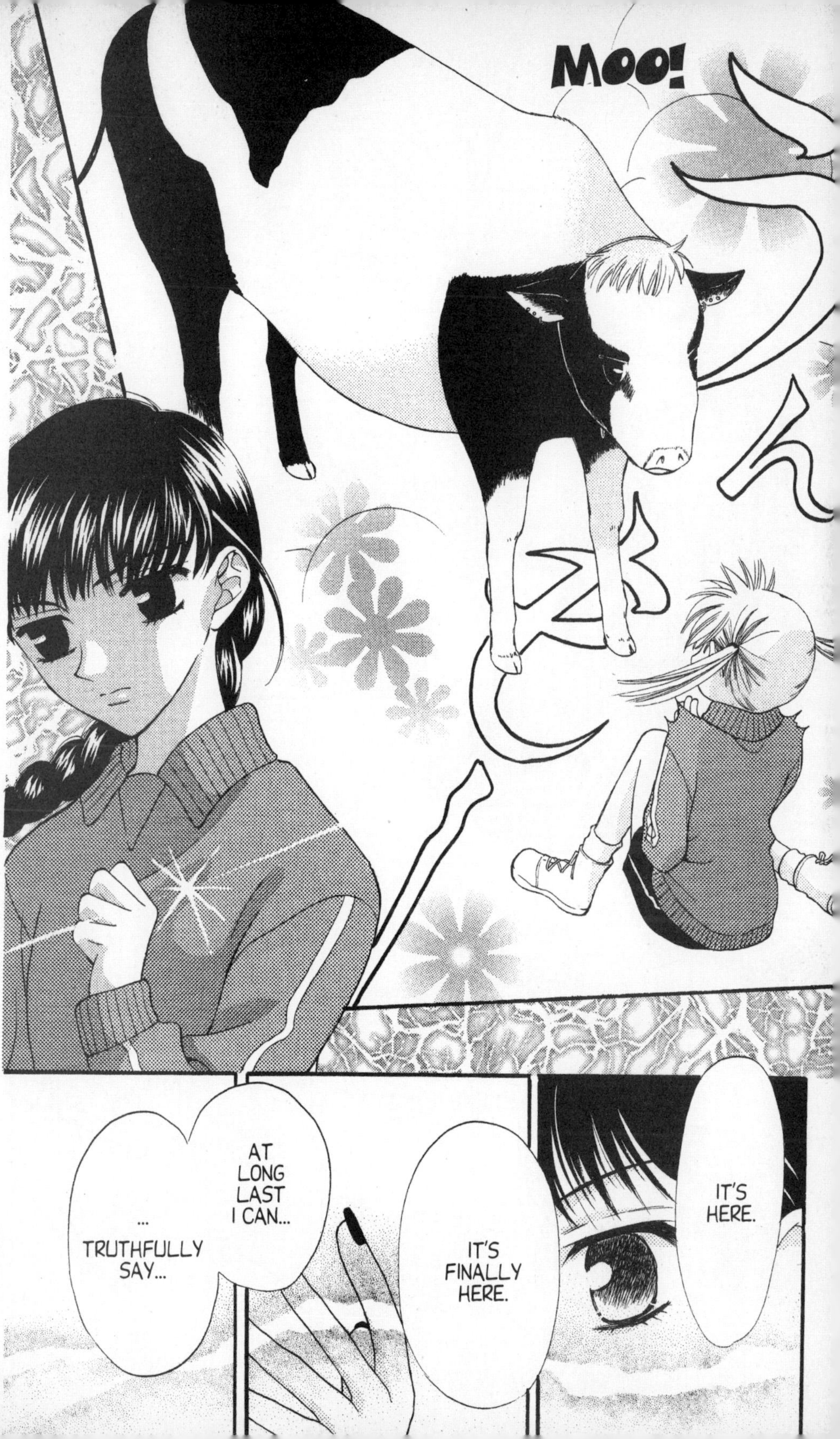
MOO!
IT'S HERE.
IT'S FINALLY HERE.
AT LONG LAST I CAN...
... TRUTHFULLY SAY...

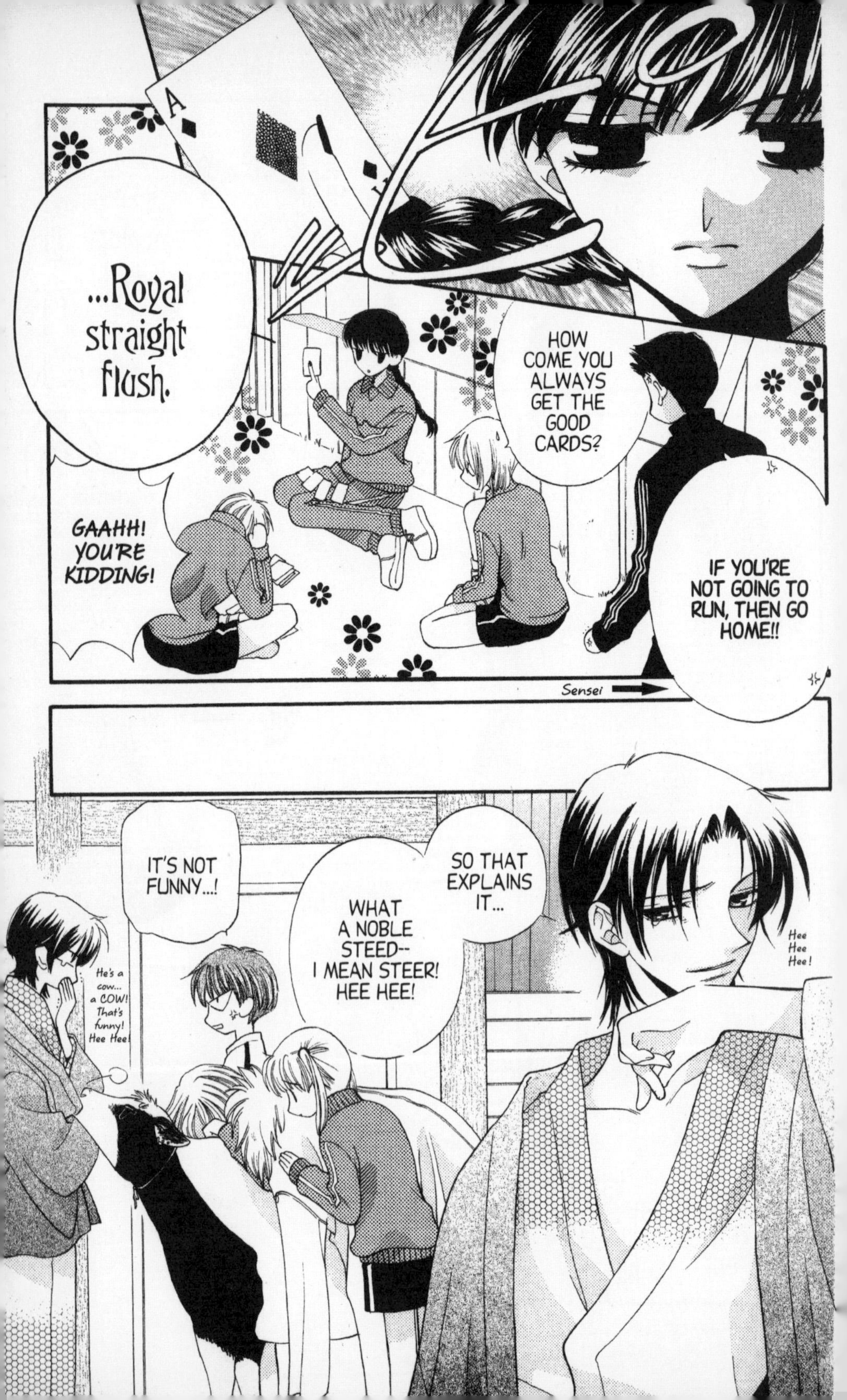
...Royal straight flush.
HOW COME YOU ALWAYS GET THE GOOD CARDS?
GAAHH! YOU'RE KIDDING!
IF YOU'RE NOT GOING TO RUN, THEN GO HOME!!
Sensei
Hee Hee Hee!
SO THAT EXPLAINS IT...
WHAT A NOBLE STEED-- I MEAN STEER! HEE HEE!
IT'S NOT FUNNY...!
He's a cow... a COW! That's funny! Hee Hee!

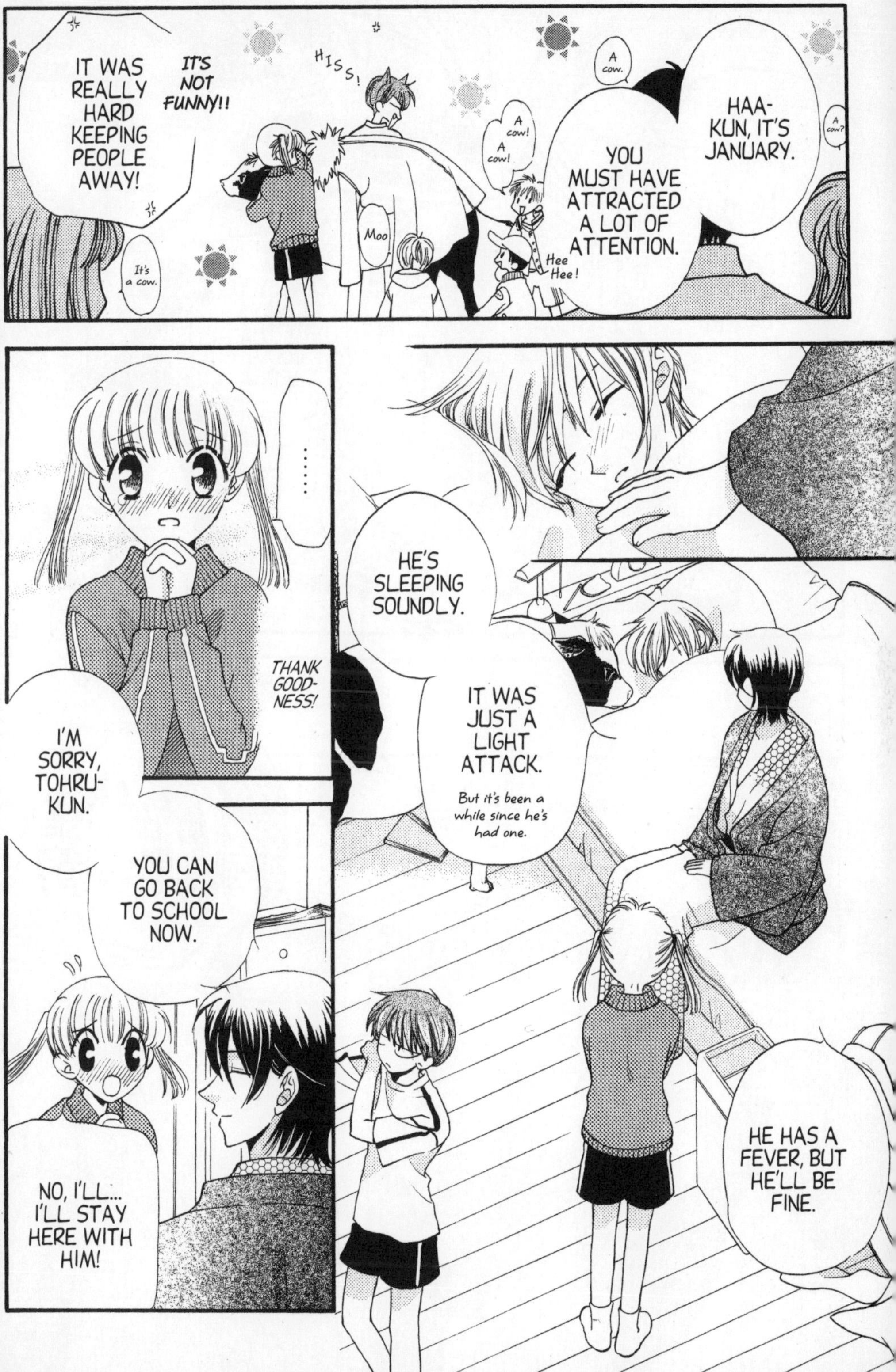
A cow?
HAA-KUN, IT'S JANUARY.
A cow.
YOU MUST HAVE ATTRACTED A LOT OF ATTENTION.
Hee Hee!
A cow! A cow!
Moo
HISS!
IT'S NOT FUNNY!!
IT WAS REALLY HARD KEEPING PEOPLE AWAY!
It's a cow.
HE'S SLEEPING SOUNDLY.
IT WAS JUST A LIGHT ATTACK.
But it's been a while since he's had one.
HE HAS A FEVER, BUT HE'LL BE FINE.
......
THANK GOODNESS!
I'M SORRY, TOHRU-KUN.
YOU CAN GO BACK TO SCHOOL NOW.
NO, I'LL... I'LL STAY HERE WITH HIM!

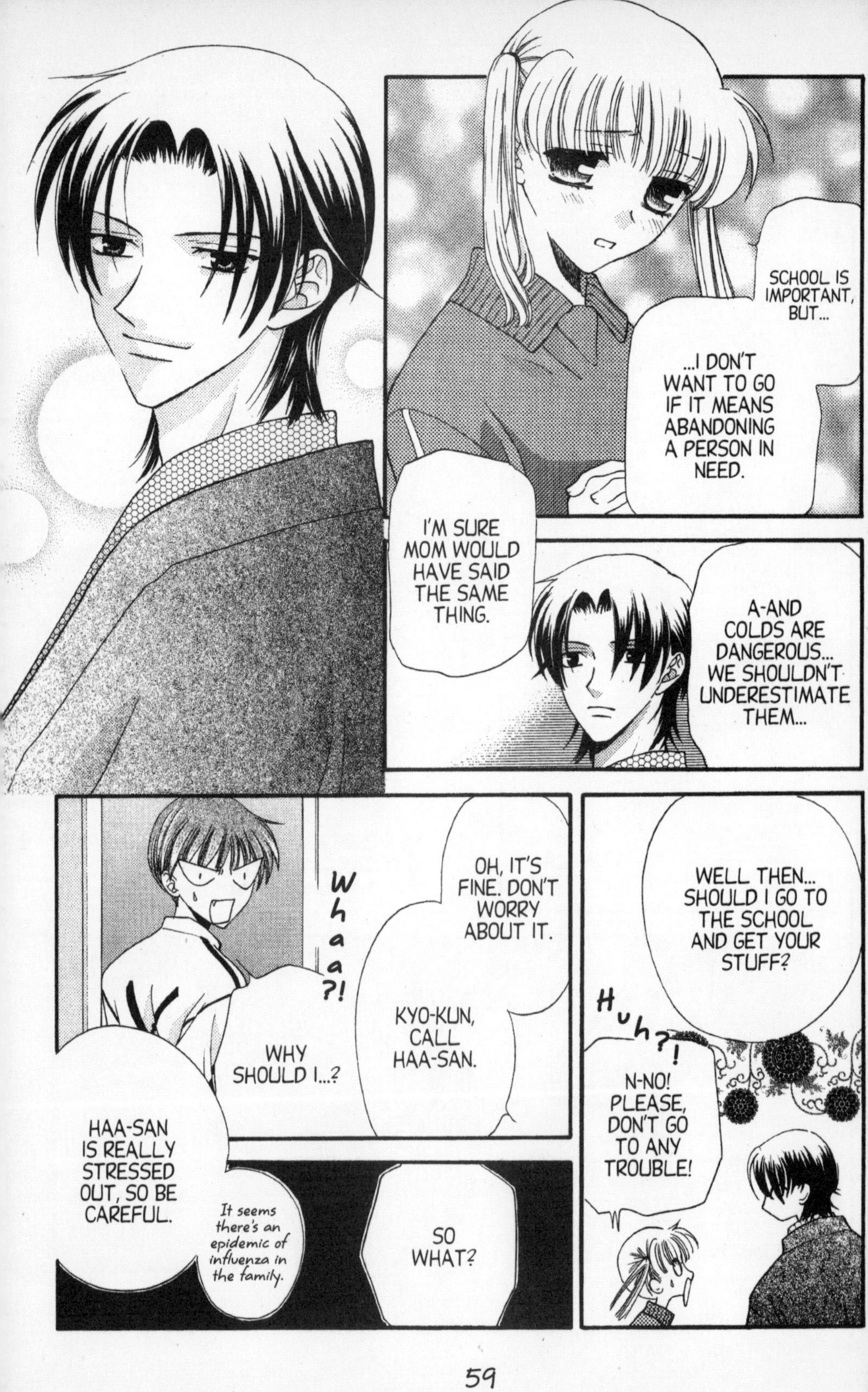
SCHOOL IS IMPORTANT, BUT...
...I DON'T WANT TO GO IF IT MEANS ABANDONING A PERSON IN NEED.
I'M SURE MOM WOULD HAVE SAID THE SAME THING.
A-AND COLDS ARE DANGEROUS... WE SHOULDN'T UNDERESTIMATE THEM...
WELL THEN... SHOULD I GO TO THE SCHOOL AND GET YOUR STUFF?
Huh?!
N-NO! PLEASE, DON'T GO TO ANY TROUBLE!
OH, IT'S FINE. DON'T WORRY ABOUT IT.
KYO-KUN, CALL HAA-SAN.
Whaaa?!
WHY SHOULD I...?
SO WHAT?
It seems there's an epidemic of influenza in the family.
HAA-SAN IS REALLY STRESSED OUT, SO BE CAREFUL.

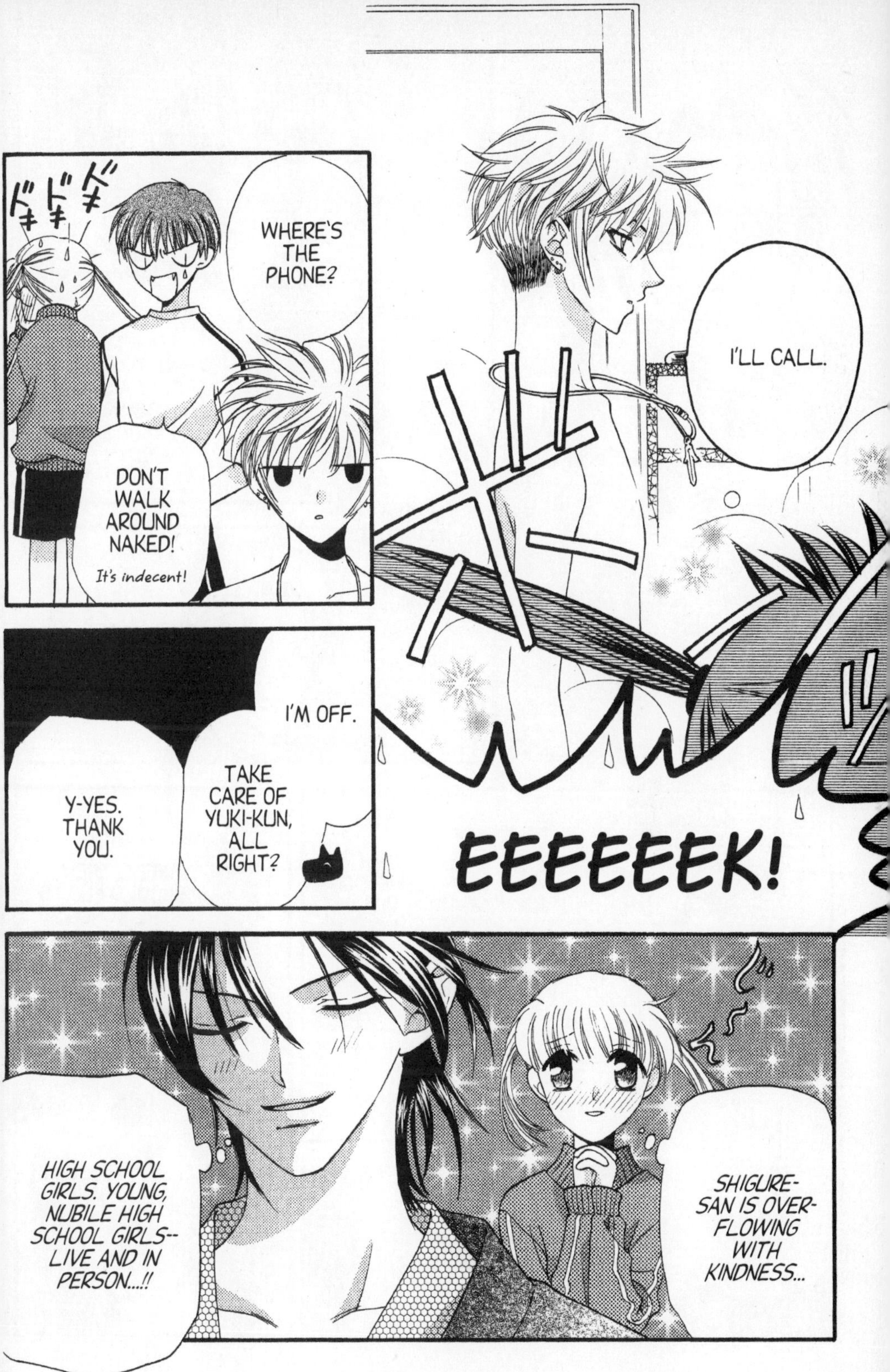
I'LL CALL.
EEEEEEEK!
ドキ ドキ ドキ
WHERE'S THE PHONE?
DON'T WALK AROUND NAKED!
It's indecent!
I'M OFF.
TAKE CARE OF YUKI-KUN, ALL RIGHT?
Y-YES. THANK YOU.
SHIGURE-SAN IS OVERFLOWING WITH KINDNESS...
HIGH SCHOOL GIRLS. YOUNG, NUBILE HIGH SCHOOL GIRLS--LIVE AND IN PERSON...!!

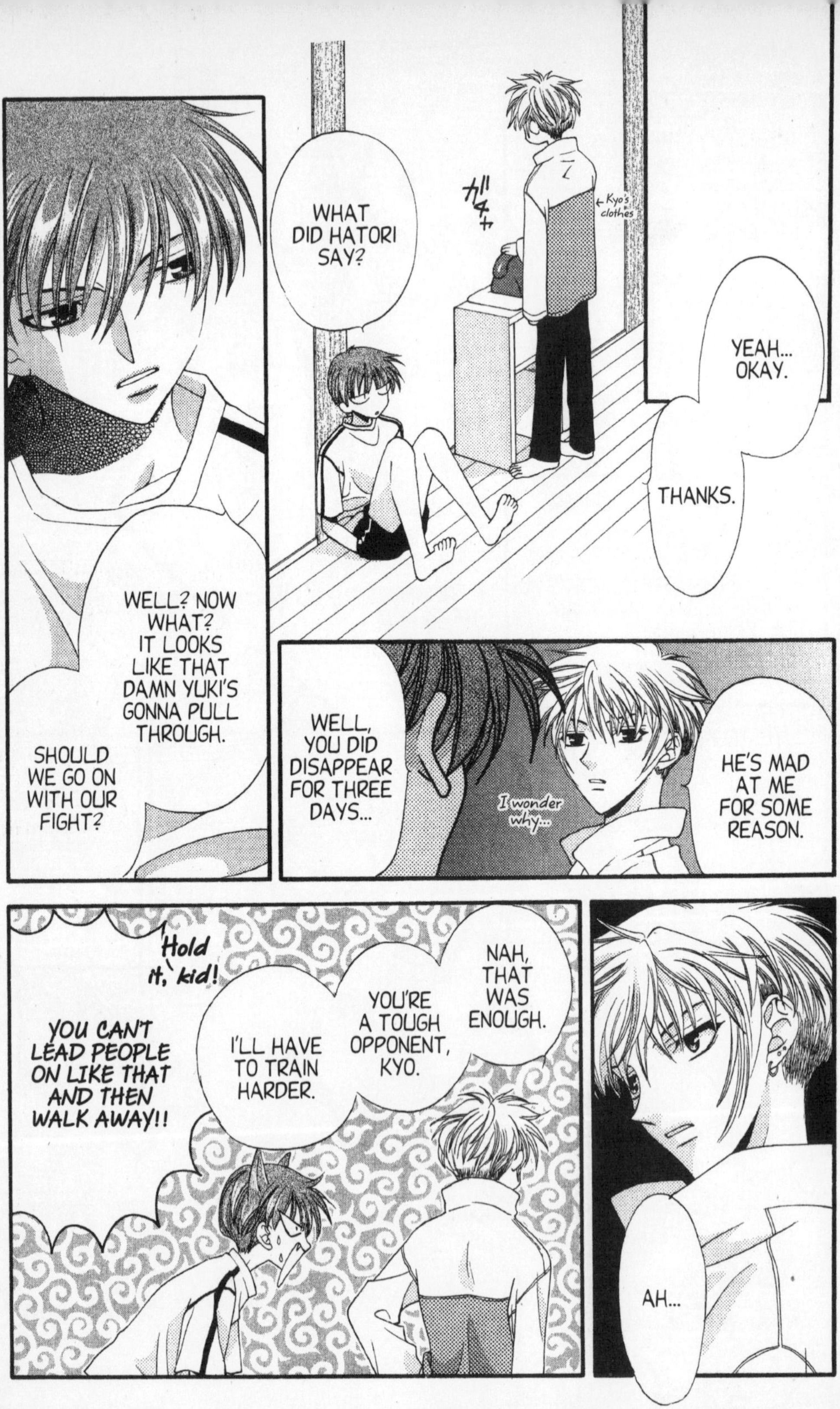

Kyo's clothes
YEAH... OKAY.
THANKS.
ガチャ
WHAT DID HATORI SAY?
HE'S MAD AT ME FOR SOME REASON.
I wonder why...
WELL, YOU DID DISAPPEAR FOR THREE DAYS...
WELL? NOW WHAT? IT LOOKS LIKE THAT DAMN YUKI'S GONNA PULL THROUGH.
SHOULD WE GO ON WITH OUR FIGHT?
AH...
NAH, THAT WAS ENOUGH.
YOU'RE A TOUGH OPPONENT, KYO.
I'LL HAVE TO TRAIN HARDER.
Hold it, kid!
YOU CAN'T LEAD PEOPLE ON LIKE THAT AND THEN WALK AWAY!!

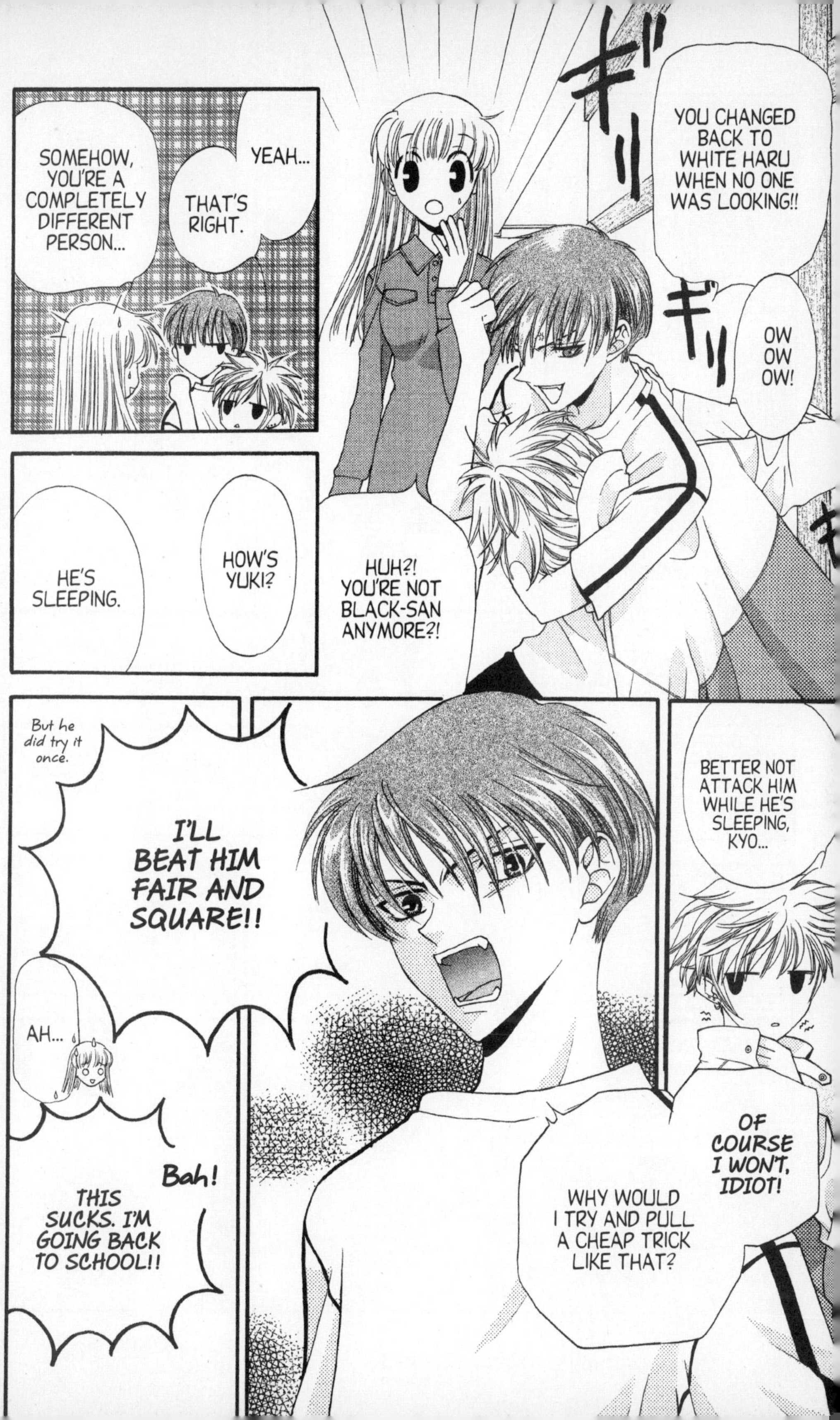
YOU CHANGED BACK TO WHITE HARU WHEN NO ONE WAS LOOKING!!
ギリ
ギリ
OW OW OW!
HUH?! YOU'RE NOT BLACK-SAN ANYMORE?!
YEAH...
THAT'S RIGHT.
SOMEHOW, YOU'RE A COMPLETELY DIFFERENT PERSON...
HOW'S YUKI?
HE'S SLEEPING.
BETTER NOT ATTACK HIM WHILE HE'S SLEEPING, KYO...
OF COURSE I WON'T, IDIOT!
WHY WOULD I TRY AND PULL A CHEAP TRICK LIKE THAT?
I'LL BEAT HIM FAIR AND SQUARE!!
But he did try it once.
AH...
Bah!
THIS SUCKS. I'M GOING BACK TO SCHOOL!!

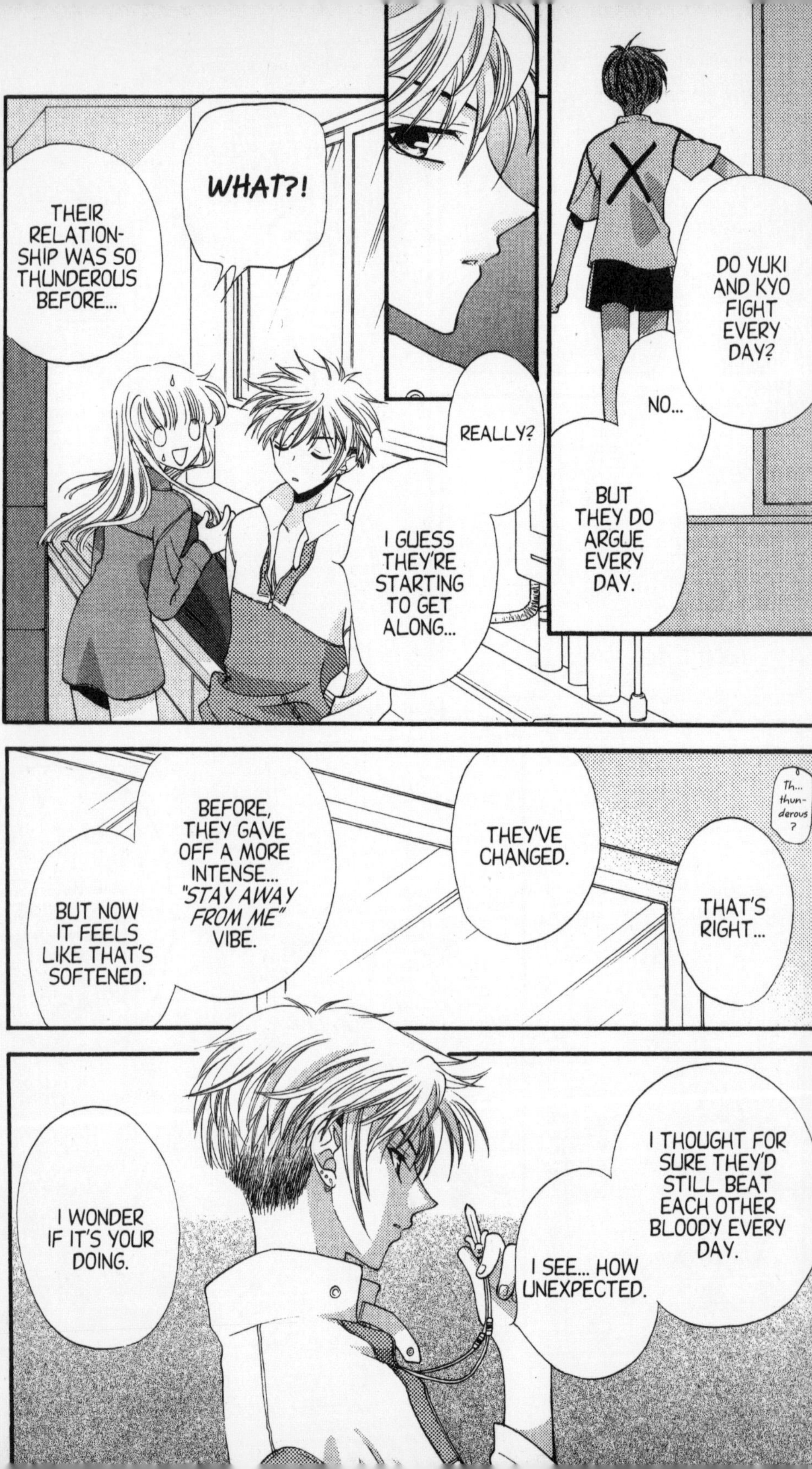
DO YUKI AND KYO FIGHT EVERY DAY?
NO...
BUT THEY DO ARGUE EVERY DAY.
REALLY?
I GUESS THEY'RE STARTING TO GET ALONG...
WHAT?!
THEIR RELATION-SHIP WAS SO THUNDEROUS BEFORE...
Th... thun-derous?
THAT'S RIGHT...
THEY'VE CHANGED.
BEFORE, THEY GAVE OFF A MORE INTENSE... *"STAY AWAY FROM ME"* VIBE.
BUT NOW IT FEELS LIKE THAT'S SOFTENED.
I THOUGHT FOR SURE THEY'D STILL BEAT EACH OTHER BLOODY EVERY DAY.
I SEE... HOW UNEXPECTED.
I WONDER IF IT'S YOUR DOING.

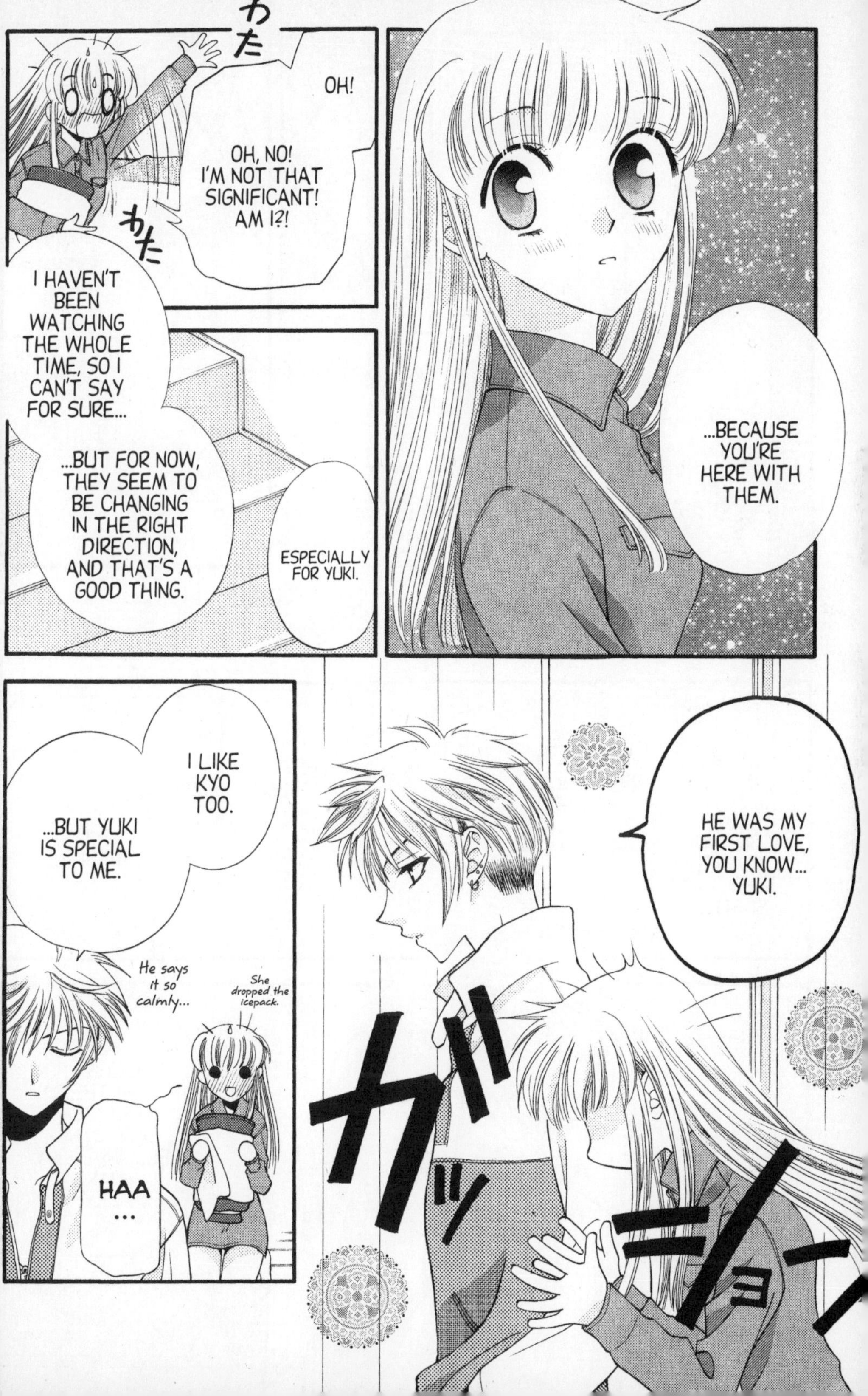
...BECAUSE YOU'RE HERE WITH THEM.
わた
OH!
OH, NO! I'M NOT THAT SIGNIFICANT! AM I?!
わた
I HAVEN'T BEEN WATCHING THE WHOLE TIME, SO I CAN'T SAY FOR SURE...
...BUT FOR NOW, THEY SEEM TO BE CHANGING IN THE RIGHT DIRECTION, AND THAT'S A GOOD THING.
ESPECIALLY FOR YUKI.
HE WAS MY FIRST LOVE, YOU KNOW... YUKI.
ガッ
I LIKE KYO TOO.
...BUT YUKI IS SPECIAL TO ME.
He says it so calmly...
She dropped the icepack.
HAA ...

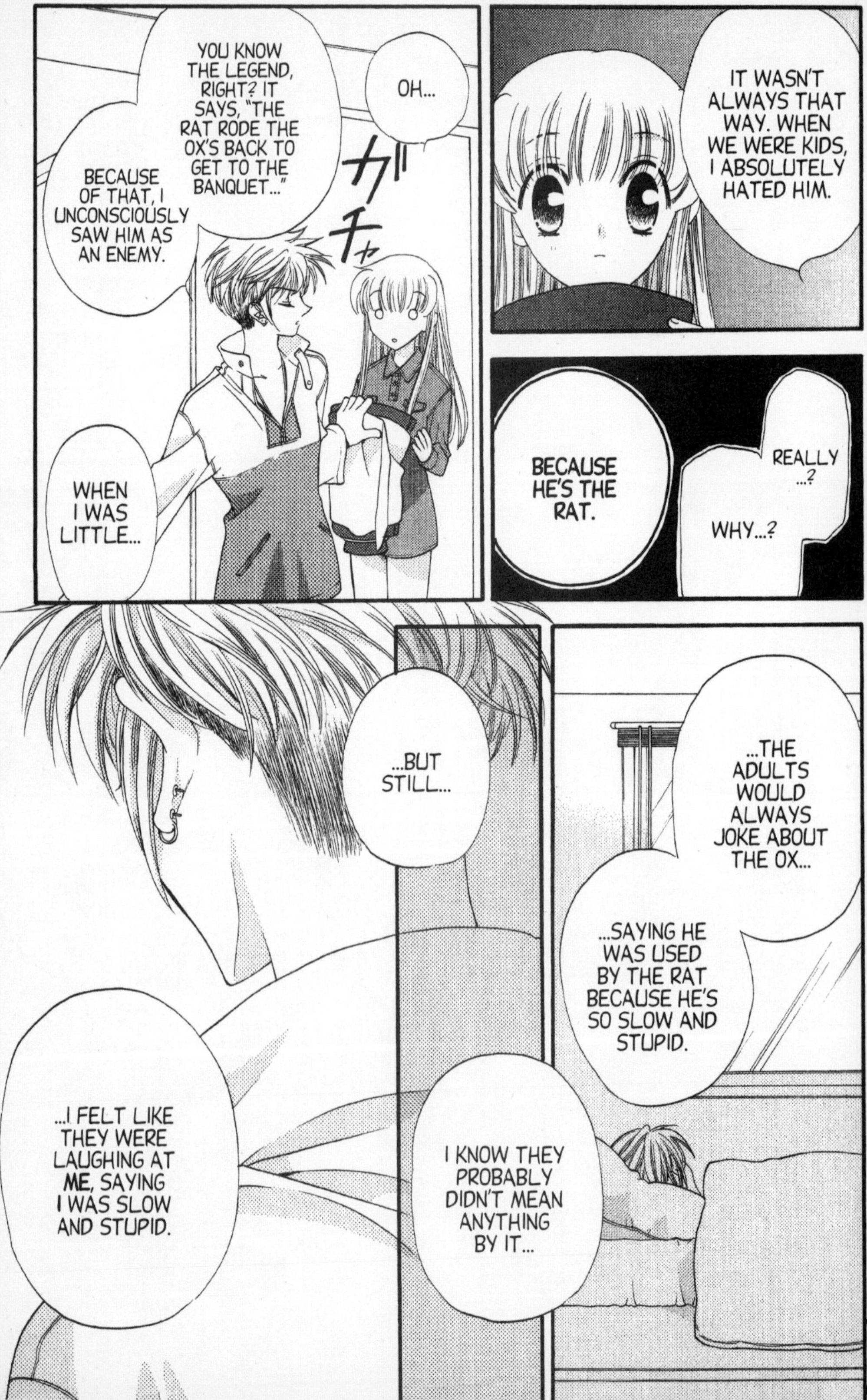

IT WASN'T ALWAYS THAT WAY. WHEN WE WERE KIDS, I ABSOLUTELY HATED HIM.
REALLY...? WHY...?
BECAUSE HE'S THE RAT.
OH...
ガチャ
YOU KNOW THE LEGEND, RIGHT? IT SAYS, "THE RAT RODE THE OX'S BACK TO GET TO THE BANQUET..."
BECAUSE OF THAT, I UNCONSCIOUSLY SAW HIM AS AN ENEMY.
WHEN I WAS LITTLE...
...THE ADULTS WOULD ALWAYS JOKE ABOUT THE OX...
...SAYING HE WAS USED BY THE RAT BECAUSE HE'S SO SLOW AND STUPID.
I KNOW THEY PROBABLY DIDN'T MEAN ANYTHING BY IT...
...BUT STILL...
...I FELT LIKE THEY WERE LAUGHING AT ME, SAYING I WAS SLOW AND STUPID.

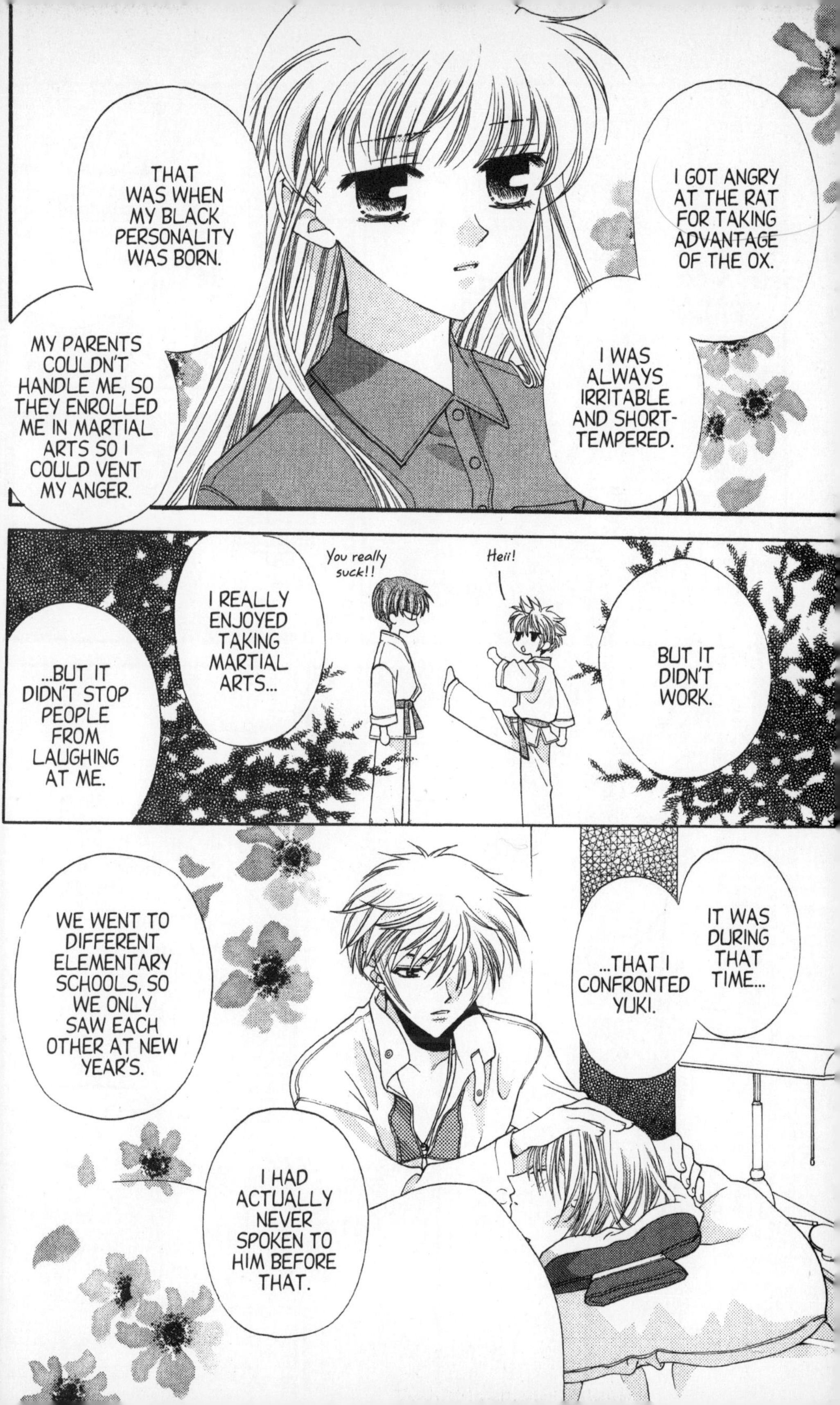
I GOT ANGRY AT THE RAT FOR TAKING ADVANTAGE OF THE OX.
THAT WAS WHEN MY BLACK PERSONALITY WAS BORN.
I WAS ALWAYS IRRITABLE AND SHORT-TEMPERED.
MY PARENTS COULDN'T HANDLE ME, SO THEY ENROLLED ME IN MARTIAL ARTS SO I COULD VENT MY ANGER.
BUT IT DIDN'T WORK.
Heii!
You really suck!!
I REALLY ENJOYED TAKING MARTIAL ARTS...
...BUT IT DIDN'T STOP PEOPLE FROM LAUGHING AT ME.
IT WAS DURING THAT TIME...
...THAT I CONFRONTED YUKI.
WE WENT TO DIFFERENT ELEMENTARY SCHOOLS, SO WE ONLY SAW EACH OTHER AT NEW YEAR'S.
I HAD ACTUALLY NEVER SPOKEN TO HIM BEFORE THAT.

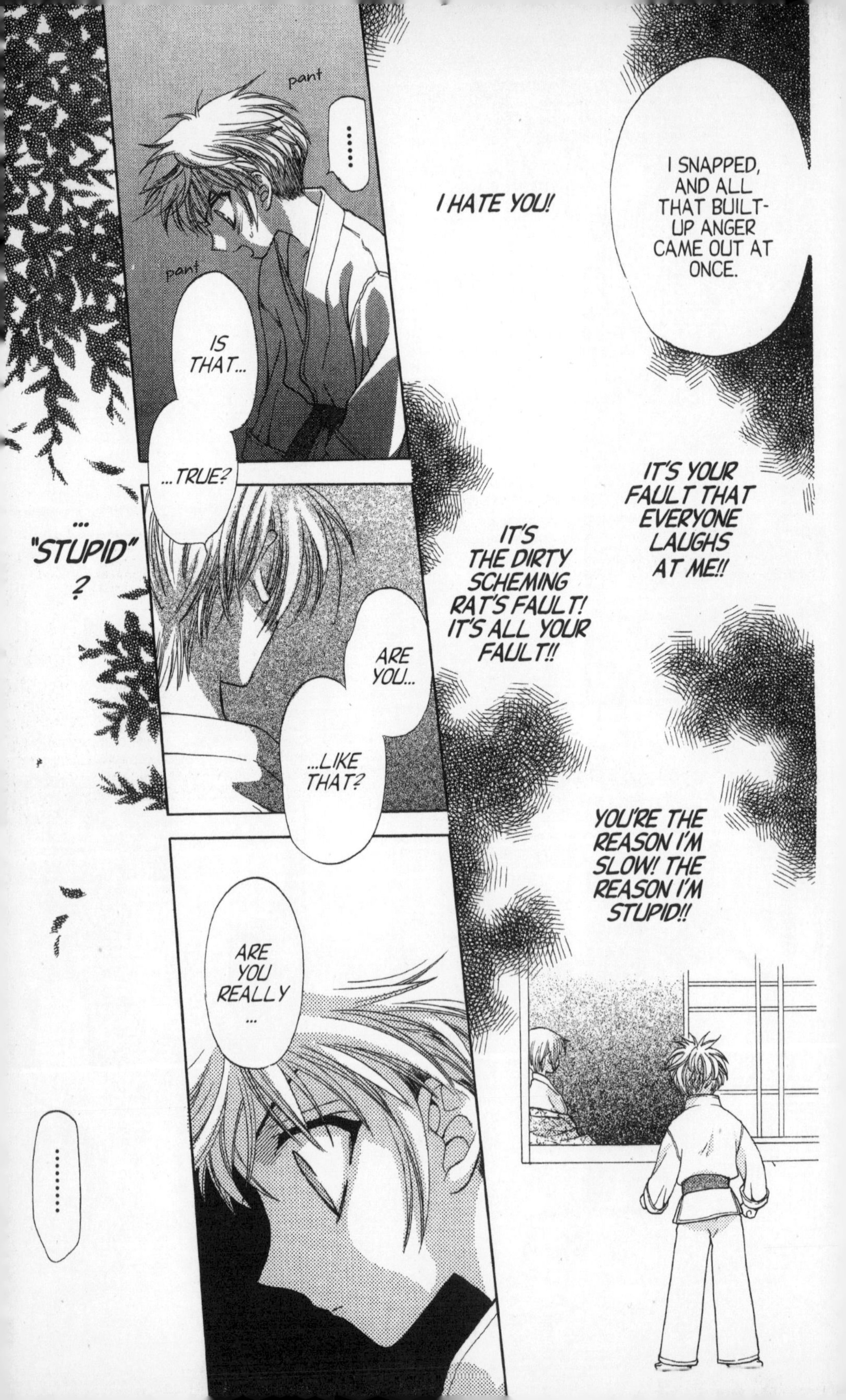

I SNAPPED, AND ALL THAT BUILT-UP ANGER CAME OUT AT ONCE.
I HATE YOU!
IT'S YOUR FAULT THAT EVERYONE LAUGHS AT ME!!
IT'S THE DIRTY SCHEMING RAT'S FAULT! IT'S ALL YOUR FAULT!!
YOU'RE THE REASON I'M SLOW! THE REASON I'M STUPID!!
pant
......
pant
IS THAT...
...TRUE?
... "STUPID" ?
ARE YOU...
...LIKE THAT?
ARE YOU REALLY ...
....

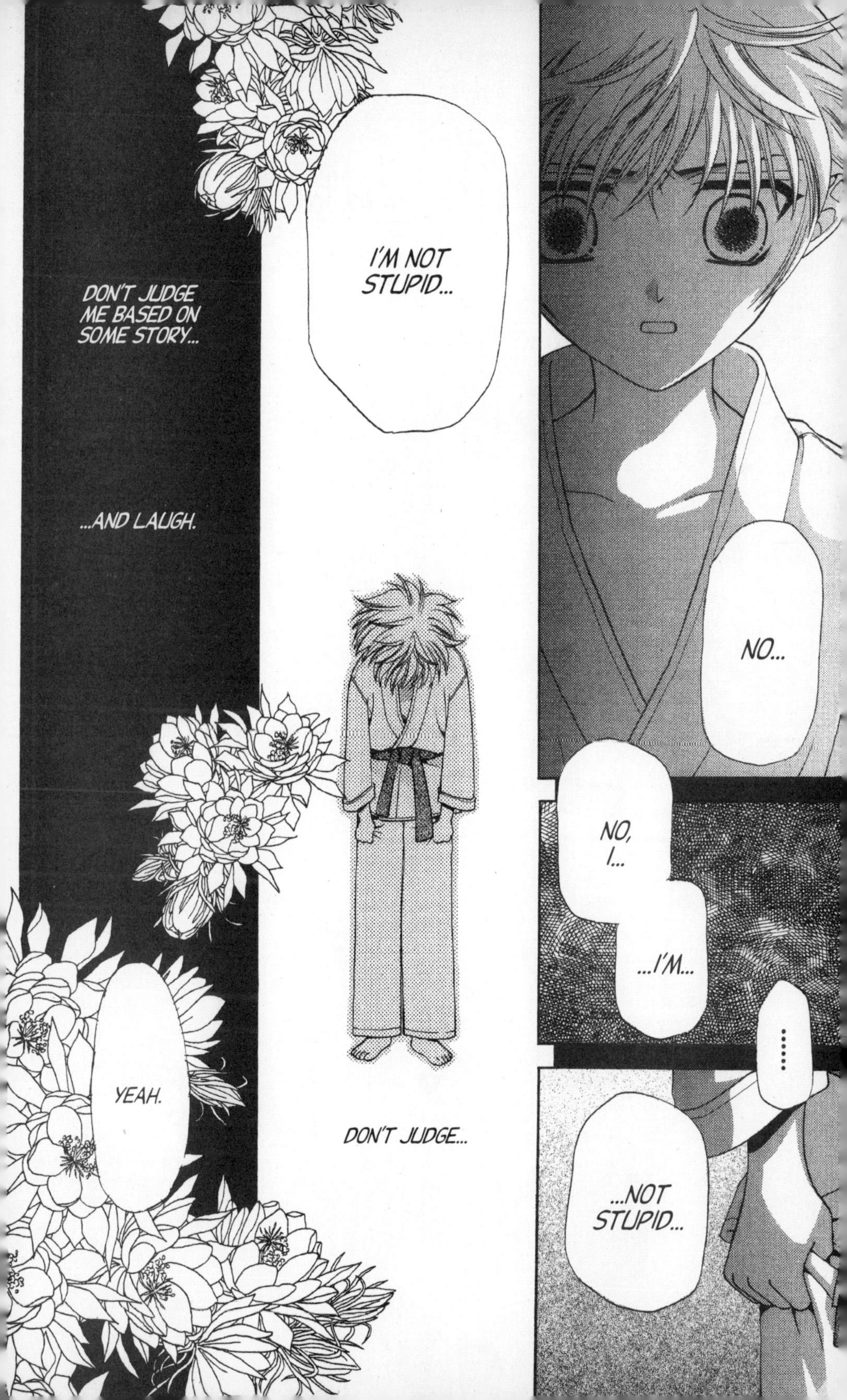
NO...
NO, I...
...I'M...
......
...NOT STUPID...
I'M NOT STUPID...
DON'T JUDGE...
DON'T JUDGE ME BASED ON SOME STORY...
...AND LAUGH.
YEAH.

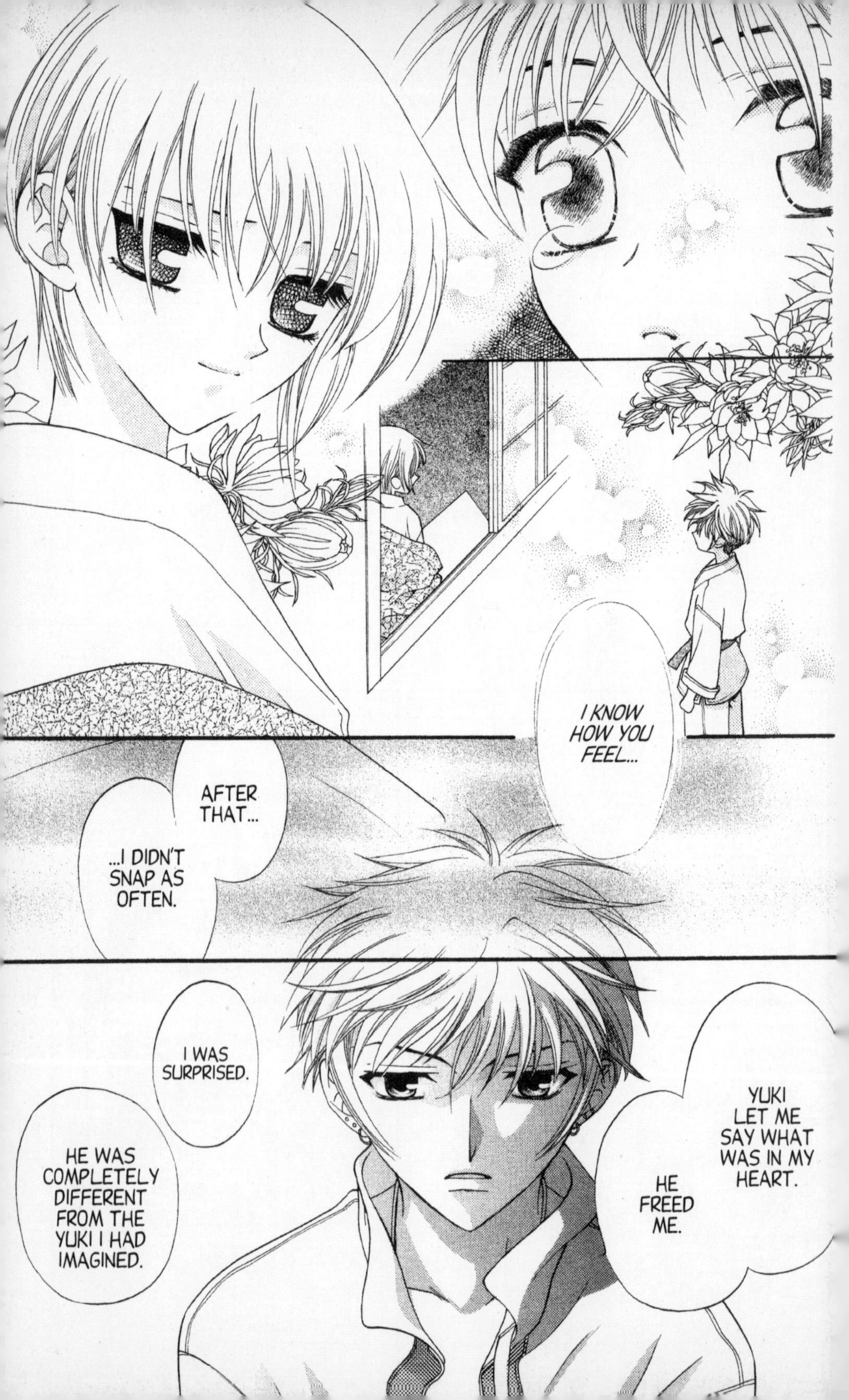
I KNOW HOW YOU FEEL...
AFTER THAT...
...I DIDN'T SNAP AS OFTEN.
YUKI LET ME SAY WHAT WAS IN MY HEART.
HE FREED ME.
I WAS SURPRISED.
HE WAS COMPLETELY DIFFERENT FROM THE YUKI I HAD IMAGINED.

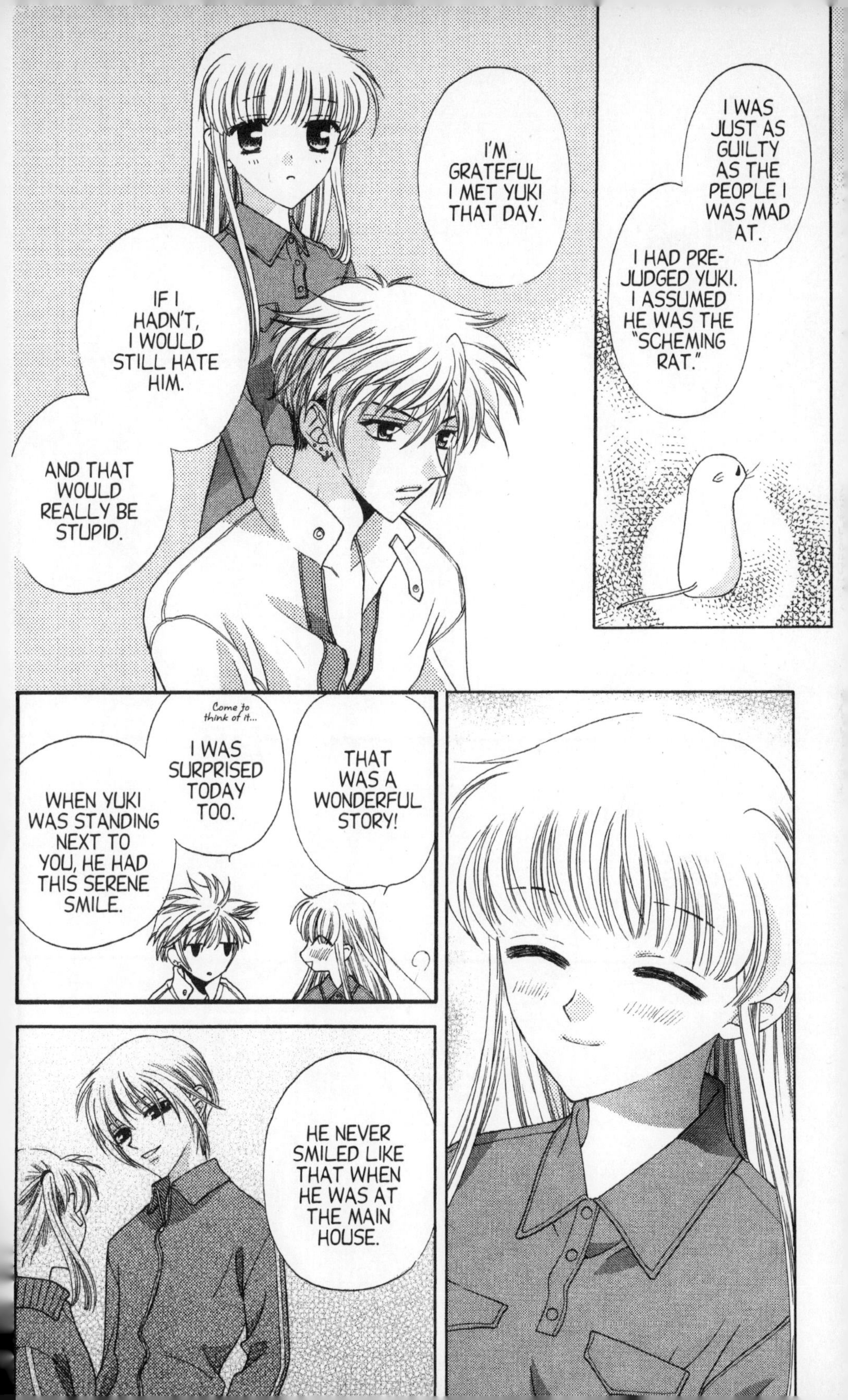
I WAS JUST AS GUILTY AS THE PEOPLE I WAS MAD AT.
I HAD PRE-JUDGED YUKI. I ASSUMED HE WAS THE "SCHEMING RAT."
I'M GRATEFUL I MET YUKI THAT DAY.
IF I HADN'T, I WOULD STILL HATE HIM.
AND THAT WOULD REALLY BE STUPID.
THAT WAS A WONDERFUL STORY!
Come to think of it...
I WAS SURPRISED TODAY TOO.
WHEN YUKI WAS STANDING NEXT TO YOU, HE HAD THIS SERENE SMILE.
HE NEVER SMILED LIKE THAT WHEN HE WAS AT THE MAIN HOUSE.

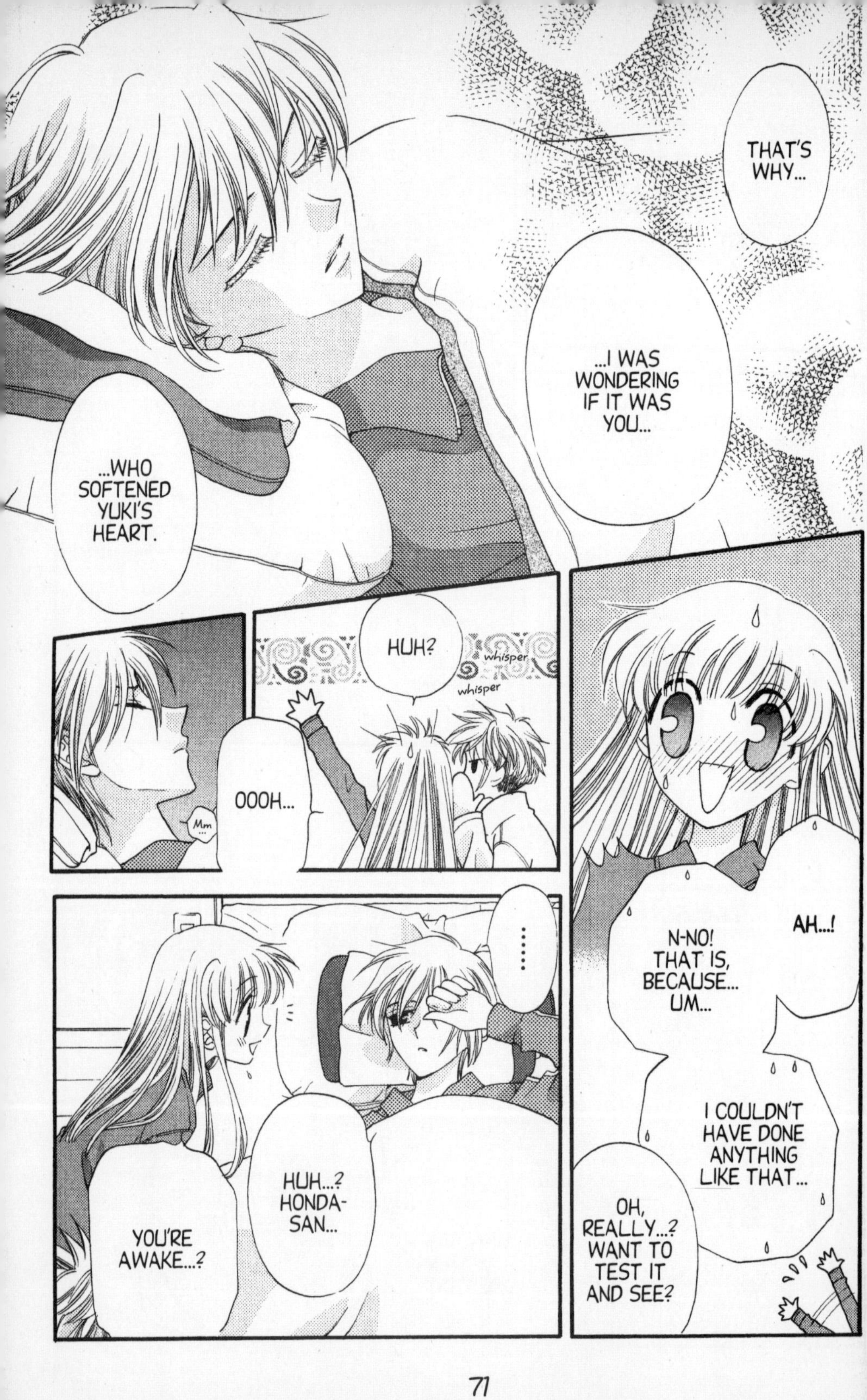
THAT'S WHY...
...I WAS WONDERING IF IT WAS YOU...
...WHO SOFTENED YUKI'S HEART.
AH...!
N-NO! THAT IS, BECAUSE... UM...
I COULDN'T HAVE DONE ANYTHING LIKE THAT...
OH, REALLY...? WANT TO TEST IT AND SEE?
HUH?
whisper
whisper
OOOH...
Mm ...
......
HUH...? HONDA-SAN...
YOU'RE AWAKE...?

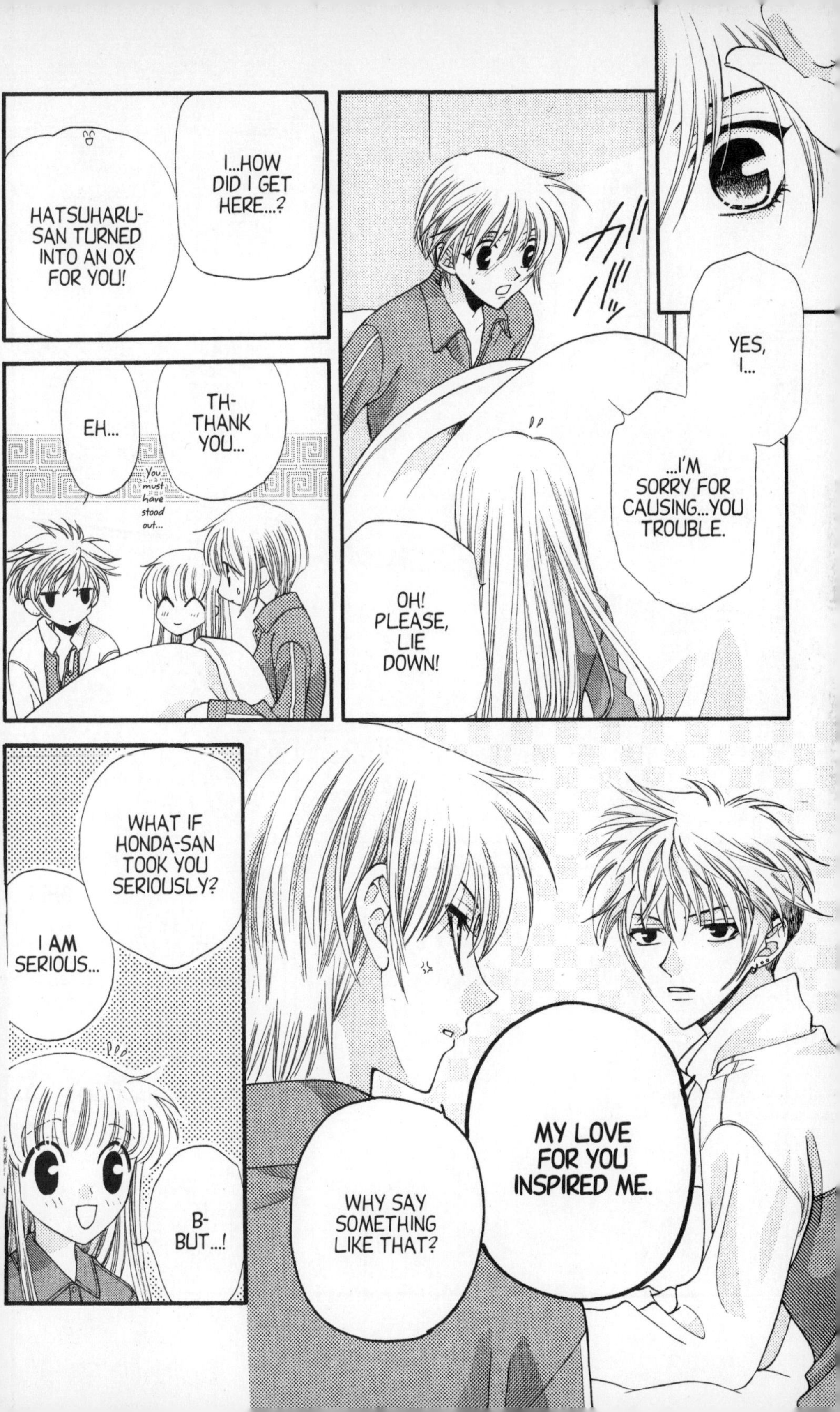
YES, I...
ガバッ
...I'M SORRY FOR CAUSING...YOU TROUBLE.
OH! PLEASE, LIE DOWN!
I...HOW DID I GET HERE...?
HATSUHARU-SAN TURNED INTO AN OX FOR YOU!
TH-THANK YOU...
EH...
You must have stood out...
MY LOVE FOR YOU INSPIRED ME.
WHY SAY SOMETHING LIKE THAT?
WHAT IF HONDA-SAN TOOK YOU SERIOUSLY?
I AM SERIOUS...
B-BUT...!

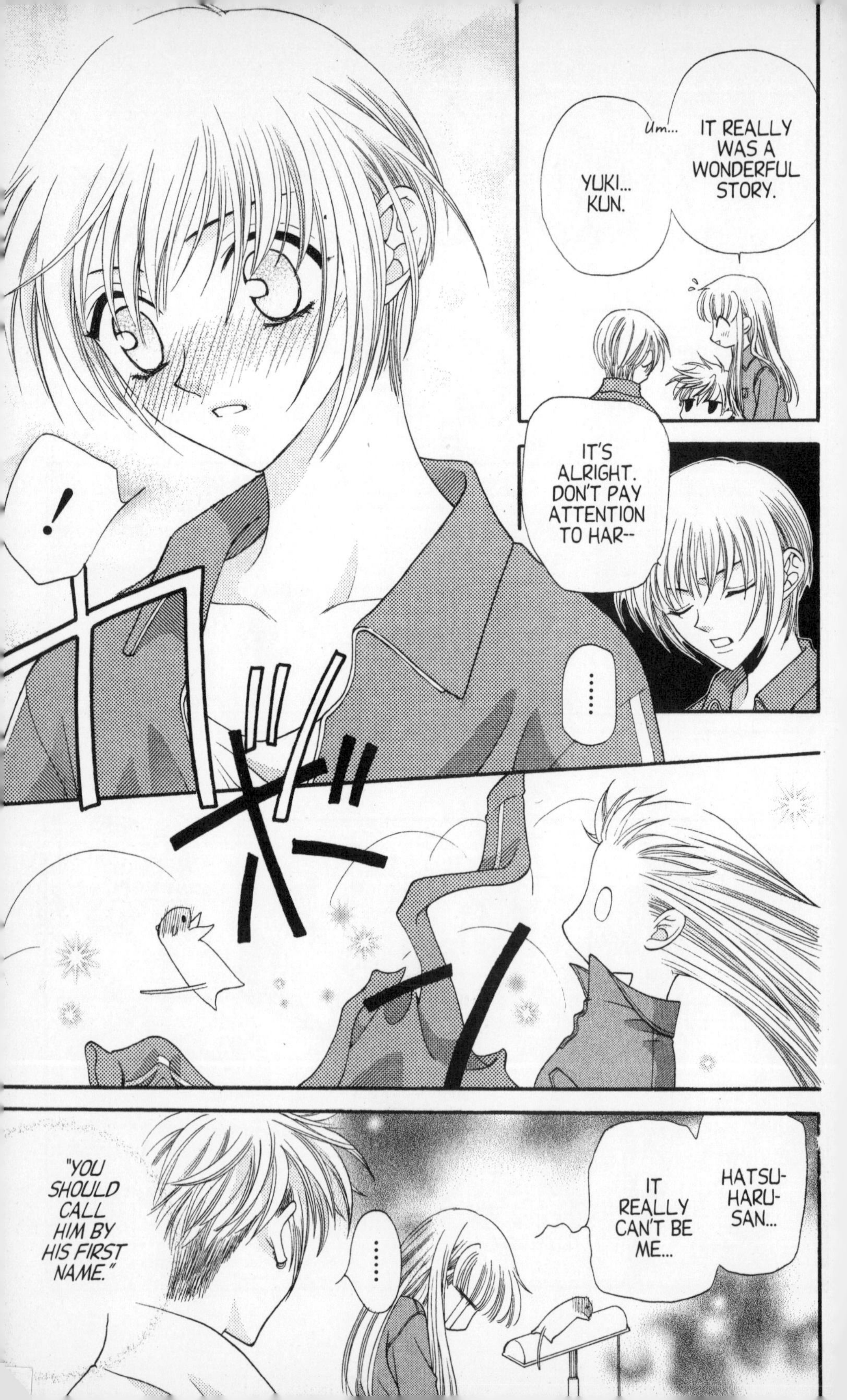
IT REALLY WAS A WONDERFUL STORY.
Um... YUKI... KUN.
IT'S ALRIGHT. DON'T PAY ATTENTION TO HAR--
!
......
HATSU-HARU-SAN...
IT REALLY CAN'T BE ME...
......
"YOU SHOULD CALL HIM BY HIS FIRST NAME."

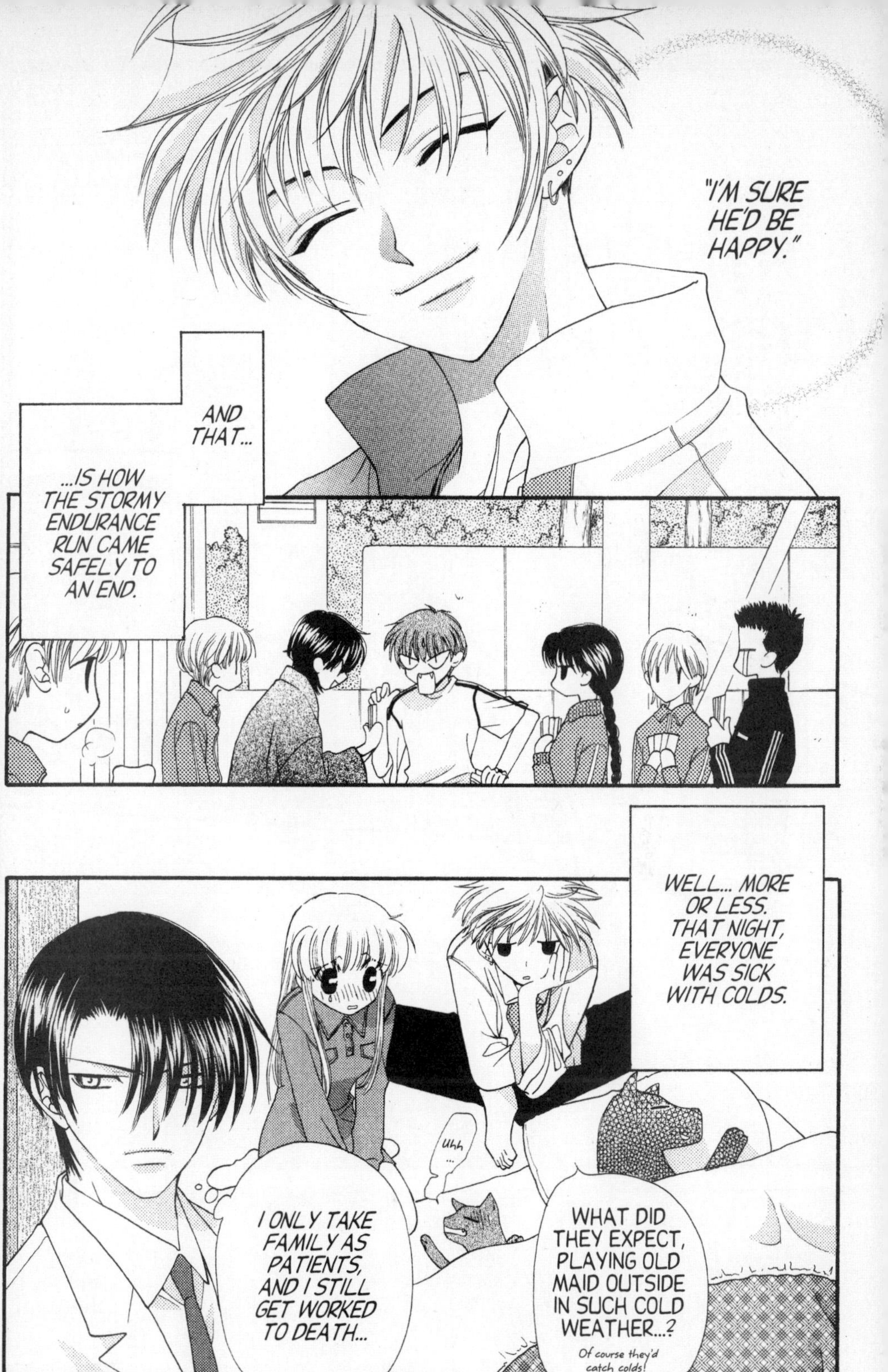
"I'M SURE HE'D BE HAPPY."
AND THAT...
...IS HOW THE STORMY ENDURANCE RUN CAME SAFELY TO AN END.
WELL... MORE OR LESS. THAT NIGHT, EVERYONE WAS SICK WITH COLDS.
Uhh ...
WHAT DID THEY EXPECT, PLAYING OLD MAID OUTSIDE IN SUCH COLD WEATHER...?
Of course they'd catch colds!
I ONLY TAKE FAMILY AS PATIENTS, AND I STILL GET WORKED TO DEATH...

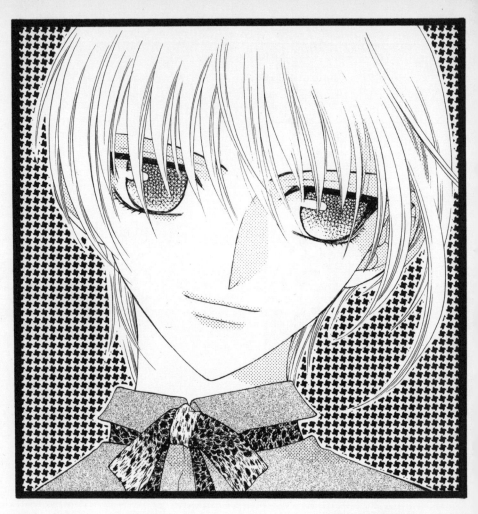

Chapter 15

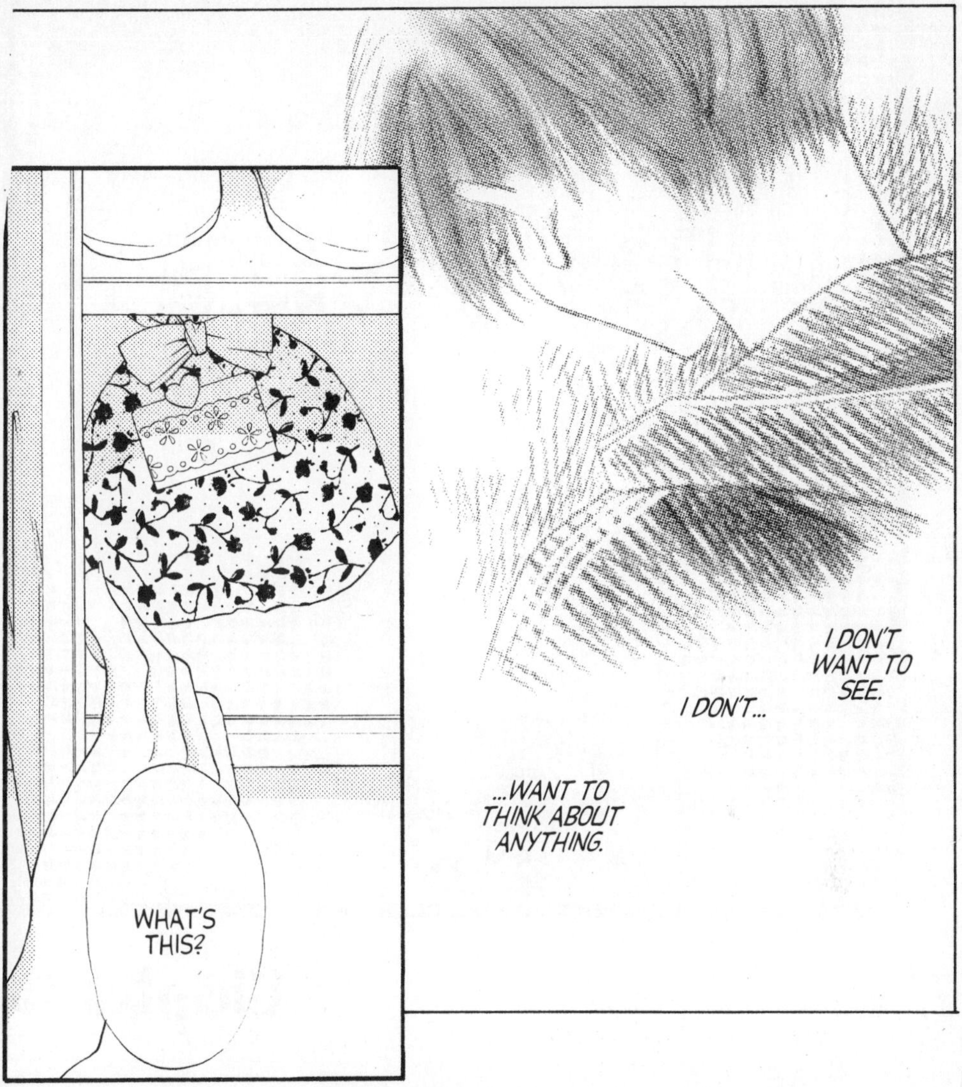
I DON'T WANT TO SEE.
I DON'T...
...WANT TO THINK ABOUT ANYTHING.
WHAT'S THIS?

ULTRA SPECIAL BLAH BLAH BLAH 3

This is a little off topic, but it's about Hatsuharu. His personality is split into Black and White. The White side represents his true self, but he retains all of his memories when he's Black too. (Of course, he probably doesn't think much besides, "Aahh... I've gone Black again!")

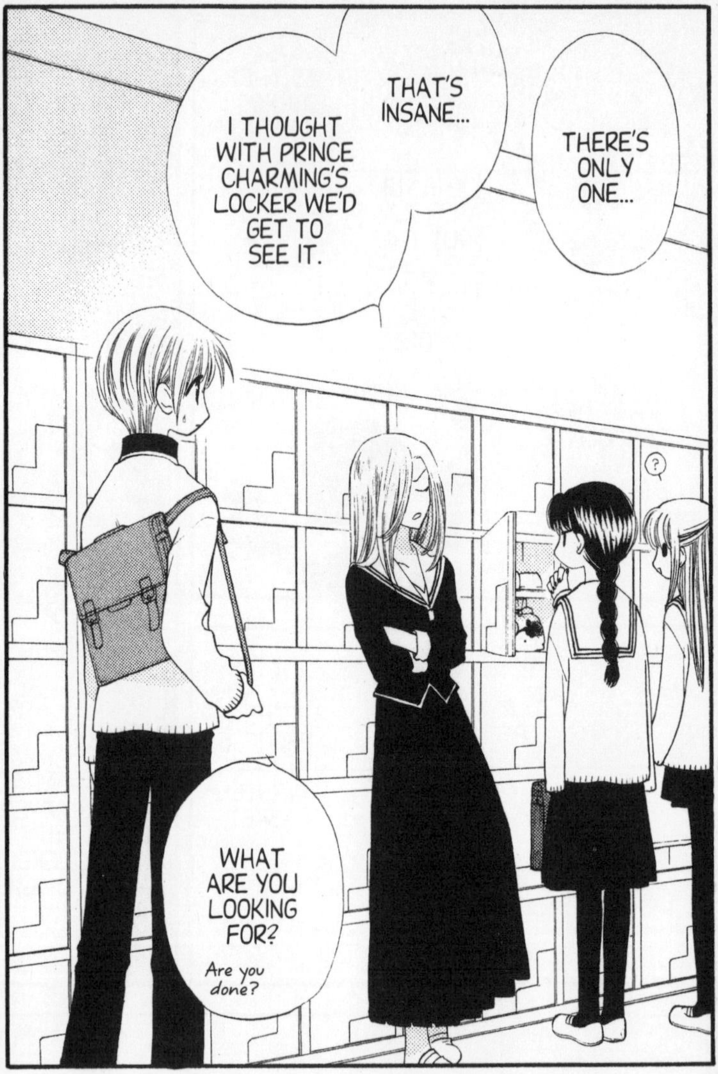
THERE'S ONLY ONE...
THAT'S INSANE...
I THOUGHT WITH PRINCE CHARMING'S LOCKER WE'D GET TO SEE IT.
?
WHAT ARE YOU LOOKING FOR?
Are you done?

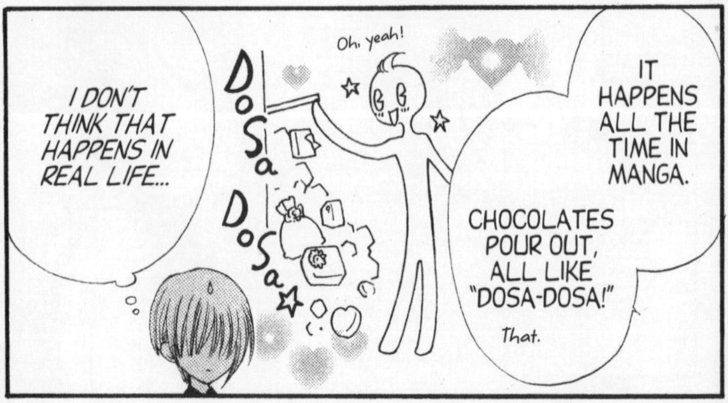
IT HAPPENS ALL THE TIME IN MANGA.
CHOCOLATES POUR OUT, ALL LIKE "DOSA-DOSA!"
That.
Oh, yeah!
DoSa DoSa
I DON'T THINK THAT HAPPENS IN REAL LIFE...

Fruits Basket 3 Part 3

The mood of manga--I know that's a very sensuous way of phrasing it--but every author has his or her own style that evokes a certain mood. Definitely. Well, what is mine like...? (Ha ha!) Anyway, a while back, Hana-Yume magazine allowed me to interview Hidaka-sensei, and I remember that she said, "I'm told I look like Sachiko-chan." * I thought, "Oohh, come to think of it, she kinda does!" (Of course I didn't say anything out loud--I just thought it.) Oh, but it was such an honor to meet her! Please accept my insane faxes (Hee hee!), Hidaka-san! And please treat Natsuki Takaya kindly...

* Sachiko is the protagonist of Hidaka Banri's SEKAI DE ICHIBAN DAIKIRAI.

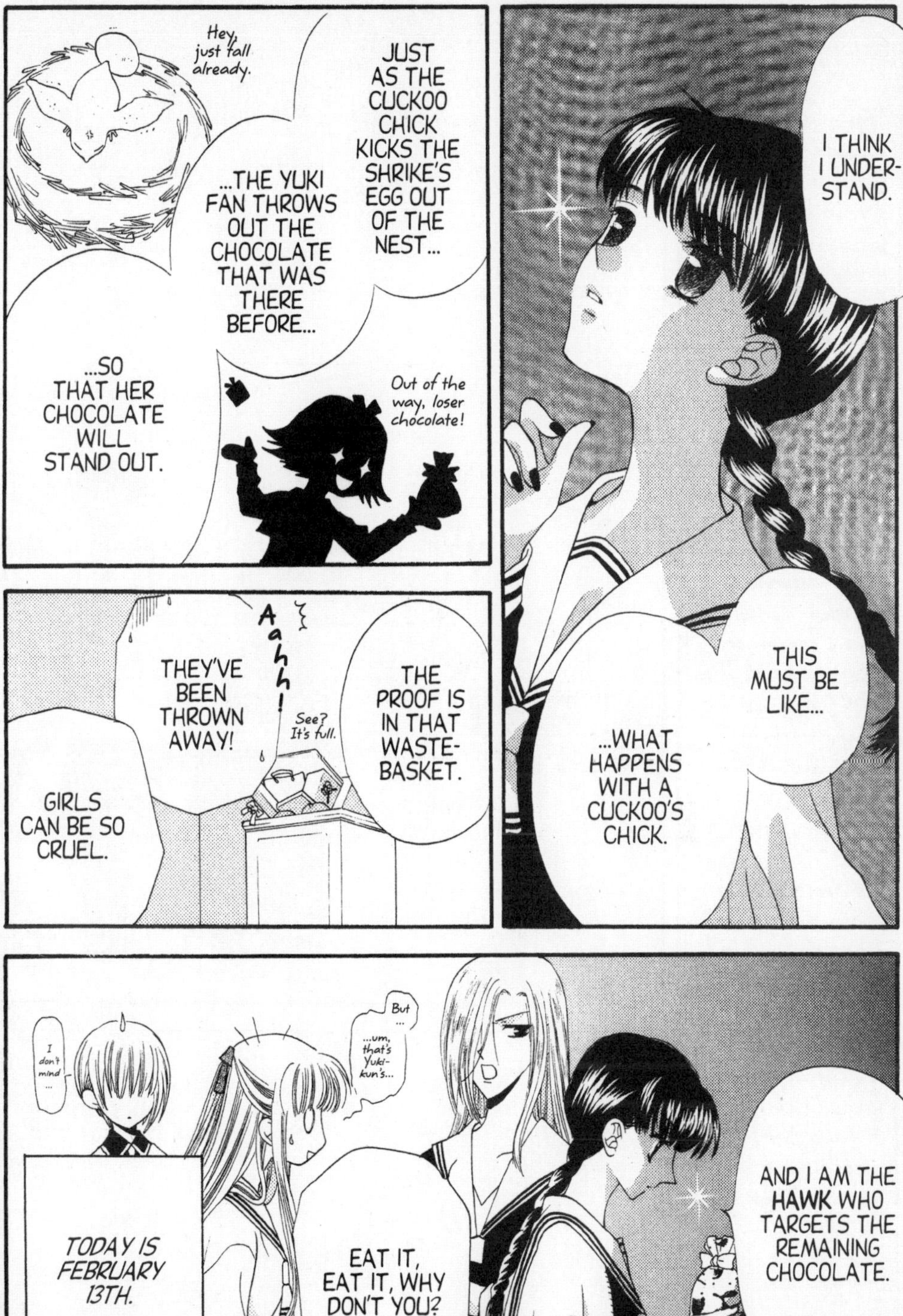
I THINK I UNDER-STAND.
THIS MUST BE LIKE...
...WHAT HAPPENS WITH A CUCKOO'S CHICK.
JUST AS THE CUCKOO CHICK KICKS THE SHRIKE'S EGG OUT OF THE NEST...
Hey, just fall already.
...THE YUKI FAN THROWS OUT THE CHOCOLATE THAT WAS THERE BEFORE...
Out of the way, loser chocolate!
...SO THAT HER CHOCOLATE WILL STAND OUT.
THE PROOF IS IN THAT WASTE-BASKET.
See? It's full.
Aahh!
THEY'VE BEEN THROWN AWAY!
GIRLS CAN BE SO CRUEL.
AND I AM THE **HAWK** WHO TARGETS THE REMAINING CHOCOLATE.
EAT IT, EAT IT, WHY DON'T YOU?
But ...
...um, that's Yuki-kun's...
I don't mind ...
TODAY IS FEBRUARY 13TH.

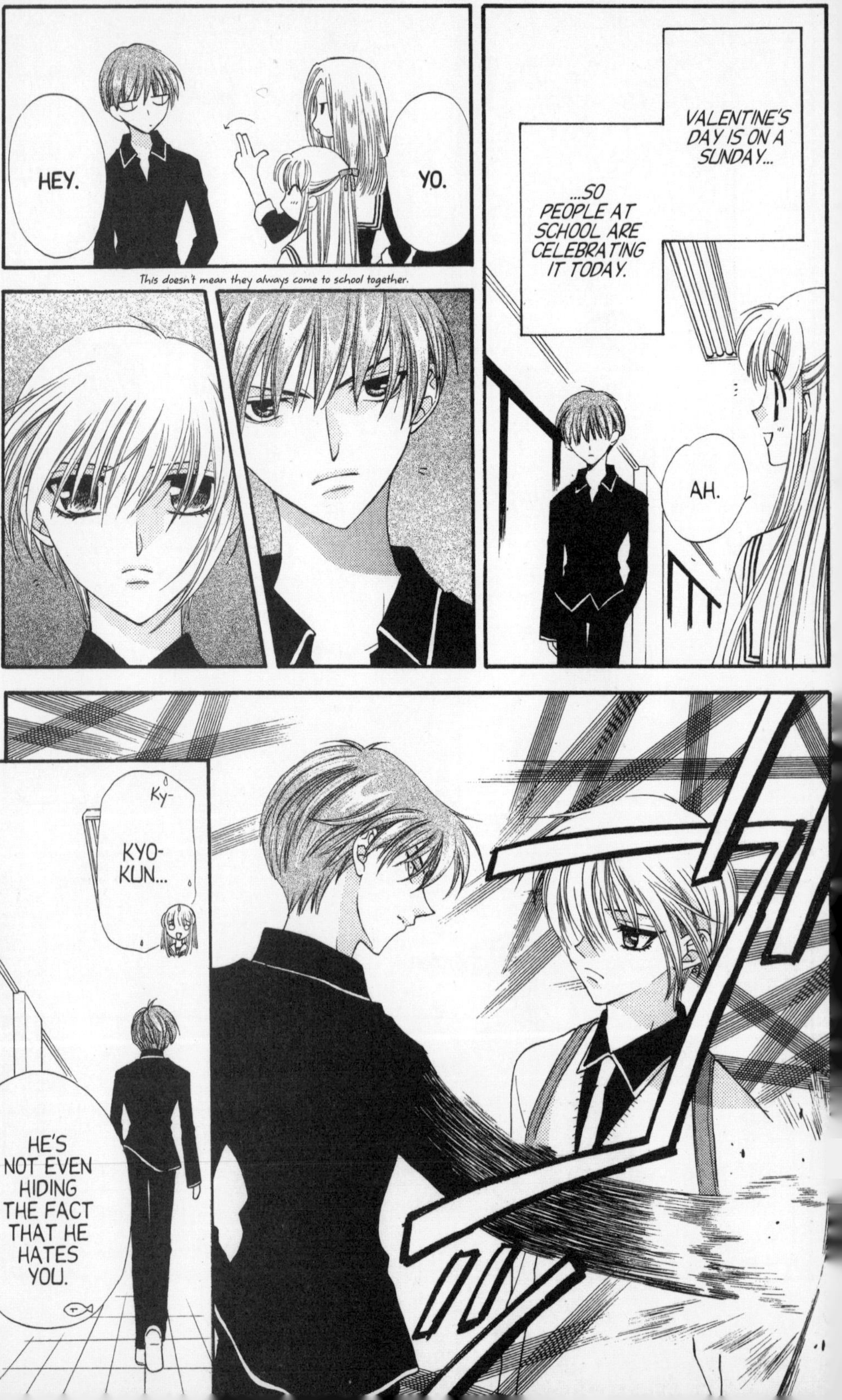
VALENTINE'S DAY IS ON A SUNDAY...
...SO PEOPLE AT SCHOOL ARE CELEBRATING IT TODAY.
AH.
YO.
HEY.
This doesn't mean they always come to school together.
Ky-
KYO-KUN...
HE'S NOT EVEN HIDING THE FACT THAT HE HATES YOU.

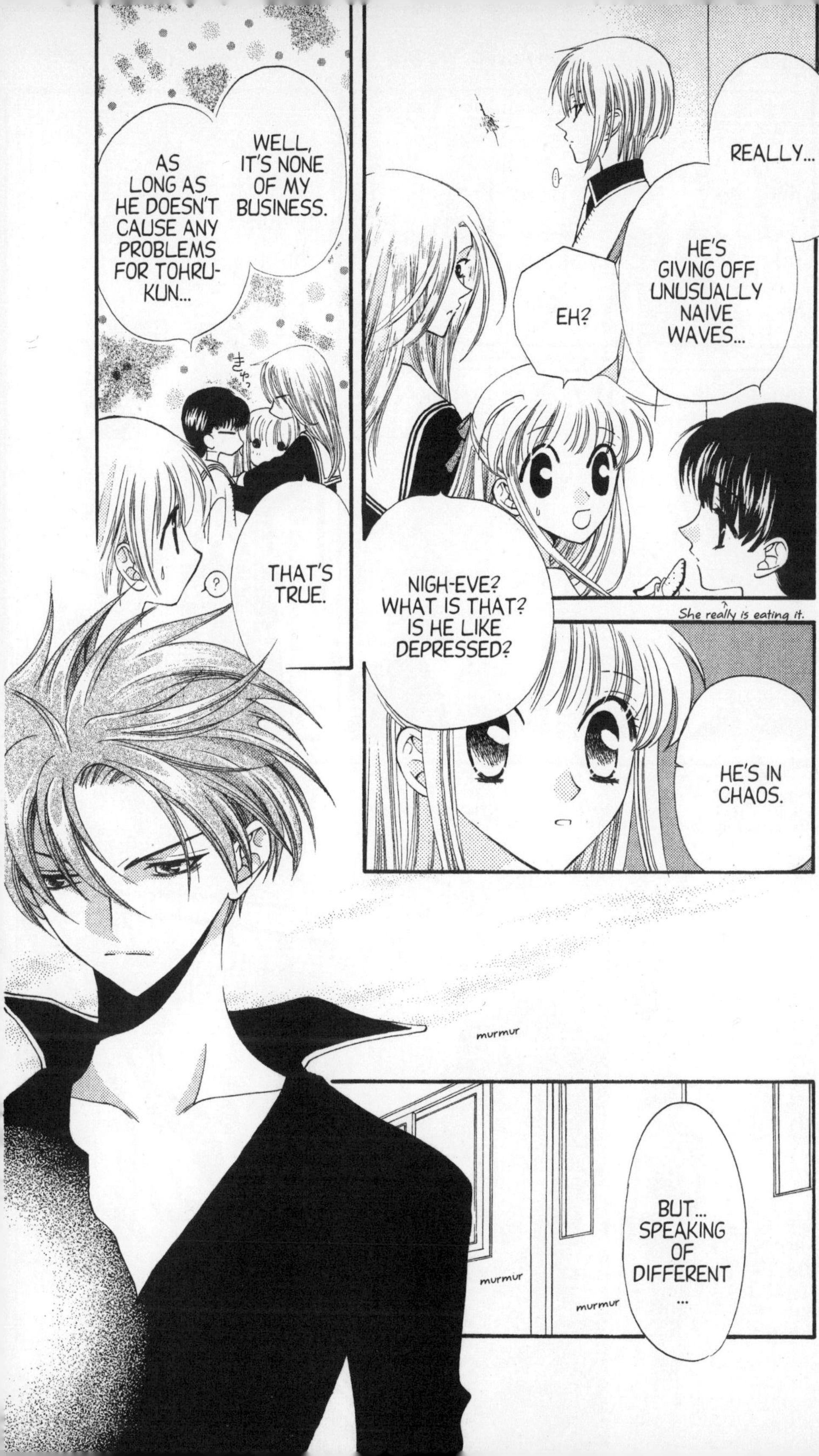
REALLY...
HE'S GIVING OFF UNUSUALLY NAIVE WAVES...
EH?
NIGH-EVE? WHAT IS THAT? IS HE LIKE DEPRESSED?
She really is eating it.
WELL, IT'S NONE OF MY BUSINESS.
AS LONG AS HE DOESN'T CAUSE ANY PROBLEMS FOR TOHRU-KUN...
きゃっ
THAT'S TRUE.
HE'S IN CHAOS.
BUT... SPEAKING OF DIFFERENT ...
murmur
murmur
murmur

THERE'S SOMETHING CREEPY ABOUT THEIR EYES.

For Sohma-kun.

Give chocolate.

Of course I'm giving some.

Of course.

To Sohma-kun.

To Yuki-kun.

GIRLS ARE REALLY SCARY THIS TIME OF YEAR.

THEY LOOK LIKE THEY'D RUSH YOU FROM A STREET CORNER.

THIS MIGHT BE THE SCARIEST DAY OF THE YEAR FOR MEMBERS OF THE CHINESE ZODIAC...

KYOOON-CHAN!!

HERE! THIS CHOCOLATE IS FOR YOU!

Aahh!

GIRLS LIKE KYO-KUN, TOO...

MR. POPULARITY.

She called him Kyon-chan.

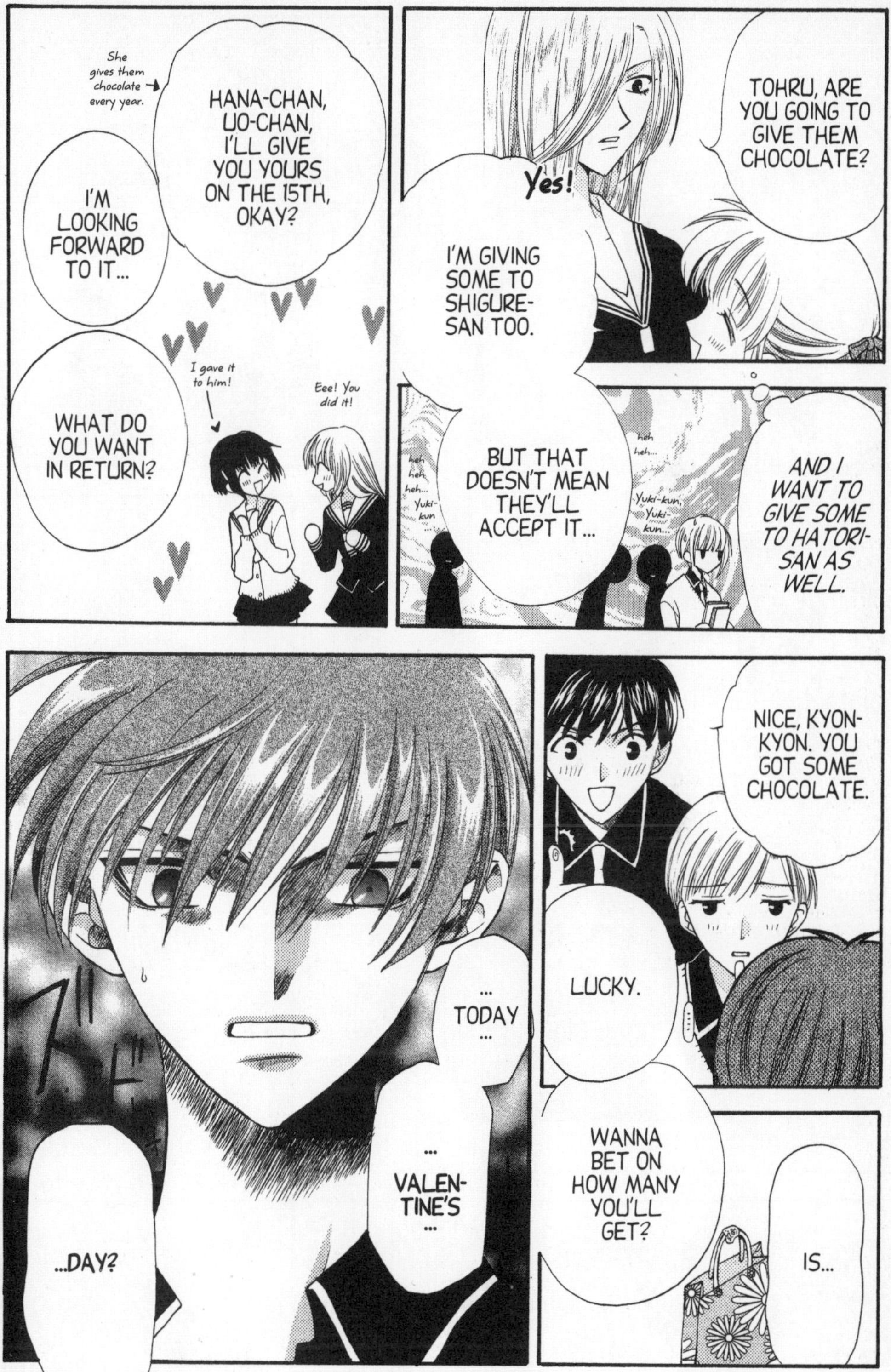
TOHRU, ARE YOU GOING TO GIVE THEM CHOCOLATE?
Yes!
I'M GIVING SOME TO SHIGURE-SAN TOO.
AND I WANT TO GIVE SOME TO HATORI-SAN AS WELL.
heh heh... Yuki-kun, Yuki-kun...
heh heh heh... Yuki-kun...
BUT THAT DOESN'T MEAN THEY'LL ACCEPT IT...
She gives them chocolate every year.
HANA-CHAN, UO-CHAN, I'LL GIVE YOU YOURS ON THE 15TH, OKAY?
I'M LOOKING FORWARD TO IT...
Eee! You did it!
I gave it to him!
WHAT DO YOU WANT IN RETURN?
NICE, KYON-KYON. YOU GOT SOME CHOCOLATE.
LUCKY.
WANNA BET ON HOW MANY YOU'LL GET?
IS...
...TODAY...
...VALENTINE'S...
...DAY?

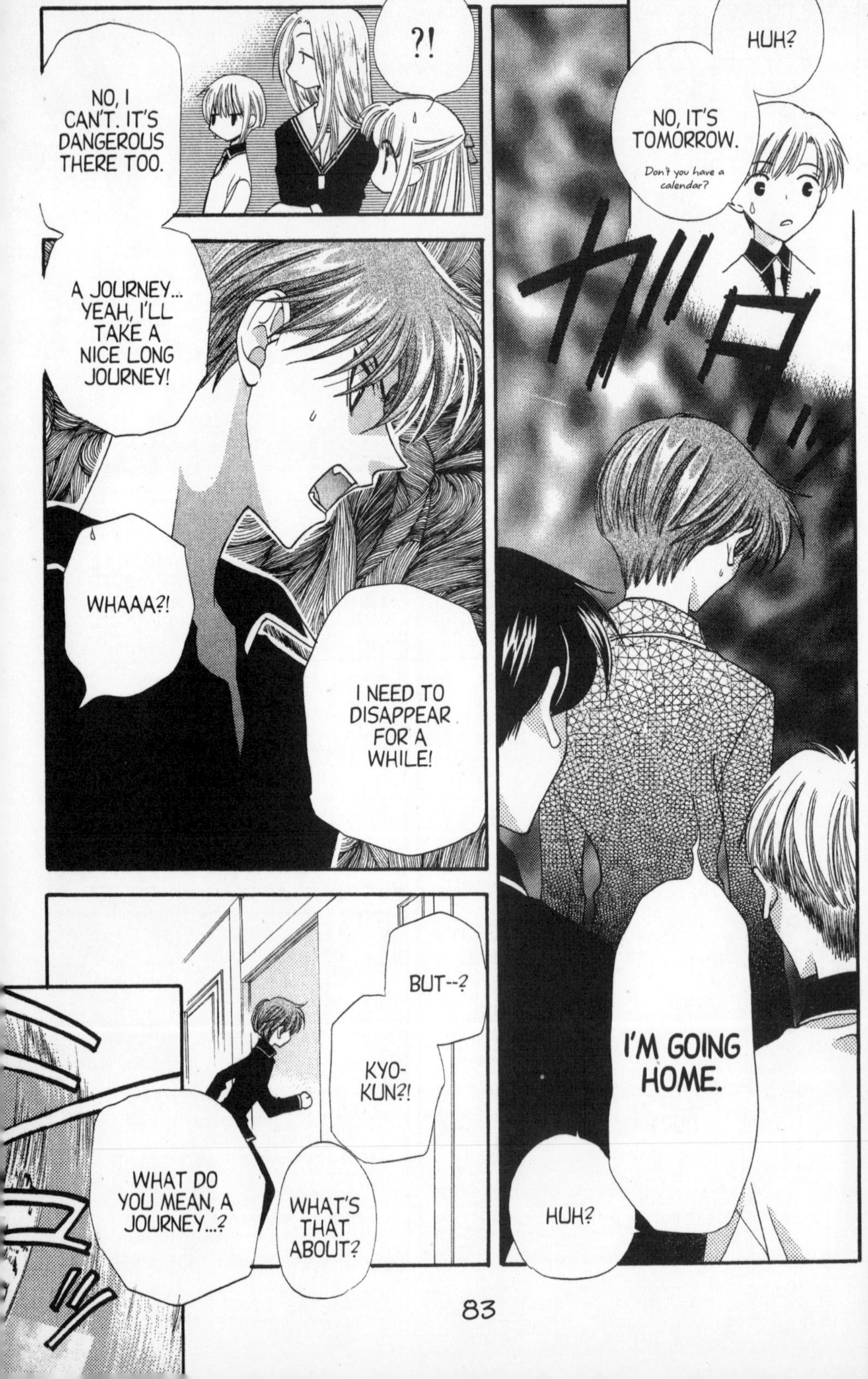
HUH?
NO, IT'S TOMORROW.
Don't you have a calendar?
I'M GOING HOME.
HUH?
?!
NO, I CAN'T. IT'S DANGEROUS THERE TOO.
A JOURNEY... YEAH, I'LL TAKE A NICE LONG JOURNEY!
WHAAA?!
I NEED TO DISAPPEAR FOR A WHILE!
BUT--?
KYO-KUN?!
WHAT'S THAT ABOUT?
WHAT DO YOU MEAN, A JOURNEY...?

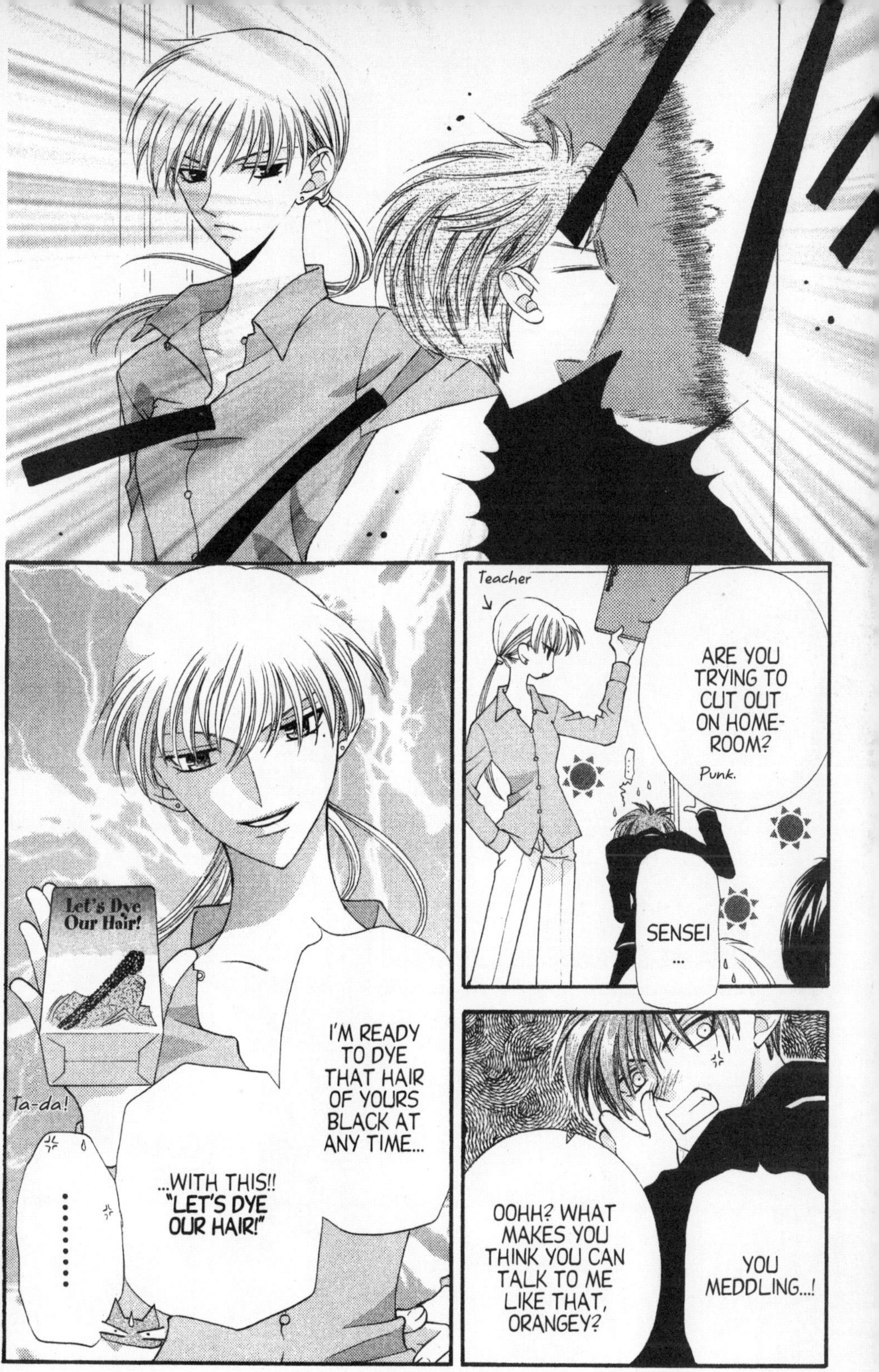
Teacher
ARE YOU TRYING TO CUT OUT ON HOME-ROOM?
Punk.
SENSEI ...
YOU MEDDLING...!
OOHH? WHAT MAKES YOU THINK YOU CAN TALK TO ME LIKE THAT, ORANGEY?
I'M READY TO DYE THAT HAIR OF YOURS BLACK AT ANY TIME...
...WITH THIS!! "LET'S DYE OUR HAIR!"
Let's Dye Our Hair!
Ta-da!
....

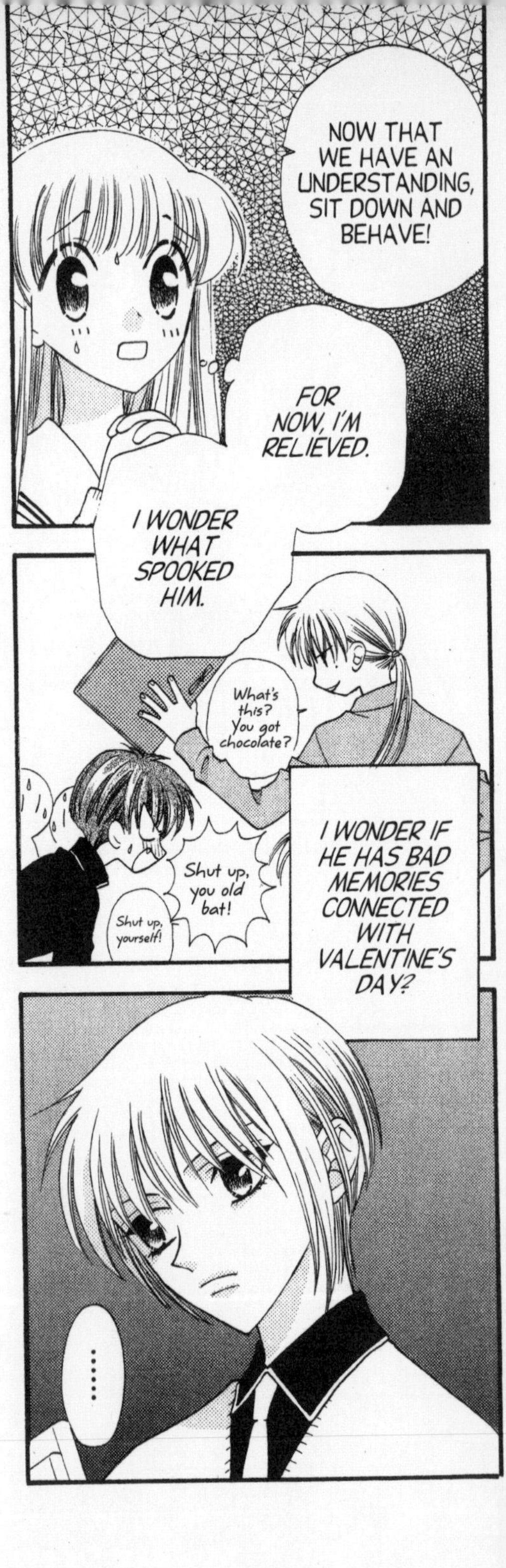
NOW THAT WE HAVE AN UNDERSTANDING, SIT DOWN AND BEHAVE!
FOR NOW, I'M RELIEVED.
I WONDER WHAT SPOOKED HIM.
What's this? You got chocolate?
Shut up, you old bat!
Shut up, yourself!
I WONDER IF HE HAS BAD MEMORIES CONNECTED WITH VALENTINE'S DAY?
......
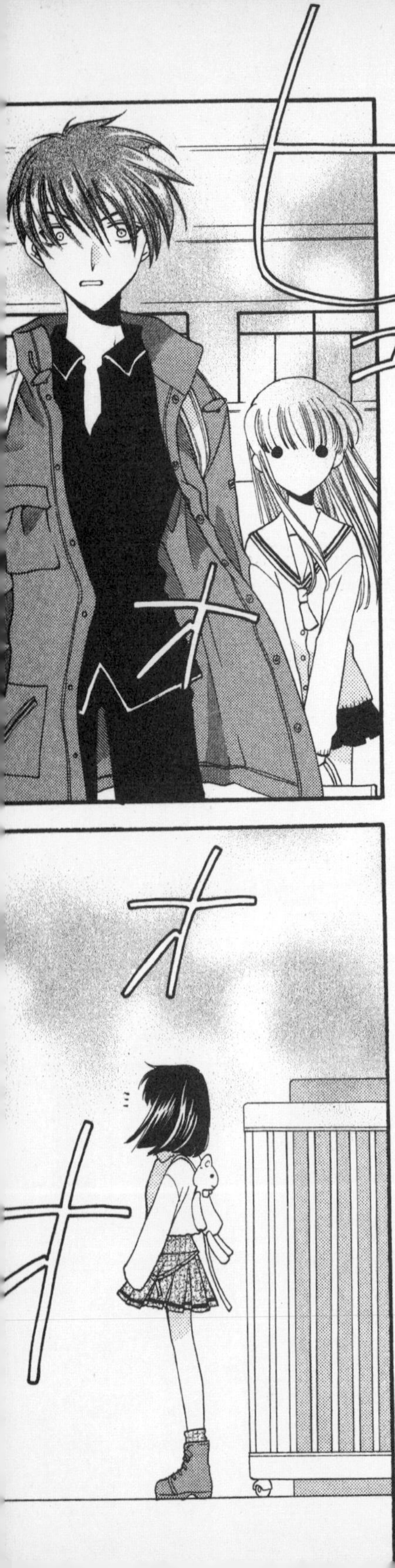

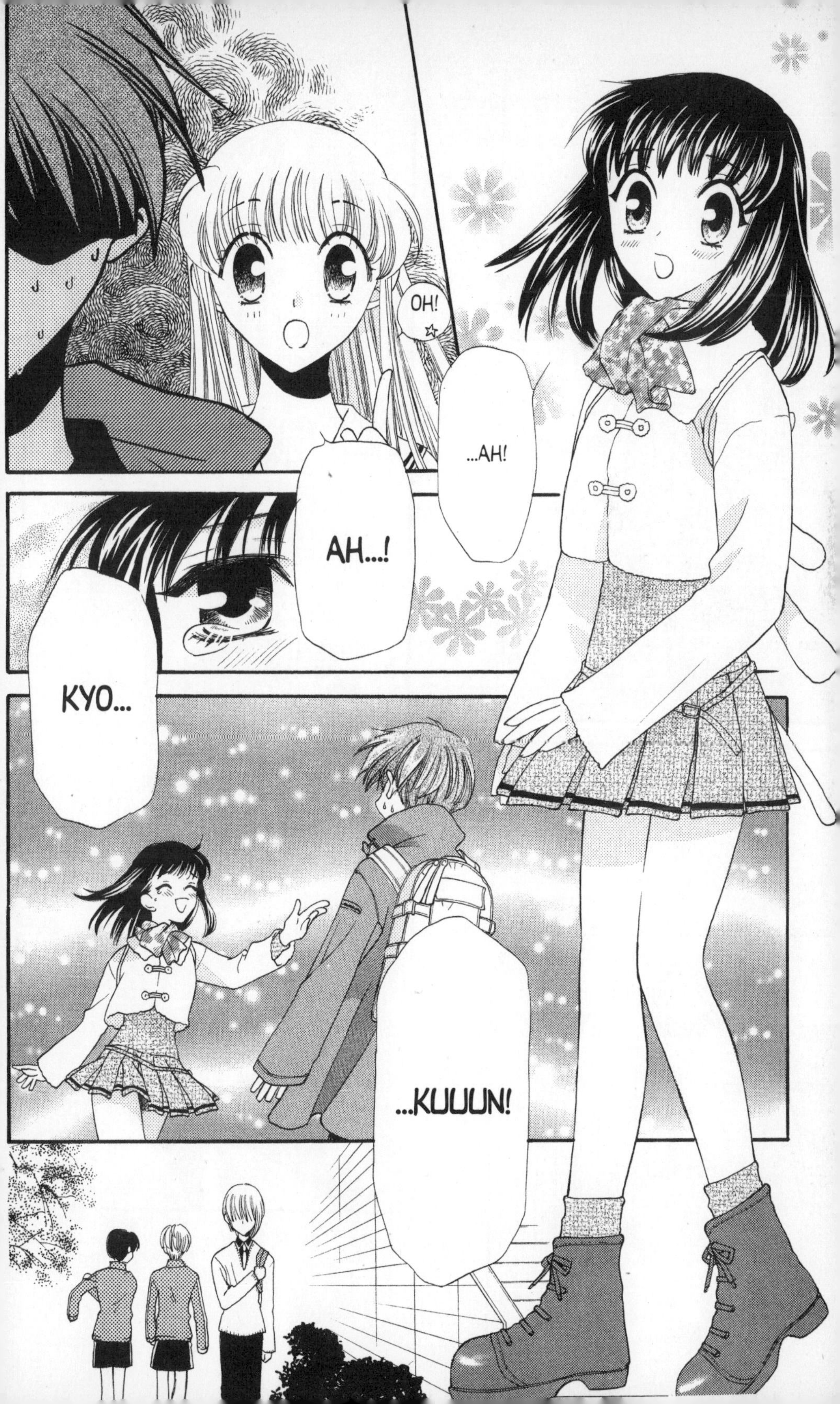

OH!
...AH!
AH...!
KYO...
...KUUUN!

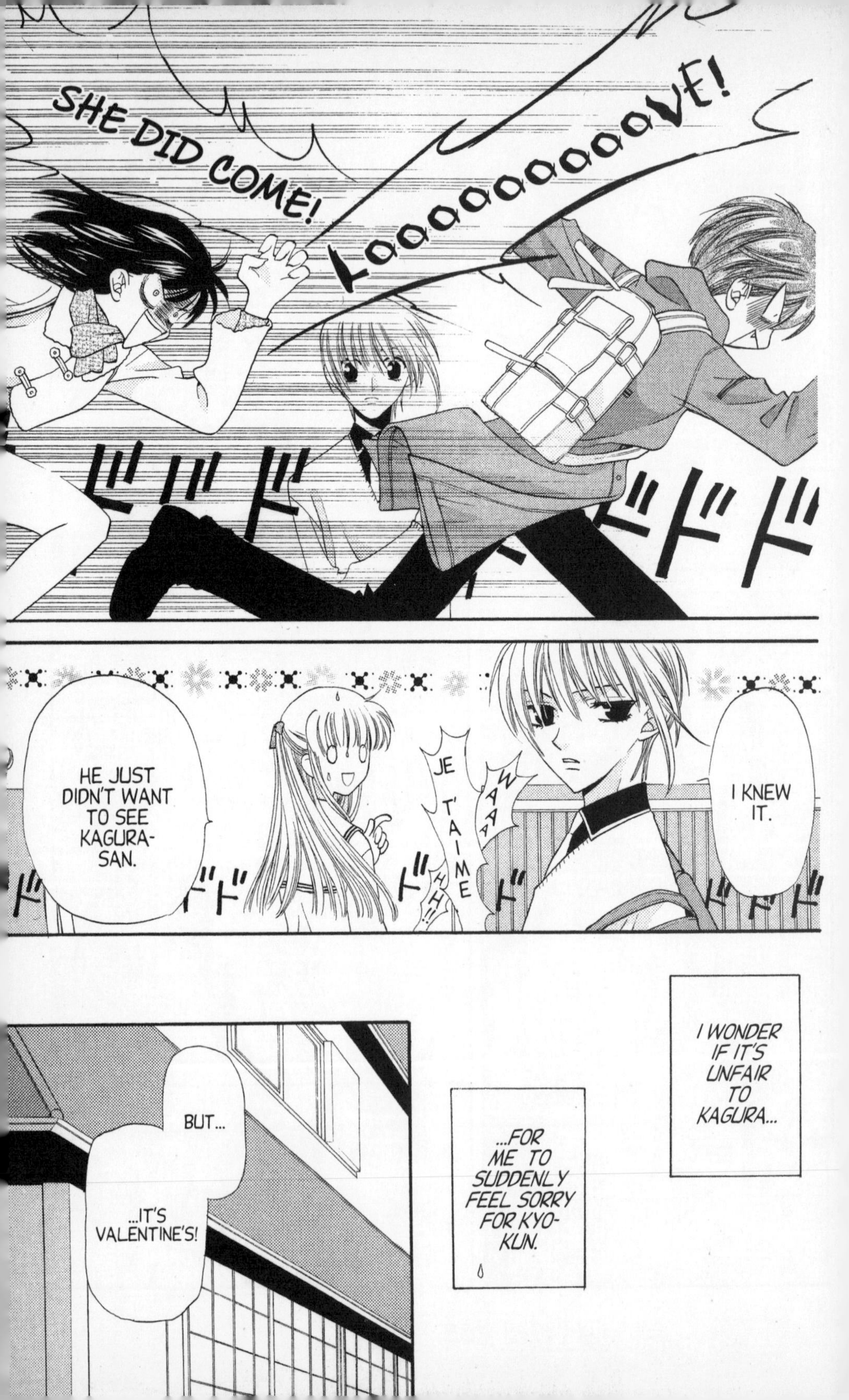
LOOOOOOOOOVE!
SHE DID COME!
ドドド
ドドド
I KNEW IT.
ドドド
WAAA
JE T'AIMEHH!!
ドド
HE JUST DIDN'T WANT TO SEE KAGURA-SAN.
ドドド
I WONDER IF IT'S UNFAIR TO KAGURA...
...FOR ME TO SUDDENLY FEEL SORRY FOR KYO-KUN.
BUT...
...IT'S VALENTINE'S!

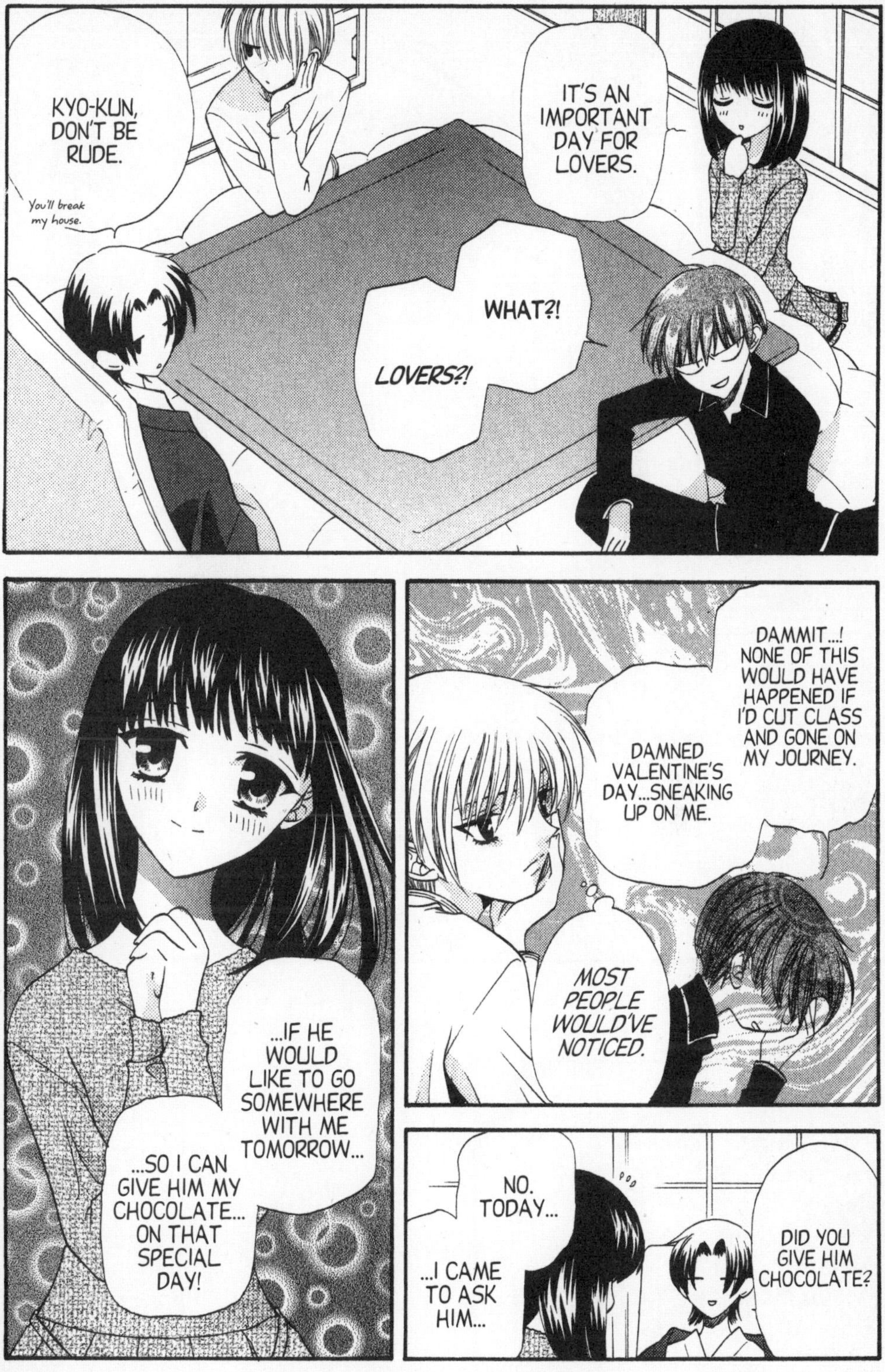
IT'S AN IMPORTANT DAY FOR LOVERS.
WHAT?!
LOVERS?!
KYO-KUN, DON'T BE RUDE.
You'll break my house.
DAMMIT...! NONE OF THIS WOULD HAVE HAPPENED IF I'D CUT CLASS AND GONE ON MY JOURNEY.
DAMNED VALENTINE'S DAY...SNEAKING UP ON ME.
MOST PEOPLE WOULD'VE NOTICED.
DID YOU GIVE HIM CHOCOLATE?
NO. TODAY...
...I CAME TO ASK HIM...
...IF HE WOULD LIKE TO GO SOMEWHERE WITH ME TOMORROW...
...SO I CAN GIVE HIM MY CHOCOLATE... ON THAT SPECIAL DAY!

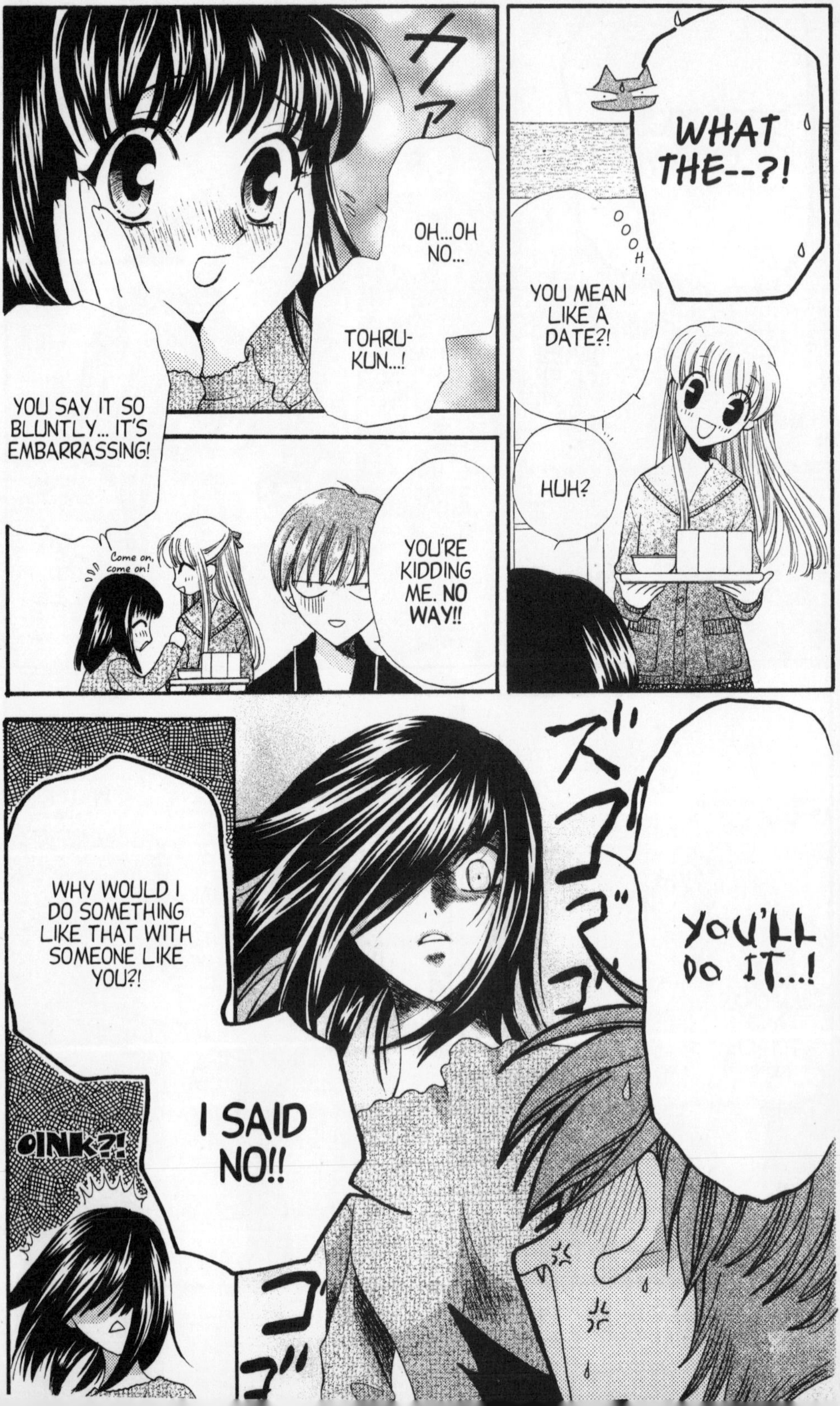
WHAT THE--?!
OOOH!
YOU MEAN LIKE A DATE?!
HUH?
OH...OH NO...
TOHRU-KUN...!
YOU SAY IT SO BLUNTLY... IT'S EMBARRASSING!
YOU'RE KIDDING ME. NO WAY!!
Come on, come on!
YOU'LL DO IT...!
WHY WOULD I DO SOMETHING LIKE THAT WITH SOMEONE LIKE YOU?!
I SAID NO!!
OINK?!

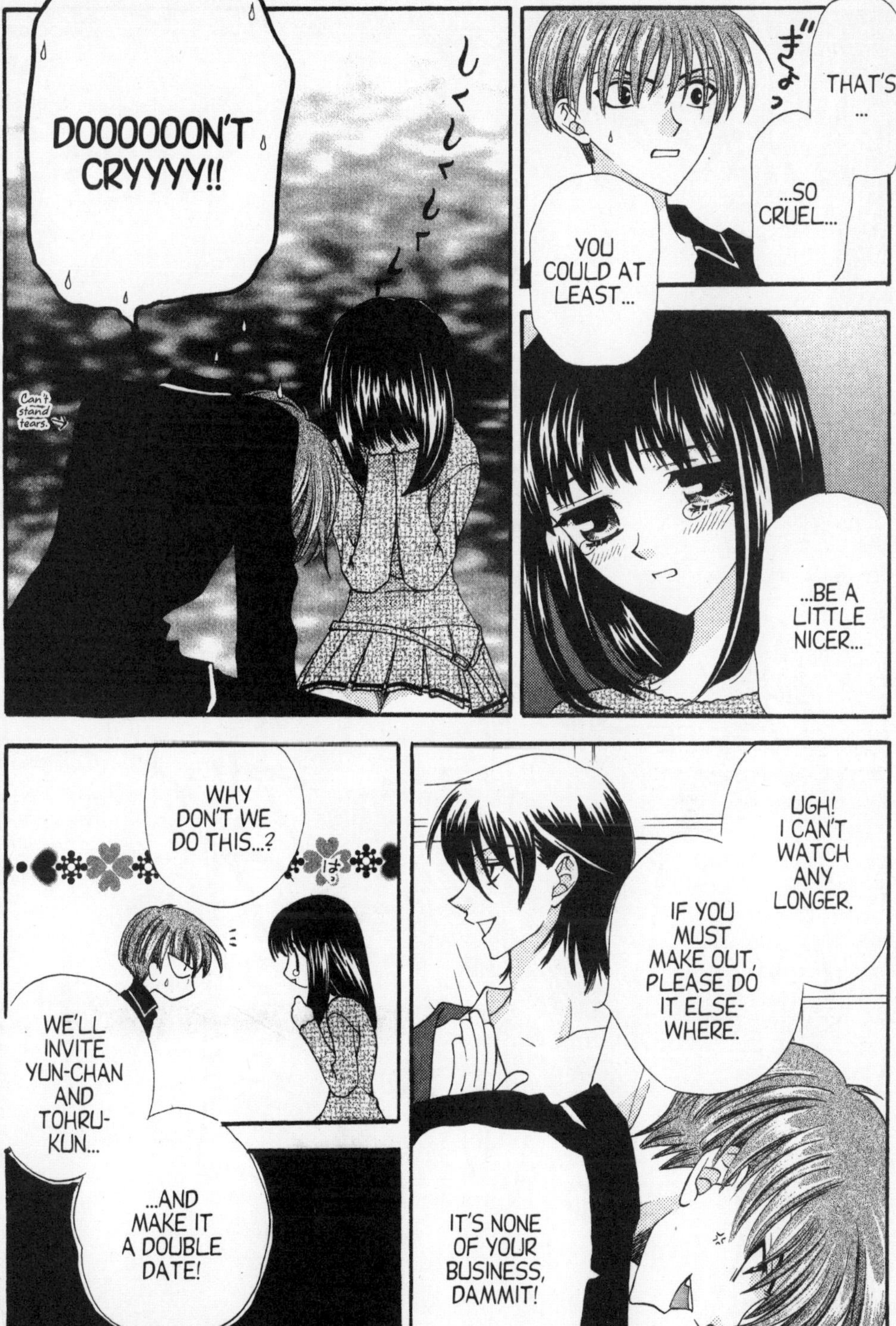
ぎょっ
THAT'S...
...SO CRUEL...
YOU COULD AT LEAST...
...BE A LITTLE NICER...
DOOOOOON'T CRYYYY!!
しくしくしく
Can't stand tears.
UGH! I CAN'T WATCH ANY LONGER.
IF YOU MUST MAKE OUT, PLEASE DO IT ELSE-WHERE.
IT'S NONE OF YOUR BUSINESS, DAMMIT!
WHY DON'T WE DO THIS...?
はっ
WE'LL INVITE YUN-CHAN AND TOHRU-KUN...
...AND MAKE IT A DOUBLE DATE!

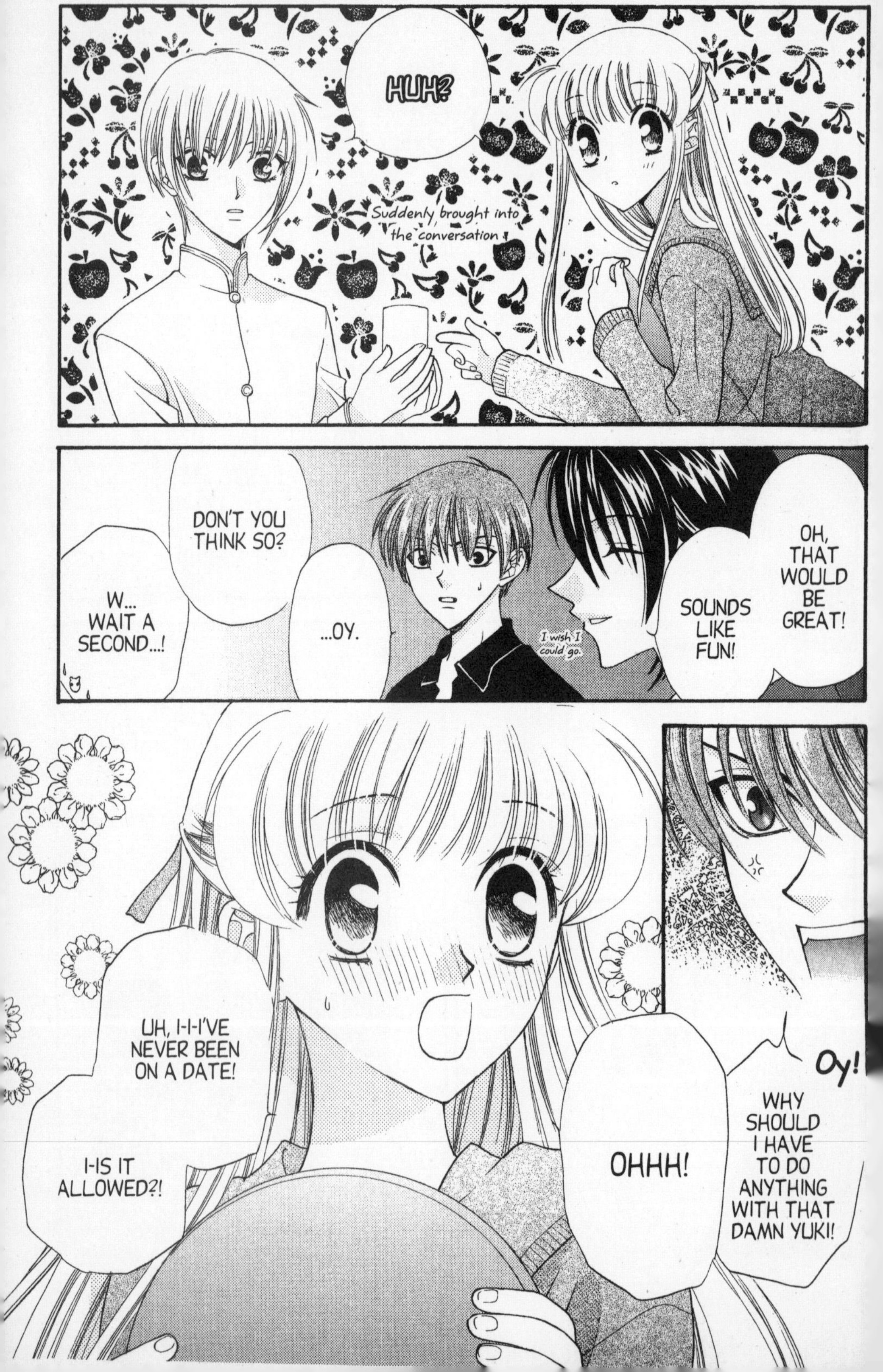
HUH?
Suddenly brought into the conversation
OH, THAT WOULD BE GREAT!
SOUNDS LIKE FUN!
I wish I could go.
...OY.
DON'T YOU THINK SO?
W... WAIT A SECOND...!
Oy!
WHY SHOULD I HAVE TO DO ANYTHING WITH THAT DAMN YUKI!
OHHH!
UH, I-I-I'VE NEVER BEEN ON A DATE!
I-IS IT ALLOWED?!

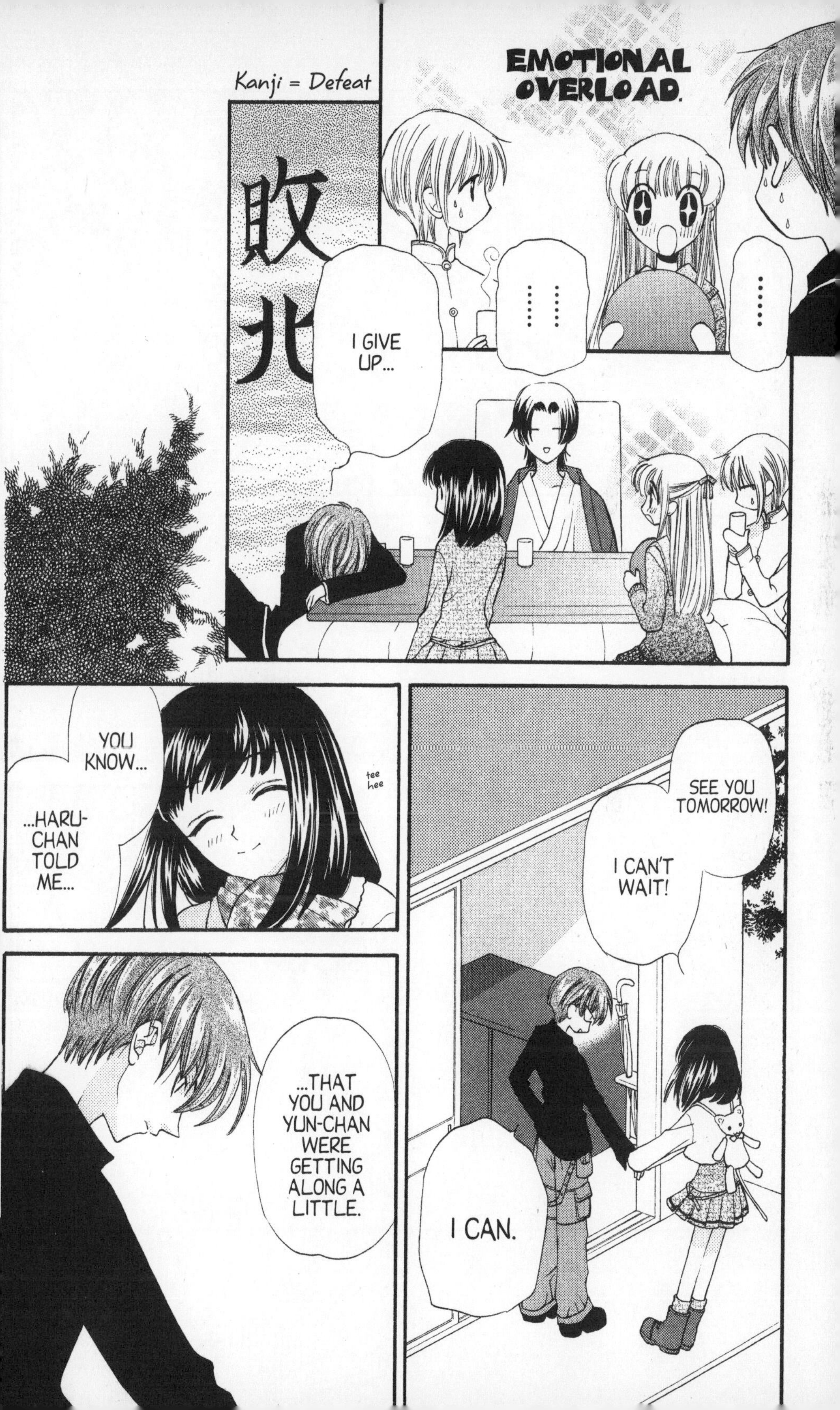
EMOTIONAL OVERLOAD.
......
......
I GIVE UP...
Kanji = Defeat
敗北
SEE YOU TOMORROW!
I CAN'T WAIT!
I CAN.
YOU KNOW...
tee hee
...HARU-CHAN TOLD ME...
...THAT YOU AND YUN-CHAN WERE GETTING ALONG A LITTLE.

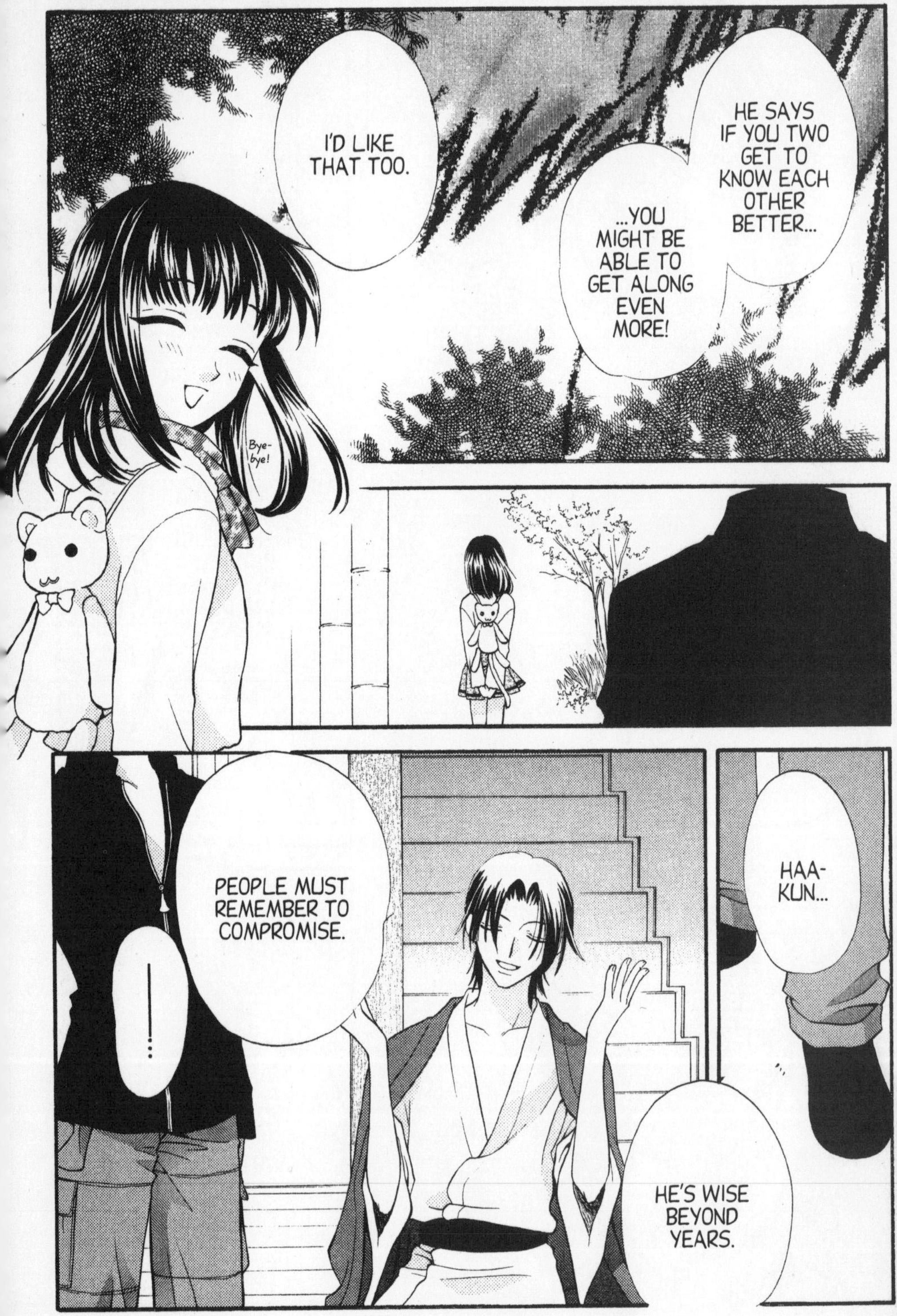
HE SAYS IF YOU TWO GET TO KNOW EACH OTHER BETTER...
...YOU MIGHT BE ABLE TO GET ALONG EVEN MORE!
I'D LIKE THAT TOO.
Bye-bye!
HAA-KUN...
PEOPLE MUST REMEMBER TO COMPROMISE.
HE'S WISE BEYOND YEARS.
......

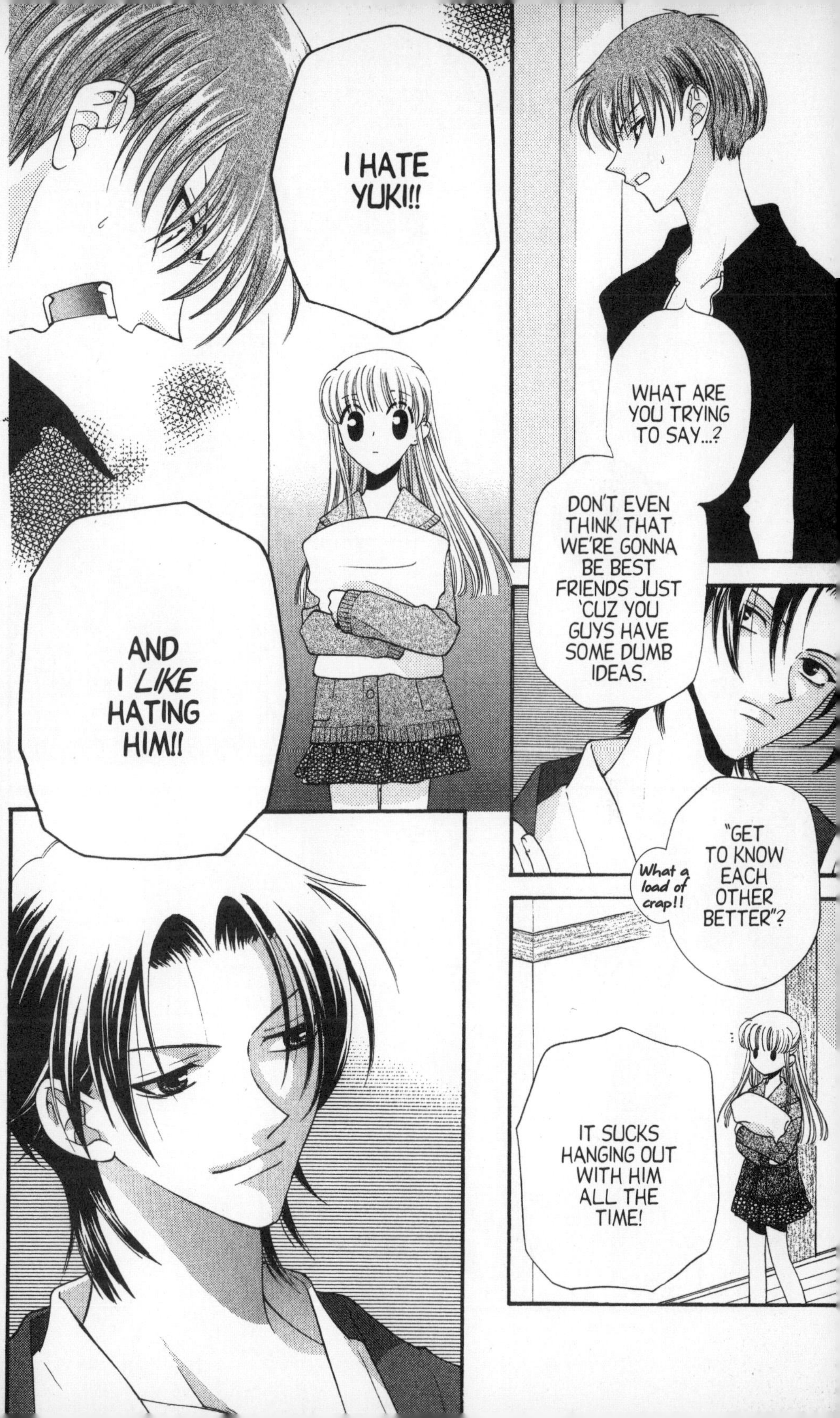
WHAT ARE YOU TRYING TO SAY...?
DON'T EVEN THINK THAT WE'RE GONNA BE BEST FRIENDS JUST 'CUZ YOU GUYS HAVE SOME DUMB IDEAS.
"GET TO KNOW EACH OTHER BETTER"?
What a load of crap!!
IT SUCKS HANGING OUT WITH HIM ALL THE TIME!
I HATE YUKI!!
AND I *LIKE* HATING HIM!!

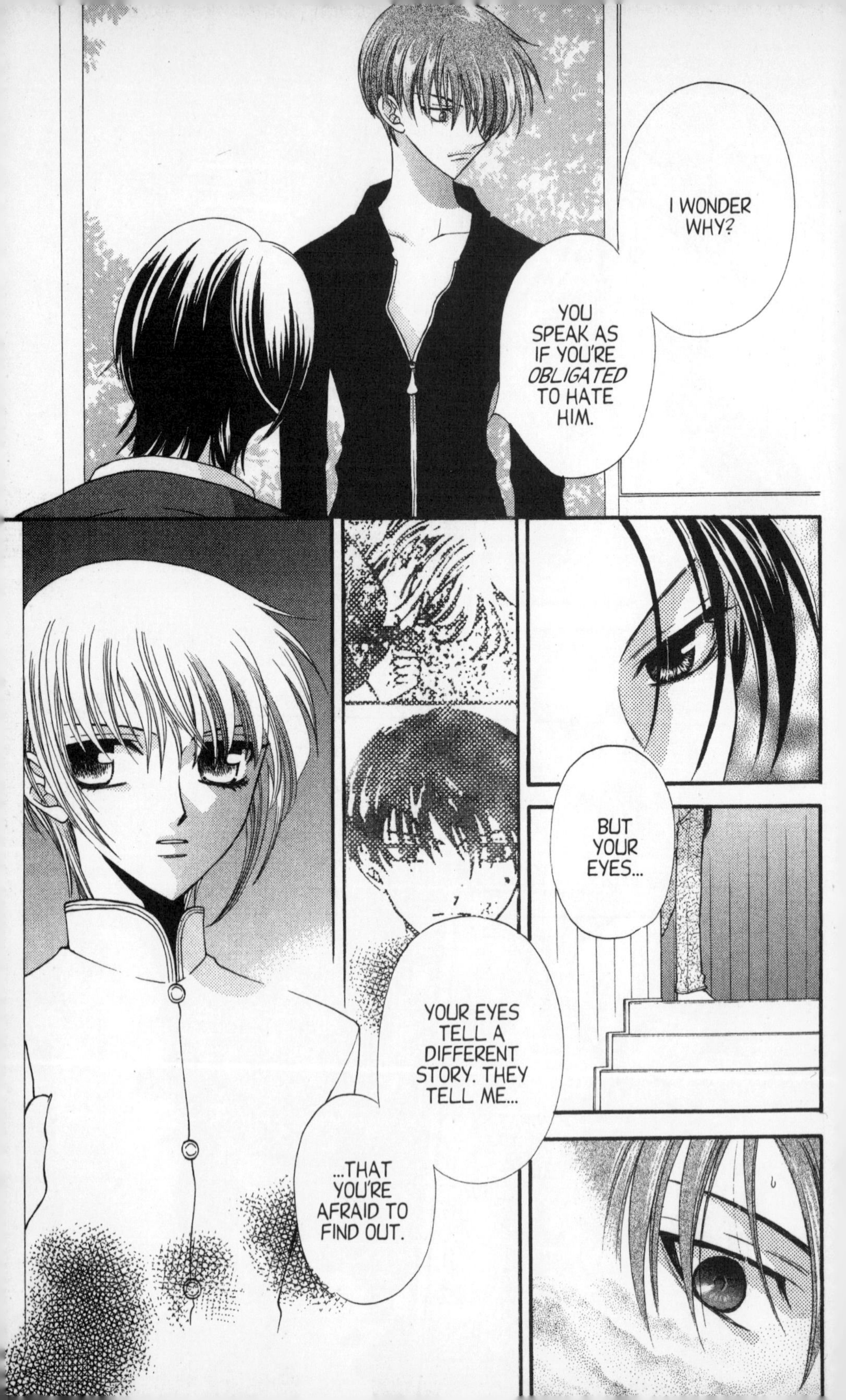
I WONDER WHY?
YOU SPEAK AS IF YOU'RE *OBLIGATED* TO HATE HIM.
BUT YOUR EYES...
YOUR EYES TELL A DIFFERENT STORY. THEY TELL ME...
...THAT YOU'RE AFRAID TO FIND OUT.

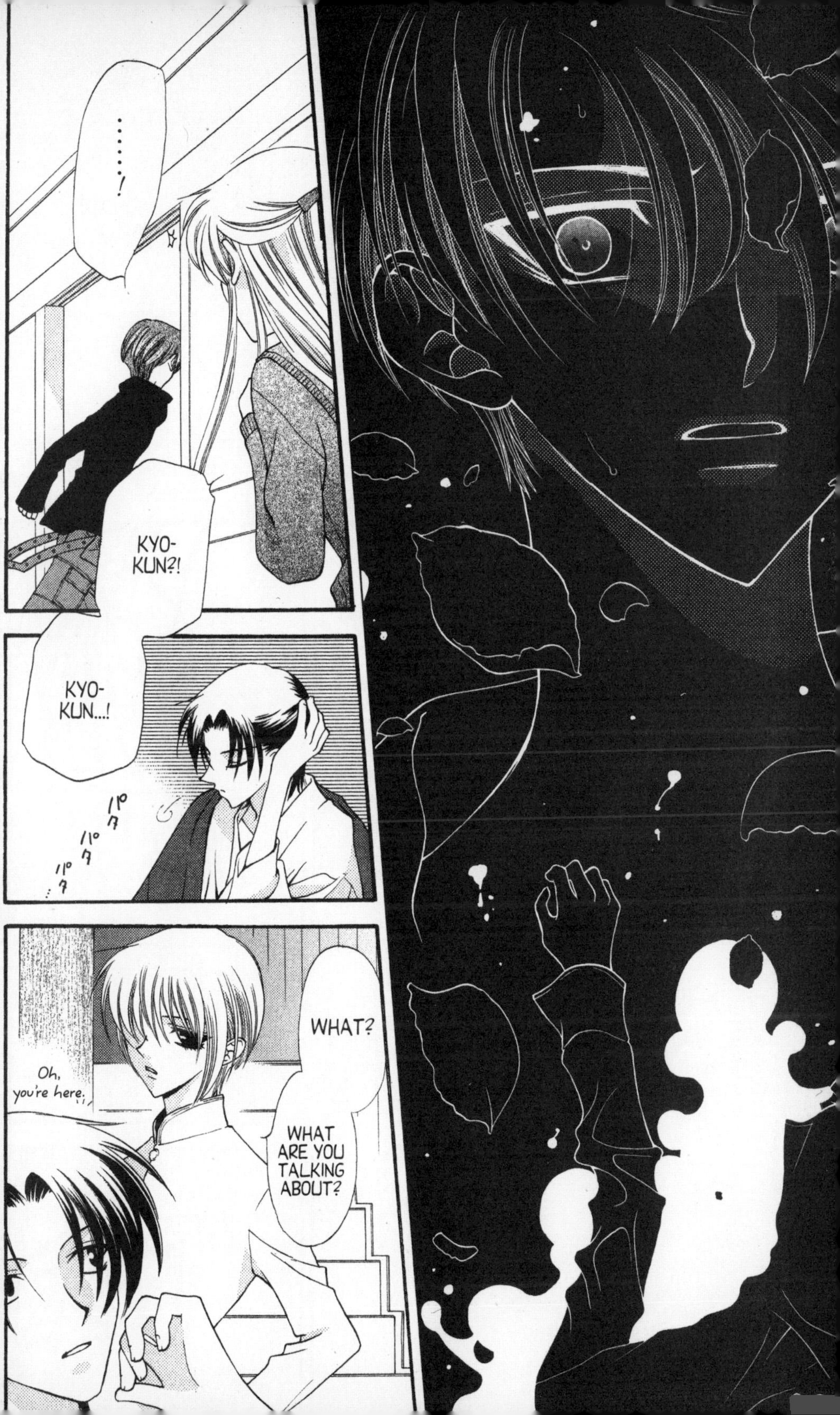
......!
KYO-KUN?!
KYO-KUN...!
パタ パタ パタ
WHAT?
WHAT ARE YOU TALKING ABOUT?
Oh, you're here.

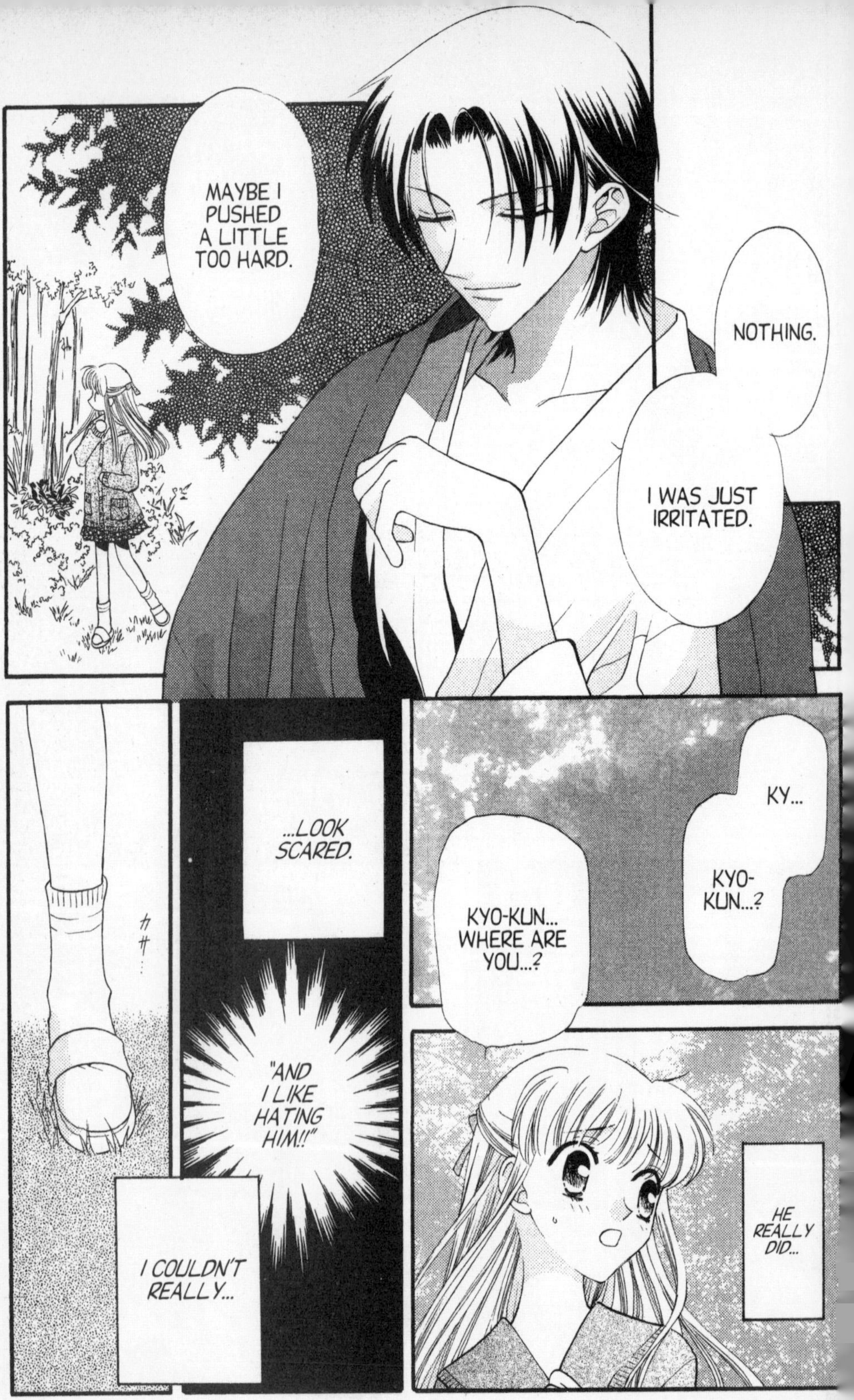
NOTHING.
I WAS JUST IRRITATED.
MAYBE I PUSHED A LITTLE TOO HARD.
KY...
KYO-KUN...?
KYO-KUN... WHERE ARE YOU...?
HE REALLY DID...
...LOOK SCARED.
"AND I LIKE HATING HIM!!"
I COULDN'T REALLY...
カサ…

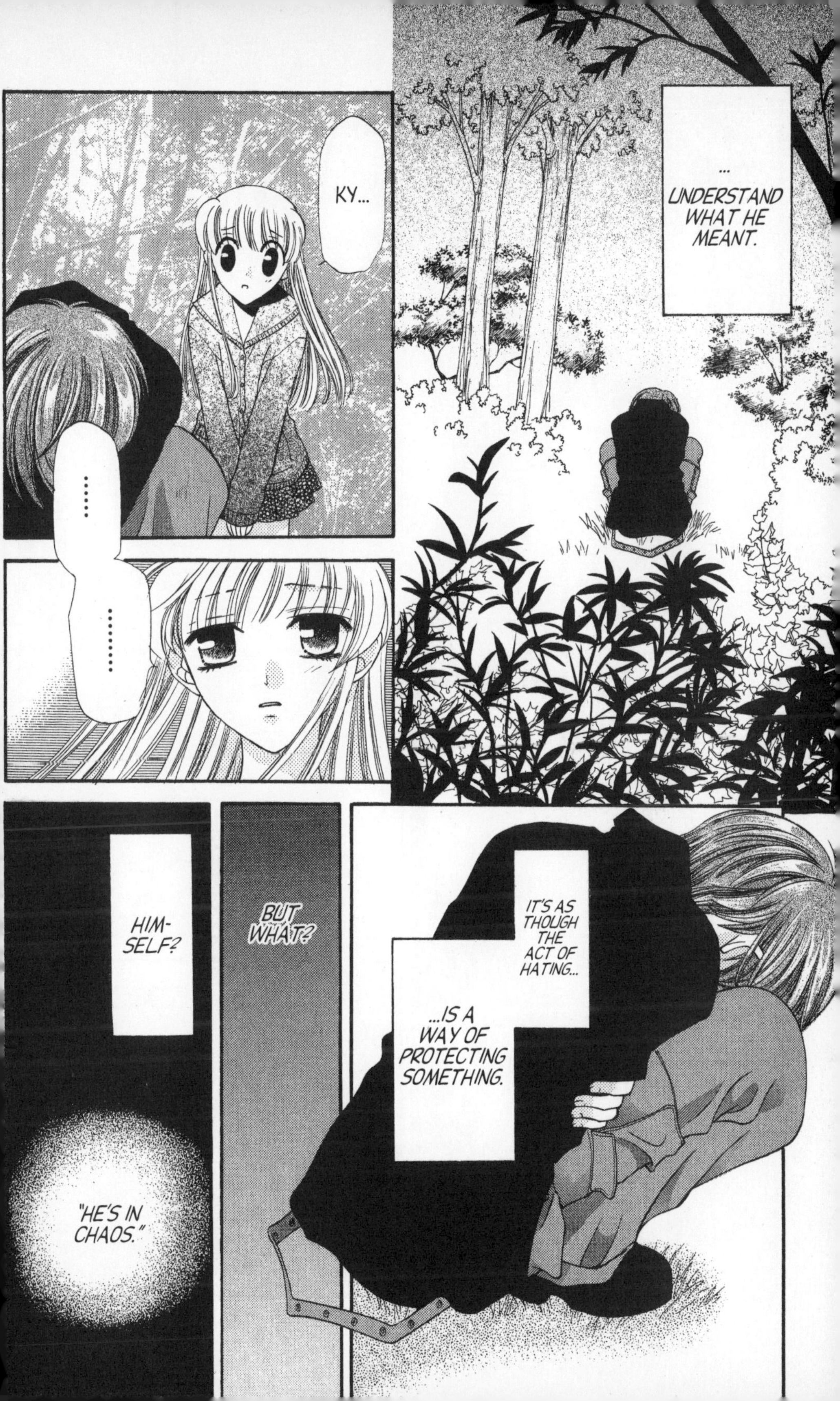

... UNDERSTAND WHAT HE MEANT.
KY...
......
....
IT'S AS THOUGH THE ACT OF HATING...
...IS A WAY OF PROTECTING SOMETHING.
BUT WHAT?
HIM-SELF?
"HE'S IN CHAOS."

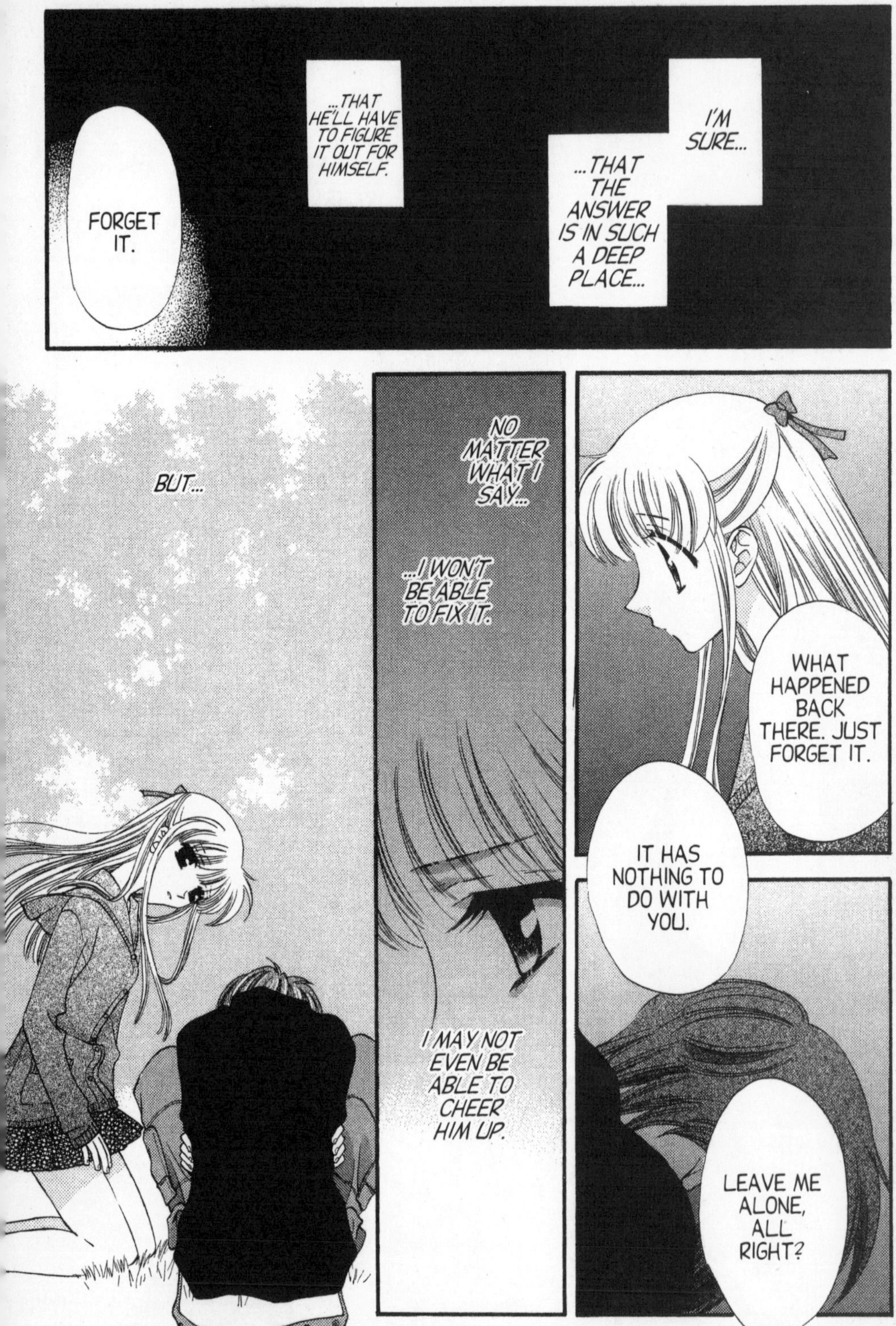
I'M SURE...
...THAT THE ANSWER IS IN SUCH A DEEP PLACE...
...THAT HE'LL HAVE TO FIGURE IT OUT FOR HIMSELF.
FORGET IT.
WHAT HAPPENED BACK THERE. JUST FORGET IT.
IT HAS NOTHING TO DO WITH YOU.
LEAVE ME ALONE, ALL RIGHT?
NO MATTER WHAT I SAY...
...I WON'T BE ABLE TO FIX IT.
I MAY NOT EVEN BE ABLE TO CHEER HIM UP.
BUT...

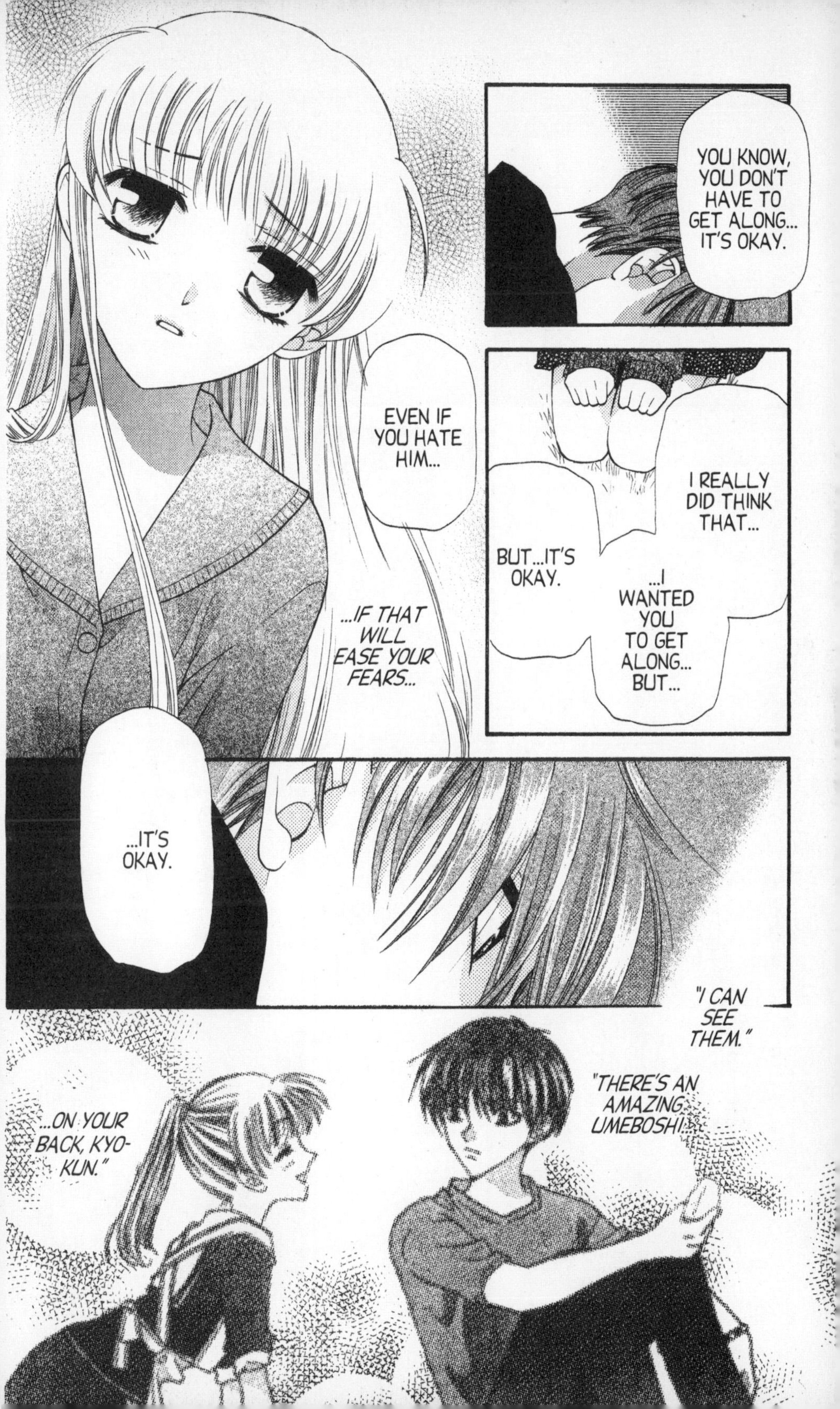
YOU KNOW, YOU DON'T HAVE TO GET ALONG... IT'S OKAY.
I REALLY DID THINK THAT...
...I WANTED YOU TO GET ALONG... BUT...
BUT...IT'S OKAY.
EVEN IF YOU HATE HIM...
...IF THAT WILL EASE YOUR FEARS...
...IT'S OKAY.
"I CAN SEE THEM."
"THERE'S AN AMAZING UMEBOSHI...
...ON YOUR BACK, KYO-KUN."

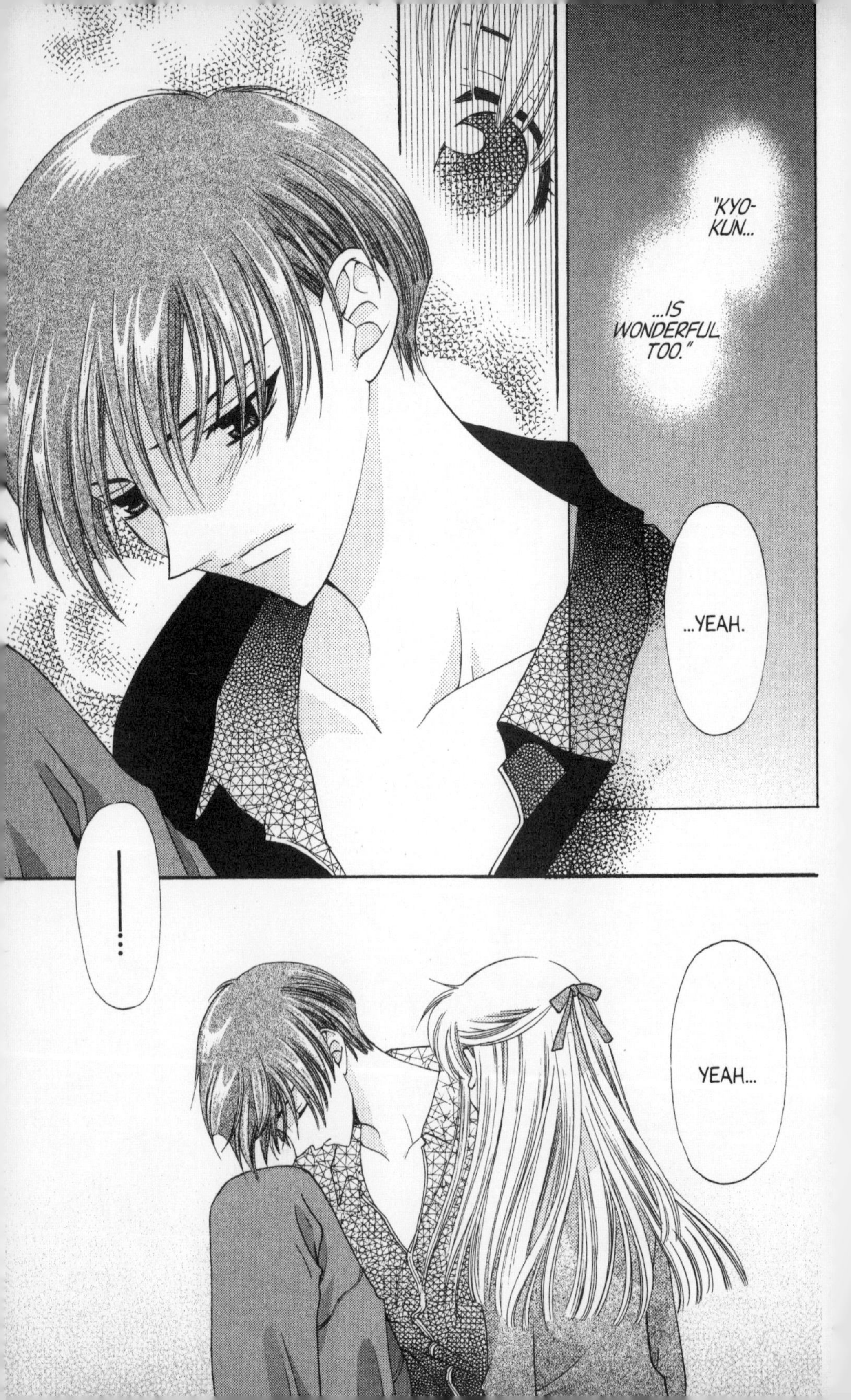
"KYO-KUN...
...IS WONDERFUL TOO."
...YEAH.
YEAH...
—...

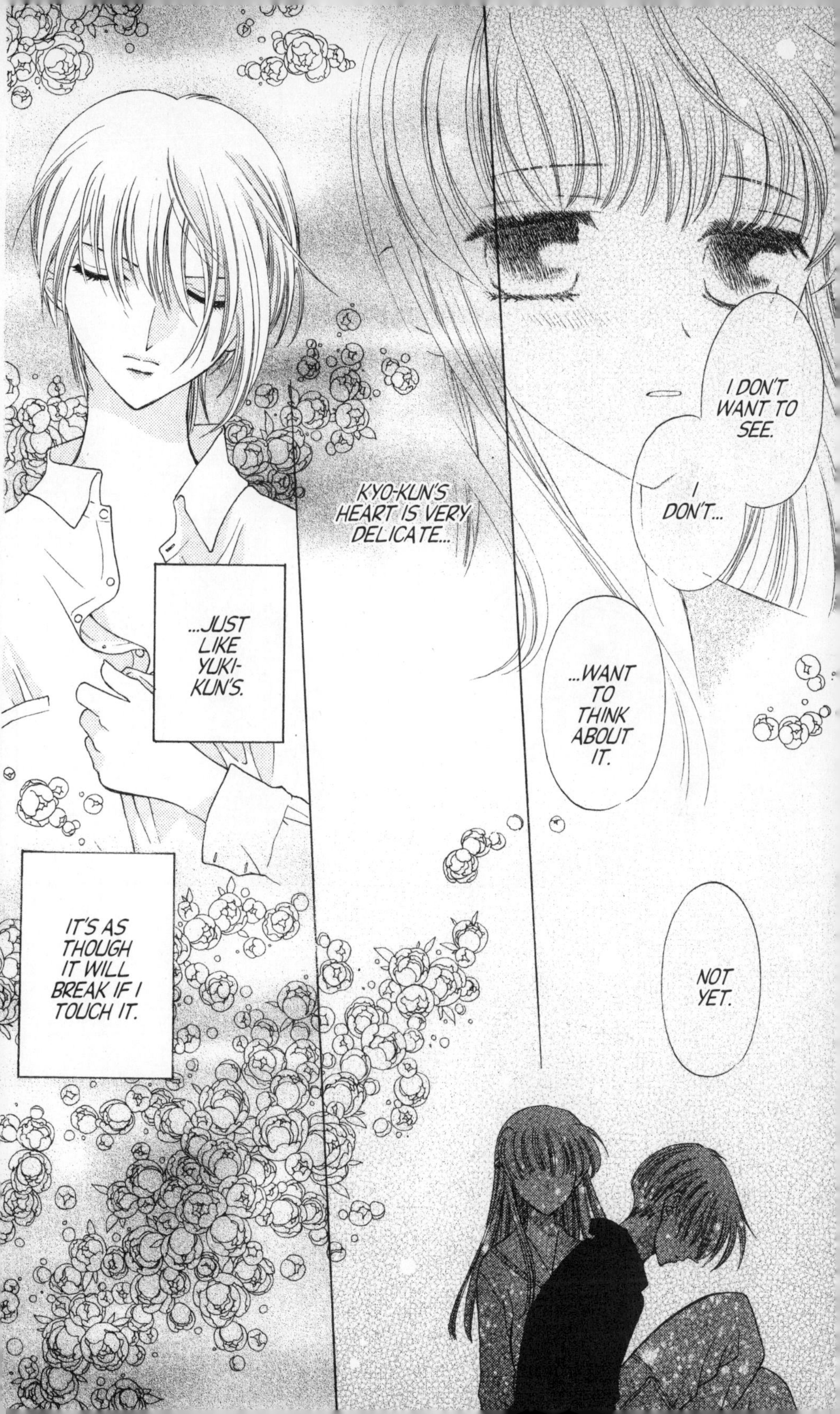
I DON'T WANT TO SEE.
I DON'T...
...WANT TO THINK ABOUT IT.
NOT YET.
KYO-KUN'S HEART IS VERY DELICATE...
...JUST LIKE YUKI-KUN'S.
IT'S AS THOUGH IT WILL BREAK IF I TOUCH IT.

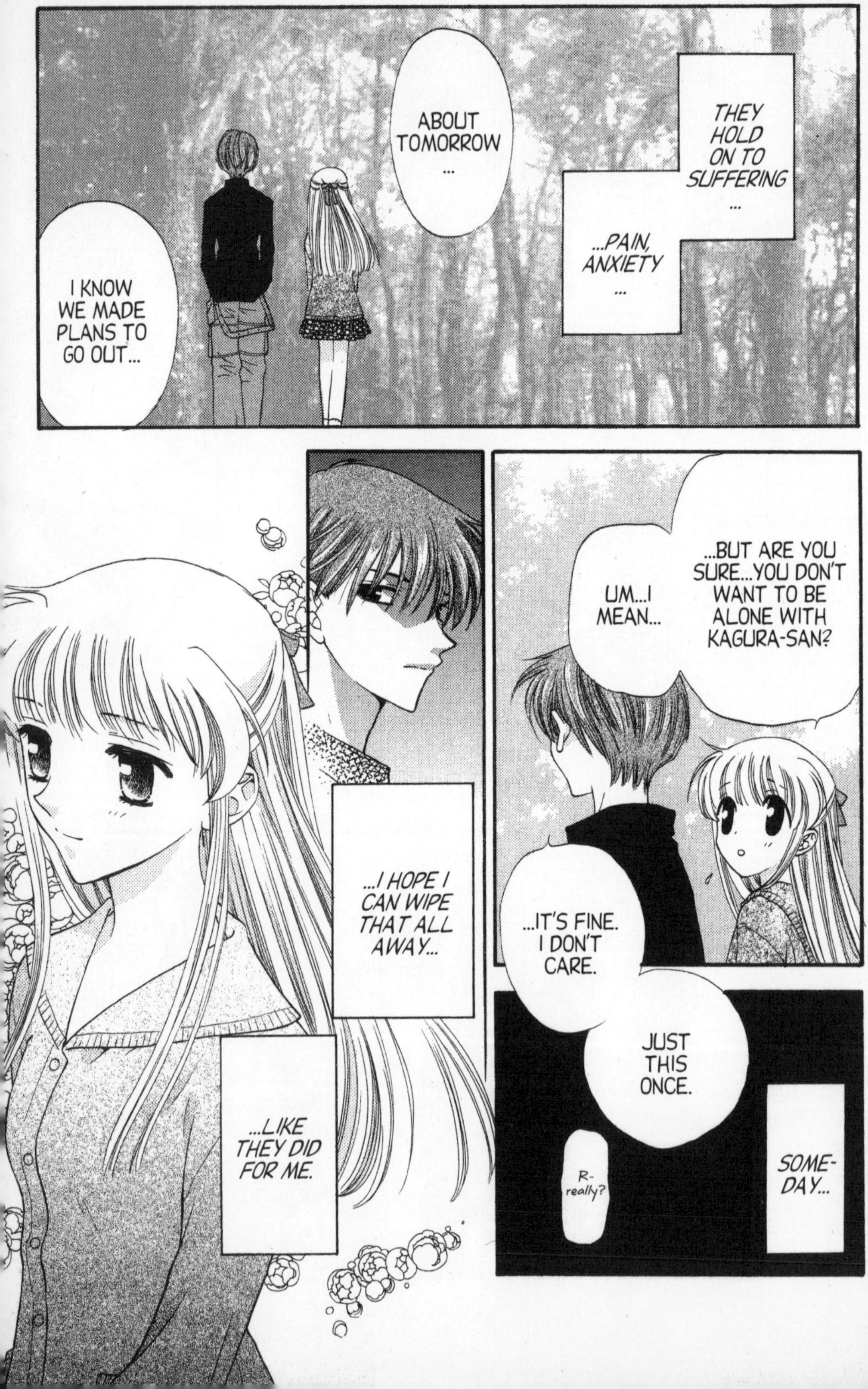
THEY HOLD ON TO SUFFERING ...
...PAIN, ANXIETY ...
ABOUT TOMORROW ...
I KNOW WE MADE PLANS TO GO OUT...
UM...I MEAN...
...BUT ARE YOU SURE...YOU DON'T WANT TO BE ALONE WITH KAGURA-SAN?
...IT'S FINE. I DON'T CARE.
JUST THIS ONCE.
R-really?
SOME-DAY...
...I HOPE I CAN WIPE THAT ALL AWAY...
...LIKE THEY DID FOR ME.

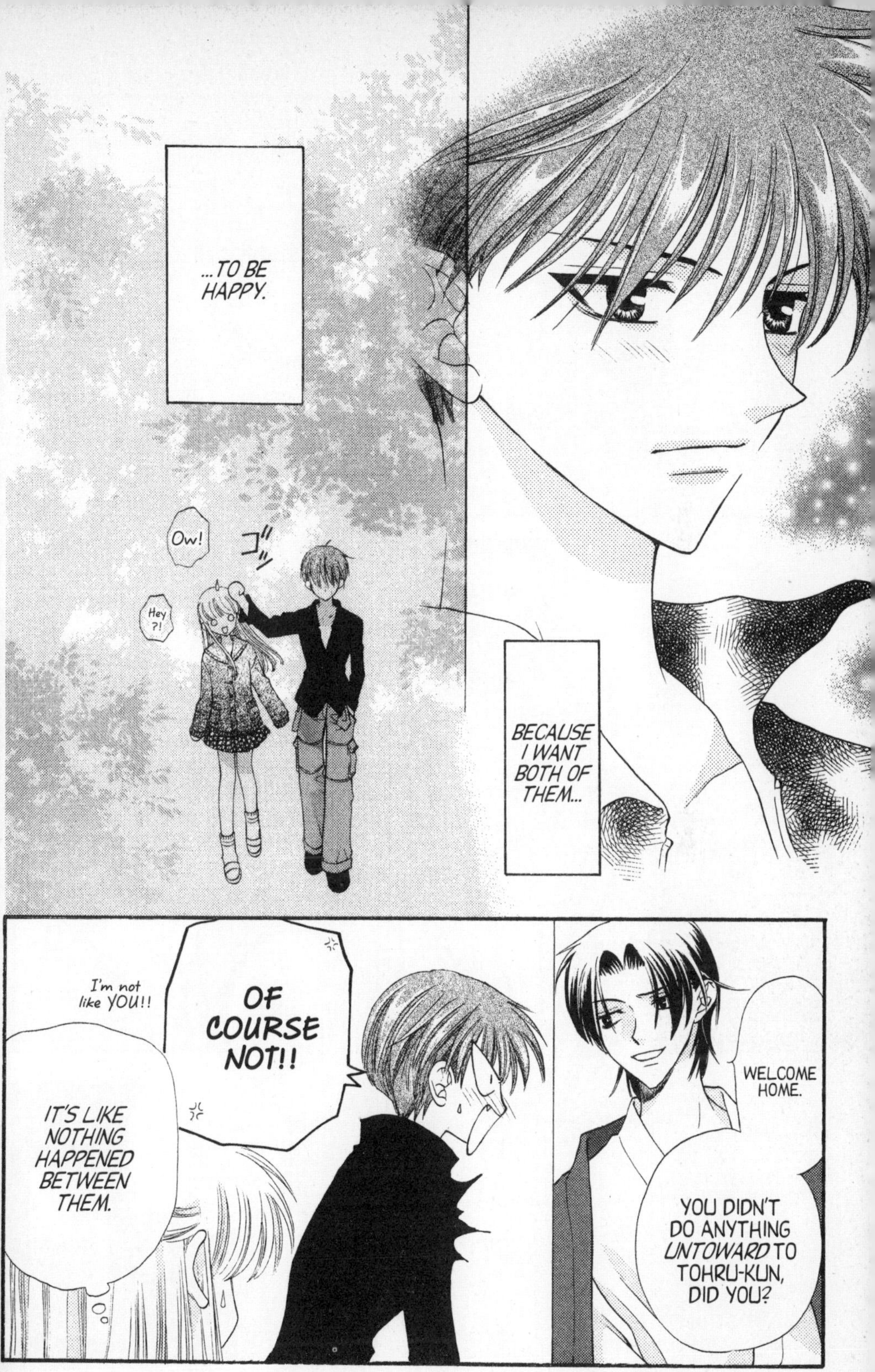
BECAUSE I WANT BOTH OF THEM...
...TO BE HAPPY.
Ow!
ゴッ
Hey ?!
WELCOME HOME.
YOU DIDN'T DO ANYTHING *UNTOWARD* TO TOHRU-KUN, DID YOU?
OF COURSE NOT!!
I'm not like YOU!!
IT'S LIKE NOTHING HAPPENED BETWEEN THEM.

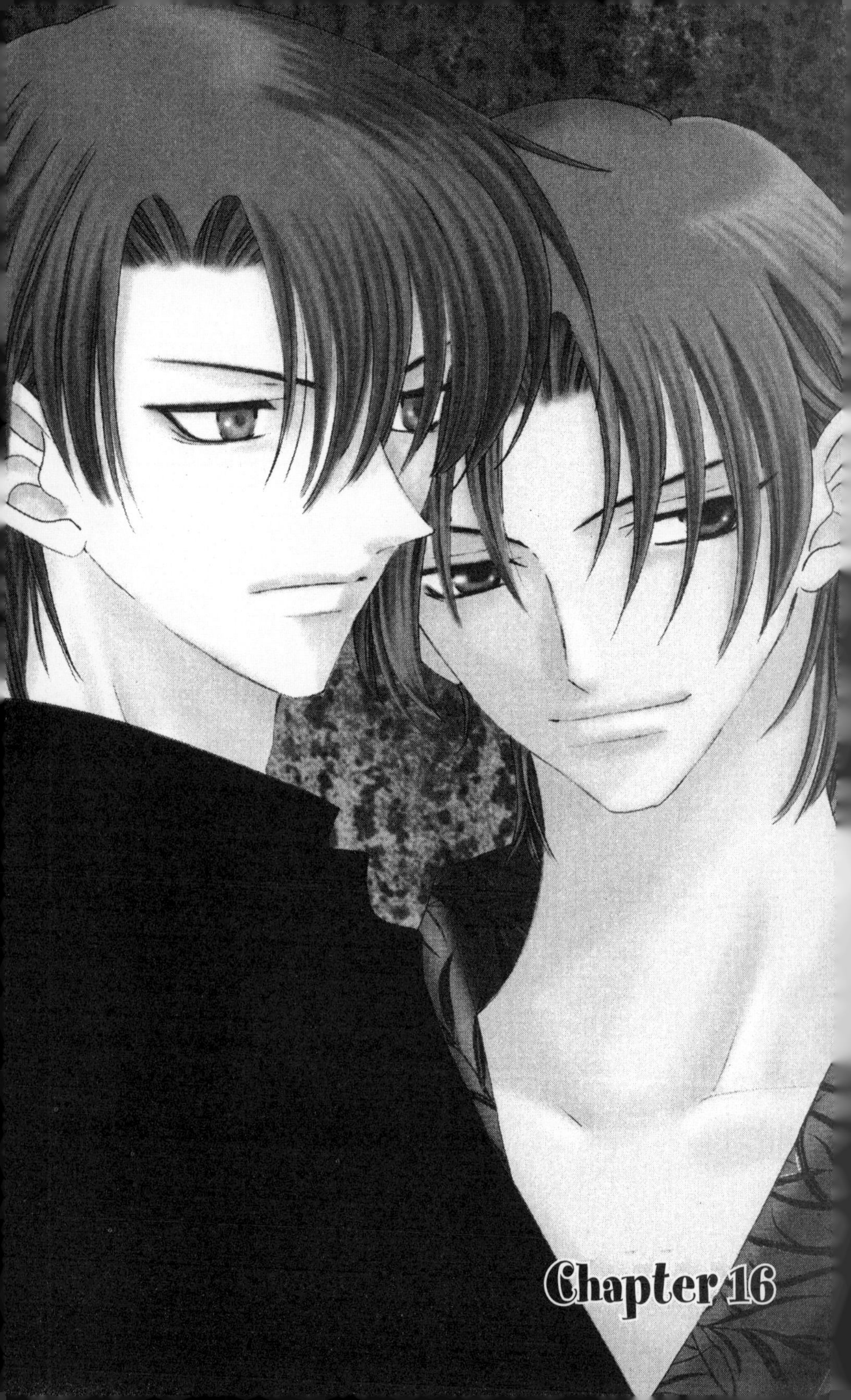
Chapter 16

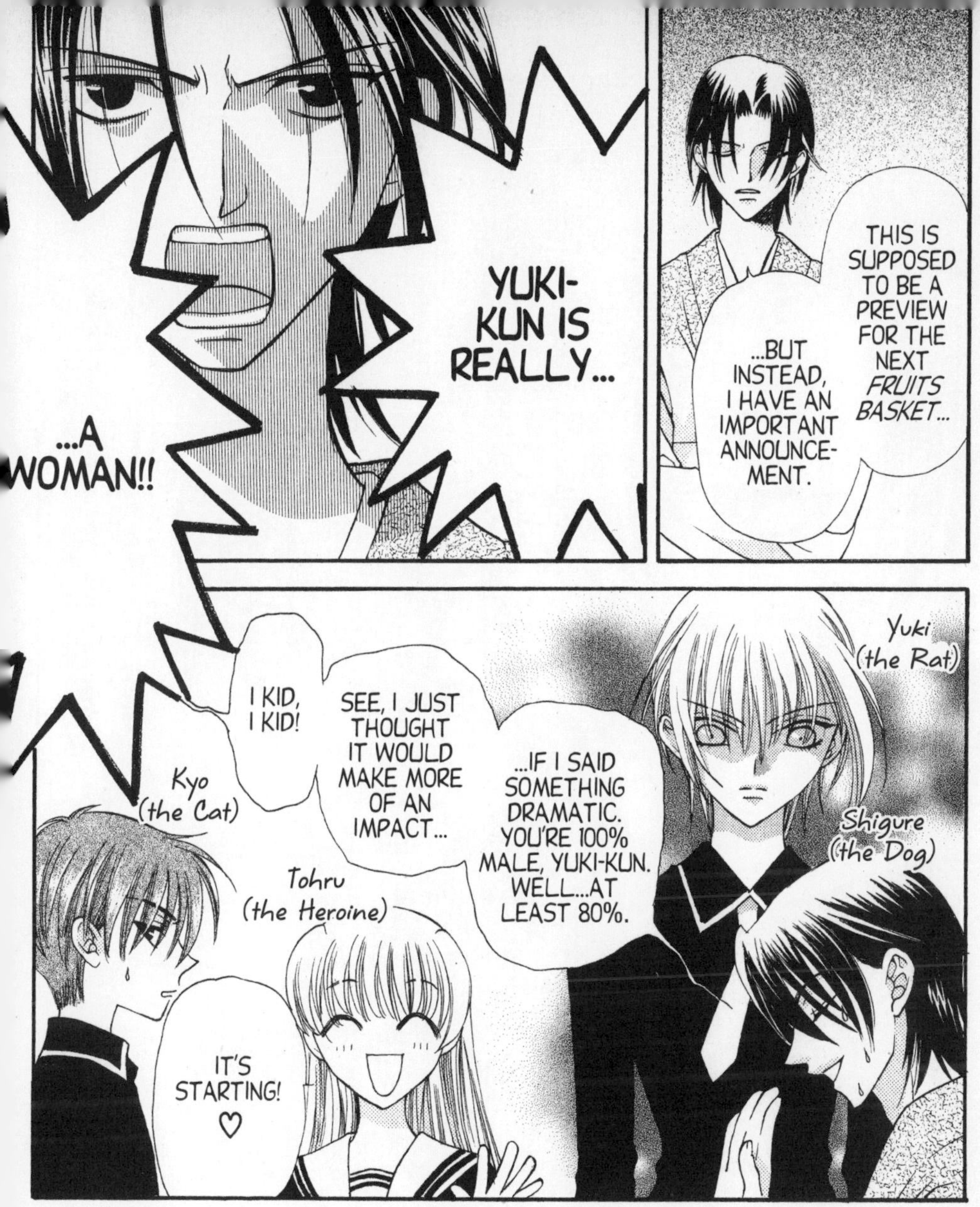
THIS IS SUPPOSED TO BE A PREVIEW FOR THE NEXT *FRUITS BASKET*...
...BUT INSTEAD, I HAVE AN IMPORTANT ANNOUNCEMENT.
YUKI-KUN IS REALLY...
...A WOMAN!!
Yuki (the Rat)
I KID, I KID!
SEE, I JUST THOUGHT IT WOULD MAKE MORE OF AN IMPACT...
...IF I SAID SOMETHING DRAMATIC. YOU'RE 100% MALE, YUKI-KUN. WELL...AT LEAST 80%.
Shigure (the Dog)
Kyo (the Cat)
Tohru (the Heroine)
IT'S STARTING! ♡

Omake Theater, Part 2

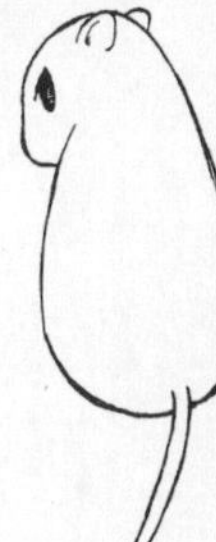

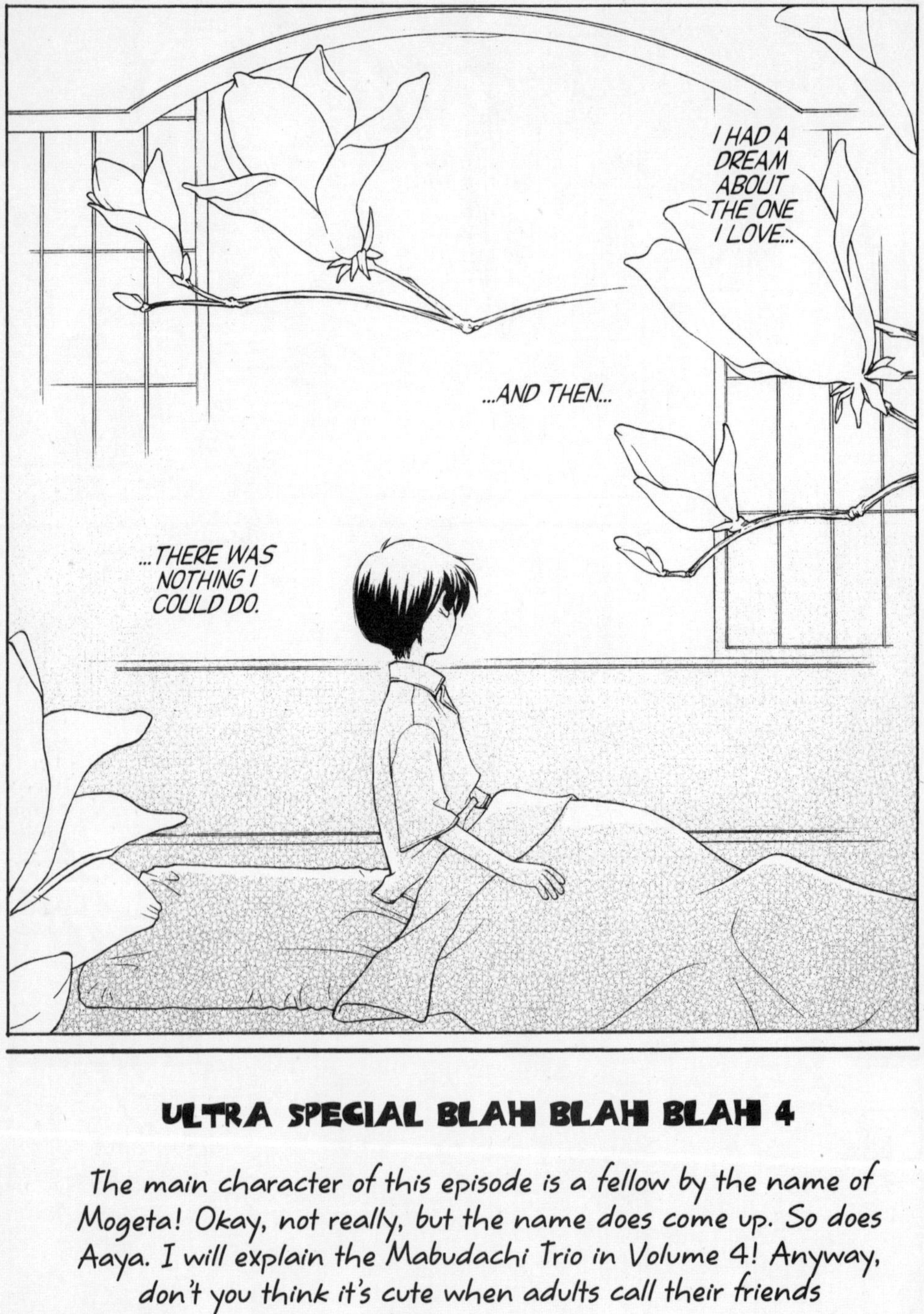
I HAD A DREAM ABOUT THE ONE I LOVE...
...AND THEN...
...THERE WAS NOTHING I COULD DO.

ULTRA SPECIAL BLAH BLAH BLAH 4

The main character of this episode is a fellow by the name of Mogeta! Okay, not really, but the name does come up. So does Aaya. I will explain the Mabudachi Trio in Volume 4! Anyway, don't you think it's cute when adults call their friends by pet names?

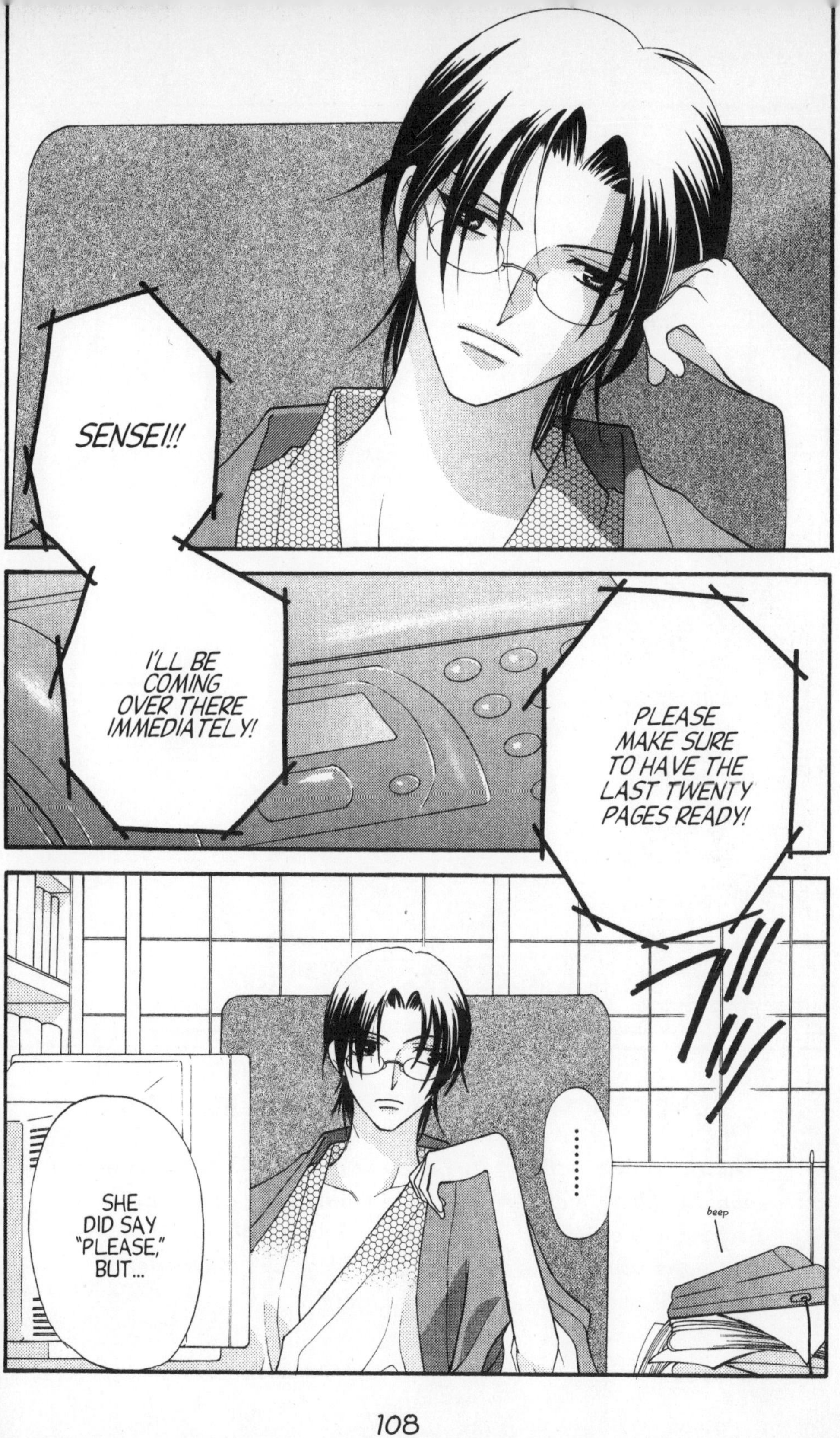
SENSEI!!
I'LL BE COMING OVER THERE IMMEDIATELY!
PLEASE MAKE SURE TO HAVE THE LAST TWENTY PAGES READY!
beep
....
SHE DID SAY "PLEASE," BUT...

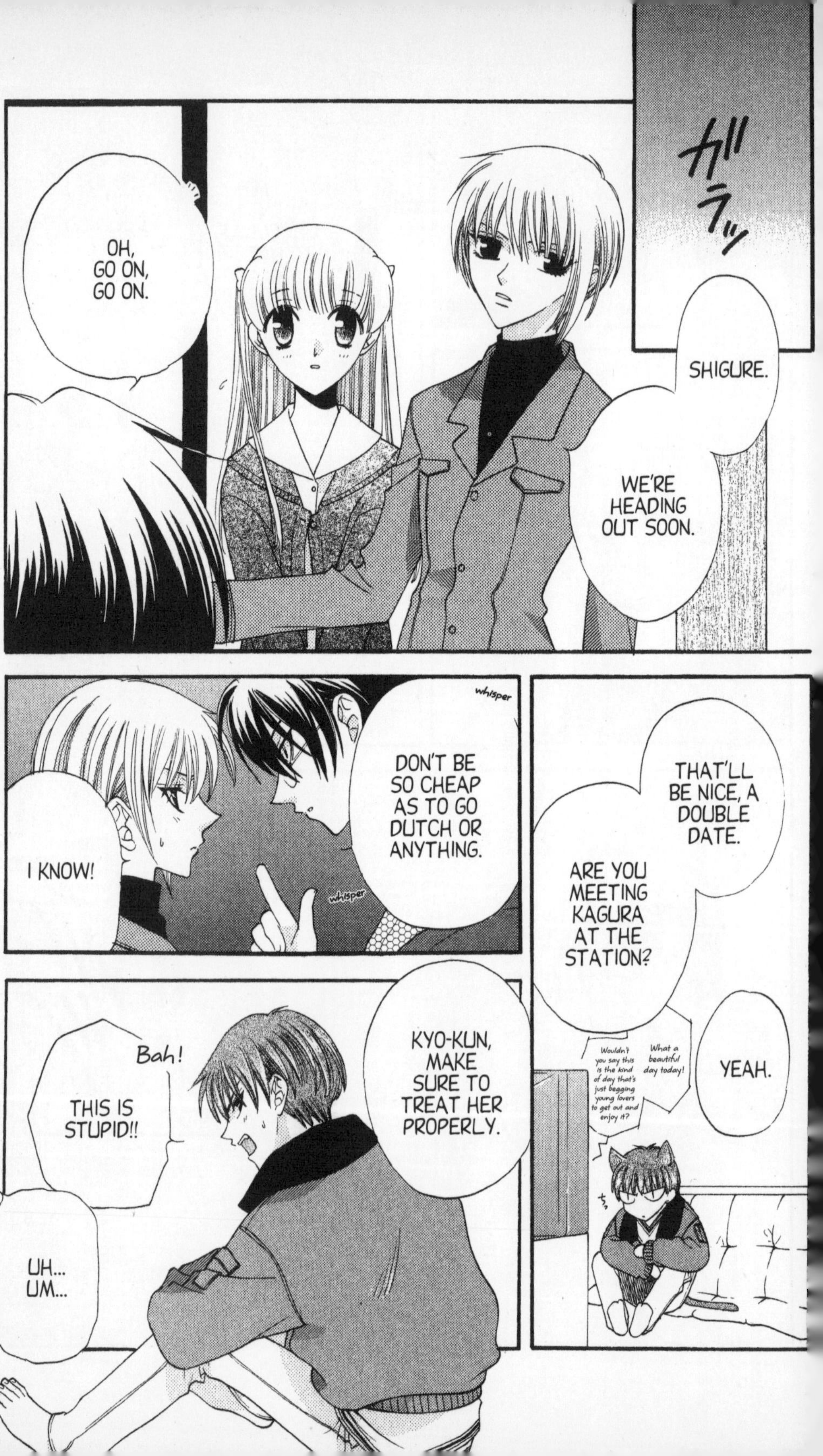

ガラッ
SHIGURE.
WE'RE HEADING OUT SOON.
OH, GO ON, GO ON.
THAT'LL BE NICE, A DOUBLE DATE.
ARE YOU MEETING KAGURA AT THE STATION?
YEAH.
What a beautiful day today!
Wouldn't you say this is the kind of day that's just begging young lovers to get out and enjoy it?
whisper
DON'T BE SO CHEAP AS TO GO DUTCH OR ANYTHING.
whisper
I KNOW!
KYO-KUN, MAKE SURE TO TREAT HER PROPERLY.
Bah!
THIS IS STUPID!!
UH... UM...

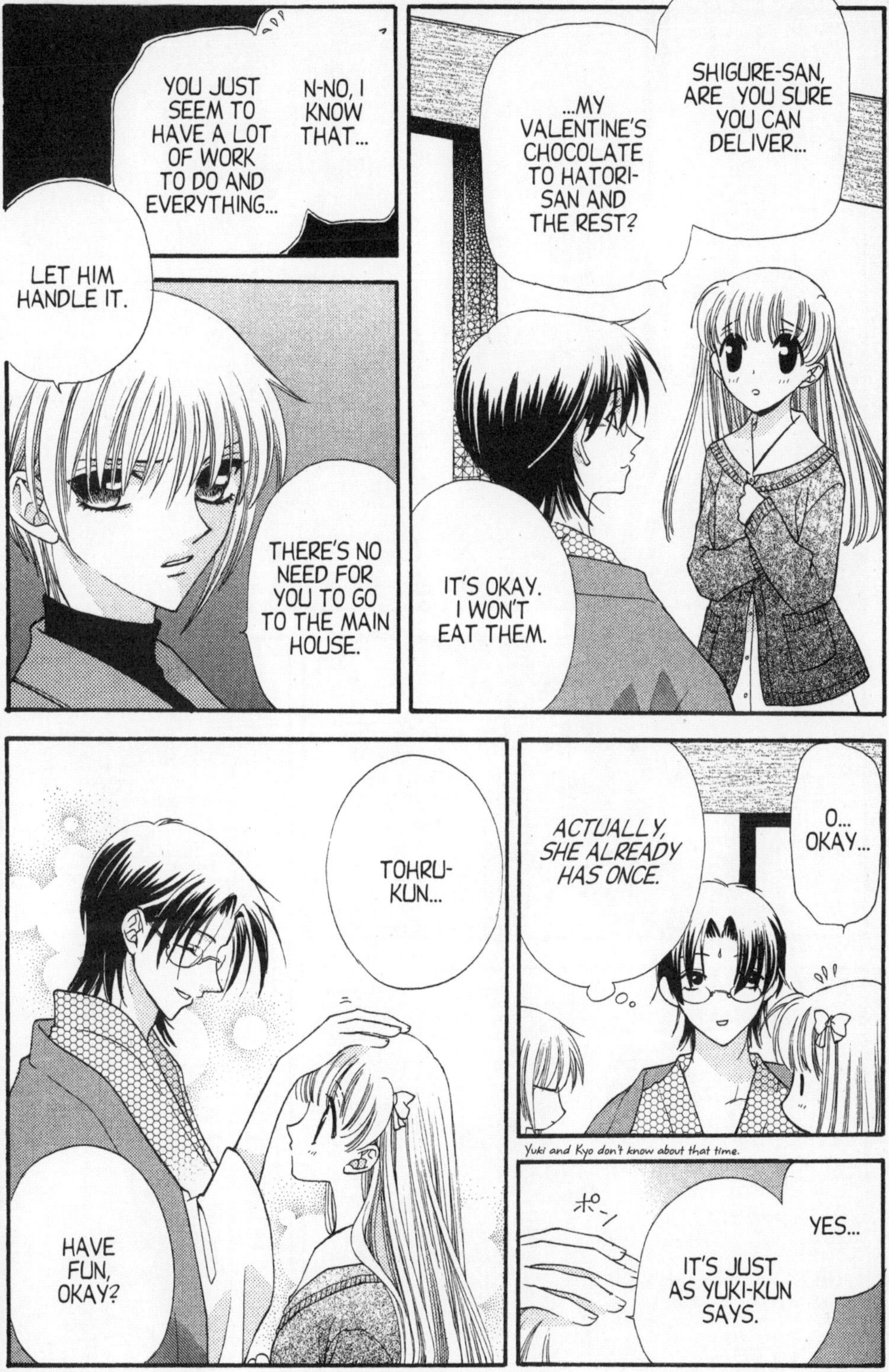
SHIGURE-SAN, ARE YOU SURE YOU CAN DELIVER...
...MY VALENTINE'S CHOCOLATE TO HATORI-SAN AND THE REST?
IT'S OKAY. I WON'T EAT THEM.
N-NO, I KNOW THAT...
YOU JUST SEEM TO HAVE A LOT OF WORK TO DO AND EVERYTHING...
THERE'S NO NEED FOR YOU TO GO TO THE MAIN HOUSE.
LET HIM HANDLE IT.
O... OKAY...
ACTUALLY, SHE ALREADY HAS ONCE.
Yuki and Kyo don't know about that time.
YES...
ポー
IT'S JUST AS YUKI-KUN SAYS.
TOHRU-KUN...
HAVE FUN, OKAY?

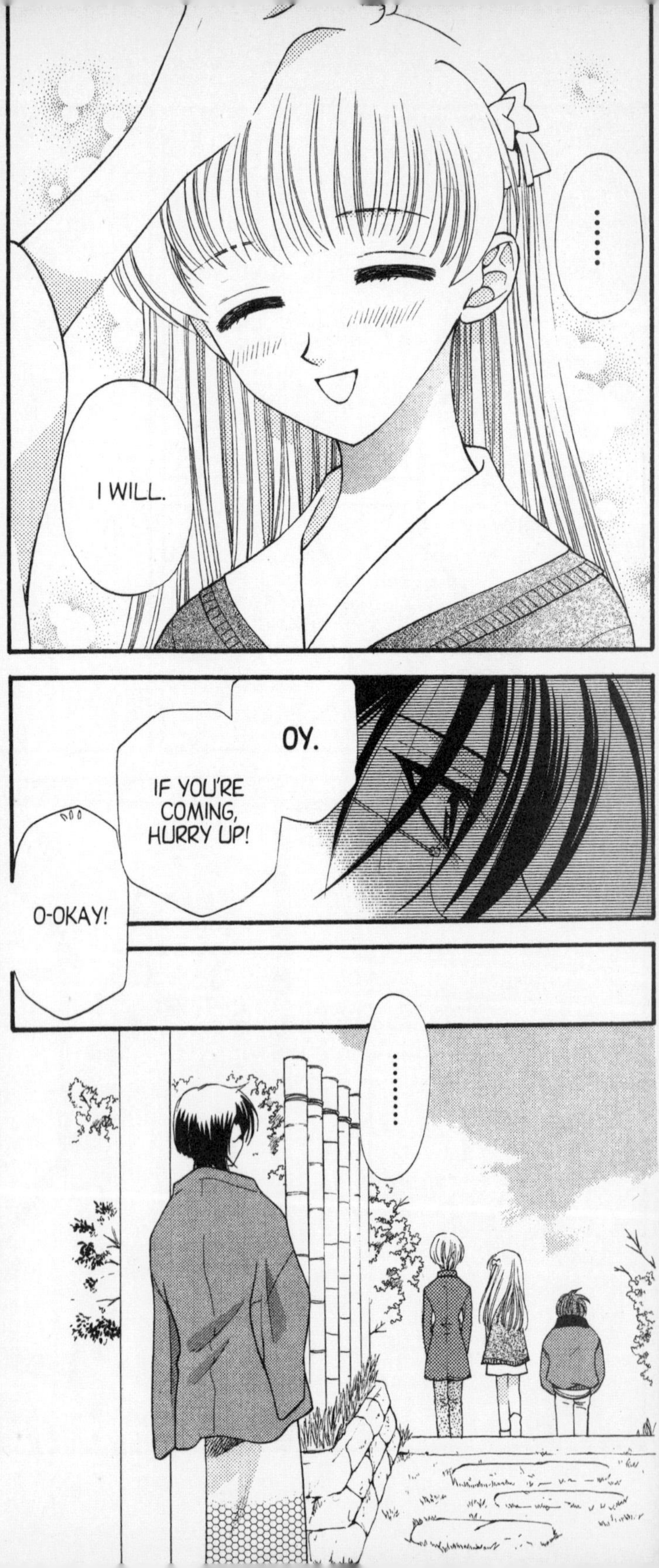
……
I WILL.
OY.
IF YOU'RE COMING, HURRY UP!
O-OKAY!
……

Fruits Basket Part 4

I think people who read the magazine already know this, but I built my own home page. It was called "Chotto Ippuku." It took forever. First, I don't understand html tags. It's like learning alien language! I gave that up pretty quickly. I got some software that helps you build a home page without knowing tags, and little by little, I learned how to do it. There was no one around I could ask about it, so it was really hard. I'm updating regularly, but...I wonder how long I can keep this up...?

Editor's note: [Chotto Ippuku went offline in September 2002]

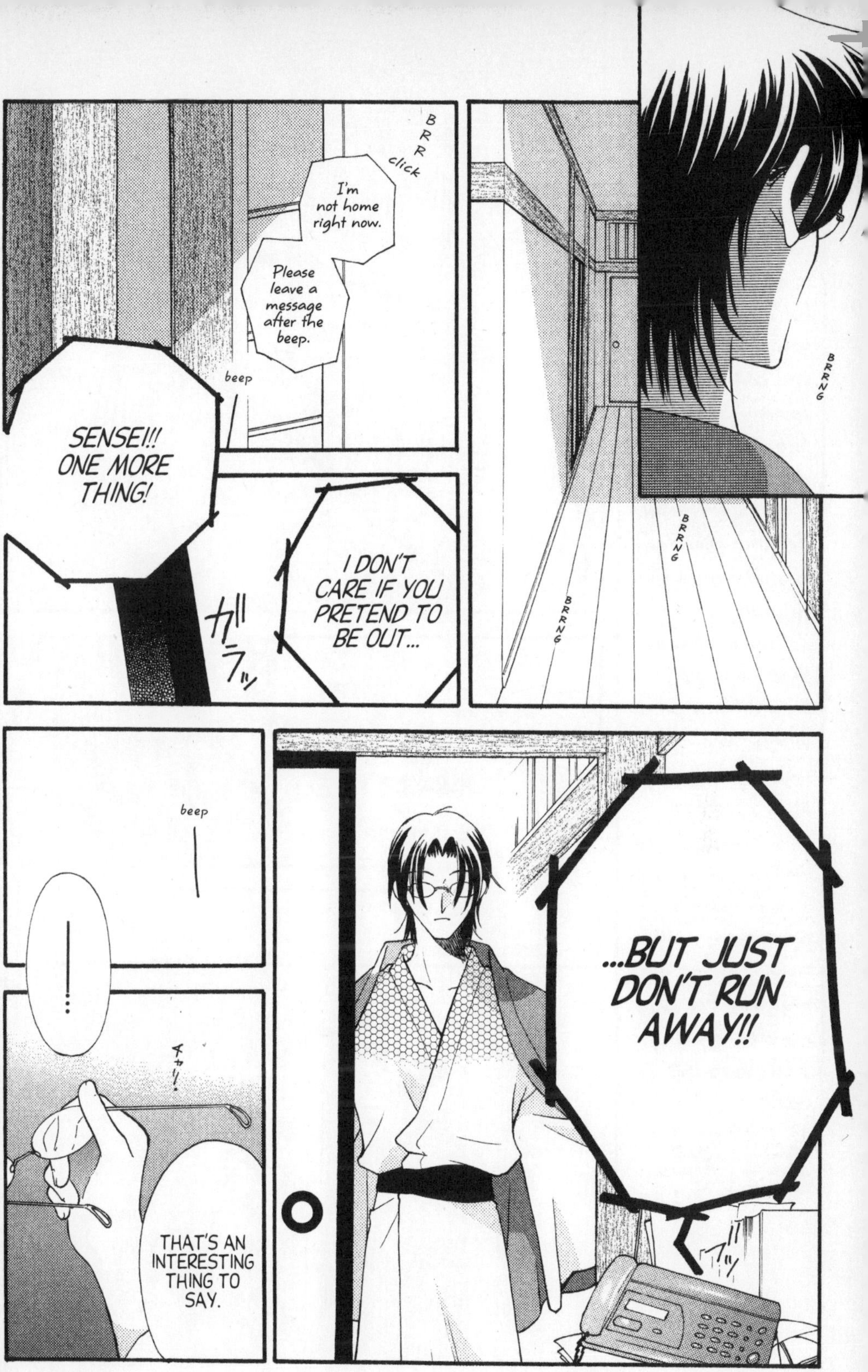
BRRNG
BRRNG
BRRNG
BRR click
I'm not home right now.
Please leave a message after the beep.
beep
SENSEI!!! ONE MORE THING!
I DON'T CARE IF YOU PRETEND TO BE OUT...
...BUT JUST DON'T RUN AWAY!!
beep
THAT'S AN INTERESTING THING TO SAY.

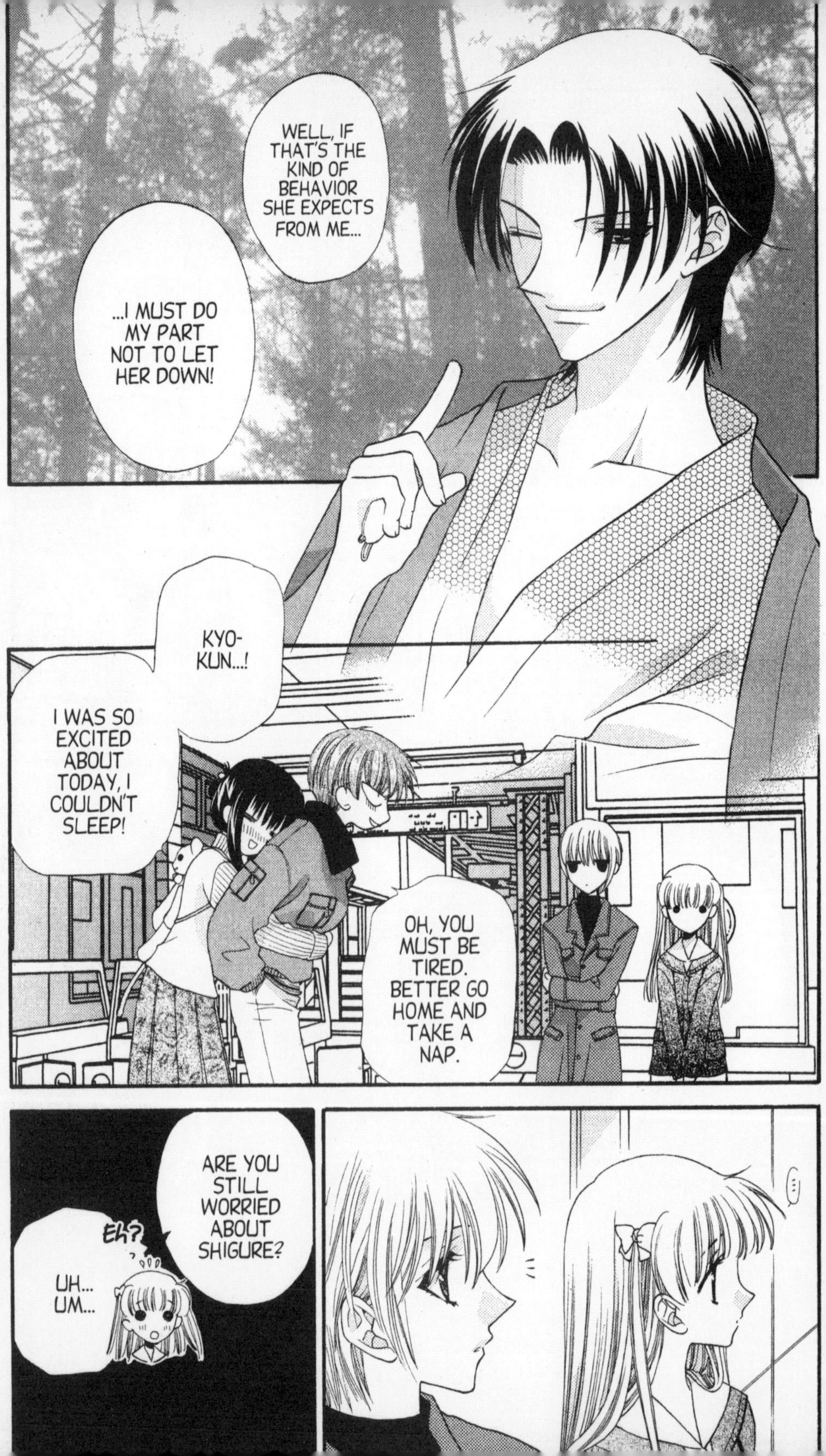
WELL, IF THAT'S THE KIND OF BEHAVIOR SHE EXPECTS FROM ME...
...I MUST DO MY PART NOT TO LET HER DOWN!
KYO-KUN...!
I WAS SO EXCITED ABOUT TODAY, I COULDN'T SLEEP!
OH, YOU MUST BE TIRED. BETTER GO HOME AND TAKE A NAP.
ARE YOU STILL WORRIED ABOUT SHIGURE?
Eh?
UH... UM...

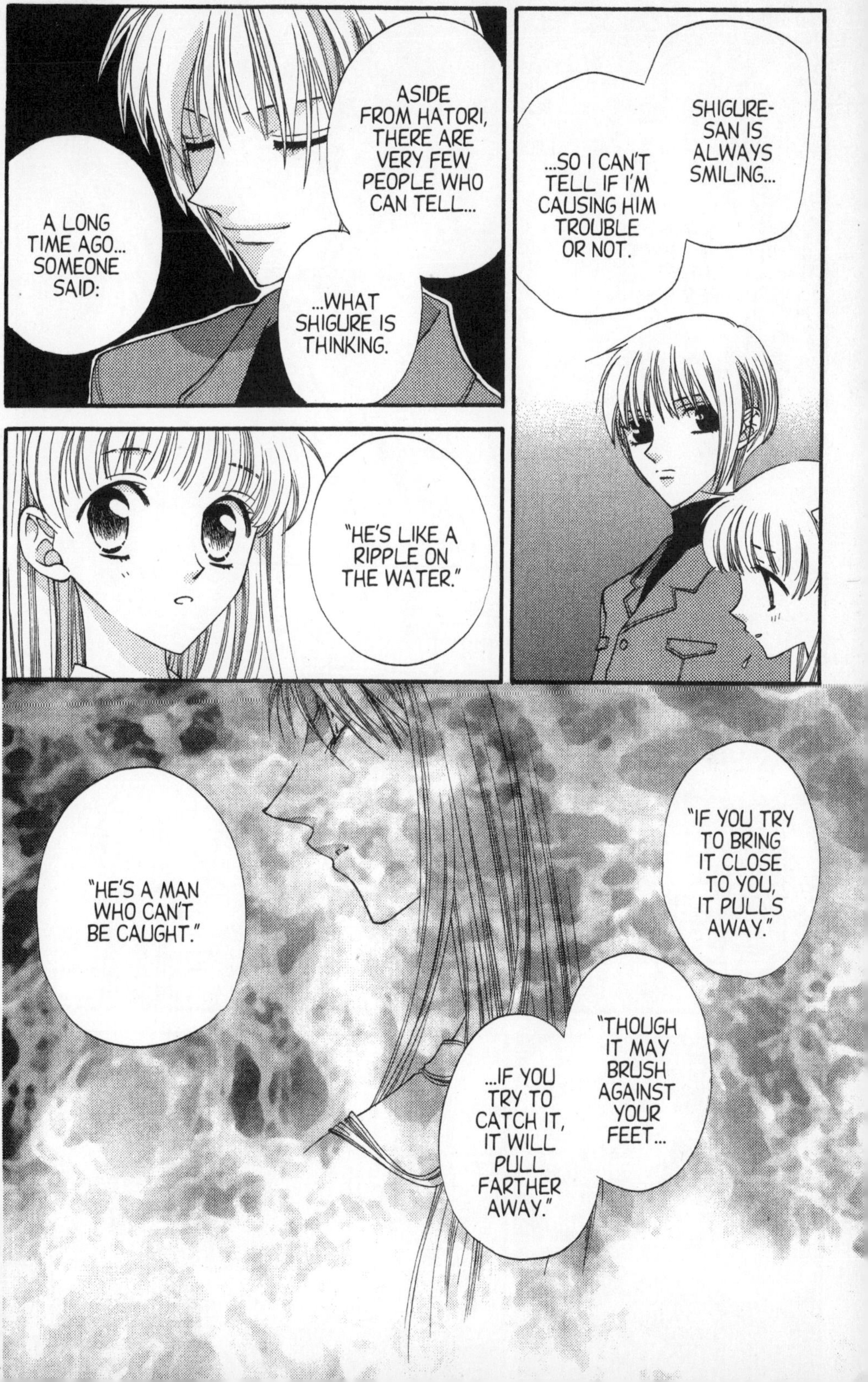
SHIGURE-SAN IS ALWAYS SMILING...
...SO I CAN'T TELL IF I'M CAUSING HIM TROUBLE OR NOT.
ASIDE FROM HATORI, THERE ARE VERY FEW PEOPLE WHO CAN TELL...
...WHAT SHIGURE IS THINKING.
A LONG TIME AGO... SOMEONE SAID:
"HE'S LIKE A RIPPLE ON THE WATER."
"IF YOU TRY TO BRING IT CLOSE TO YOU, IT PULLS AWAY."
"THOUGH IT MAY BRUSH AGAINST YOUR FEET...
...IF YOU TRY TO CATCH IT, IT WILL PULL FARTHER AWAY."
"HE'S A MAN WHO CAN'T BE CAUGHT."

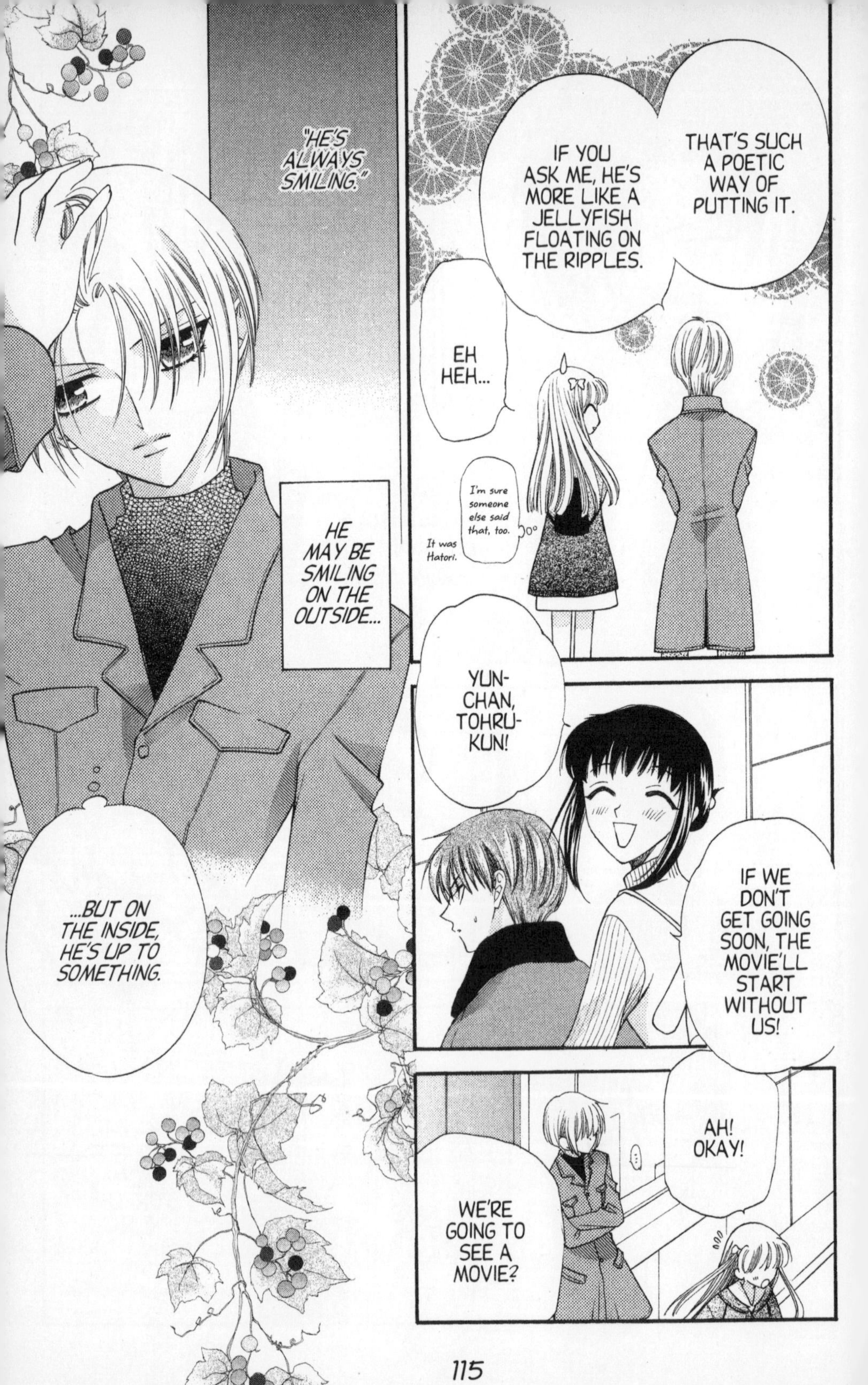
THAT'S SUCH A POETIC WAY OF PUTTING IT.
IF YOU ASK ME, HE'S MORE LIKE A JELLYFISH FLOATING ON THE RIPPLES.
EH HEH...
I'm sure someone else said that, too.
It was Hatori.
YUN-CHAN, TOHRU-KUN!
IF WE DON'T GET GOING SOON, THE MOVIE'LL START WITHOUT US!
AH! OKAY!
...
WE'RE GOING TO SEE A MOVIE?
"HE'S ALWAYS SMILING."
HE MAY BE SMILING ON THE OUTSIDE...
...BUT ON THE INSIDE, HE'S UP TO SOMETHING.

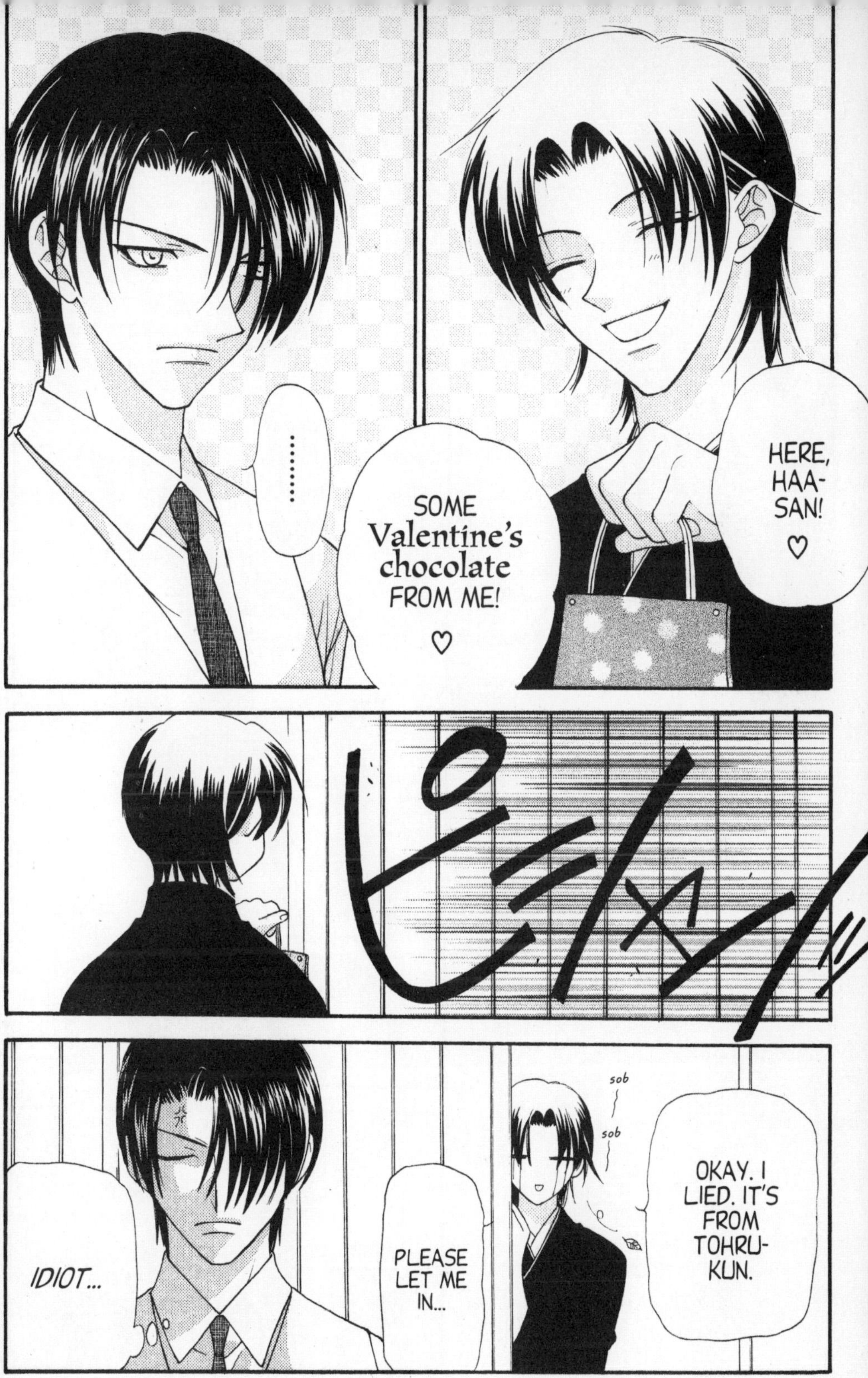
HERE, HAA-SAN! ♡
SOME Valentine's chocolate FROM ME! ♡
......
sob sob
OKAY. I LIED. IT'S FROM TOHRU-KUN.
PLEASE LET ME IN...
IDIOT...

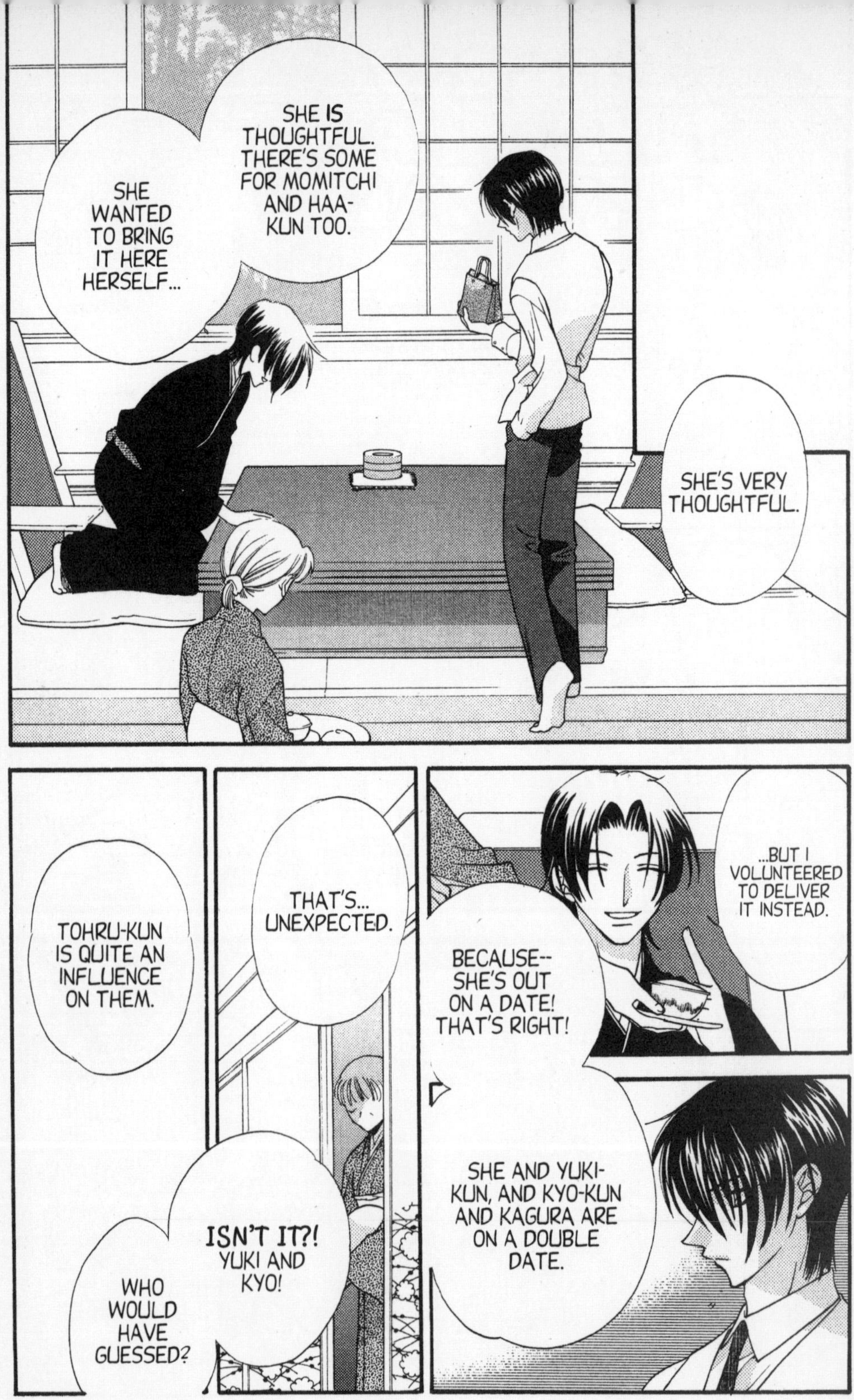
SHE'S VERY THOUGHTFUL.
SHE IS THOUGHTFUL. THERE'S SOME FOR MOMITCHI AND HAA-KUN TOO.
SHE WANTED TO BRING IT HERE HERSELF...
...BUT I VOLUNTEERED TO DELIVER IT INSTEAD.
BECAUSE-- SHE'S OUT ON A DATE! THAT'S RIGHT!
SHE AND YUKI-KUN, AND KYO-KUN AND KAGURA ARE ON A DOUBLE DATE.
THAT'S... UNEXPECTED.
ISN'T IT?! YUKI AND KYO!
WHO WOULD HAVE GUESSED?
TOHRU-KUN IS QUITE AN INFLUENCE ON THEM.

MOGETA: THE LAST CRUSADE

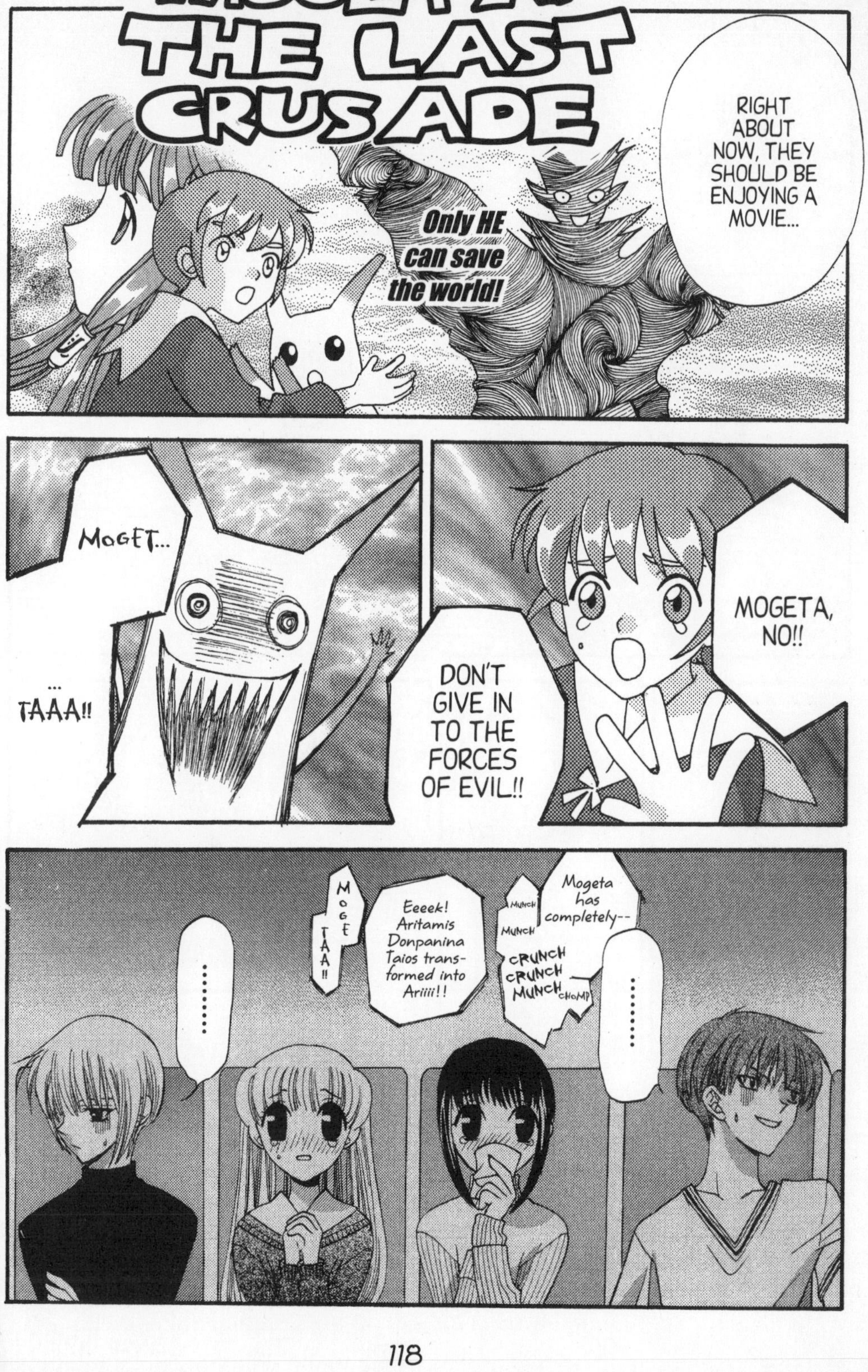

RIGHT ABOUT NOW, THEY SHOULD BE ENJOYING A MOVIE...
Only HE can save the world!
MOGETA, NO!!
DON'T GIVE IN TO THE FORCES OF EVIL!!
MOGET...
...TAAA!!
....
Mogeta has completely--
MUNCH MUNCH CRUNCH CRUNCH MUNCH CHOMP
Eeeek! Aritamis Donpanina Taios transformed into Ariiii!!
MOGE TAAA!!
....

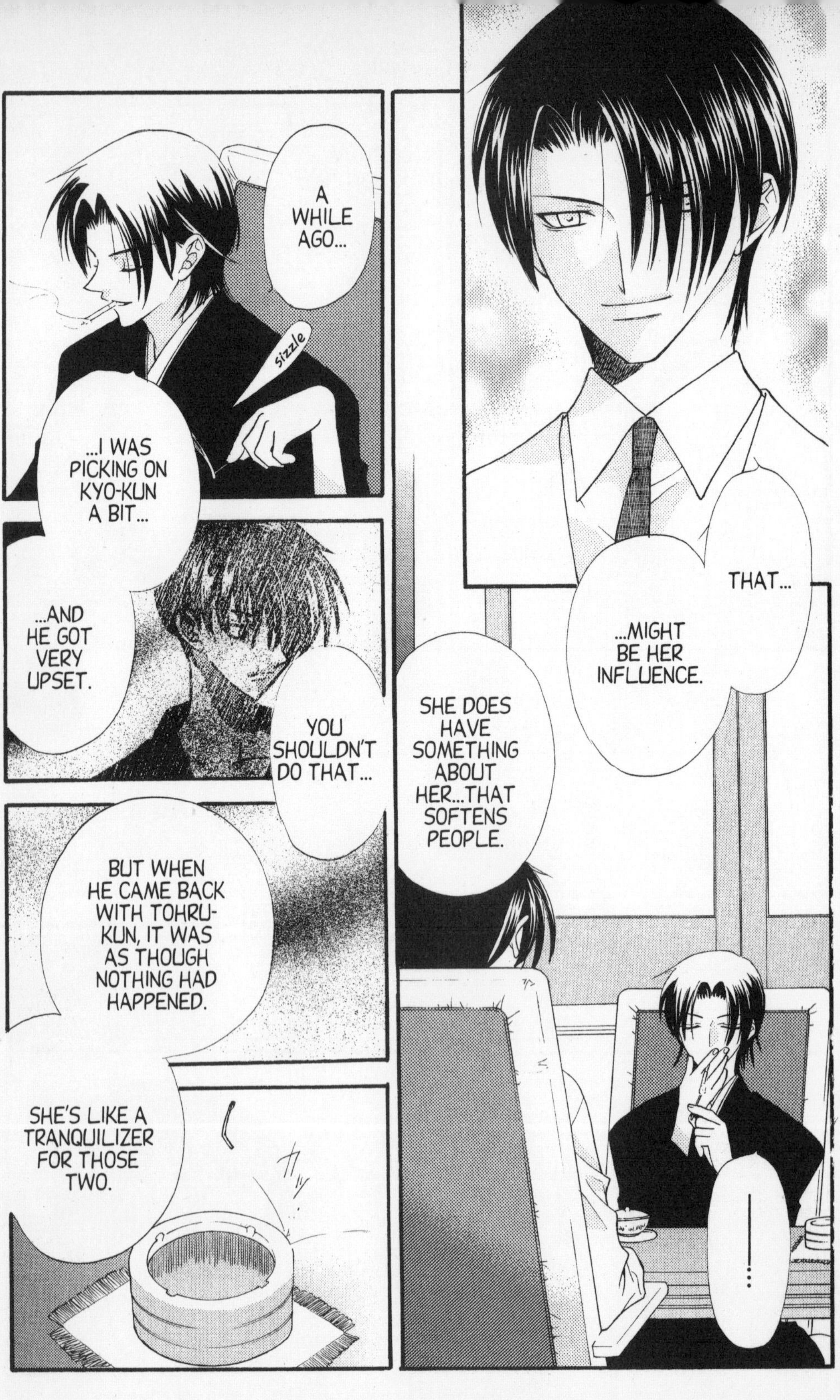
THAT...
...MIGHT BE HER INFLUENCE.
SHE DOES HAVE SOMETHING ABOUT HER...THAT SOFTENS PEOPLE.
......
A WHILE AGO...
sizzle
...I WAS PICKING ON KYO-KUN A BIT...
...AND HE GOT VERY UPSET.
YOU SHOULDN'T DO THAT...
BUT WHEN HE CAME BACK WITH TOHRU-KUN, IT WAS AS THOUGH NOTHING HAD HAPPENED.
SHE'S LIKE A TRANQUILIZER FOR THOSE TWO.

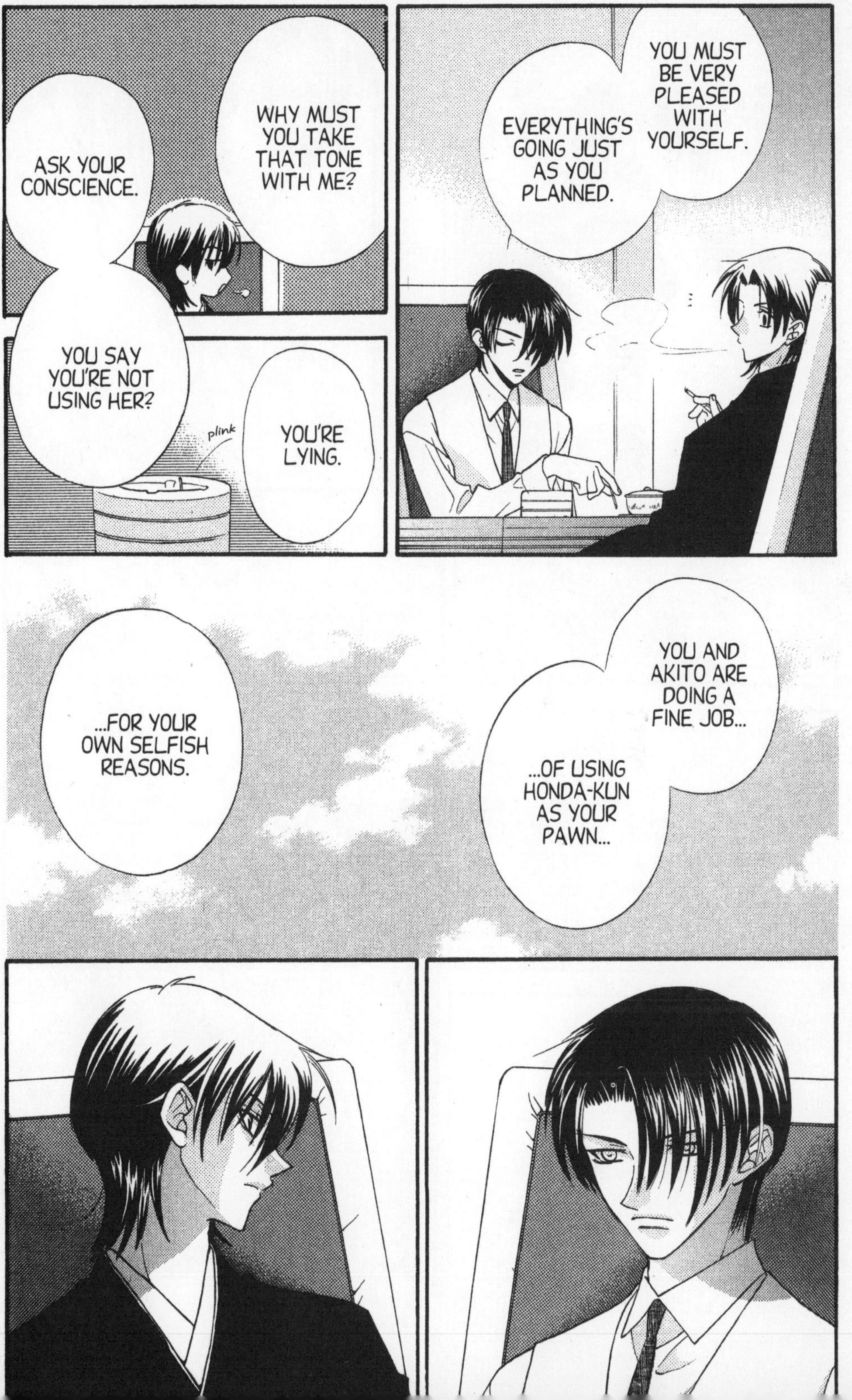
YOU MUST BE VERY PLEASED WITH YOURSELF.
EVERYTHING'S GOING JUST AS YOU PLANNED.
WHY MUST YOU TAKE THAT TONE WITH ME?
ASK YOUR CONSCIENCE.
YOU SAY YOU'RE NOT USING HER?
plink
YOU'RE LYING.
YOU AND AKITO ARE DOING A FINE JOB...
...OF USING HONDA-KUN AS YOUR PAWN...
...FOR YOUR OWN SELFISH REASONS.

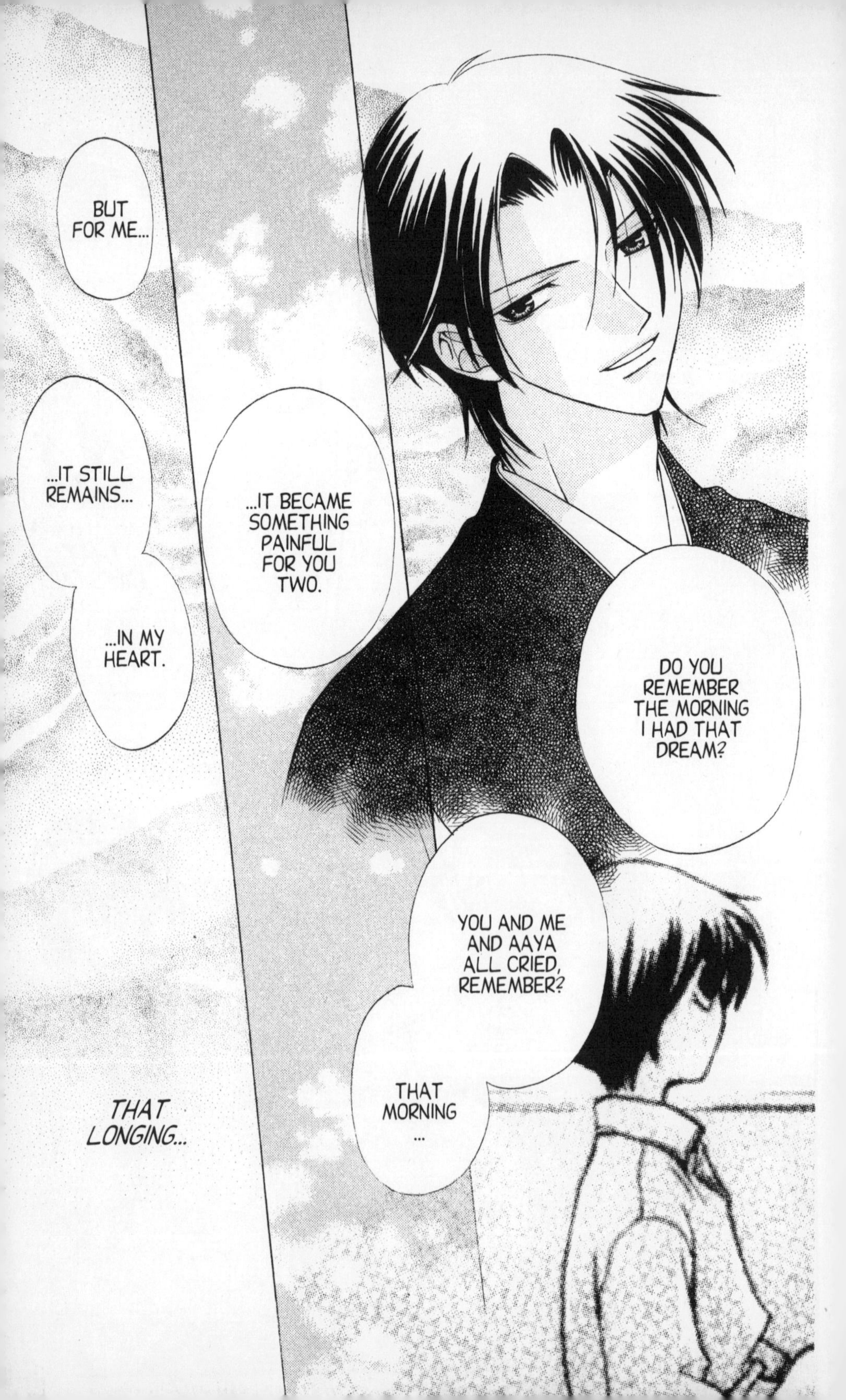
DO YOU REMEMBER THE MORNING I HAD THAT DREAM?
YOU AND ME AND AAYA ALL CRIED, REMEMBER?
THAT MORNING ...
...IT BECAME SOMETHING PAINFUL FOR YOU TWO.
BUT FOR ME...
...IT STILL REMAINS...
...IN MY HEART.
THAT LONGING...

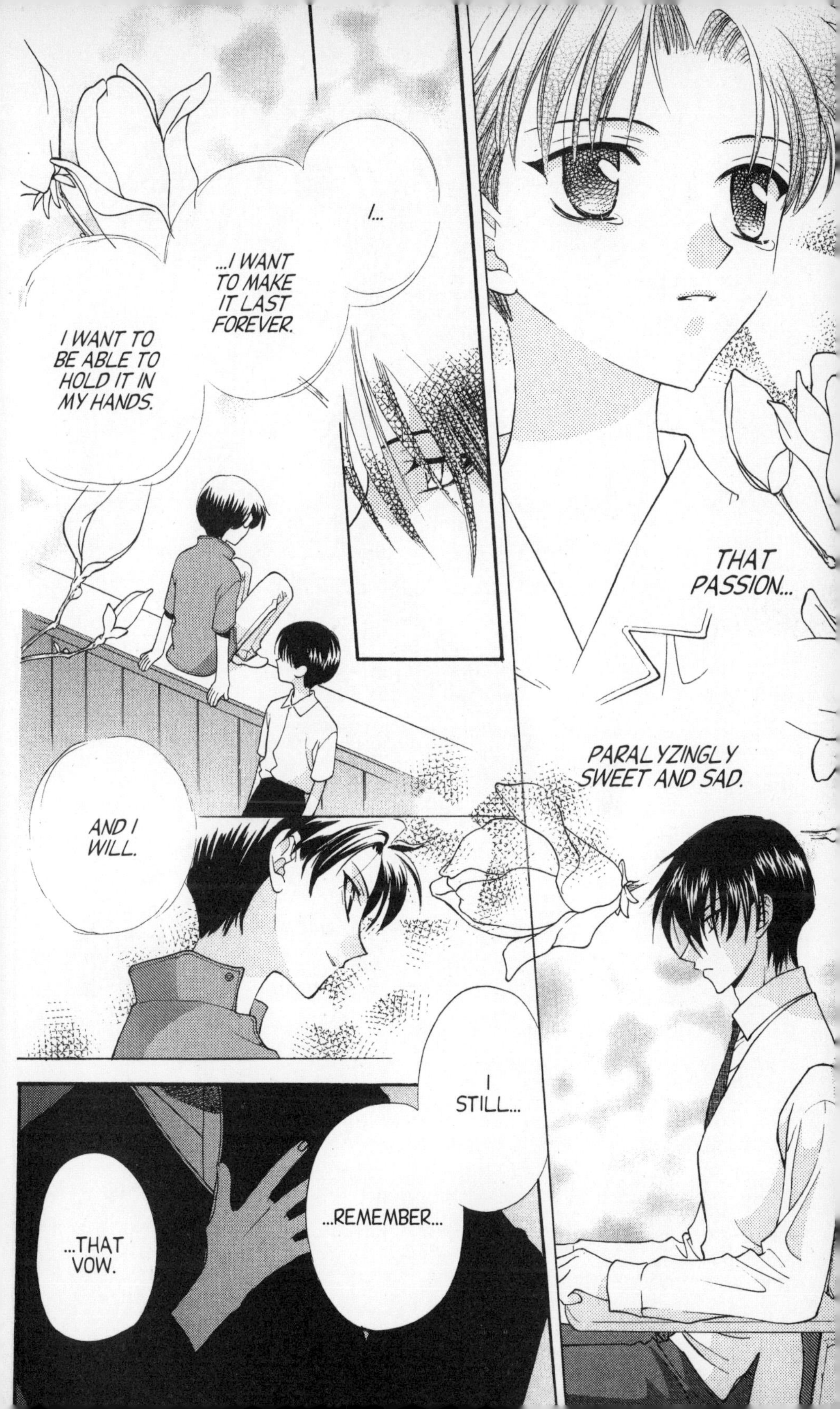
THAT PASSION...
PARALYZINGLY SWEET AND SAD.
I...
...I WANT TO MAKE IT LAST FOREVER.
I WANT TO BE ABLE TO HOLD IT IN MY HANDS.
AND I WILL.
I STILL...
...REMEMBER...
...THAT VOW.

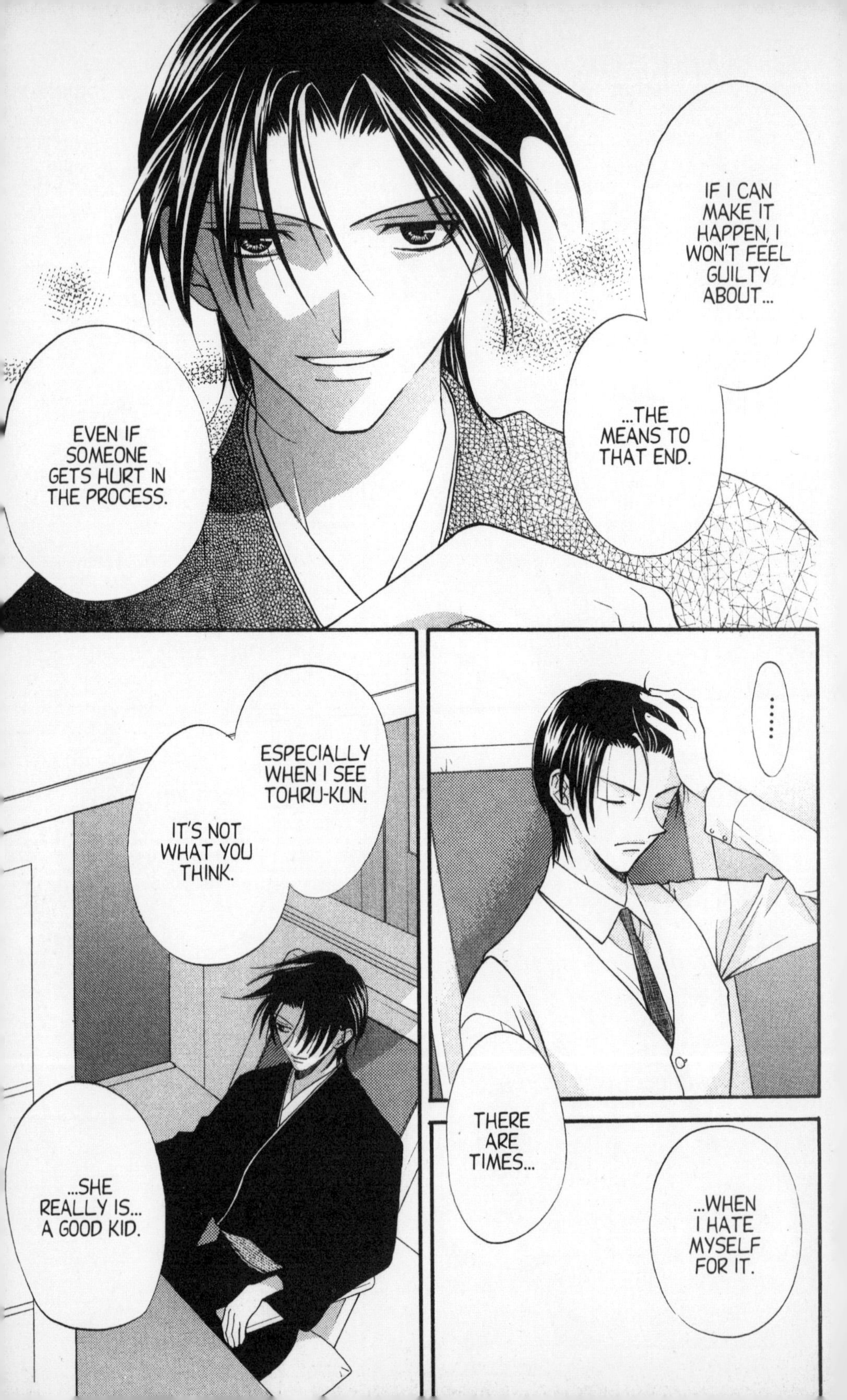
IF I CAN MAKE IT HAPPEN, I WON'T FEEL GUILTY ABOUT...
...THE MEANS TO THAT END.
EVEN IF SOMEONE GETS HURT IN THE PROCESS.
......
THERE ARE TIMES...
...WHEN I HATE MYSELF FOR IT.
ESPECIALLY WHEN I SEE TOHRU-KUN.
IT'S NOT WHAT YOU THINK.
...SHE REALLY IS... A GOOD KID.

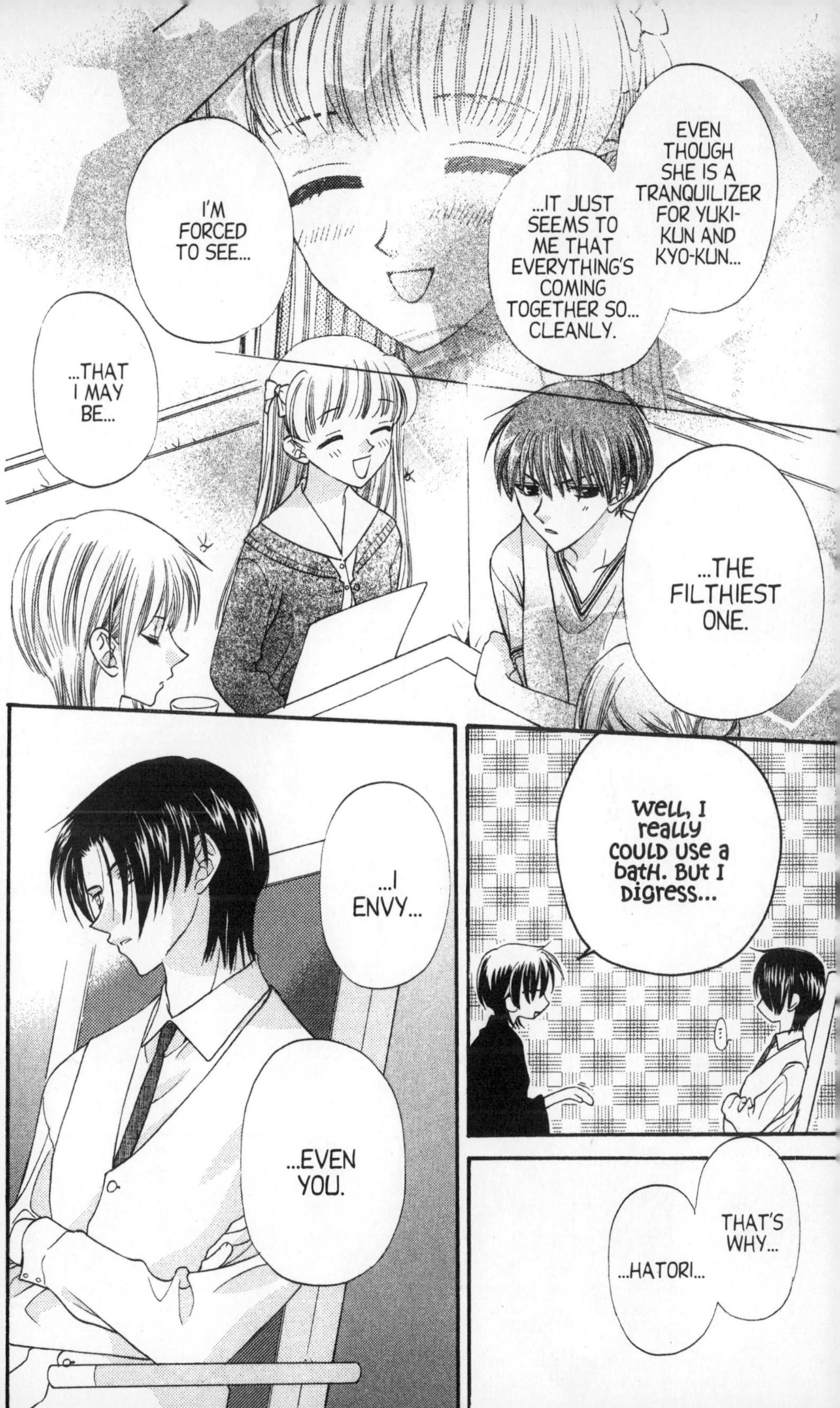
EVEN THOUGH SHE IS A TRANQUILIZER FOR YUKI-KUN AND KYO-KUN...
...IT JUST SEEMS TO ME THAT EVERYTHING'S COMING TOGETHER SO... CLEANLY.
I'M FORCED TO SEE...
...THAT I MAY BE...
...THE FILTHIEST ONE.
Well, I really could use a bath. But I digress...
...
THAT'S WHY...
...HATORI...
...I ENVY...
...EVEN YOU.

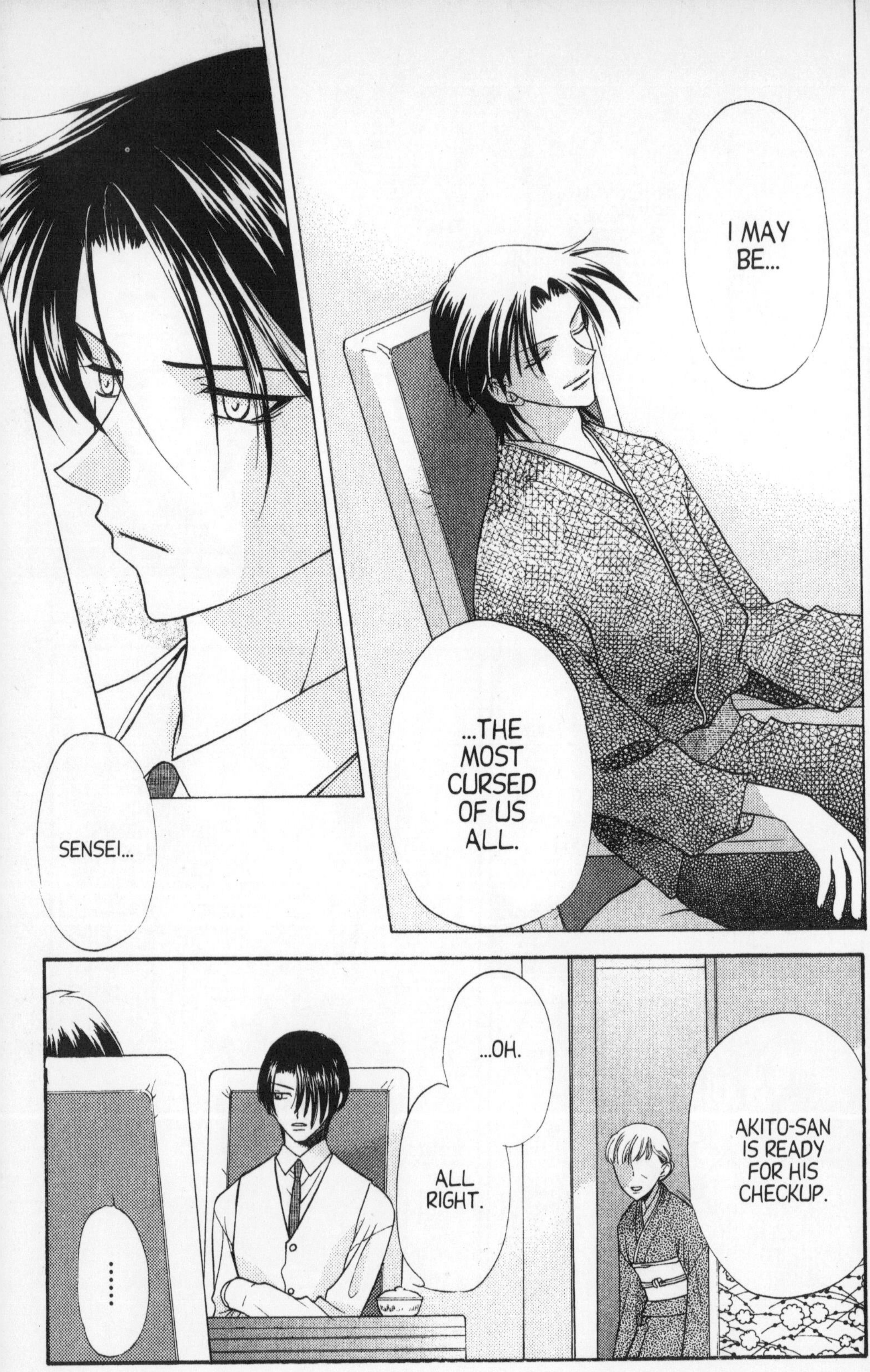
I MAY BE...
...THE MOST CURSED OF US ALL.
SENSEI...
AKITO-SAN IS READY FOR HIS CHECKUP.
...OH.
ALL RIGHT.
......

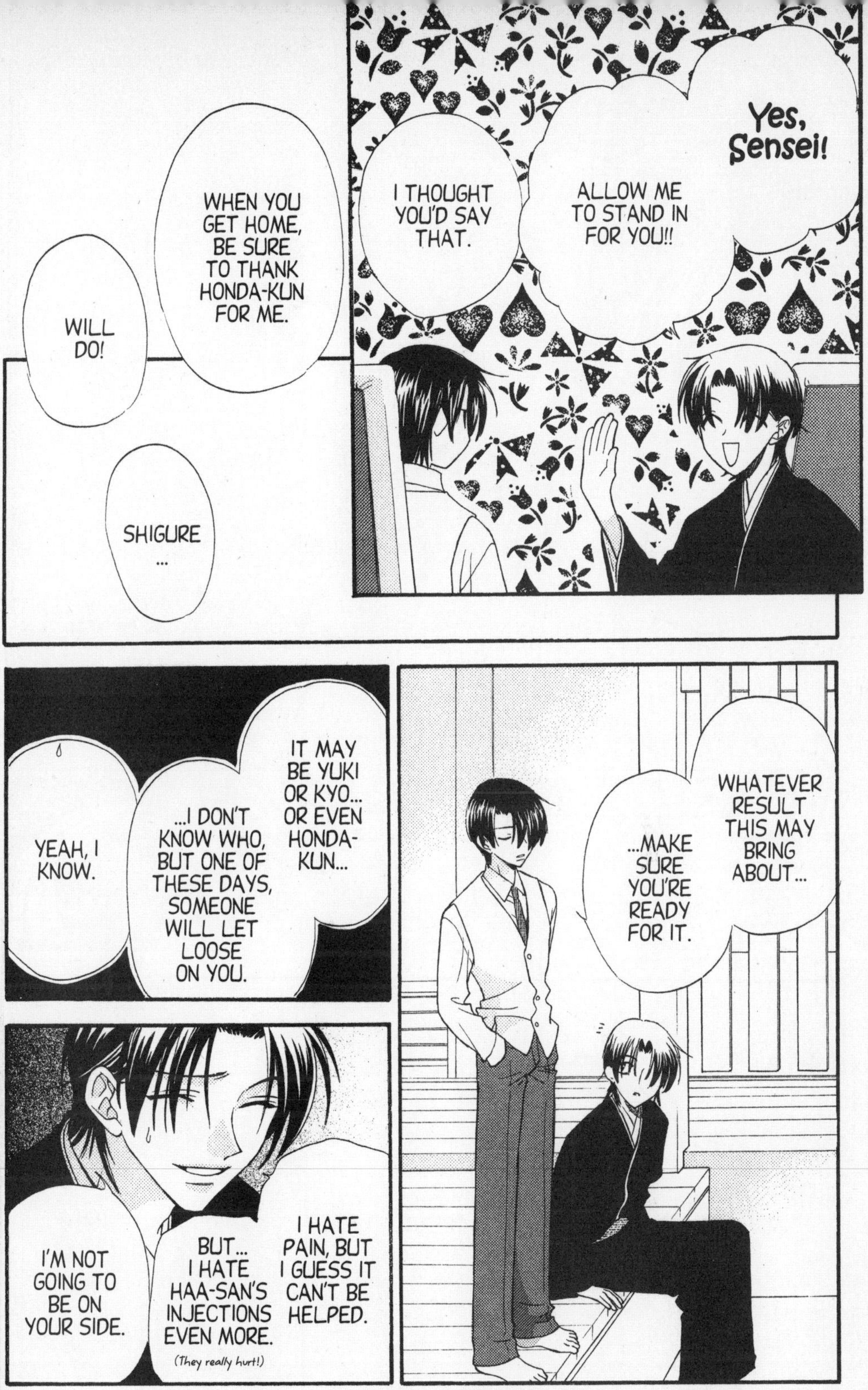

Yes, Sensei!
ALLOW ME TO STAND IN FOR YOU!!
I THOUGHT YOU'D SAY THAT.
WHEN YOU GET HOME, BE SURE TO THANK HONDA-KUN FOR ME.
WILL DO!
SHIGURE ...
WHATEVER RESULT THIS MAY BRING ABOUT...
...MAKE SURE YOU'RE READY FOR IT.
IT MAY BE YUKI OR KYO... OR EVEN HONDA-KUN...
...I DON'T KNOW WHO, BUT ONE OF THESE DAYS, SOMEONE WILL LET LOOSE ON YOU.
YEAH, I KNOW.
I HATE PAIN, BUT I GUESS IT CAN'T BE HELPED.
BUT... I HATE HAA-SAN'S INJECTIONS EVEN MORE.
(They really hurt!)
I'M NOT GOING TO BE ON YOUR SIDE.

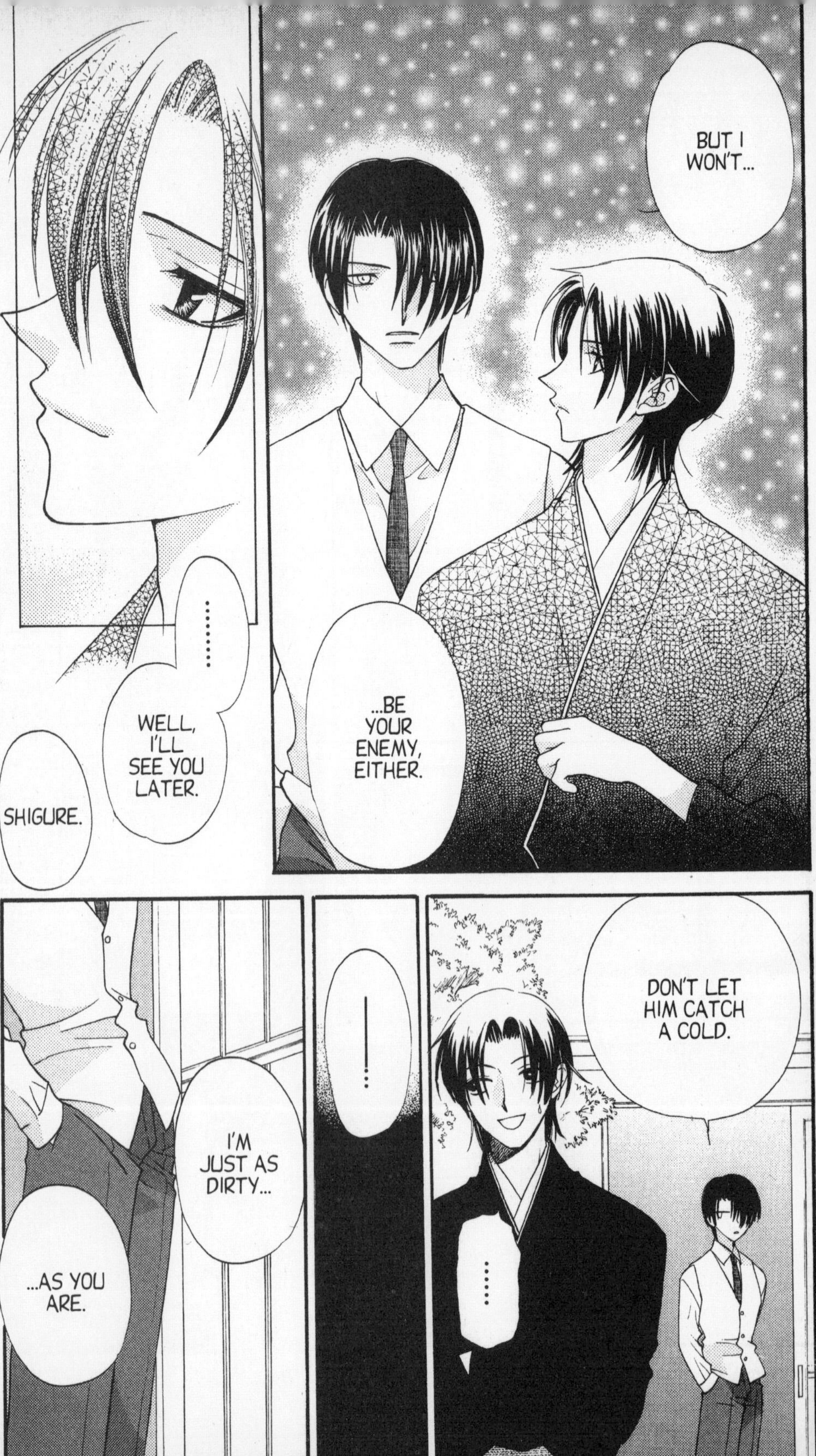
BUT I WON'T...
...BE YOUR ENEMY, EITHER.
......
WELL, I'LL SEE YOU LATER.
SHIGURE.
DON'T LET HIM CATCH A COLD.
......
—......
I'M JUST AS DIRTY...
...AS YOU ARE.

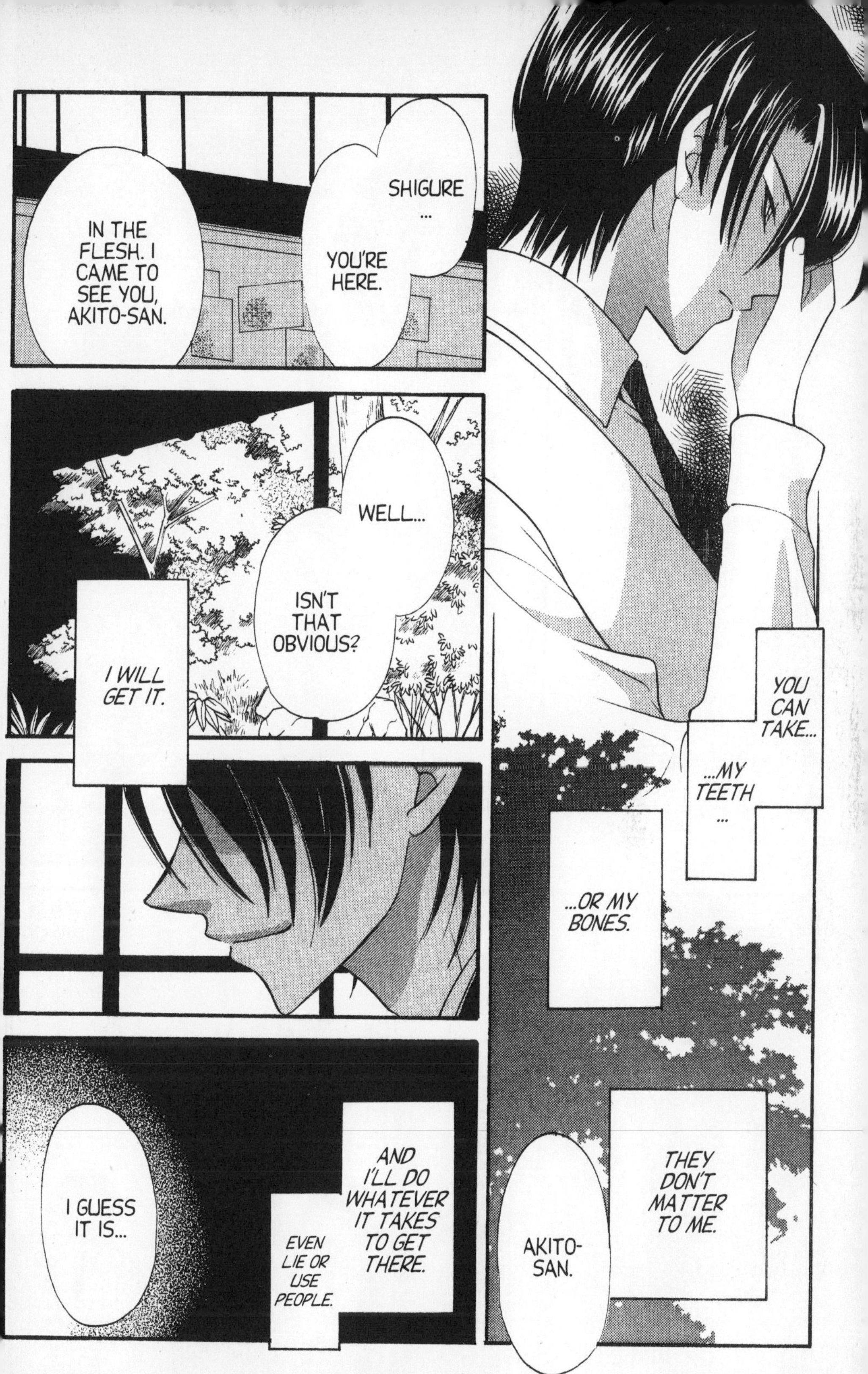
YOU CAN TAKE...
...MY TEETH ...
...OR MY BONES.
THEY DON'T MATTER TO ME.
AKITO-SAN.
SHIGURE ... YOU'RE HERE.
IN THE FLESH. I CAME TO SEE YOU, AKITO-SAN.
WELL... ISN'T THAT OBVIOUS?
I WILL GET IT.
AND I'LL DO WHATEVER IT TAKES TO GET THERE.
EVEN LIE OR USE PEOPLE.
I GUESS IT IS...

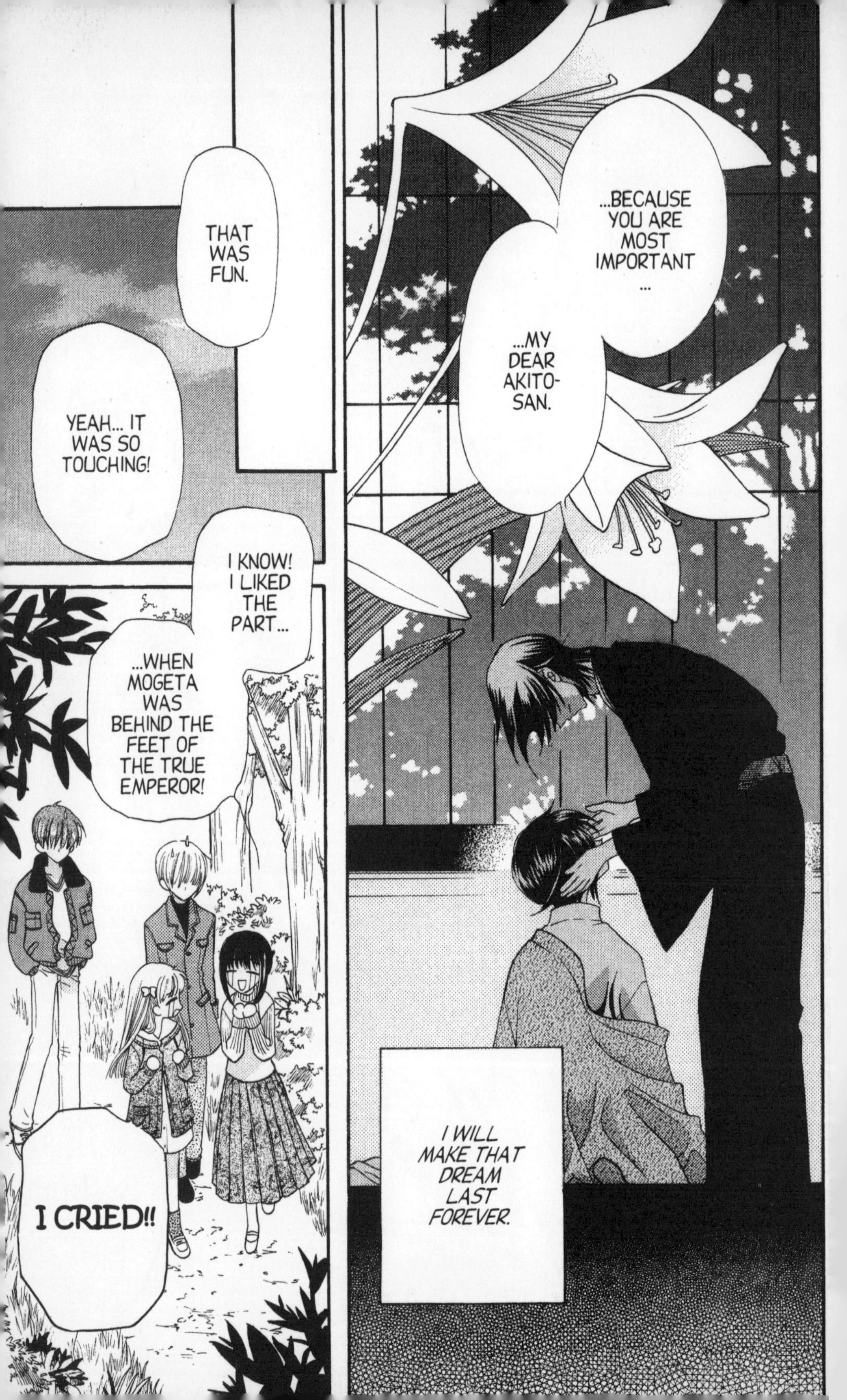
...BECAUSE YOU ARE MOST IMPORTANT ...
...MY DEAR AKITO-SAN.
I WILL MAKE THAT DREAM LAST FOREVER.
THAT WAS FUN.
YEAH... IT WAS SO TOUCHING!
I KNOW! I LIKED THE PART...
...WHEN MOGETA WAS BEHIND THE FEET OF THE TRUE EMPEROR!
I CRIED!!

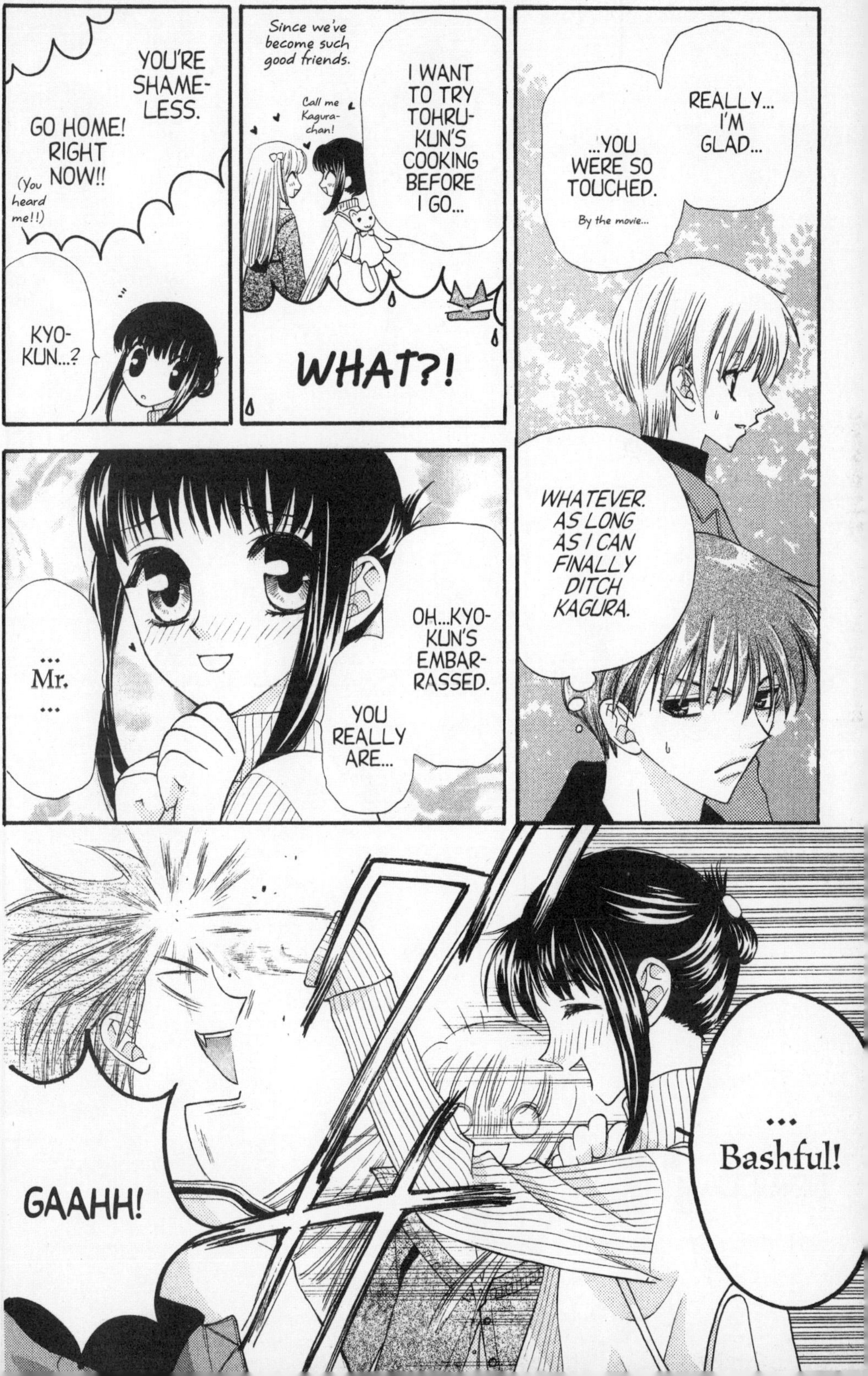
REALLY... I'M GLAD...
...YOU WERE SO TOUCHED.
By the movie...
WHATEVER. AS LONG AS I CAN FINALLY DITCH KAGURA.
Since we've become such good friends.
I WANT TO TRY TOHRU-KUN'S COOKING BEFORE I GO...
Call me Kagura-chan!
WHAT?!
YOU'RE SHAME-LESS.
GO HOME! RIGHT NOW!!
(You heard me!!)
KYO-KUN...?
OH...KYO-KUN'S EMBAR-RASSED.
YOU REALLY ARE...
... Mr. ...
... Bashful!
GAAHH!

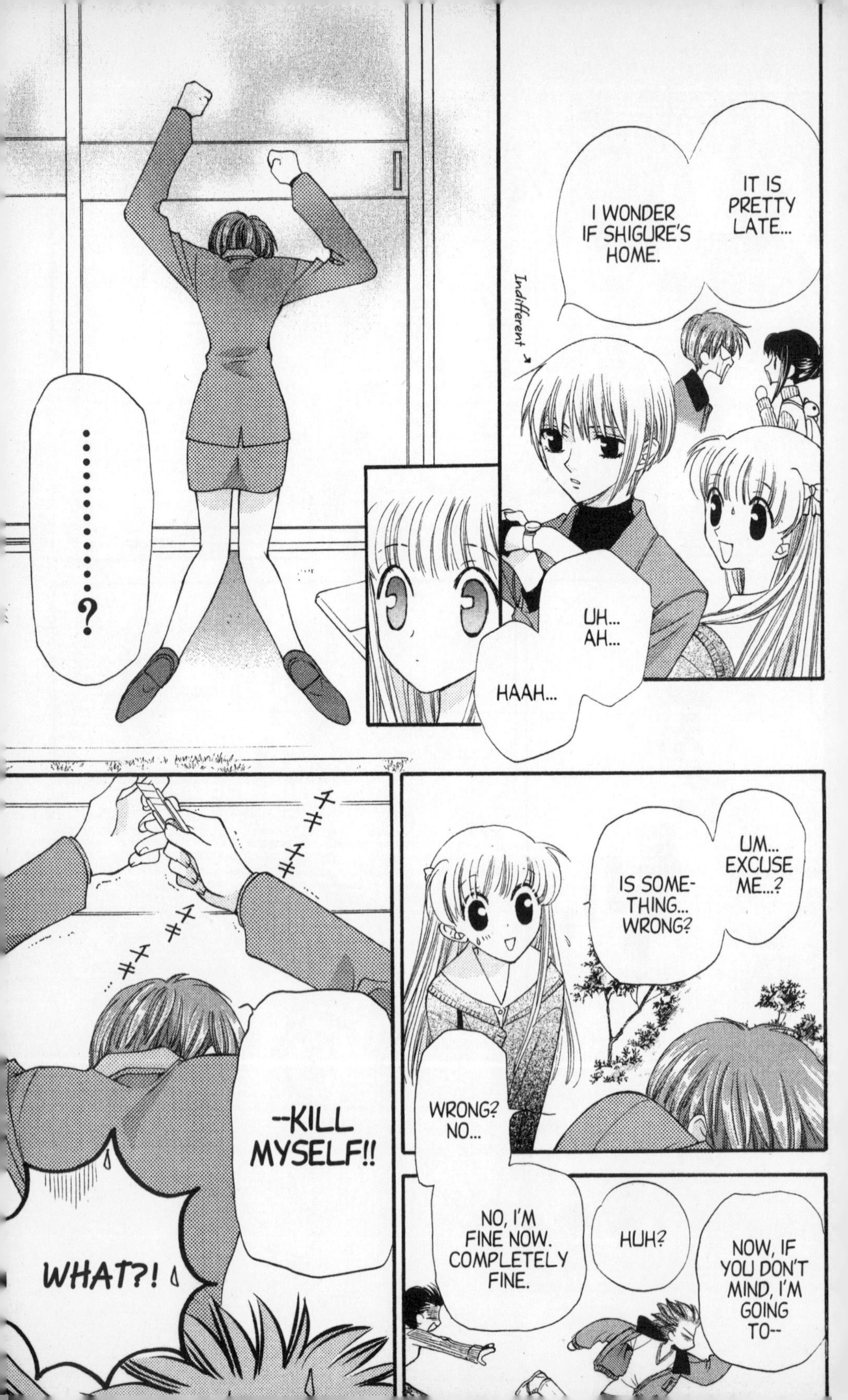
IT IS PRETTY LATE...
I WONDER IF SHIGURE'S HOME.
Indifferent
UH... AH...
HAAH...
.........?
UM... EXCUSE ME...?
IS SOME-THING... WRONG?
WRONG? NO...
NO, I'M FINE NOW. COMPLETELY FINE.
HUH?
NOW, IF YOU DON'T MIND, I'M GOING TO--
チキ
チキ
チキ
チキ
--KILL MYSELF!!
WHAT?!

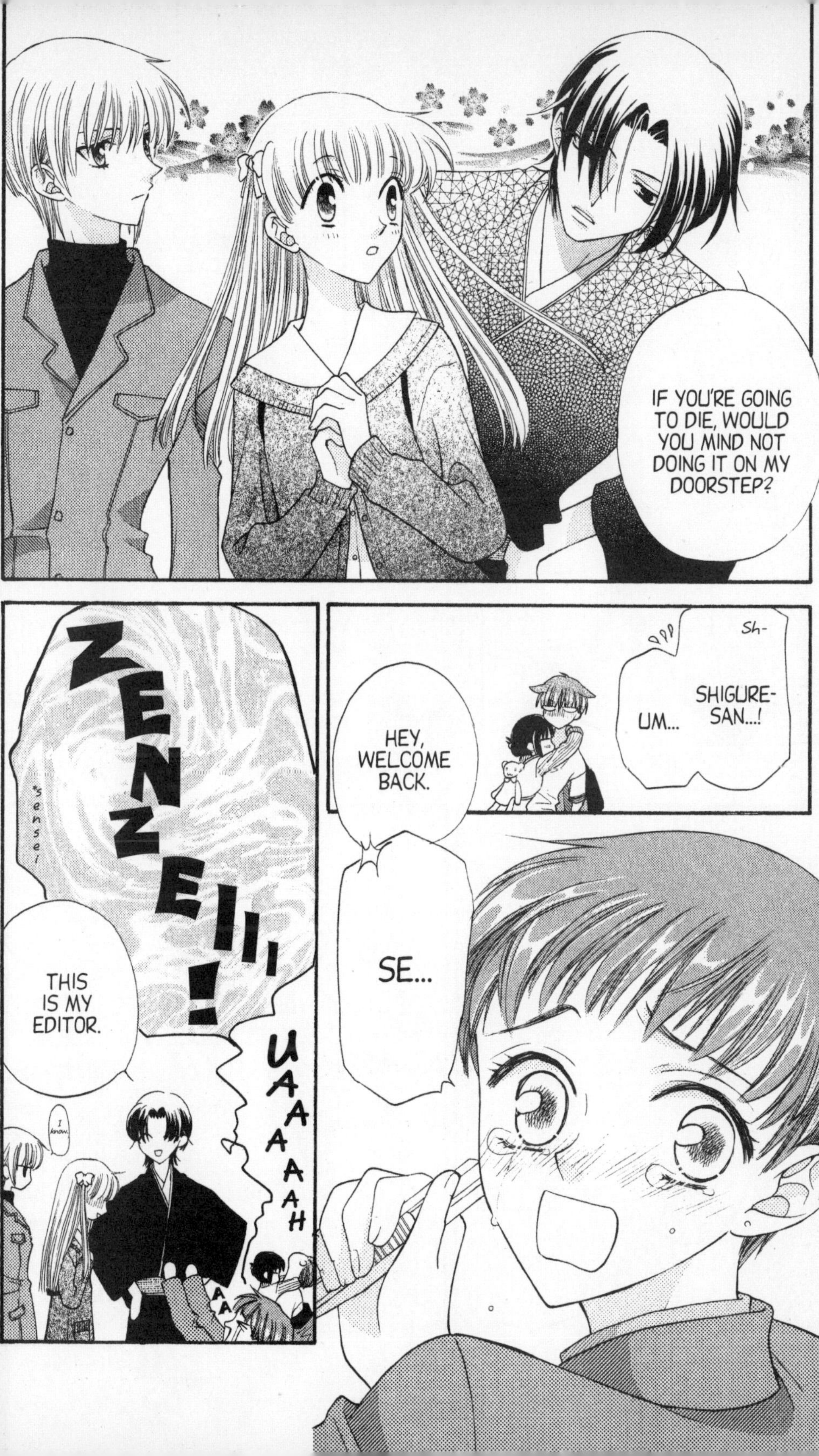

IF YOU'RE GOING TO DIE, WOULD YOU MIND NOT DOING IT ON MY DOORSTEP?
Sh-
SHIGURE-SAN...!
UM...
HEY, WELCOME BACK.
SE...
ZENZEIII!
*sensei
UAAAAAAH
THIS IS MY EDITOR.
I know.

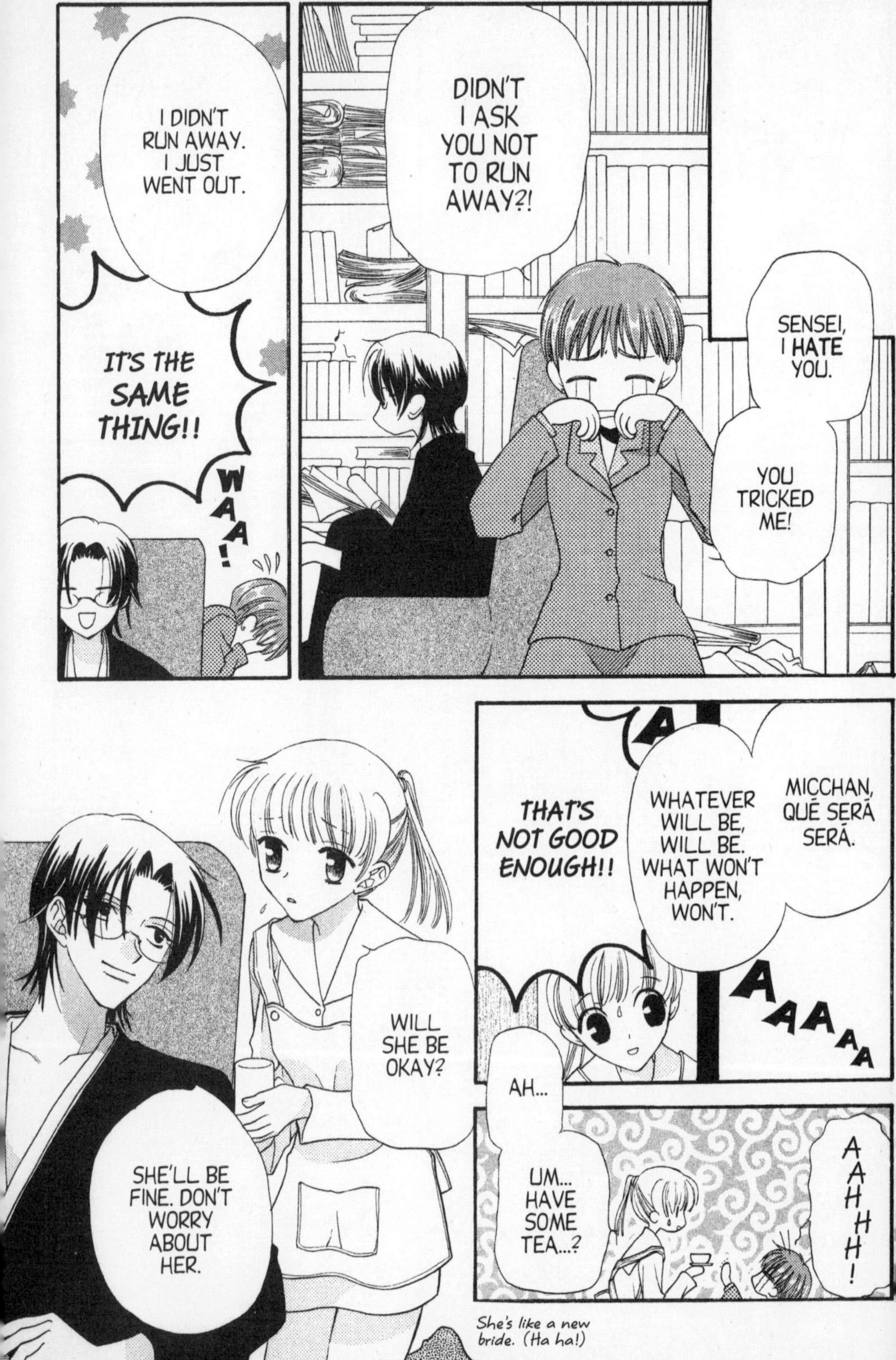
SENSEI, I HATE YOU.
YOU TRICKED ME!
DIDN'T I ASK YOU NOT TO RUN AWAY?!
I DIDN'T RUN AWAY. I JUST WENT OUT.
IT'S THE SAME THING!!
WAAA!
MICCHAN, QUÉ SERÁ SERÁ.
WHATEVER WILL BE, WILL BE. WHAT WON'T HAPPEN, WON'T.
THAT'S NOT GOOD ENOUGH!!
A
AAAAAA
AAHHH!
AH...
UM... HAVE SOME TEA...?
WILL SHE BE OKAY?
SHE'LL BE FINE. DON'T WORRY ABOUT HER.

She's like a new bride. (Ha ha!)

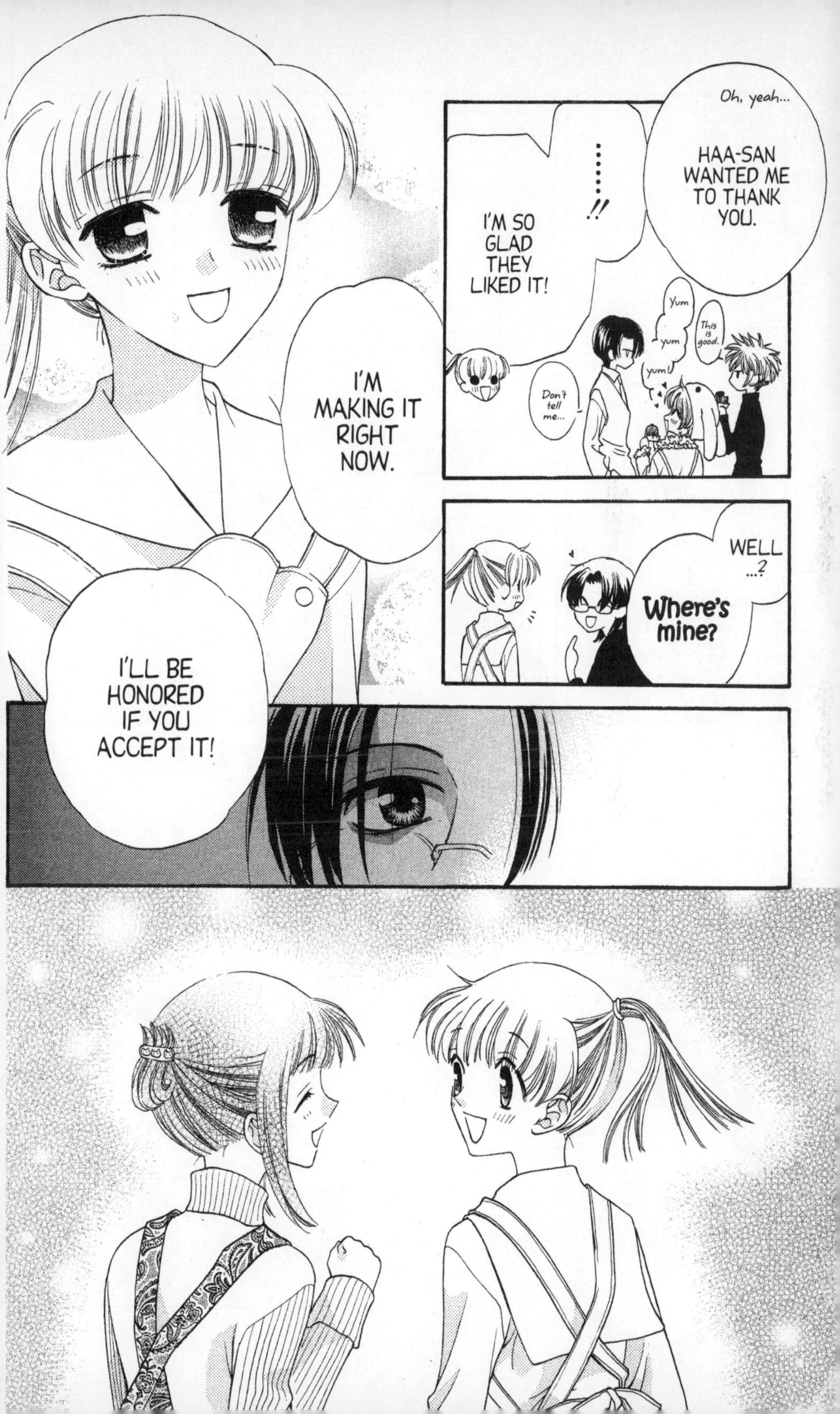
Oh, yeah...
HAA-SAN WANTED ME TO THANK YOU.
......!!
I'M SO GLAD THEY LIKED IT!
This is good.
Yum yum yum!
Don't tell me...
WELL ...?
Where's mine?
I'M MAKING IT RIGHT NOW.
I'LL BE HONORED IF YOU ACCEPT IT!

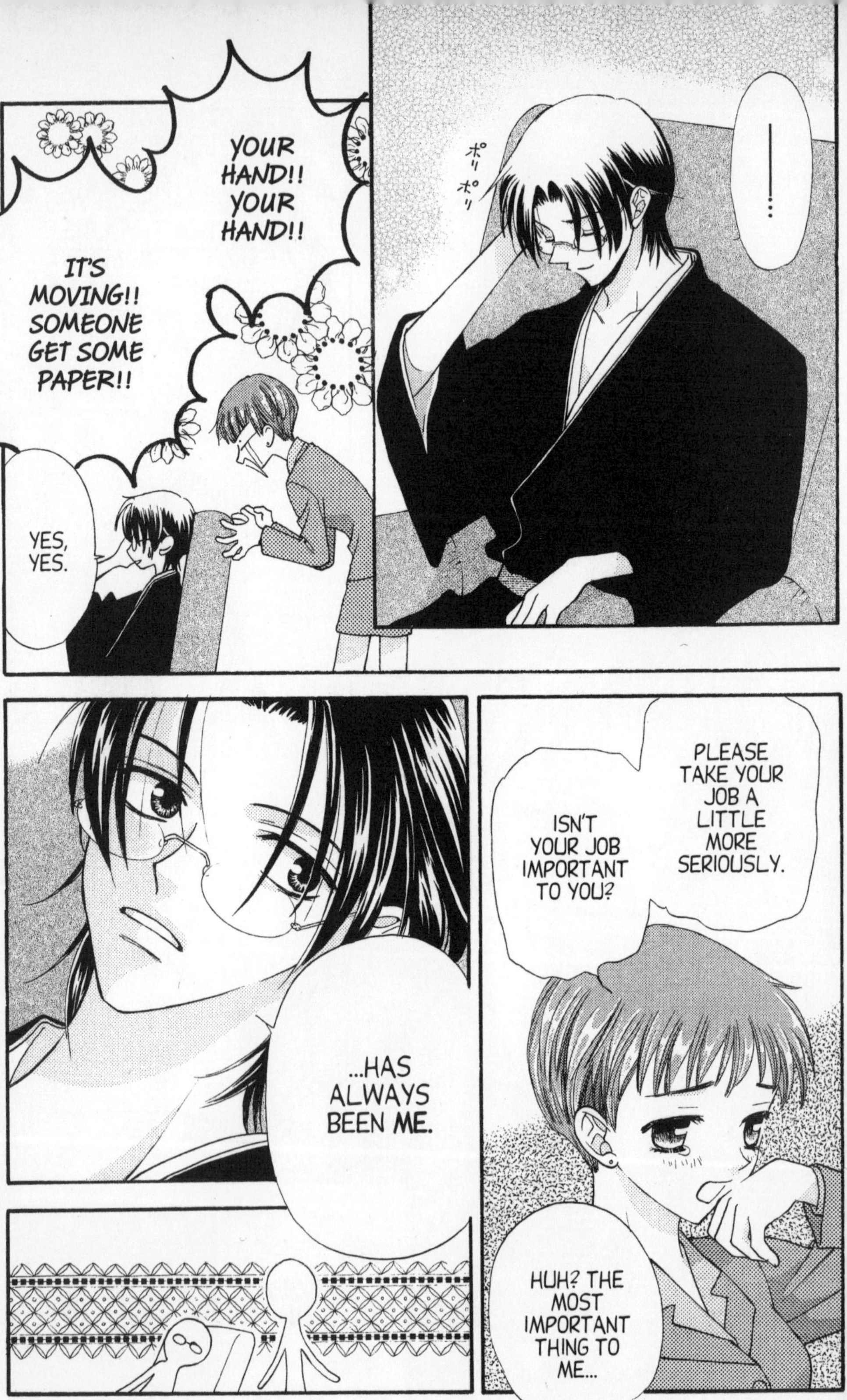

—...
ポリ ポリ
YOUR HAND!! YOUR HAND!!
IT'S MOVING!! SOMEONE GET SOME PAPER!!
YES, YES.
PLEASE TAKE YOUR JOB A LITTLE MORE SERIOUSLY.
ISN'T YOUR JOB IMPORTANT TO YOU?
HUH? THE MOST IMPORTANT THING TO ME...
...HAS ALWAYS BEEN ME.

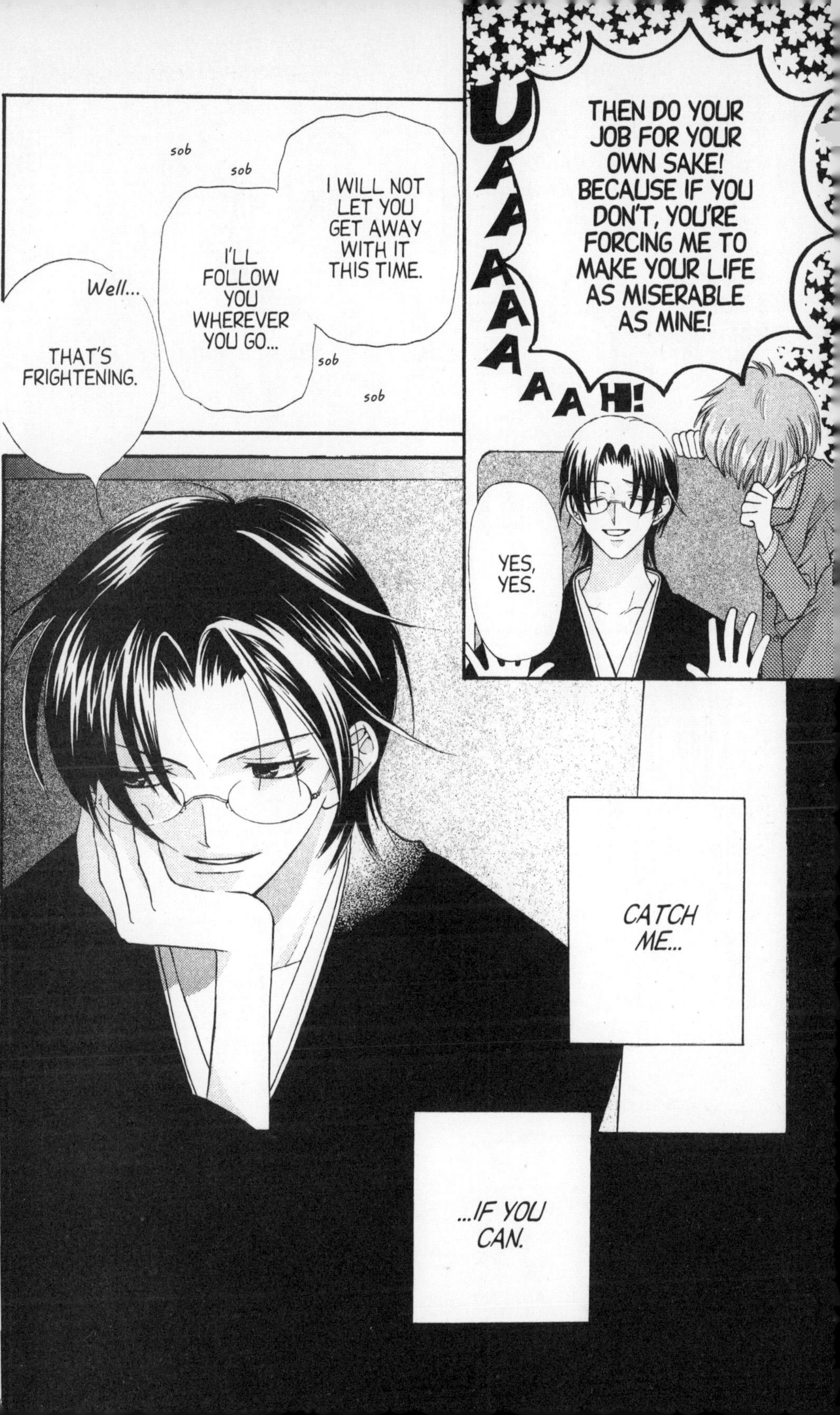
THEN DO YOUR JOB FOR YOUR OWN SAKE! BECAUSE IF YOU DON'T, YOU'RE FORCING ME TO MAKE YOUR LIFE AS MISERABLE AS MINE!
UAAAAAAAAH!
YES, YES.
I WILL NOT LET YOU GET AWAY WITH IT THIS TIME.
sob
sob
I'LL FOLLOW YOU WHEREVER YOU GO...
sob
sob
Well...
THAT'S FRIGHTENING.
CATCH ME...
...IF YOU CAN.

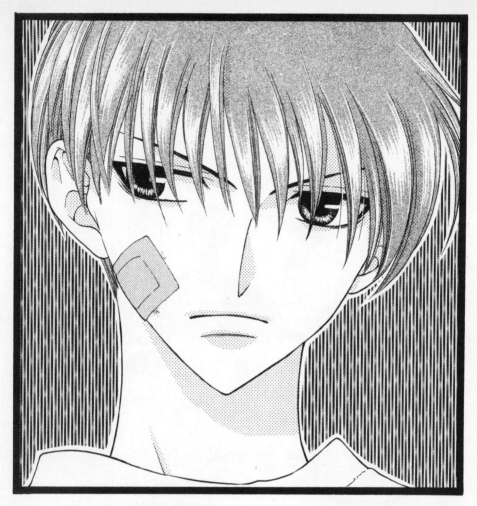

Chapter 17

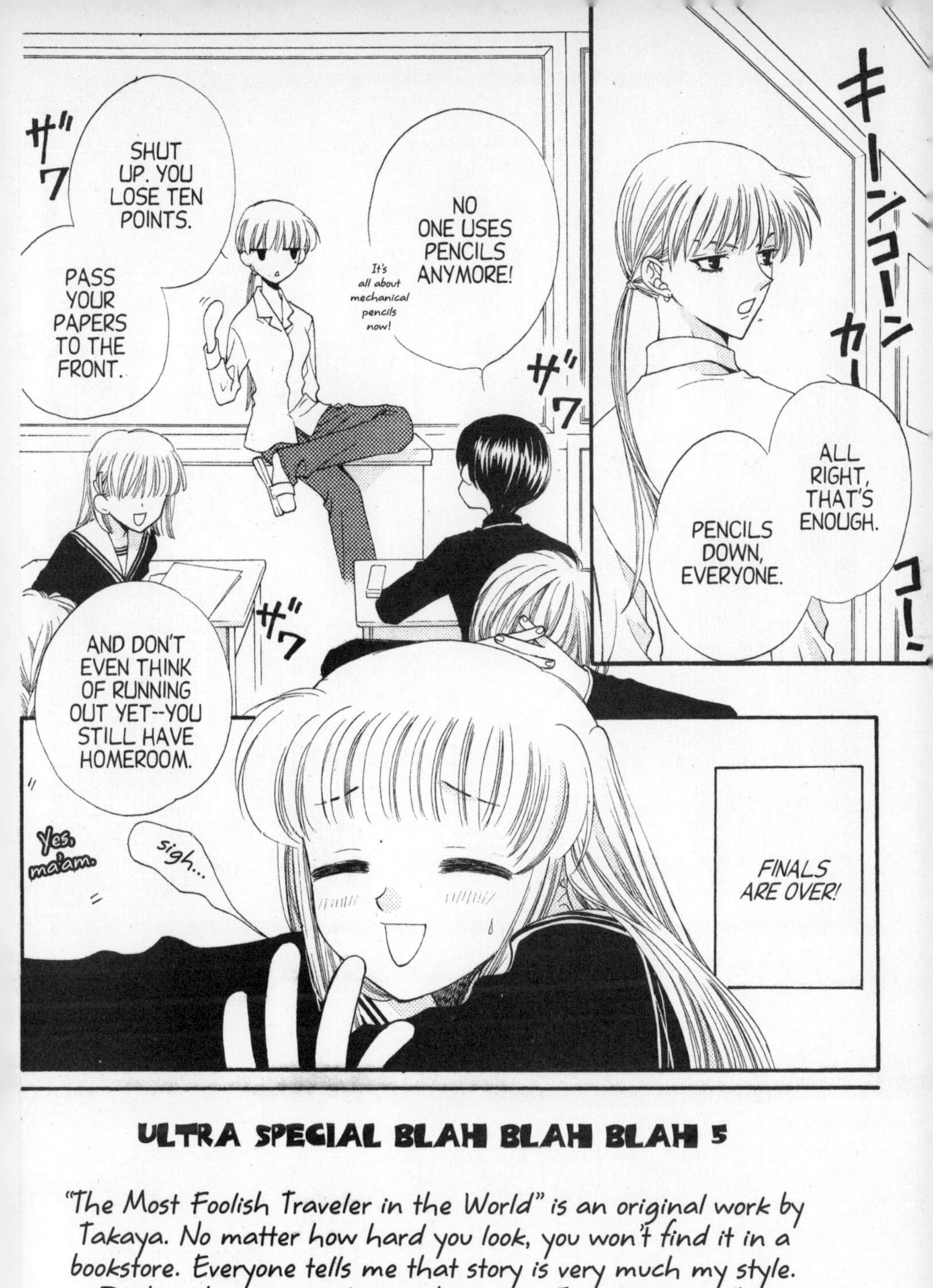
キーンコーン
カー
コー!
ALL RIGHT, THAT'S ENOUGH.
PENCILS DOWN, EVERYONE.
NO ONE USES PENCILS ANYMORE!
It's all about mechanical pencils now!
ザワ
ザワ
SHUT UP. YOU LOSE TEN POINTS.
PASS YOUR PAPERS TO THE FRONT.
ザワ
AND DON'T EVEN THINK OF RUNNING OUT YET--YOU STILL HAVE HOMEROOM.
FINALS ARE OVER!
sigh...
Yes, ma'am.

ULTRA SPECIAL BLAH BLAH BLAH 5

"The Most Foolish Traveler in the World" is an original work by Takaya. No matter how hard you look, you won't find it in a bookstore. Everyone tells me that story is very much my style. Rather than try to elicit a cheap cry, I really wanted to make readers face their own emotions.

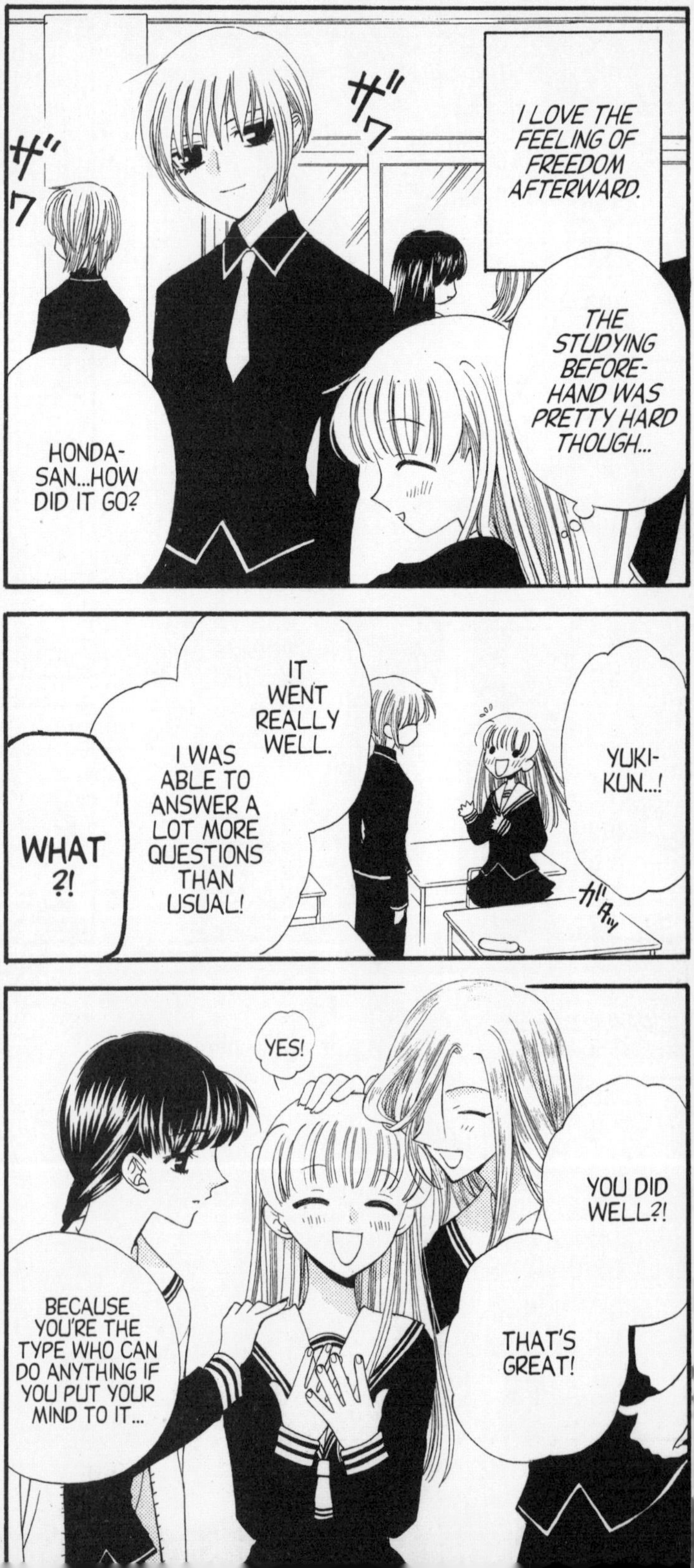
I LOVE THE FEELING OF FREEDOM AFTERWARD.
ザワ
ザワ
THE STUDYING BEFORE-HAND WAS PRETTY HARD THOUGH...
HONDA-SAN...HOW DID IT GO?
YUKI-KUN...!
IT WENT REALLY WELL.
I WAS ABLE TO ANSWER A LOT MORE QUESTIONS THAN USUAL!
WHAT?!
YOU DID WELL?!
YES!
THAT'S GREAT!
BECAUSE YOU'RE THE TYPE WHO CAN DO ANYTHING IF YOU PUT YOUR MIND TO IT...

**Fruits Basket 3
Part 5**

In Vol. 2 I said there weren't any plans for it, but a Furuba CD drama is coming out after all! It's a special offer, so it's not being sold to the public. These things happen suddenly, so it might be a good idea to check the magazine. Currently, the script isn't even done, but I hope it turns out to be fun! It's an oasis in the desert of my heart!! King of MidoriXXXX-san (it probably won't mean anything to censor his name at this point...) is... not in it. Sometimes I hate myself because I get serious at strange times. I really like all the voice actors who have agreed to be in Furuba, so I'm still very happy! I'm looking forward to it!

To be continued...

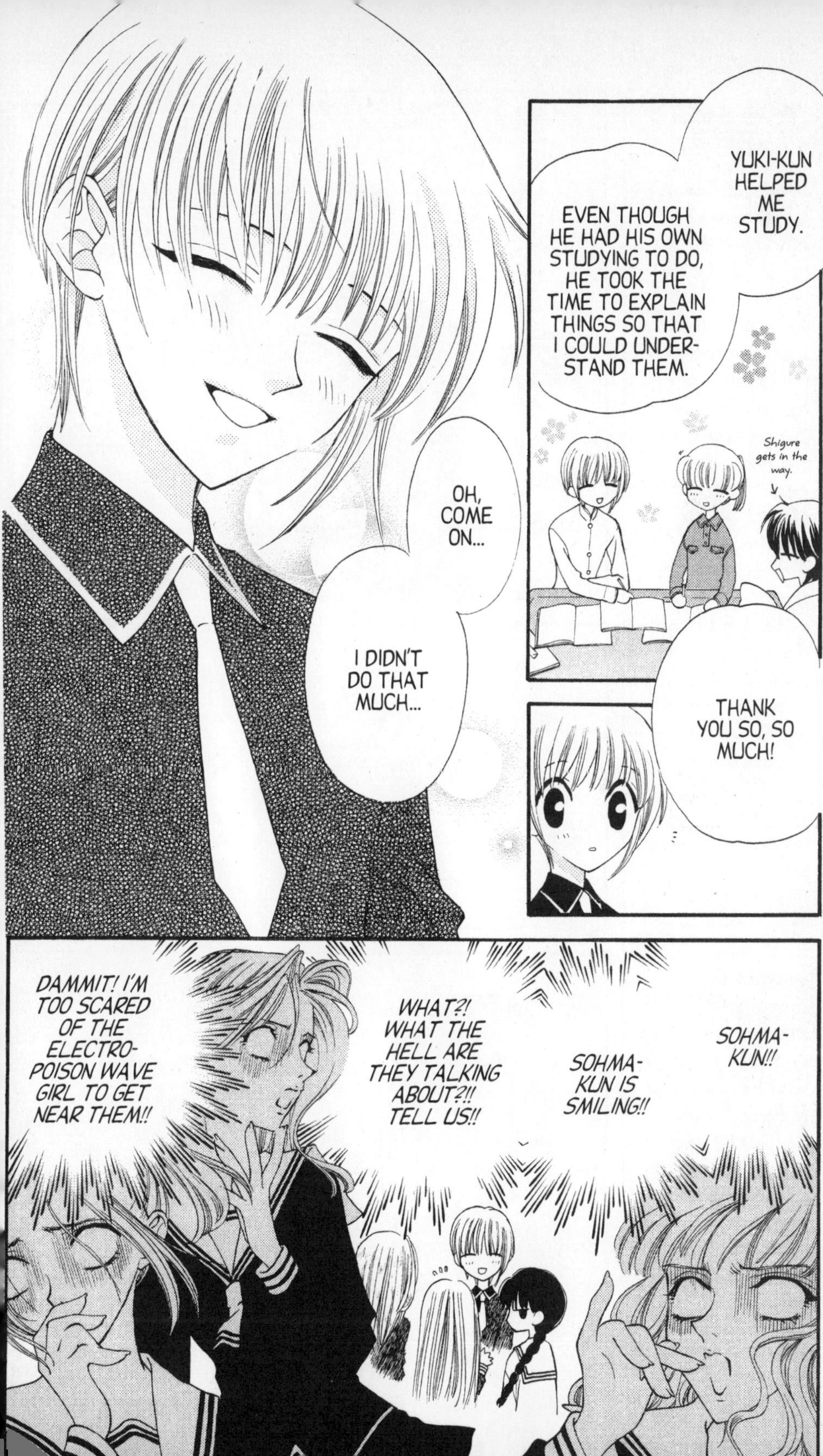
YUKI-KUN HELPED ME STUDY.
EVEN THOUGH HE HAD HIS OWN STUDYING TO DO, HE TOOK THE TIME TO EXPLAIN THINGS SO THAT I COULD UNDER-STAND THEM.
Shigure gets in the way.
THANK YOU SO, SO MUCH!
OH, COME ON...
I DIDN'T DO THAT MUCH...
SOHMA-KUN!!
SOHMA-KUN IS SMILING!!
WHAT?! WHAT THE HELL ARE THEY TALKING ABOUT?!! TELL US!!
DAMMIT! I'M TOO SCARED OF THE ELECTRO-POISON WAVE GIRL TO GET NEAR THEM!!

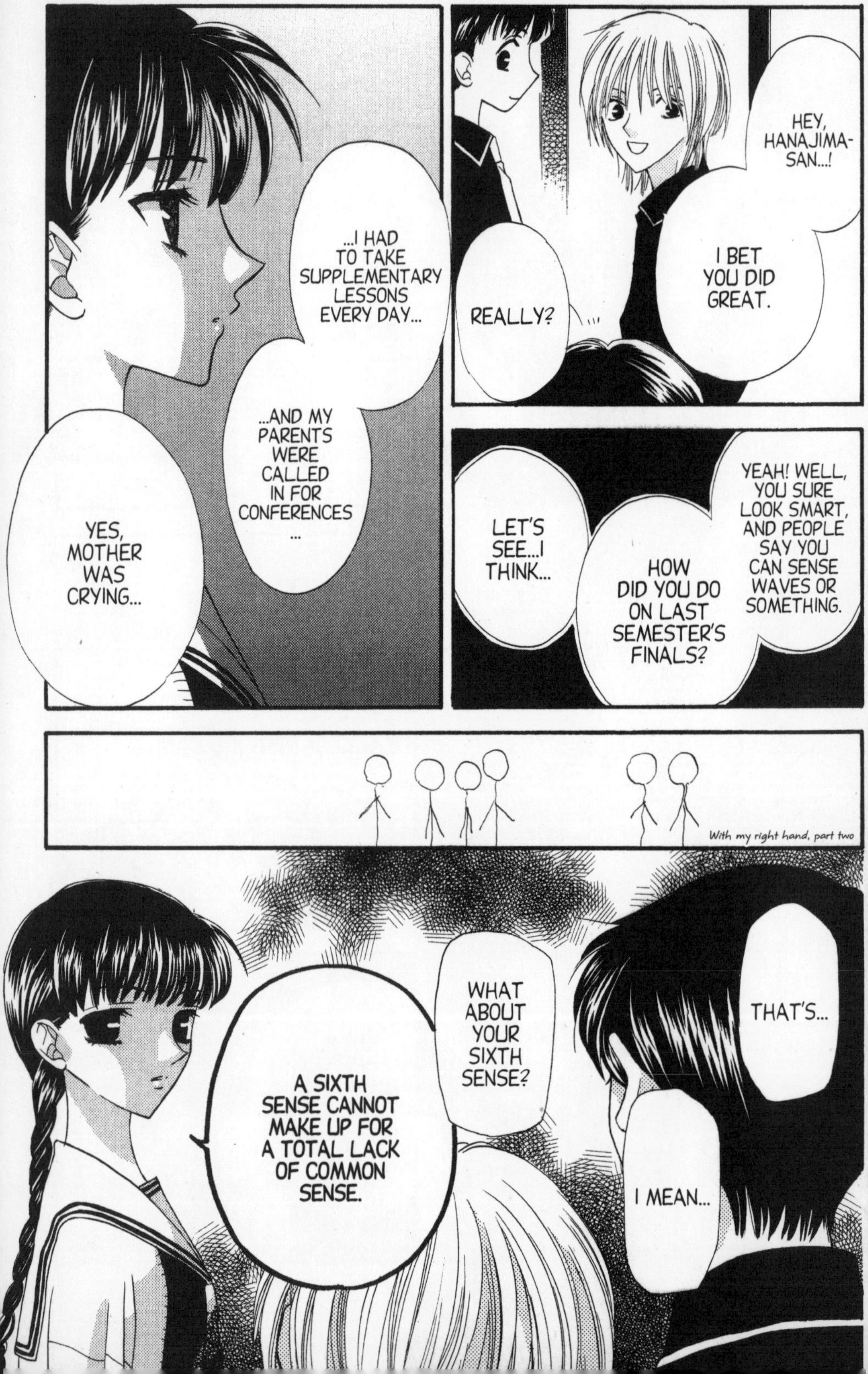
HEY, HANAJIMA-SAN...!
I BET YOU DID GREAT.
REALLY?
YEAH! WELL, YOU SURE LOOK SMART, AND PEOPLE SAY YOU CAN SENSE WAVES OR SOMETHING.
HOW DID YOU DO ON LAST SEMESTER'S FINALS?
LET'S SEE...I THINK...
...I HAD TO TAKE SUPPLEMENTARY LESSONS EVERY DAY...
...AND MY PARENTS WERE CALLED IN FOR CONFERENCES ...
YES, MOTHER WAS CRYING...
With my right hand, part two
THAT'S...
I MEAN...
WHAT ABOUT YOUR SIXTH SENSE?
A SIXTH SENSE CANNOT MAKE UP FOR A TOTAL LACK OF COMMON SENSE.

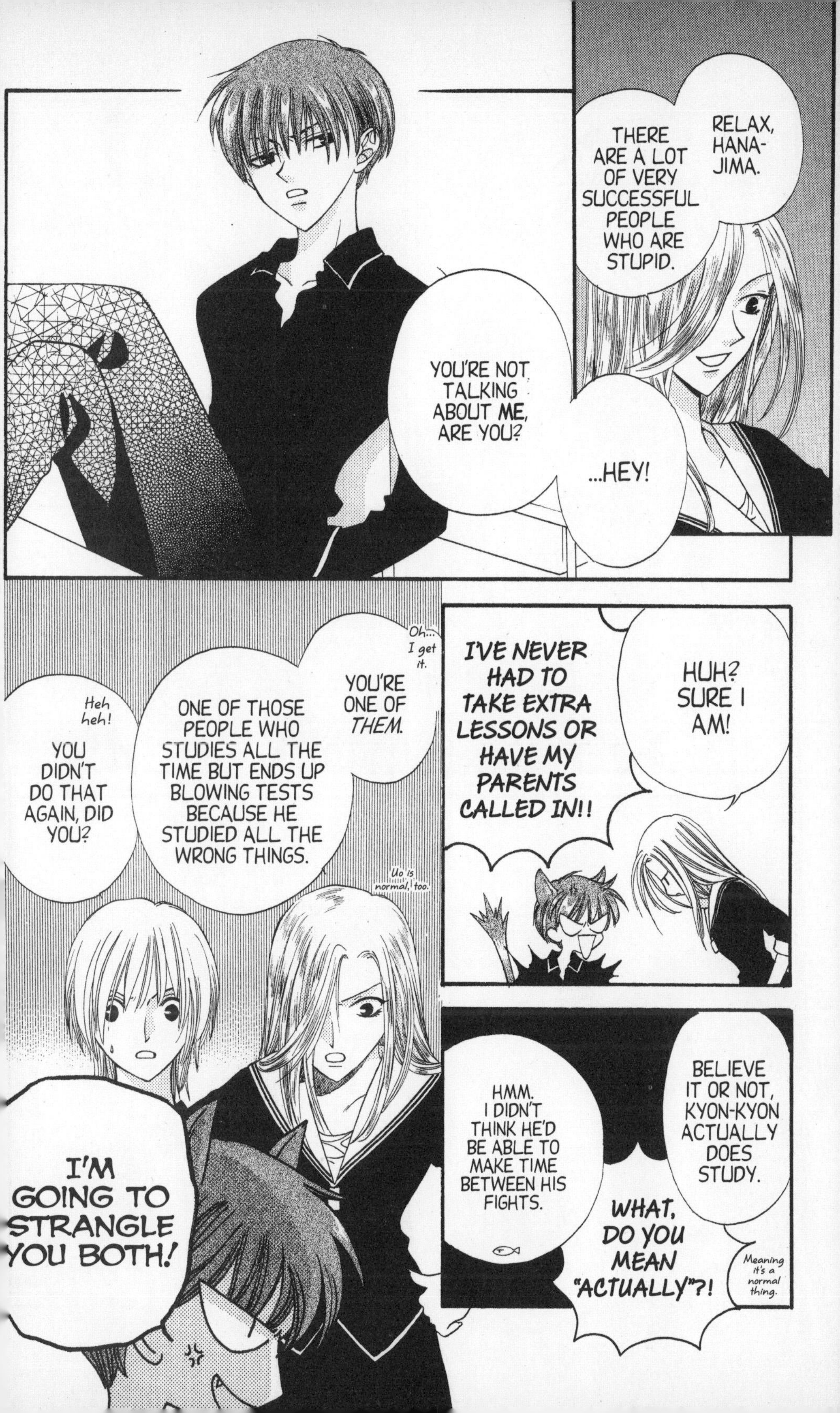
RELAX, HANA-JIMA.
THERE ARE A LOT OF VERY SUCCESSFUL PEOPLE WHO ARE STUPID.
...HEY!
YOU'RE NOT TALKING ABOUT ME, ARE YOU?
HUH? SURE I AM!
I'VE NEVER HAD TO TAKE EXTRA LESSONS OR HAVE MY PARENTS CALLED IN!!
BELIEVE IT OR NOT, KYON-KYON ACTUALLY DOES STUDY.
Meaning it's a normal thing.
HMM. I DIDN'T THINK HE'D BE ABLE TO MAKE TIME BETWEEN HIS FIGHTS.
WHAT, DO YOU MEAN "ACTUALLY"?!
Oh... I get it.
YOU'RE ONE OF THEM.
ONE OF THOSE PEOPLE WHO STUDIES ALL THE TIME BUT ENDS UP BLOWING TESTS BECAUSE HE STUDIED ALL THE WRONG THINGS.
Heh heh!
YOU DIDN'T DO THAT AGAIN, DID YOU?
Uo is normal, too.
I'M GOING TO STRANGLE YOU BOTH!

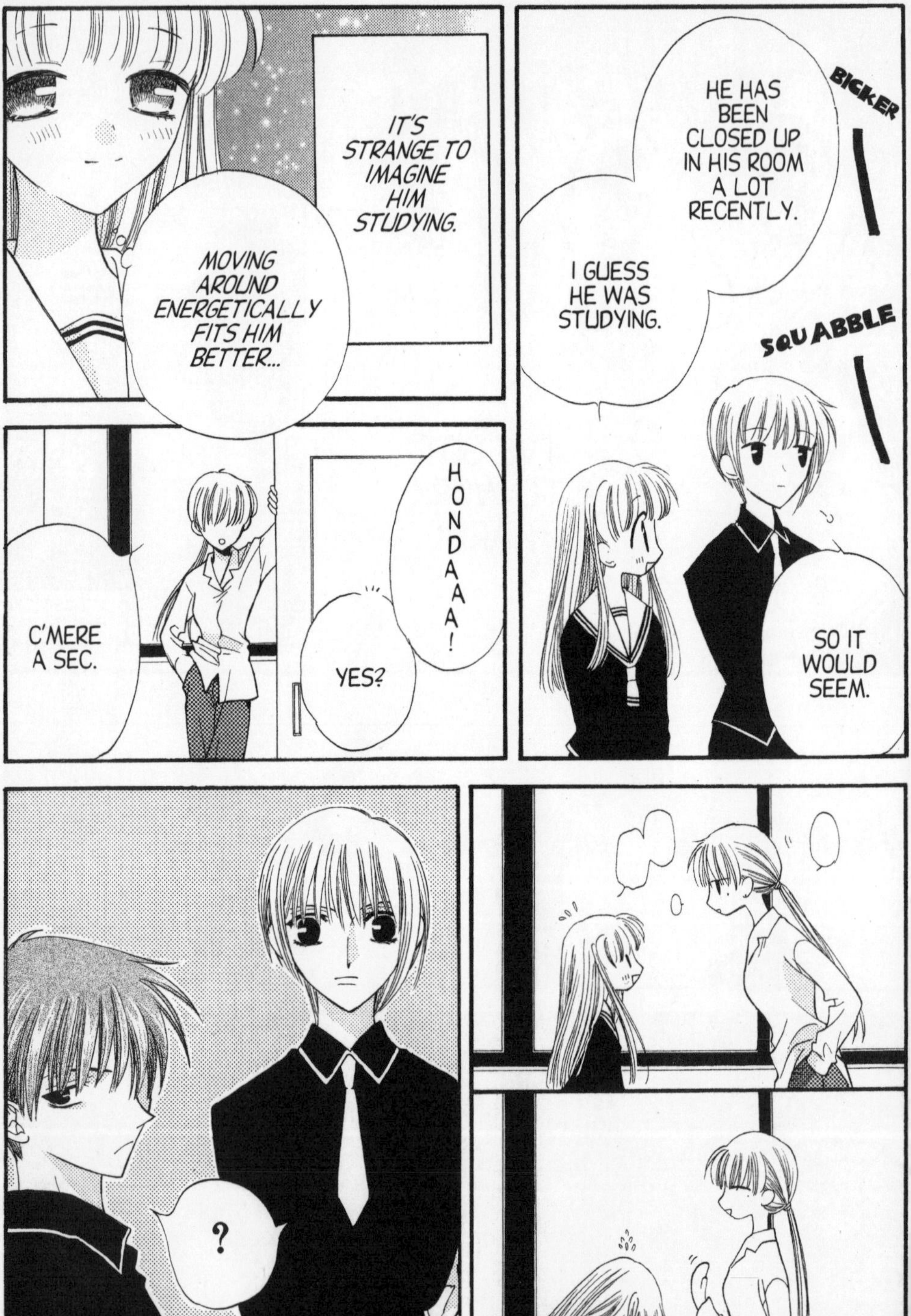
BICKER
HE HAS BEEN CLOSED UP IN HIS ROOM A LOT RECENTLY.
I GUESS HE WAS STUDYING.
SQUABBLE
SO IT WOULD SEEM.
IT'S STRANGE TO IMAGINE HIM STUDYING.
MOVING AROUND ENERGETICALLY FITS HIM BETTER...
HONDAAAA!
YES?
C'MERE A SEC.
?

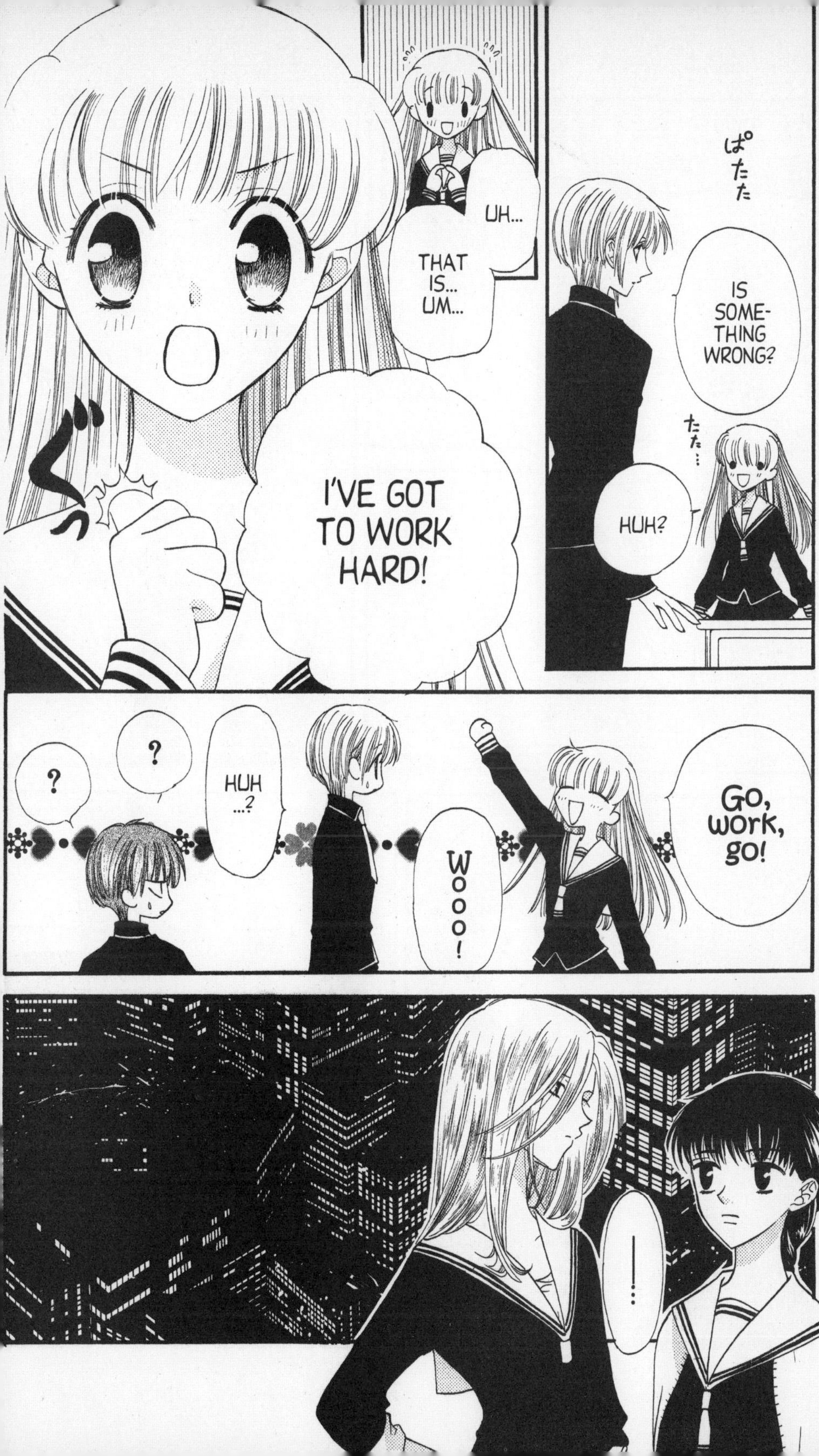
ぱたた
IS SOMETHING WRONG?
たた…
HUH?
UH...
THAT IS... UM...
ぐっ
I'VE GOT TO WORK HARD!
Go, work, go!
Wooo!
HUH ...?
?
?
—...

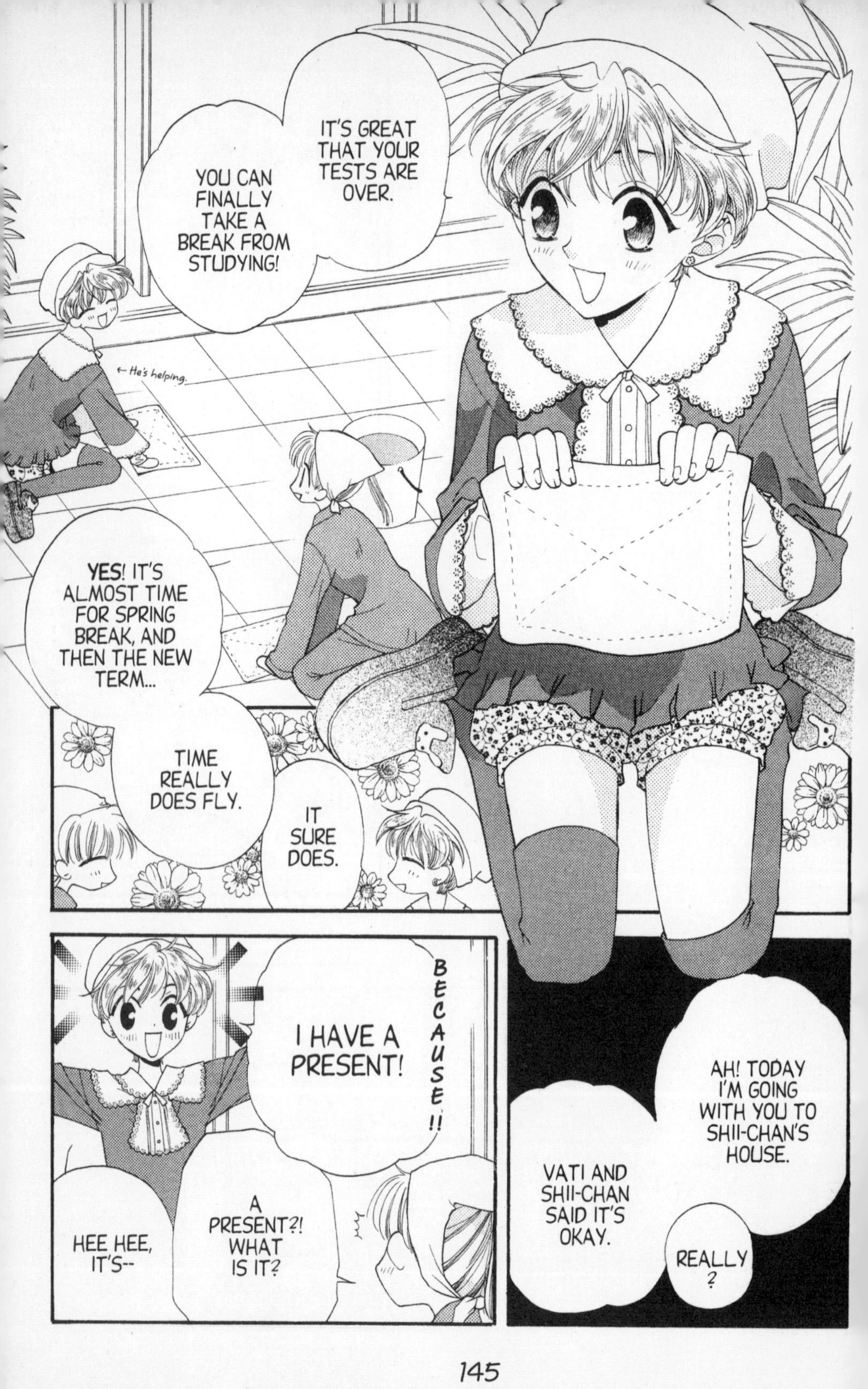
IT'S GREAT THAT YOUR TESTS ARE OVER.
YOU CAN FINALLY TAKE A BREAK FROM STUDYING!
← He's helping.
YES! IT'S ALMOST TIME FOR SPRING BREAK, AND THEN THE NEW TERM...
TIME REALLY DOES FLY.
IT SURE DOES.
AH! TODAY I'M GOING WITH YOU TO SHII-CHAN'S HOUSE.
VATI AND SHII-CHAN SAID IT'S OKAY.
REALLY?
BECAUSE!!
I HAVE A PRESENT!
A PRESENT?! WHAT IS IT?
HEE HEE, IT'S--

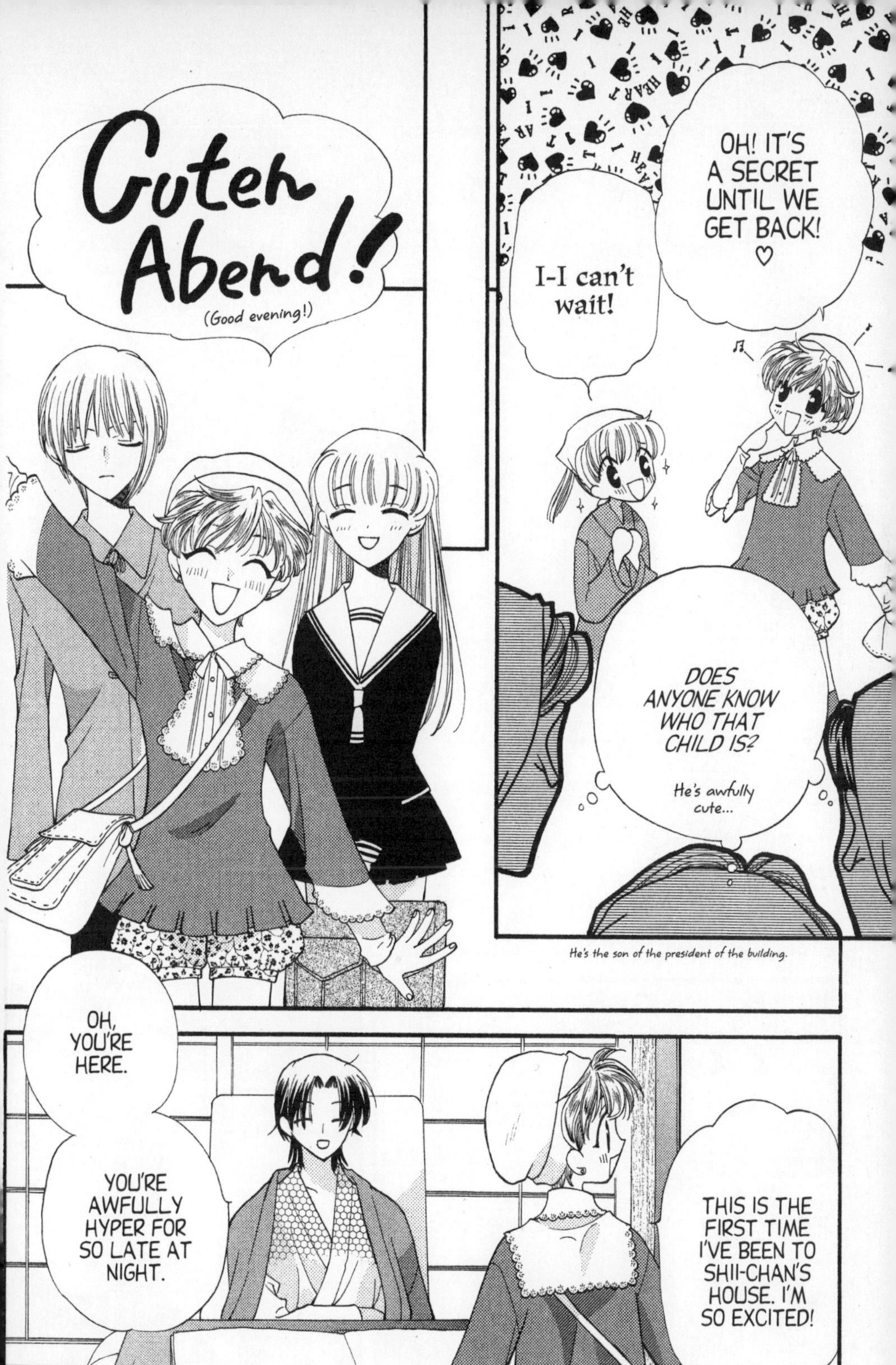
OH! IT'S A SECRET UNTIL WE GET BACK! ♡
I-I can't wait!
DOES ANYONE KNOW WHO THAT CHILD IS?
He's awfully cute...
He's the son of the president of the building.
Guten Abend!
(Good evening!)
THIS IS THE FIRST TIME I'VE BEEN TO SHII-CHAN'S HOUSE. I'M SO EXCITED!
OH, YOU'RE HERE.
YOU'RE AWFULLY HYPER FOR SO LATE AT NIGHT.

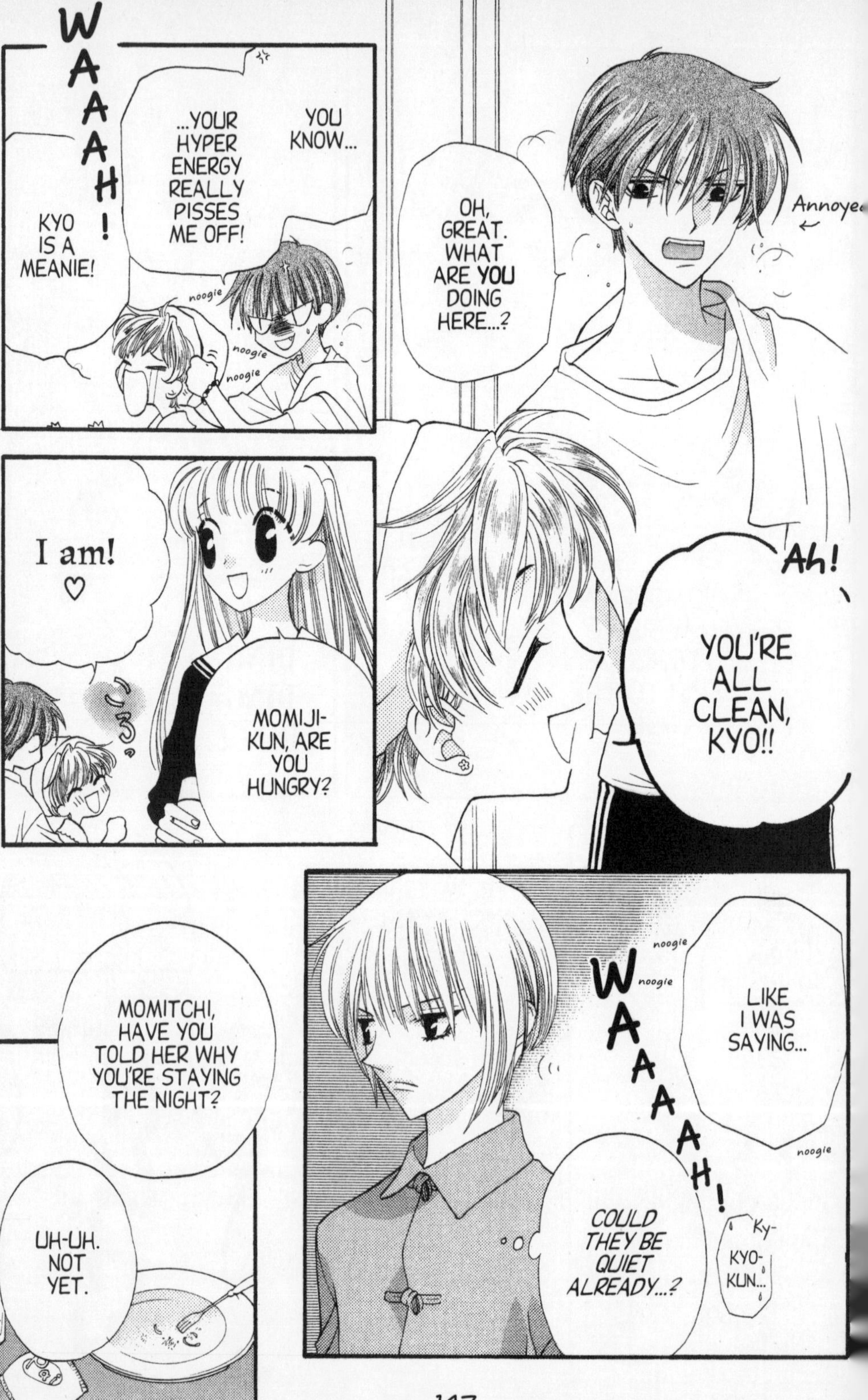
Annoye
OH, GREAT. WHAT ARE YOU DOING HERE...?
Ah!
YOU'RE ALL CLEAN, KYO!!
YOU KNOW...
...YOUR HYPER ENERGY REALLY PISSES ME OFF!
WAAAAH!
KYO IS A MEANIE!
noogie
noogie
noogie
MOMIJI-KUN, ARE YOU HUNGRY?
I am! ♡
LIKE I WAS SAYING...
noogie
noogie
noogie
WAAAAAH!
Ky-KYO-KUN...
COULD THEY BE QUIET ALREADY...?
MOMITCHI, HAVE YOU TOLD HER WHY YOU'RE STAYING THE NIGHT?
UH-UH. NOT YET.

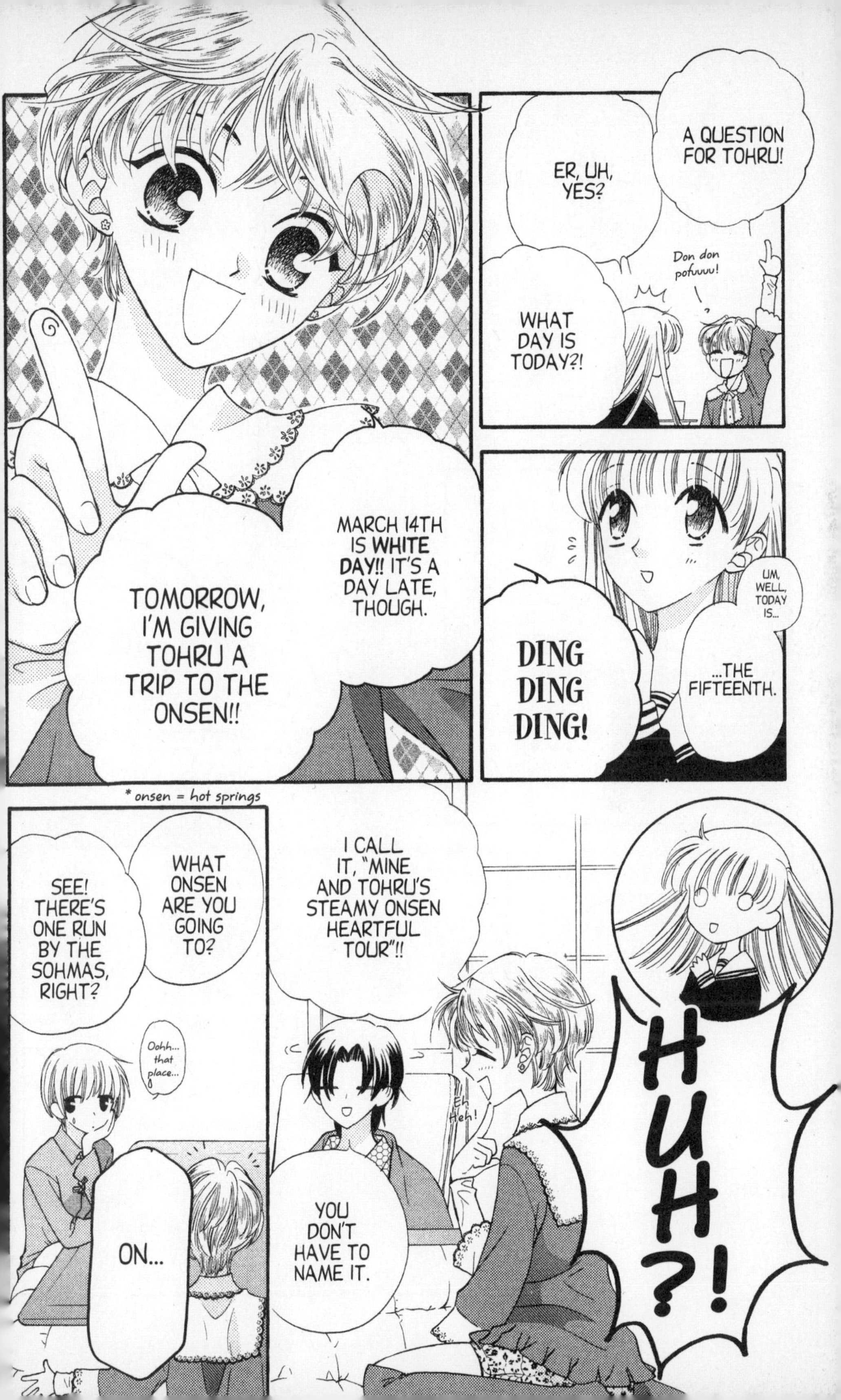
A QUESTION FOR TOHRU!
Don don pofuuuu!
ER, UH, YES?
WHAT DAY IS TODAY?!
UM, WELL, TODAY IS...
...THE FIFTEENTH.
DING DING DING!
MARCH 14TH IS WHITE DAY!! IT'S A DAY LATE, THOUGH.
TOMORROW, I'M GIVING TOHRU A TRIP TO THE ONSEN!!
HUH?!
I CALL IT, "MINE AND TOHRU'S STEAMY ONSEN HEARTFUL TOUR"!!
Eh Heh!
YOU DON'T HAVE TO NAME IT.
WHAT ONSEN ARE YOU GOING TO?
SEE! THERE'S ONE RUN BY THE SOHMAS, RIGHT?
Oohh... that place...
ON...

* onsen = hot springs

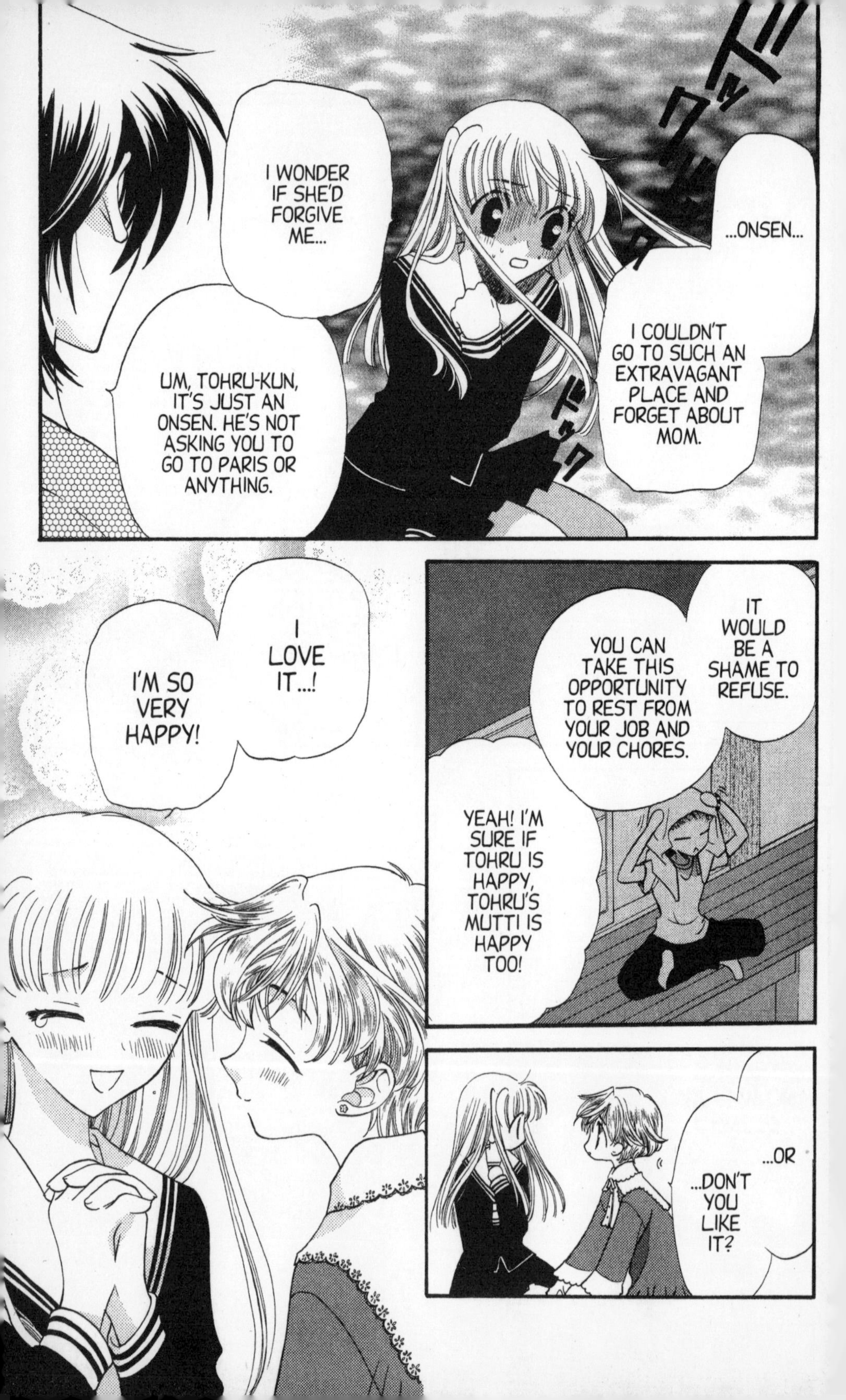
...ONSEN...
I COULDN'T GO TO SUCH AN EXTRAVAGANT PLACE AND FORGET ABOUT MOM.
I WONDER IF SHE'D FORGIVE ME...
UM, TOHRU-KUN, IT'S JUST AN ONSEN. HE'S NOT ASKING YOU TO GO TO PARIS OR ANYTHING.
IT WOULD BE A SHAME TO REFUSE.
YOU CAN TAKE THIS OPPORTUNITY TO REST FROM YOUR JOB AND YOUR CHORES.
YEAH! I'M SURE IF TOHRU IS HAPPY, TOHRU'S MUTTI IS HAPPY TOO!
...OR
...DON'T YOU LIKE IT?
I LOVE IT...!
I'M SO VERY HAPPY!

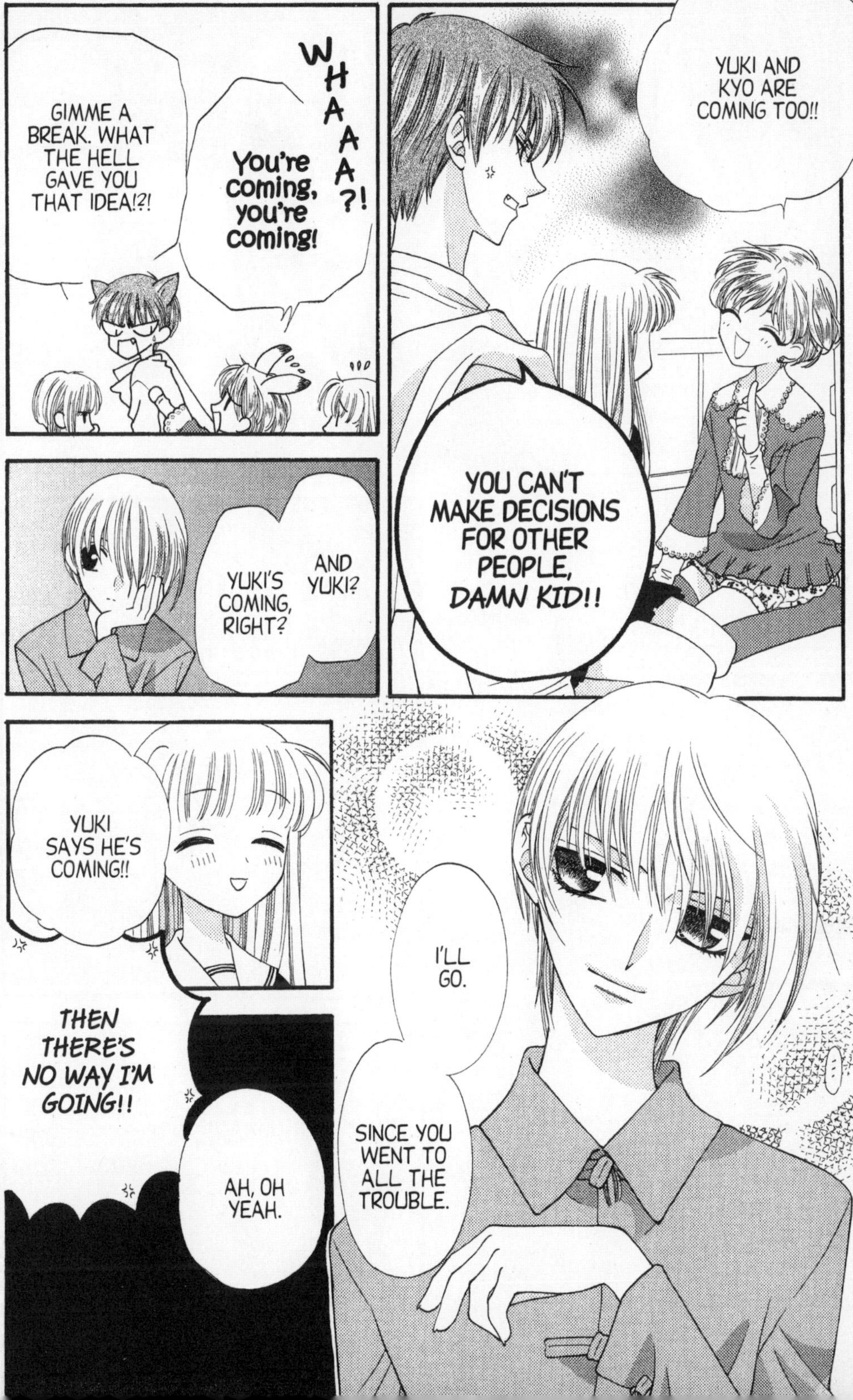
YUKI AND KYO ARE COMING TOO!!
YOU CAN'T MAKE DECISIONS FOR OTHER PEOPLE, DAMN KID!!
WHAAAA?!
You're coming, you're coming!
GIMME A BREAK. WHAT THE HELL GAVE YOU THAT IDEA!?!
AND YUKI?
YUKI'S COMING, RIGHT?
I'LL GO.
SINCE YOU WENT TO ALL THE TROUBLE.
...
YUKI SAYS HE'S COMING!!
THEN THERE'S NO WAY I'M GOING!!
AH, OH YEAH.

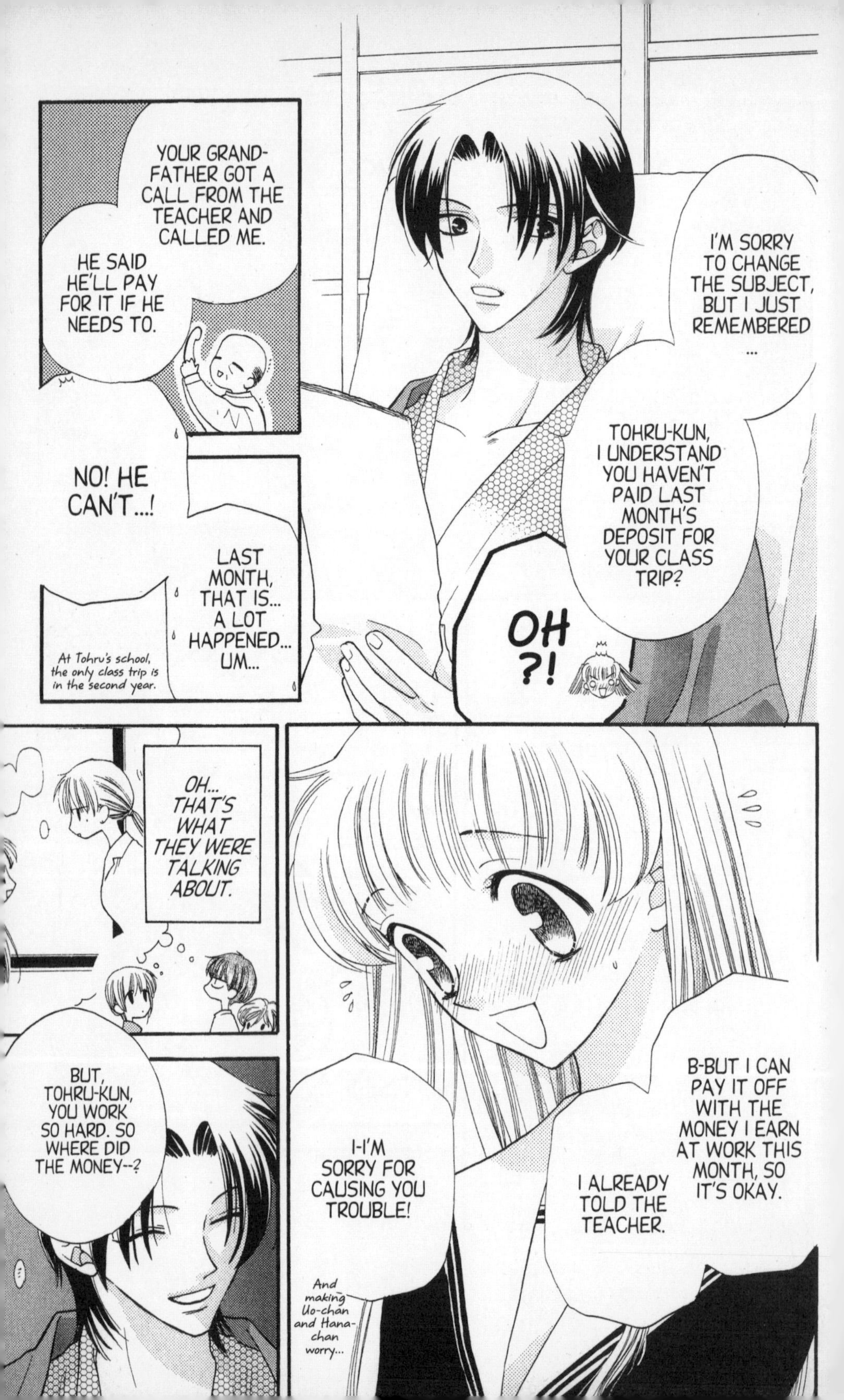
I'M SORRY TO CHANGE THE SUBJECT, BUT I JUST REMEMBERED ...
TOHRU-KUN, I UNDERSTAND YOU HAVEN'T PAID LAST MONTH'S DEPOSIT FOR YOUR CLASS TRIP?
OH ?!
YOUR GRAND-FATHER GOT A CALL FROM THE TEACHER AND CALLED ME.
HE SAID HE'LL PAY FOR IT IF HE NEEDS TO.
NO! HE CAN'T...!
LAST MONTH, THAT IS... A LOT HAPPENED... UM...
At Tohru's school, the only class trip is in the second year.
B-BUT I CAN PAY IT OFF WITH THE MONEY I EARN AT WORK THIS MONTH, SO IT'S OKAY.
I ALREADY TOLD THE TEACHER.
I-I'M SORRY FOR CAUSING YOU TROUBLE!
And making Uo-chan and Hana-chan worry...
OH... THAT'S WHAT THEY WERE TALKING ABOUT.
BUT, TOHRU-KUN, YOU WORK SO HARD. SO WHERE DID THE MONEY--?

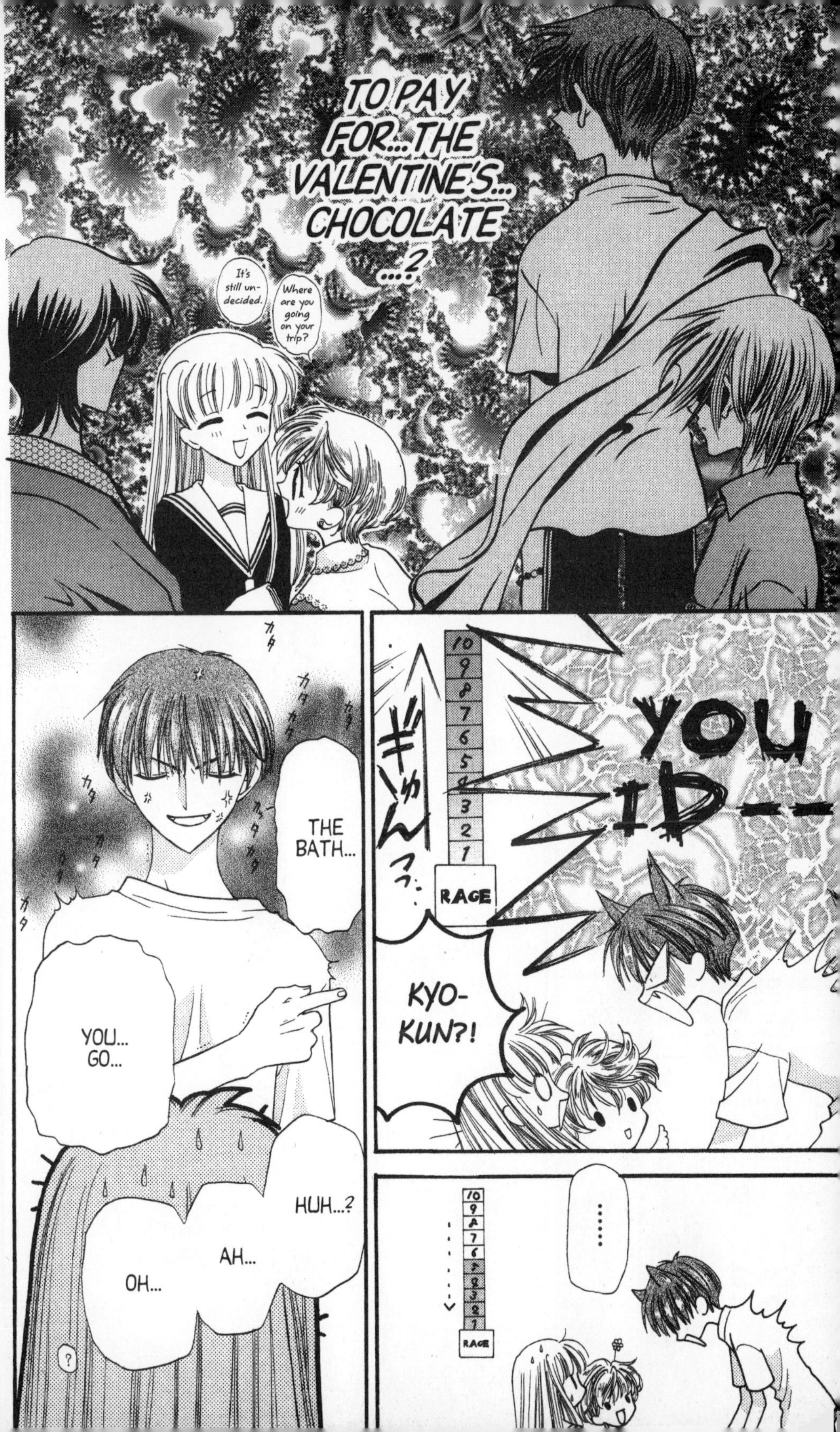
TO PAY FOR...THE VALENTINE'S... CHOCOLATE ...?
Where are you going on your trip?
It's still un-decided.
RAGE
YOU ID--
KYO-KUN?!
......
RAGE
THE BATH...
YOU... GO...
HUH...?
AH...
OH...
?

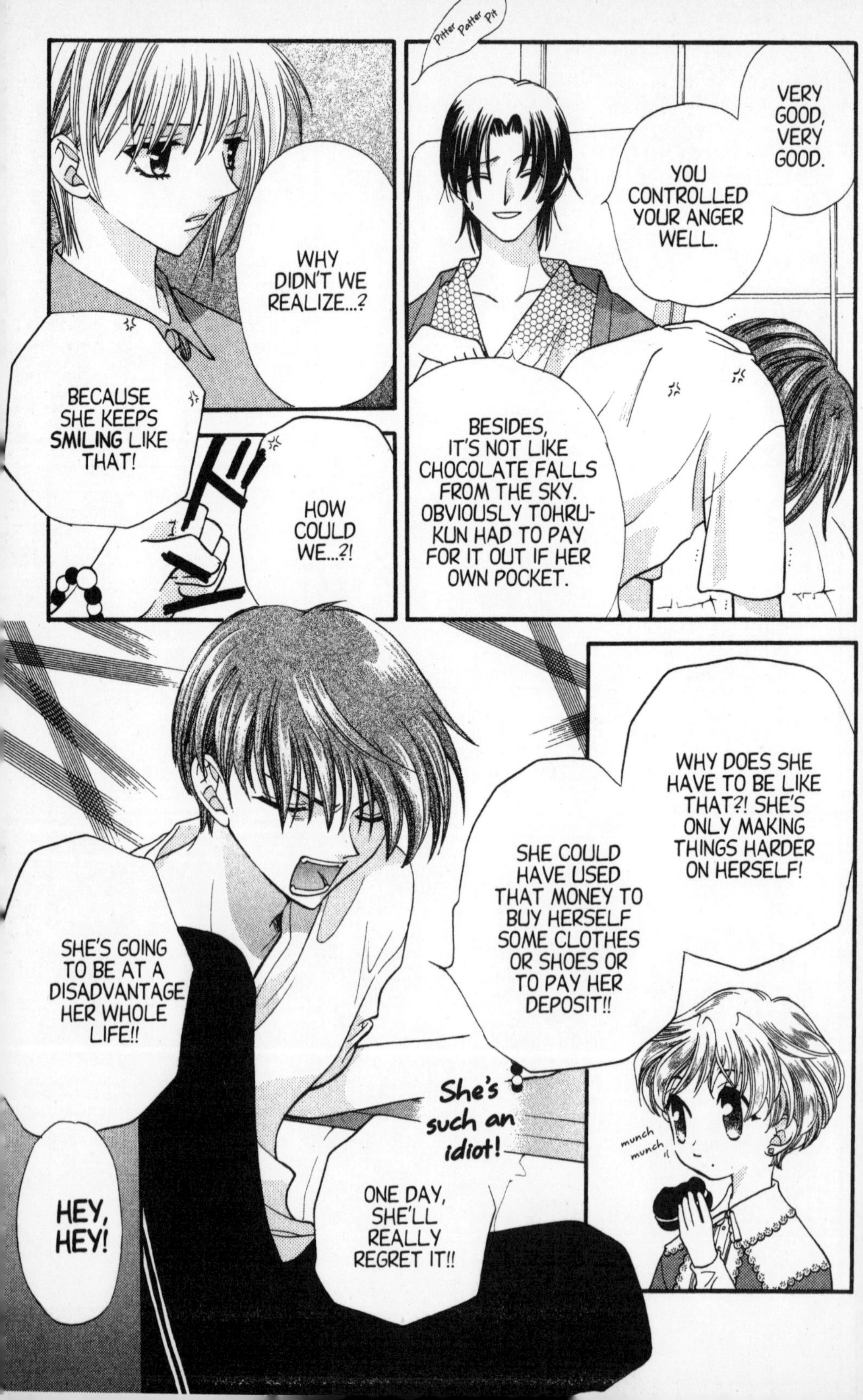
Pitter Patter Pit
VERY GOOD, VERY GOOD.
YOU CONTROLLED YOUR ANGER WELL.
BESIDES, IT'S NOT LIKE CHOCOLATE FALLS FROM THE SKY. OBVIOUSLY TOHRU-KUN HAD TO PAY FOR IT OUT IF HER OWN POCKET.
WHY DIDN'T WE REALIZE...?
HOW COULD WE...?!
BECAUSE SHE KEEPS SMILING LIKE THAT!
WHY DOES SHE HAVE TO BE LIKE THAT?! SHE'S ONLY MAKING THINGS HARDER ON HERSELF!
SHE COULD HAVE USED THAT MONEY TO BUY HERSELF SOME CLOTHES OR SHOES OR TO PAY HER DEPOSIT!!
munch munch
SHE'S GOING TO BE AT A DISADVANTAGE HER WHOLE LIFE!!
She's such an idiot!
ONE DAY, SHE'LL REALLY REGRET IT!!
HEY, HEY!

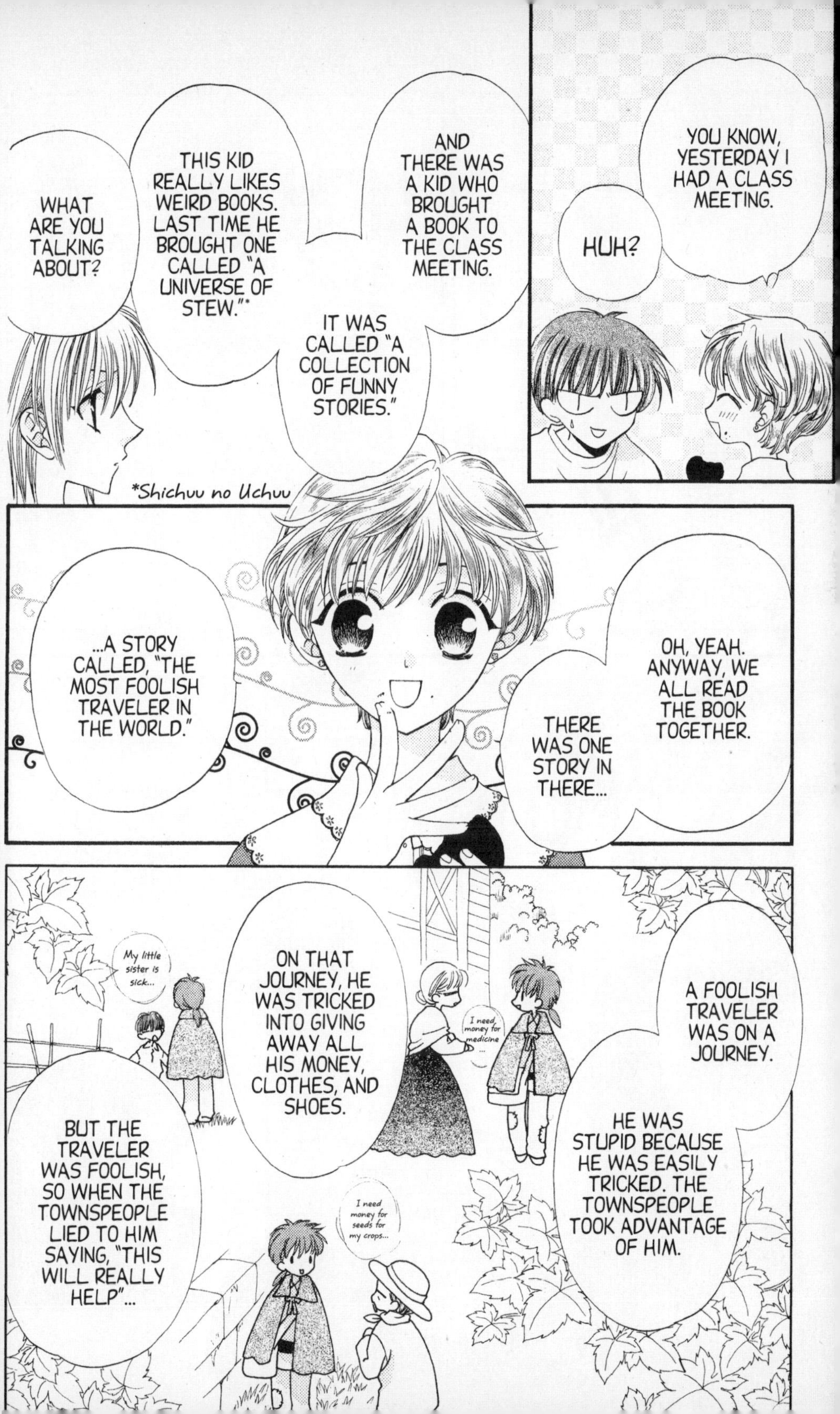

YOU KNOW, YESTERDAY I HAD A CLASS MEETING.
HUH?
AND THERE WAS A KID WHO BROUGHT A BOOK TO THE CLASS MEETING.
THIS KID REALLY LIKES WEIRD BOOKS. LAST TIME HE BROUGHT ONE CALLED "A UNIVERSE OF STEW."*
WHAT ARE YOU TALKING ABOUT?
IT WAS CALLED "A COLLECTION OF FUNNY STORIES."
*Shichuu no Uchuu
OH, YEAH. ANYWAY, WE ALL READ THE BOOK TOGETHER.
THERE WAS ONE STORY IN THERE...
...A STORY CALLED, "THE MOST FOOLISH TRAVELER IN THE WORLD."
A FOOLISH TRAVELER WAS ON A JOURNEY.
I need money for medicine...
ON THAT JOURNEY, HE WAS TRICKED INTO GIVING AWAY ALL HIS MONEY, CLOTHES, AND SHOES.
My little sister is sick...
HE WAS STUPID BECAUSE HE WAS EASILY TRICKED. THE TOWNSPEOPLE TOOK ADVANTAGE OF HIM.
I need money for seeds for my crops...
BUT THE TRAVELER WAS FOOLISH, SO WHEN THE TOWNSPEOPLE LIED TO HIM SAYING, "THIS WILL REALLY HELP"...

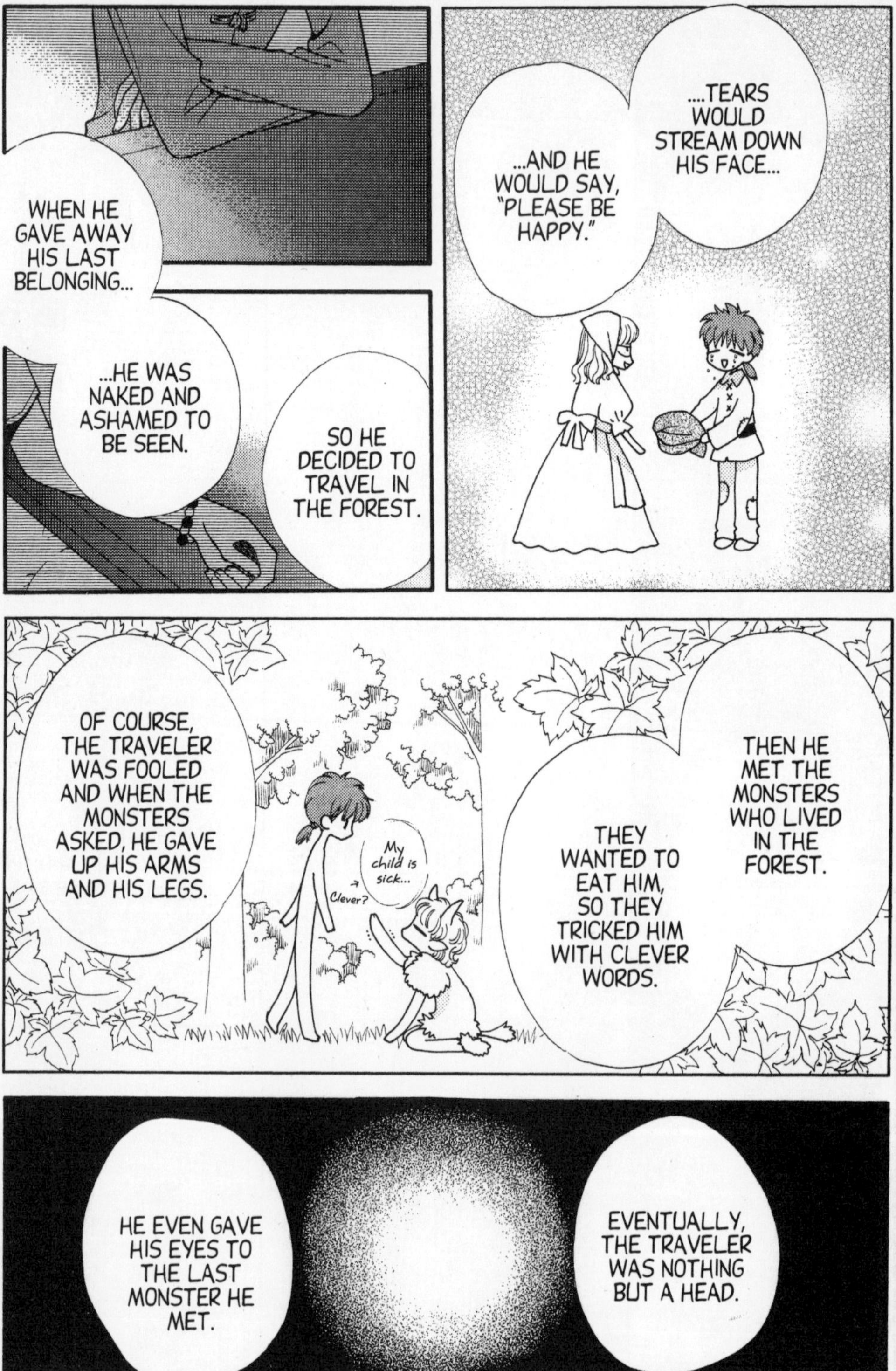
....TEARS WOULD STREAM DOWN HIS FACE...
...AND HE WOULD SAY, "PLEASE BE HAPPY."
WHEN HE GAVE AWAY HIS LAST BELONGING...
...HE WAS NAKED AND ASHAMED TO BE SEEN.
SO HE DECIDED TO TRAVEL IN THE FOREST.
THEN HE MET THE MONSTERS WHO LIVED IN THE FOREST.
THEY WANTED TO EAT HIM, SO THEY TRICKED HIM WITH CLEVER WORDS.
My child is sick...
Clever?
OF COURSE, THE TRAVELER WAS FOOLED AND WHEN THE MONSTERS ASKED, HE GAVE UP HIS ARMS AND HIS LEGS.
EVENTUALLY, THE TRAVELER WAS NOTHING BUT A HEAD.
HE EVEN GAVE HIS EYES TO THE LAST MONSTER HE MET.

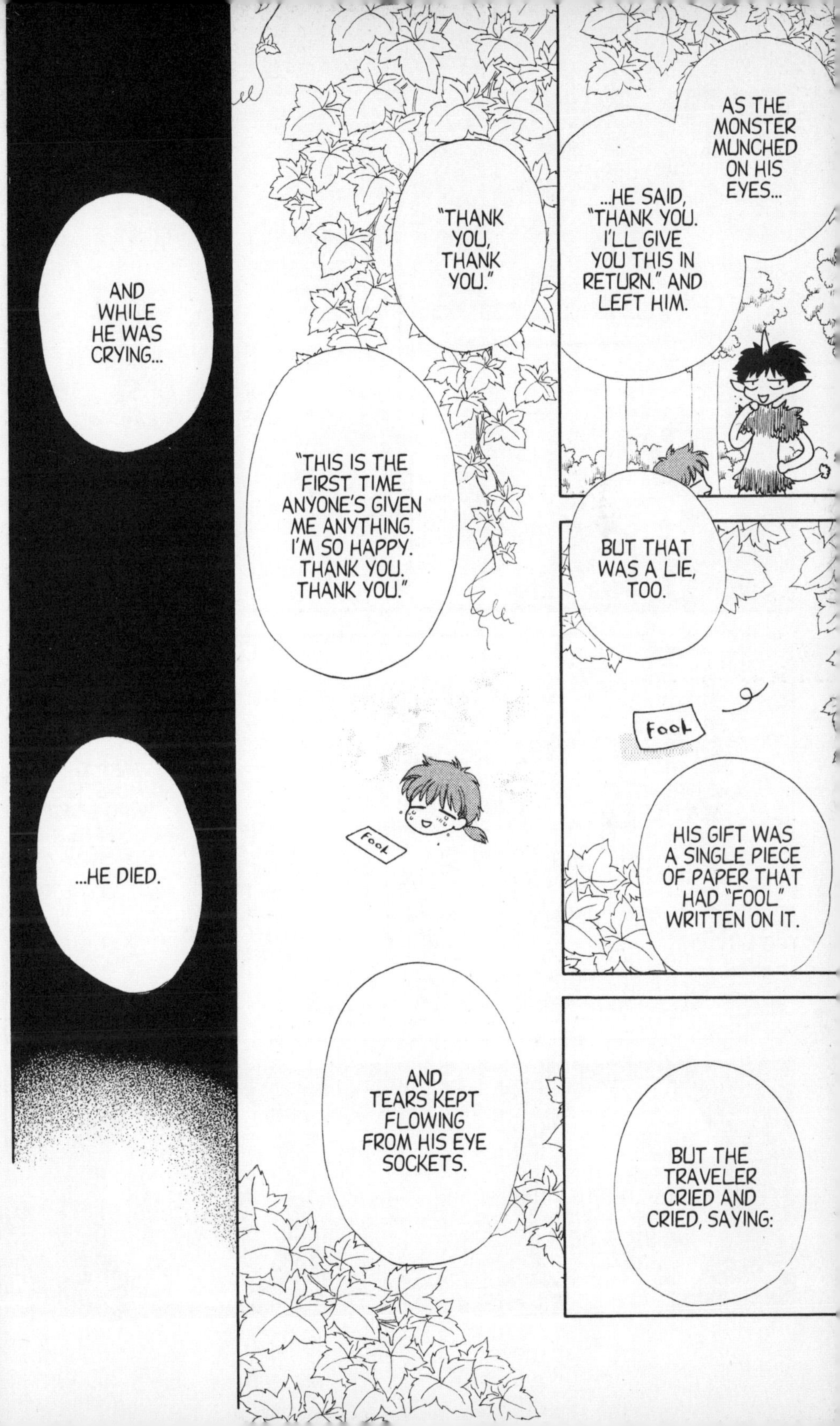
AS THE MONSTER MUNCHED ON HIS EYES...
...HE SAID, "THANK YOU. I'LL GIVE YOU THIS IN RETURN." AND LEFT HIM.
BUT THAT WAS A LIE, TOO.
Fool
HIS GIFT WAS A SINGLE PIECE OF PAPER THAT HAD "FOOL" WRITTEN ON IT.
BUT THE TRAVELER CRIED AND CRIED, SAYING:
"THANK YOU, THANK YOU."
"THIS IS THE FIRST TIME ANYONE'S GIVEN ME ANYTHING. I'M SO HAPPY. THANK YOU. THANK YOU."
Fool
AND TEARS KEPT FLOWING FROM HIS EYE SOCKETS.
AND WHILE HE WAS CRYING...
...HE DIED.

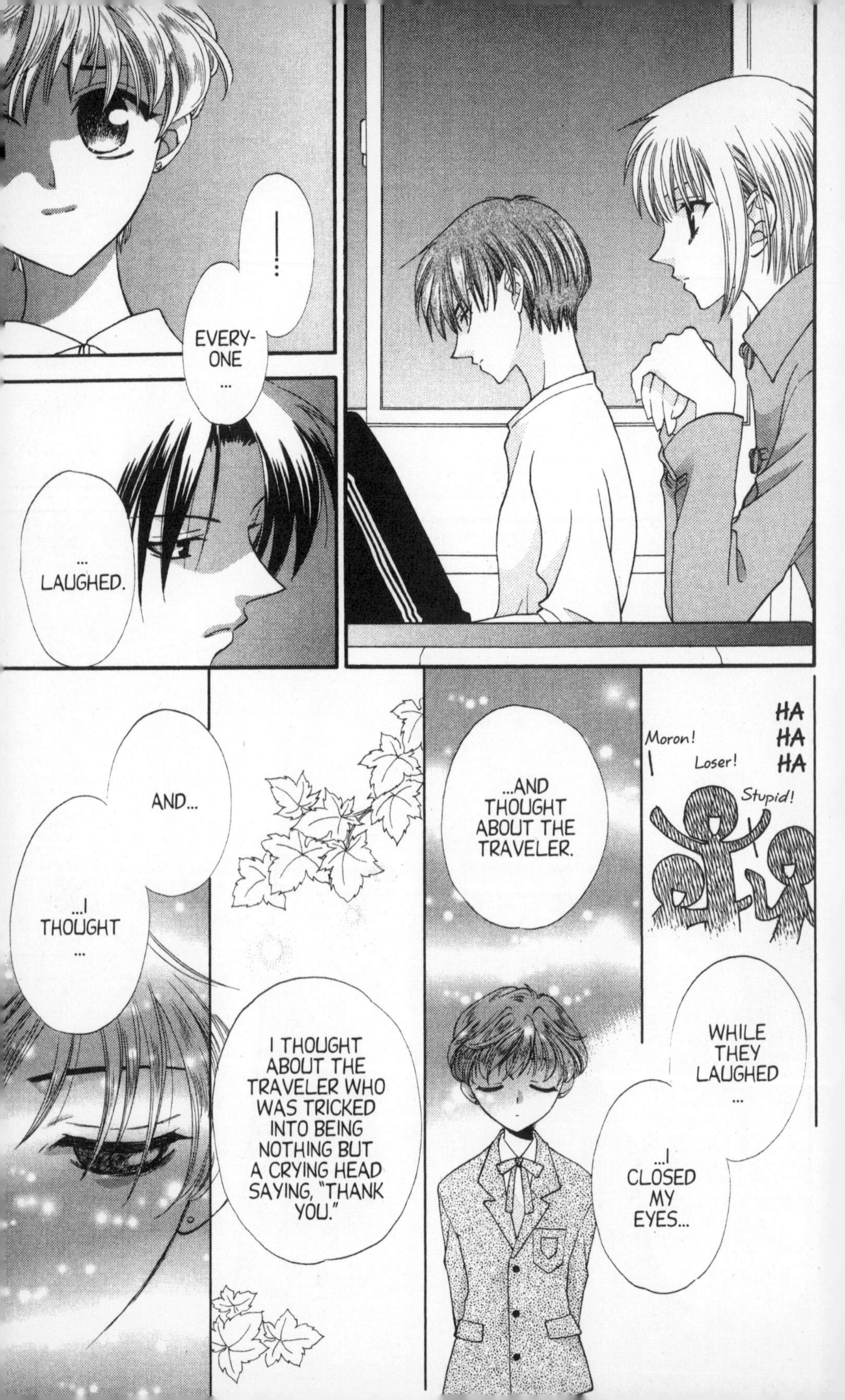

...!
EVERY-ONE ...
... LAUGHED.
HA HA HA
Moron!
Loser!
Stupid!
WHILE THEY LAUGHED ...
...I CLOSED MY EYES...
...AND THOUGHT ABOUT THE TRAVELER.
AND...
...I THOUGHT ...
I THOUGHT ABOUT THE TRAVELER WHO WAS TRICKED INTO BEING NOTHING BUT A CRYING HEAD SAYING, "THANK YOU."

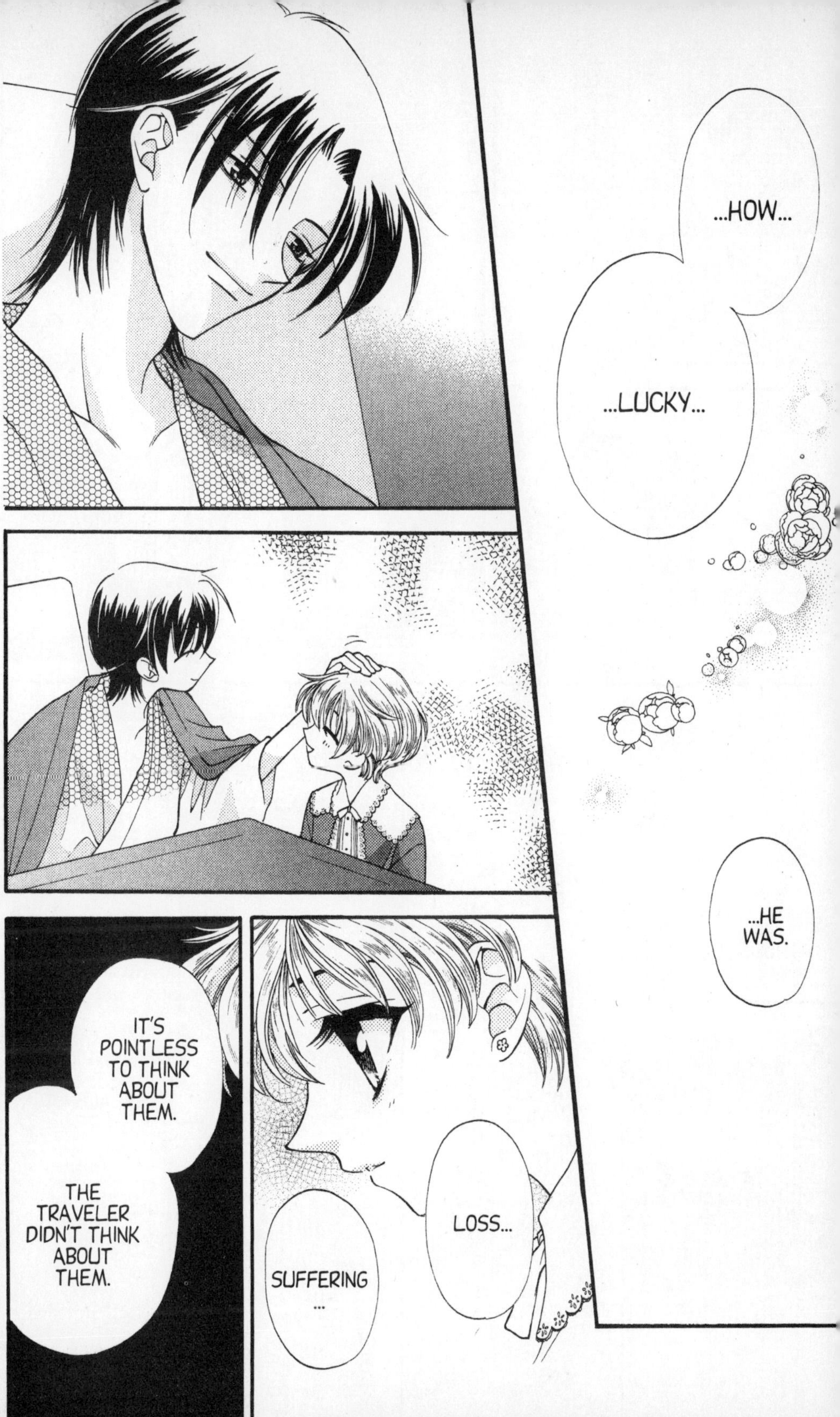
...HOW...
...LUCKY...
...HE WAS.
LOSS...
SUFFERING...
IT'S POINTLESS TO THINK ABOUT THEM.
THE TRAVELER DIDN'T THINK ABOUT THEM.

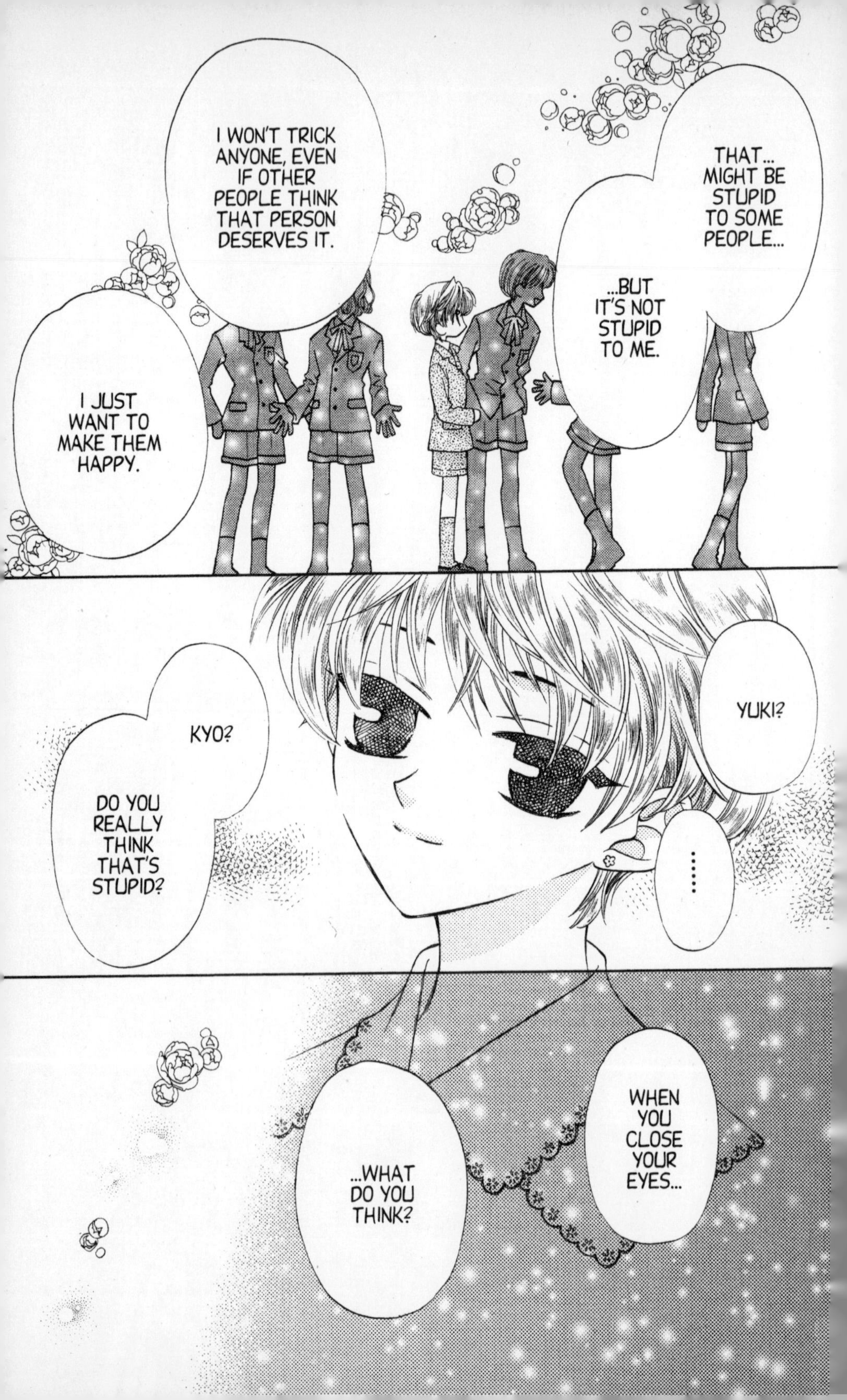
THAT... MIGHT BE STUPID TO SOME PEOPLE...
...BUT IT'S NOT STUPID TO ME.
I WON'T TRICK ANYONE, EVEN IF OTHER PEOPLE THINK THAT PERSON DESERVES IT.
I JUST WANT TO MAKE THEM HAPPY.
YUKI?
......
KYO?
DO YOU REALLY THINK THAT'S STUPID?
WHEN YOU CLOSE YOUR EYES...
...WHAT DO YOU THINK?

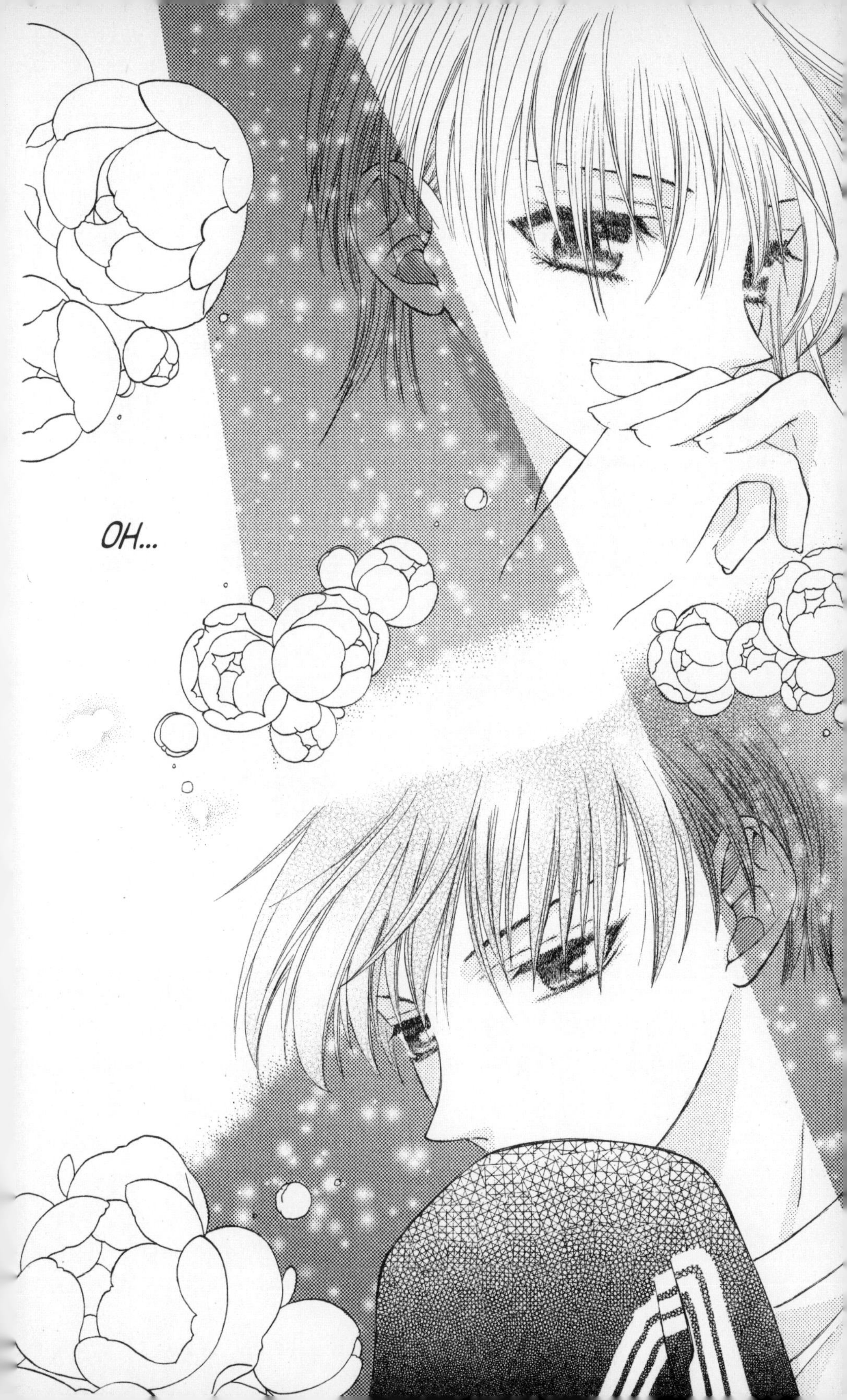
OH...

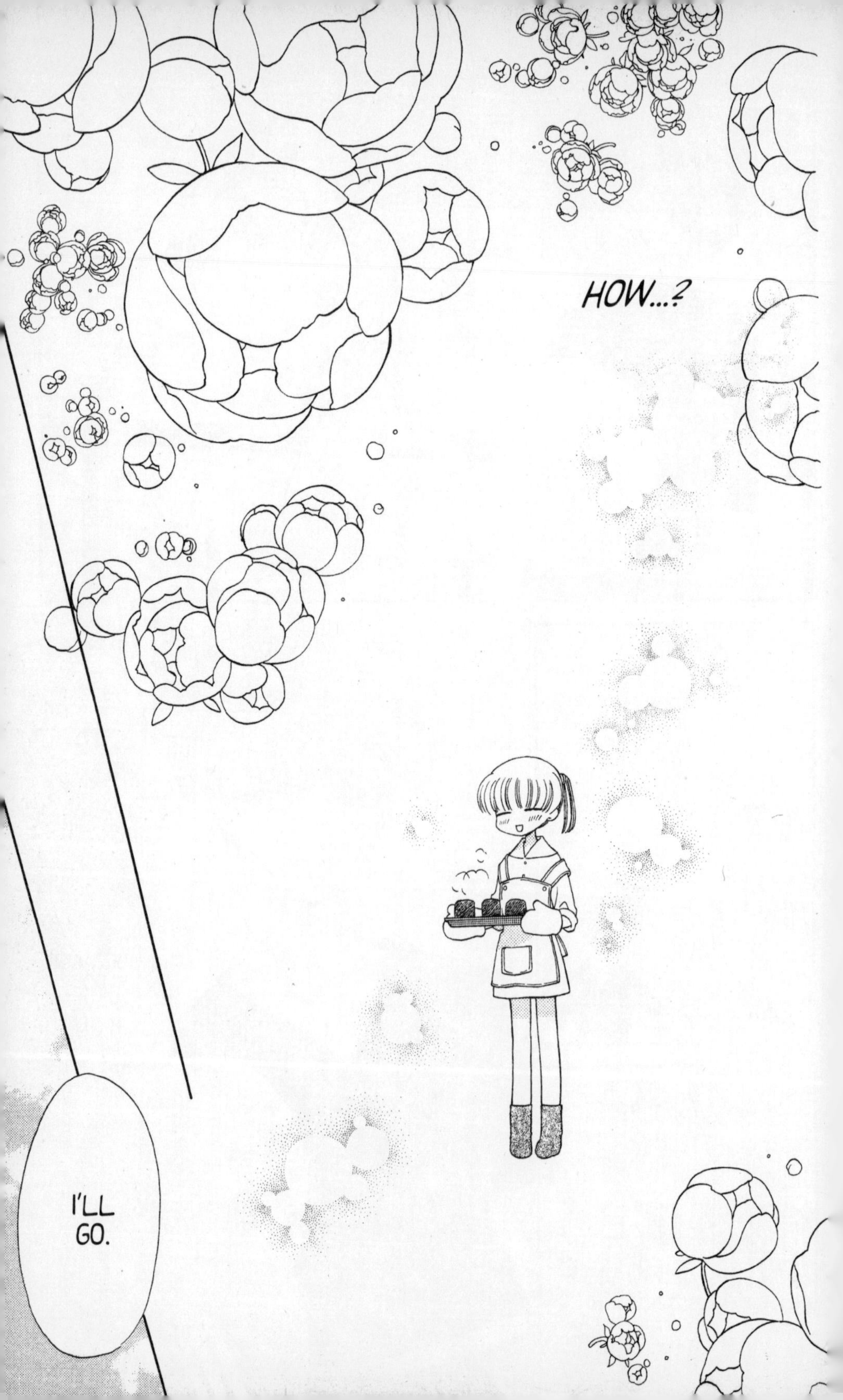
HOW...?
I'LL GO.

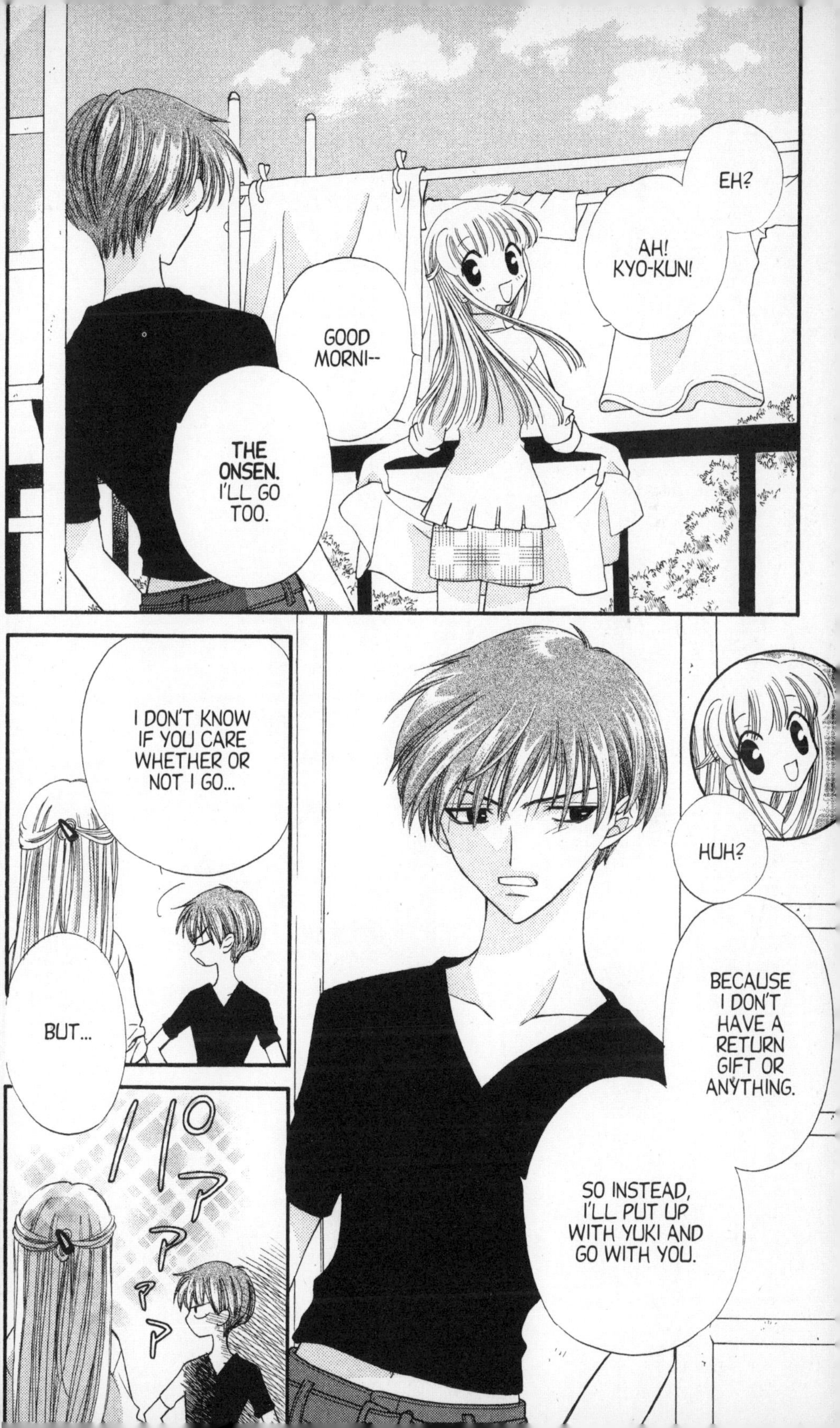
EH?
AH! KYO-KUN!
GOOD MORNI--
THE ONSEN. I'LL GO TOO.
HUH?
BECAUSE I DON'T HAVE A RETURN GIFT OR ANYTHING.
SO INSTEAD, I'LL PUT UP WITH YUKI AND GO WITH YOU.
I DON'T KNOW IF YOU CARE WHETHER OR NOT I GO...
BUT...
パァァァ

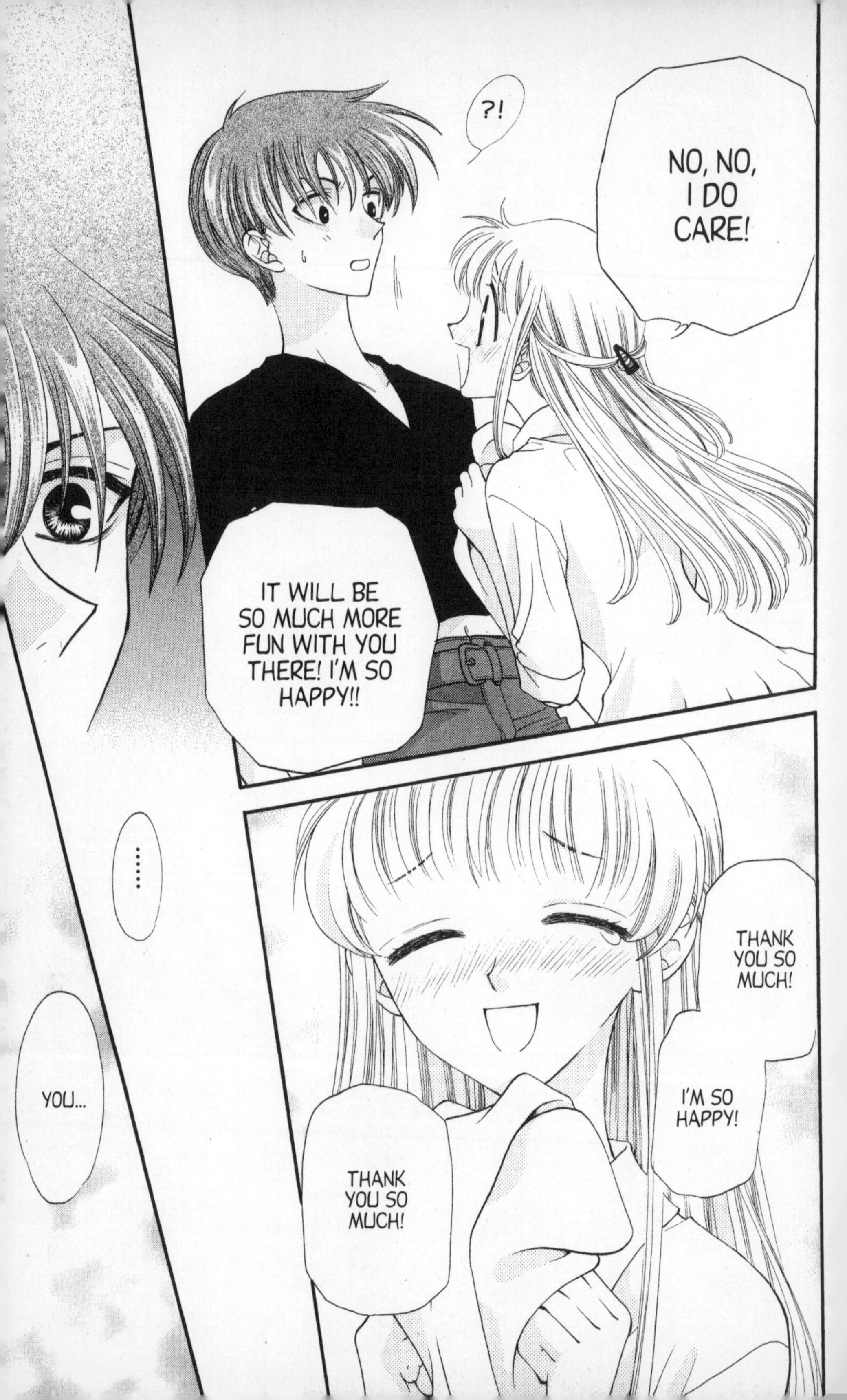
NO, NO, I DO CARE!
?!
IT WILL BE SO MUCH MORE FUN WITH YOU THERE! I'M SO HAPPY!!
THANK YOU SO MUCH!
I'M SO HAPPY!
THANK YOU SO MUCH!
......
YOU...

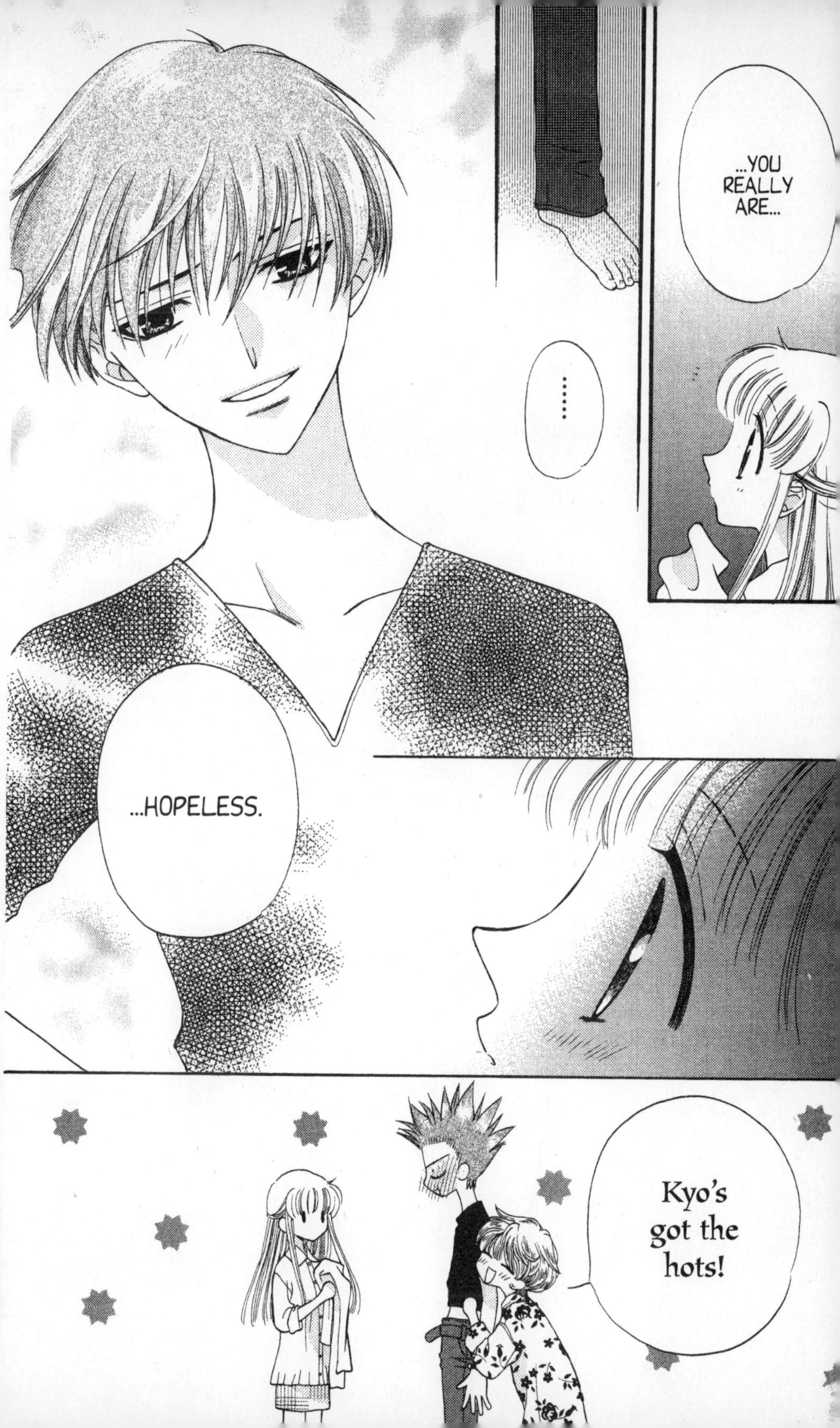

...YOU REALLY ARE...
......
...HOPELESS.
Kyo's got the hots!

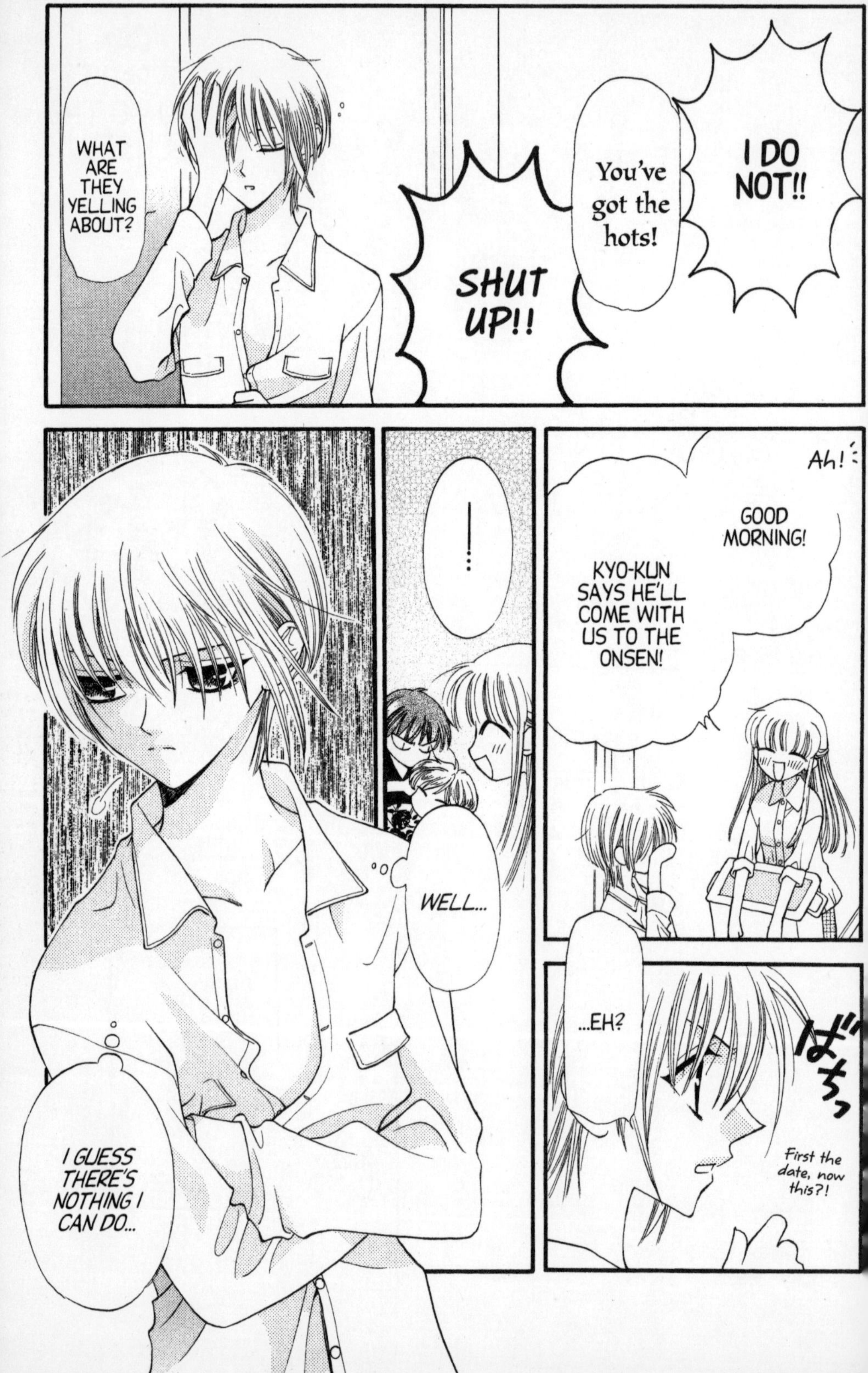

I DO NOT!!
You've got the hots!
SHUT UP!!
WHAT ARE THEY YELLING ABOUT?
Ah!
GOOD MORNING!
KYO-KUN SAYS HE'LL COME WITH US TO THE ONSEN!
ばちっ
...EH?
First the date, now this?!
!...
WELL...
I GUESS THERE'S NOTHING I CAN DO...

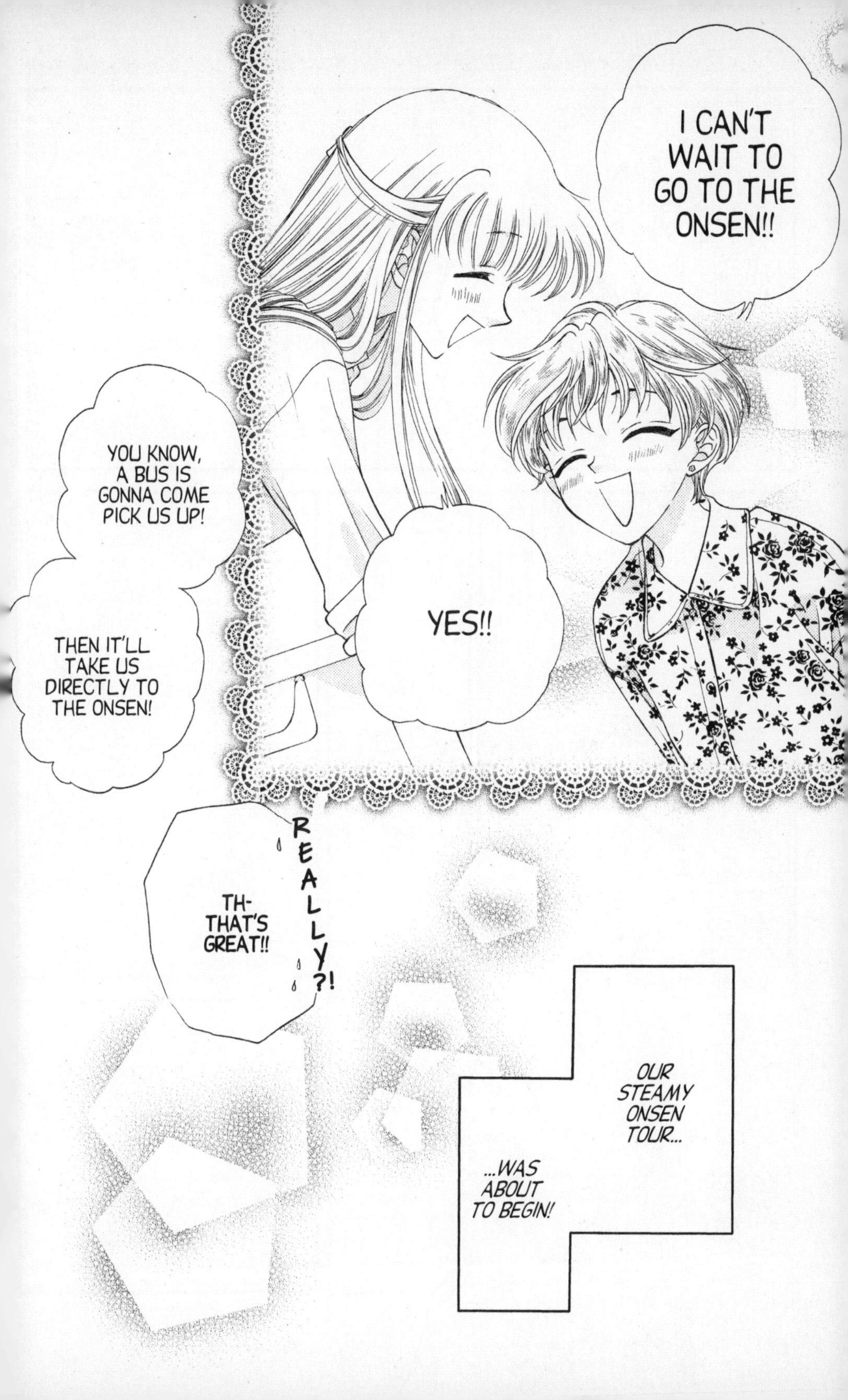
I CAN'T WAIT TO GO TO THE ONSEN!!
YES!!
YOU KNOW, A BUS IS GONNA COME PICK US UP!
THEN IT'LL TAKE US DIRECTLY TO THE ONSEN!
REALLY?!
TH- THAT'S GREAT!!
OUR STEAMY ONSEN TOUR...
...WAS ABOUT TO BEGIN!

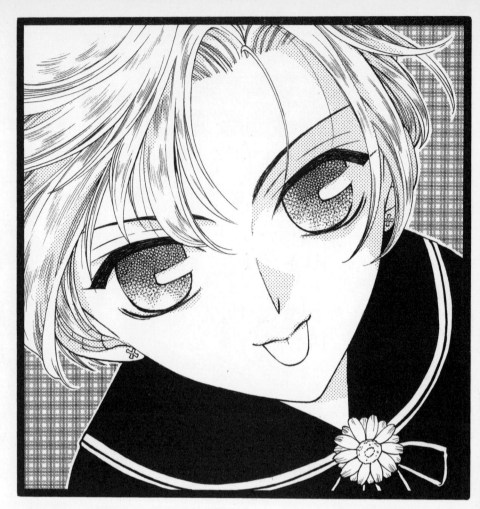

Chapter 18

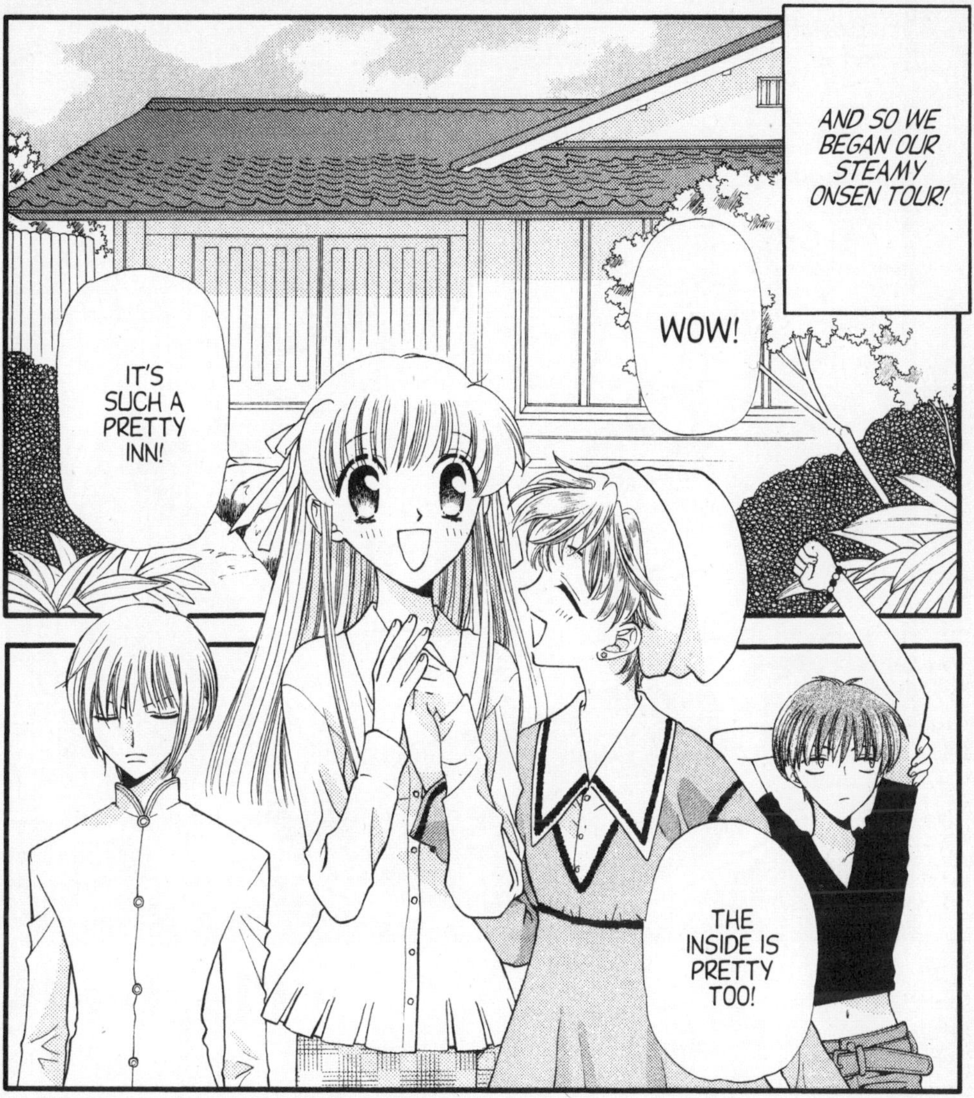
AND SO WE BEGAN OUR STEAMY ONSEN TOUR!
WOW!
IT'S SUCH A PRETTY INN!
THE INSIDE IS PRETTY TOO!

ULTRA SPECIAL BLAH BLAH BLAH 6

The people who have read my other manga will know--the hostess is actually a revival of the ghost woman from "Tsubasa o Motsu Mono." I thought it would be a waste to not use this character anymore...so I brought her back. It's very rare. Normally, I don't do that kind of thing.

Fruits Basket 3 Part 6

Maybe because I said I really, really like King Of-san is why I get a lot of information about him and a lot of people saying, "I like him too ♥ !" So, I guess he really is popular! I think... I really must have been lucky to have him play Raimon. So I support him as a fan too. Anyway, since I started using the 'net, I've had the opportunity to meet a lot of people; for someone like me who spends all her time closed up inside working, it's kind of a sensational feeling. Maybe next I'll get a driver's license?! (Nah, that will never happen.) Someone as careless as me should not be allowed to drive. I'm sure I'd get into an accident.
Oh no... Ah!!! I haven't talked about video games!! I'm almost done with Persona 2: Tsumi (AKA Persona 2: Eternal Punishment), and then I'll finish Ore no Shikabane (not available in the US).

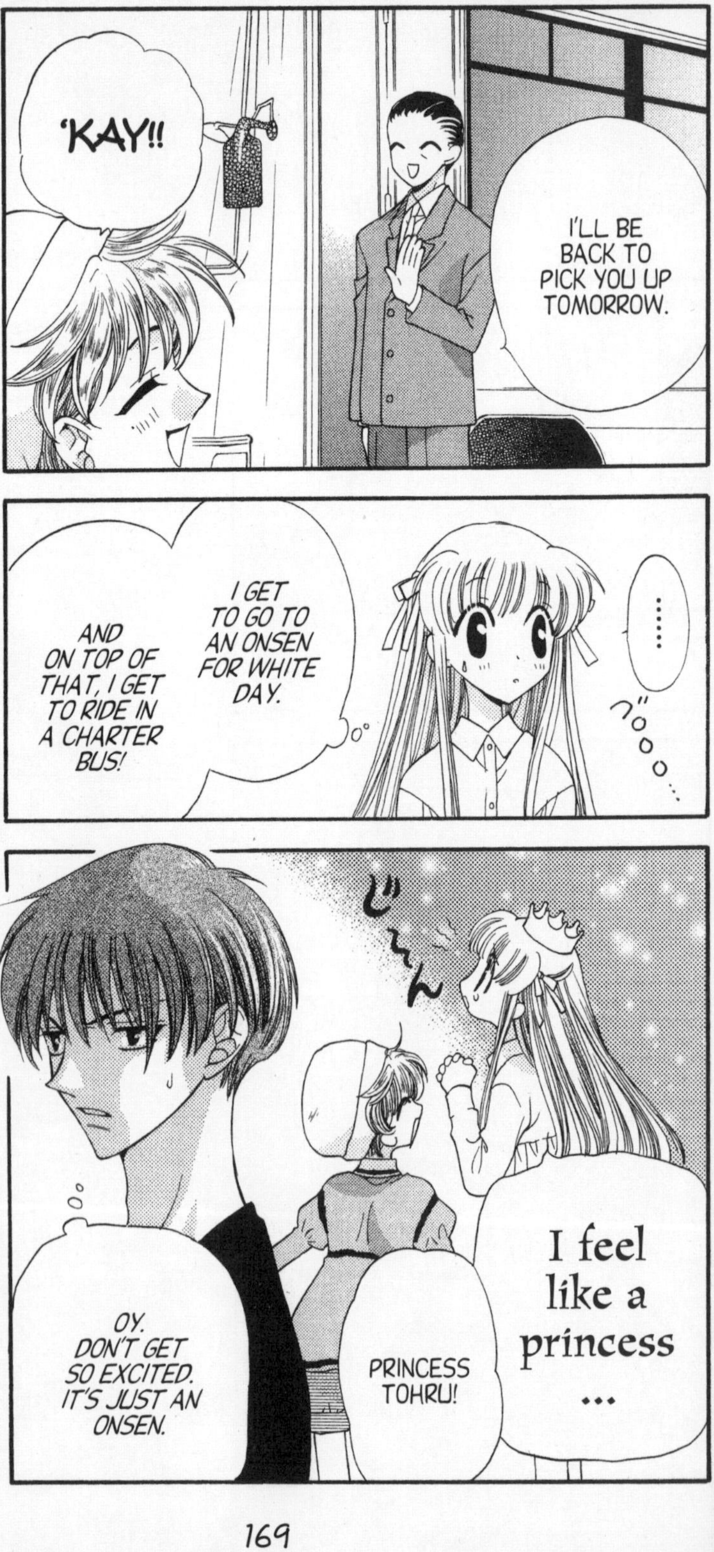
I'LL BE BACK TO PICK YOU UP TOMORROW.
'KAY!!
......
I GET TO GO TO AN ONSEN FOR WHITE DAY.
AND ON TOP OF THAT, I GET TO RIDE IN A CHARTER BUS!
I feel like a princess ...
PRINCESS TOHRU!
OY. DON'T GET SO EXCITED. IT'S JUST AN ONSEN.

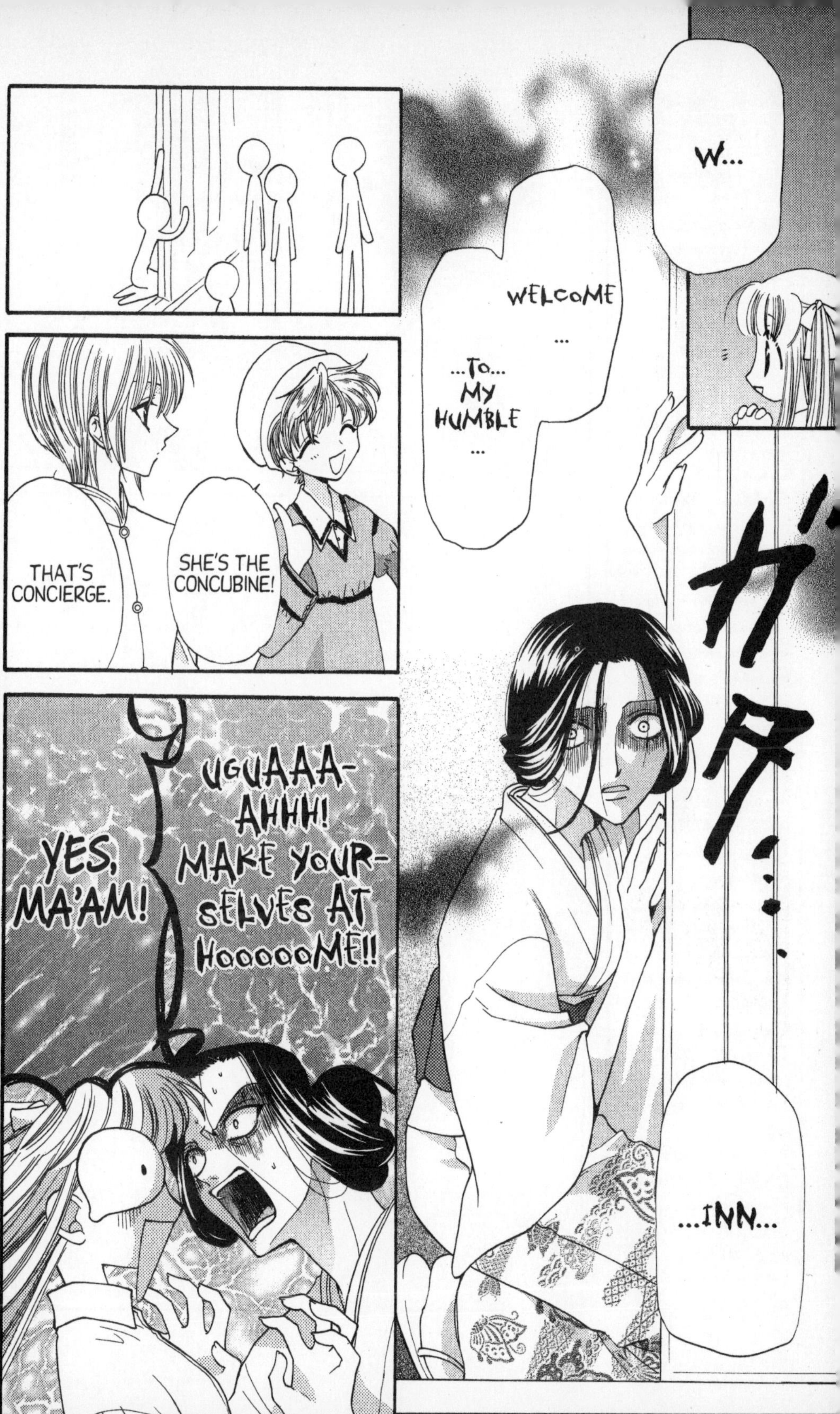

W...
WELCOME ... ...TO... MY HUMBLE ...
ガタ…
...INN...
SHE'S THE CONCUBINE!
THAT'S CONCIERGE.
UGUAAA-AHHH! MAKE YOUR-SELVES AT HOOOOOME!!
YES, MA'AM!

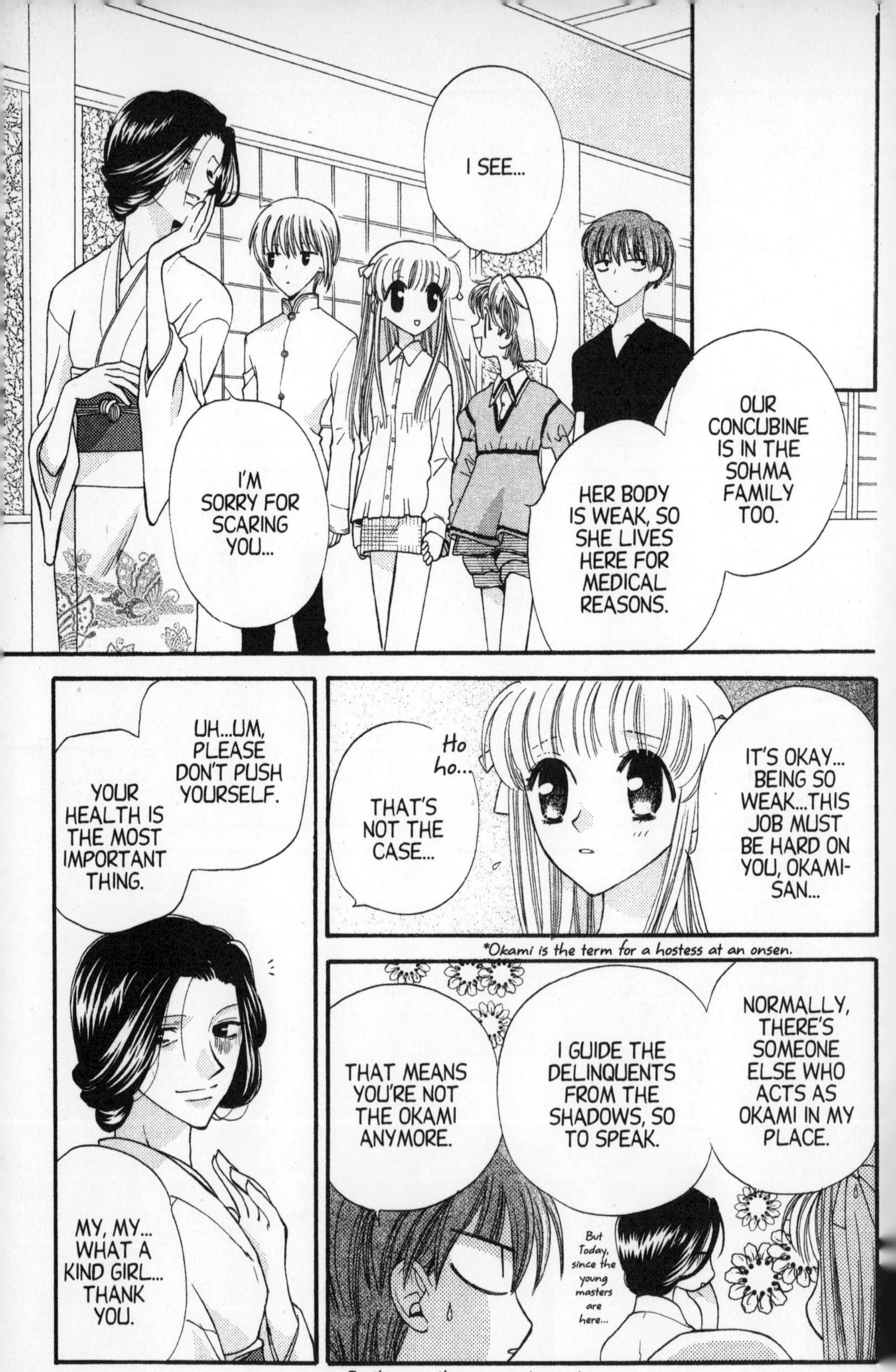
OUR CONCUBINE IS IN THE SOHMA FAMILY TOO.
HER BODY IS WEAK, SO SHE LIVES HERE FOR MEDICAL REASONS.
I SEE...
I'M SORRY FOR SCARING YOU...
IT'S OKAY... BEING SO WEAK...THIS JOB MUST BE HARD ON YOU, OKAMI-SAN...
Ho ho...
THAT'S NOT THE CASE...
*Okami is the term for a hostess at an onsen.
NORMALLY, THERE'S SOMEONE ELSE WHO ACTS AS OKAMI IN MY PLACE.
I GUIDE THE DELINQUENTS FROM THE SHADOWS, SO TO SPEAK.
THAT MEANS YOU'RE NOT THE OKAMI ANYMORE.
But Today, since the young masters are here...
UH...UM, PLEASE DON'T PUSH YOURSELF.
YOUR HEALTH IS THE MOST IMPORTANT THING.
MY, MY... WHAT A KIND GIRL... THANK YOU.

By the way, there are waitresses too.

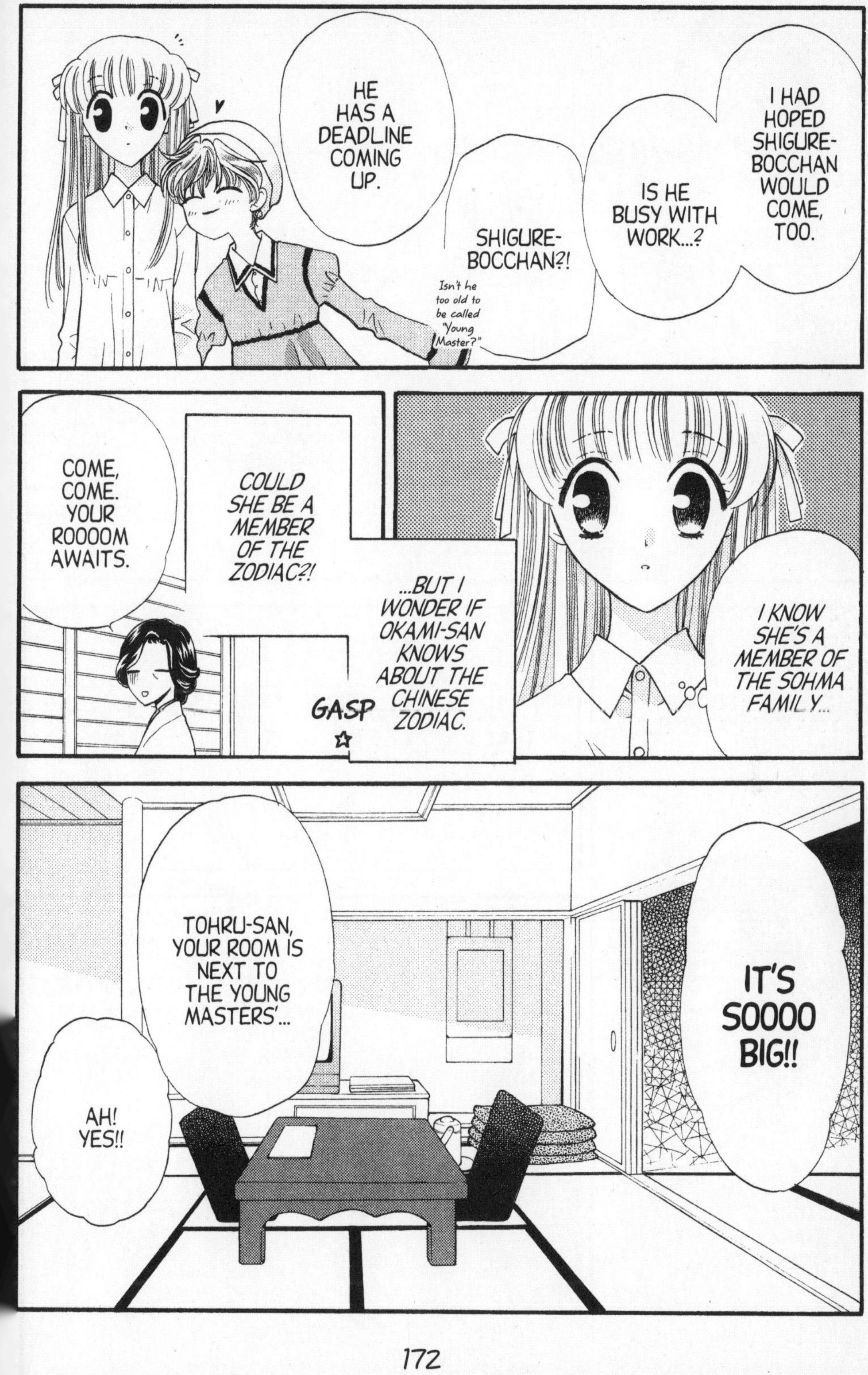
I HAD HOPED SHIGURE-BOCCHAN WOULD COME, TOO.
IS HE BUSY WITH WORK...?
SHIGURE-BOCCHAN?!
Isn't he too old to be called "Young Master?"
HE HAS A DEADLINE COMING UP.
I KNOW SHE'S A MEMBER OF THE SOHMA FAMILY...
...BUT I WONDER IF OKAMI-SAN KNOWS ABOUT THE CHINESE ZODIAC.
GASP
COULD SHE BE A MEMBER OF THE ZODIAC?!
COME, COME. YOUR ROOOOM AWAITS.
IT'S SOOOO BIG!!
TOHRU-SAN, YOUR ROOM IS NEXT TO THE YOUNG MASTERS'...
AH! YES!!

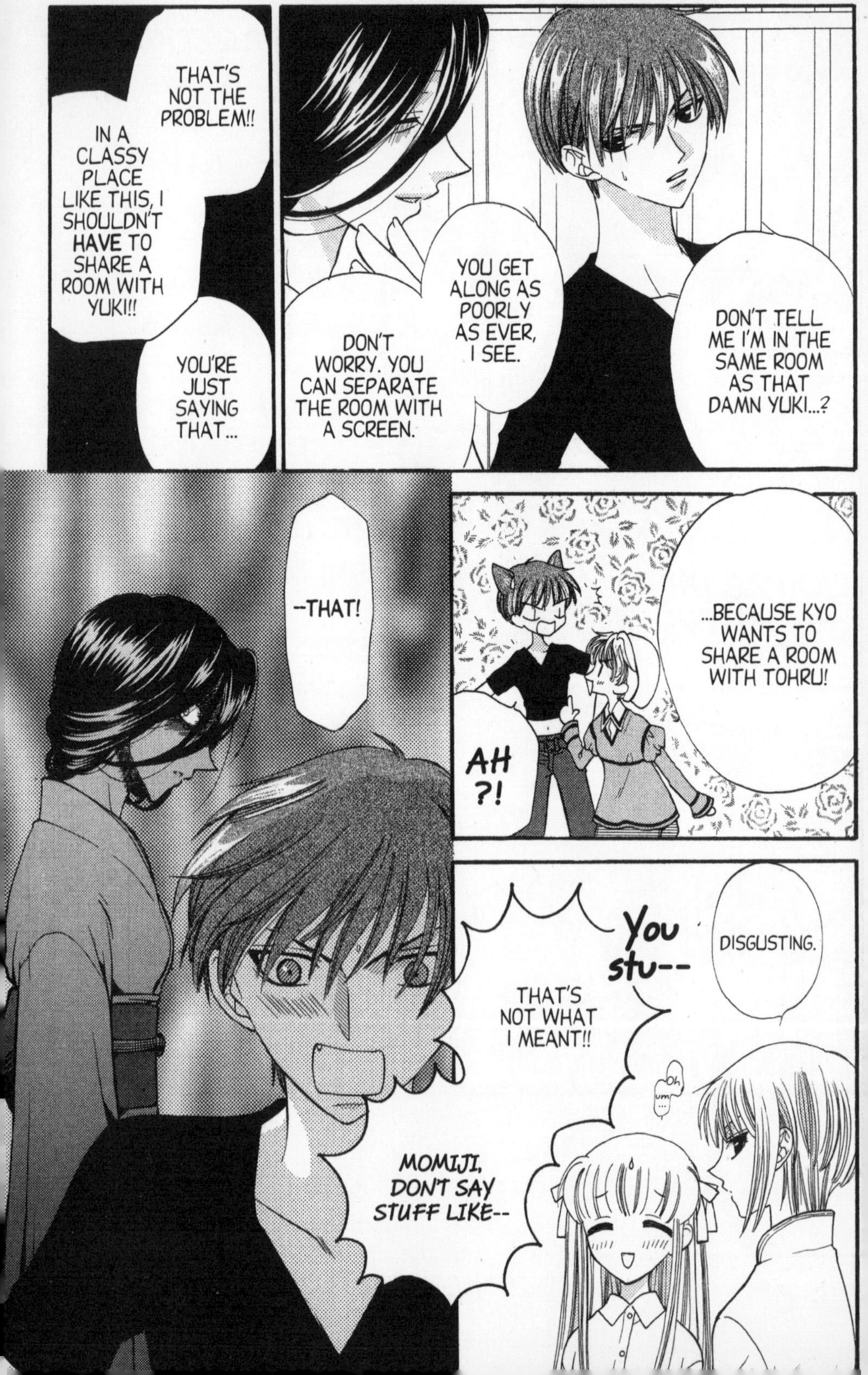
DON'T TELL ME I'M IN THE SAME ROOM AS THAT DAMN YUKI...?
YOU GET ALONG AS POORLY AS EVER, I SEE.
DON'T WORRY. YOU CAN SEPARATE THE ROOM WITH A SCREEN.
THAT'S NOT THE PROBLEM!!
IN A CLASSY PLACE LIKE THIS, I SHOULDN'T **HAVE** TO SHARE A ROOM WITH YUKI!!
YOU'RE JUST SAYING THAT...
...BECAUSE KYO WANTS TO SHARE A ROOM WITH TOHRU!
AH ?!
DISGUSTING.
You stu--
THAT'S NOT WHAT I MEANT!!
Oh um...
MOMIJI, DON'T SAY STUFF LIKE--
--THAT!

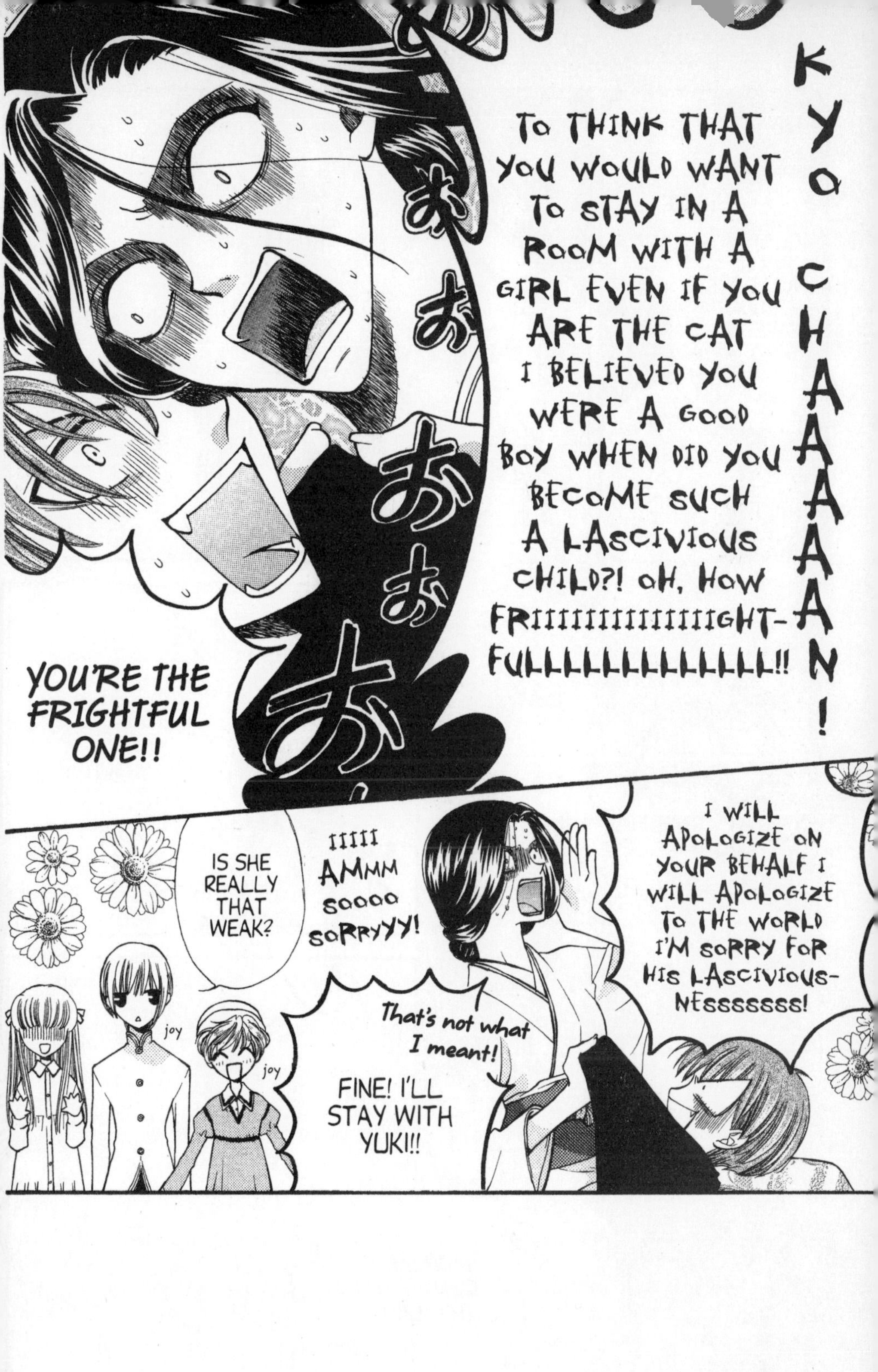
KYO CHAAAAAAAN!
TO THINK THAT YOU WOULD WANT TO STAY IN A ROOM WITH A GIRL EVEN IF YOU ARE THE CAT I BELIEVED YOU WERE A GOOD BOY WHEN DID YOU BECOME SUCH A LASCIVIOUS CHILD?! OH, HOW FRIIIIIIIIIIIIIIGHT-FULLLLLLLLLLLLLL!!
おぉおぉお
YOU'RE THE FRIGHTFUL ONE!!
I WILL APOLOGIZE ON YOUR BEHALF I WILL APOLOGIZE TO THE WORLD I'M SORRY FOR HIS LASCIVIOUS-NESSSSSSS!
IIIII AMMM SOOOO SORRYYY!
That's not what I meant!
FINE! I'LL STAY WITH YUKI!!
IS SHE REALLY THAT WEAK?
joy
joy

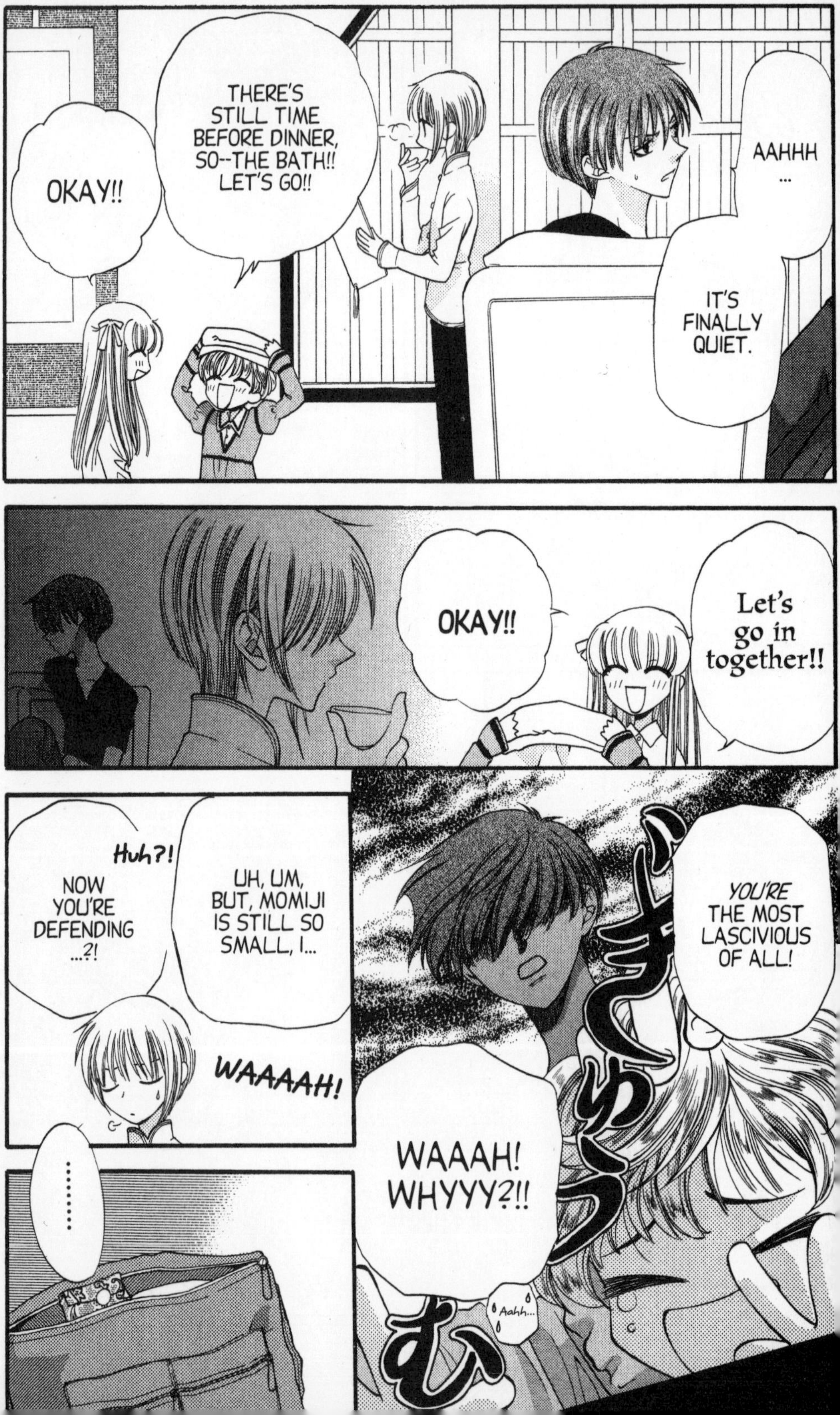

AAHHH ...
IT'S FINALLY QUIET.
THERE'S STILL TIME BEFORE DINNER, SO--THE BATH!! LET'S GO!!
OKAY!!
Let's go in together!!
OKAY!!
YOU'RE THE MOST LASCIVIOUS OF ALL!
WAAAH! WHYYY?!!
Aahh...
UH, UM, BUT, MOMIJI IS STILL SO SMALL, I...
Huh?!
NOW YOU'RE DEFENDING ...?!
WAAAAH!
....

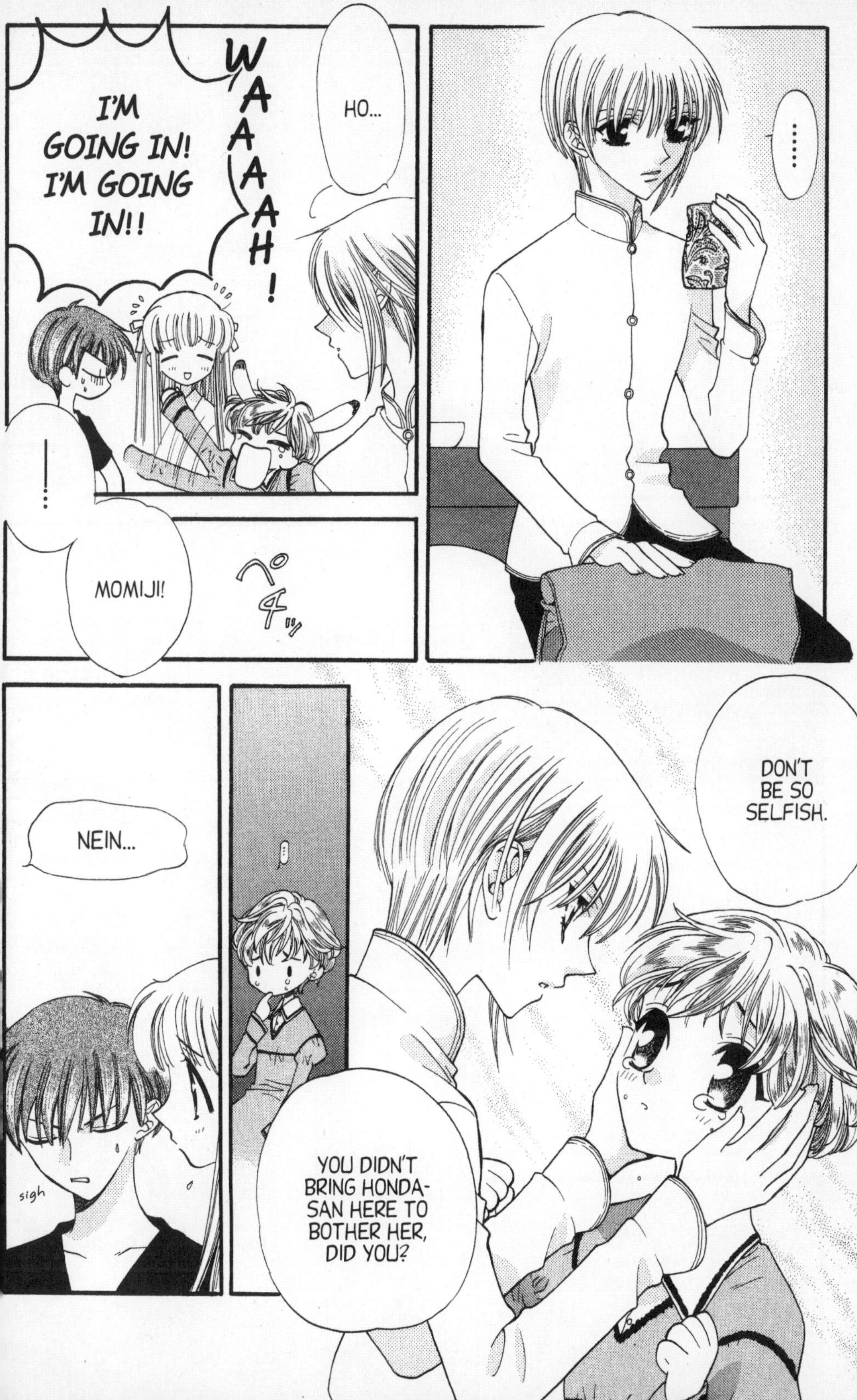
......
HO...
WAAAAAH!
I'M GOING IN! I'M GOING IN!!
......
MOMIJI!
DON'T BE SO SELFISH.
YOU DIDN'T BRING HONDA-SAN HERE TO BOTHER HER, DID YOU?
...
NEIN...
sigh

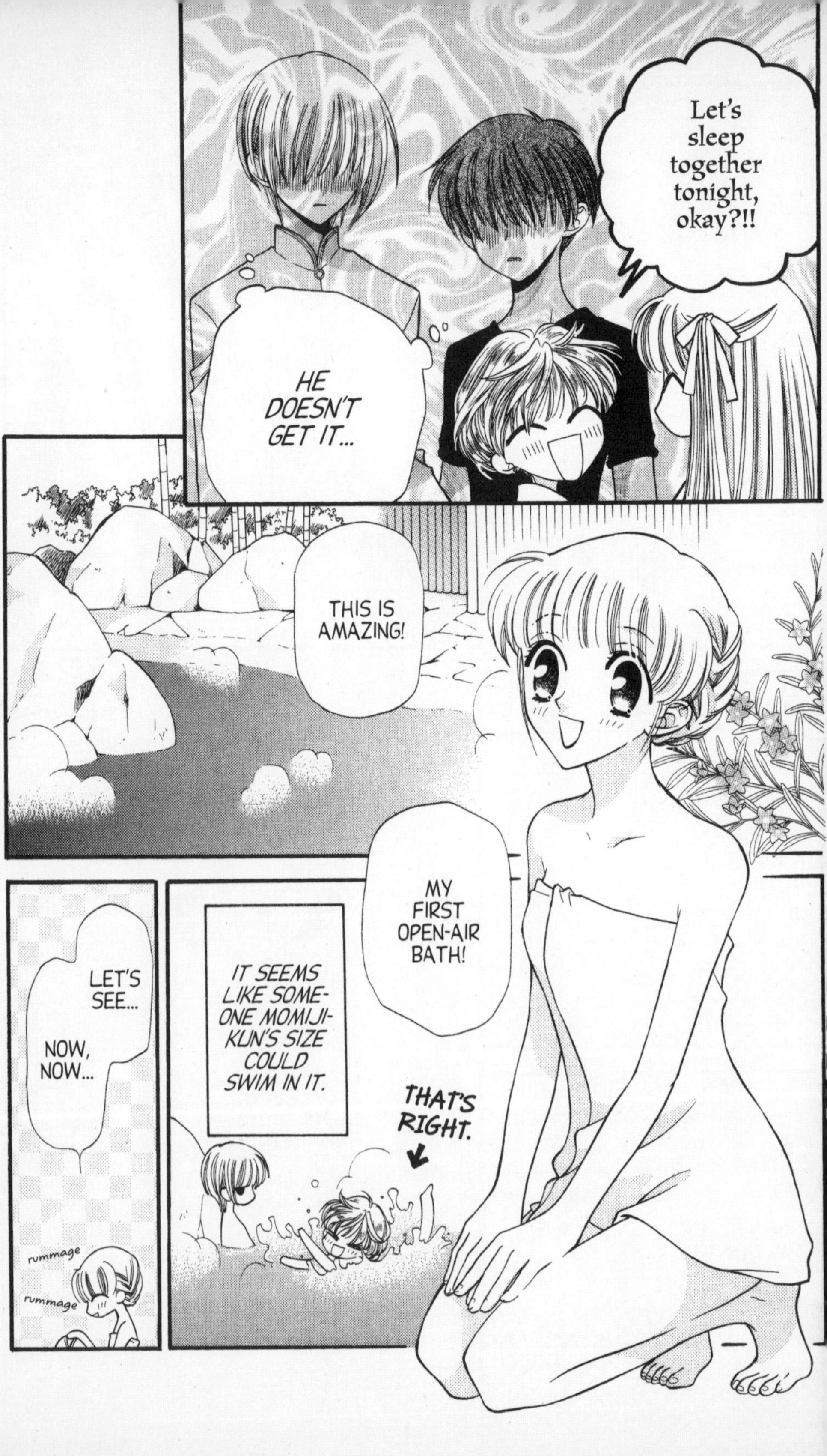
Let's sleep together tonight, okay?!!
HE DOESN'T GET IT...
THIS IS AMAZING!
MY FIRST OPEN-AIR BATH!
IT SEEMS LIKE SOME-ONE MOMIJI-KUN'S SIZE COULD SWIM IN IT.
THAT'S RIGHT.
LET'S SEE...
NOW, NOW...
rummage
rummage

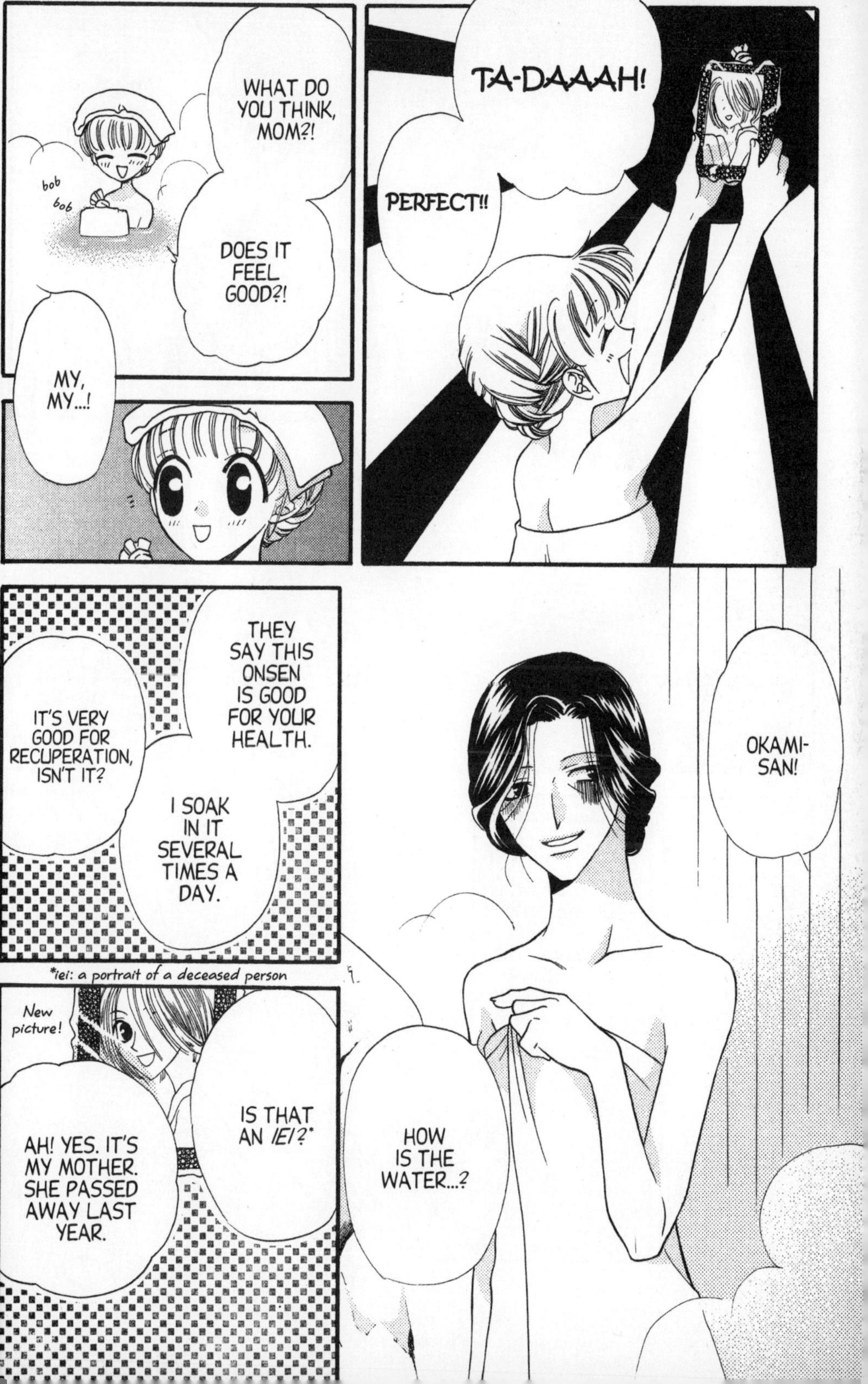
TA-DAAAH!
PERFECT!!
WHAT DO YOU THINK, MOM?!
bob bob
DOES IT FEEL GOOD?!
MY, MY...!
OKAMI-SAN!
HOW IS THE WATER...?
THEY SAY THIS ONSEN IS GOOD FOR YOUR HEALTH.
IT'S VERY GOOD FOR RECUPERATION, ISN'T IT?
I SOAK IN IT SEVERAL TIMES A DAY.
*iei: a portrait of a deceased person
New picture!
IS THAT AN IEI?*
AH! YES. IT'S MY MOTHER. SHE PASSED AWAY LAST YEAR.

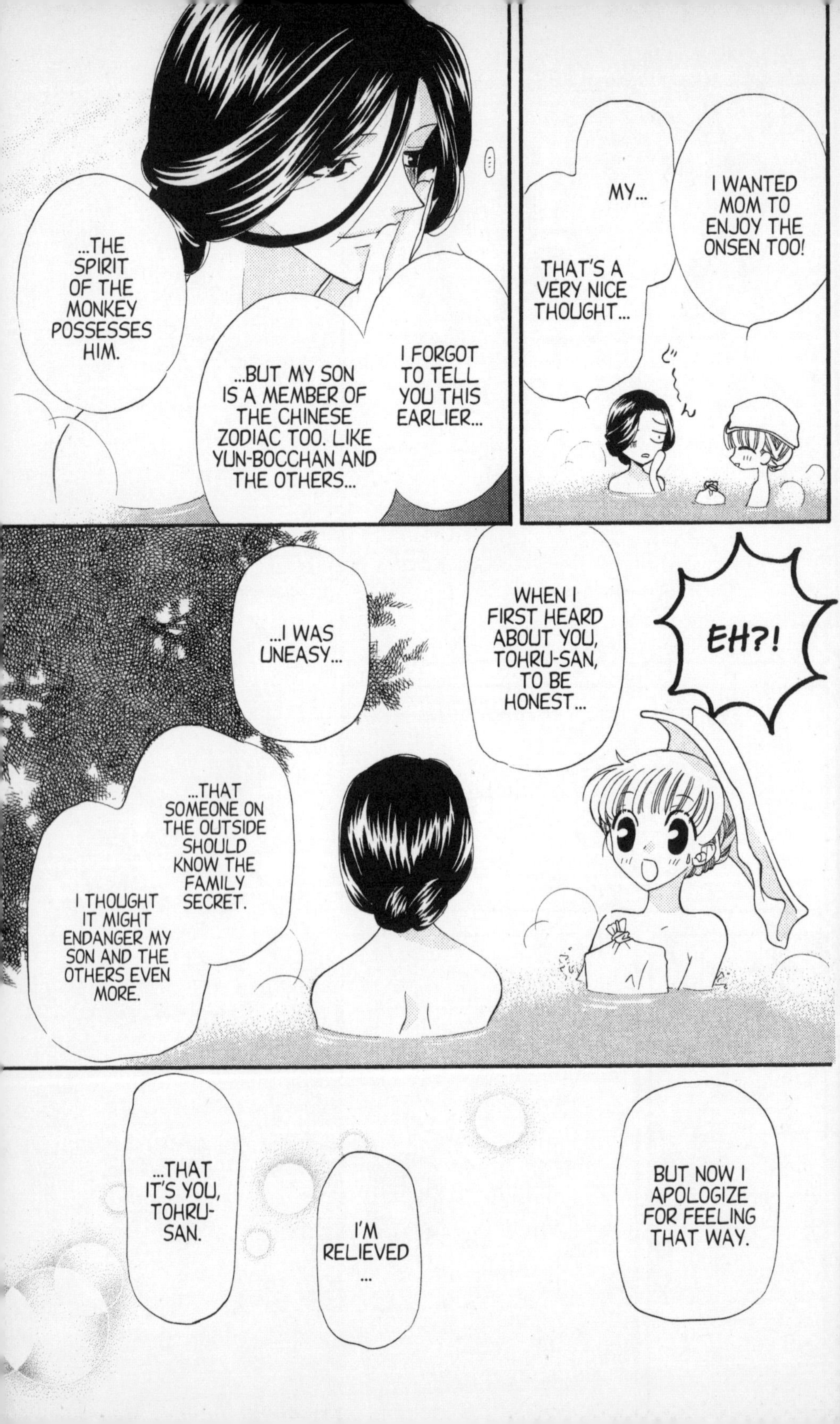
I WANTED MOM TO ENJOY THE ONSEN TOO!
MY...
THAT'S A VERY NICE THOUGHT...
I FORGOT TO TELL YOU THIS EARLIER...
...BUT MY SON IS A MEMBER OF THE CHINESE ZODIAC TOO. LIKE YUN-BOCCHAN AND THE OTHERS...
...THE SPIRIT OF THE MONKEY POSSESSES HIM.
EH?!
WHEN I FIRST HEARD ABOUT YOU, TOHRU-SAN, TO BE HONEST...
...I WAS UNEASY...
...THAT SOMEONE ON THE OUTSIDE SHOULD KNOW THE FAMILY SECRET.
I THOUGHT IT MIGHT ENDANGER MY SON AND THE OTHERS EVEN MORE.
BUT NOW I APOLOGIZE FOR FEELING THAT WAY.
I'M RELIEVED ...
...THAT IT'S YOU, TOHRU-SAN.

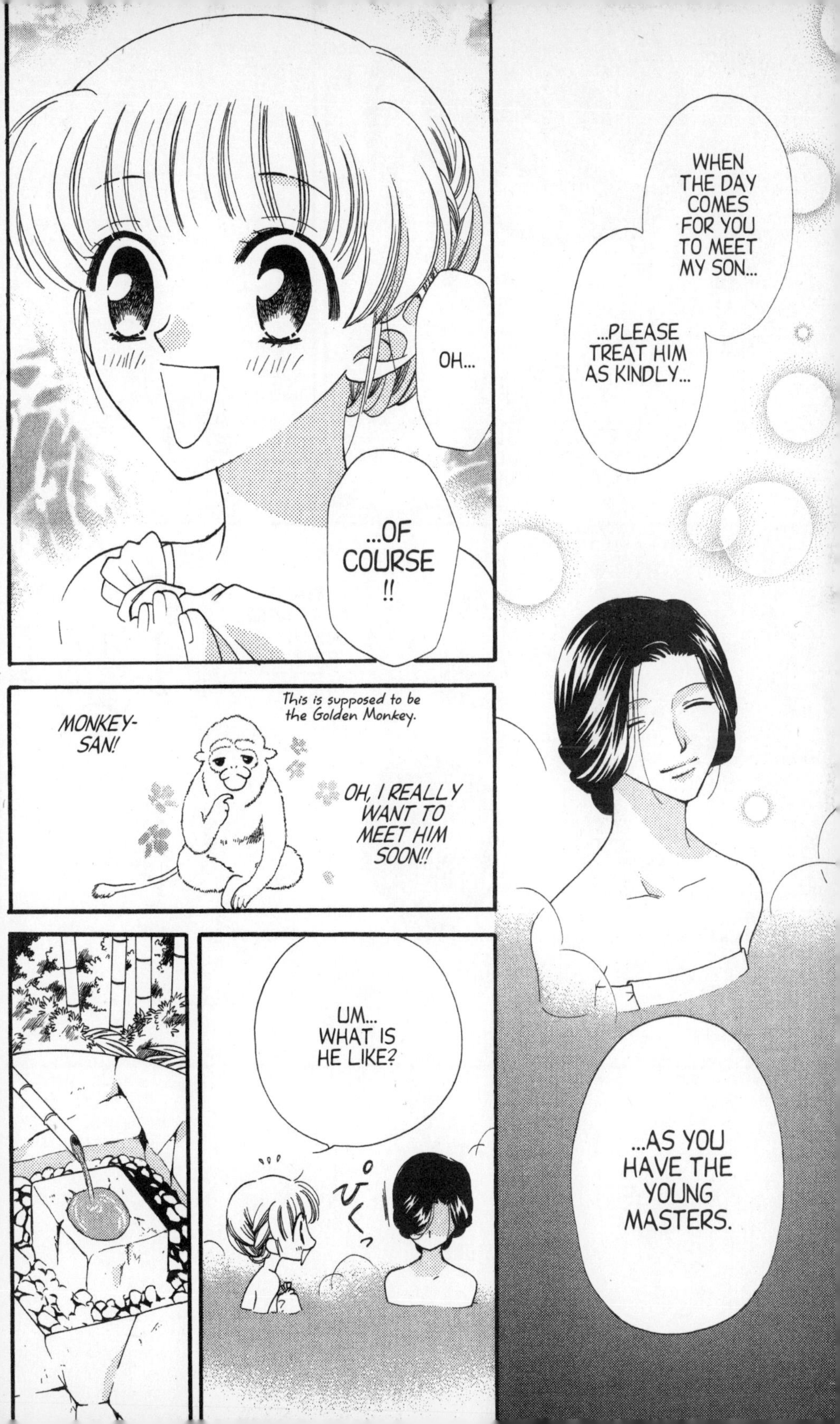
WHEN THE DAY COMES FOR YOU TO MEET MY SON...
...PLEASE TREAT HIM AS KINDLY...
...AS YOU HAVE THE YOUNG MASTERS.
OH...
...OF COURSE !!
This is supposed to be the Golden Monkey.
MONKEY-SAN!
OH, I REALLY WANT TO MEET HIM SOON!!
UM... WHAT IS HE LIKE?
ぴくっ

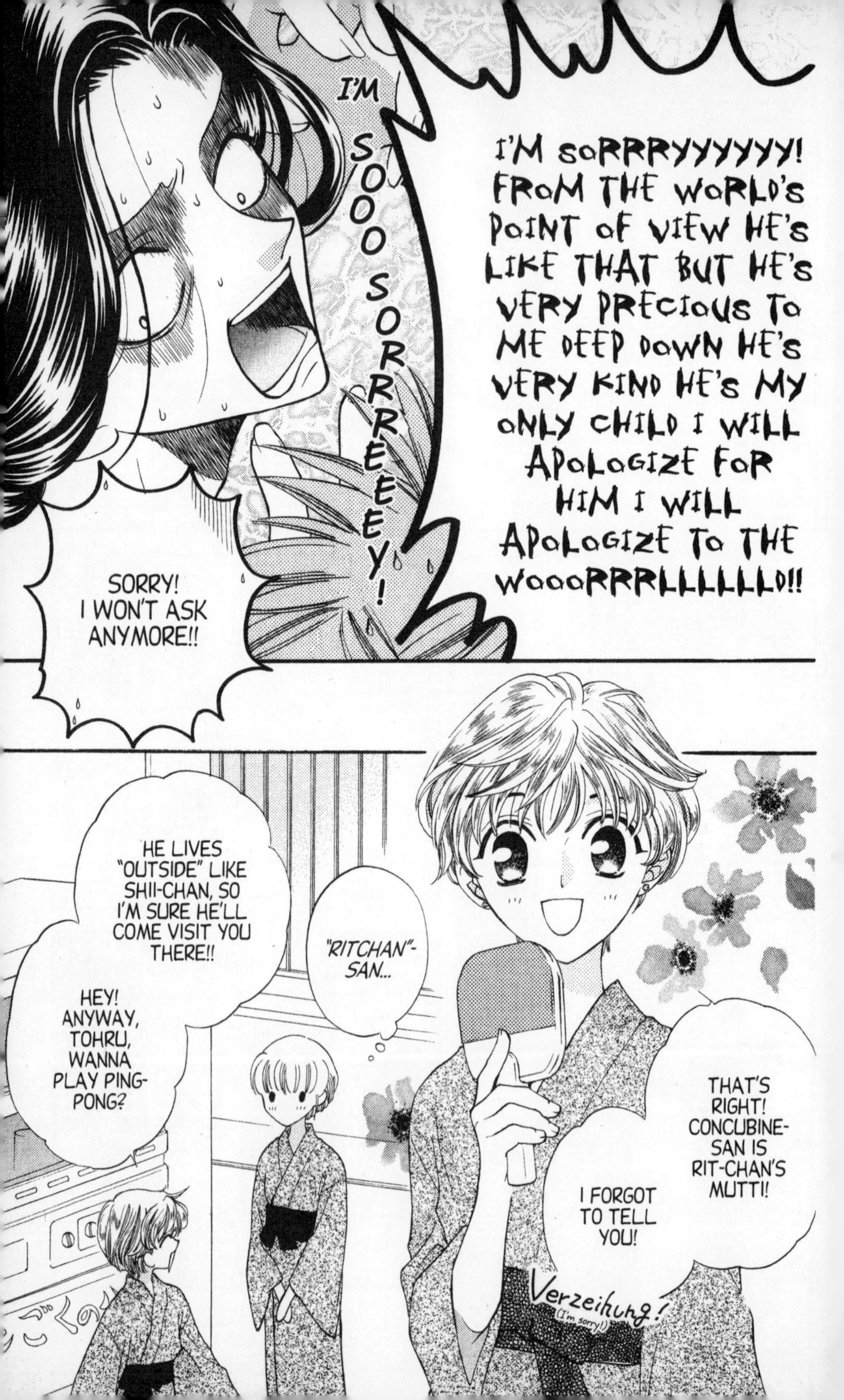
I'M SORRRYYYYYY! FROM THE WORLD'S POINT OF VIEW HE'S LIKE THAT BUT HE'S VERY PRECIOUS TO ME DEEP DOWN HE'S VERY KIND HE'S MY ONLY CHILD I WILL APOLOGIZE FOR HIM I WILL APOLOGIZE TO THE WOOORRRLLLLLLD!!
I'M SOOOO SORRREEEY!
SORRY! I WON'T ASK ANYMORE!!
THAT'S RIGHT! CONCUBINE-SAN IS RIT-CHAN'S MUTTI!
I FORGOT TO TELL YOU!
Verzeihung!
(I'm sorry!)
"RITCHAN"-SAN...
HE LIVES "OUTSIDE" LIKE SHII-CHAN, SO I'M SURE HE'LL COME VISIT YOU THERE!!
HEY! ANYWAY, TOHRU, WANNA PLAY PING-PONG?

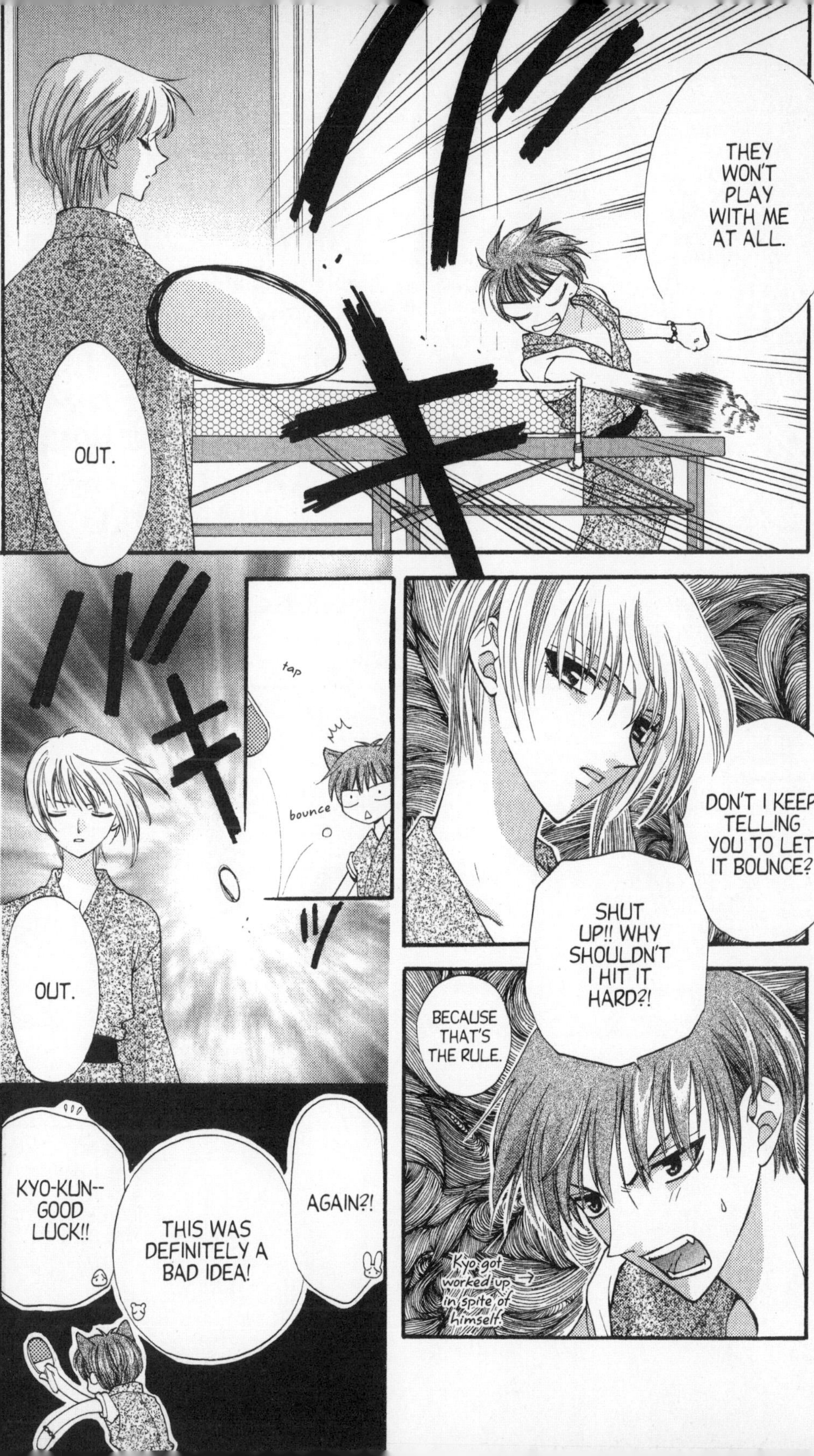
THEY WON'T PLAY WITH ME AT ALL.
OUT.
DON'T I KEEP TELLING YOU TO LET IT BOUNCE?
tap
bounce
OUT.
SHUT UP!! WHY SHOULDN'T I HIT IT HARD?!
BECAUSE THAT'S THE RULE.
Kyo got worked up in spite of himself.
AGAIN?!
THIS WAS DEFINITELY A BAD IDEA!
KYO-KUN-- GOOD LUCK!!

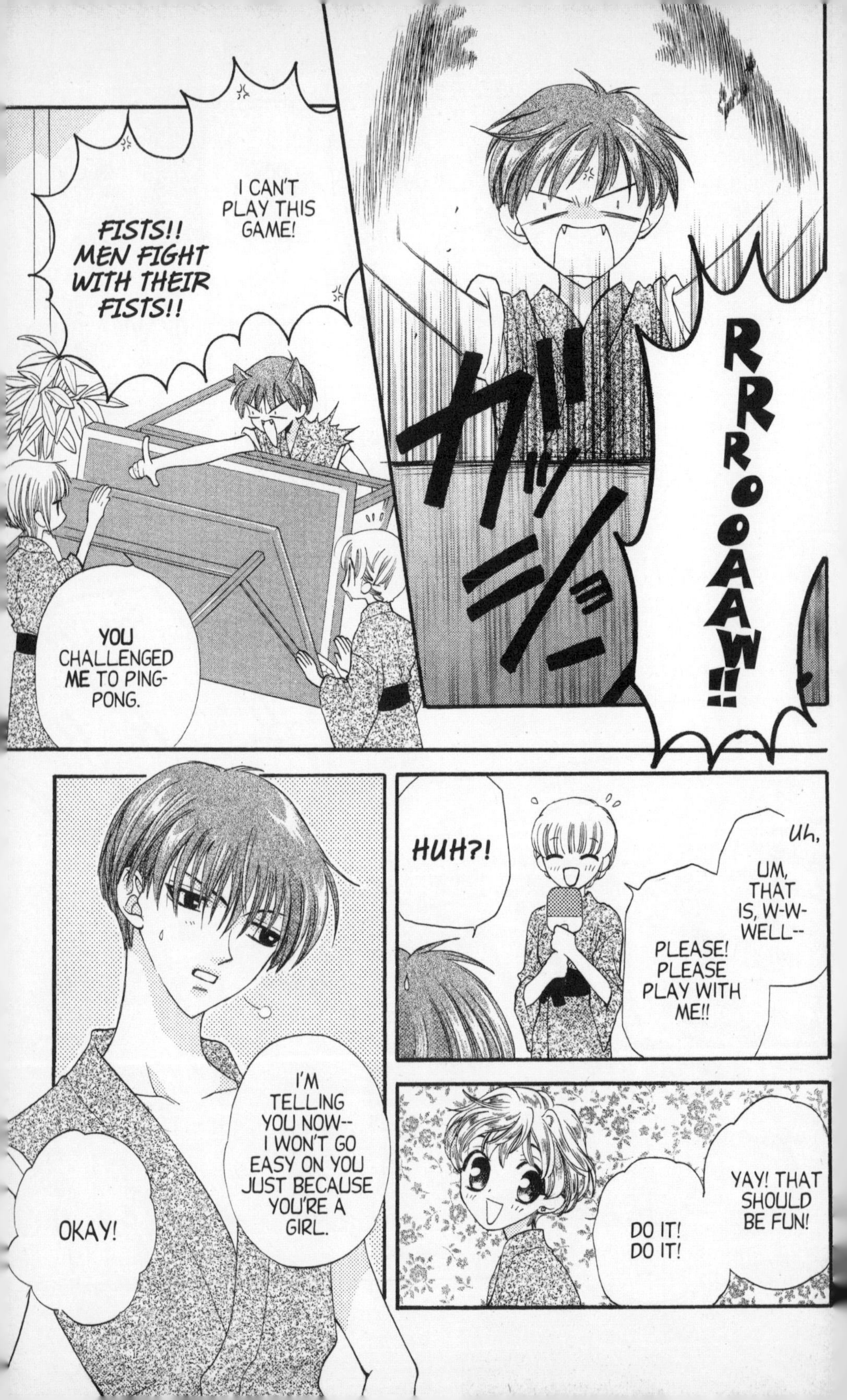
RRROOAAAW!!
I CAN'T PLAY THIS GAME!
FISTS!! MEN FIGHT WITH THEIR FISTS!!
YOU CHALLENGED ME TO PING-PONG.
Uh, UM, THAT IS, W-W-WELL--
PLEASE! PLEASE PLAY WITH ME!!
HUH?!
YAY! THAT SHOULD BE FUN!
DO IT! DO IT!
I'M TELLING YOU NOW-- I WON'T GO EASY ON YOU JUST BECAUSE YOU'RE A GIRL.
OKAY!

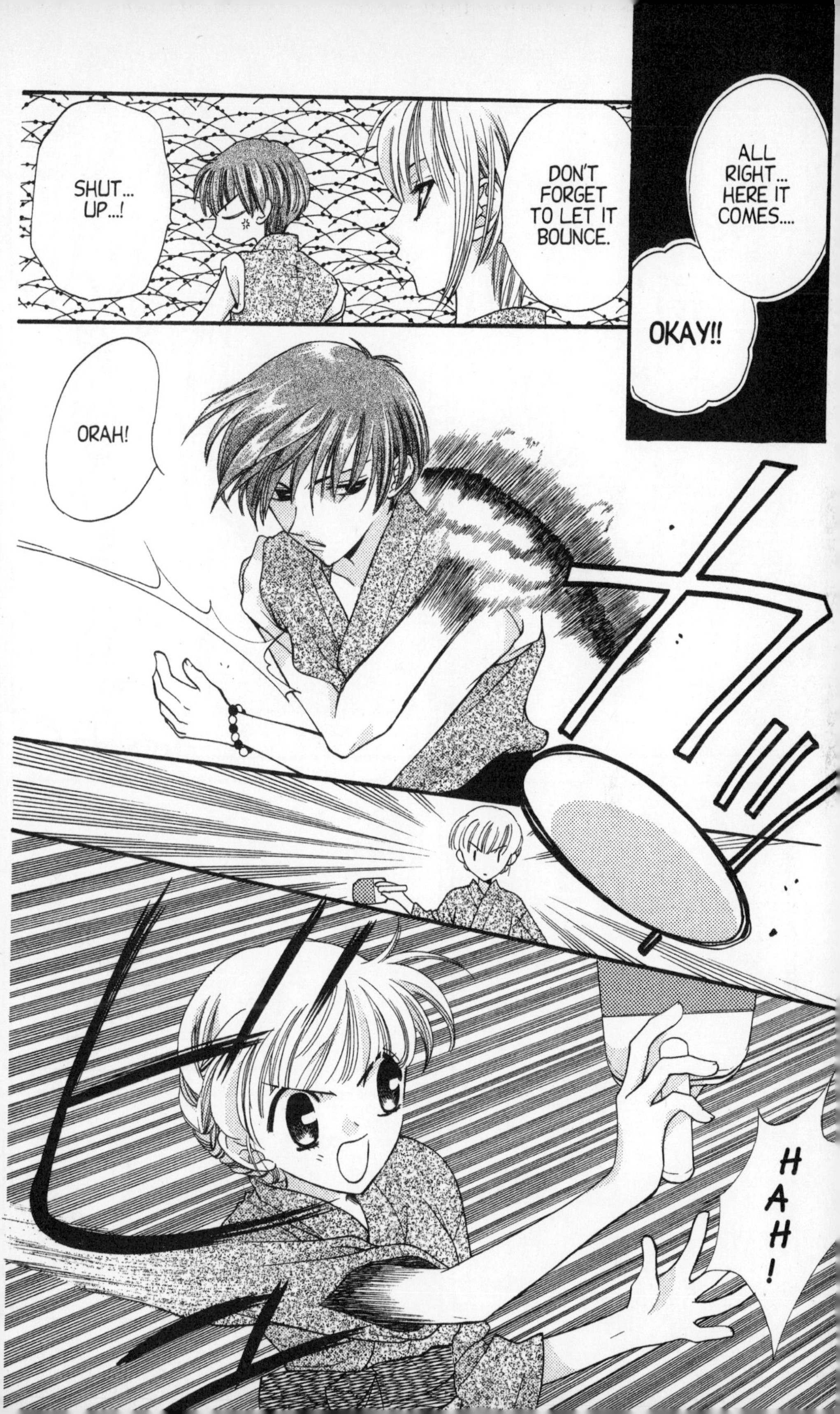
ALL RIGHT... HERE IT COMES....
OKAY!!
DON'T FORGET TO LET IT BOUNCE.
SHUT... UP...!
ORAH!
HAH!

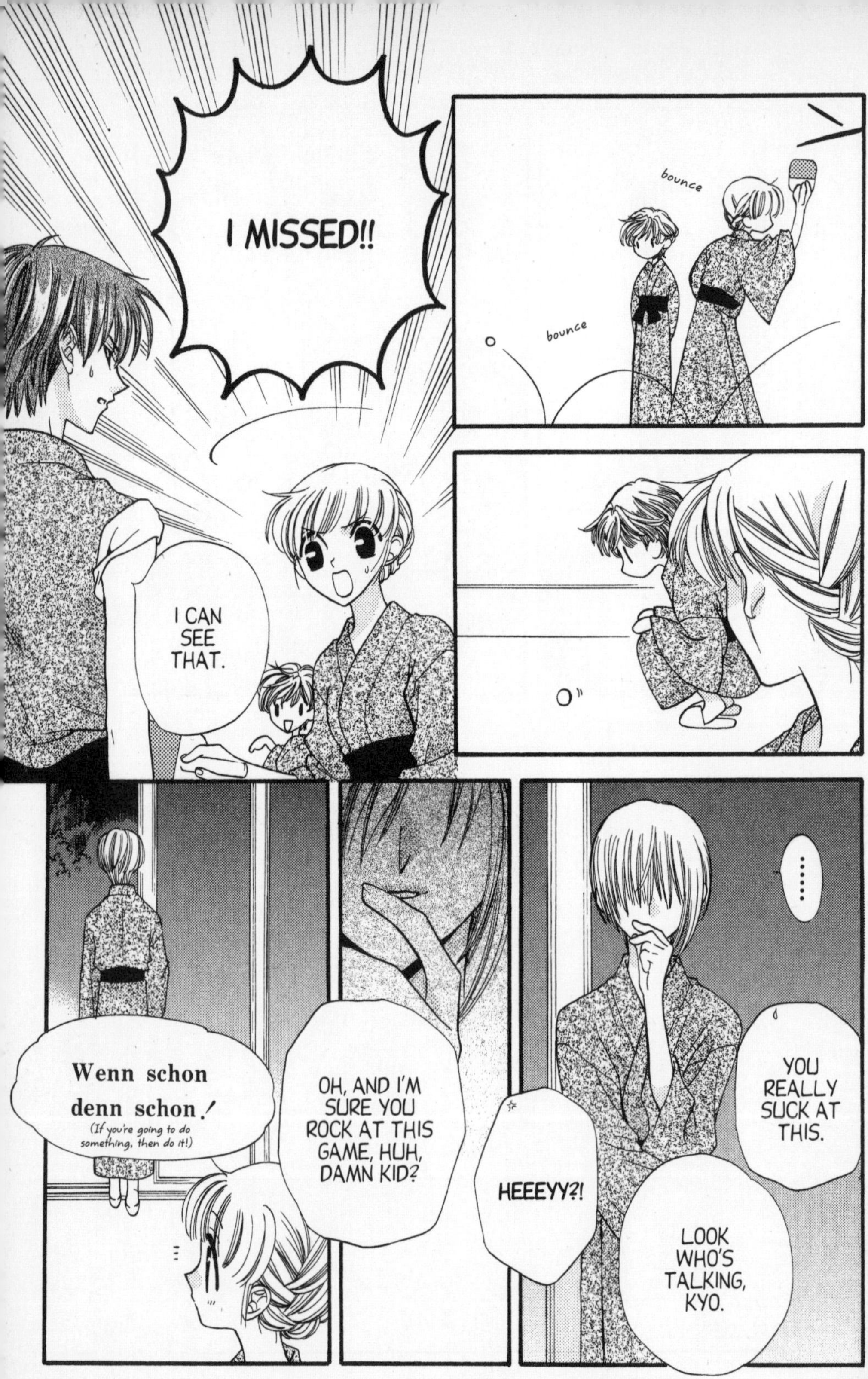
bounce
bounce
I MISSED!!
I CAN SEE THAT.
......
YOU REALLY SUCK AT THIS.
HEEEYY?!
LOOK WHO'S TALKING, KYO.
OH, AND I'M SURE YOU ROCK AT THIS GAME, HUH, DAMN KID?
Wenn schon denn schon!
(If you're going to do something, then do it!)

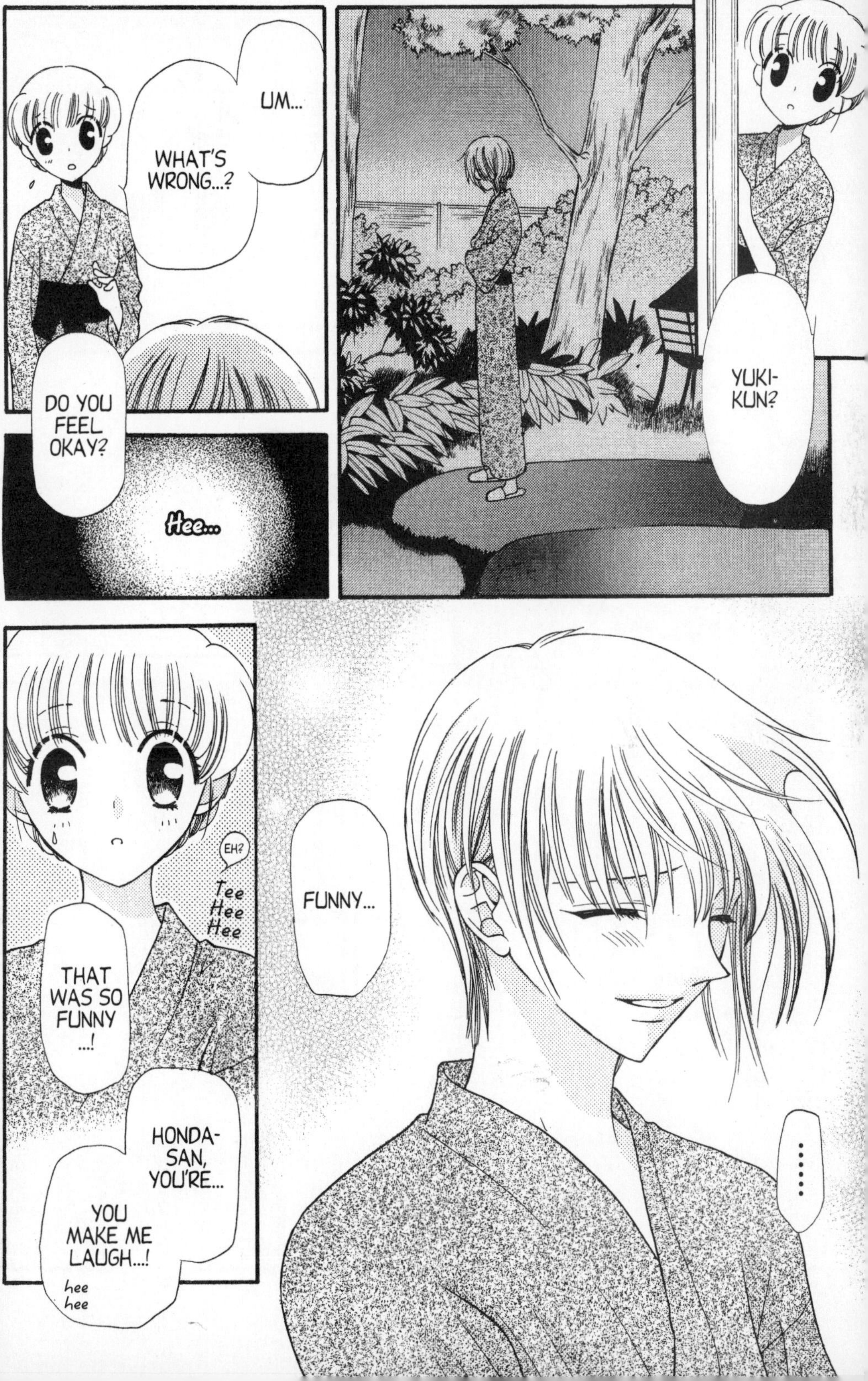
YUKI-KUN?
UM... WHAT'S WRONG...?
DO YOU FEEL OKAY?
Hee...
FUNNY...
......
EH?
Tee Hee Hee
THAT WAS SO FUNNY ...!
HONDA-SAN, YOU'RE...
YOU MAKE ME LAUGH...!
hee hee

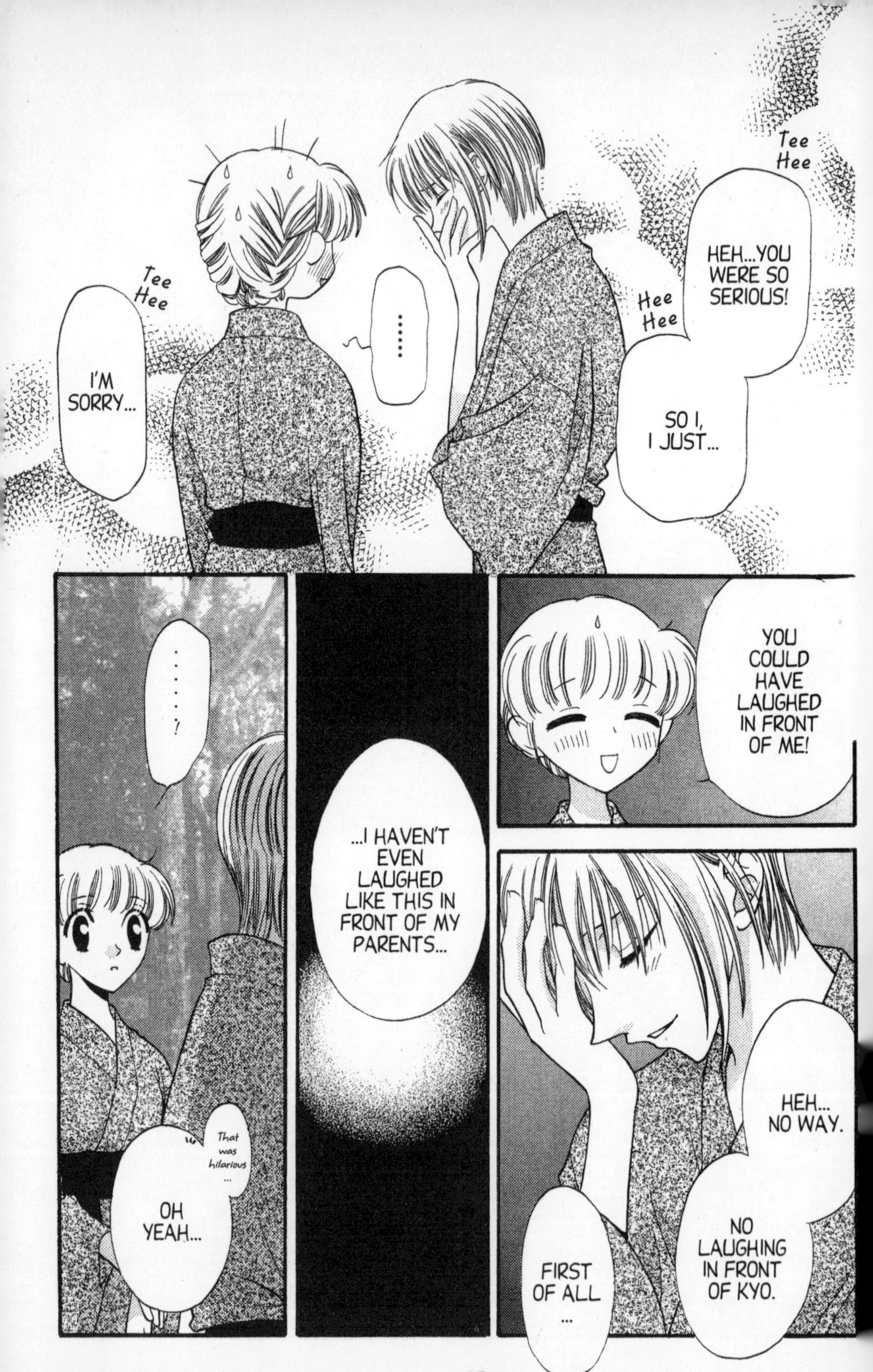
Tee Hee
HEH...YOU WERE SO SERIOUS!
Hee Hee
SO I, I JUST...
......
Tee Hee
I'M SORRY...
YOU COULD HAVE LAUGHED IN FRONT OF ME!
HEH... NO WAY.
NO LAUGHING IN FRONT OF KYO.
FIRST OF ALL ...
...I HAVEN'T EVEN LAUGHED LIKE THIS IN FRONT OF MY PARENTS...
......!
That was hilarious ...
OH YEAH...

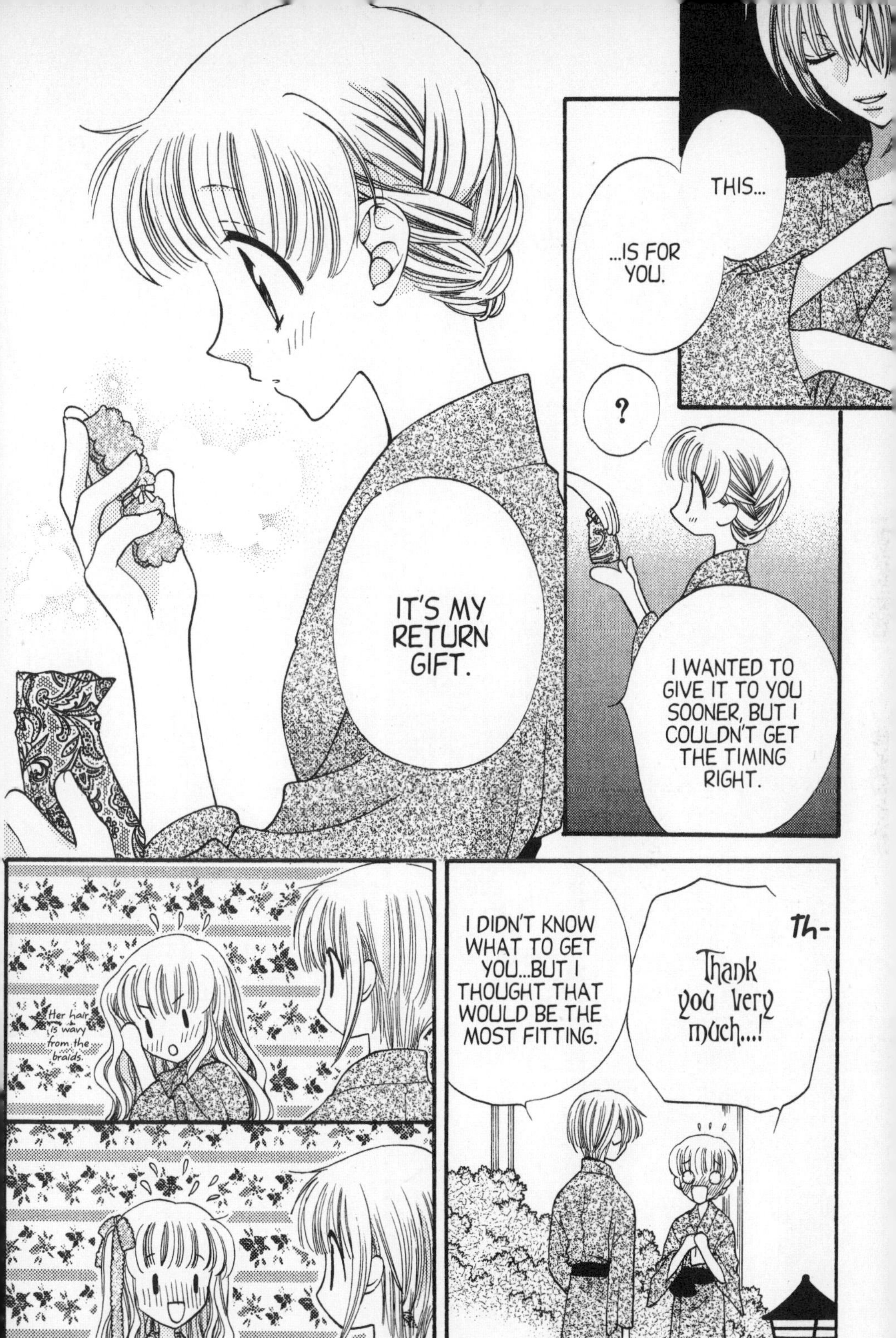
THIS...
...IS FOR YOU.
?
I WANTED TO GIVE IT TO YOU SOONER, BUT I COULDN'T GET THE TIMING RIGHT.
IT'S MY RETURN GIFT.
Th-
Thank you very much...!
I DIDN'T KNOW WHAT TO GET YOU...BUT I THOUGHT THAT WOULD BE THE MOST FITTING.
Her hair is wavy from the braids.

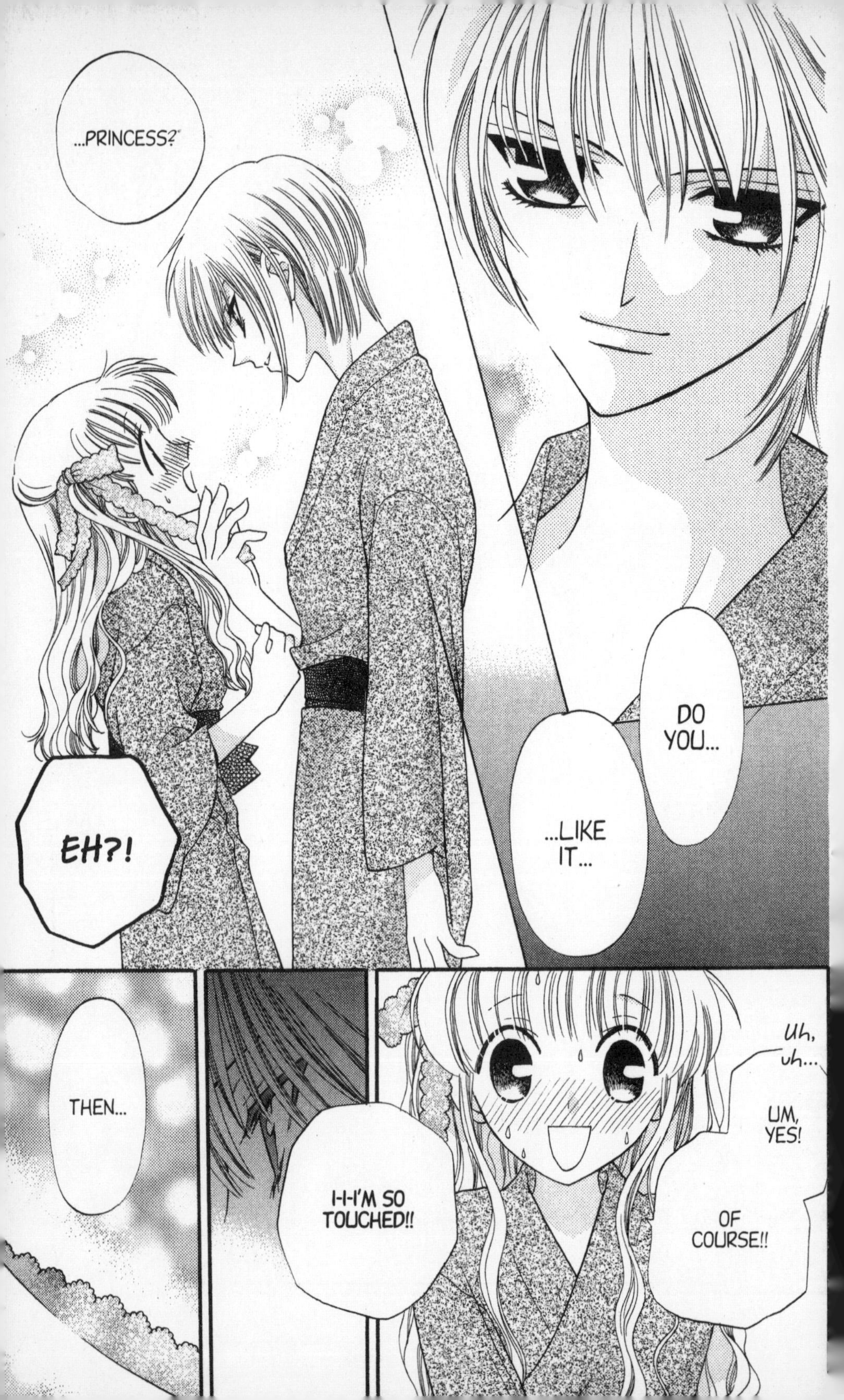
DO YOU...
...LIKE IT...
...PRINCESS?
EH?!
Uh, uh...
UM, YES!
OF COURSE!!
I-I-I'M SO TOUCHED!!
THEN...

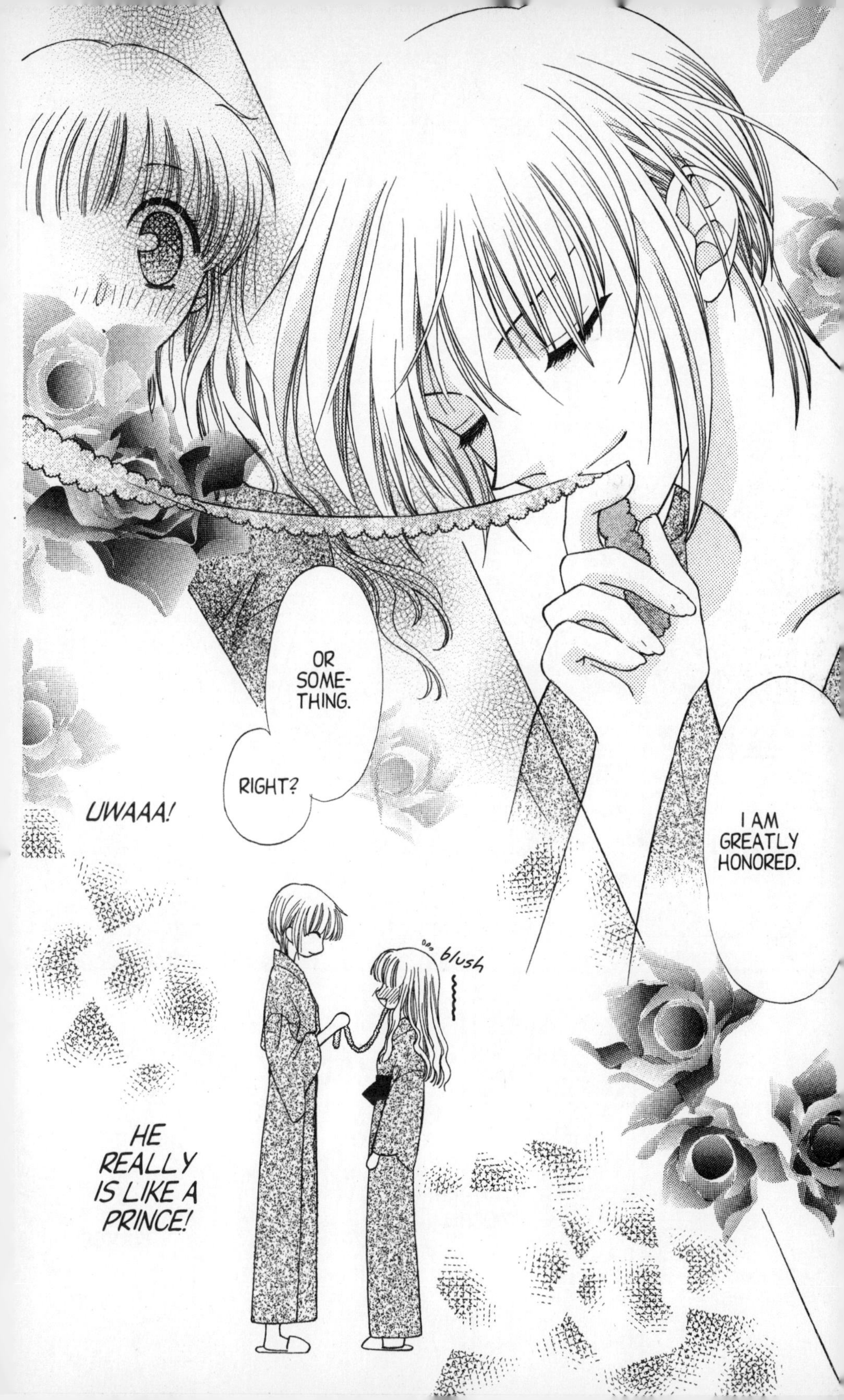
I AM GREATLY HONORED.
OR SOMETHING.
RIGHT?
blush
UWAAA!
HE REALLY IS LIKE A PRINCE!

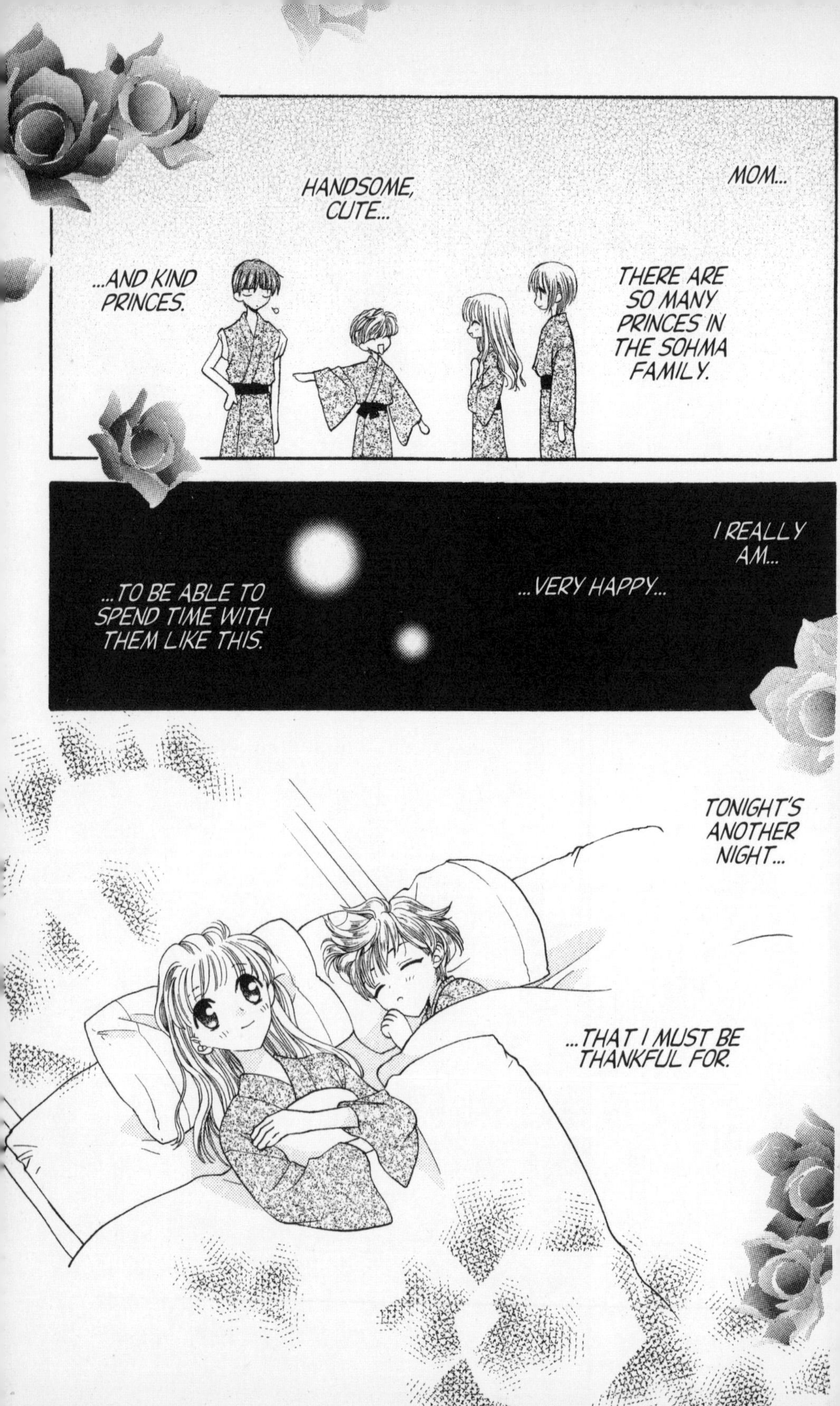
MOM...
THERE ARE SO MANY PRINCES IN THE SOHMA FAMILY.
HANDSOME, CUTE...
...AND KIND PRINCES.
I REALLY AM...
...VERY HAPPY...
...TO BE ABLE TO SPEND TIME WITH THEM LIKE THIS.
TONIGHT'S ANOTHER NIGHT...
...THAT I MUST BE THANKFUL FOR.

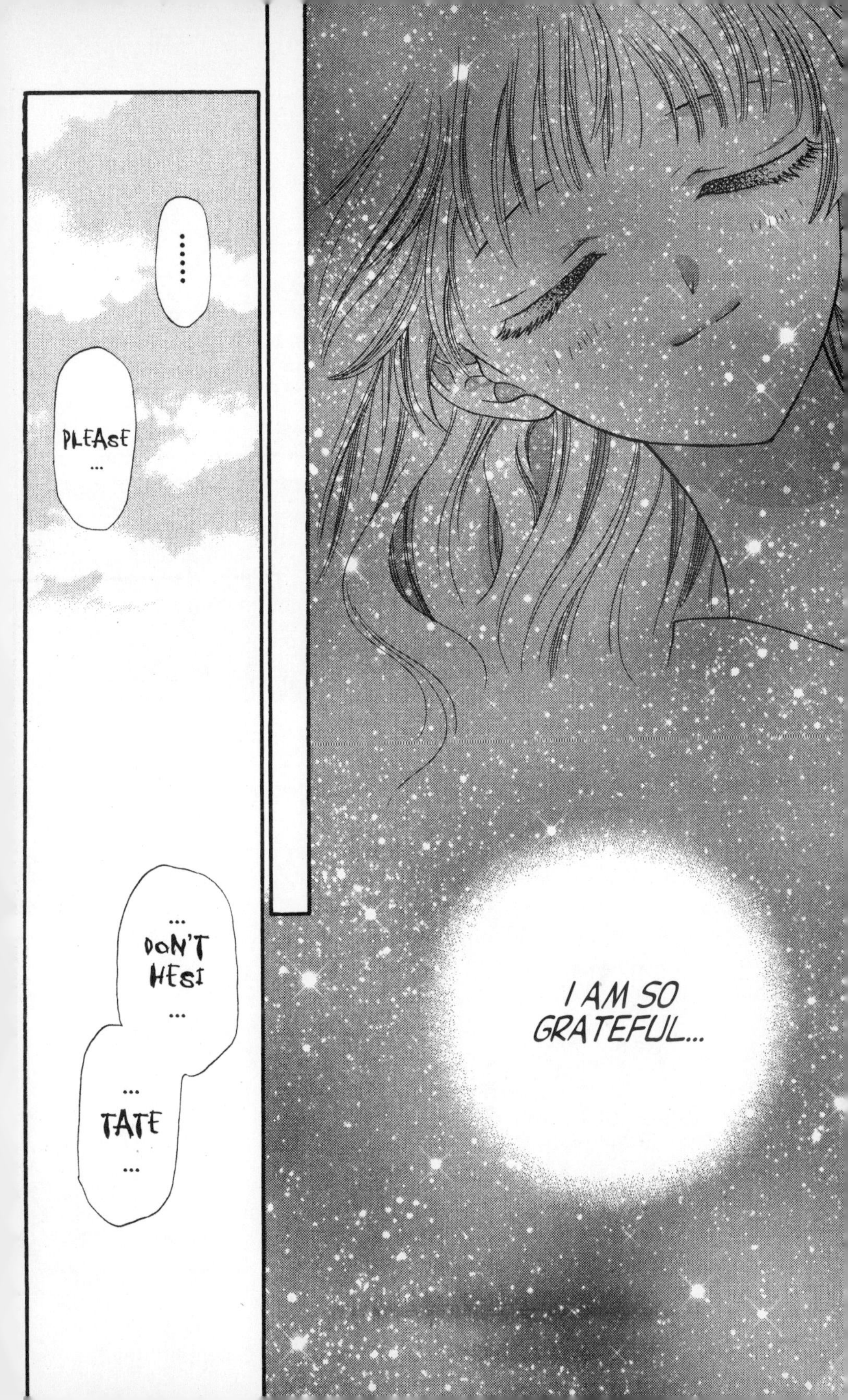
I AM SO GRATEFUL...
......
PLEASE ...
... DON'T HESI ...
... TATE ...

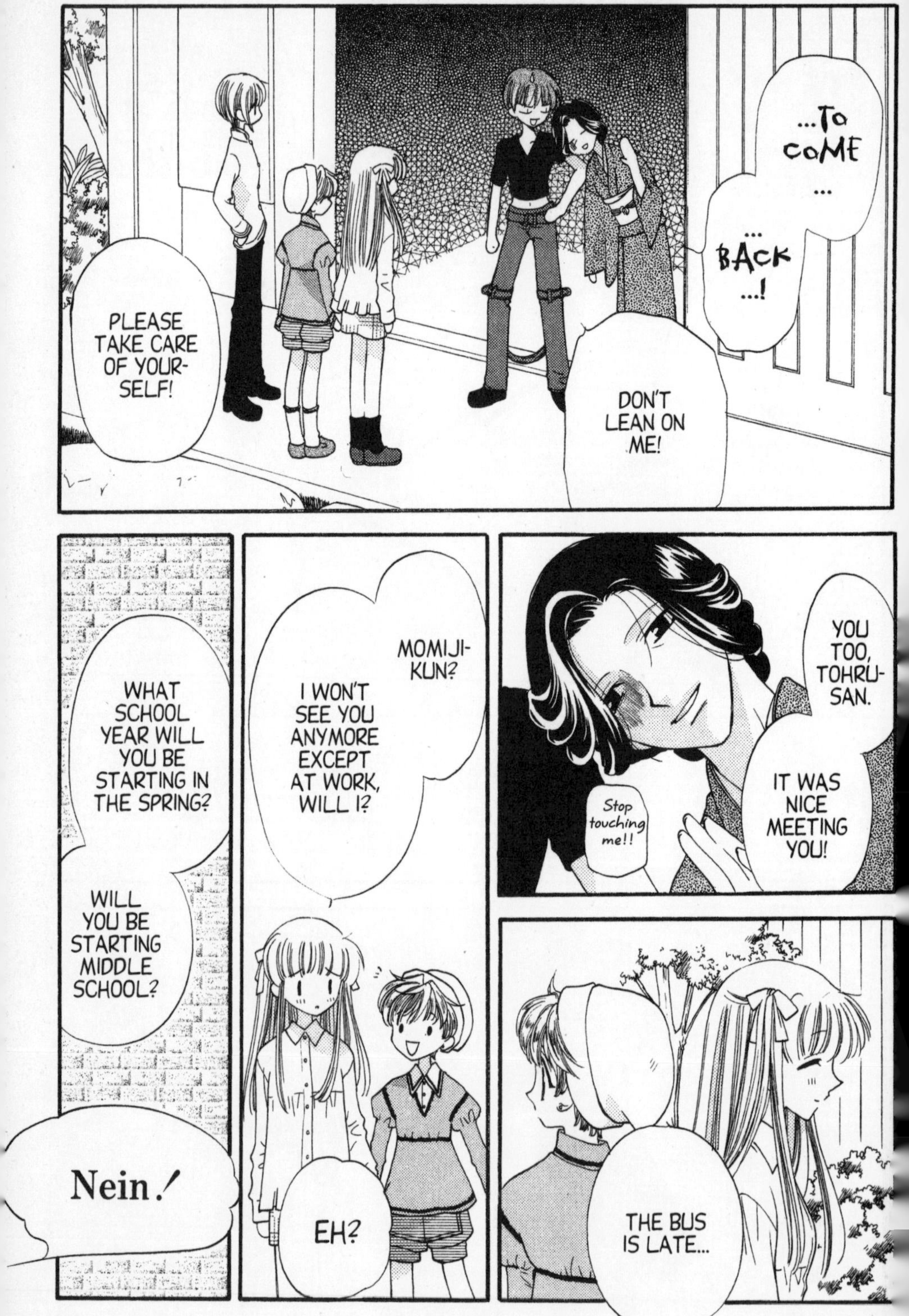
...TO COME... ...BACK...!
DON'T LEAN ON ME!
PLEASE TAKE CARE OF YOURSELF!
YOU TOO, TOHRU-SAN.
IT WAS NICE MEETING YOU!
Stop touching me!!
THE BUS IS LATE...
MOMIJI-KUN?
I WON'T SEE YOU ANYMORE EXCEPT AT WORK, WILL I?
EH?
WHAT SCHOOL YEAR WILL YOU BE STARTING IN THE SPRING?
WILL YOU BE STARTING MIDDLE SCHOOL?
Nein.!

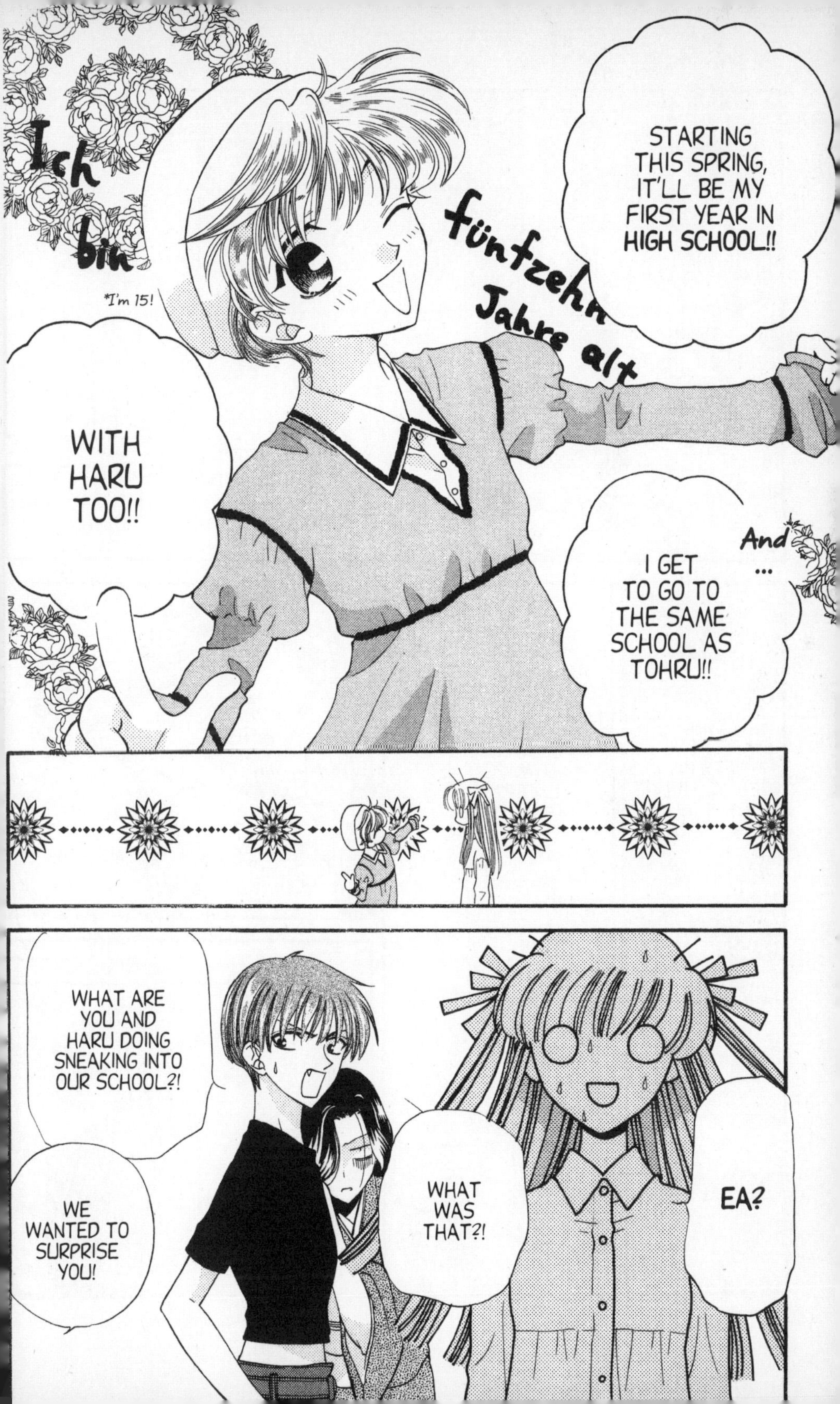
STARTING THIS SPRING, IT'LL BE MY FIRST YEAR IN HIGH SCHOOL!!
Ich bin fünfzehn Jahre alt
*I'm 15!
WITH HARU TOO!!
And ...
I GET TO GO TO THE SAME SCHOOL AS TOHRU!!
EA?
WHAT WAS THAT?!
WHAT ARE YOU AND HARU DOING SNEAKING INTO OUR SCHOOL?!
WE WANTED TO SURPRISE YOU!

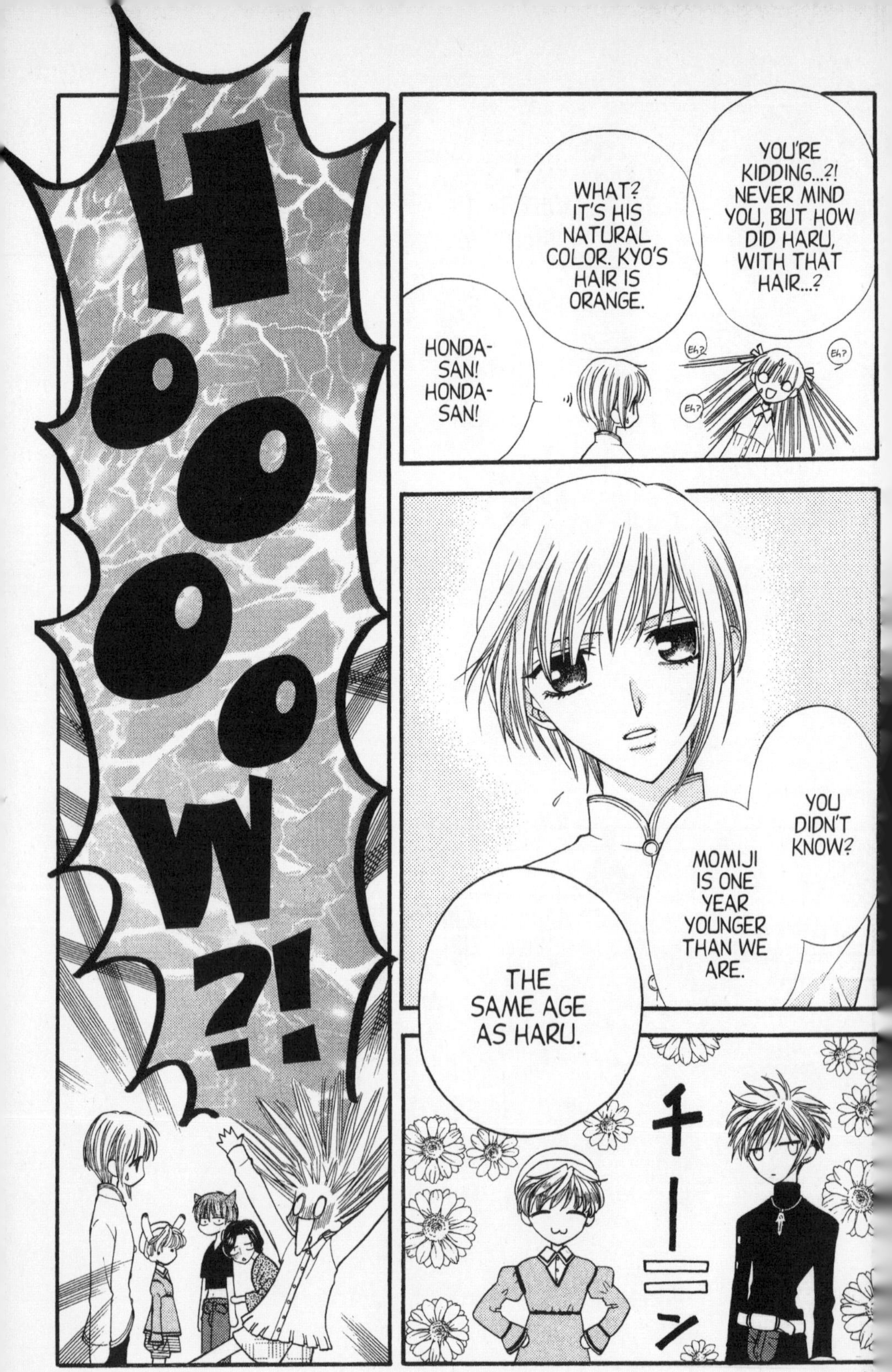
YOU'RE KIDDING...?! NEVER MIND YOU, BUT HOW DID HARU, WITH THAT HAIR...?
Eh?
Eh?
Eh?
WHAT? IT'S HIS NATURAL COLOR. KYO'S HAIR IS ORANGE.
HONDA-SAN! HONDA-SAN!
YOU DIDN'T KNOW?
MOMIJI IS ONE YEAR YOUNGER THAN WE ARE.
THE SAME AGE AS HARU.
チーン
HOOOOW?!

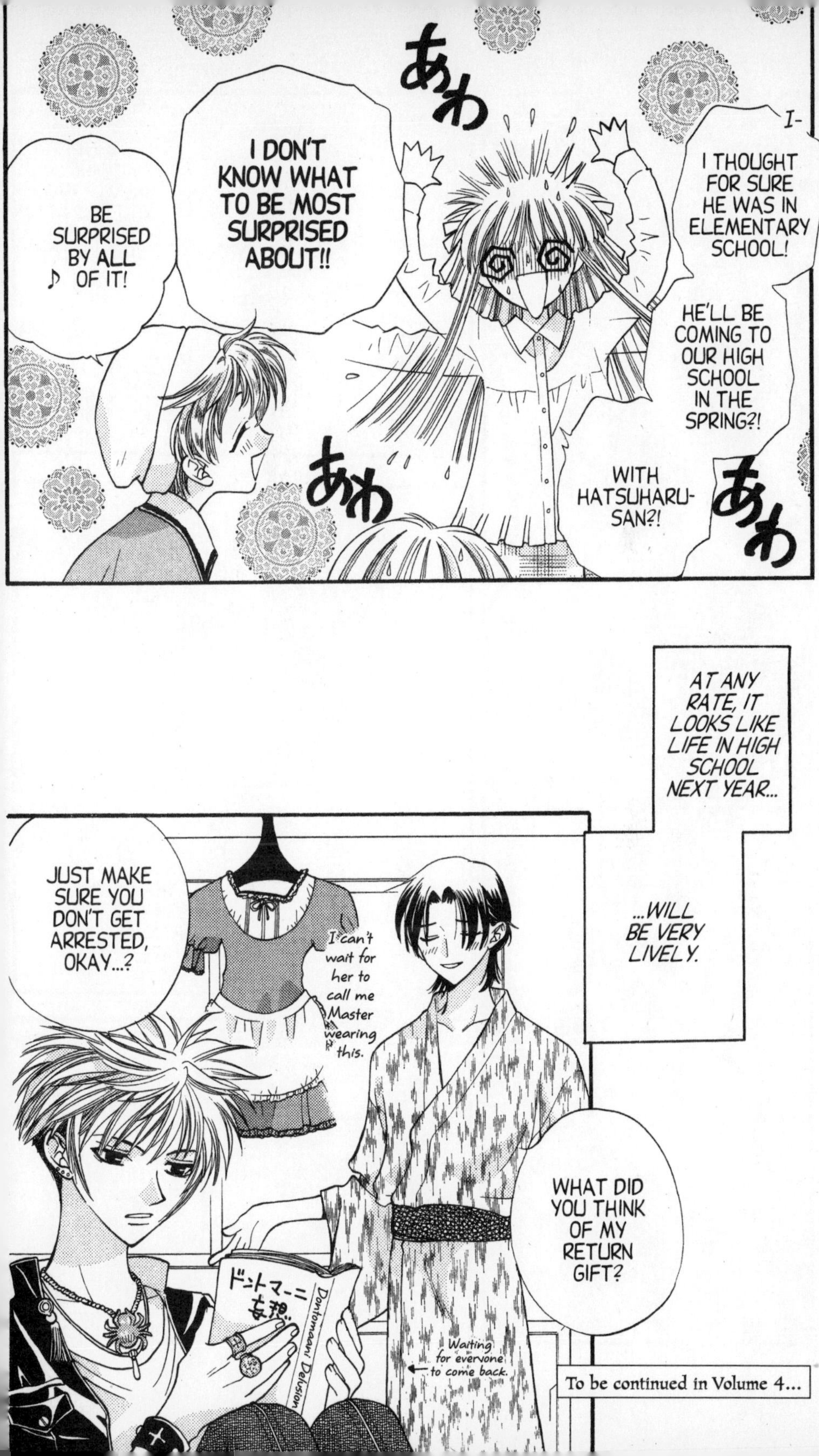
あわ
I-
I THOUGHT FOR SURE HE WAS IN ELEMENTARY SCHOOL!
HE'LL BE COMING TO OUR HIGH SCHOOL IN THE SPRING?!
WITH HATSUHARU-SAN?!
あわ
I DON'T KNOW WHAT TO BE MOST SURPRISED ABOUT!!
あわ
BE SURPRISED BY ALL ♪ OF IT!
AT ANY RATE, IT LOOKS LIKE LIFE IN HIGH SCHOOL NEXT YEAR...
...WILL BE VERY LIVELY.
WHAT DID YOU THINK OF MY RETURN GIFT?
I can't wait for her to call me Master wearing this.
JUST MAKE SURE YOU DON'T GET ARRESTED, OKAY...?
Waiting for everyone to come back.
ドントマーニ妄想
Dontomaani Delusion

To be continued in Volume 4...

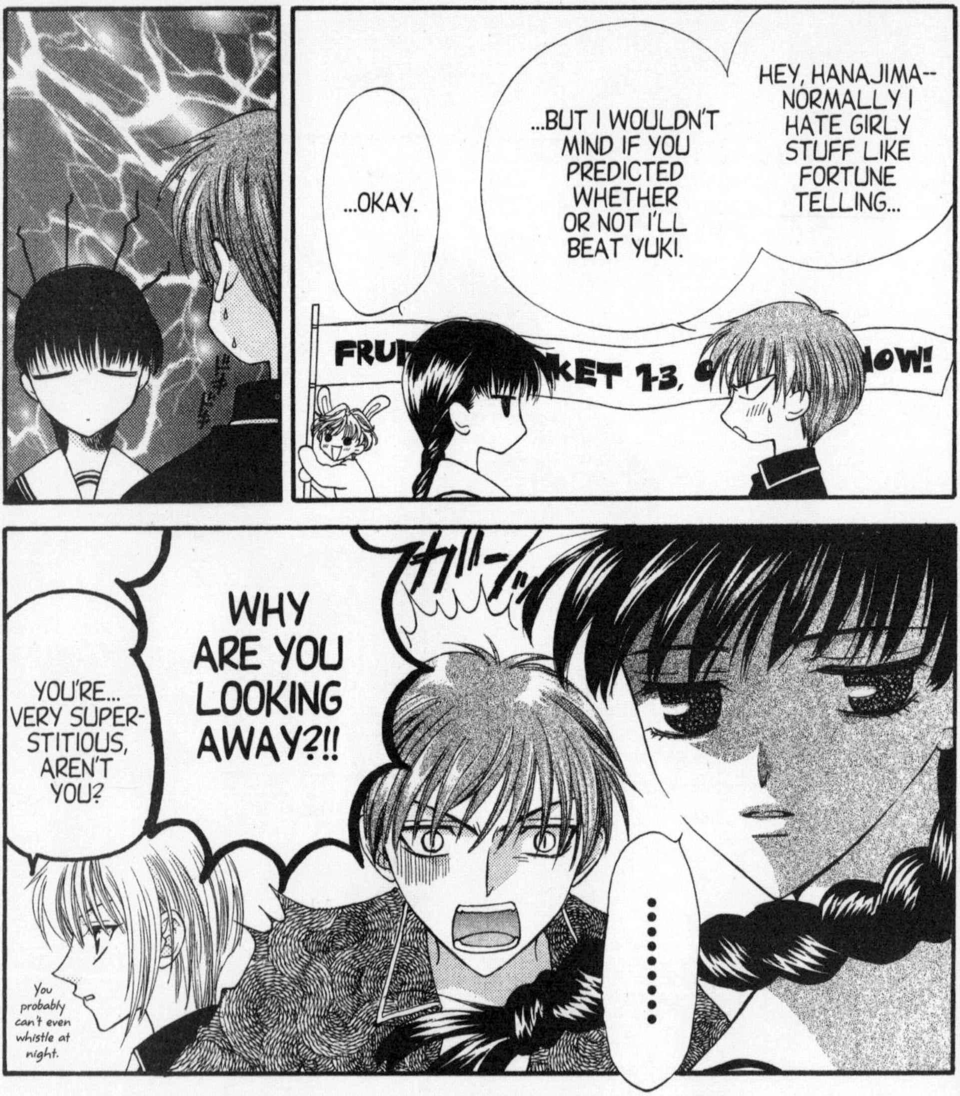
HEY, HANAJIMA-- NORMALLY I HATE GIRLY STUFF LIKE FORTUNE TELLING...
...BUT I WOULDN'T MIND IF YOU PREDICTED WHETHER OR NOT I'LL BEAT YUKI.
...OKAY.
......
WHY ARE YOU LOOKING AWAY?!!
YOU'RE... VERY SUPER-STITIOUS, AREN'T YOU?
You probably can't even whistle at night.

Omake Theater, Part 3

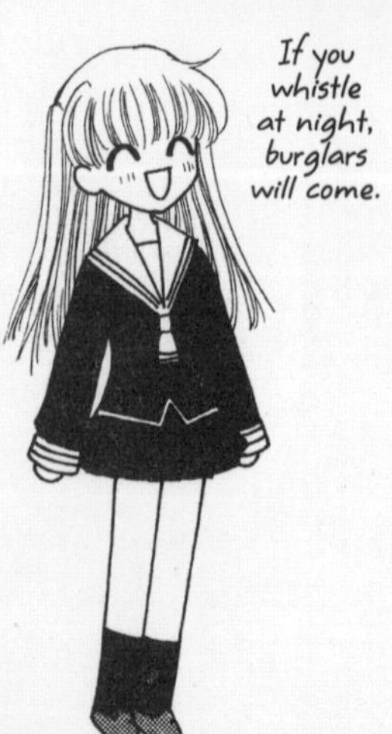
If you whistle at night, burglars will come.

Thank you so much!

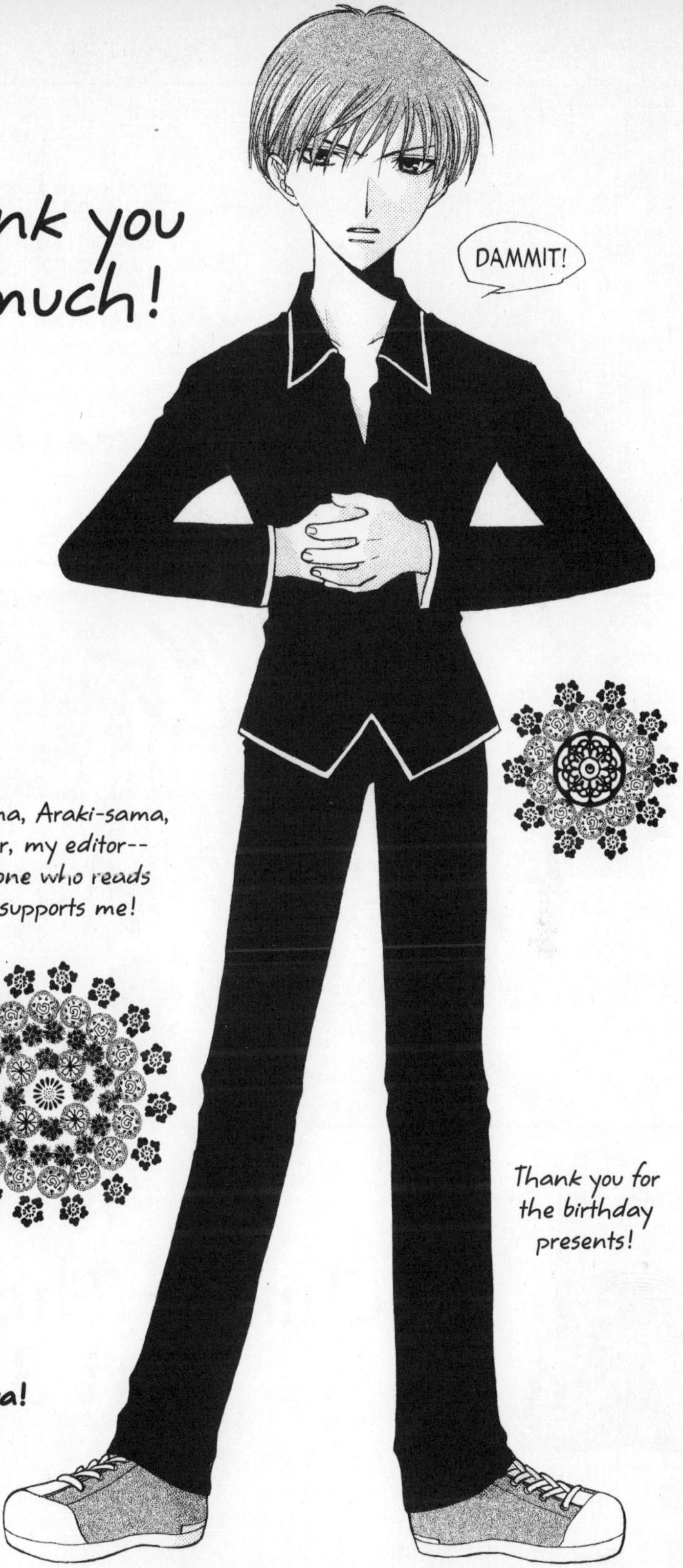
DAMMIT!

Harada-sama, Araki-sama, my mother, my editor-- and everyone who reads this and supports me!

Thank you for the birthday presents!

Next time is Gure-san! This has been **Natsuki Takaya!**

Next time in...

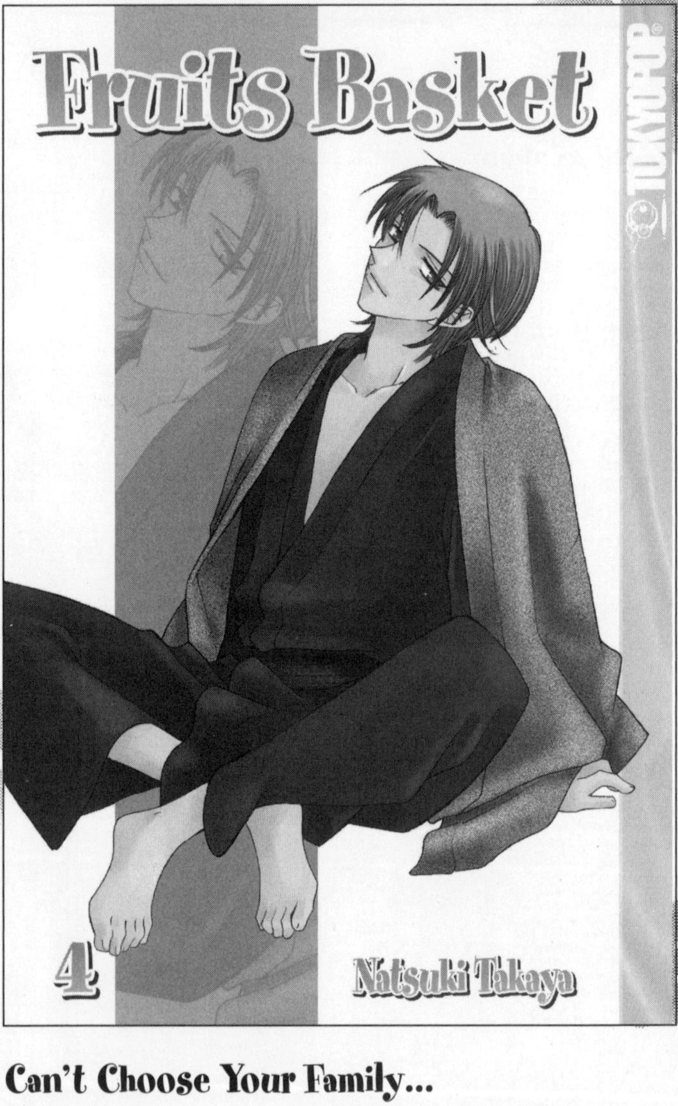
Fruits Basket
TOKYOPOP
4
Natsuki Takaya

You Can't Choose Your Family...

When the infamous Akito makes an in-class appearance at the start of the school year, the Sohma family worries that his arrival will be an uncensored exercise of show-and-tell about Yuki's past. Meanwhile, when Ayame vows to rekindle his brother's lost friendship, he begins to realize that you can choose your friends but you can't choose your family—especially when they're acting like animals!

Interview with Takaya-sensei

First, please tell us about yourself.

- Birthday: July 7
- Horoscope: Cancer
- Blood type: A
- Place of birth: Born in Shizuoka, raised in Tokyo
- Motto: I have about three, but… They're secret.
- Hobbies: Video Games
- Favorite color-Light colors, especially green and blue. Lately I've been into pastels.
- Favorite food: Abalone (because I rarely get to eat it). I love gum! I eat it so much they call me a gum monster. I don't like green peppers.

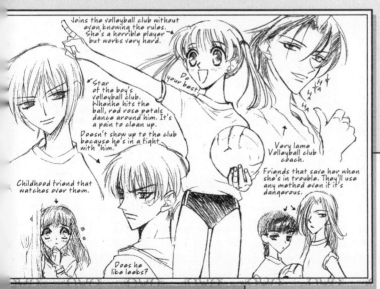

Joins the volleyball club without even knowing the rules. She's a horrible player but works very hard.
Do your best!
HA HA HA HA
Very lame Volleyball club coach.
Star of the boy's volleyball club. Whenhe hits the ball, red rose petals dance around him. It's a pain to clean up.
Doesn't show up to the club because he's in a fight with "him."
Friends that save her when she's in trouble. They'll use any method even if it's dangerous.
Childhood friend that watches over them.
Does he like leeks?

SPORTS FURUBA

What if Fruits Basket was a sports manga? That was the idea behind these sketches. Yuki's dancing rose petals are amazing but what about Kyo being the son of a green grocer? Minagawa Motoko's family also runs a produce store... Why am I so obsessed with them?

SPOTLIGHT ON THE KAIBARA HIGH SCHOOL UNIFORMS!!
The back is long too.
Summer
There's no school pin.
Spotlight on the Kaibara High School Uniforms!!
Here are my model sheets for the male and female Kaibara High uniforms.
The sleeves were long in book 1 but not now. (Ha ha!) Now they end about 3cm from the elbow.
The tie is pretty much just for looks. (back of tie)
Hidden Buttons
You button the tie here. (back)
The skirt is short. If you wear one as short as Tohru then remember to wear shorts underneath.
The sailor collars end about 5cm under the bust.
The skirt is dark blue in summer and winter.
Length of sleeves is same as girls. The boy's uniform sure is boring. (laughs)
It's basically the same as the girls.
Follow the Kaibara High School Uniform!! (There's an ocean nearby?) (Kai=ocean)
Why am I using Yuki? He's the only male who actually wears the school uniform!
The summer tie has a colored tip. It's a normal tie but short. Hangs down just below the bust. (do guys have a bust?)
Very similar to the girl's uniform.
Pants are thin.
The buttons are gold.
White
The lines are a dark purple.
The shirt covers about half of the butt.
The winter uniform isn't all that different.
Hana-chan is taller than normal.
Winter.
Her manicure is in black. And the nails are a square cut.
Wants to say something but doesn't have the chance to.
The sleeves are long and have gold buttons.
And the boy's ties are all white now.
But the boy's trim color is now white and the girl's trim color around their waist is white. Watch out for that...
You can see the winter uniforms on one of the book covers.

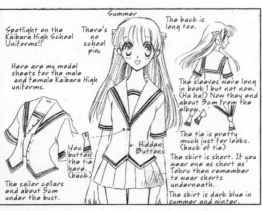

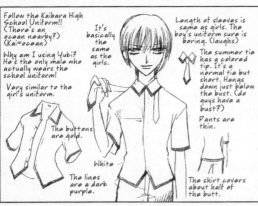

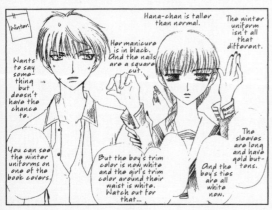

2) Tell us about your work schedule.

I don't write out a full scrip Well, I'm just not able to d well, so I go straight from notes (which only I can decip to the rough draft. It's much ea to get the rough draft done r off the bat, but the downside have to correct it over and ov but that's still easier for m seems I'm the "draw it first decide if it's good or not" typ

So getting back to the questic it takes me about 3-5 days the rough draft. Then I sho to my editor and discuss it, rect problems, and when I ge OK I start the real drawings. sketches take about 2 and a days, then another 2 and a days to ink it. Then the tones the rest take another 2 days o

3) Tell us about your daily schedule.

I work all day long, stopping for meals. When I have a s moment I take a bath or video games.

4) What tools and supplies you use for your work?

Nothing particularly specia paper, various brands of Zebra no Maru pens and a cutter. And currency ink.

5) When did you start using your Macintosh for work? What do you use it for?

Around the final chapter of Genei Musou. I used it mainly for the color art. I've always been bad at coloring since I was a child. My mother once told me, "I'm not going to buy you any more coloring books!" That's how bad I was. Coloring with the Mac is so helpful. Plus it's so fun to use! Although I still can't do anything complicated with it.

6) When you're working on the plot or rough draft, do you ever get writer's block? How do you cope with that?

Yes, that does happen… My biggest problem is working out how to fit the story into the allotted pages. When I'm stuck I take a break. Sometimes I'll talk it over with my editor, other times I play a video game and get my head away from the problem. That usually helps.

7) When did you decide you wanted to be a manga-ka? What made you decide to pursue that career?

Around first grade, I think. At that time my sister wanted to become a manga-ka too, and that influenced me. I don't know… I just really wanted to become one for some reason.

) What kind of work was your first manga?

It was a Sci-Fi comedy with a female duo… I think. I was in grade school so don't remember too well.

See more Questions with Takaya-sensei in volume 4!

Fans Basket

Thao-Linh N.
Blaine, MN

Oh look! There really is a place for an onigiri in a fruits basket!

Katlin M.
Lisle, IL

Beautiful picture, Katlin. I lik the way you use depth of fiel with the feathers. Kyo is H-O

Even though my mother died
I was never alone
The ancestors of the Zodiac
were my family and home
They gave me so much
Needed so little in return
The least I could do
is give my gratitude to them
Yuki and Kyo
may always fight
but each of them
Is truly nice
Shigure is welcoming
warm and kind
he may be a perv
but he's still nice
I guess that sometimes
a truly bad thing
can change in front
of your very eyes
from something horrible
to something nice
all just in
the blink of an eye

SO
WOND
DRAWI
ME A
FRIEND
CAN
REPA
THOSE

A poem and a picture! Thanks a bunch, Sophia!

Sophia X.
Buffalo Grove, IL

Do you want to share your love for Fruits Basket with fans around the world? "Fans Basket" is taking submissions of fan art, poetry, cosplay photos, or any other Furuaba fun you'd like to share!

How to submit:

1)Send your work via regular mail (NOT e-mail) to:

"Fans Basket"
c/o TOKYOPOP
5900 Wilshire Blvd.
Suite 2000
Los Angeles, CA 90036

2) All work should be in black and white and no larger than 8.5" x 11". (And try not to fold it too many times!)

3) Anything you send will not be returned. If you want to keep your original, it's fine to send us a copy.

4) Please include your full name, age, city and state for us to print with your work. If you'd rather us use a pen name, please include that too.

5) IMPORTANT: If you're under the age of 18, you must have your parent's permission in order for us to print your work. Any submissions without a signed note of parental consent cannot be used.

6) For full details, please check out our website.http://www.tokyopop.com/aboutus/fanart.php

Disclaimer: Anything you send to us becomes the exclusive property of TOKYOPOP Inc. and, as we said before, will not be returned to you. We will have the right to print, reproduce, distribute, or modify the artwork for use in future volumes of Fruits Basket or on the web royalty-free.

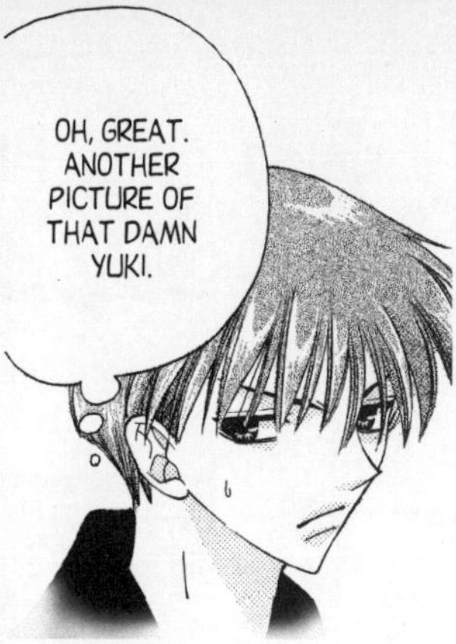
OH, GREAT. ANOTHER PICTURE OF THAT DAMN YUKI.

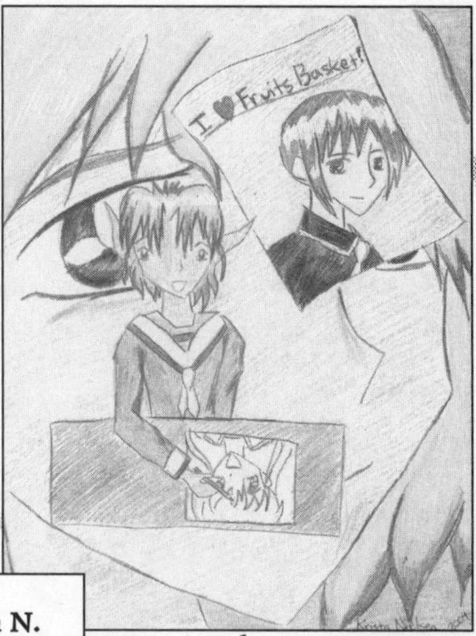
I ♥ Fruits Basket!

Krista N.
Kingwood, TX

Picture's within pictures... neat idea! Thanks for the self-portrait.

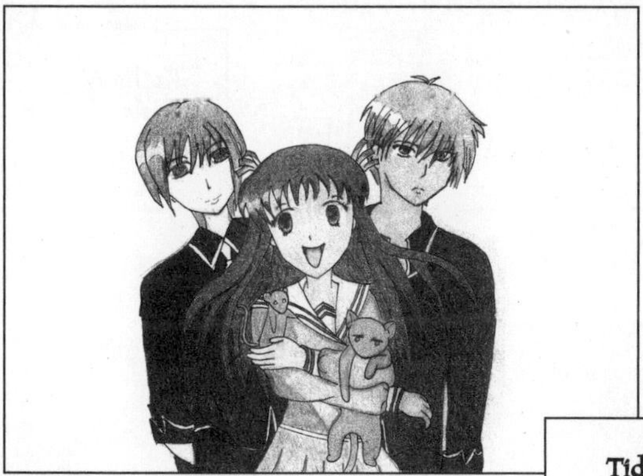

Tida J.
Van Nuys, CA

Kawaii! The animals are so adorable! The people are cute too.

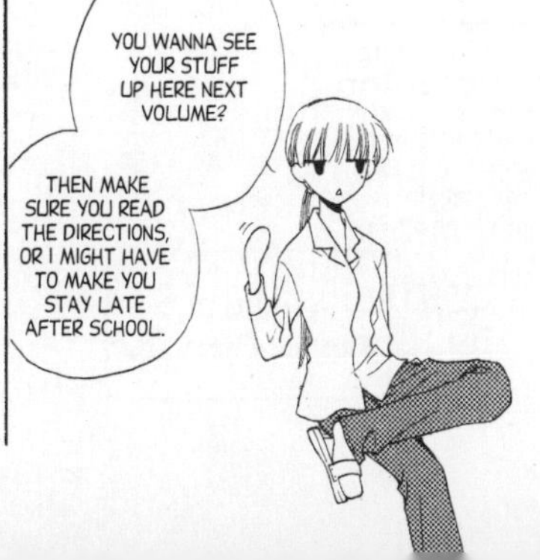
YOU WANNA SEE YOUR STUFF UP HERE NEXT VOLUME?
THEN MAKE SURE YOU READ THE DIRECTIONS, OR I MIGHT HAVE TO MAKE YOU STAY LATE AFTER SCHOOL.

SOUND EFFECT INDEX

THE FOLLOWING IS A LIST OF THE SOUND EFFECTS USED IN FRUITS BASKET. EACH SOUND IS LABELED BY PAGE AND PANEL NUMBER, SEPARATED BY A PERIOD. THE FIRST DESCRIPTION IS THE PHONETIC READING OF THE JAPANESE, AND IS FOLLOWED BY THE EQUIVALENT ENGLISH SOUND OR A DESCRIPTION.

23.2	gakuh: stagger
26.2	dopyuun: zoom
27.1	ze: wheeze x3
27.3	piku: twitch
27.4	suku: rise
27.5	suta suta: stride
28.2	kyuu: tug
28.3	shyuru shyuru: wiggle
28.4	dota dota: (approaching footsteps)
28.5a	batan!: crash
28.5b	bishi: twang
28.5c	zusa: skid
29.3	gaba: surge
29.4	doku doku: dribble (blood)
31.1	goshi goshi: rub rub
31.5	peko peko: bow
32.6	gyaa gyaa: bicker
33.3	Gan!: whack
33.5	gishi: snap
34.1	zun: (fanfare)
34.4	doh!: kick
35.3	su: slip
36.1	giri giri: struggle
38.1-2	gogogogo: thunder
42.2	za!: (drama!)
42.4	gakii: snap
43.1	muka: (anger)
43.3	buchi: snap
43.4	Goh!: wham
43.5	doka baki: whack, bam
45.3	Zuru: slump
45.6	su: fall
46.4	suku: rise
46.5	ga: grab
48.5	ji: stare
49.2	Gyuu: hug
49.3a	bon: poof

9.1, 9.2	zawa zawa: chatter
10.1	Sucha: strap
10.2	gyu: squeeze
10.3	za!: (drama!)
10.4	don!: (impact!)
10.5	charin charin: ring ring
12.2	Sha: slide
12.3	fu: fume x2
13.5	gyaa: bicker
14.1	Ki: anger
14.2	za!: (strike a pose!)
14.3	zuppo: shoop
14.4	Agaaa: gag

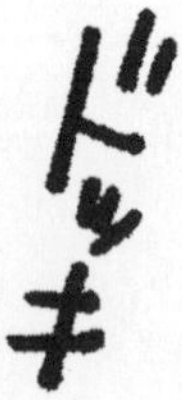

DOKI-DOKI

ONE OF THE MOST COMMON SOUND EFFECTS IN MANGA, "DOKI-DOKI" IS THE SOUND (A POUNDING HEARTBEAT. IT' USED TO INDICATE A TENSE, EMOTIONAL SITUATION.

15.3	kara kara: rattle (sliding door)
16.2	Biku: wince
17.3	Zudoon!: (meanacing fanfare)
18.1	Mera: burn
18.4	Zugogoon: (meanacing fanfare)
21.4	Gaiin: wham
21.5	zuru zuru: slide
22.1a	zawa zawa: chatter
22.1b	hero hero: wobble
22.2	don!: (impact!)
22.3	zawa zawa: chatter
23.1a	paan: (starting gun)
23.1b	zaa...: chatter (cut off)

2.2 zawa zawa: chatter
3.1 zawa zawa: chatter
3.2 gata: clatter
8.1 patata: pitter patter
8.3 guu: clench
1.3 koro: turn

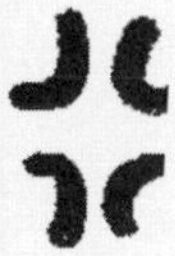

ANGER MARKS

THESE LITTLE "PLUS SIGNS" ARE MEANT TO REPRESENT A THROBBING VEIN. OVER THE YEARS, THESE HAVE BECOME A VISUAL SHORTCUT IN MANGA FOR ANGER. IN THE FRUITS BASKET ANIME, SHIGURE POKES FUN AT HIS EASY GOING PERSONALITY BY HOLDING AN ANGER MARK IN FRONT OF HIS FACE TO SHOW HIS RANGE.

3.1 doku doku (pounding heartbeat)
6.2 gyuun: shoom
6.3 kata kata: (surpressing anger)
7.3 don: bam
5.4 paaa: brighten
.3 bachi: snap
3.2 gororo: vroom
3.3 jiiin: stare
4.2 gata: clatter
3.1 aaaa: moaning
.3 gyuumu: (the grab of doom!)
.3 pecha: grab
.1 jiiin: stare
.4 piku: bright
.1 baki!: whack
.5 baki!: whack
.1 gashyon: upheave!
.3 kah: smack
.5 byu: swing
.3 chiin: ching!
.1 awa awa: panic
.2 doki doki: (heartbeat)
.3 gaan: shock

49.3b Bari Biri Bori: (ripping clothes)
51.1 pi:shing
54.1 bon: poof
54.2 doki doki: (heartbeat)
54.4 jiiin: stare
55.1 gacha: click
56.1 giri giri: struggle
58.2 wata wata: flap flap
58.4 gashyon: shock
59.3 gacha: click
66.1 gaba: jolt
67.3 Ka: blush
67.4 bon: poof
73.5 Goh!: slam
74.4 zawa zawa: chatter
74.3 kya: grab
76.6 Zudoon!: horror

ZAWA-ZAWA

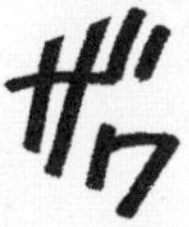
ザワ

THE SOUND OF A CROWD. IF YOU SEE "ZAWA"S IN A CLASSROOM, IT PROBABLY MEANS THAT CLASS HASN'T STARTED YET. EITHER THAT, OR A TEACHER CAN'T CONTROL HIS OR HER STUDENTS!

77.1 gata: clatter
77.5 shuu: shoop
78.1 ban!: bam!
79.4-5 Hyuoooo:wind
81.1-2 do-do-do-do: stomp stomp...
83.2 kaa: blush
83.4 zugogogogo: (menacing presence)
84.1 gyo: irk
84.3 shiku shiku: sob sob
90.3 pata pata: stomp stomp
91.5 kasa: step
98.2 gotsu: smack
102.3 butsu: click
103.1 gara: rattle
104.5 pon: pat
106.3 gara: rattle
106.5 butsu: click
106.7 chari: (remove)
110.3 Pishan!: Slam!
113.5 kah: tink
124.5 gusa: poke
125.6 chiki chiki: click click
129.1 pori pori: scratch scratch
132.1 kiin kon kan kon: (school bells)

Fruits Basket

Volume 4

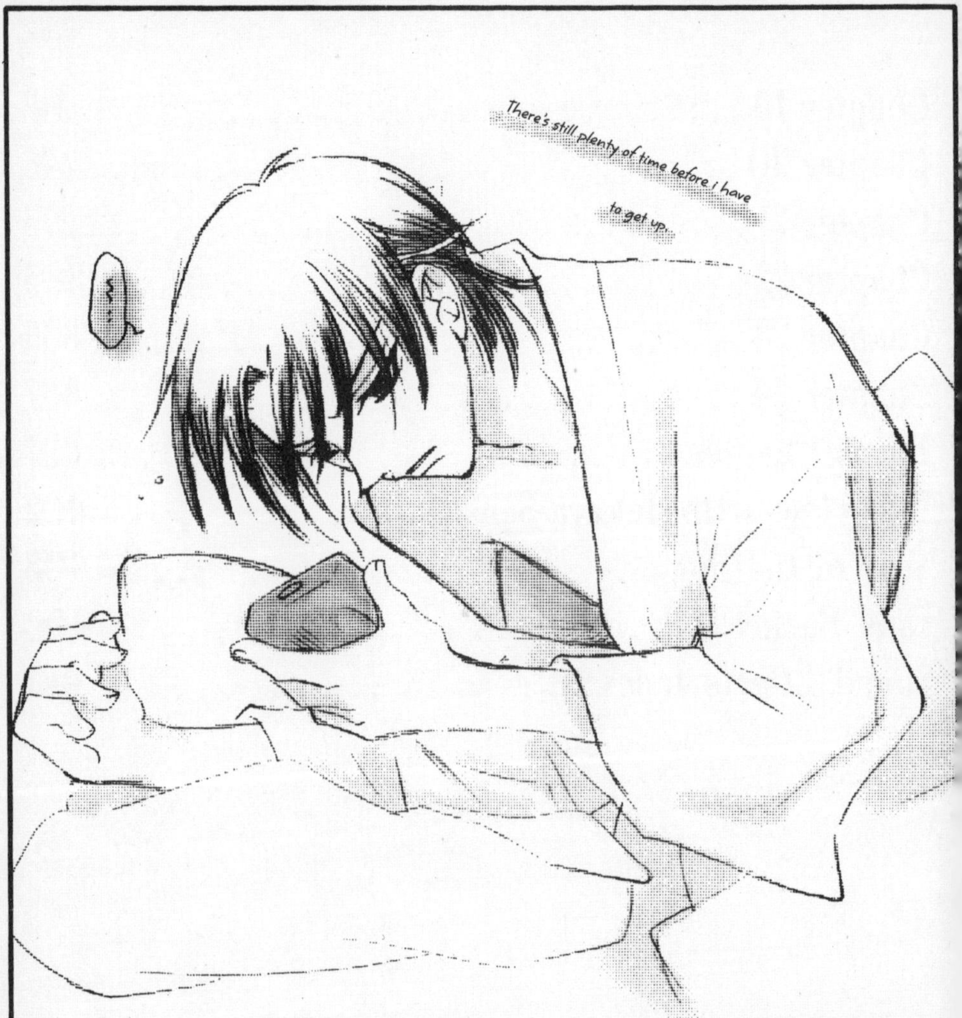
There's still plenty of time before i have
to get up...

Natsuki Takaya

Fruits Basket

Volume 4

Table of Contents

STORY SO FAR...

Hello, I'm Tohru Honda, and I have come to know a terrible secret. After the death of my mother, I was living by myself in a tent when the Sohma family took me in. I soon learned that the Sohma family lives with a curse! Each family member is possessed by the vengeful spirit of an animal from the Chinese Zodiac. Whenever one of them becomes weak or is hugged by a member of the opposite sex, they change into their Zodiac animal!

TODAY YUKI-KUN, KYO-KUN AND I START OUR SECOND YEAR OF HIGH SCHOOL.
MOMIJI-KUN AND HATSUHARU-SAN WILL BE ATTENDING OUR SCHOOL, TOO. LIFE IS SURE TO GET EXCITING!
I WONDER WHICH MEMBERS OF THE ZODIAC I'LL ENCOUNTER THIS TIME...?

Tohru Honda

The ever-optimistic hero of our story. Recently orphaned, Tohru has taken up residence in Shigure Sohma's house, along with Yuki and Kyo. She's the only person outside of the Sohma family who knows about their Zodiac curse.

Yuki Sohma

At school he's known as Prince Charming. Polite and soft-spoken, he's the polar opposite of Kyo. Yuki is possessed by the spirit of the Rat.

Kyo Sohma

Just as the Cat of legend (whose spirit possesses him) was left out of the Zodiac, Kyo is ostracized by the Sohma family. His greatest wish in life is to defeat Yuki in battle and win his rightful place in the Zodiac.

Shigure Sohma

The enigmatic Shigure keeps a house outside of the Sohma estate where he lives with Yuki, Kyo and Tohru. He may act perverted at times, but he has a good heart. His Zodiac spirit is the Dog.

Hatori Sohma

The family doctor of the Sohma clan and one of the Juunishi (his symbol is the Dragon, which manifests as a seahorse). When Akito wills it, he erases the memories of those who stumble upon the family's secret. Hatori once had to erase the memories of the woman he loved, and ever since has been firmly against letting anyone else know the secret--even Tohru.

Fruits Basket Characters

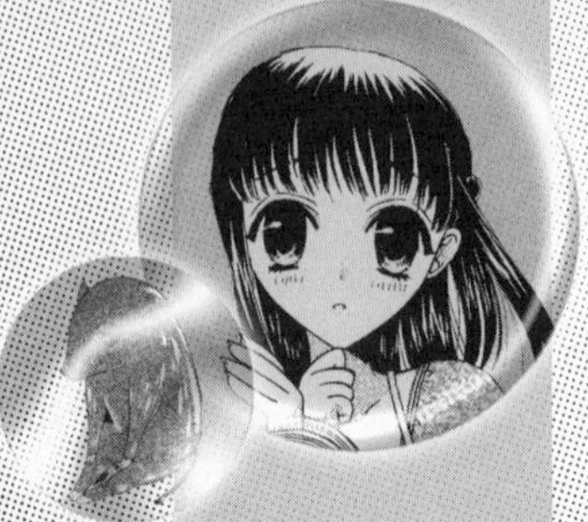

Kagura Sohma

Stubborn and jealous as her Zodiac symbol, the Boar, Kagura is determined to marry Kyo. even if she kills him in the process.

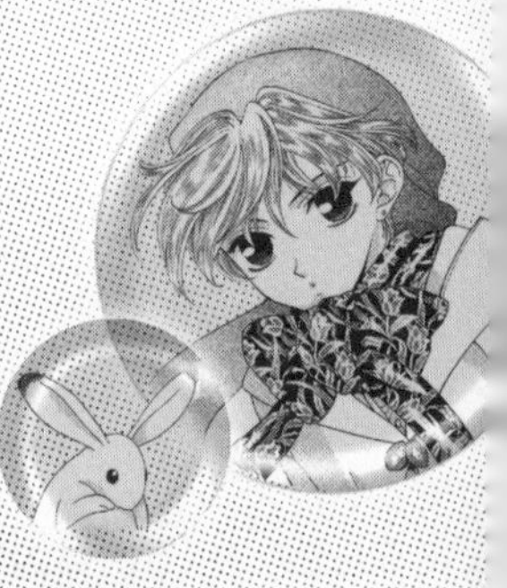

Momiji Sohma

Playful and carefree as the Rabbit he turns into, Momiji is the youngest member of the Sohma family that Tohru has met. He's half German and half Japanese, and switches casually between the two languages. His father owns the building where Tohru works.

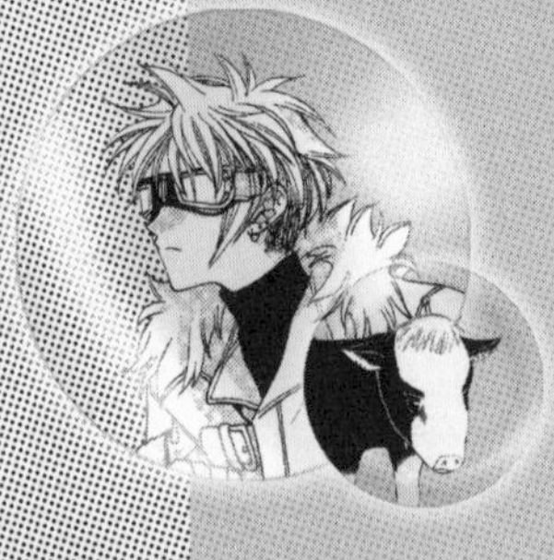

Hatsuharu Sohma

Usually cool, calm and collected, like a cow, Haru turns into a raging bull when his "Black" personalit comes out. He's a rival to Kyo and a friend to Yuki (after years of unfounded animosity). Believe it or not, Haru and Momiji are in the same grade!

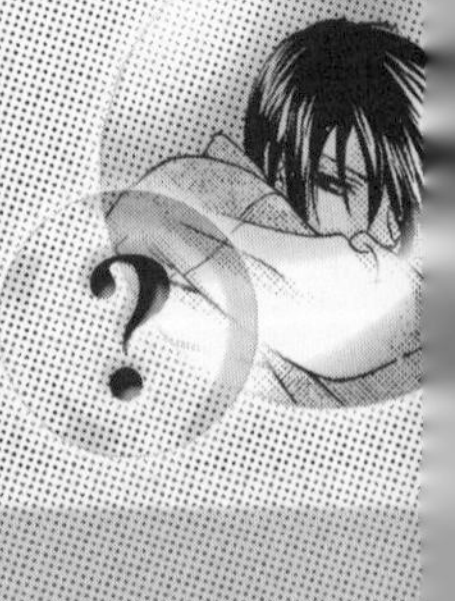

?

Akito Sohma

The mysterious leader of the Sohma clan, the other family members treat him with equal measures of fear and reverence. Tohru hasn't met him...yet.

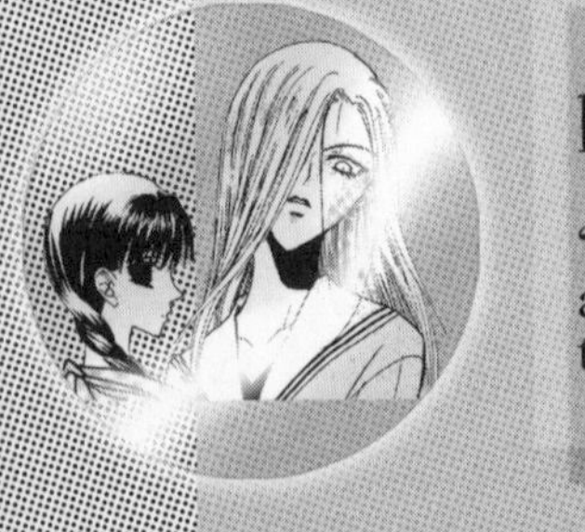

Hanajima & Arisa

"A psychic freak and a yankee thug." The two best frien a girl could hope for. They always look out for Tohru; they've become friends with Yuki and Kyo as well.

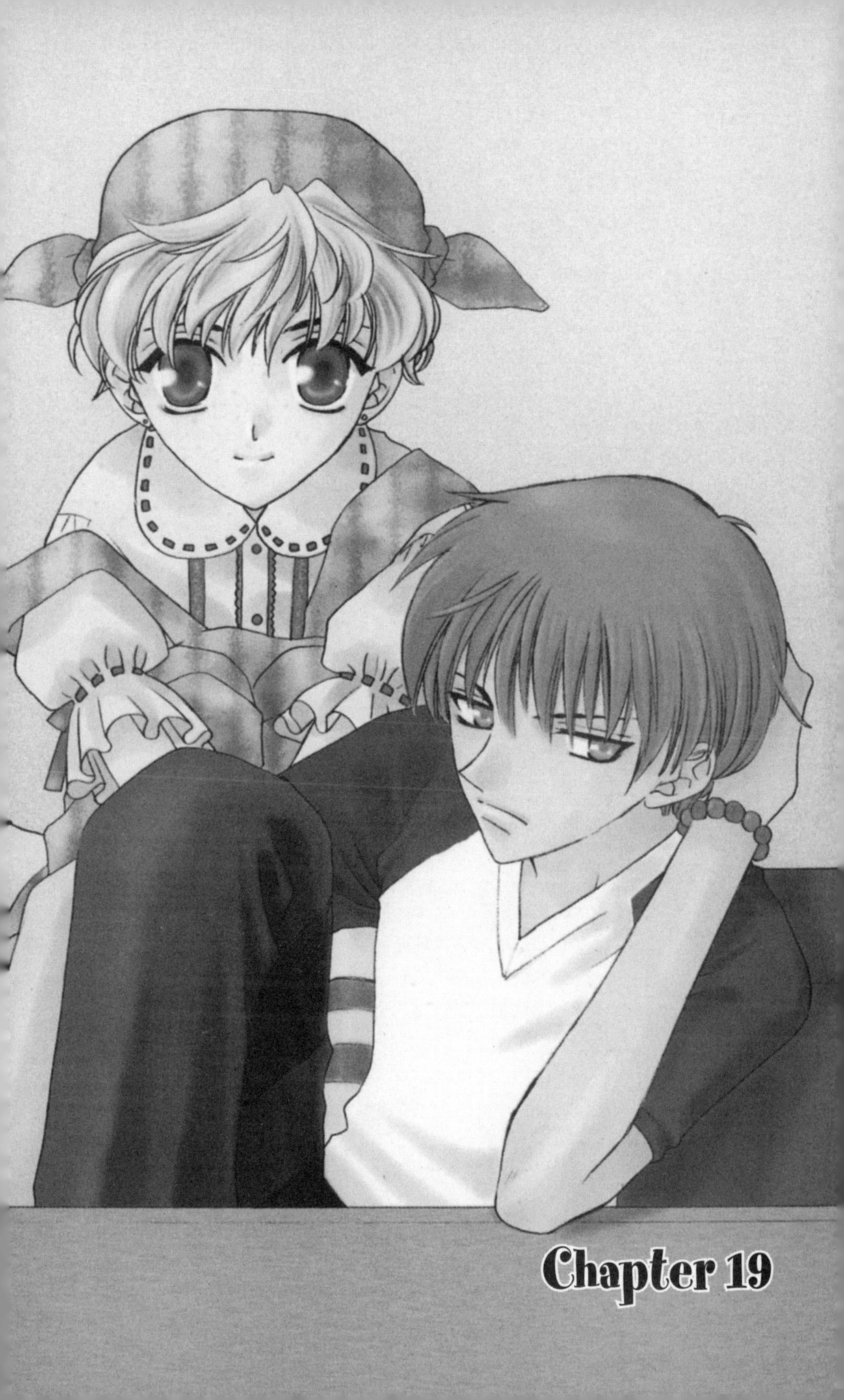
Chapter 19

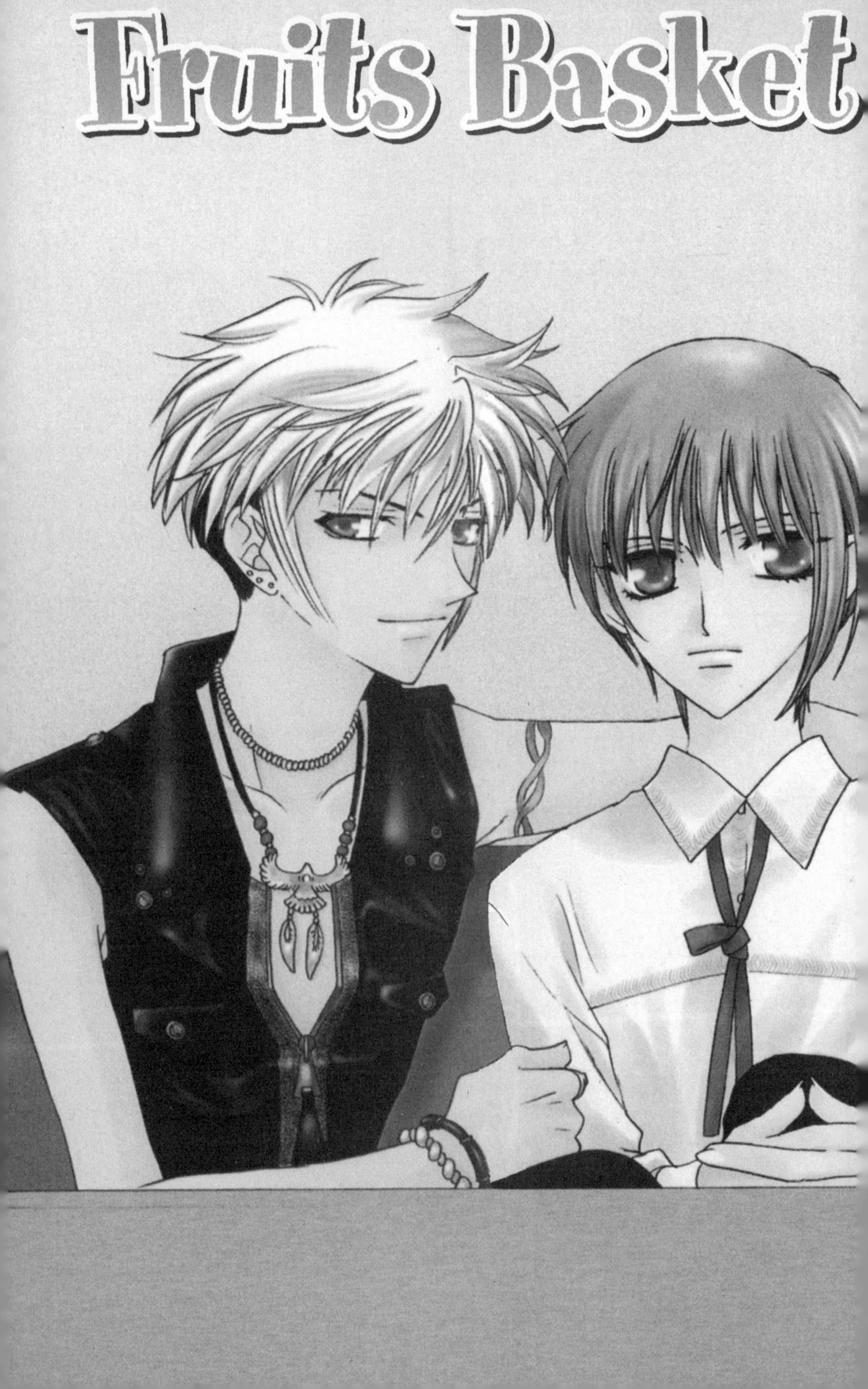
Fruits Basket

A story that's near and dear to my heart.

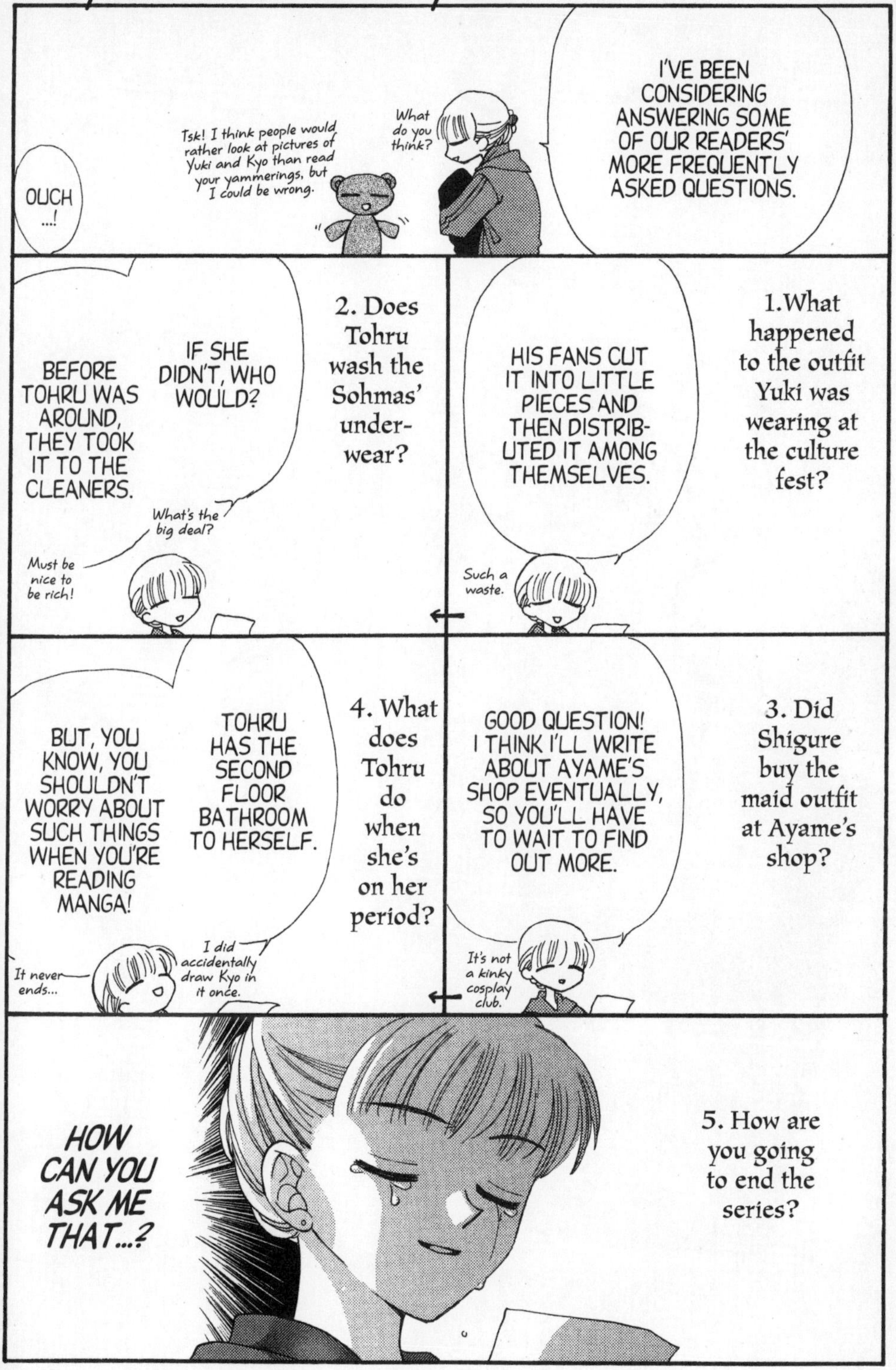
I'VE BEEN CONSIDERING ANSWERING SOME OF OUR READERS' MORE FREQUENTLY ASKED QUESTIONS.
What do you think?
Tsk! I think people would rather look at pictures of Yuki and Kyo than read your yammerings, but I could be wrong.
OUCH ...!
1.What happened to the outfit Yuki was wearing at the culture fest?
HIS FANS CUT IT INTO LITTLE PIECES AND THEN DISTRIB-UTED IT AMONG THEMSELVES.
Such a waste.
2. Does Tohru wash the Sohmas' under-wear?
IF SHE DIDN'T, WHO WOULD?
BEFORE TOHRU WAS AROUND, THEY TOOK IT TO THE CLEANERS.
What's the big deal?
Must be nice to be rich!
3. Did Shigure buy the maid outfit at Ayame's shop?
GOOD QUESTION! I THINK I'LL WRITE ABOUT AYAME'S SHOP EVENTUALLY, SO YOU'LL HAVE TO WAIT TO FIND OUT MORE.
It's not a kinky cosplay club.
4. What does Tohru do when she's on her period?
TOHRU HAS THE SECOND FLOOR BATHROOM TO HERSELF.
BUT, YOU KNOW, YOU SHOULDN'T WORRY ABOUT SUCH THINGS WHEN YOU'RE READING MANGA!
I did accidentally draw Kyo in it once.
It never ends...
5. How are you going to end the series?
HOW CAN YOU ASK ME THAT...?

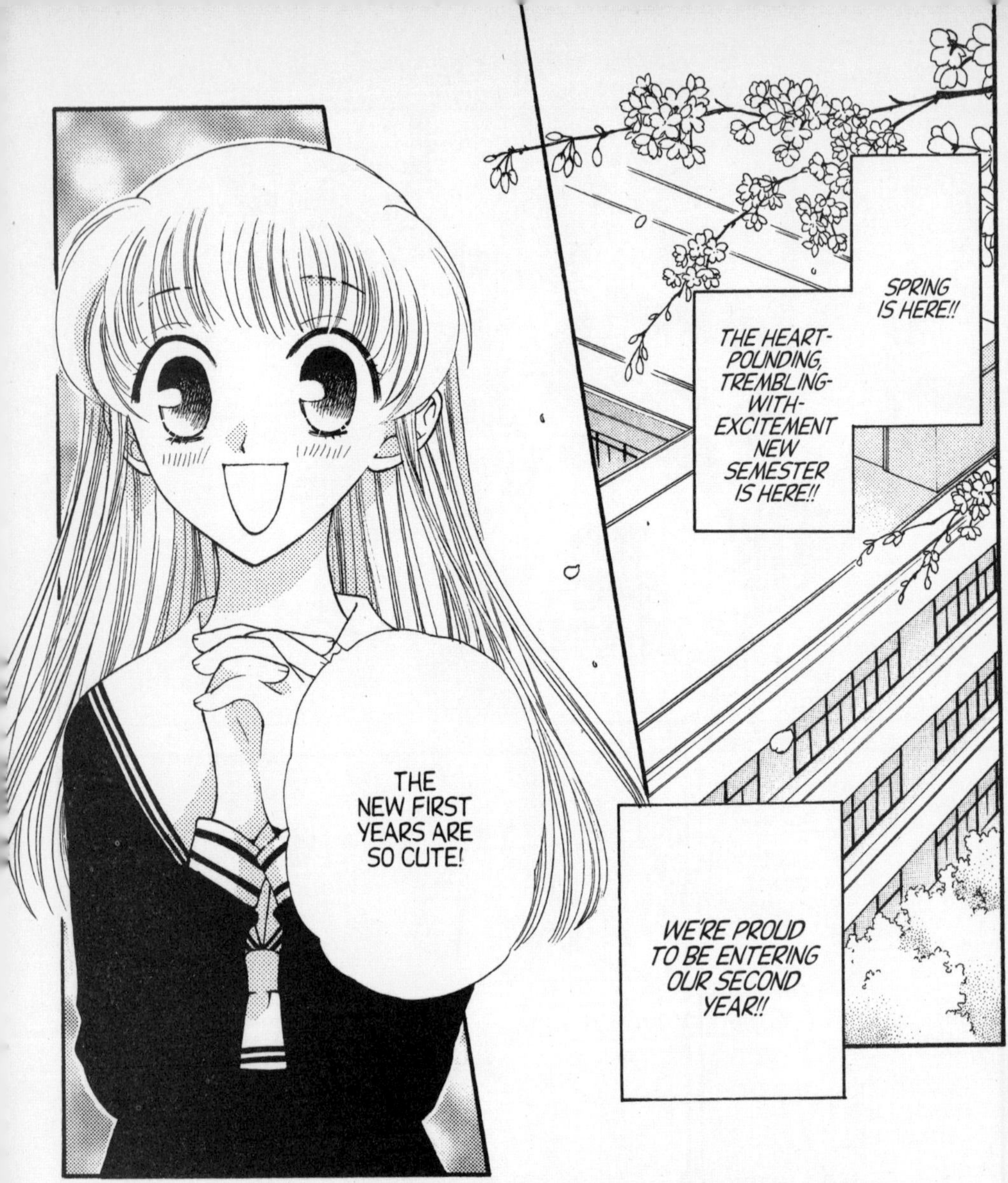
SPRING IS HERE!!
THE HEART-POUNDING, TREMBLING-WITH-EXCITEMENT NEW SEMESTER IS HERE!!
WE'RE PROUD TO BE ENTERING OUR SECOND YEAR!!
THE NEW FIRST YEARS ARE SO CUTE!

ULTRA SPECIAL BLAH BLAH BLAH 1

I forgot to mention it last time, but starting with volume 3, there will be character introductions and summaries at the beginning of each volume. I mean, there already are! I meant to do it earlier, but I just didn't have the time. At last, another Takaya dream is realized! (ha ha!)

NOTE: These features were added in Vol. 2 of the English edition.

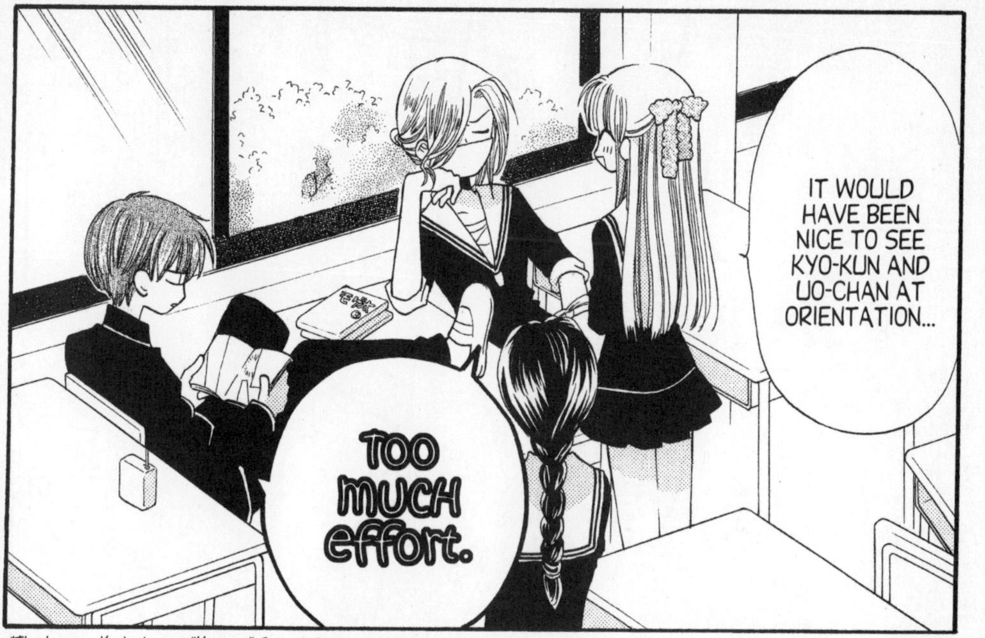
IT WOULD HAVE BEEN NICE TO SEE KYO-KUN AND UO-CHAN AT ORIENTATION...
TOO MUCH effort.

*The book on Kyo's desk is "Mogeta." See vol. 3.

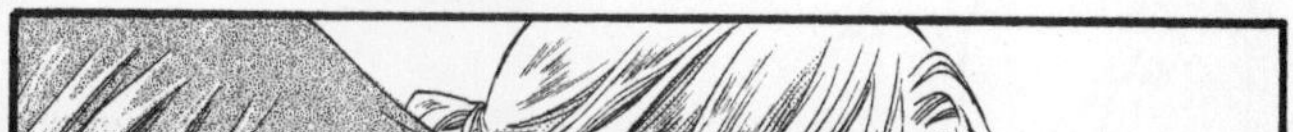
sigh
AND EVEN IF IT WASN'T, THERE'S TOO MUCH POLLEN OUTSIDE.
IF I HAD TO SIT STILL OUT THERE, I'D GO NUTS.
JUST TAKE A PILL.

So close the window!

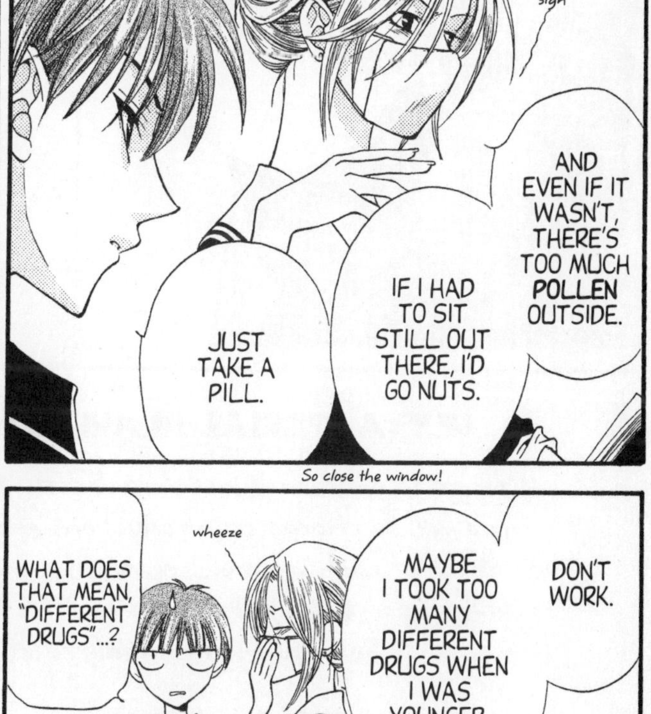
DON'T WORK.
MAYBE I TOOK TOO MANY DIFFERENT DRUGS WHEN I WAS YOUNGER.
wheeze
WHAT DOES THAT MEAN, "DIFFERENT DRUGS"...?

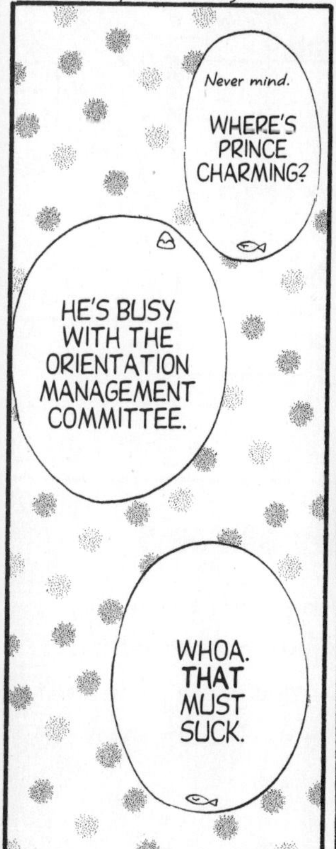
Never mind.
WHERE'S PRINCE CHARMING?
HE'S BUSY WITH THE ORIENTATION MANAGEMENT COMMITTEE.
WHOA. THAT MUST SUCK.

Fruits Basket 4 Part 1:

Hajimemashite! (That's Japanese for "how do you do.") Takaya here. Furuba has made it to volume 4! As each volume is released, the big picture starts to reveal itself. Until now, I've had to keep my gloating to myself! It feels so much better to let it out! (Ha!) But "Guretchi." Guretchi the jellyfish: I keep getting letters begging, "please say he isn't over 25!" Sorry. Shigure is 27. Don't worry--a man's stock only goes up as he gets older! Oh yeah, Shigure's name is pronounced without an accent--the intonation doesn't go up **or** down. So now you know. Okay, as usual I'm exhausted, but Furuba is raring to go--so let's get on with it!

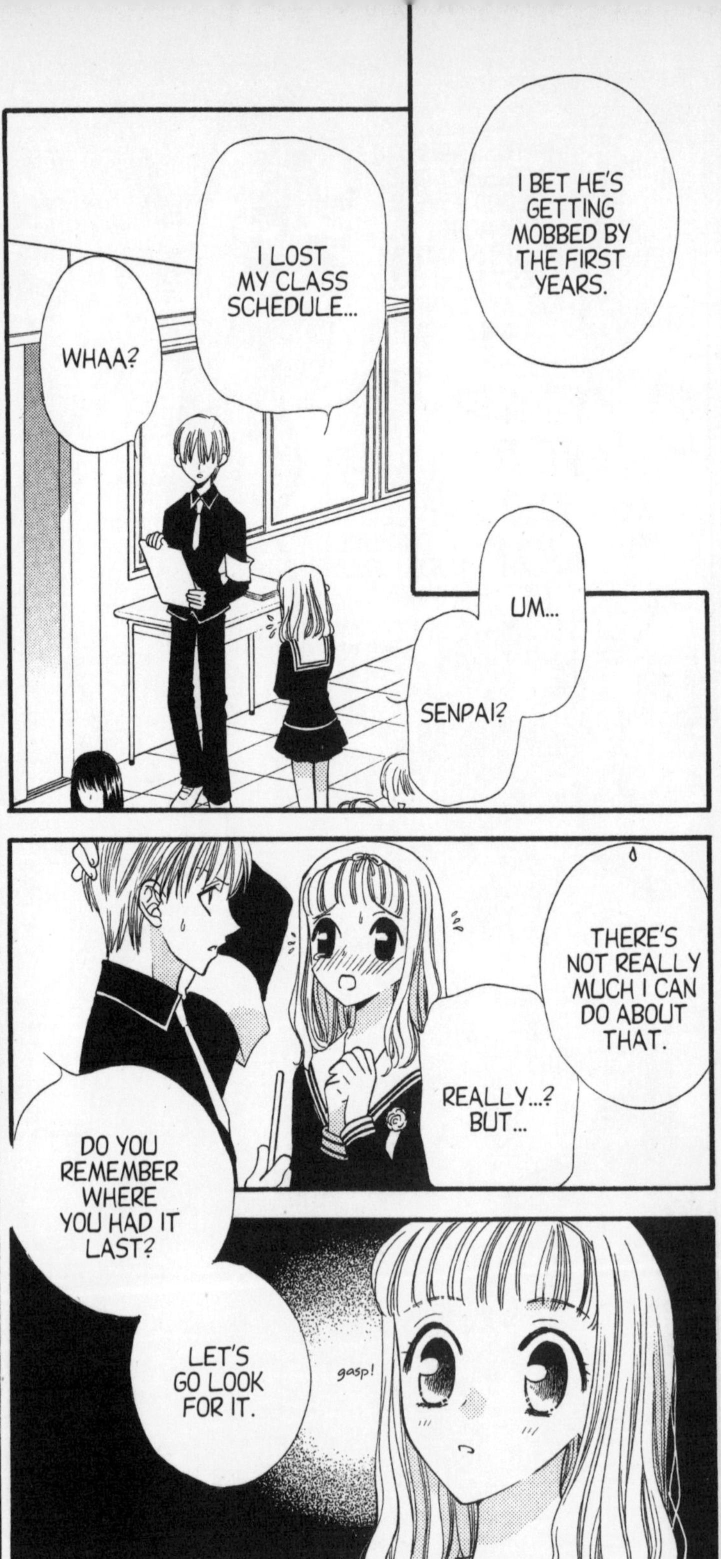

I BET HE'S GETTING MOBBED BY THE FIRST YEARS.
I LOST MY CLASS SCHEDULE...
WHAA?
UM... SENPAI?
THERE'S NOT REALLY MUCH I CAN DO ABOUT THAT.
REALLY...? BUT...
DO YOU REMEMBER WHERE YOU HAD IT LAST?
LET'S GO LOOK FOR IT.
gasp!

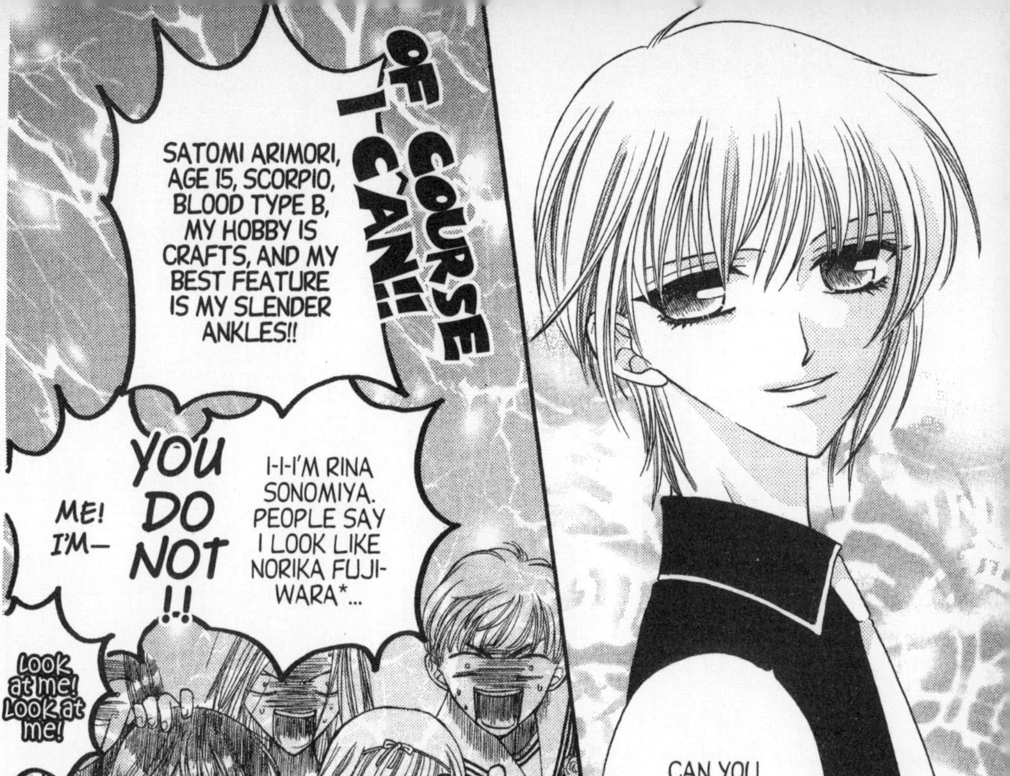
CAN YOU TELL ME YOUR NAME AND WHICH CLASS YOU'RE IN?
OF COURSE I—CAN!!
SATOMI ARIMORI, AGE 15, SCORPIO, BLOOD TYPE B, MY HOBBY IS CRAFTS, AND MY BEST FEATURE IS MY SLENDER ANKLES!!
I-I-I'M RINA SONOMIYA. PEOPLE SAY I LOOK LIKE NORIKA FUJI-WARA*...
YOU DO NOT!!
ME! I'M—
Look at me! Look at me!
I'M TOO FREAKED OUT TO BE JEALOUS, SOHMA...

* A famous actress who starred in the GTO drama, she's also a model. Her official web site is: www.norikanesque.com

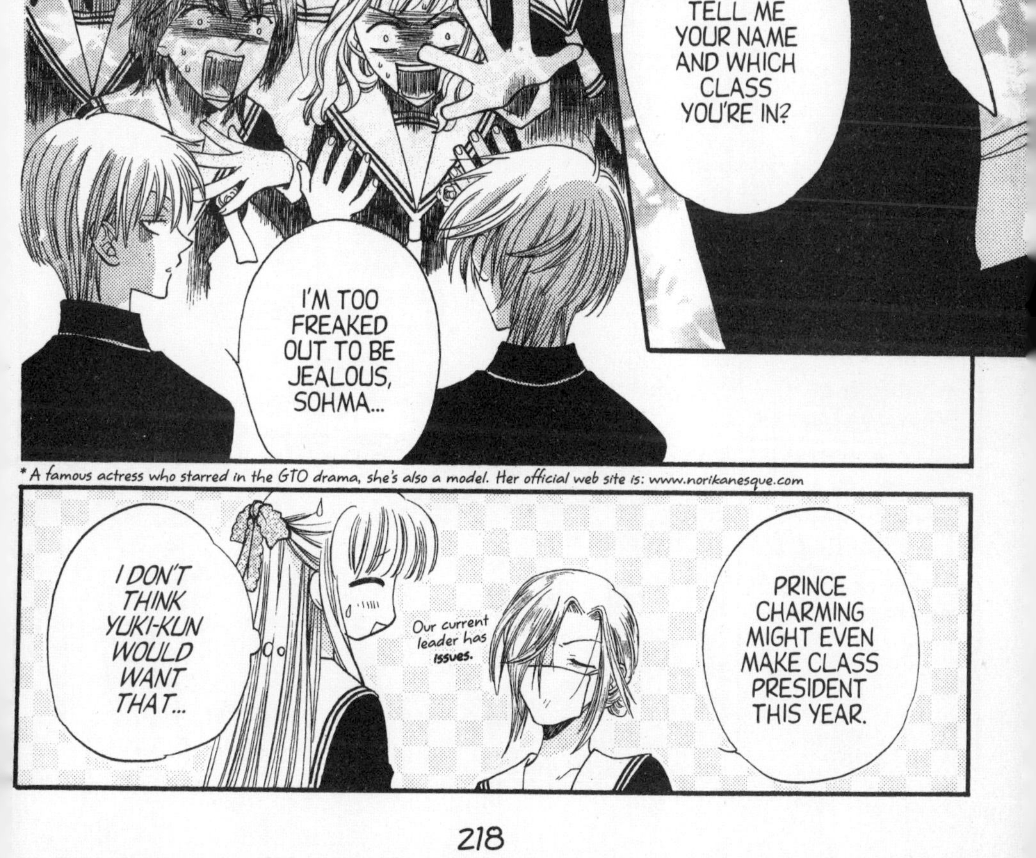
PRINCE CHARMING MIGHT EVEN MAKE CLASS PRESIDENT THIS YEAR.
Our current leader has issues.
I DON'T THINK YUKI-KUN WOULD WANT THAT...

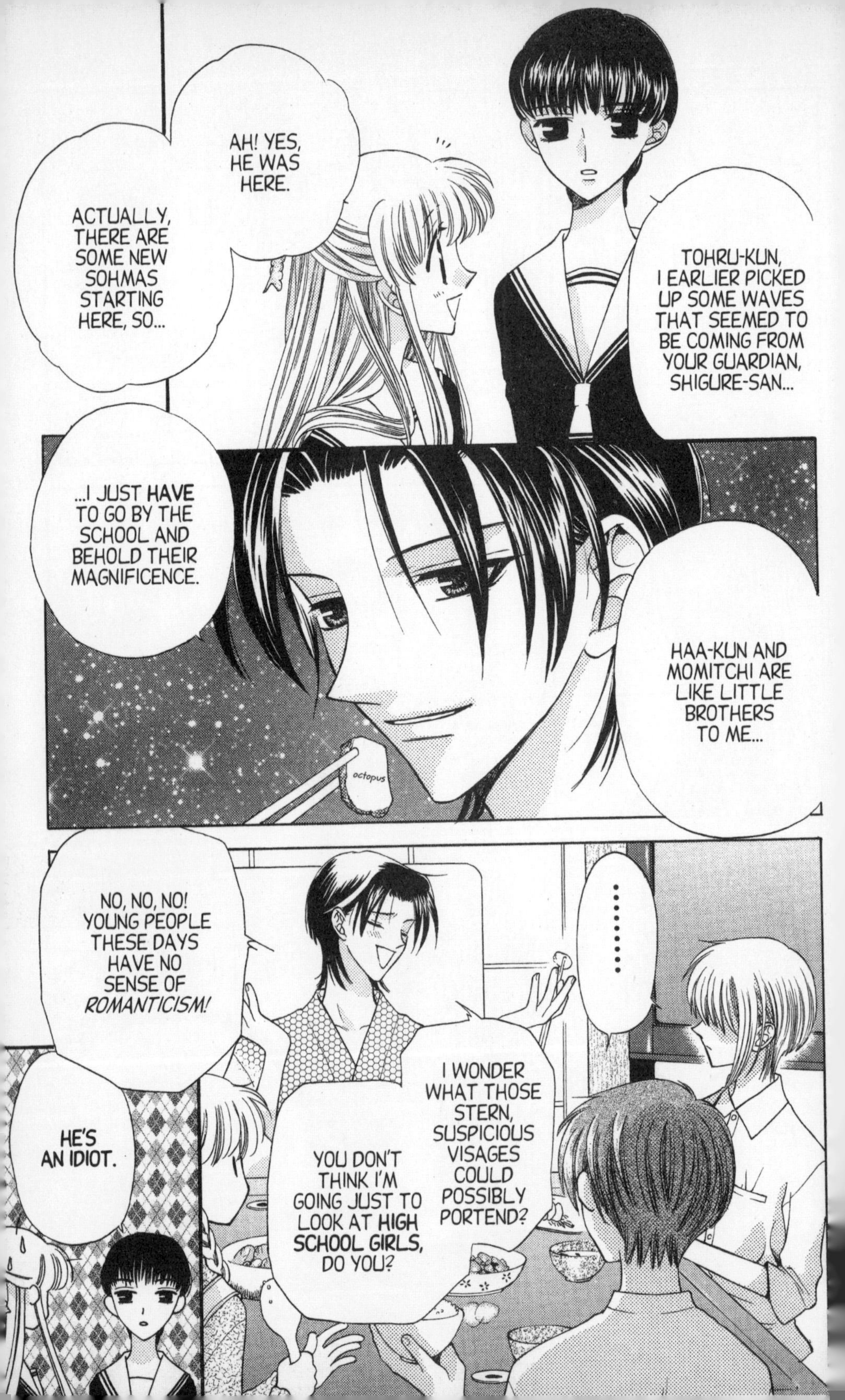
TOHRU-KUN, I EARLIER PICKED UP SOME WAVES THAT SEEMED TO BE COMING FROM YOUR GUARDIAN, SHIGURE-SAN...
AH! YES, HE WAS HERE.
ACTUALLY, THERE ARE SOME NEW SOHMAS STARTING HERE, SO...
HAA-KUN AND MOMITCHI ARE LIKE LITTLE BROTHERS TO ME...
...I JUST **HAVE** TO GO BY THE SCHOOL AND BEHOLD THEIR MAGNIFICENCE.
octopus
......
I WONDER WHAT THOSE STERN, SUSPICIOUS VISAGES COULD POSSIBLY PORTEND?
NO, NO, NO! YOUNG PEOPLE THESE DAYS HAVE NO SENSE OF *ROMANTICISM!*
YOU DON'T THINK I'M GOING JUST TO LOOK AT **HIGH SCHOOL GIRLS**, DO YOU?
HE'S AN IDIOT.

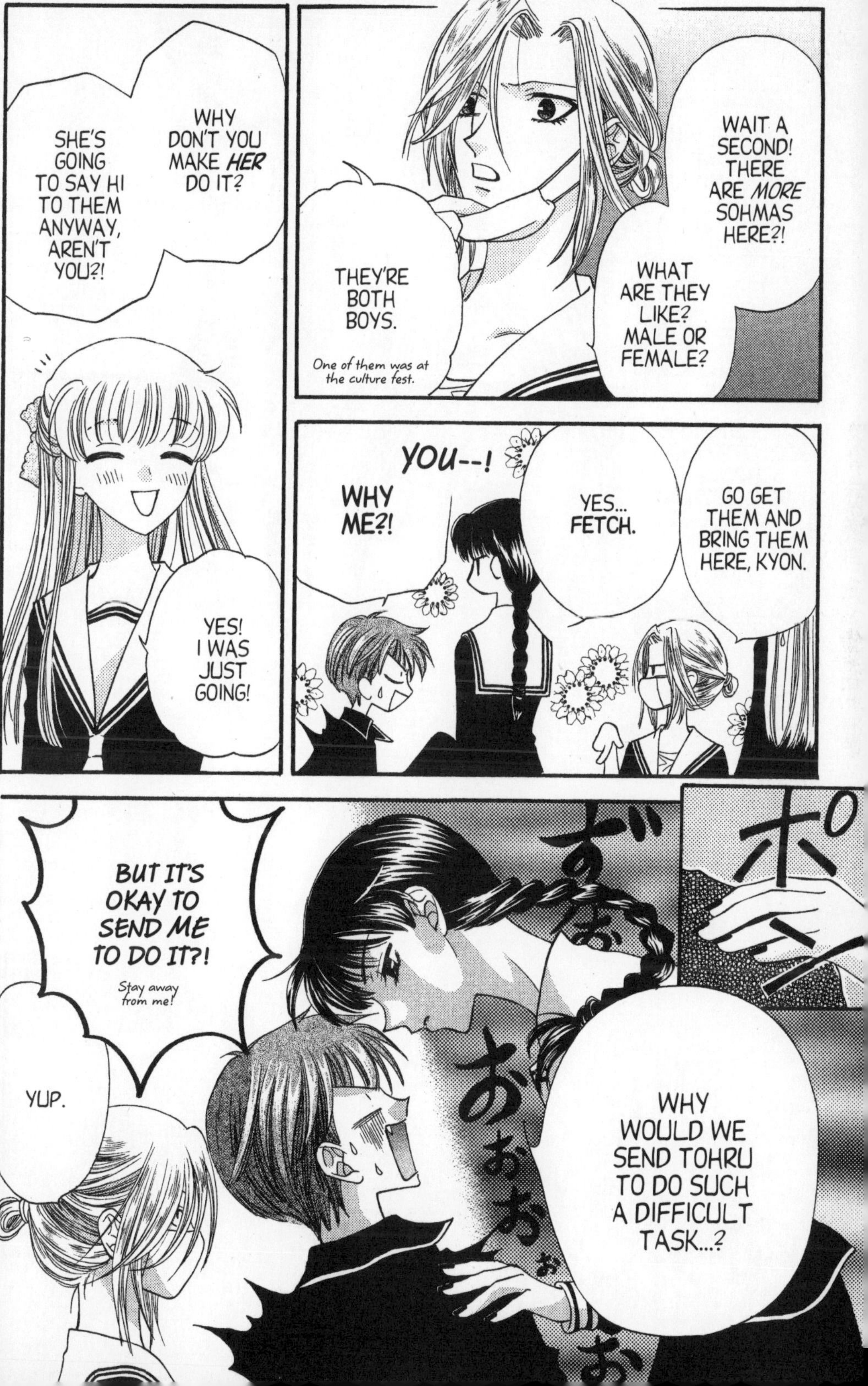
WAIT A SECOND! THERE ARE *MORE* SOHMAS HERE?!
WHAT ARE THEY LIKE? MALE OR FEMALE?
THEY'RE BOTH BOYS.
One of them was at the culture fest.
GO GET THEM AND BRING THEM HERE, KYON.
YES... FETCH.
WHY ME?!
YOU--!
WHY DON'T YOU MAKE *HER* DO IT?
SHE'S GOING TO SAY HI TO THEM ANYWAY, AREN'T YOU?!
YES! I WAS JUST GOING!
WHY WOULD WE SEND TOHRU TO DO SUCH A DIFFICULT TASK...?
BUT IT'S OKAY TO SEND ME TO DO IT?!
Stay away from me!
YUP.

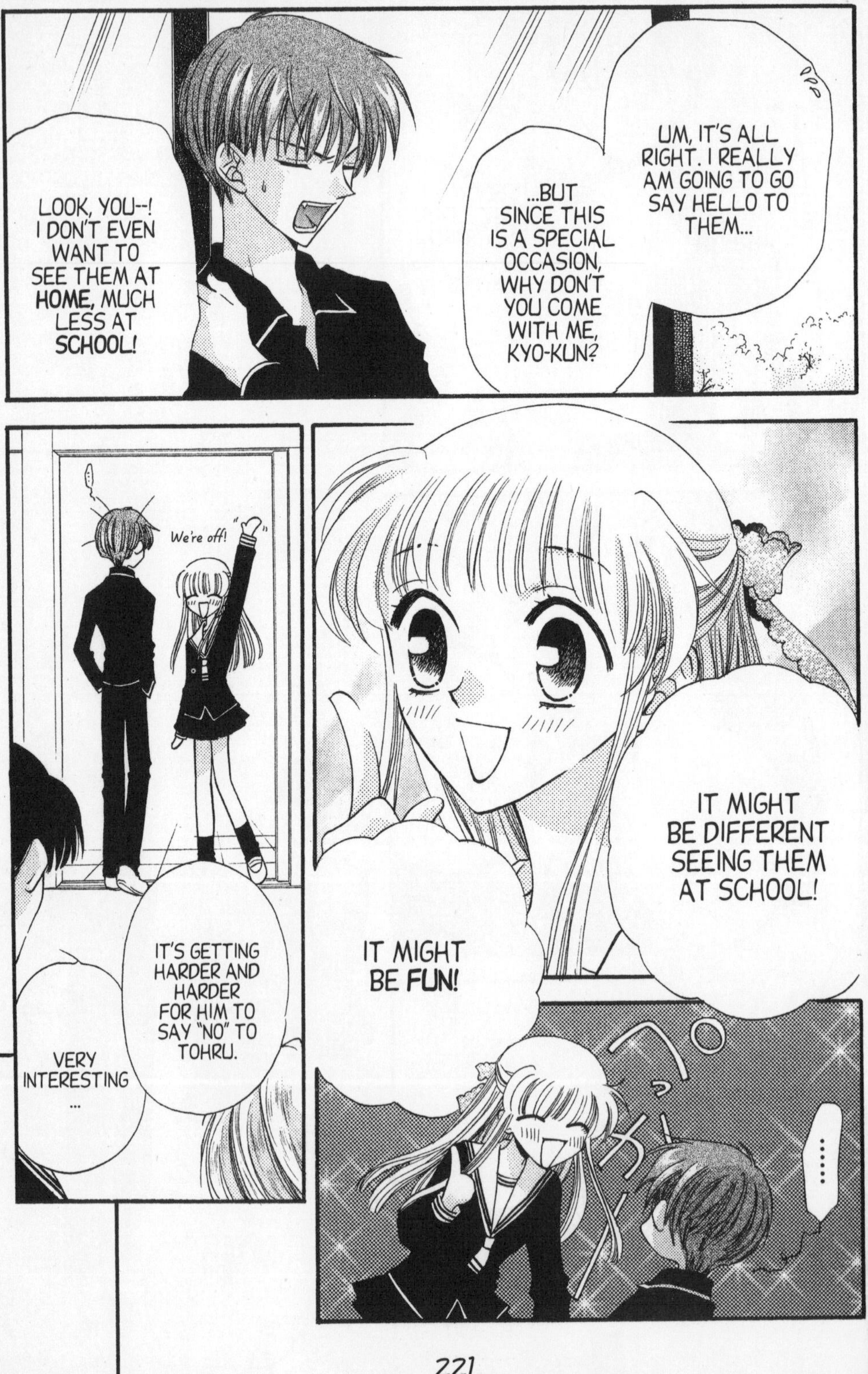
UM, IT'S ALL RIGHT. I REALLY AM GOING TO GO SAY HELLO TO THEM...
...BUT SINCE THIS IS A SPECIAL OCCASION, WHY DON'T YOU COME WITH ME, KYO-KUN?
LOOK, YOU--! I DON'T EVEN WANT TO SEE THEM AT HOME, MUCH LESS AT SCHOOL!
IT MIGHT BE DIFFERENT SEEING THEM AT SCHOOL!
IT MIGHT BE FUN!
......
!
We're off!
IT'S GETTING HARDER AND HARDER FOR HIM TO SAY "NO" TO TOHRU.
VERY INTERESTING ...

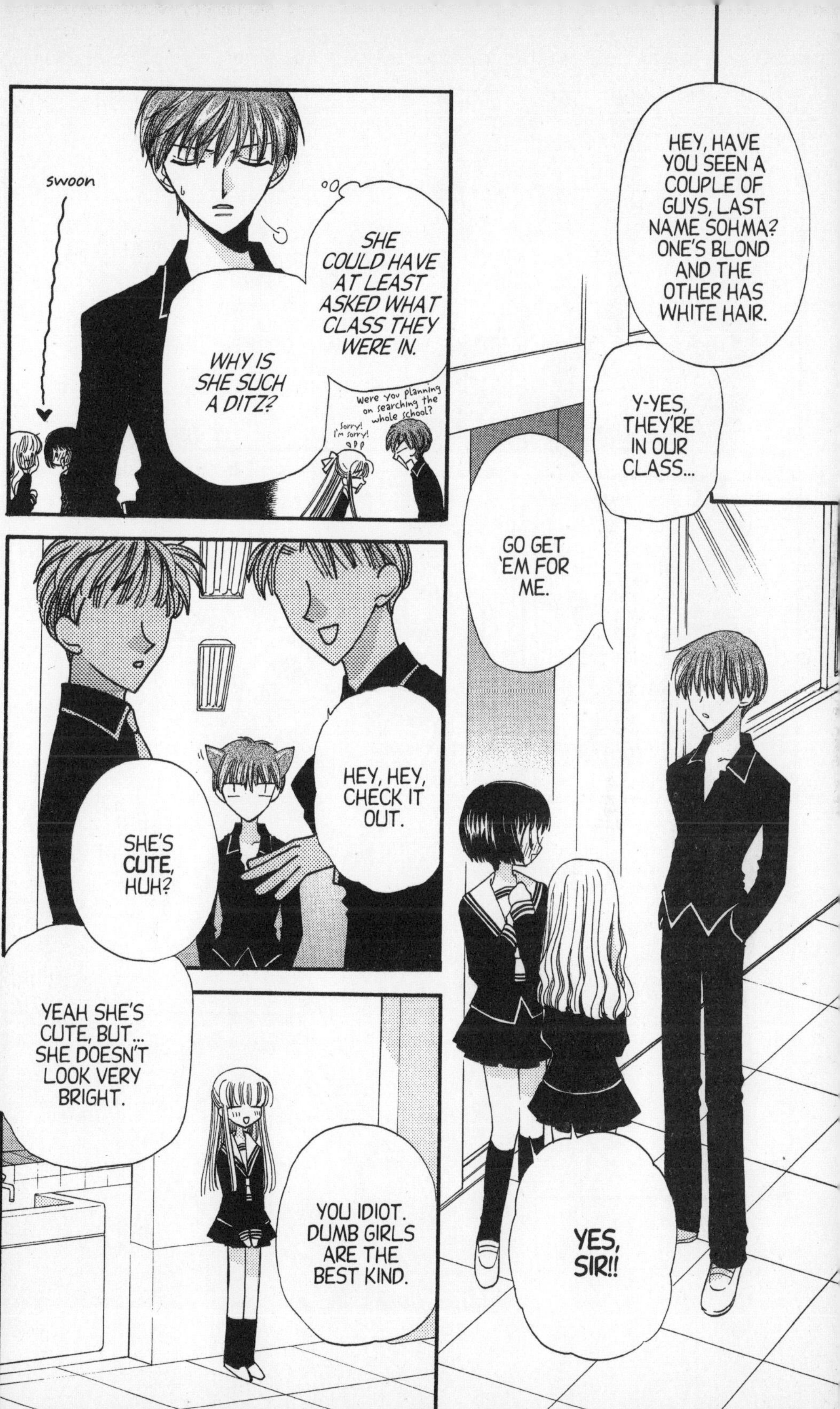
HEY, HAVE YOU SEEN A COUPLE OF GUYS, LAST NAME SOHMA? ONE'S BLOND AND THE OTHER HAS WHITE HAIR.
Y-YES, THEY'RE IN OUR CLASS...
GO GET 'EM FOR ME.
YES, SIR!!
swoon
SHE COULD HAVE AT LEAST ASKED WHAT CLASS THEY WERE IN.
WHY IS SHE SUCH A DITZ?
Were you planning on searching the whole school?
Sorry! I'm sorry!
HEY, HEY, CHECK IT OUT.
SHE'S CUTE, HUH?
YEAH SHE'S CUTE, BUT... SHE DOESN'T LOOK VERY BRIGHT.
YOU IDIOT. DUMB GIRLS ARE THE BEST KIND.

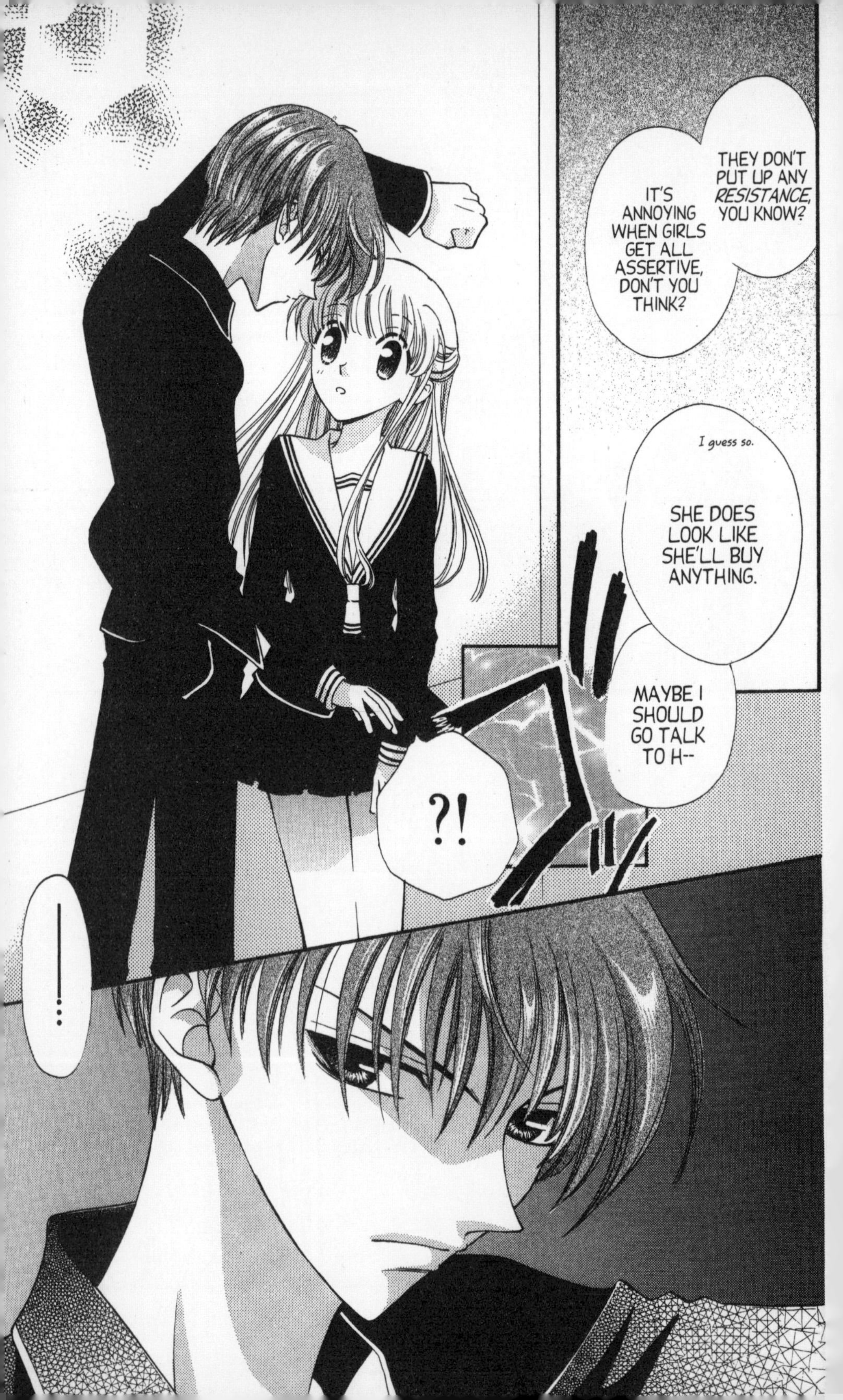
THEY DON'T PUT UP ANY *RESISTANCE*, YOU KNOW?
IT'S ANNOYING WHEN GIRLS GET ALL ASSERTIVE, DON'T YOU THINK?
I guess so.
SHE DOES LOOK LIKE SHE'LL BUY ANYTHING.
MAYBE I SHOULD GO TALK TO H--
?!
...!

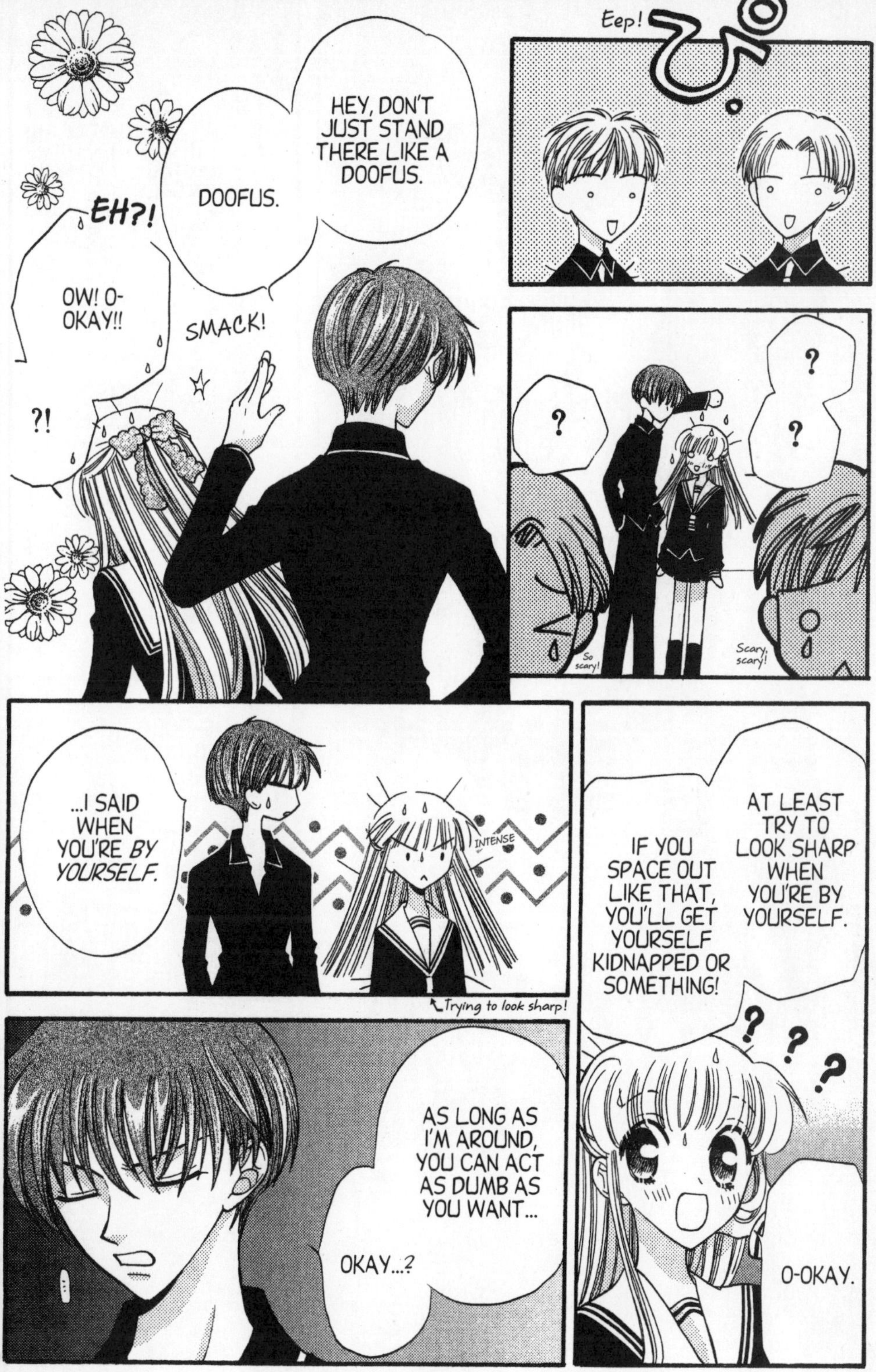
Eep!
?
?
?
Scary, scary!
So scary!
HEY, DON'T JUST STAND THERE LIKE A DOOFUS.
DOOFUS.
EH?!
SMACK!
OW! O-OKAY!!
?!
AT LEAST TRY TO LOOK SHARP WHEN YOU'RE BY YOURSELF.
IF YOU SPACE OUT LIKE THAT, YOU'LL GET YOURSELF KIDNAPPED OR SOMETHING!
? ? ?
O-OKAY.
INTENSE
...I SAID WHEN YOU'RE *BY YOURSELF*.
Trying to look sharp!
AS LONG AS I'M AROUND, YOU CAN ACT AS DUMB AS YOU WANT...
OKAY...?
...

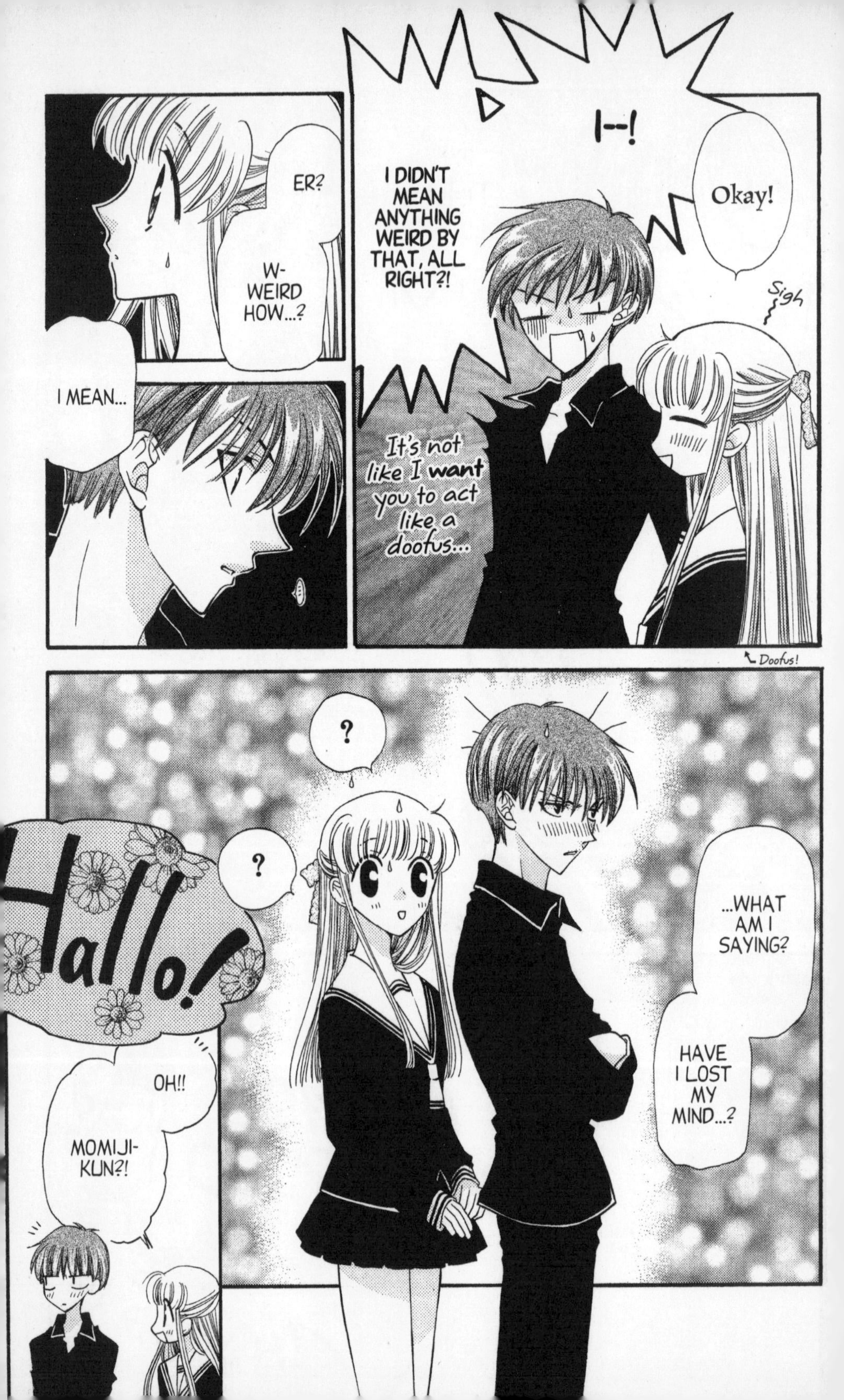
I--!
I DIDN'T MEAN ANYTHING WEIRD BY THAT, ALL RIGHT?!
Okay!
Sigh
It's not like I want you to act like a doofus...
Doofus!
ER?
W-WEIRD HOW...?
I MEAN...
...WHAT AM I SAYING?
HAVE I LOST MY MIND...?
?
?
Hallo!
OH!!
MOMIJI-KUN?!

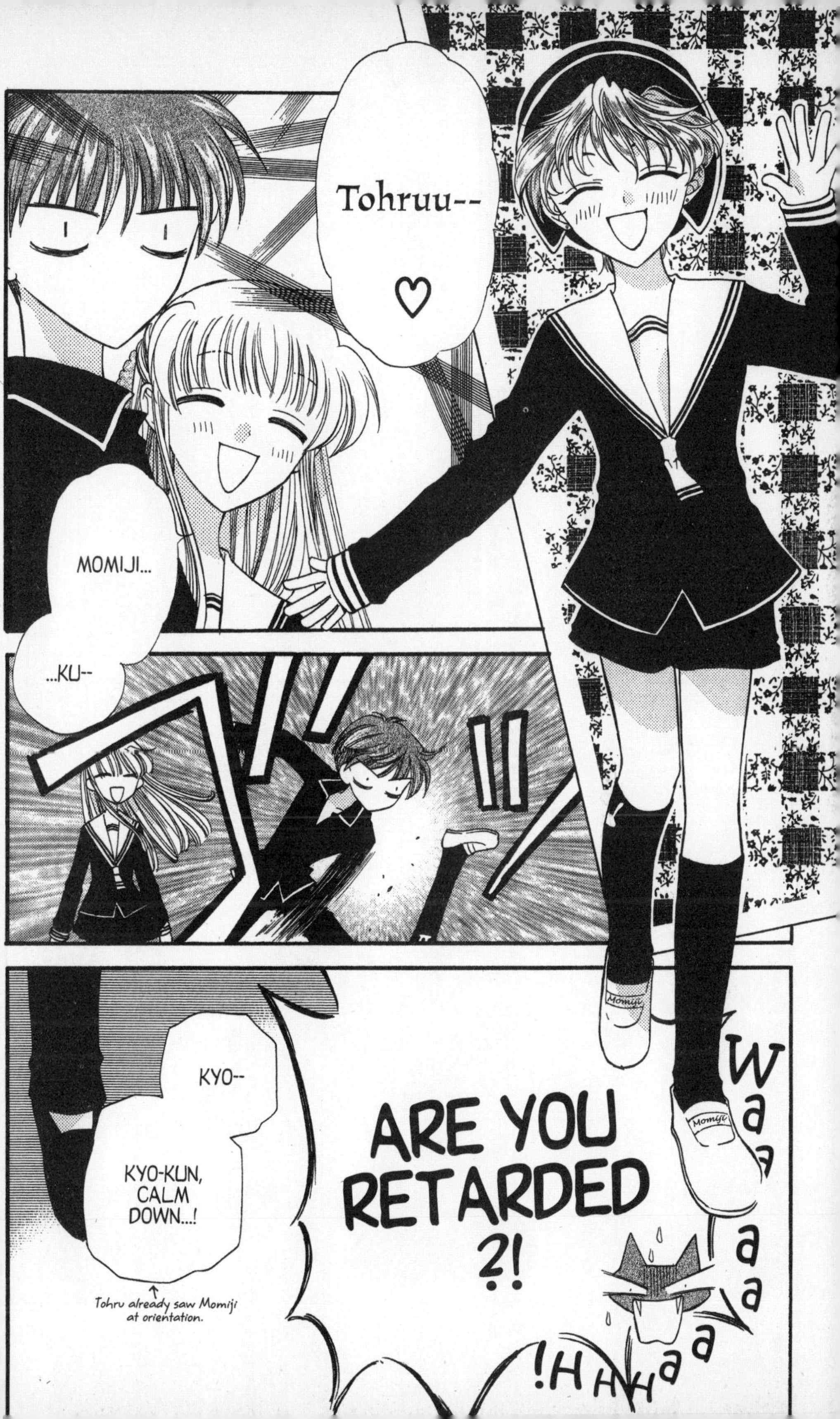
Tohruu-- ♡
MOMIJI...
...KU--
WaaaaaaaHHH!
ARE YOU RETARDED?!
KYO--
KYO-KUN, CALM DOWN...!
Tohru already saw Momiji at orientation.

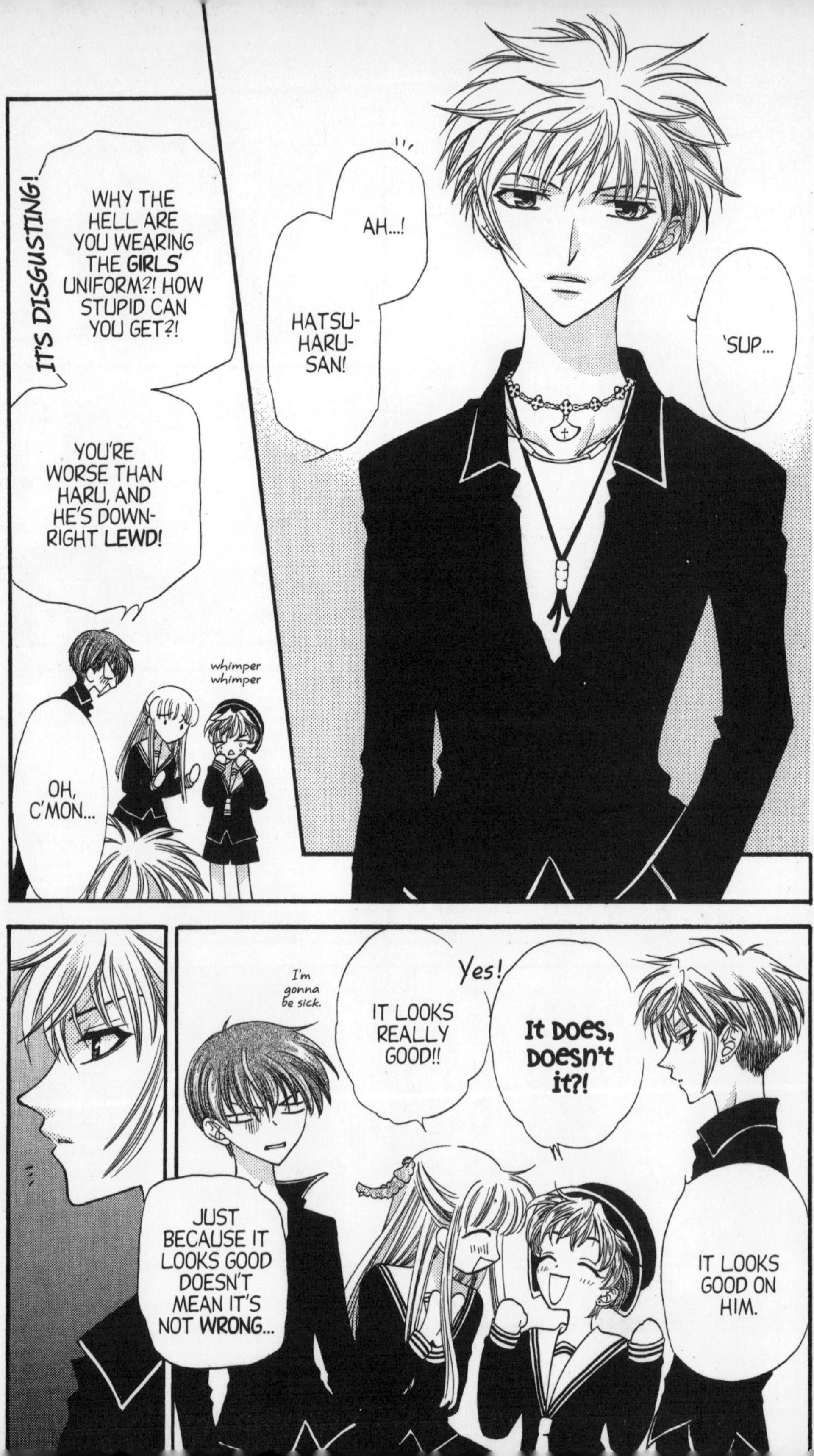
AH...!
HATSU-HARU-SAN!
'SUP...
WHY THE HELL ARE YOU WEARING THE GIRLS' UNIFORM?! HOW STUPID CAN YOU GET?!
IT'S DISGUSTING!
YOU'RE WORSE THAN HARU, AND HE'S DOWN-RIGHT LEWD!
whimper whimper
OH, C'MON...
IT LOOKS GOOD ON HIM.
It DOES, DOESN'T it?!
Yes!
IT LOOKS REALLY GOOD!!
I'm gonna be sick.
JUST BECAUSE IT LOOKS GOOD DOESN'T MEAN IT'S NOT WRONG...

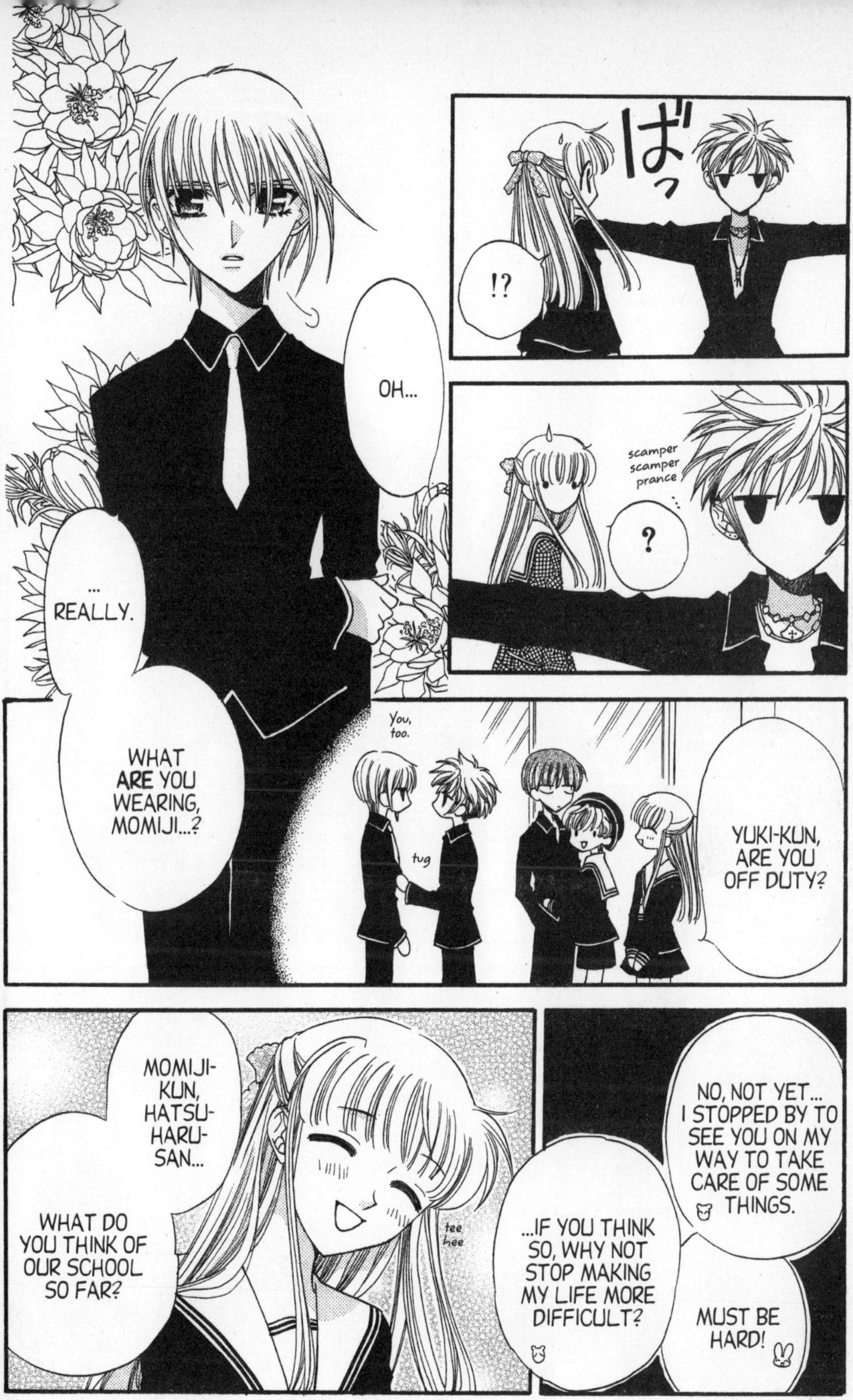
ばっ
!?
scamper scamper prance
...
?
OH...
...REALLY.
WHAT ARE YOU WEARING, MOMIJI...?
YUKI-KUN, ARE YOU OFF DUTY?
You, too.
tug
NO, NOT YET... I STOPPED BY TO SEE YOU ON MY WAY TO TAKE CARE OF SOME THINGS.
MUST BE HARD!
...IF YOU THINK SO, WHY NOT STOP MAKING MY LIFE MORE DIFFICULT?
MOMIJI-KUN, HATSU-HARU-SAN...
tee hee
WHAT DO YOU THINK OF OUR SCHOOL SO FAR?

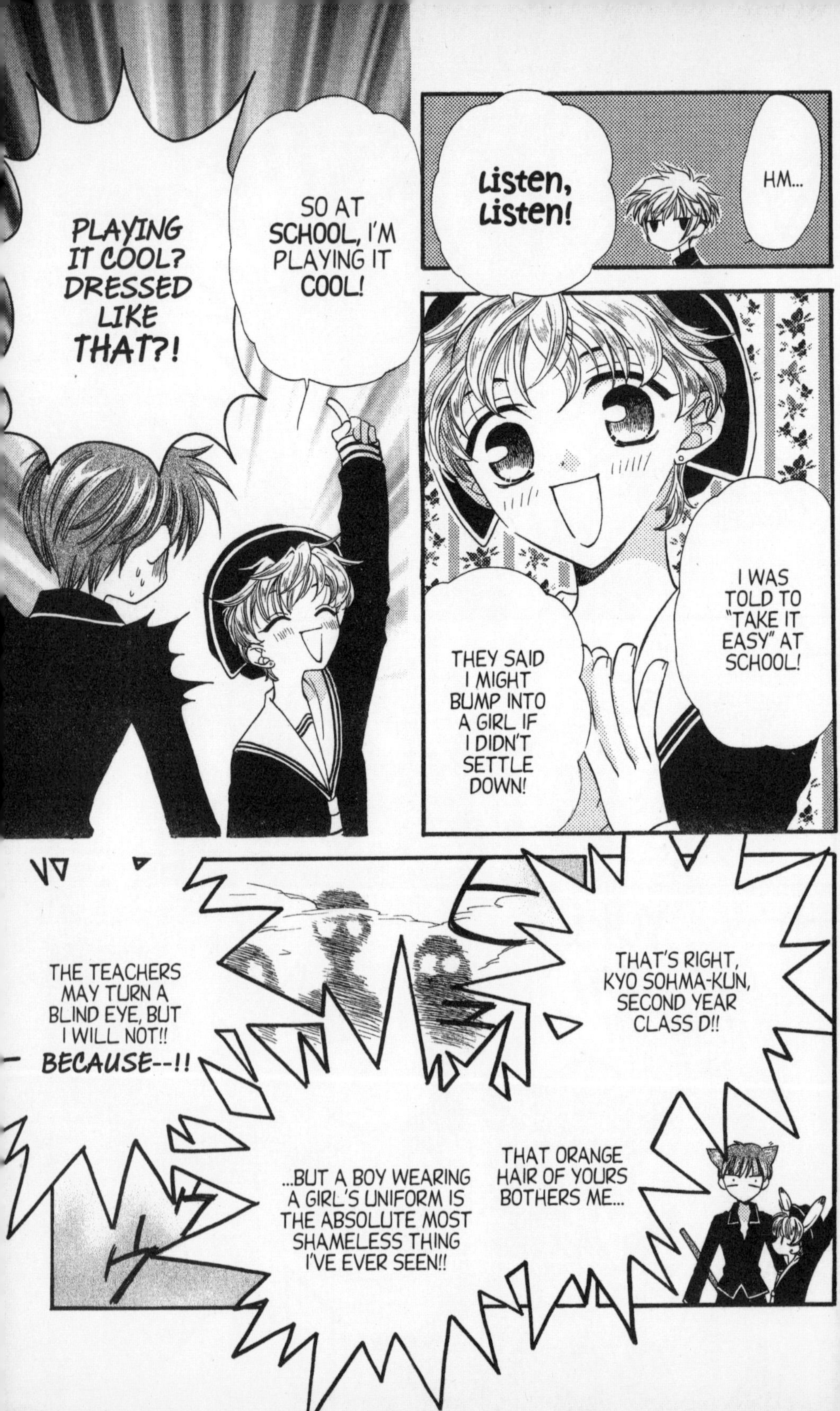
HM...
Listen, Listen!
I WAS TOLD TO "TAKE IT EASY" AT SCHOOL!
THEY SAID I MIGHT BUMP INTO A GIRL IF I DIDN'T SETTLE DOWN!
SO AT SCHOOL, I'M PLAYING IT COOL!
PLAYING IT COOL? DRESSED LIKE THAT?!
THAT'S RIGHT, KYO SOHMA-KUN, SECOND YEAR CLASS D!!
THE TEACHERS MAY TURN A BLIND EYE, BUT I WILL NOT!! BECAUSE--!!
THAT ORANGE HAIR OF YOURS BOTHERS ME...
...BUT A BOY WEARING A GIRL'S UNIFORM IS THE ABSOLUTE MOST SHAMELESS THING I'VE EVER SEEN!!

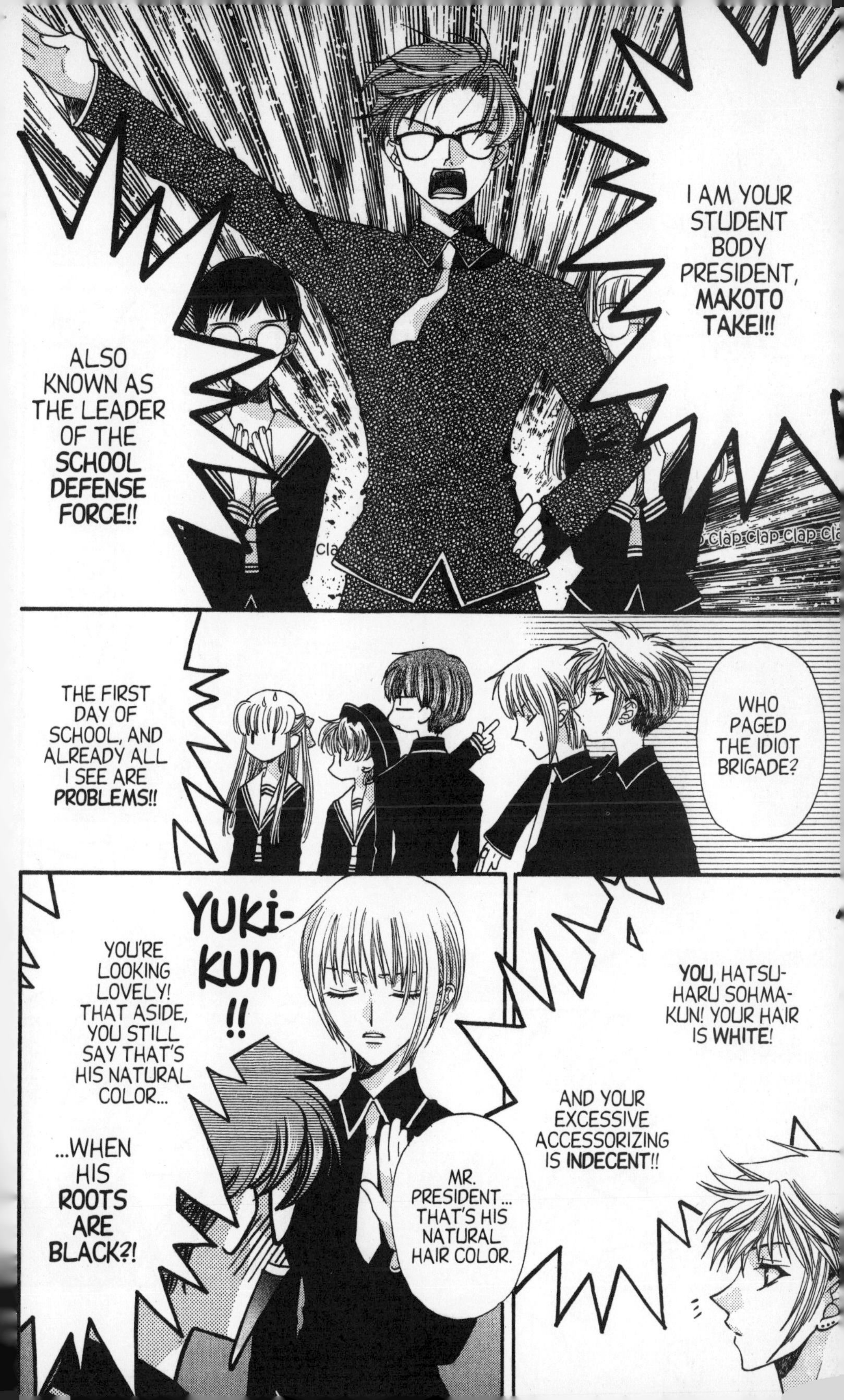
I AM YOUR STUDENT BODY PRESIDENT, MAKOTO TAKEI!!
ALSO KNOWN AS THE LEADER OF THE SCHOOL DEFENSE FORCE!!
WHO PAGED THE IDIOT BRIGADE?
THE FIRST DAY OF SCHOOL, AND ALREADY ALL I SEE ARE PROBLEMS!!
YOU, HATSUHARU SOHMA-KUN! YOUR HAIR IS WHITE!
AND YOUR EXCESSIVE ACCESSORIZING IS INDECENT!!
MR. PRESIDENT... THAT'S HIS NATURAL HAIR COLOR.
YUKI-KUN!!
YOU'RE LOOKING LOVELY! THAT ASIDE, YOU STILL SAY THAT'S HIS NATURAL COLOR...
...WHEN HIS ROOTS ARE BLACK?!

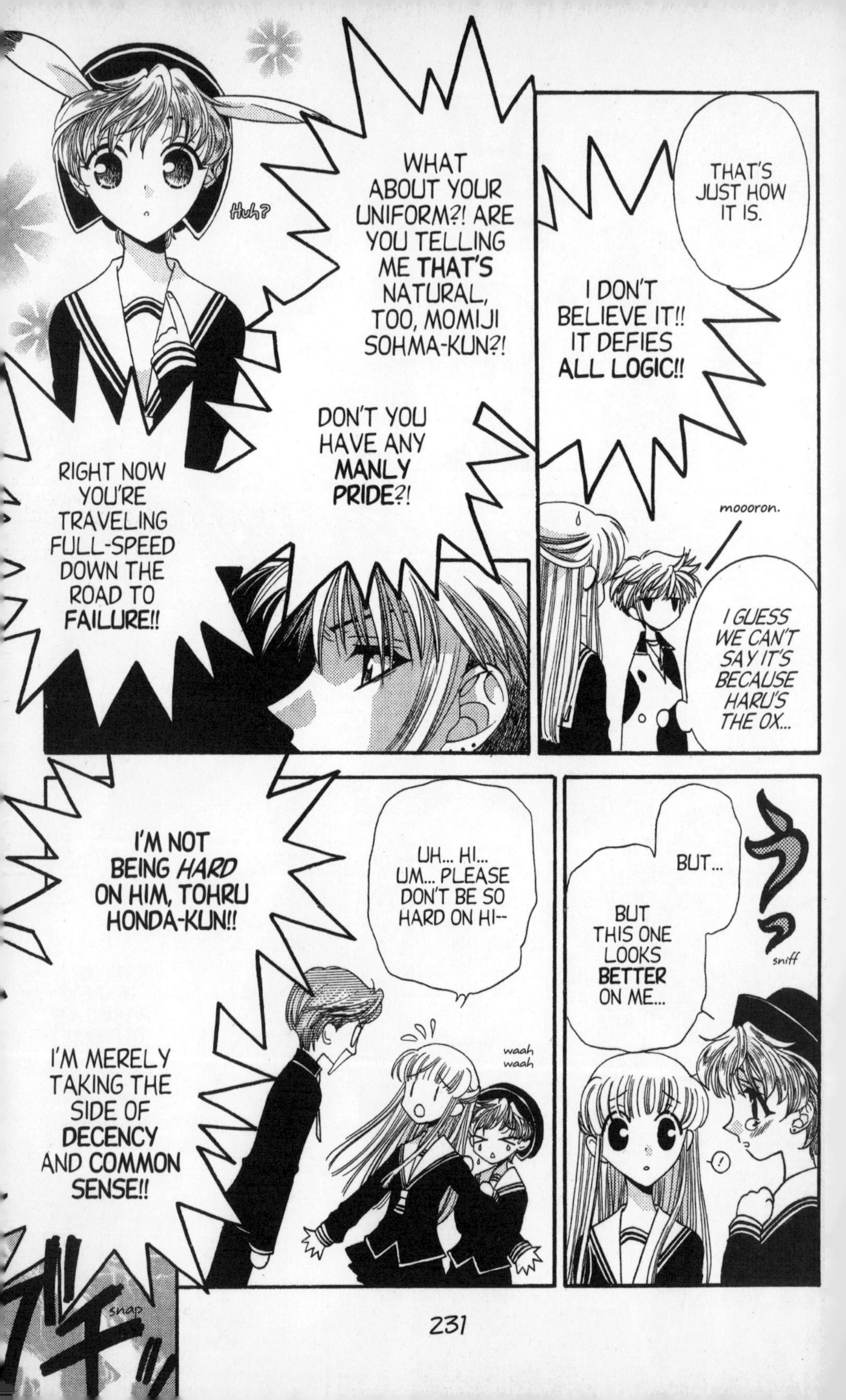

THAT'S JUST HOW IT IS.
I DON'T BELIEVE IT!! IT DEFIES **ALL LOGIC!!**
moooron.
I GUESS WE CAN'T SAY IT'S BECAUSE HARU'S THE OX...
WHAT ABOUT YOUR UNIFORM?! ARE YOU TELLING ME **THAT'S** NATURAL, TOO, MOMIJI SOHMA-KUN?!
Huh?
DON'T YOU HAVE ANY **MANLY PRIDE**?!
RIGHT NOW YOU'RE TRAVELING FULL-SPEED DOWN THE ROAD TO **FAILURE!!**
BUT...
BUT THIS ONE LOOKS **BETTER** ON ME...
sniff
UH... HI... UM... PLEASE DON'T BE SO HARD ON HI--
waah waah
I'M NOT BEING ***HARD*** ON HIM, TOHRU HONDA-KUN!!
I'M MERELY TAKING THE SIDE OF **DECENCY** AND COMMON **SENSE!!**
snap

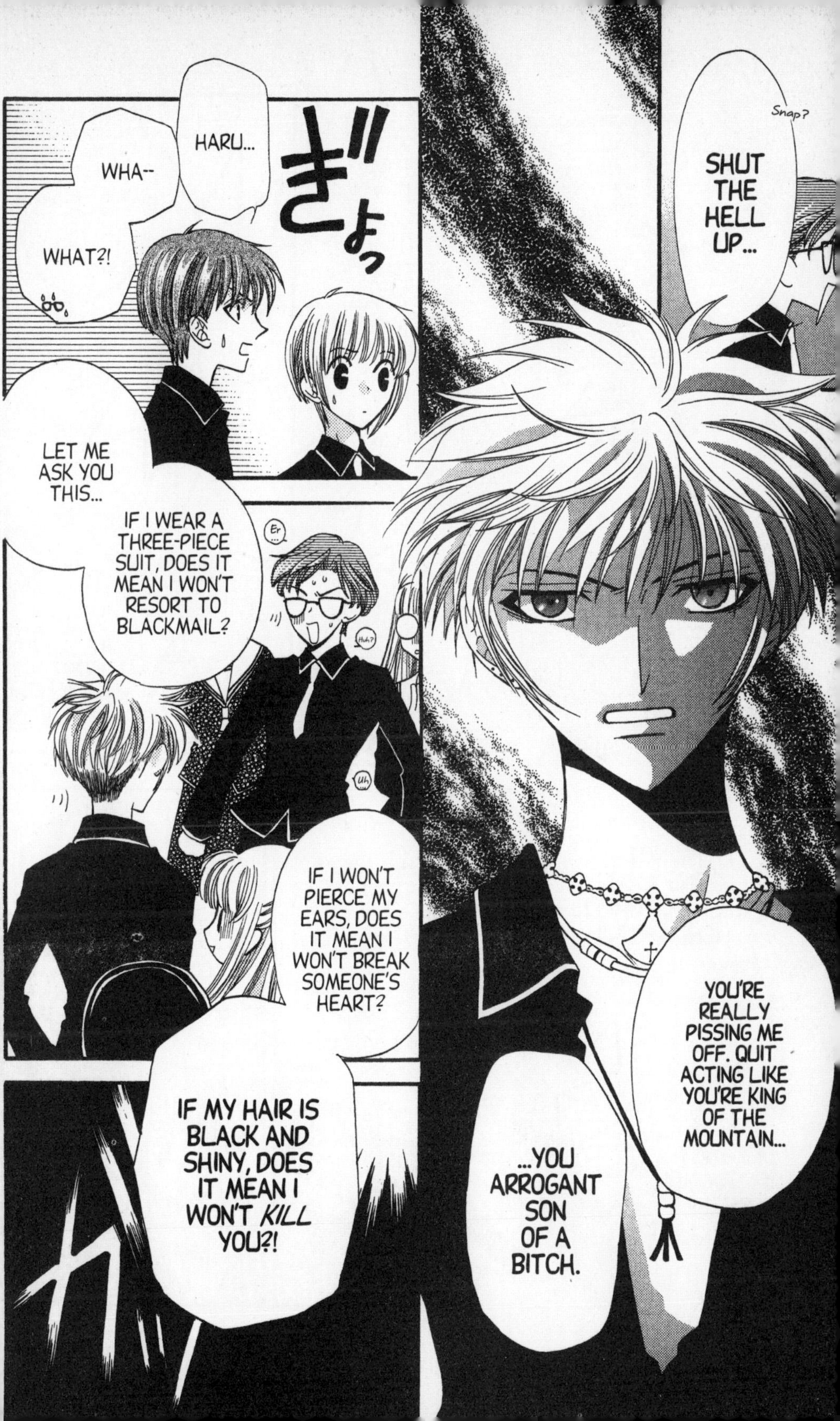
Snap?
SHUT THE HELL UP...
YOU'RE REALLY PISSING ME OFF. QUIT ACTING LIKE YOU'RE KING OF THE MOUNTAIN...
...YOU ARROGANT SON OF A BITCH.
ぎょっ
HARU...
WHA--
WHAT?!
LET ME ASK YOU THIS...
IF I WEAR A THREE-PIECE SUIT, DOES IT MEAN I WON'T RESORT TO BLACKMAIL?
Er...
Huh?
Uh
IF I WON'T PIERCE MY EARS, DOES IT MEAN I WON'T BREAK SOMEONE'S HEART?
IF MY HAIR IS BLACK AND SHINY, DOES IT MEAN I WON'T *KILL* YOU?!

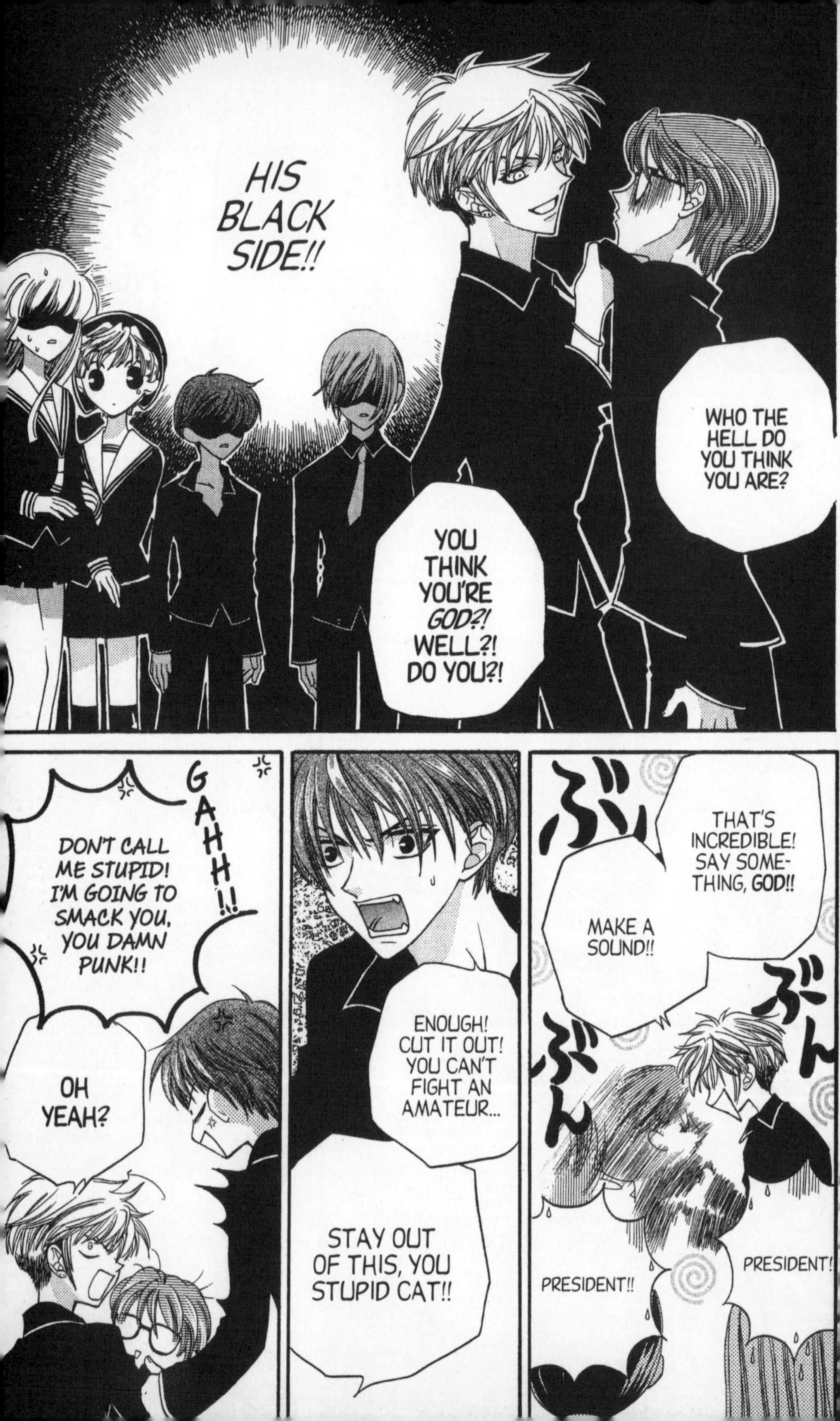
WHO THE HELL DO YOU THINK YOU ARE?
YOU THINK YOU'RE *GOD?!* WELL?! DO YOU?!
HIS BLACK SIDE!!
ぶん
THAT'S INCREDIBLE! SAY SOME-THING, GOD!!
MAKE A SOUND!!
ぶん
ぶん
PRESIDENT!
PRESIDENT!!
ENOUGH! CUT IT OUT! YOU CAN'T FIGHT AN AMATEUR...
STAY OUT OF THIS, YOU STUPID CAT!!
GAHH!!
DON'T CALL ME STUPID! I'M GOING TO SMACK YOU, YOU DAMN PUNK!!
OH YEAH?

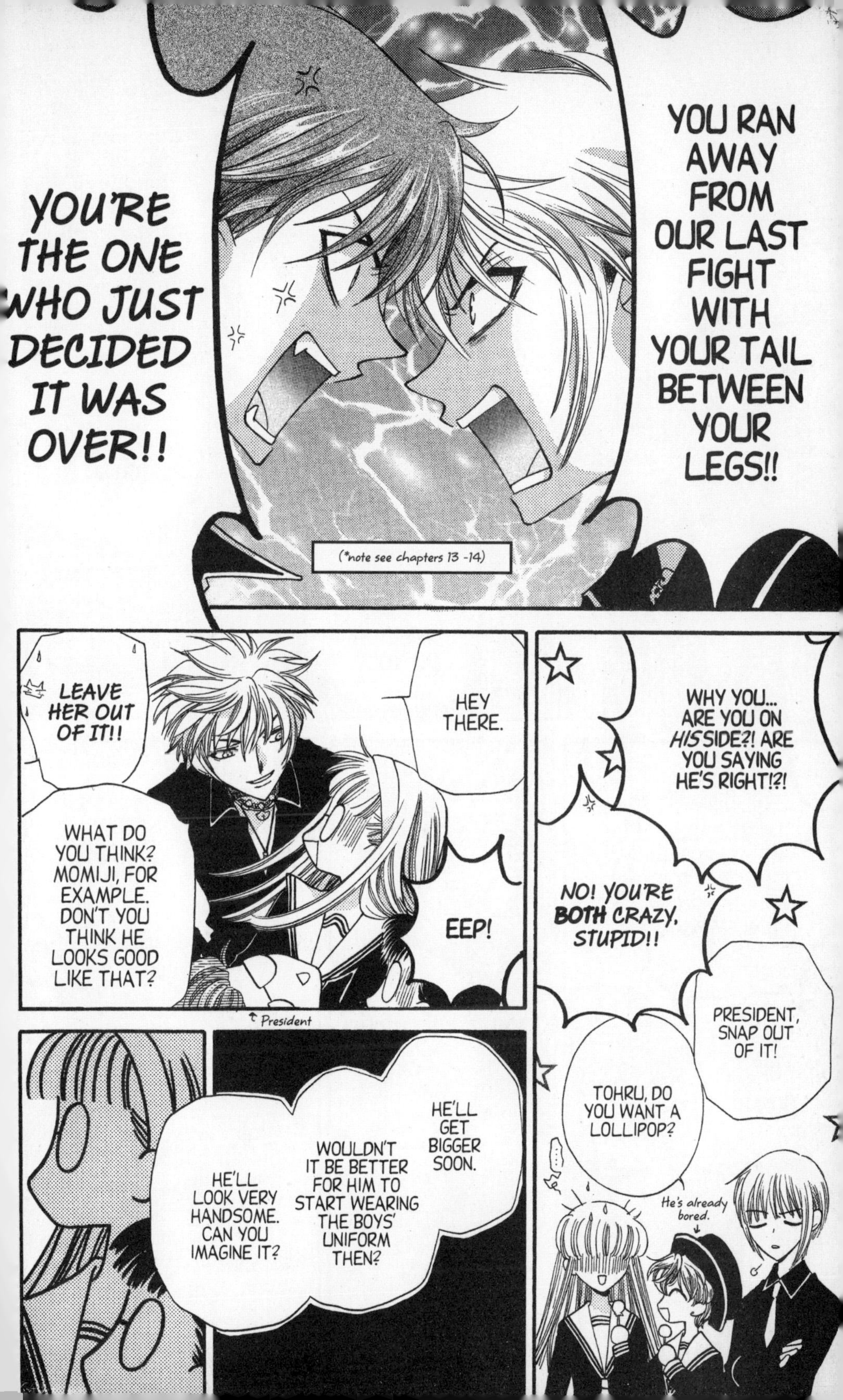
YOU RAN AWAY FROM OUR LAST FIGHT WITH YOUR TAIL BETWEEN YOUR LEGS!!
YOU'RE THE ONE WHO JUST DECIDED IT WAS OVER!!
(*note see chapters 13 -14)
WHY YOU... ARE YOU ON *HIS* SIDE?! ARE YOU SAYING HE'S RIGHT!?!
NO! YOU'RE **BOTH** CRAZY, STUPID!!
PRESIDENT, SNAP OUT OF IT!
TOHRU, DO YOU WANT A LOLLIPOP?
...
He's already bored.
HEY THERE.
EEP!
LEAVE HER OUT OF IT!!
WHAT DO YOU THINK? MOMIJI, FOR EXAMPLE. DON'T YOU THINK HE LOOKS GOOD LIKE THAT?
President
HE'LL GET BIGGER SOON.
WOULDN'T IT BE BETTER FOR HIM TO START WEARING THE BOYS' UNIFORM THEN?
HE'LL LOOK VERY HANDSOME. CAN YOU IMAGINE IT?

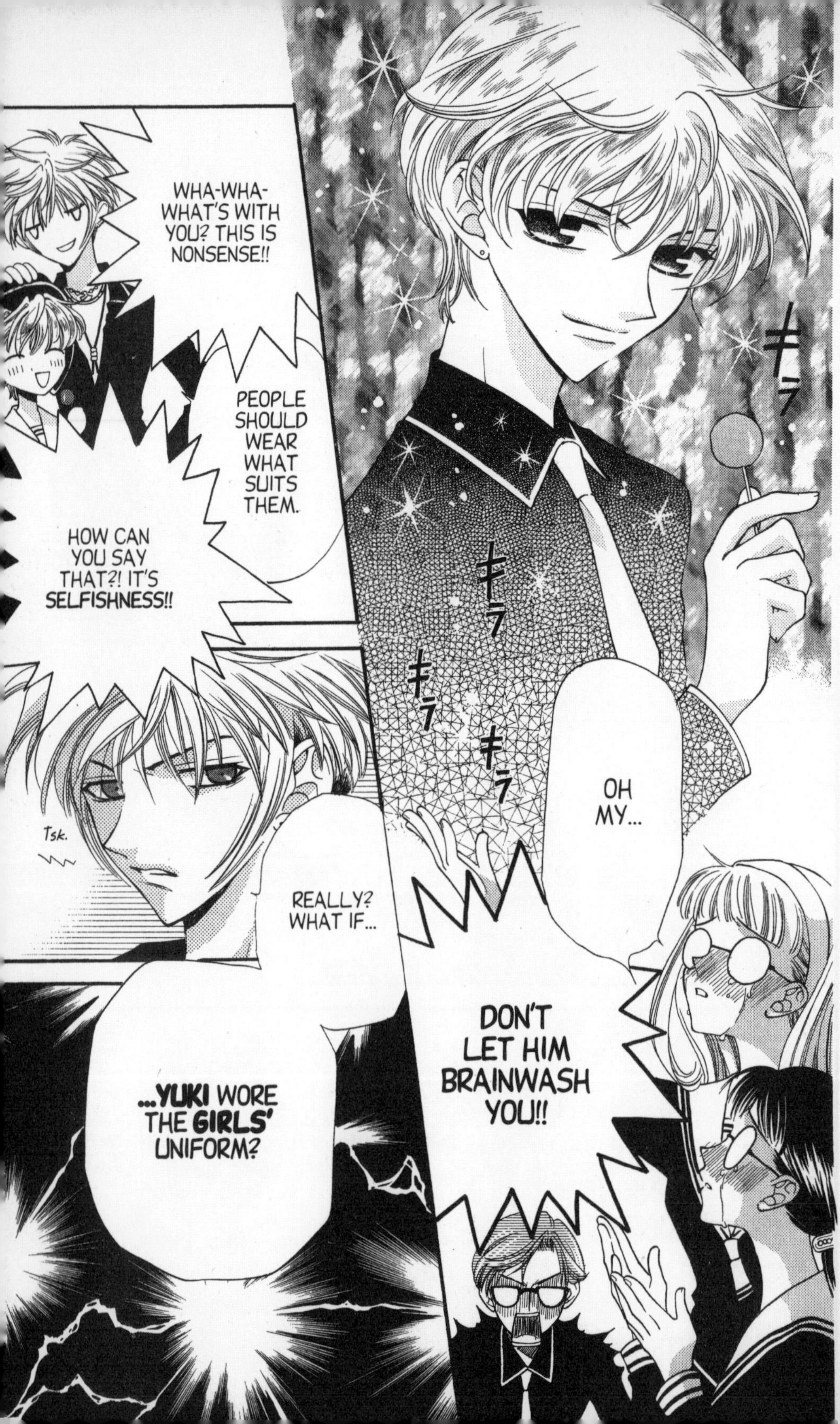
キラ
キラ
キラ
キラ
OH MY...
WHA-WHA-WHAT'S WITH YOU? THIS IS NONSENSE!!
PEOPLE SHOULD WEAR WHAT SUITS THEM.
HOW CAN YOU SAY THAT?! IT'S SELFISHNESS!!
Tsk.
REALLY? WHAT IF...
...YUKI WORE THE GIRLS' UNIFORM?
DON'T LET HIM BRAINWASH YOU!!

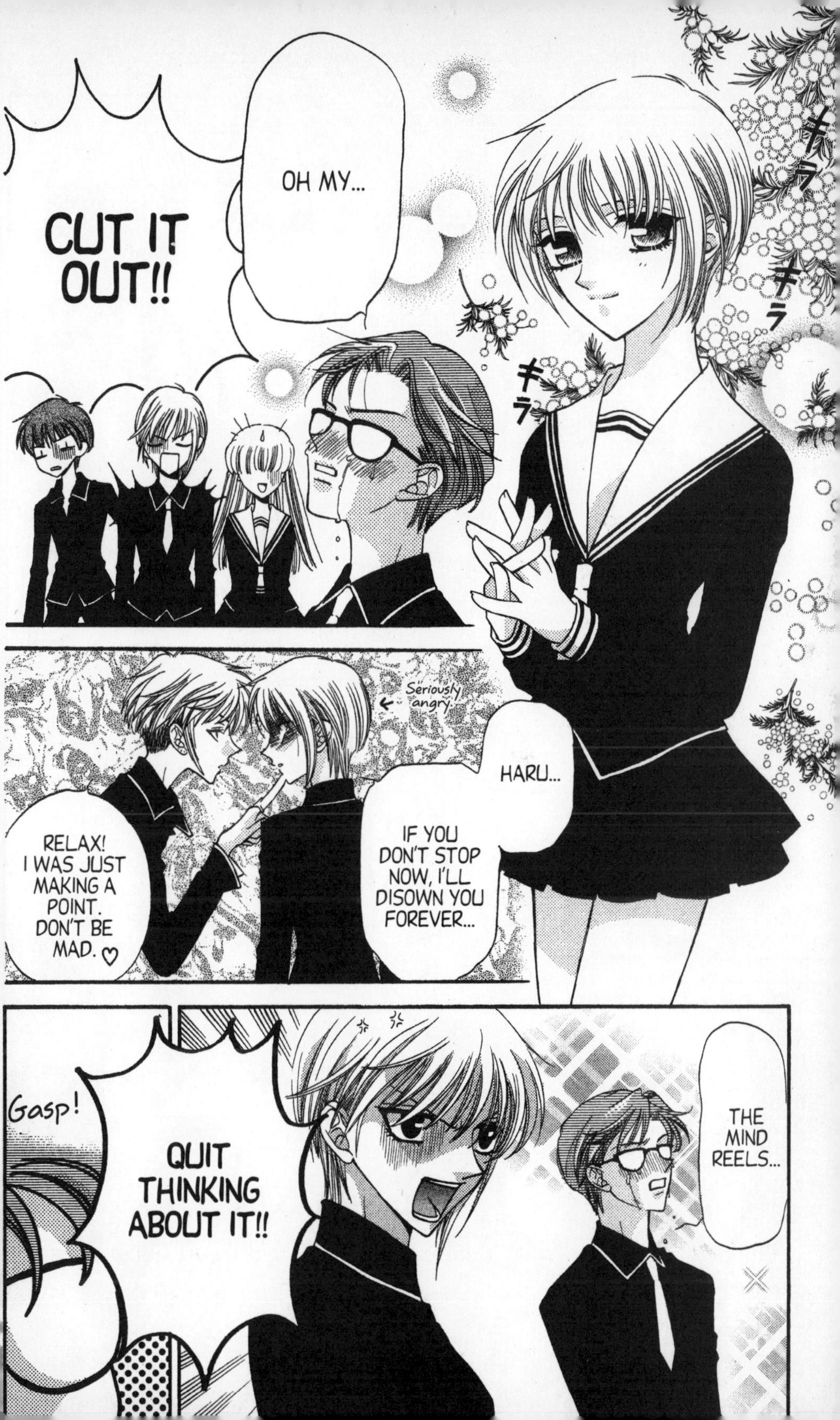
OH MY...
キラ
キラ
キラ
CUT IT OUT!!
Seriously angry.
HARU...
IF YOU DON'T STOP NOW, I'LL DISOWN YOU FOREVER...
RELAX! I WAS JUST MAKING A POINT. DON'T BE MAD. ♡
THE MIND REELS...
Gasp!
QUIT THINKING ABOUT IT!!

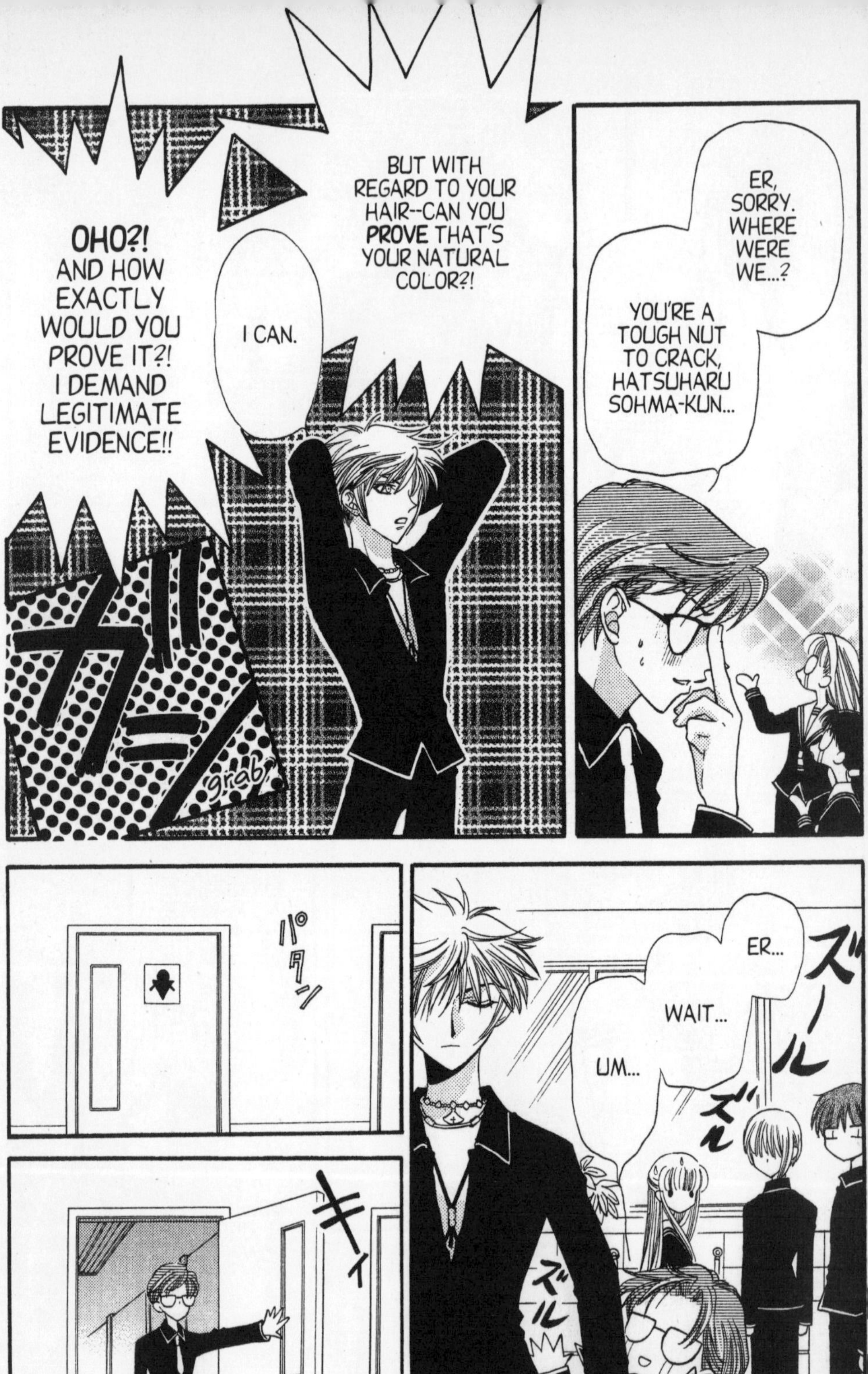
ER, SORRY. WHERE WERE WE...?
YOU'RE A TOUGH NUT TO CRACK, HATSUHARU SOHMA-KUN...
BUT WITH REGARD TO YOUR HAIR--CAN YOU **PROVE** THAT'S YOUR NATURAL COLOR?!
I CAN.
OHO?! AND HOW EXACTLY WOULD YOU PROVE IT?! I DEMAND LEGITIMATE EVIDENCE!!
grab
ズール
ER...
WAIT...
UM...
ズル
ズル
パタン
キィ

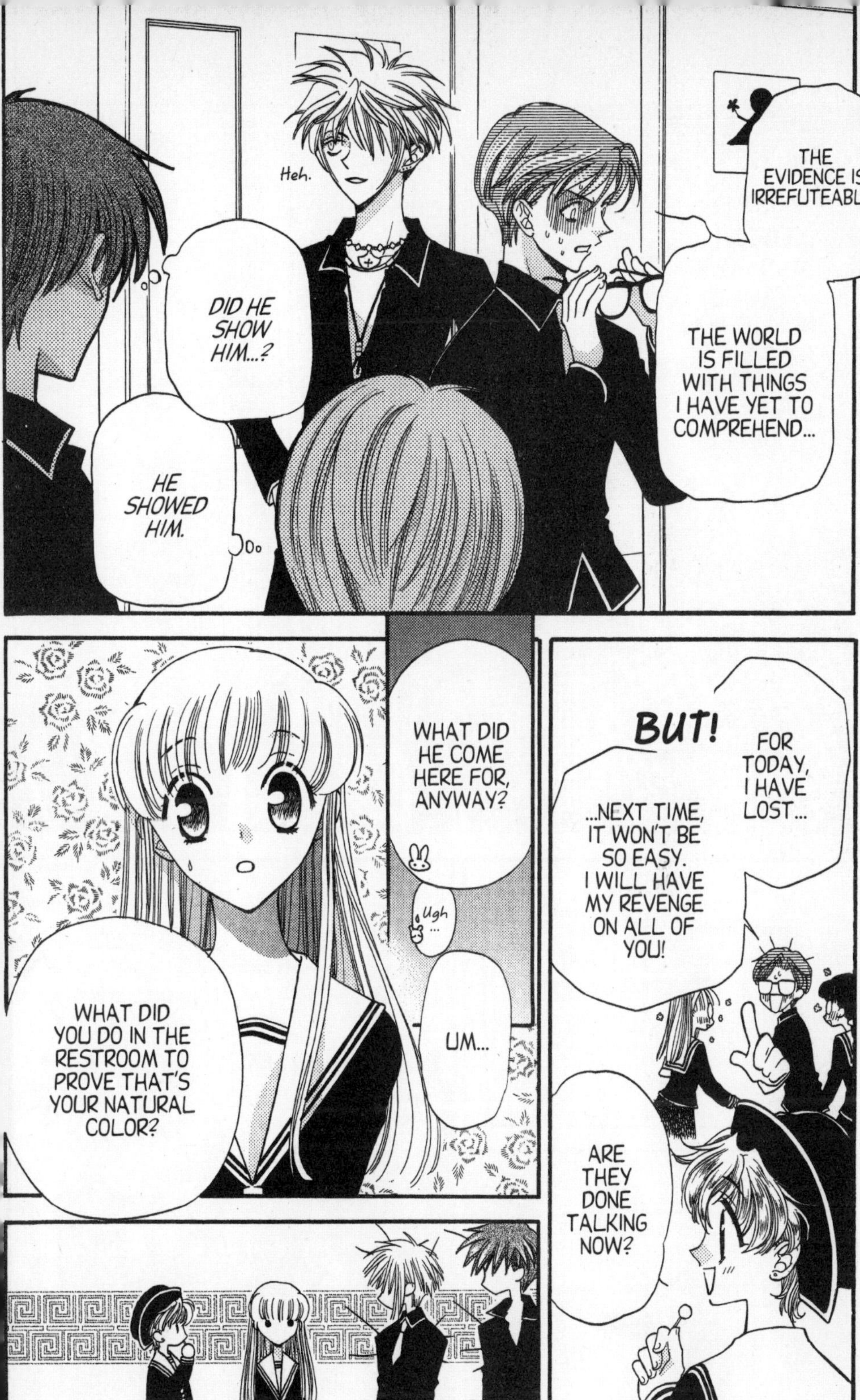
THE EVIDENCE IS IRREFUTEABLE.
THE WORLD IS FILLED WITH THINGS I HAVE YET TO COMPREHEND...
Heh.
DID HE SHOW HIM...?
HE SHOWED HIM.
FOR TODAY, I HAVE LOST...
BUT!
...NEXT TIME, IT WON'T BE SO EASY. I WILL HAVE MY REVENGE ON ALL OF YOU!
ARE THEY DONE TALKING NOW?
WHAT DID HE COME HERE FOR, ANYWAY?
Ugh...
UM...
WHAT DID YOU DO IN THE RESTROOM TO PROVE THAT'S YOUR NATURAL COLOR?

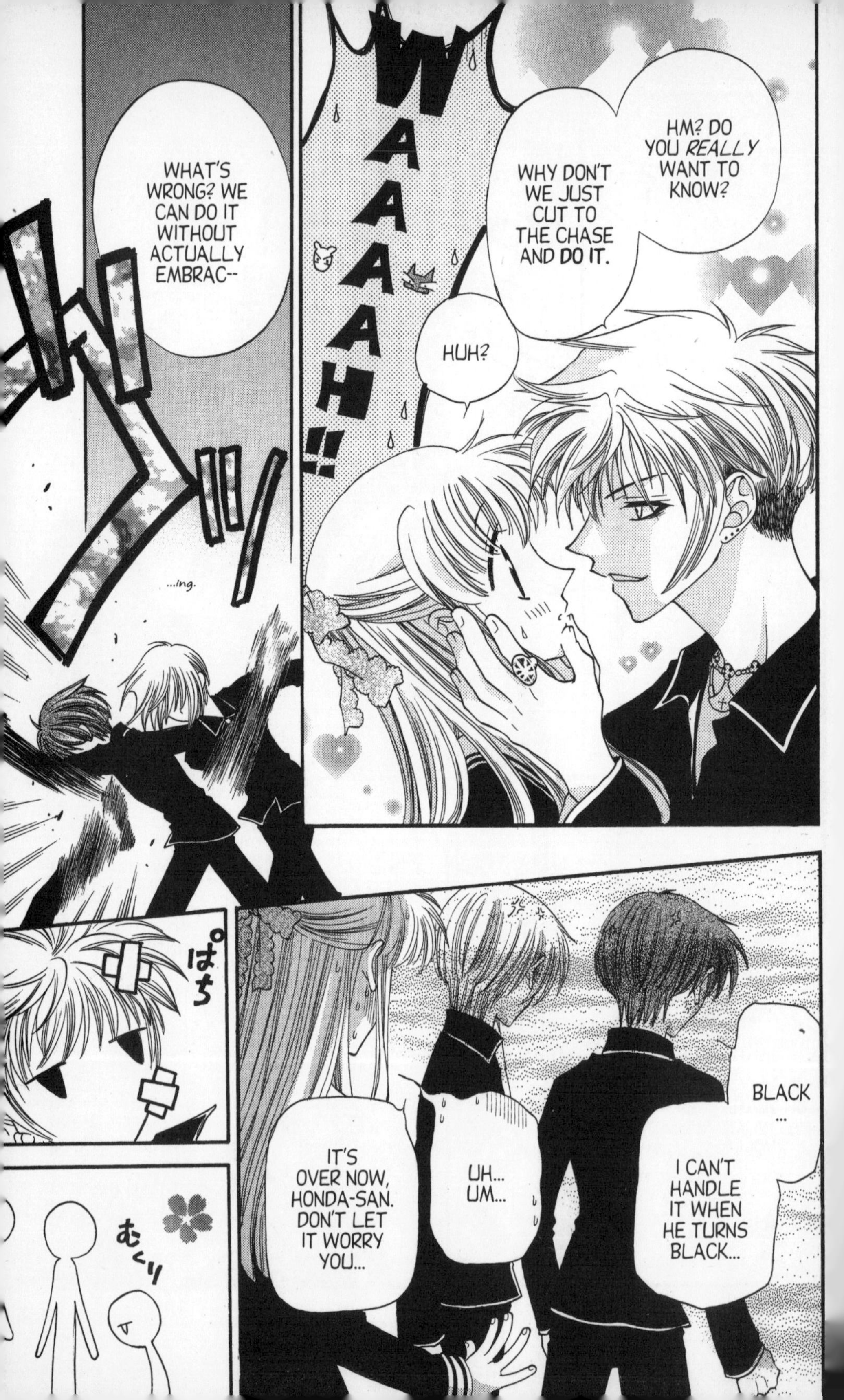
HM? DO YOU *REALLY* WANT TO KNOW?
WHY DON'T WE JUST CUT TO THE CHASE AND **DO IT**.
HUH?
WAAAAAH!!
WHAT'S WRONG? WE CAN DO IT WITHOUT ACTUALLY EMBRAC--
...ing.
BLACK ...
I CAN'T HANDLE IT WHEN HE TURNS BLACK...
UH... UM...
IT'S OVER NOW, HONDA-SAN. DON'T LET IT WORRY YOU...
ぱち
むくり

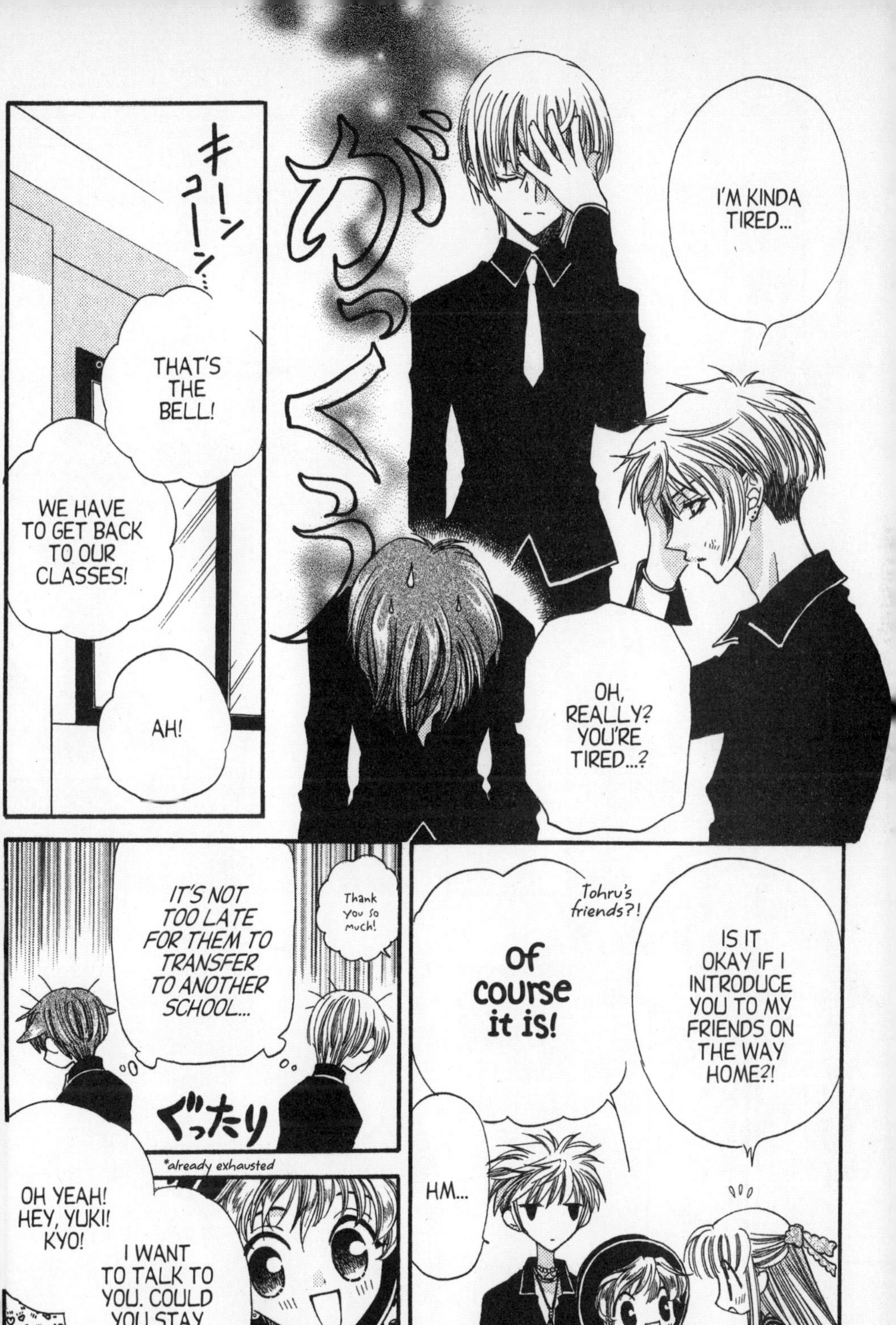

I'M KINDA TIRED...
OH, REALLY? YOU'RE TIRED...?
キーンコーン...
THAT'S THE BELL!
WE HAVE TO GET BACK TO OUR CLASSES!
AH!
IS IT OKAY IF I INTRODUCE YOU TO MY FRIENDS ON THE WAY HOME?!
Tohru's friends?!
Of course it is!
HM...
Thank you so much!
IT'S NOT TOO LATE FOR THEM TO TRANSFER TO ANOTHER SCHOOL...
ぐったり
*already exhausted
OH YEAH! HEY, YUKI! KYO!
I WANT TO TALK TO YOU. COULD YOU STAY HERE?

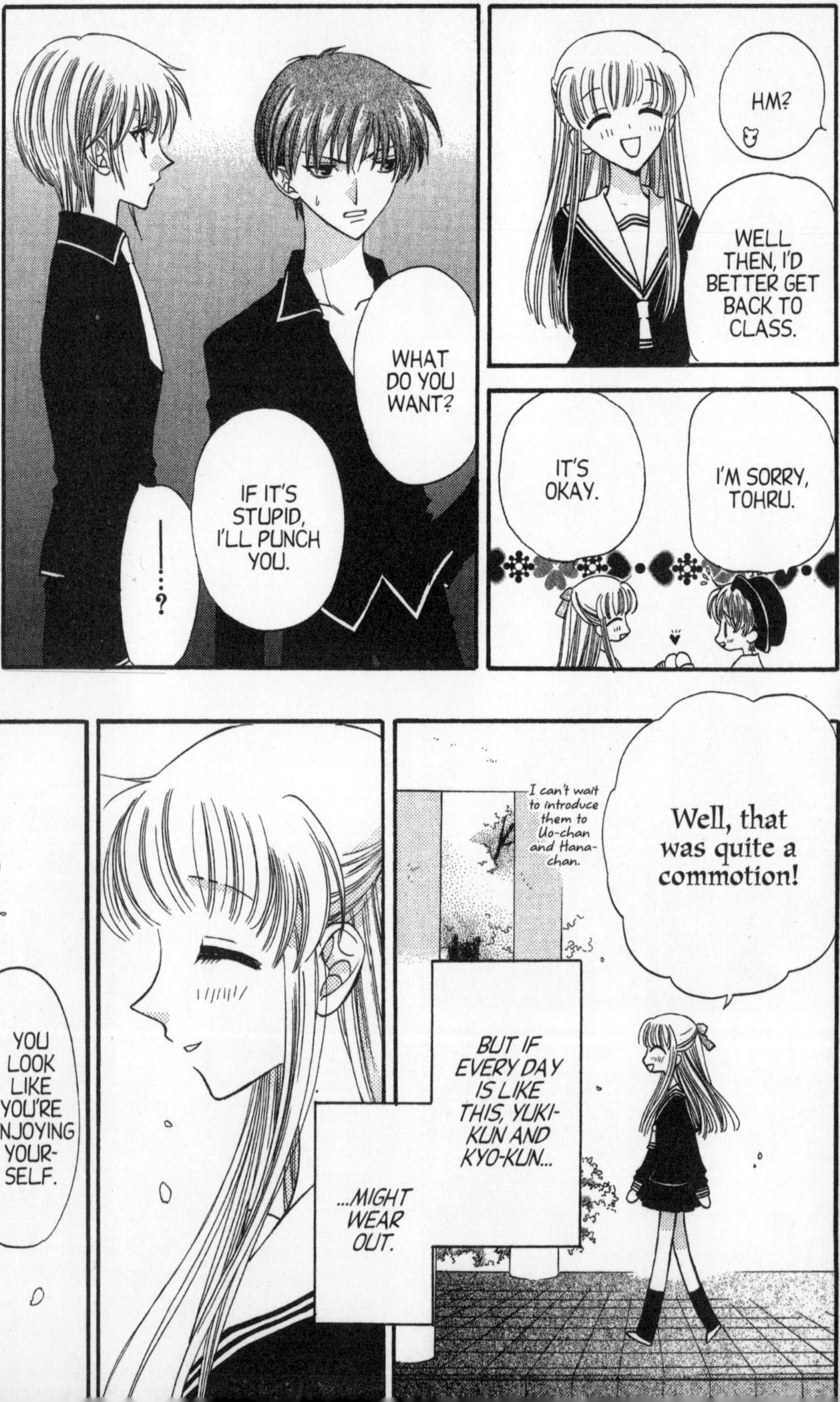
HM?
WELL THEN, I'D BETTER GET BACK TO CLASS.
I'M SORRY, TOHRU.
IT'S OKAY.
WHAT DO YOU WANT?
IF IT'S STUPID, I'LL PUNCH YOU.
!...?
Well, that was quite a commotion!
I can't wait to introduce them to Uo-chan and Hana-chan.
BUT IF EVERY DAY IS LIKE THIS, YUKI-KUN AND KYO-KUN...
...MIGHT WEAR OUT.
YOU LOOK LIKE YOU'RE ENJOYING YOURSELF.

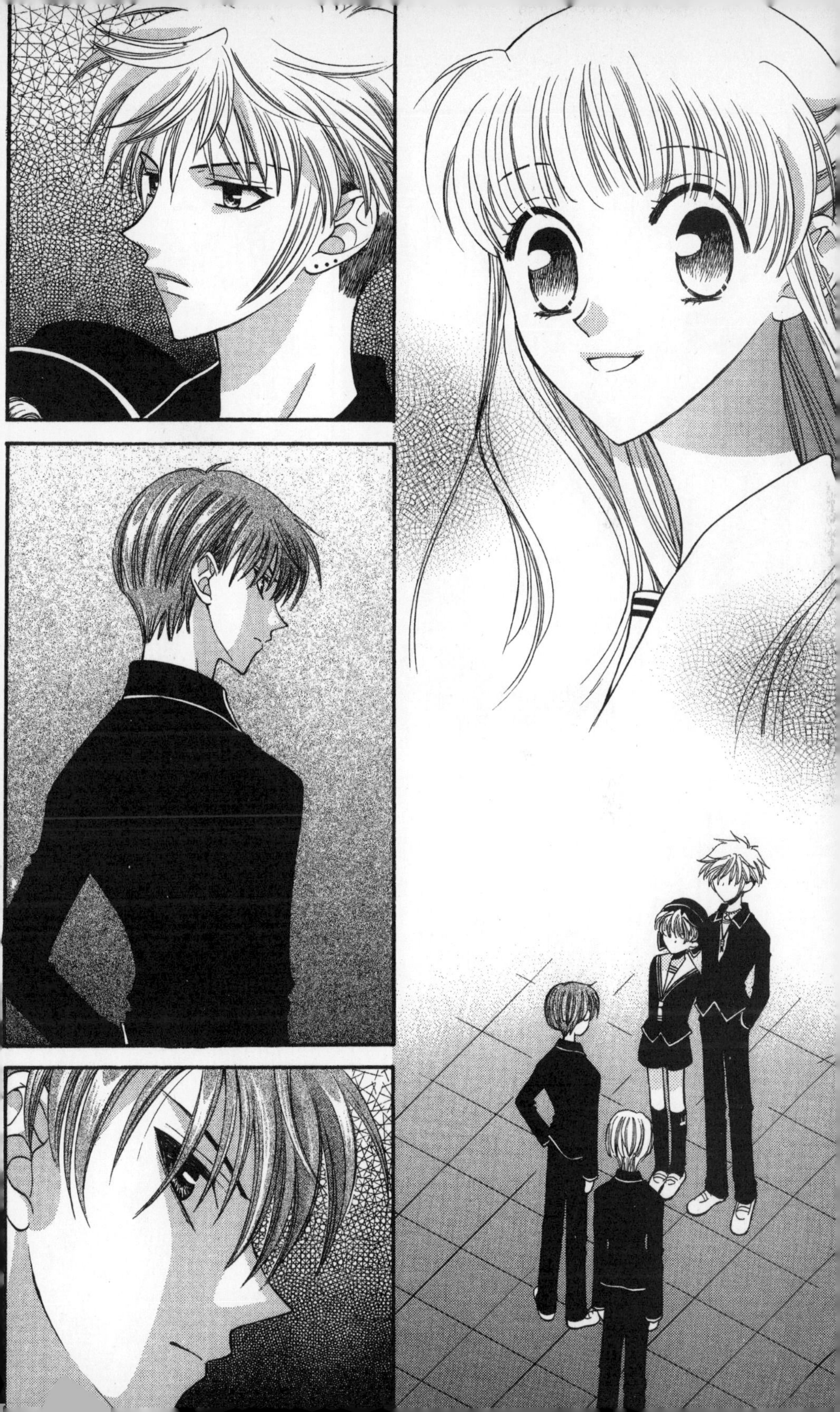

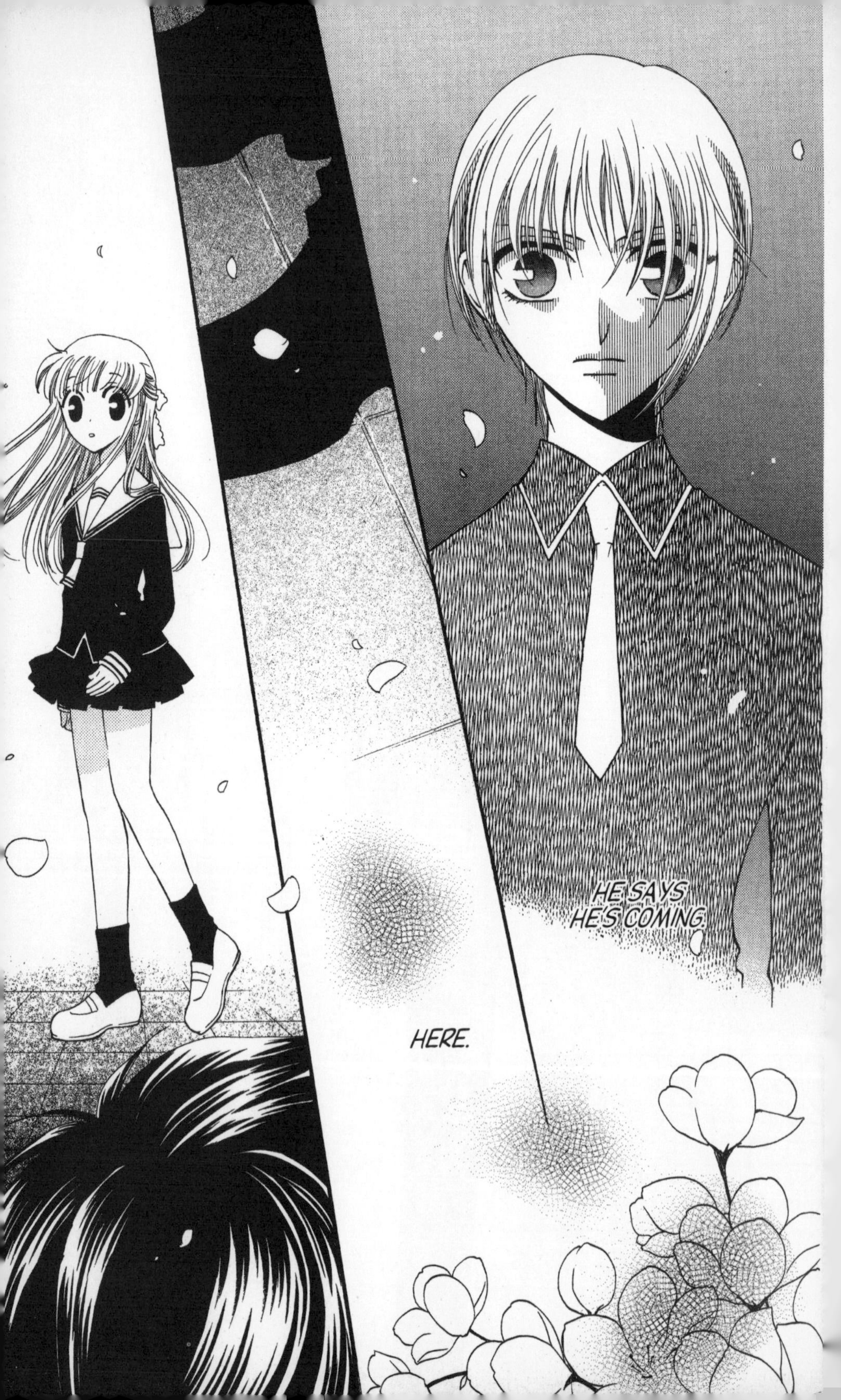
HE SAYS HE'S COMING.
HERE.

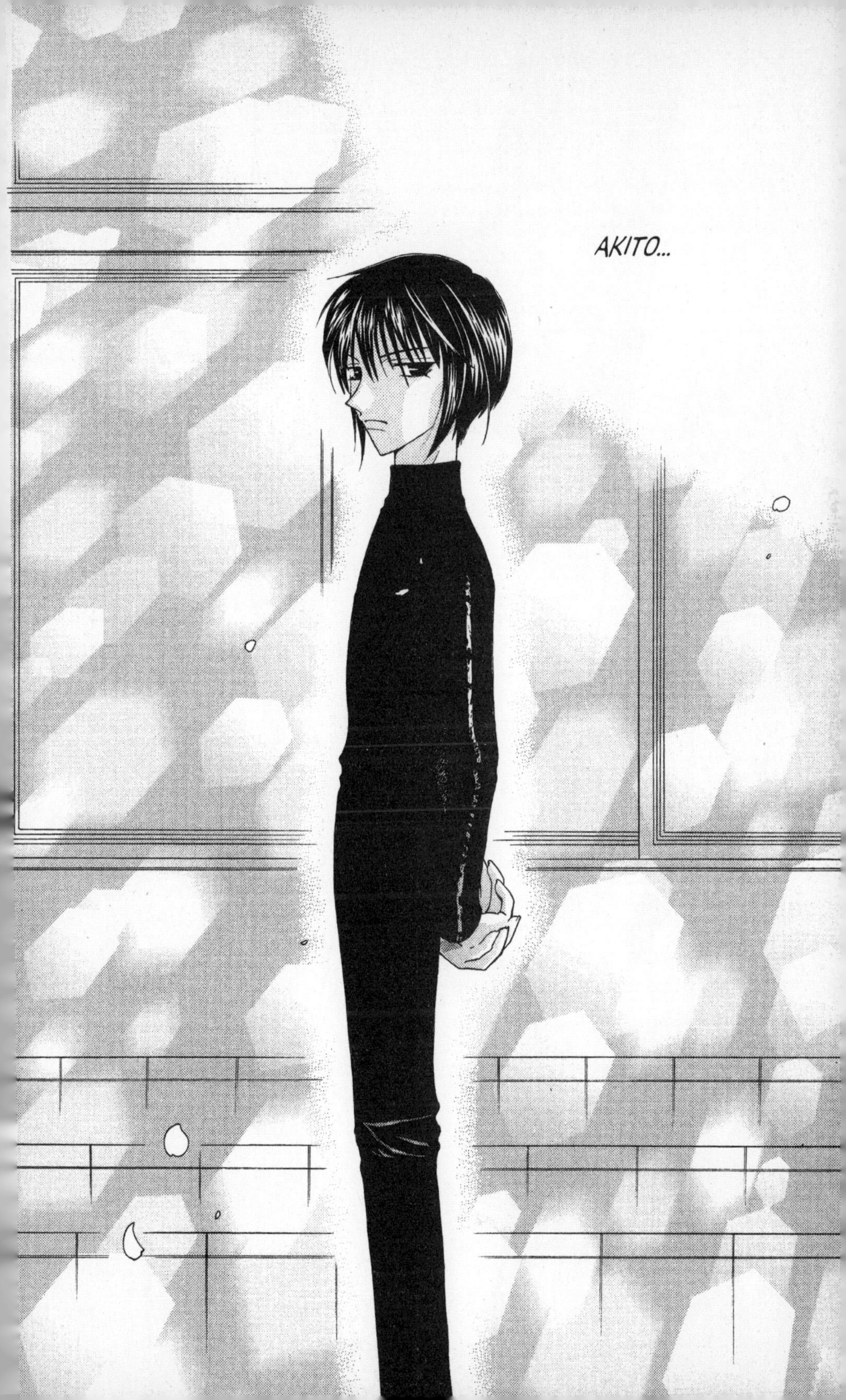
AKITO...

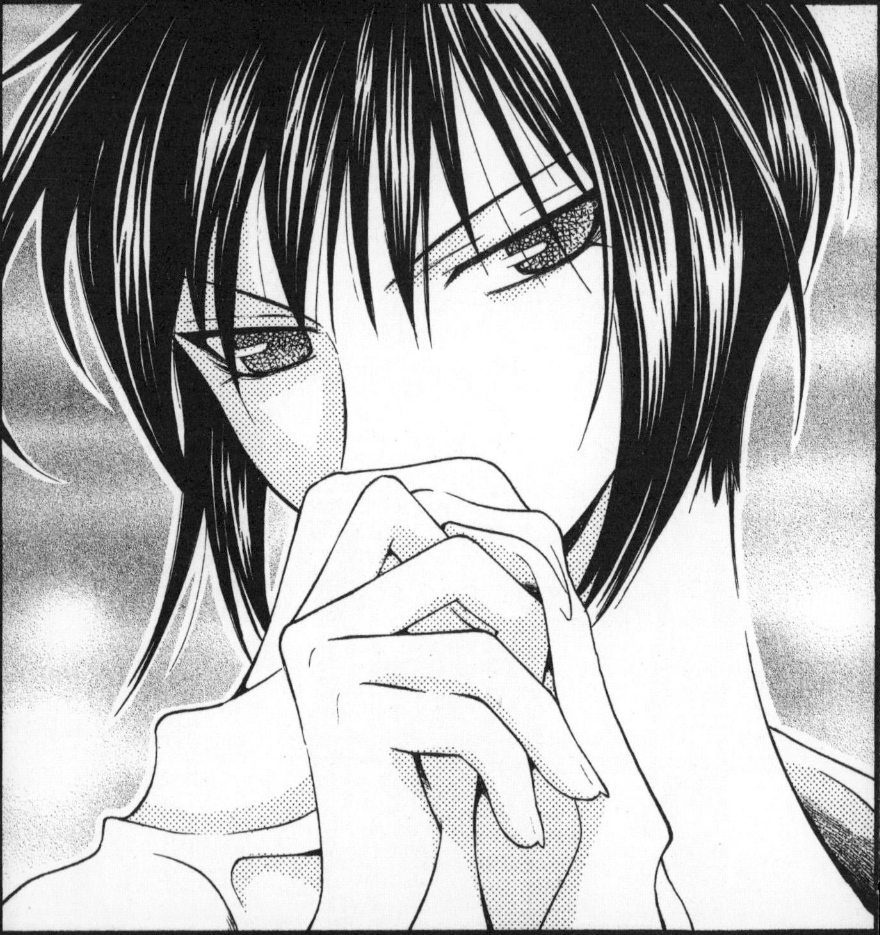

Chapter 20

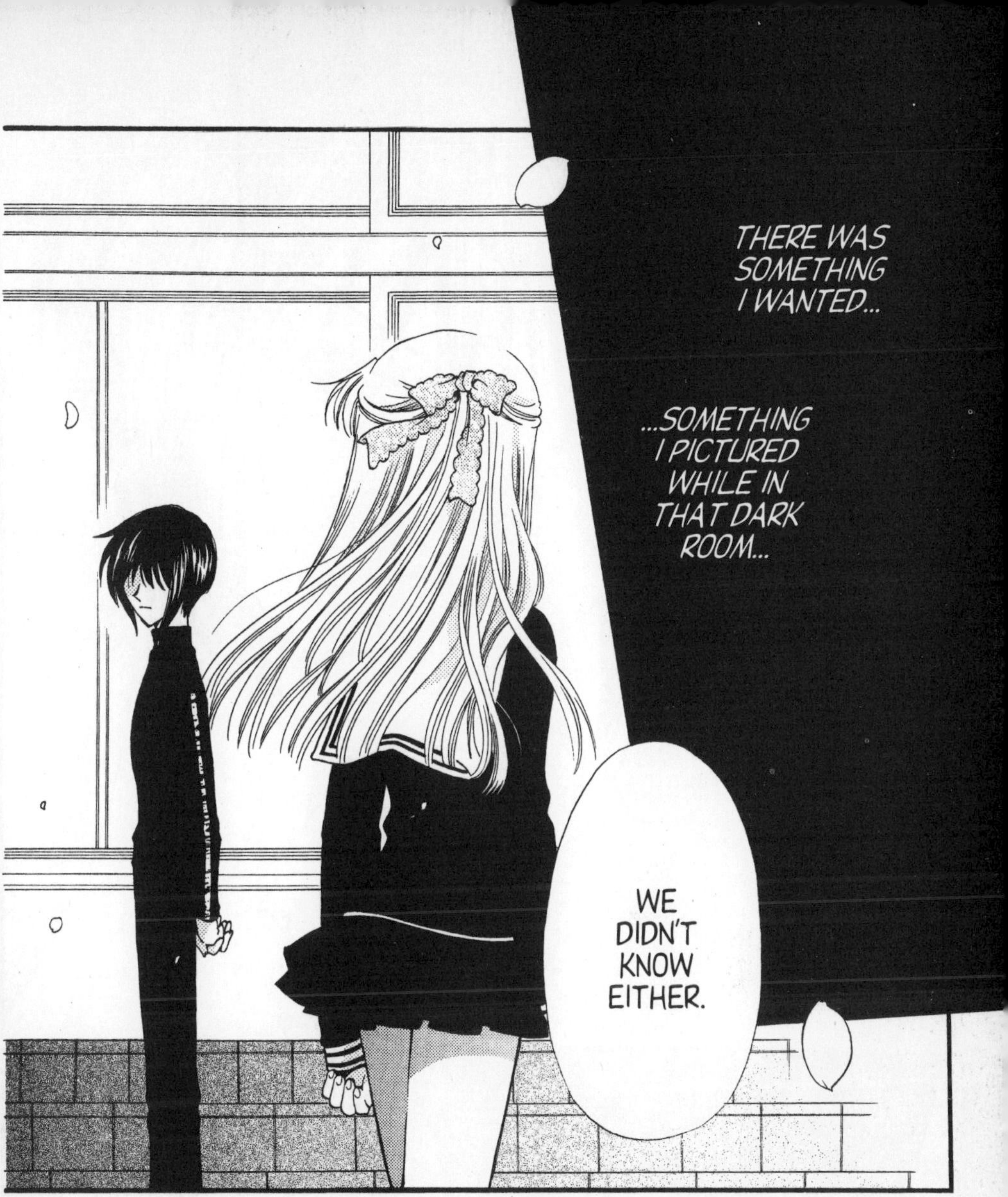
THERE WAS SOMETHING I WANTED...
...SOMETHING I PICTURED WHILE IN THAT DARK ROOM...
WE DIDN'T KNOW EITHER.

ULTRA SPECIAL BLAH BLAH BLAH 2

Akkii, Akkii, poisonous Akkii... My Mabudachi Akkii! Ha ha! (Er...sorry, inside joke.) I'm sure he slaps a cynical smile on the faces of the people who like him and the people who hate him. Mmm, poison. I actually meant to have him show up in the first volume, but looking back at it now, I'm glad I didn't. Better to draw things out...

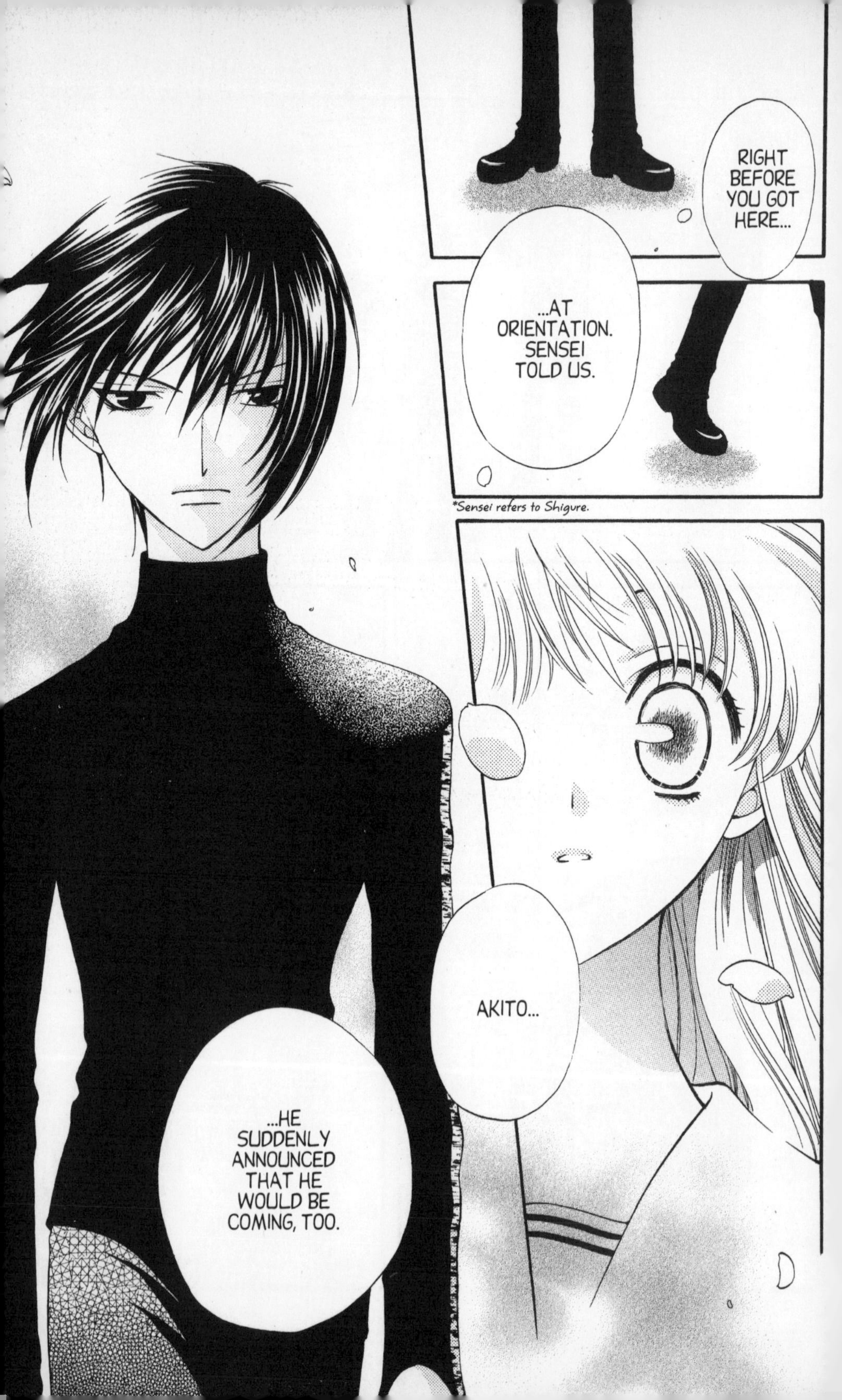
RIGHT BEFORE YOU GOT HERE...
...AT ORIENTATION. SENSEI TOLD US.
*Sensei refers to Shigure.
AKITO...
...HE SUDDENLY ANNOUNCED THAT HE WOULD BE COMING, TOO.

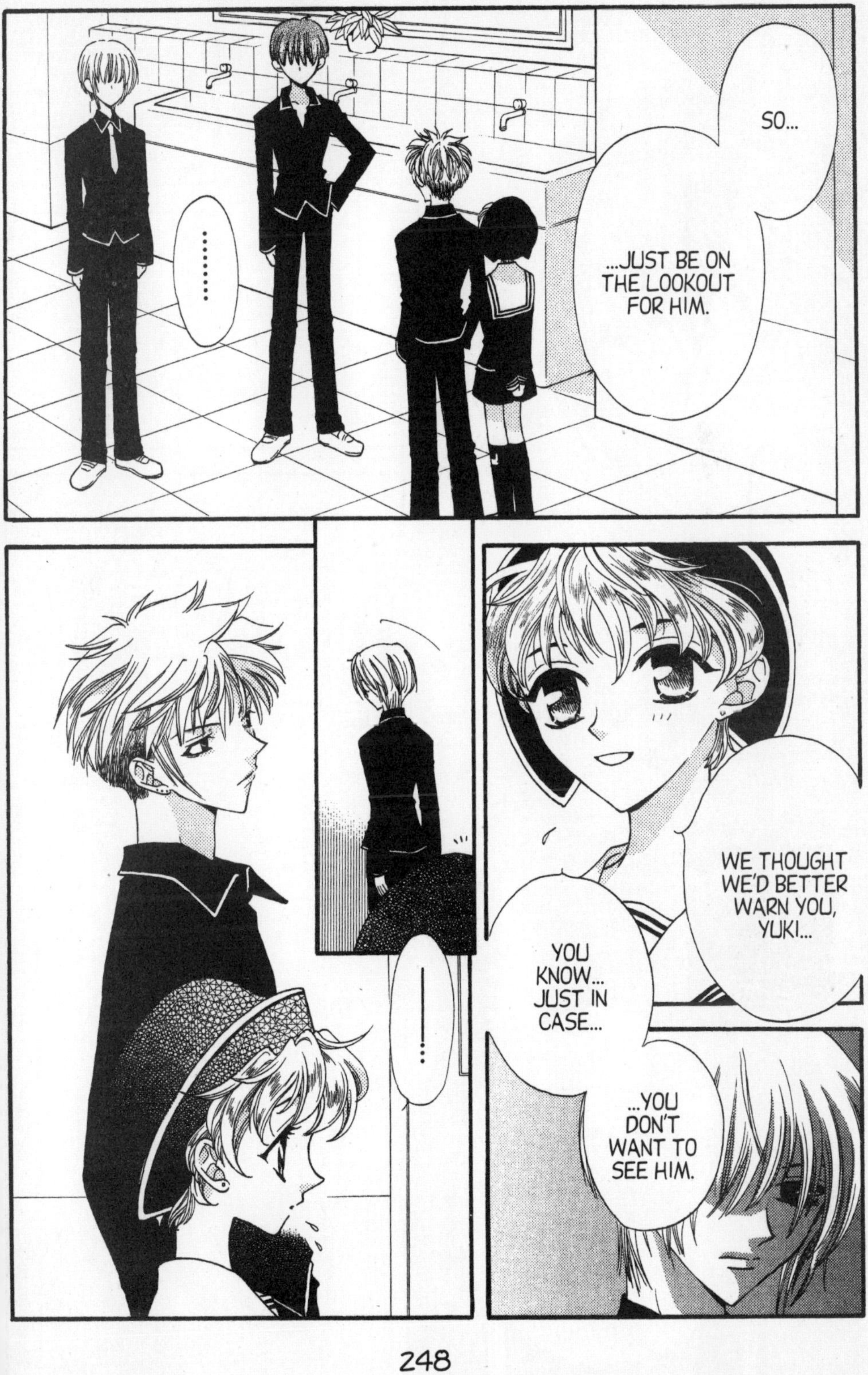
SO...
...JUST BE ON THE LOOKOUT FOR HIM.
......
WE THOUGHT WE'D BETTER WARN YOU, YUKI...
YOU KNOW... JUST IN CASE...
...YOU DON'T WANT TO SEE HIM.
......

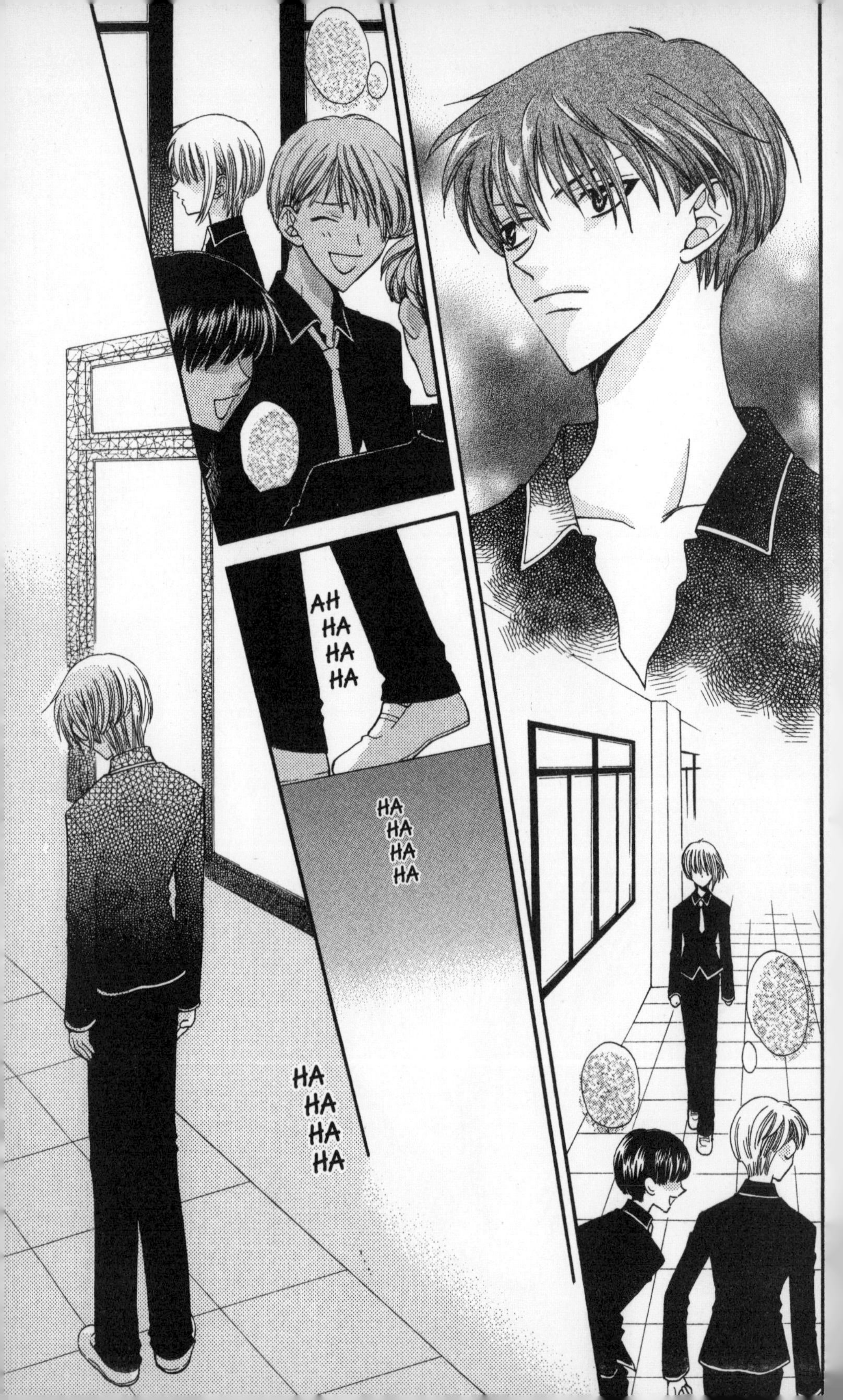
AH HA HA HA
HA HA HA HA
HA HA HA HA

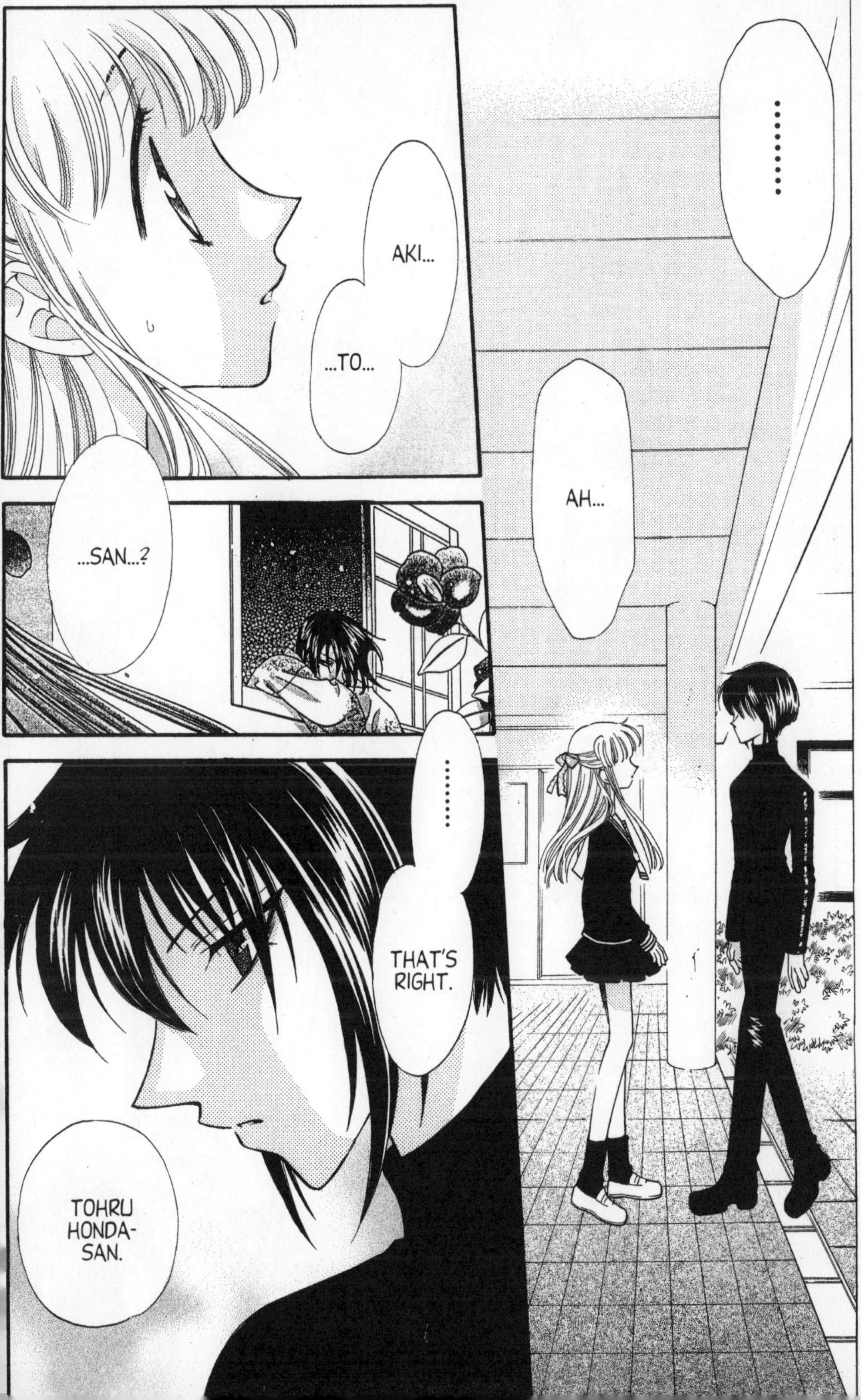
....
AH...
AKI...
...TO...
...SAN...?
....
THAT'S RIGHT.
TOHRU HONDA-SAN.

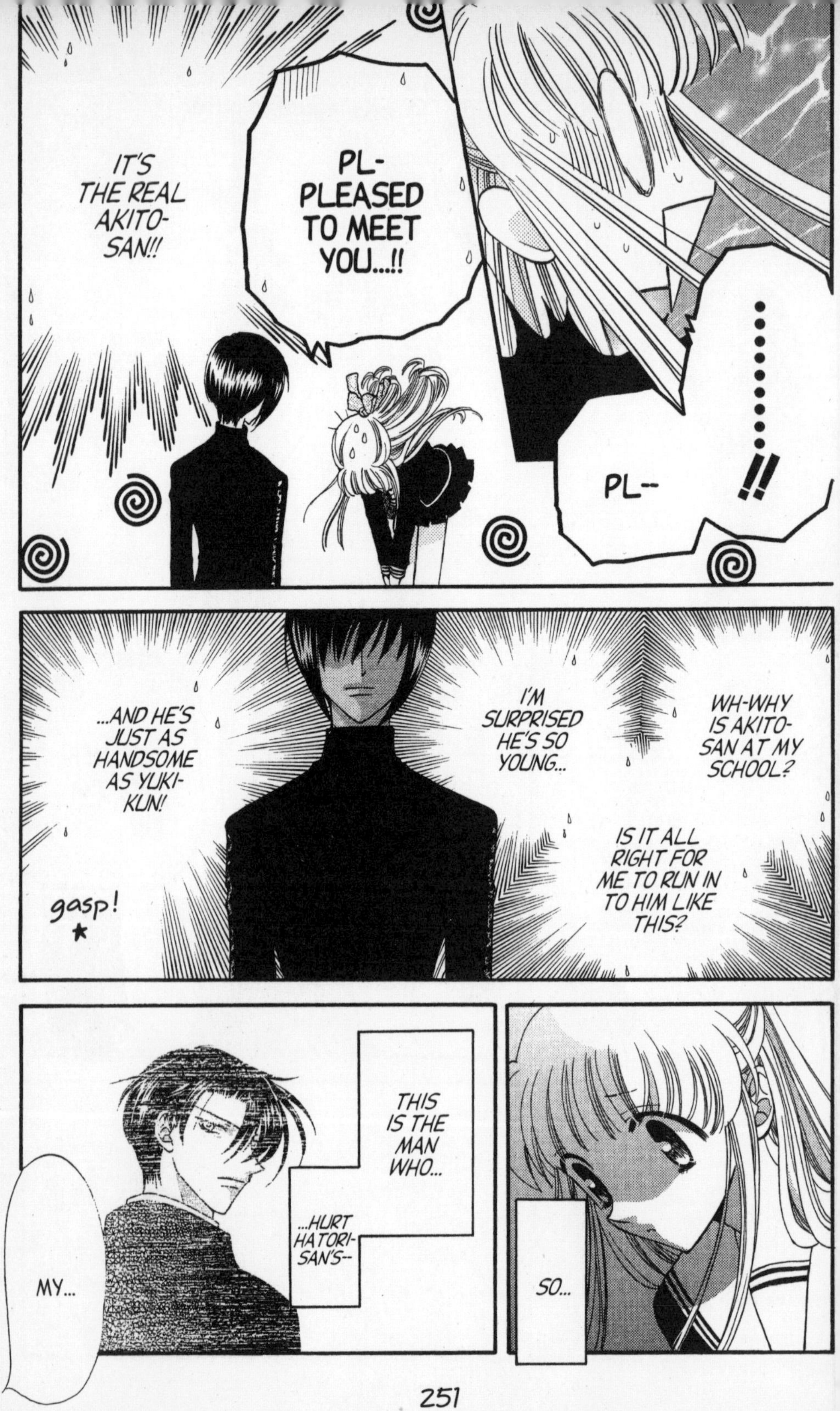
PL--
........!!
PL- PLEASED TO MEET YOU...!!
IT'S THE REAL AKITO-SAN!!
WH-WHY IS AKITO-SAN AT MY SCHOOL?
I'M SURPRISED HE'S SO YOUNG...
IS IT ALL RIGHT FOR ME TO RUN IN TO HIM LIKE THIS?
...AND HE'S JUST AS HANDSOME AS YUKI-KUN!
gasp!
SO...
THIS IS THE MAN WHO...
...HURT HATORI-SAN'S--
MY...

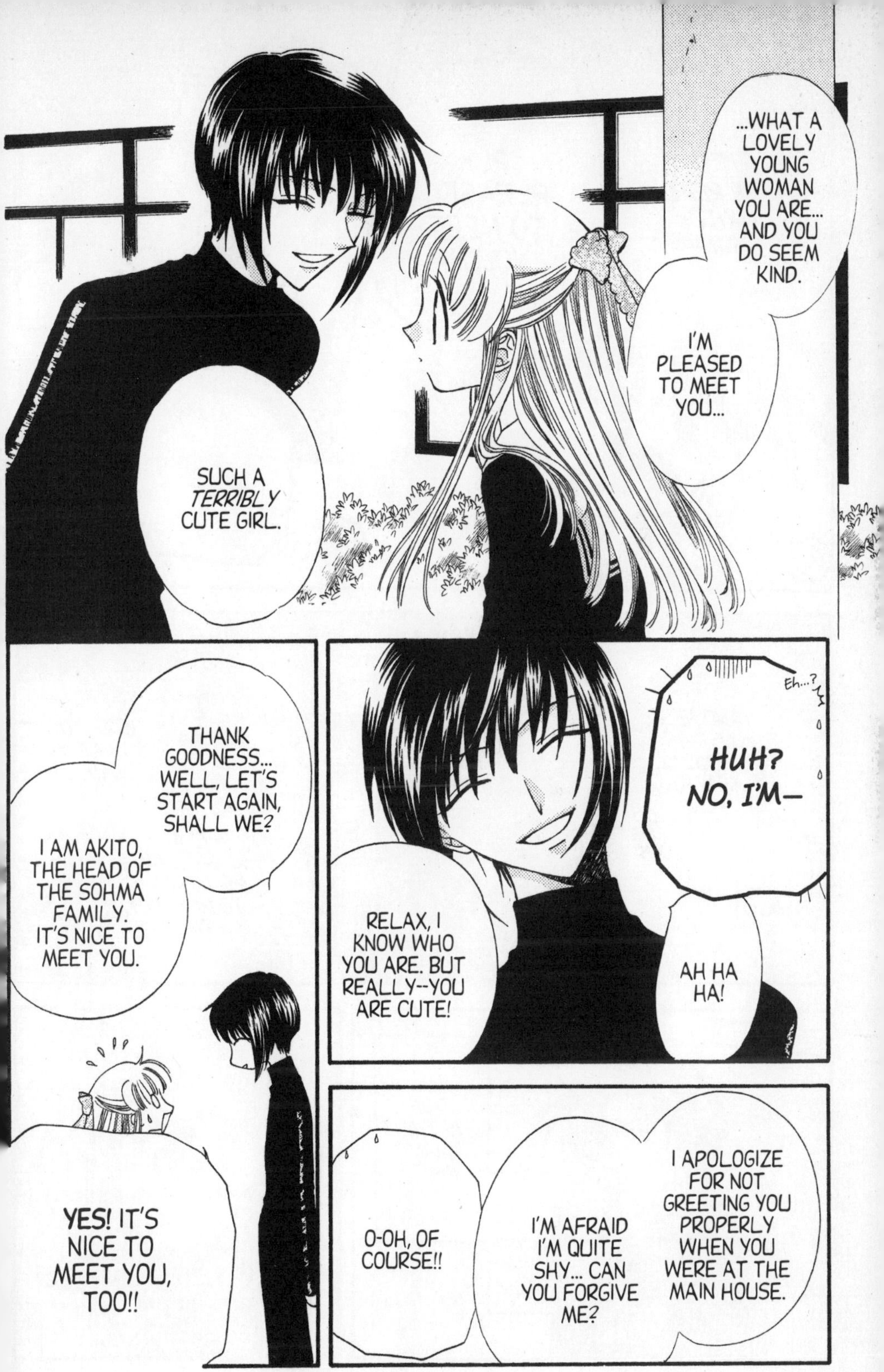
...WHAT A LOVELY YOUNG WOMAN YOU ARE... AND YOU DO SEEM KIND.
I'M PLEASED TO MEET YOU...
SUCH A *TERRIBLY* CUTE GIRL.
Eh...?
HUH? NO, I'M—
AH HA HA!
RELAX, I KNOW WHO YOU ARE. BUT REALLY--YOU ARE CUTE!
I APOLOGIZE FOR NOT GREETING YOU PROPERLY WHEN YOU WERE AT THE MAIN HOUSE.
I'M AFRAID I'M QUITE SHY... CAN YOU FORGIVE ME?
O-OH, OF COURSE!!
THANK GOODNESS... WELL, LET'S START AGAIN, SHALL WE?
I AM AKITO, THE HEAD OF THE SOHMA FAMILY. IT'S NICE TO MEET YOU.
YES! IT'S NICE TO MEET YOU, TOO!!

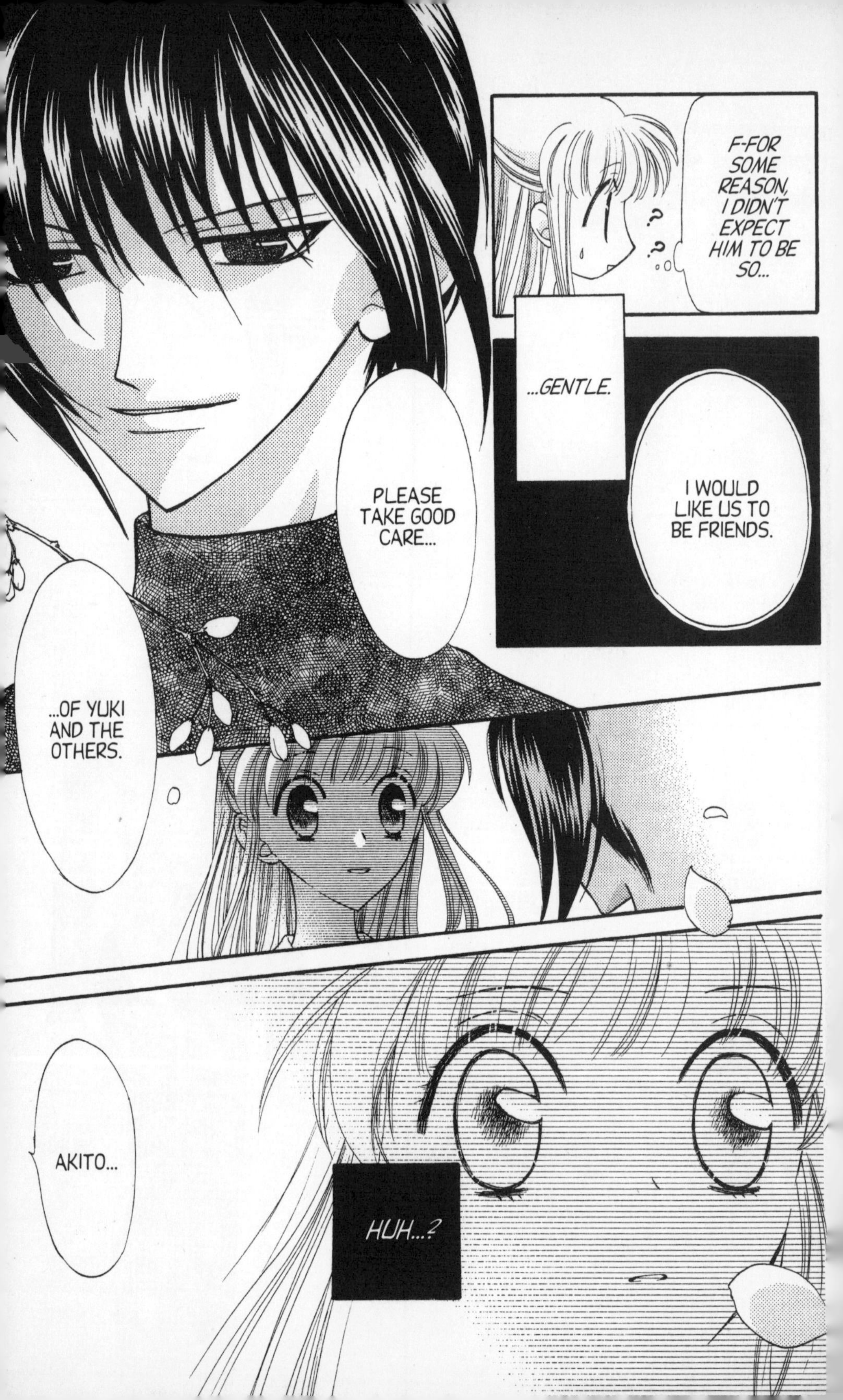
F-FOR SOME REASON, I DIDN'T EXPECT HIM TO BE SO...
...GENTLE.
I WOULD LIKE US TO BE FRIENDS.
PLEASE TAKE GOOD CARE...
...OF YUKI AND THE OTHERS.
AKITO...
HUH...?

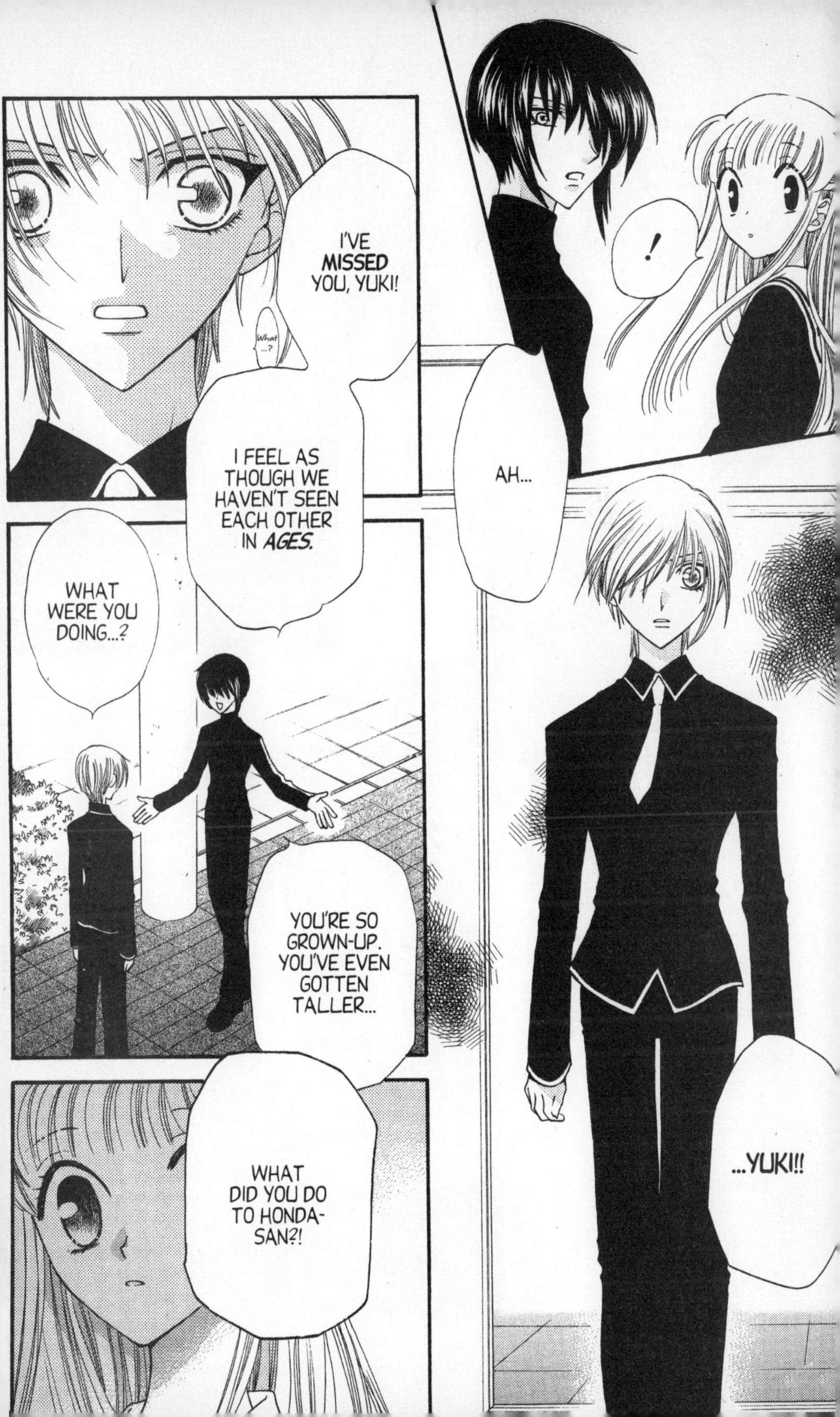
!
AH...
...YUKI!!
I'VE MISSED YOU, YUKI!
What ...?
I FEEL AS THOUGH WE HAVEN'T SEEN EACH OTHER IN AGES.
WHAT WERE YOU DOING...?
YOU'RE SO GROWN-UP. YOU'VE EVEN GOTTEN TALLER...
WHAT DID YOU DO TO HONDA-SAN?!

Fruits Basket 4 Part 2:

At the end of this book, I inserted a manga advertising the CD drama. It's a special offer, so it won't be on sale to the general public. And it's past the deadline to apply! Ha ha! Thank you very much for sending so many applications. I'll say clearly that I am in **love** with the Furuba CD. It's such a fun CD! I can't thank the voice actors who performed in it enough. I've shed so many tears of gratitude that my eyes have just about gone dry. What I find interesting is that even while listening to the lines, I split them into panels. I wonder if this is what they call an occupational hazard. I even break things into panels when I'm watching TV!

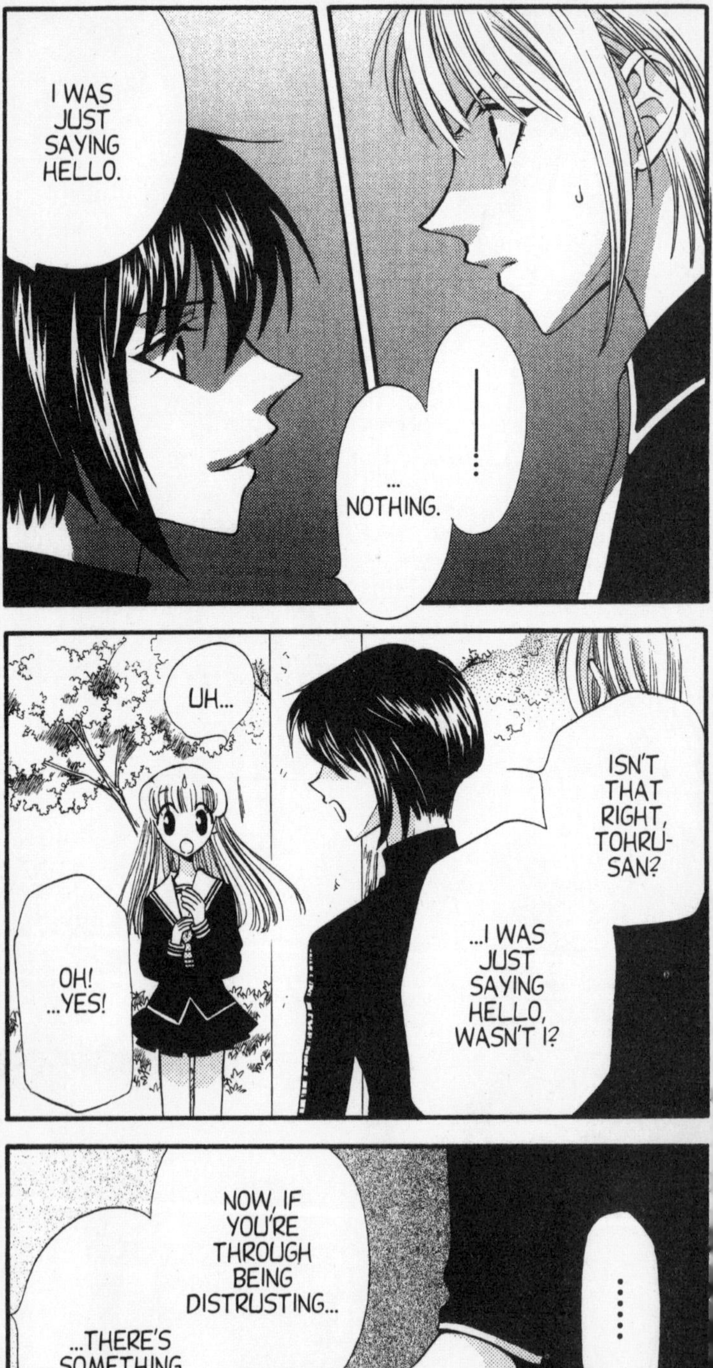
—... NOTHING.
I WAS JUST SAYING HELLO.
ISN'T THAT RIGHT, TOHRU-SAN?
...I WAS JUST SAYING HELLO, WASN'T I?
UH...
OH! ...YES!
......
NOW, IF YOU'RE THROUGH BEING DISTRUSTING...
...THERE'S SOMETHING I NEED TO ASK YOU.

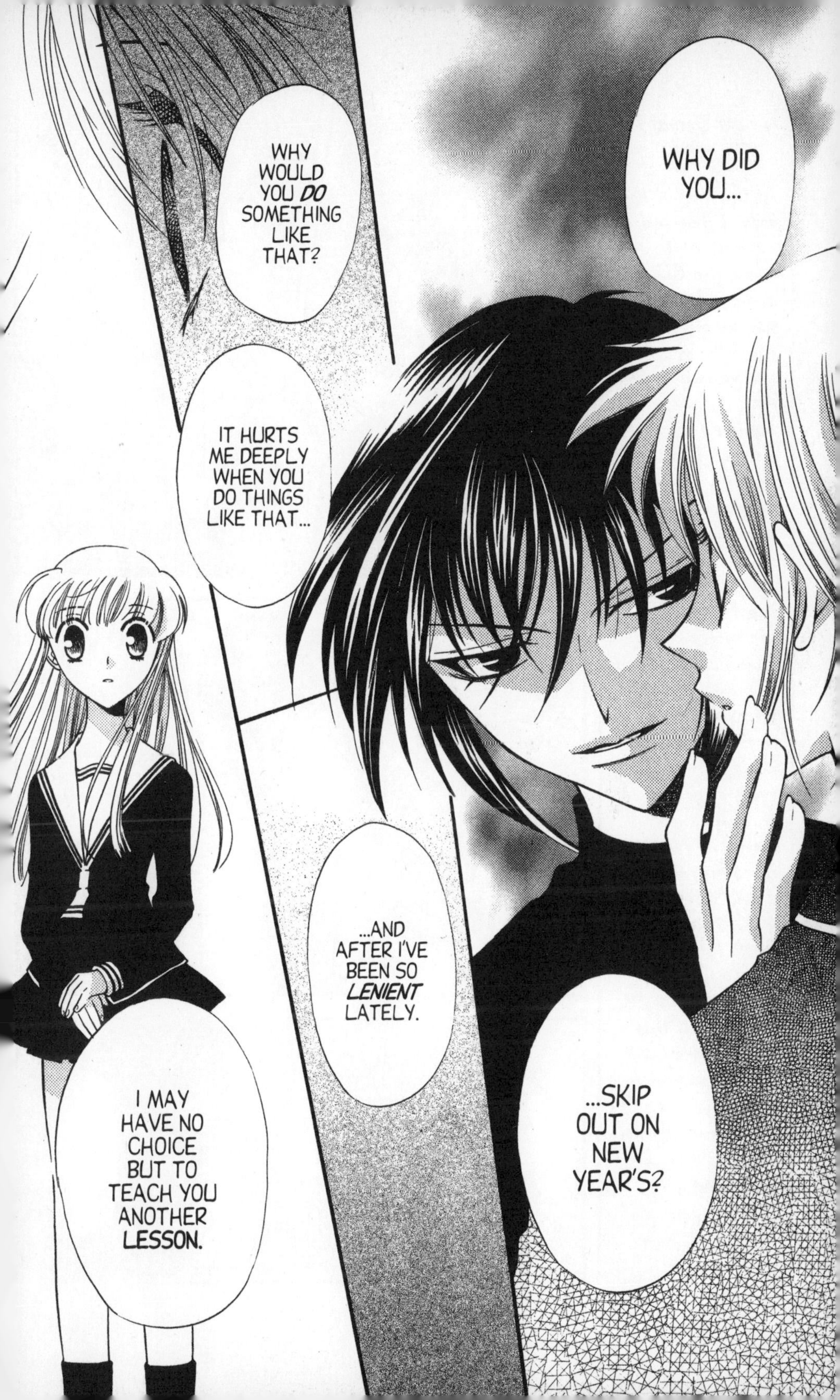
WHY DID YOU...
...SKIP OUT ON NEW YEAR'S?
WHY WOULD YOU *DO* SOMETHING LIKE THAT?
IT HURTS ME DEEPLY WHEN YOU DO THINGS LIKE THAT...
...AND AFTER I'VE BEEN SO *LENIENT* LATELY.
I MAY HAVE NO CHOICE BUT TO TEACH YOU ANOTHER **LESSON.**

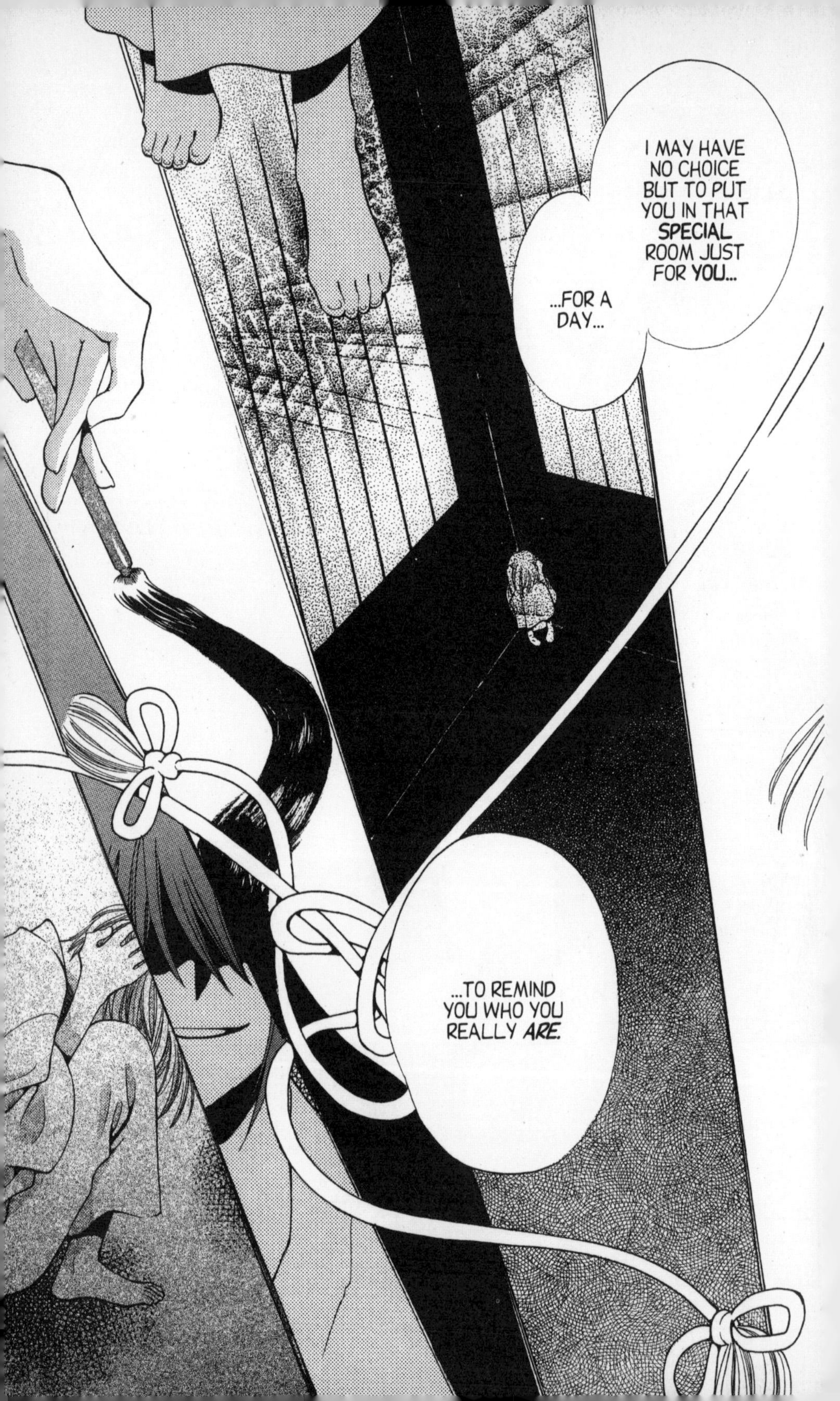
I MAY HAVE NO CHOICE BUT TO PUT YOU IN THAT **SPECIAL** ROOM JUST FOR **YOU**...
...FOR A DAY...
...TO REMIND YOU WHO YOU REALLY ***ARE.***

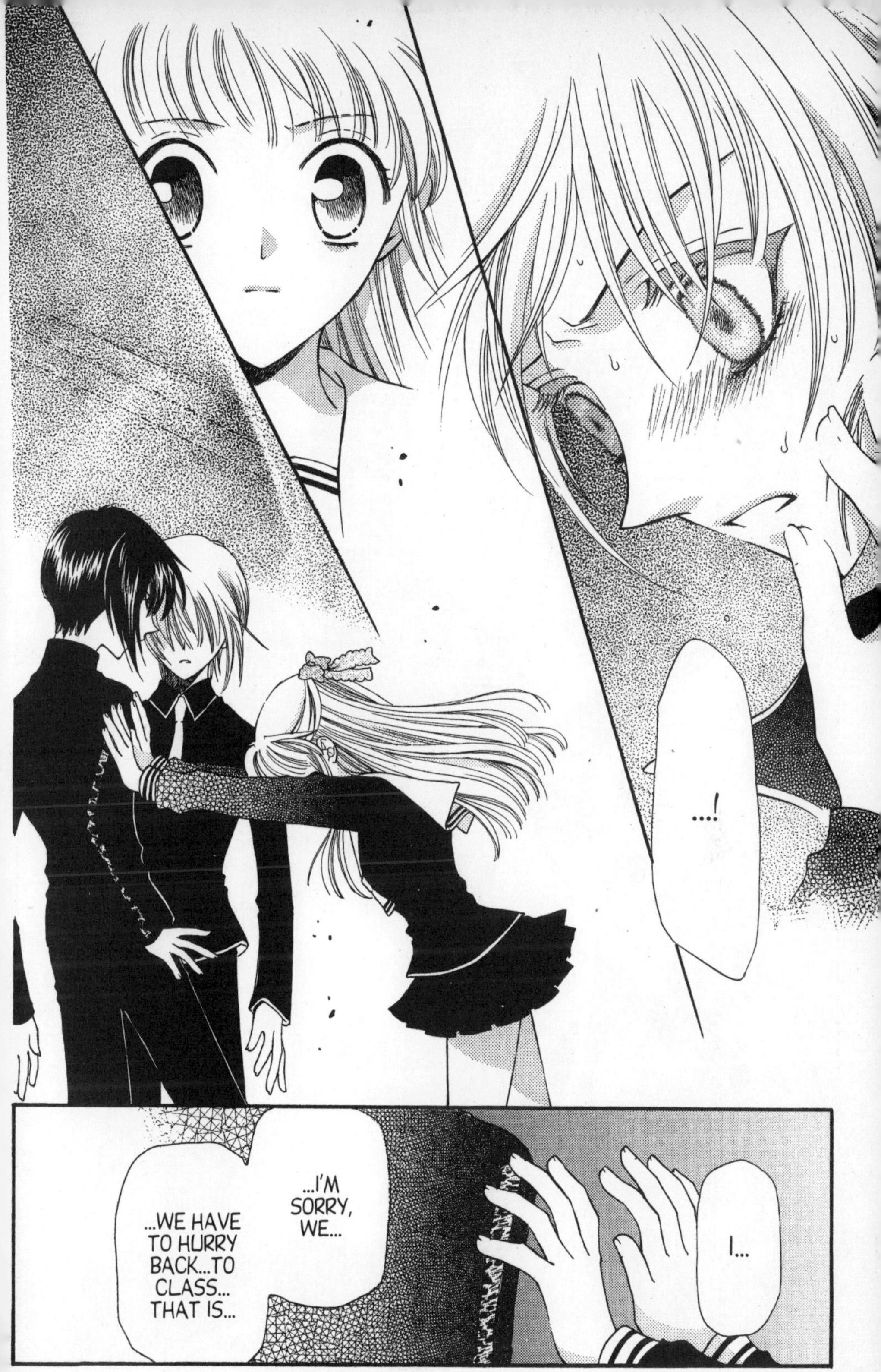
...!
I...
...I'M SORRY, WE...
...WE HAVE TO HURRY BACK...TO CLASS... THAT IS...

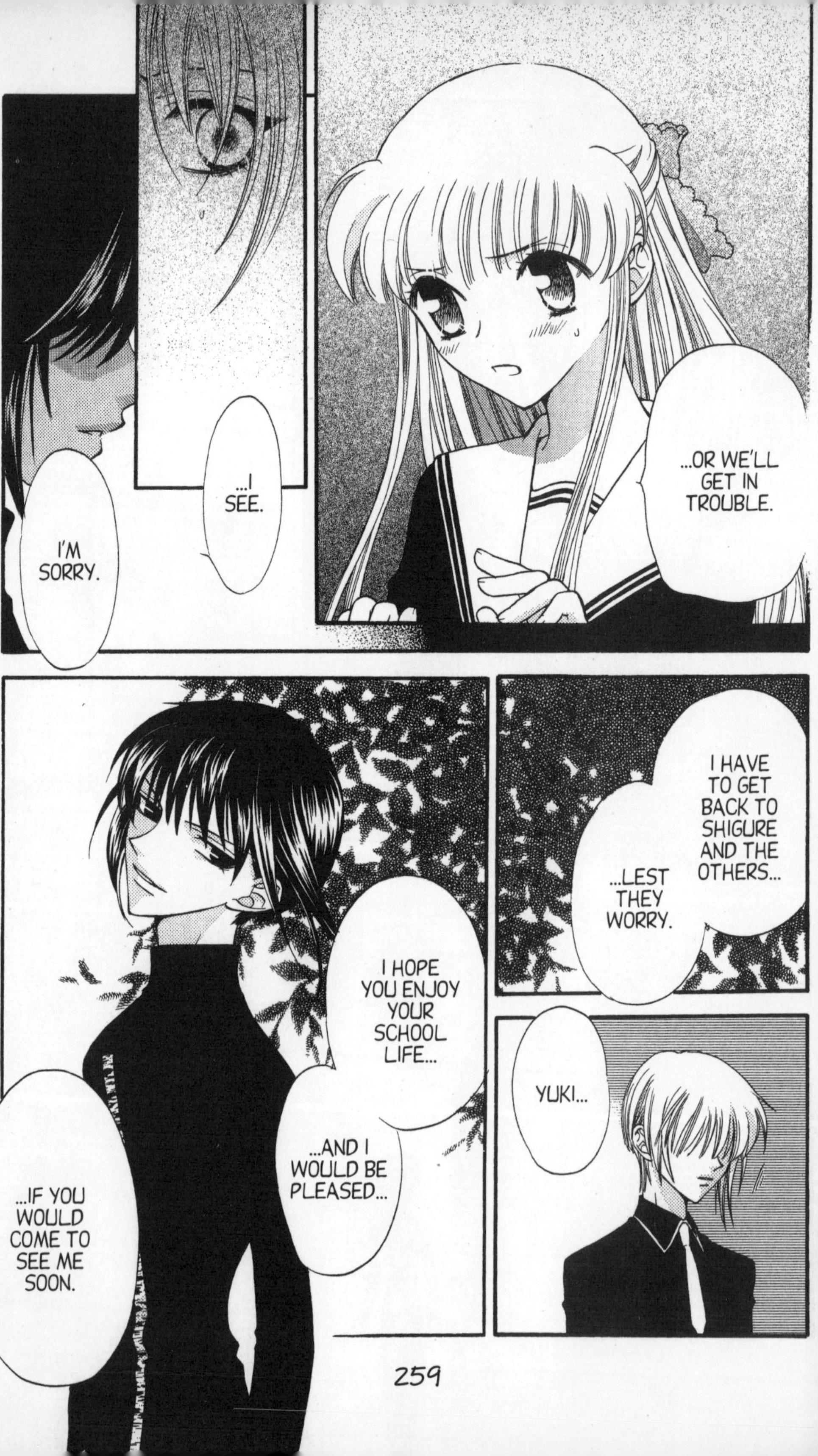
...OR WE'LL GET IN TROUBLE.
...I SEE.
I'M SORRY.
I HAVE TO GET BACK TO SHIGURE AND THE OTHERS...
...LEST THEY WORRY.
YUKI...
I HOPE YOU ENJOY YOUR SCHOOL LIFE...
...AND I WOULD BE PLEASED...
...IF YOU WOULD COME TO SEE ME SOON.

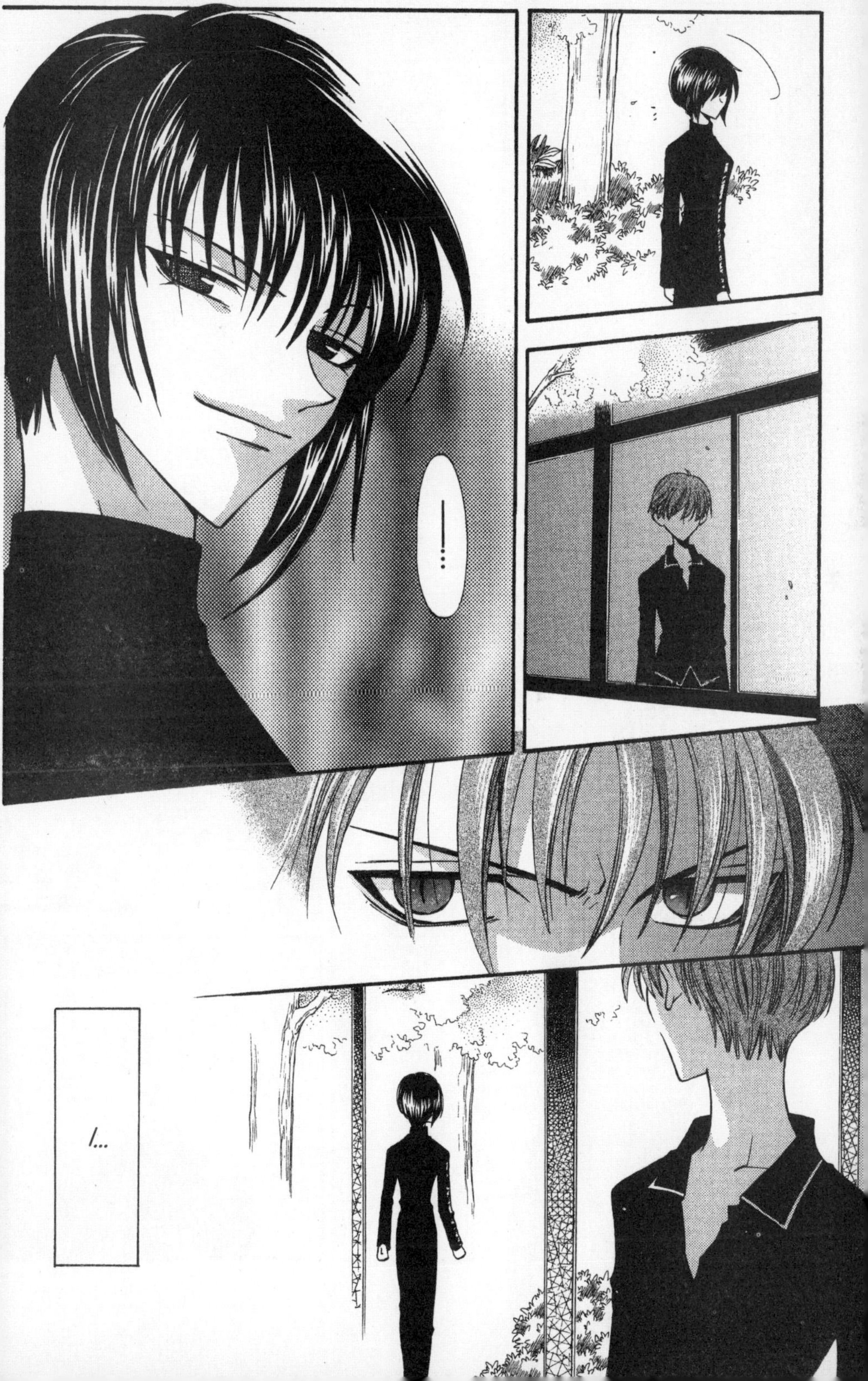
!...
I...

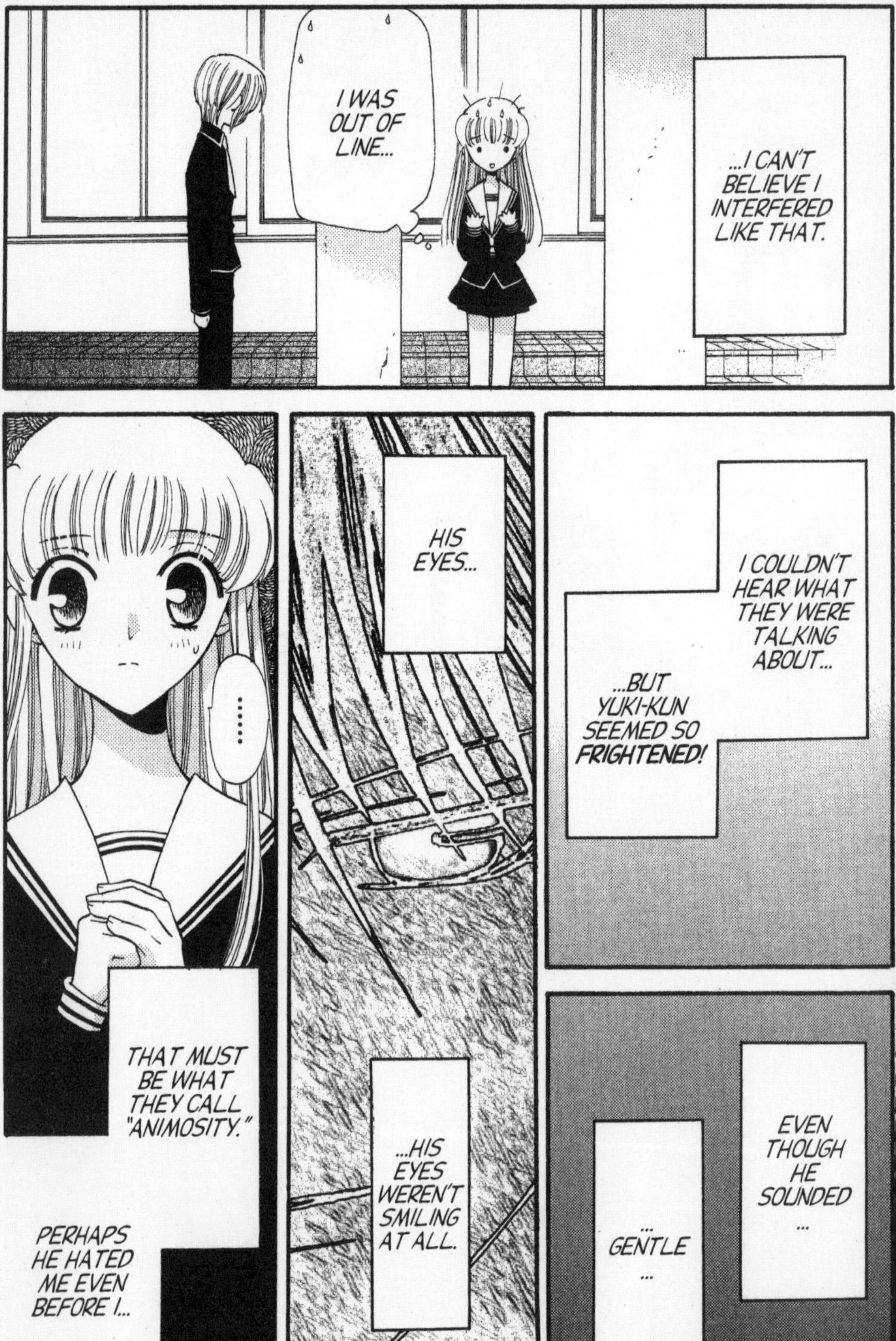
...I CAN'T BELIEVE I INTERFERED LIKE THAT.
I WAS OUT OF LINE...
I COULDN'T HEAR WHAT THEY WERE TALKING ABOUT...
...BUT YUKI-KUN SEEMED SO FRIGHTENED!
EVEN THOUGH HE SOUNDED...
...GENTLE...
HIS EYES...
...HIS EYES WEREN'T SMILING AT ALL.
......
THAT MUST BE WHAT THEY CALL "ANIMOSITY."
PERHAPS HE HATED ME EVEN BEFORE I...

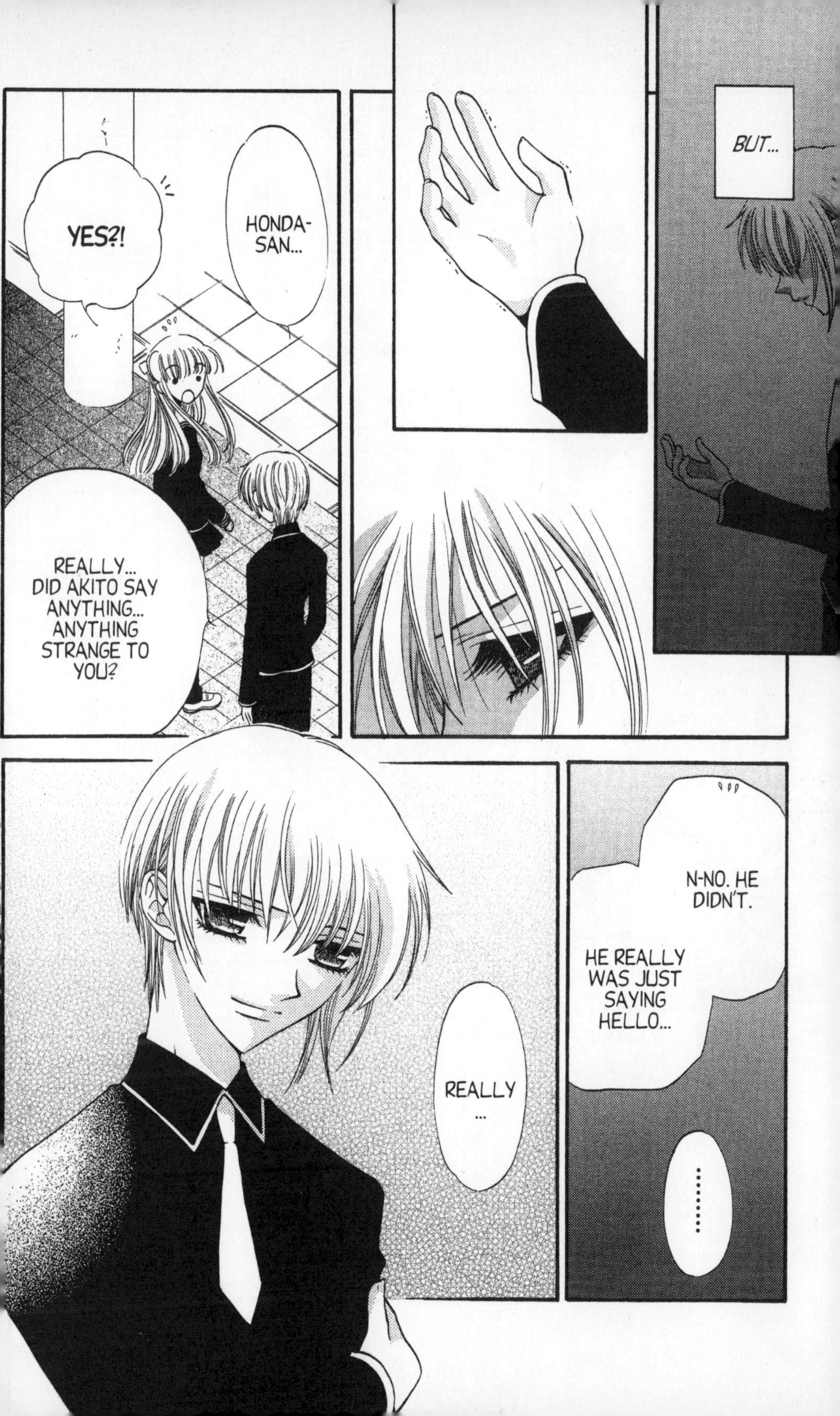
BUT...
HONDA-SAN...
YES?!
REALLY... DID AKITO SAY ANYTHING... ANYTHING STRANGE TO YOU?
N-NO. HE DIDN'T.
HE REALLY WAS JUST SAYING HELLO...
......
REALLY...

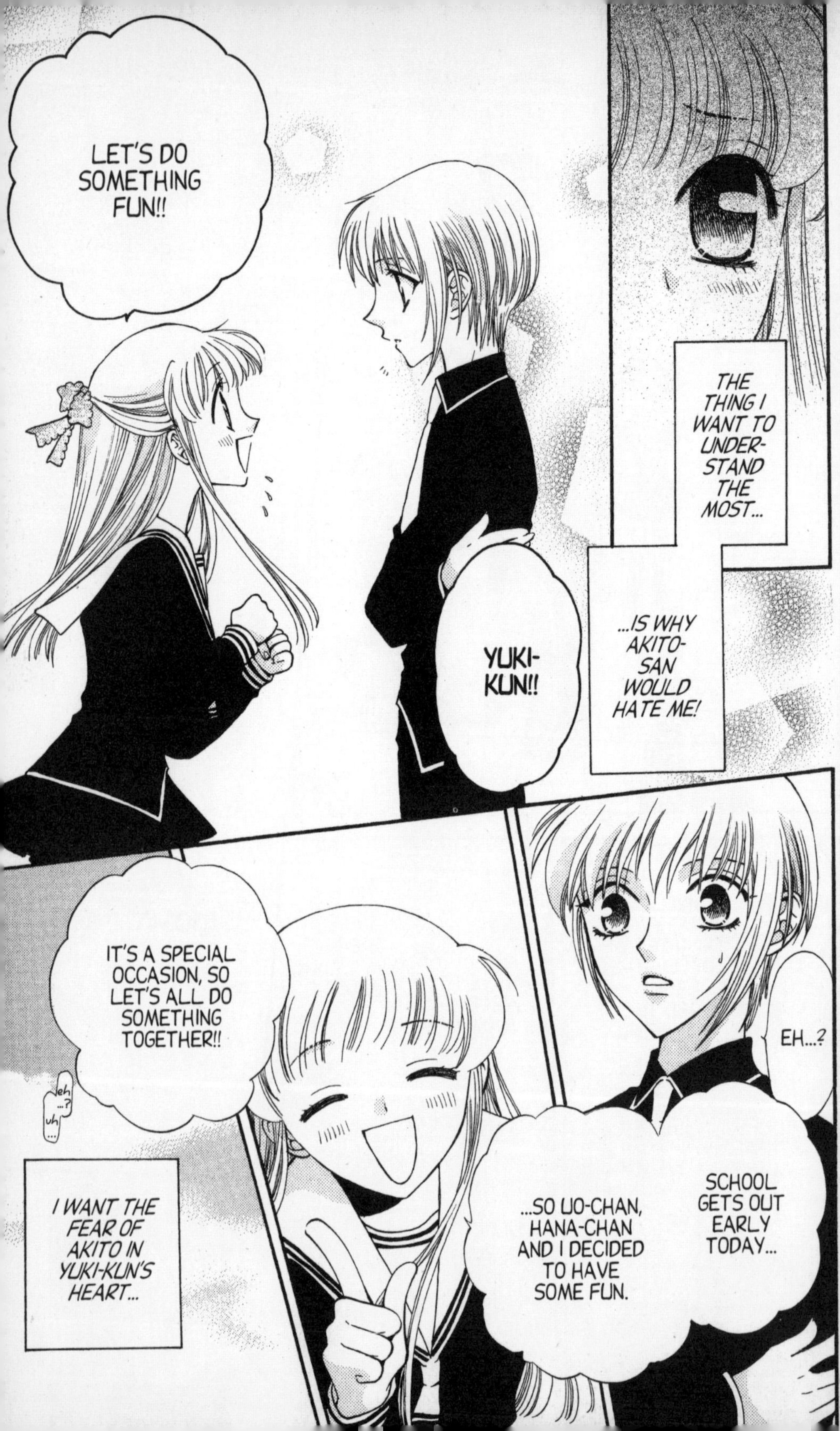
THE THING I WANT TO UNDERSTAND THE MOST...
...IS WHY AKITO-SAN WOULD HATE ME!
YUKI-KUN!!
LET'S DO SOMETHING FUN!!
EH...?
SCHOOL GETS OUT EARLY TODAY...
...SO UO-CHAN, HANA-CHAN AND I DECIDED TO HAVE SOME FUN.
IT'S A SPECIAL OCCASION, SO LET'S ALL DO SOMETHING TOGETHER!!
eh ...? uh ...
I WANT THE FEAR OF AKITO IN YUKI-KUN'S HEART...

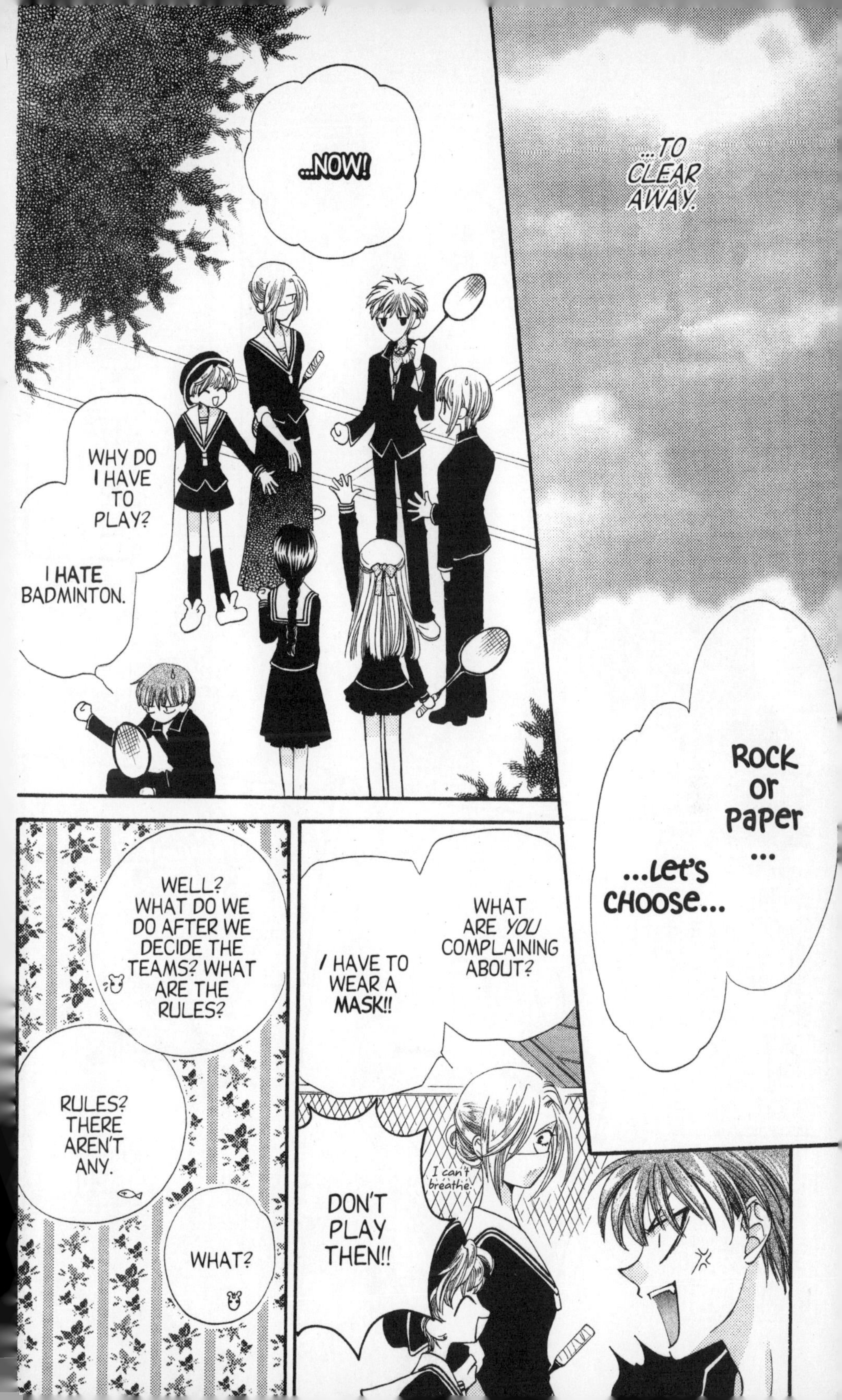
...TO CLEAR AWAY.
...LET'S CHOOSE...
ROCK OR PAPER ...
...NOW!
WHY DO I HAVE TO PLAY?
I HATE BADMINTON.
WHAT ARE *YOU* COMPLAINING ABOUT?
I HAVE TO WEAR A MASK!!
I can't breathe.
DON'T PLAY THEN!!
WELL? WHAT DO WE DO AFTER WE DECIDE THE TEAMS? WHAT ARE THE RULES?
RULES? THERE AREN'T ANY.
WHAT?

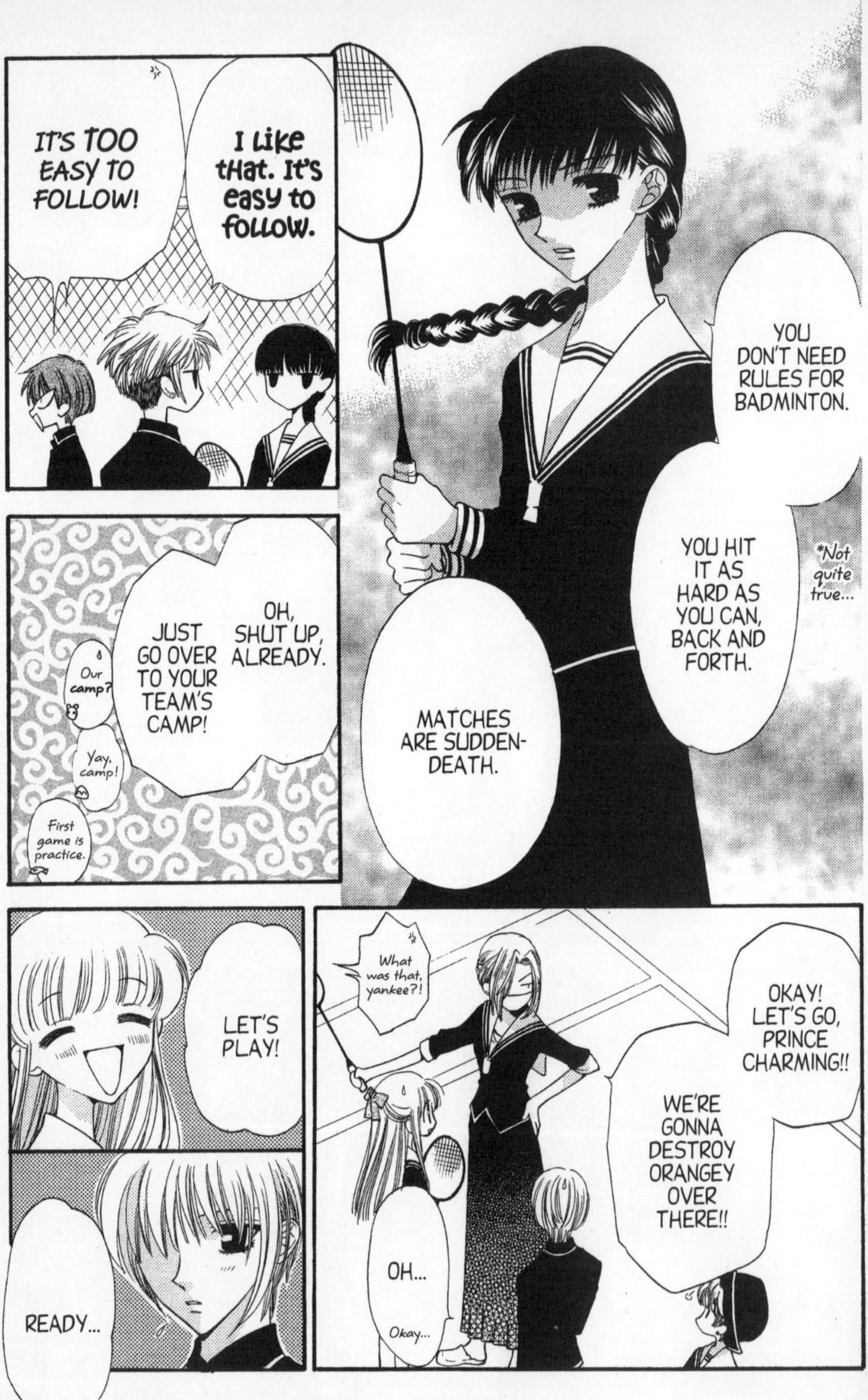
YOU DON'T NEED RULES FOR BADMINTON.
YOU HIT IT AS HARD AS YOU CAN, BACK AND FORTH.
*Not quite true...
MATCHES ARE SUDDEN-DEATH.
I like that. It's easy to follow.
IT'S TOO EASY TO FOLLOW!
OH, SHUT UP, ALREADY.
JUST GO OVER TO YOUR TEAM'S CAMP!
Our camp?
Yay, camp!
First game is practice.
OKAY! LET'S GO, PRINCE CHARMING!!
WE'RE GONNA DESTROY ORANGEY OVER THERE!!
What was that, yankee?!
OH...
Okay...
LET'S PLAY!
READY...

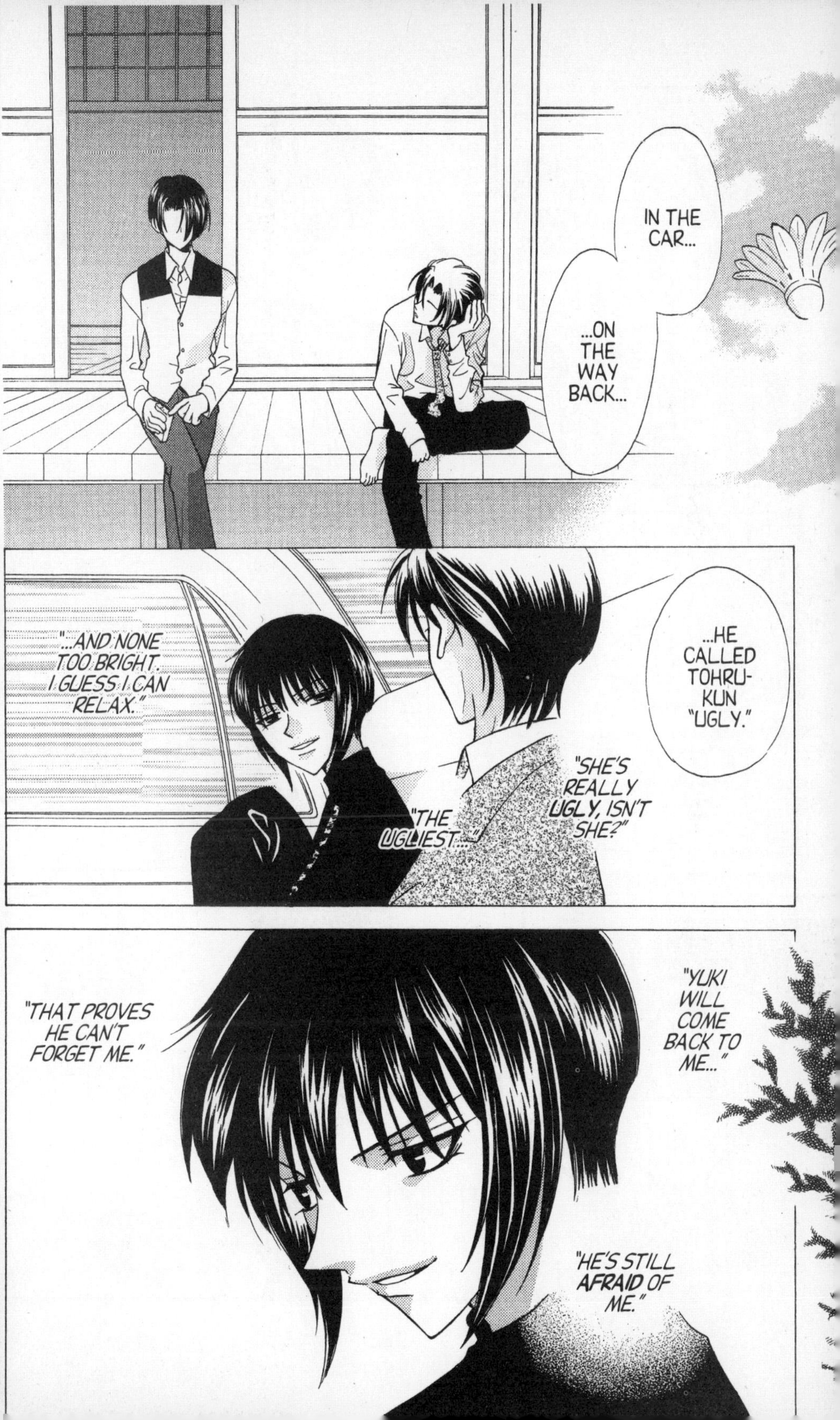
IN THE CAR...
...ON THE WAY BACK...
...HE CALLED TOHRU-KUN "UGLY."
"SHE'S REALLY UGLY, ISN'T SHE?"
"THE UGLIEST..."
"...AND NONE TOO BRIGHT. I GUESS I CAN RELAX."
"YUKI WILL COME BACK TO ME..."
"THAT PROVES HE CAN'T FORGET ME."
"HE'S STILL AFRAID OF ME."

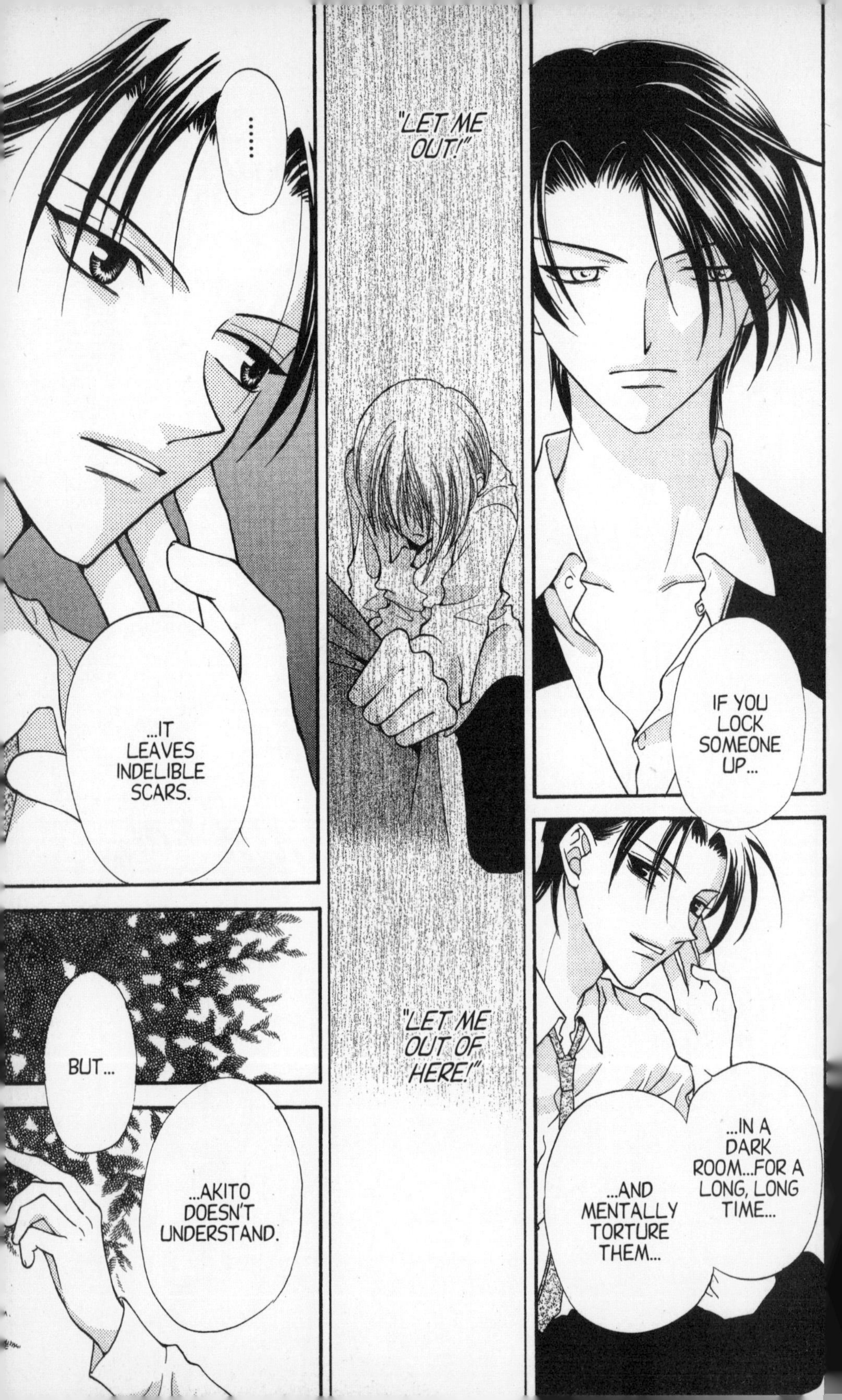
IF YOU LOCK SOMEONE UP...
...IN A DARK ROOM...FOR A LONG, LONG TIME...
...AND MENTALLY TORTURE THEM...
"LET ME OUT!"
"LET ME OUT OF HERE!"
......
...IT LEAVES INDELIBLE SCARS.
BUT...
...AKITO DOESN'T UNDERSTAND.

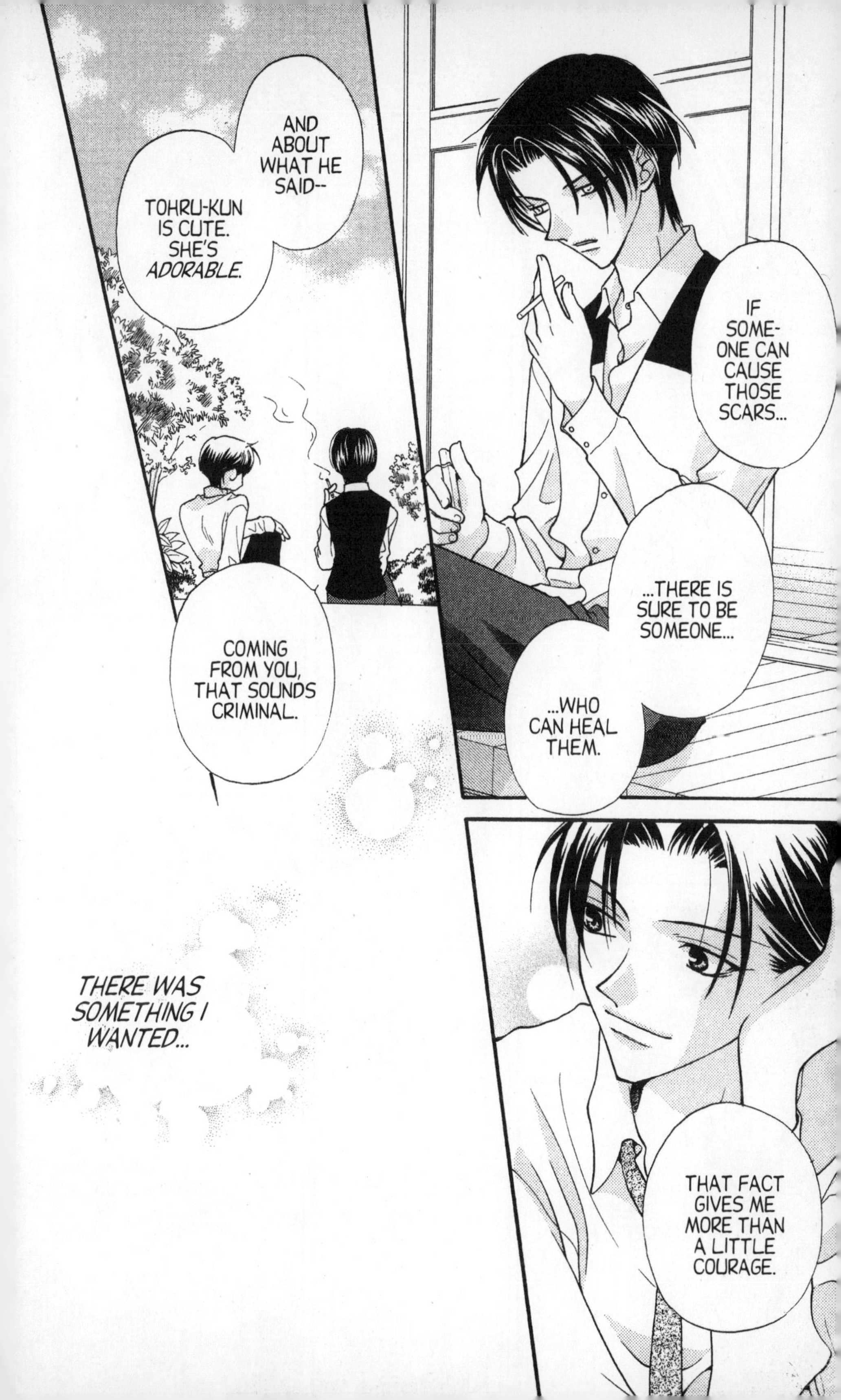
IF SOME-ONE CAN CAUSE THOSE SCARS...
...THERE IS SURE TO BE SOMEONE...
...WHO CAN HEAL THEM.
AND ABOUT WHAT HE SAID--
TOHRU-KUN IS CUTE. SHE'S *ADORABLE.*
COMING FROM YOU, THAT SOUNDS CRIMINAL.
THAT FACT GIVES ME MORE THAN A LITTLE COURAGE.
THERE WAS SOMETHING I WANTED...

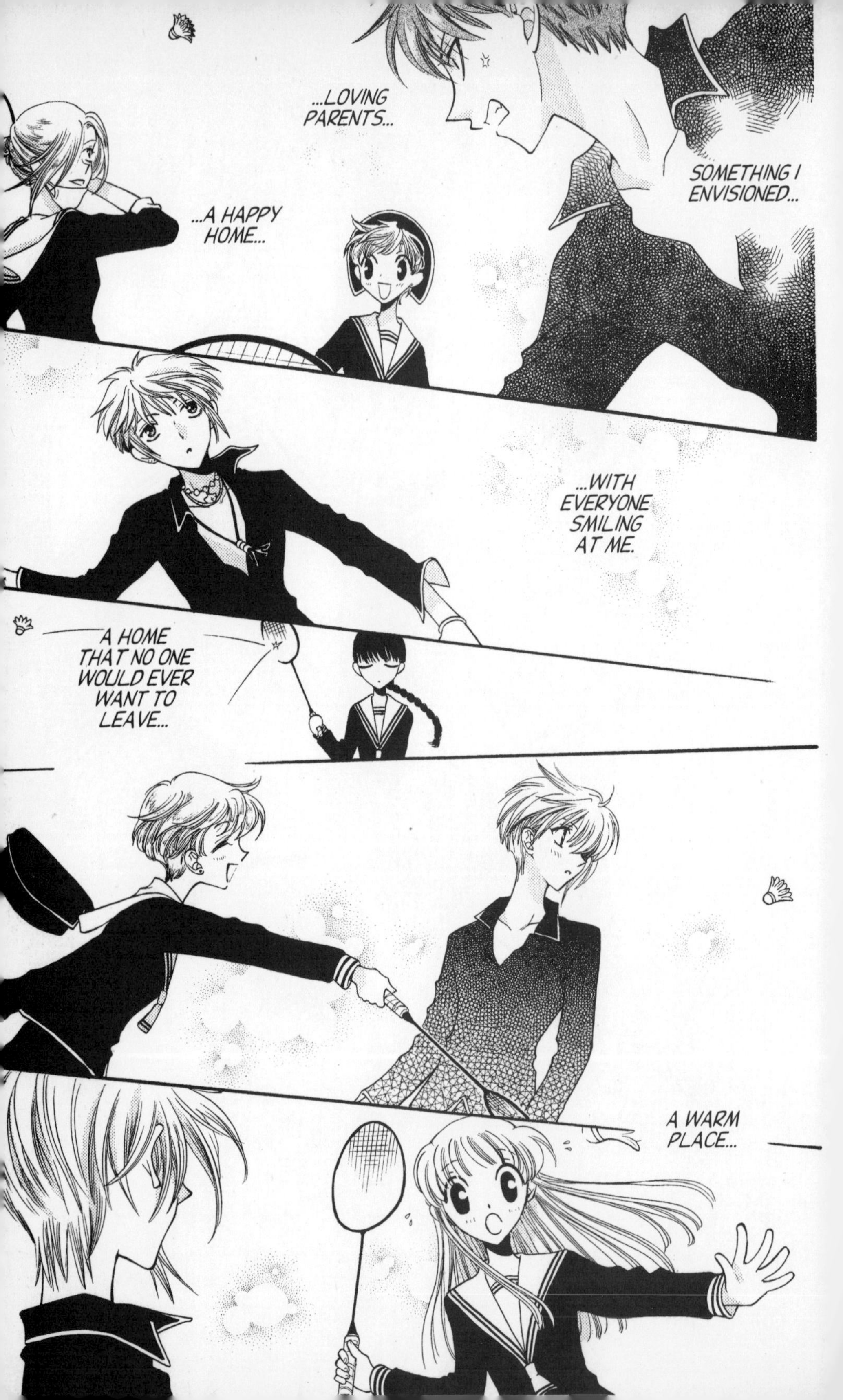
SOMETHING I ENVISIONED...
...LOVING PARENTS...
...A HAPPY HOME...
...WITH EVERYONE SMILING AT ME.
A HOME THAT NO ONE WOULD EVER WANT TO LEAVE...
A WARM PLACE...

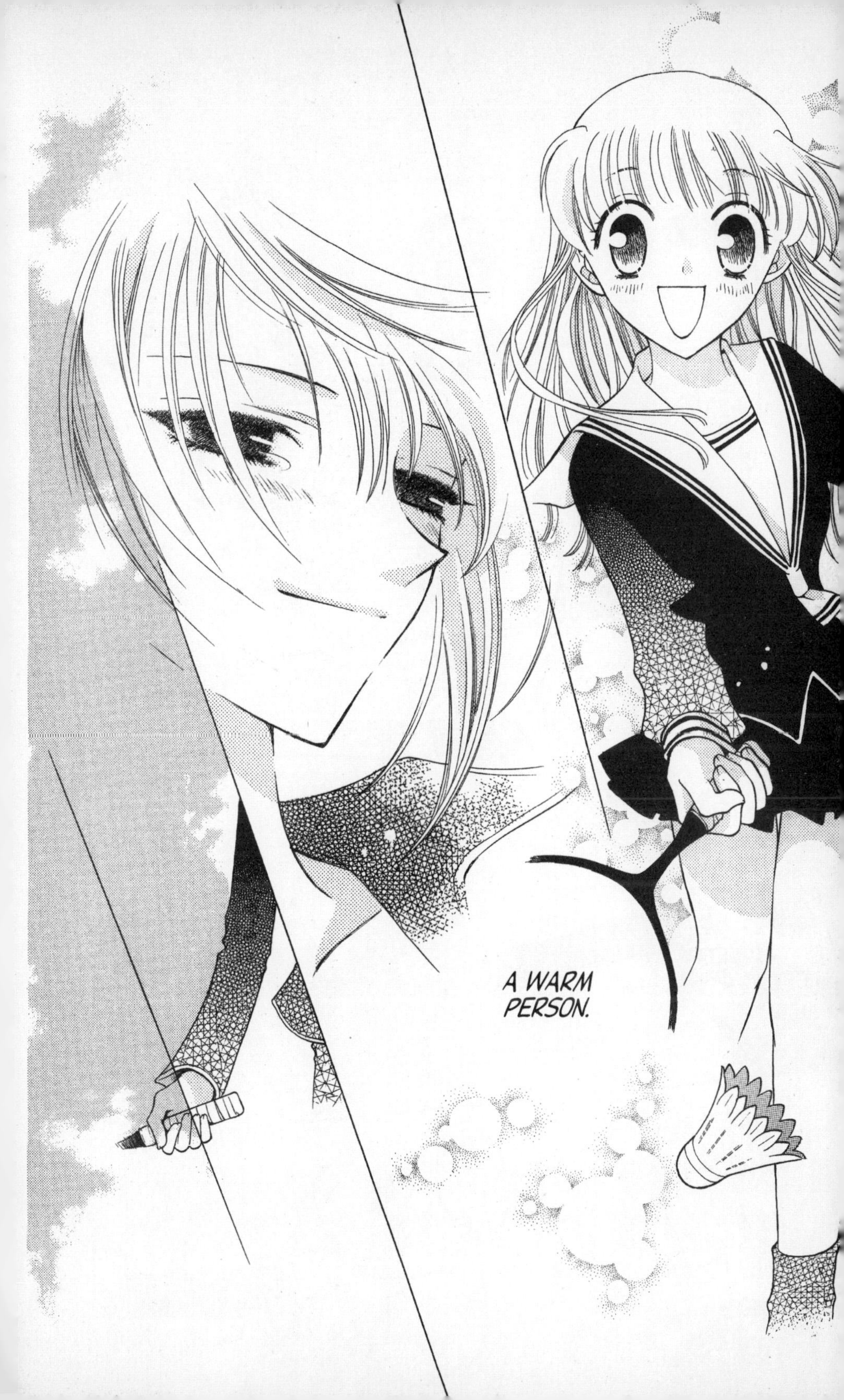
A WARM PERSON.

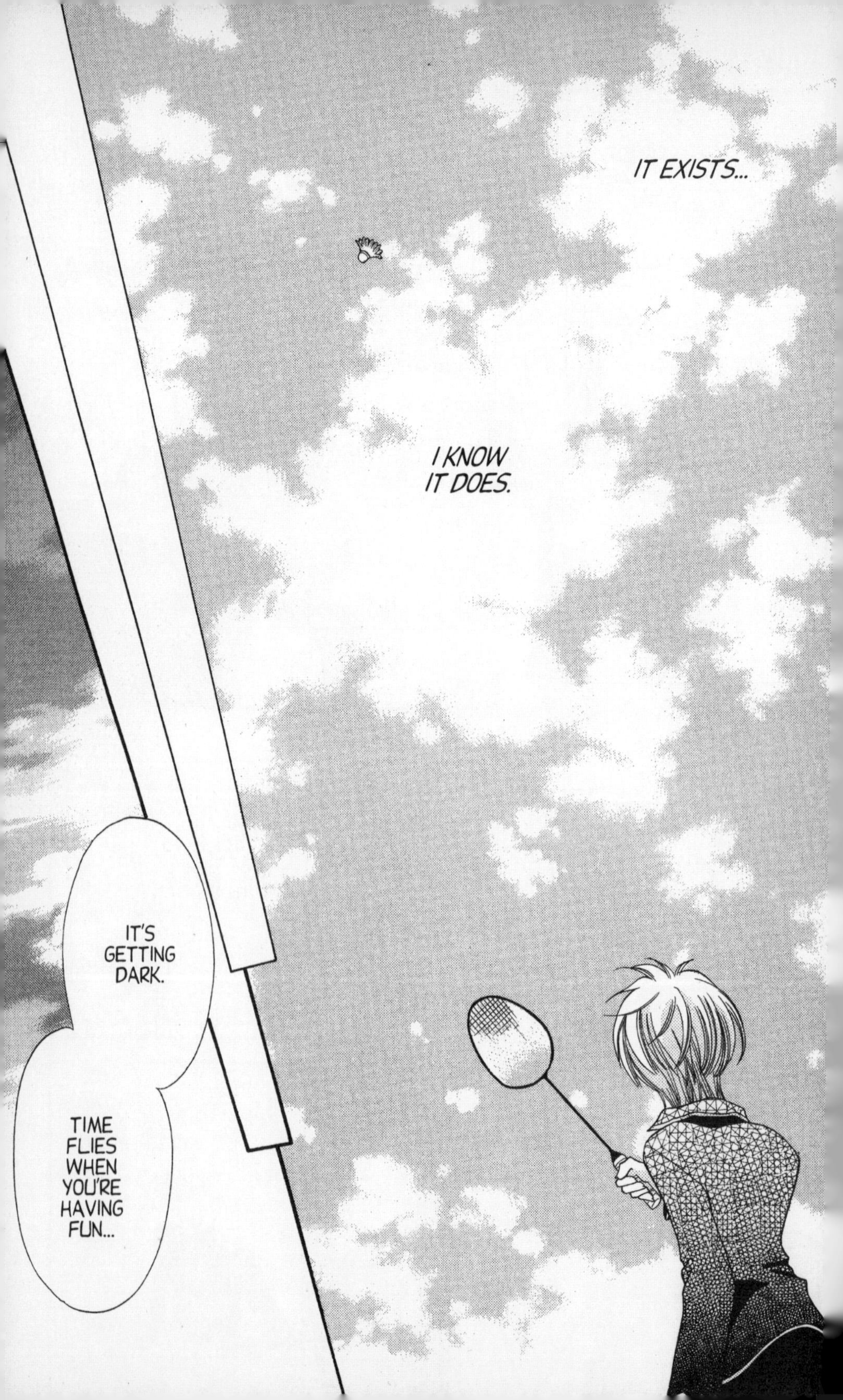
IT EXISTS...
I KNOW IT DOES.
IT'S GETTING DARK.
TIME FLIES WHEN YOU'RE HAVING FUN...

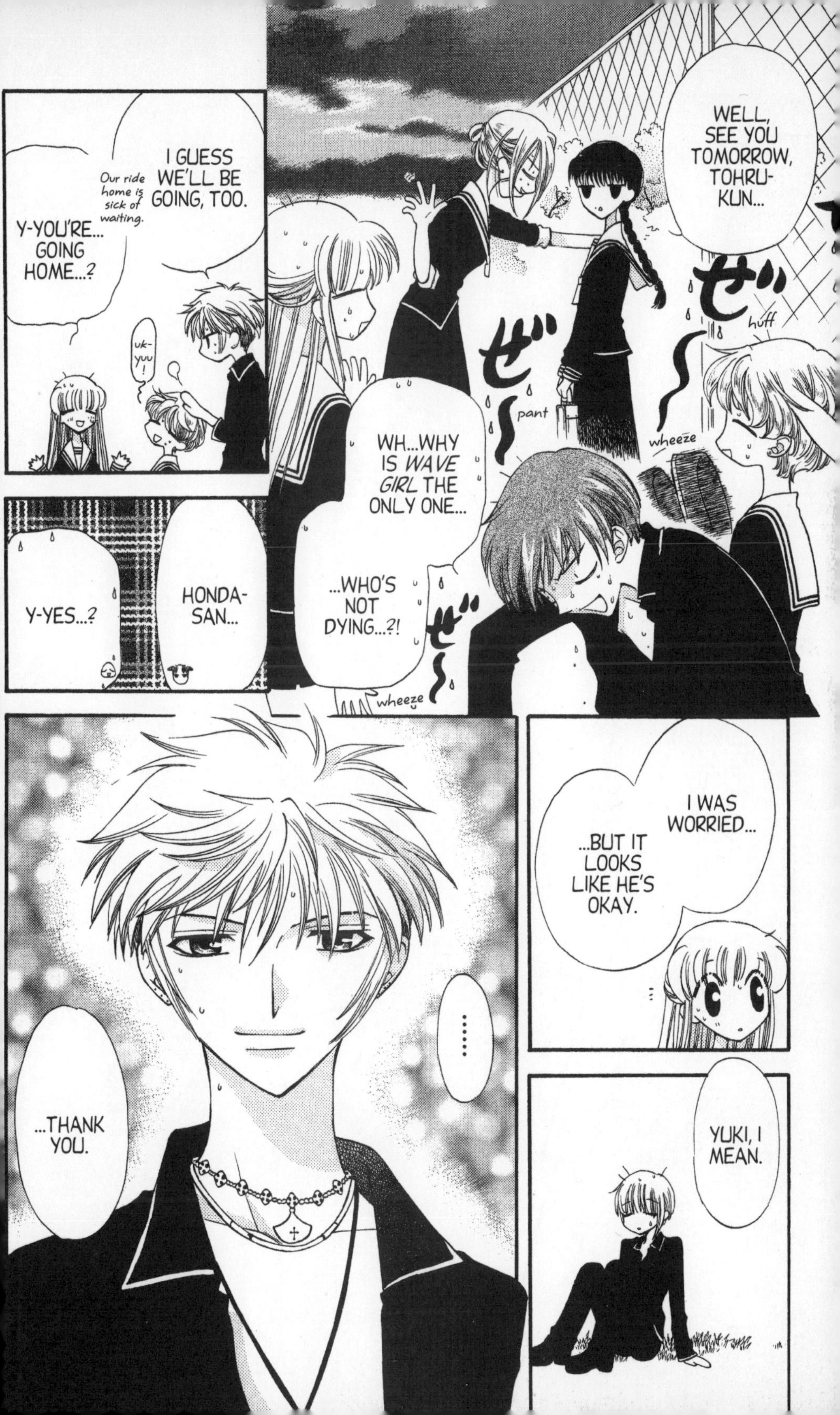
WELL, SEE YOU TOMORROW, TOHRU-KUN...
ぜい
huff
ぜ~
pant
wheeze
WH...WHY IS *WAVE GIRL* THE ONLY ONE...
...WHO'S NOT DYING...?!
ぜ~
wheeze
I GUESS WE'LL BE GOING, TOO.
Our ride home is sick of waiting.
Y-YOU'RE... GOING HOME...?
uk-yuu!
HONDA-SAN...
Y-YES...?
I WAS WORRIED...
...BUT IT LOOKS LIKE HE'S OKAY.
YUKI, I MEAN.
......
...THANK YOU.

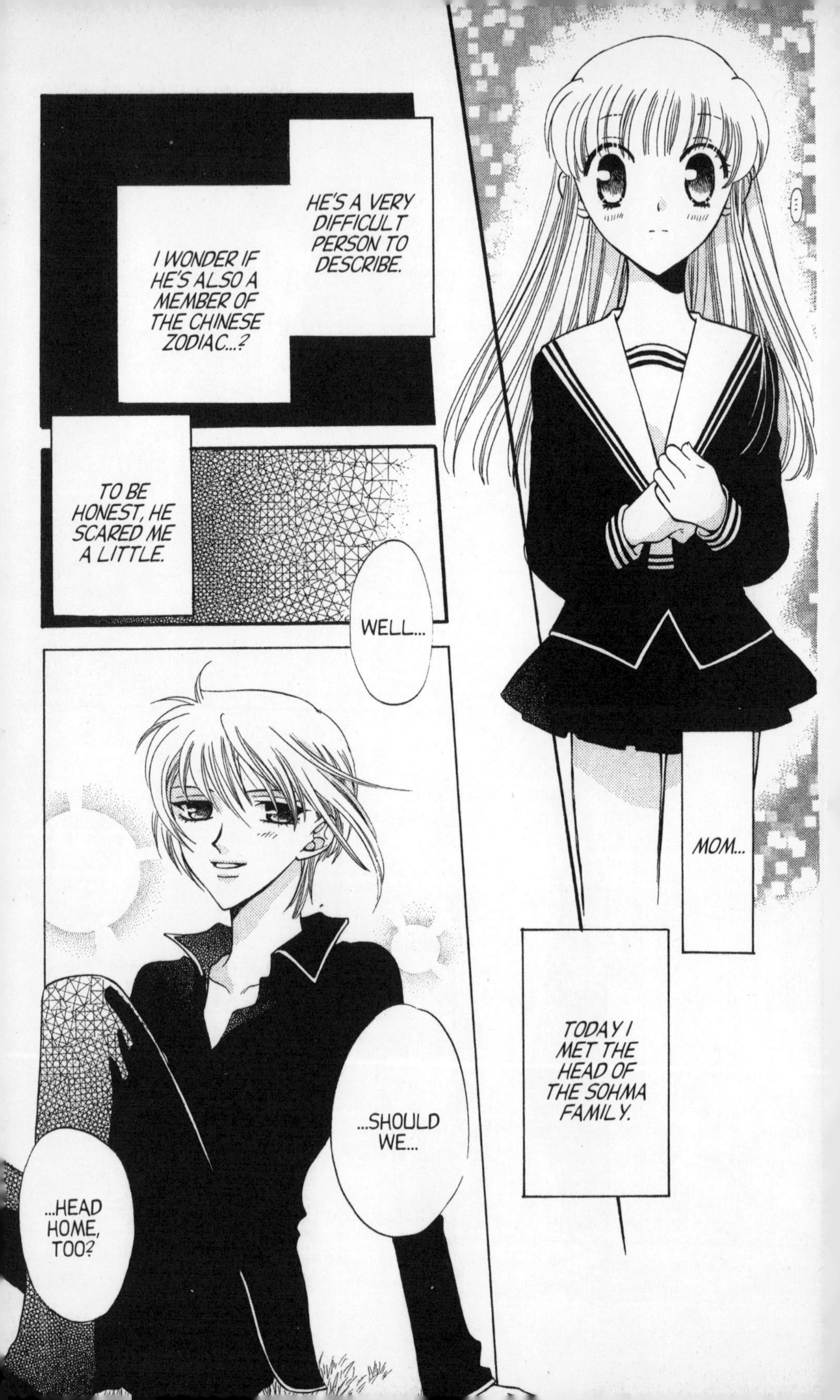
...
MOM...
TODAY I MET THE HEAD OF THE SOHMA FAMILY.
HE'S A VERY DIFFICULT PERSON TO DESCRIBE.
I WONDER IF HE'S ALSO A MEMBER OF THE CHINESE ZODIAC...?
TO BE HONEST, HE SCARED ME A LITTLE.
WELL...
...SHOULD WE...
...HEAD HOME, TOO?

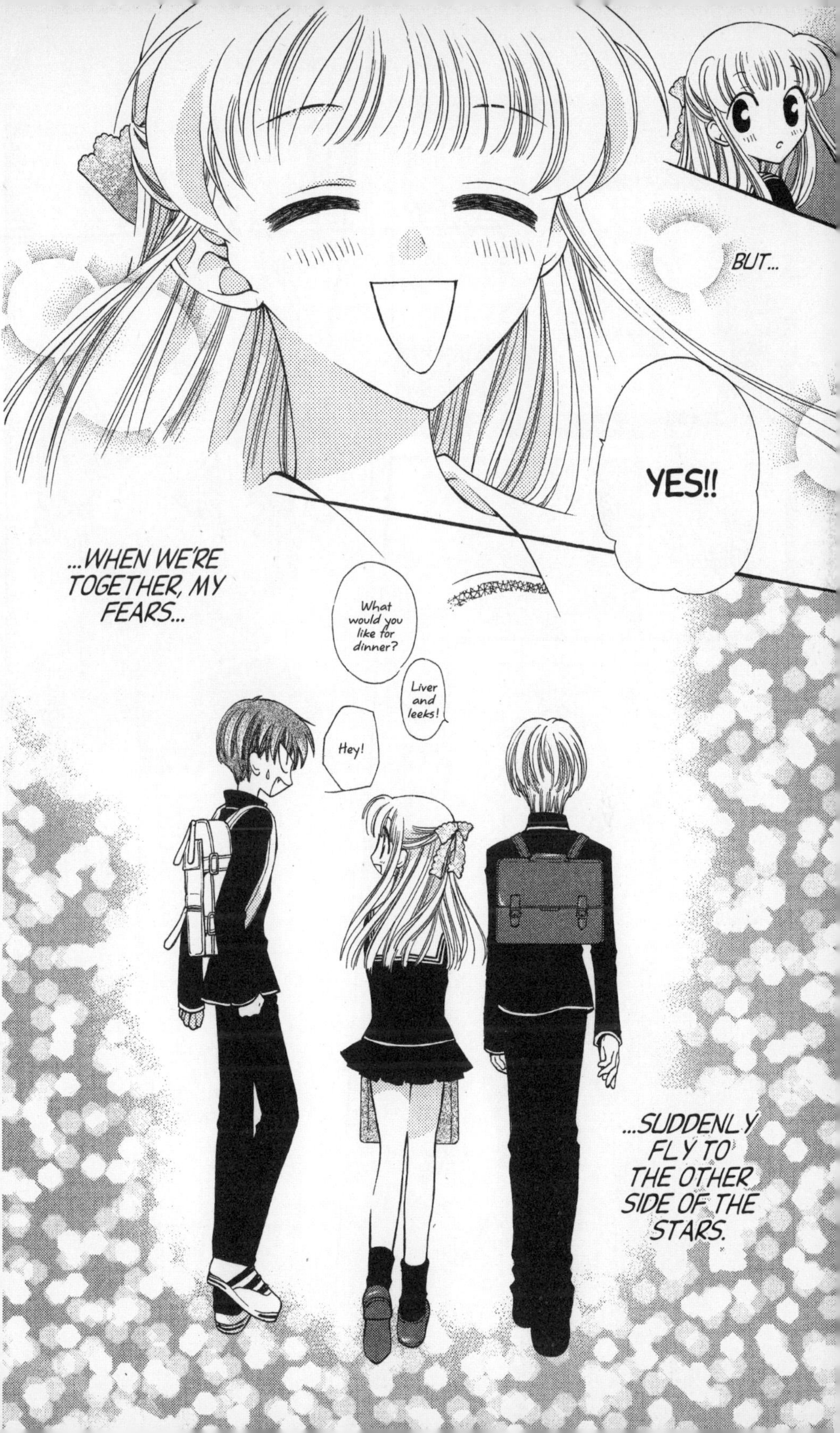
BUT...
YES!!
...WHEN WE'RE TOGETHER, MY FEARS...
What would you like for dinner?
Liver and leeks!
Hey!
...SUDDENLY FLY TO THE OTHER SIDE OF THE STARS.

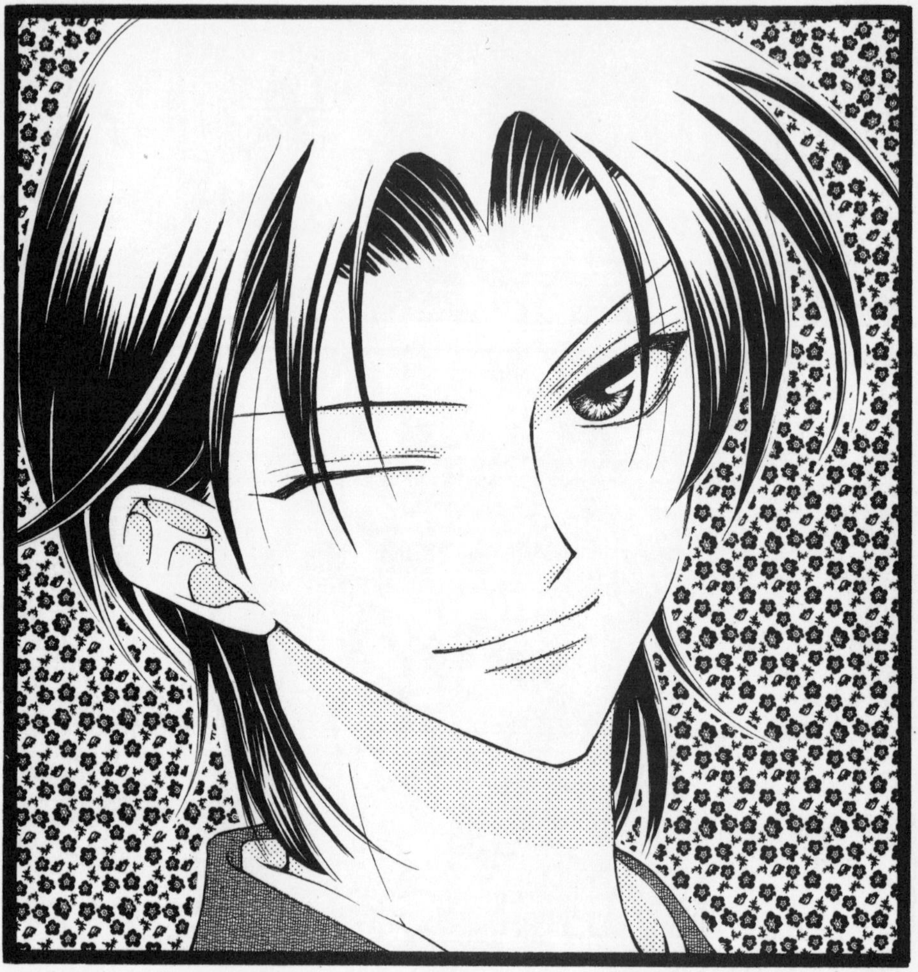

Chapter 21

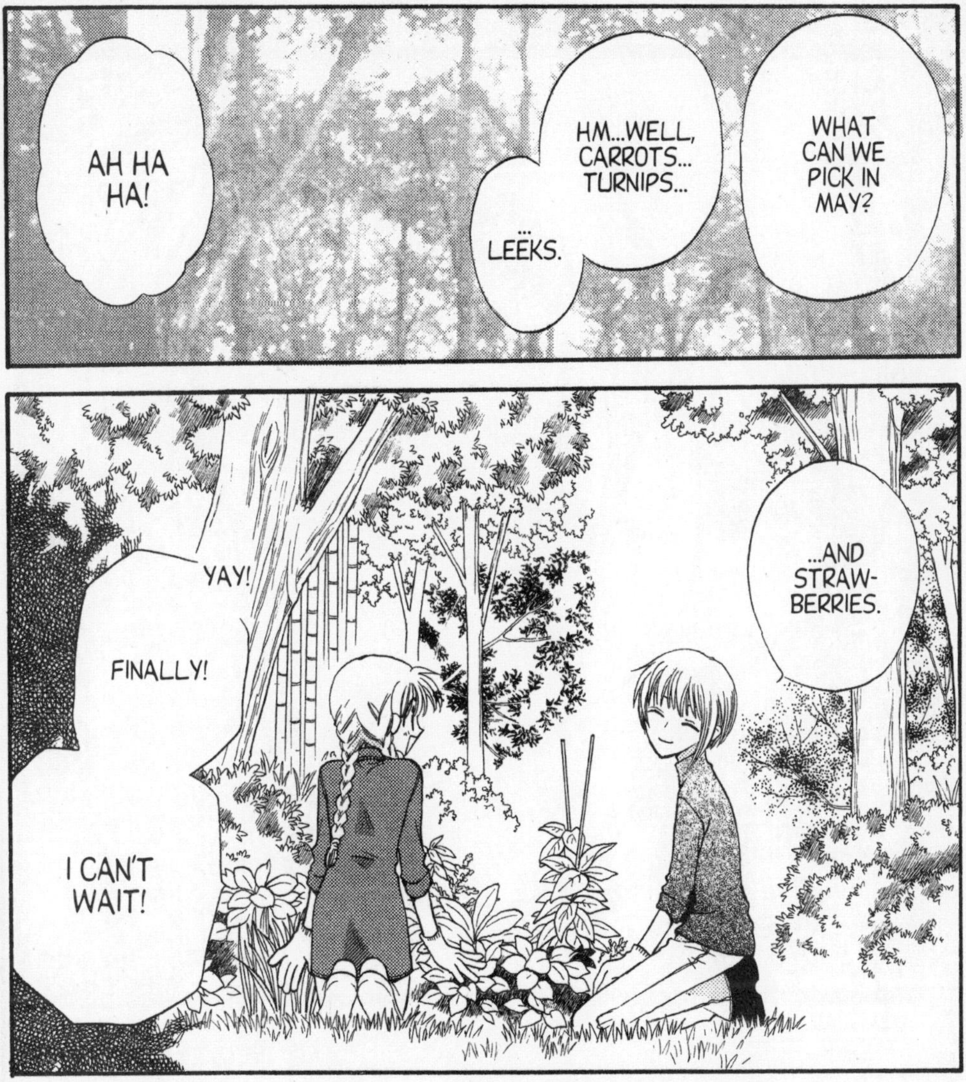
WHAT CAN WE PICK IN MAY?
HM...WELL, CARROTS... TURNIPS...
... LEEKS.
AH HA HA!
...AND STRAW-BERRIES.
YAY!
FINALLY!
I CAN'T WAIT!

ULTRA SPECIAL BLAH BLAH BLAH 3

Enter the moron...er, I mean--the older brother! He was dragged into the story pretty late, huh? He's very popular, though not as popular as the Mabudachi Trio! Sometimes people tell me that a character of mine looks like some famous person and it kind of hurts my feelings because I work so hard to create original characters! For some reason, it doesn't bother me if people compare my characters to each other, though.

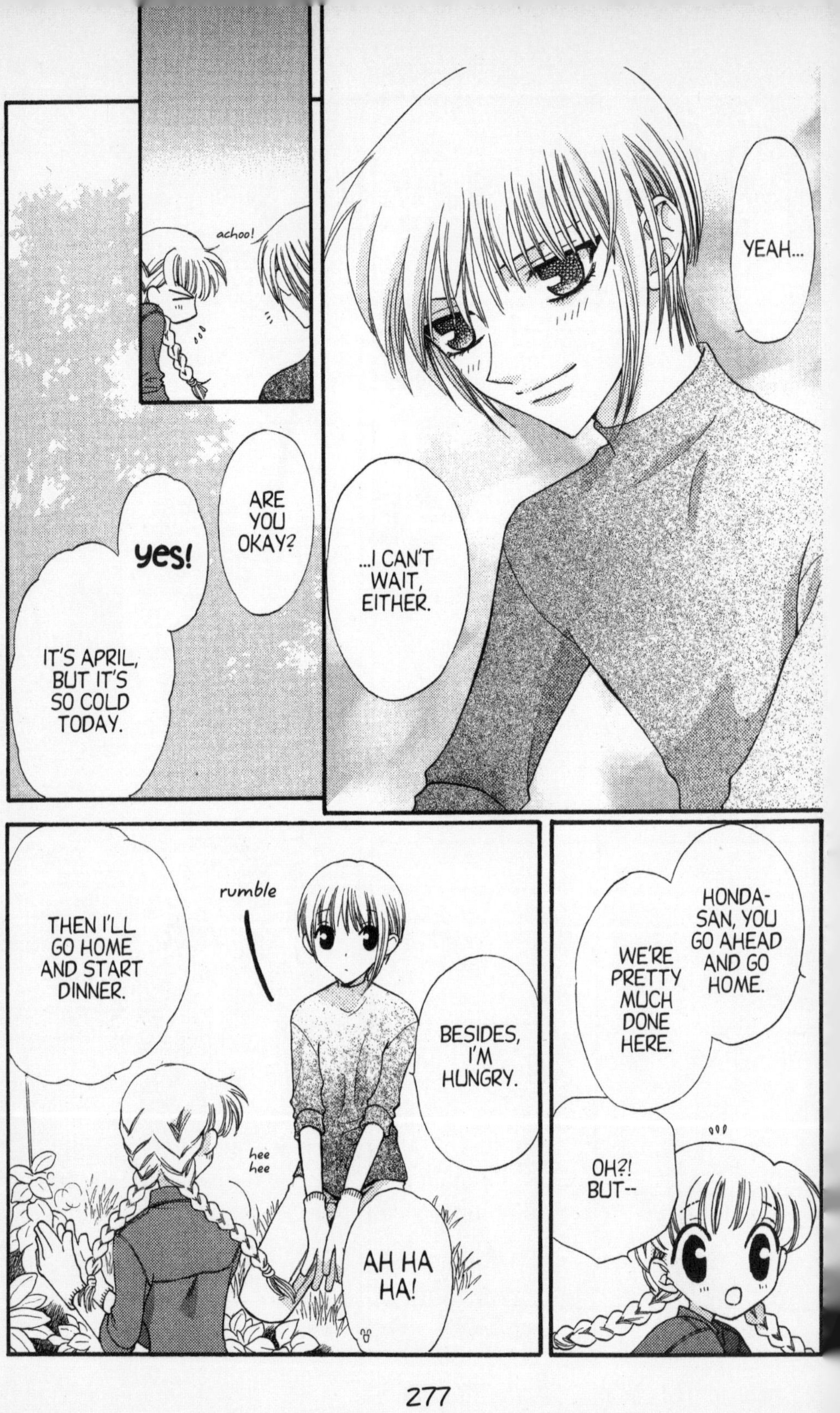
YEAH...
...I CAN'T WAIT, EITHER.
achoo!
ARE YOU OKAY?
yes!
IT'S APRIL, BUT IT'S SO COLD TODAY.
HONDA-SAN, YOU GO AHEAD AND GO HOME.
WE'RE PRETTY MUCH DONE HERE.
OH?! BUT--
BESIDES, I'M HUNGRY.
rumble
AH HA HA!
hee hee
THEN I'LL GO HOME AND START DINNER.

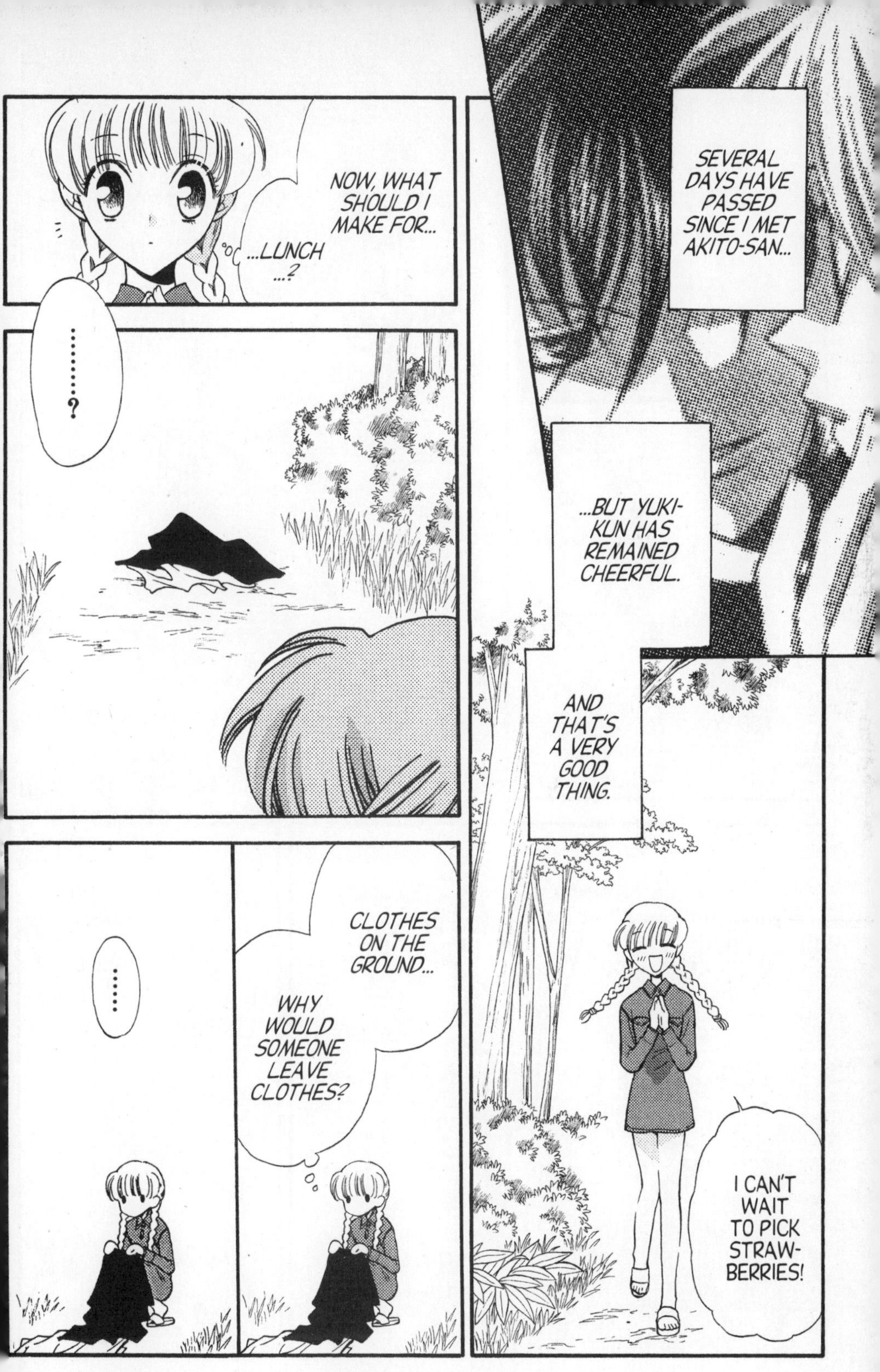
SEVERAL DAYS HAVE PASSED SINCE I MET AKITO-SAN...
...BUT YUKI-KUN HAS REMAINED CHEERFUL.
AND THAT'S A VERY GOOD THING.
I CAN'T WAIT TO PICK STRAW-BERRIES!
NOW, WHAT SHOULD I MAKE FOR...
...LUNCH ...?
......?
CLOTHES ON THE GROUND...
WHY WOULD SOMEONE LEAVE CLOTHES?
......

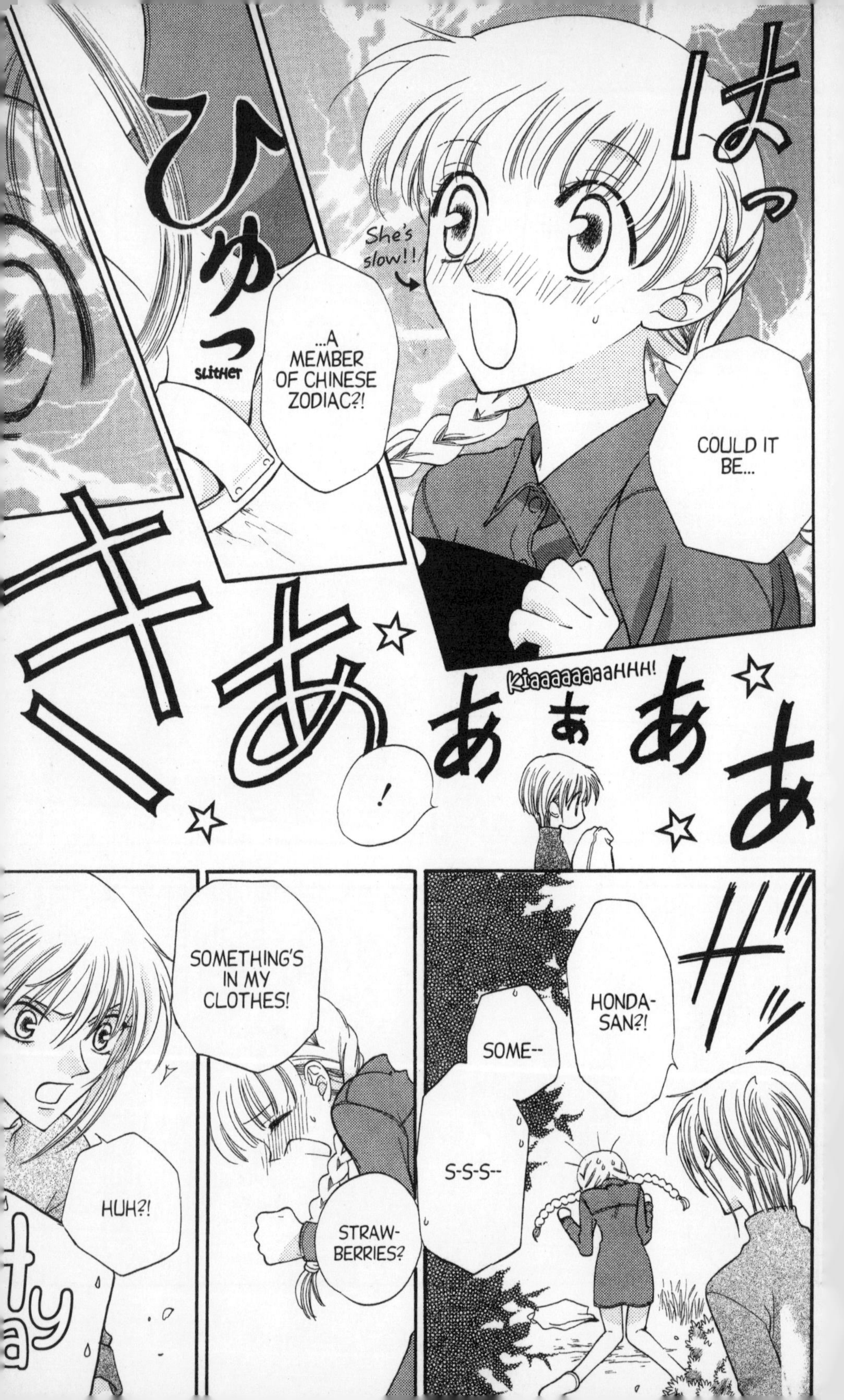
はっ
COULD IT BE...
She's slow!!
...A MEMBER OF CHINESE ZODIAC?!
ひゅっ
SLITHER
キャあ☆あぁああ
KiaaaaaaaaHHH!
!
ザッ
HONDA-SAN?!
SOME--
S-S-S--
SOMETHING'S IN MY CLOTHES!
STRAW-BERRIES?
HUH?!

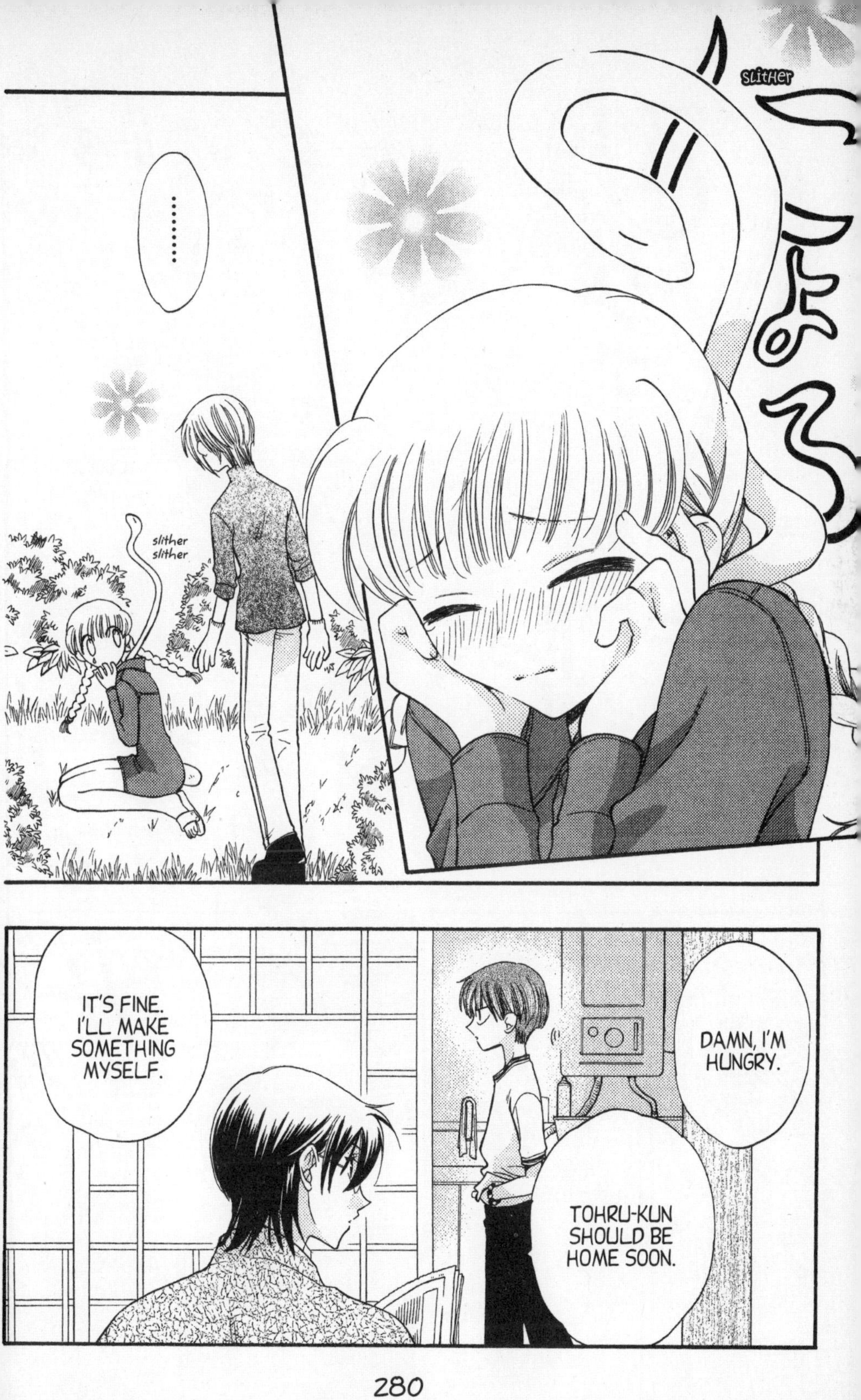
SLITHER
......
slither slither
DAMN, I'M HUNGRY.
TOHRU-KUN SHOULD BE HOME SOON.
IT'S FINE. I'LL MAKE SOMETHING MYSELF.

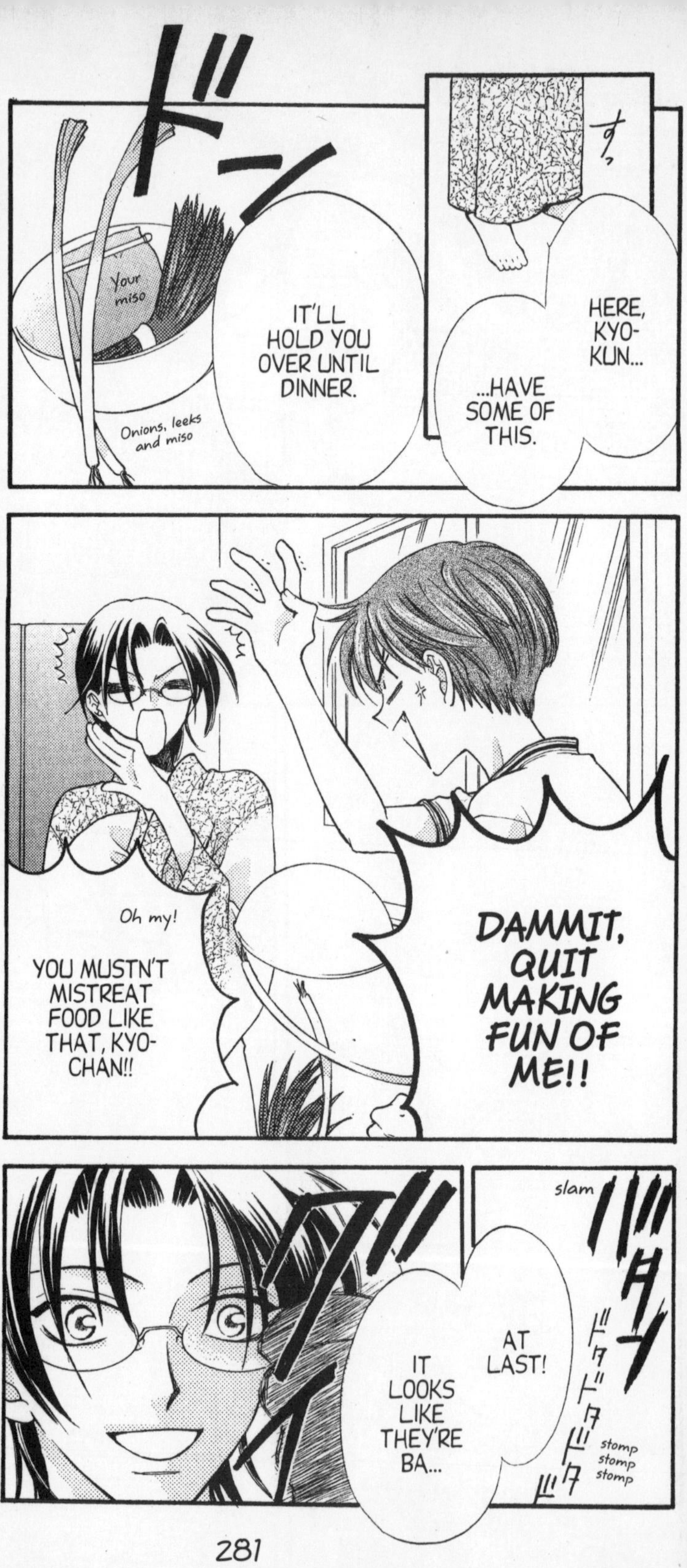
HERE, KYO-KUN...
...HAVE SOME OF THIS.
IT'LL HOLD YOU OVER UNTIL DINNER.
Your miso
Onions, leeks and miso
DAMMIT, QUIT MAKING FUN OF ME!!
Oh my!
YOU MUSTN'T MISTREAT FOOD LIKE THAT, KYO-CHAN!!
slam
stomp stomp stomp
AT LAST!
IT LOOKS LIKE THEY'RE BA...

Fruits Basket 4 Part 3:

I went to my first autograph session—at the HanaYume festival. There were so many people, I got nervous! I wanted to say, "I'm not that great," you know? (I'm really not.) I even got presents. Thank you.
I thought of getting a Furuba print club, too, but the line was so long I gave up. (By the way, I've never taken a print club picture. There actually are people who haven't.) But I was very happy to have people thank me so sincerely. I really felt they meant it.
Anyway, did you enjoy the Hana-Yume festival? I'm very happy because I got a Hanya* plush toy! (Ha ha!)

*A character from the Hana to Yume comic, "Uchuu no Hate kara Konnichi wa"

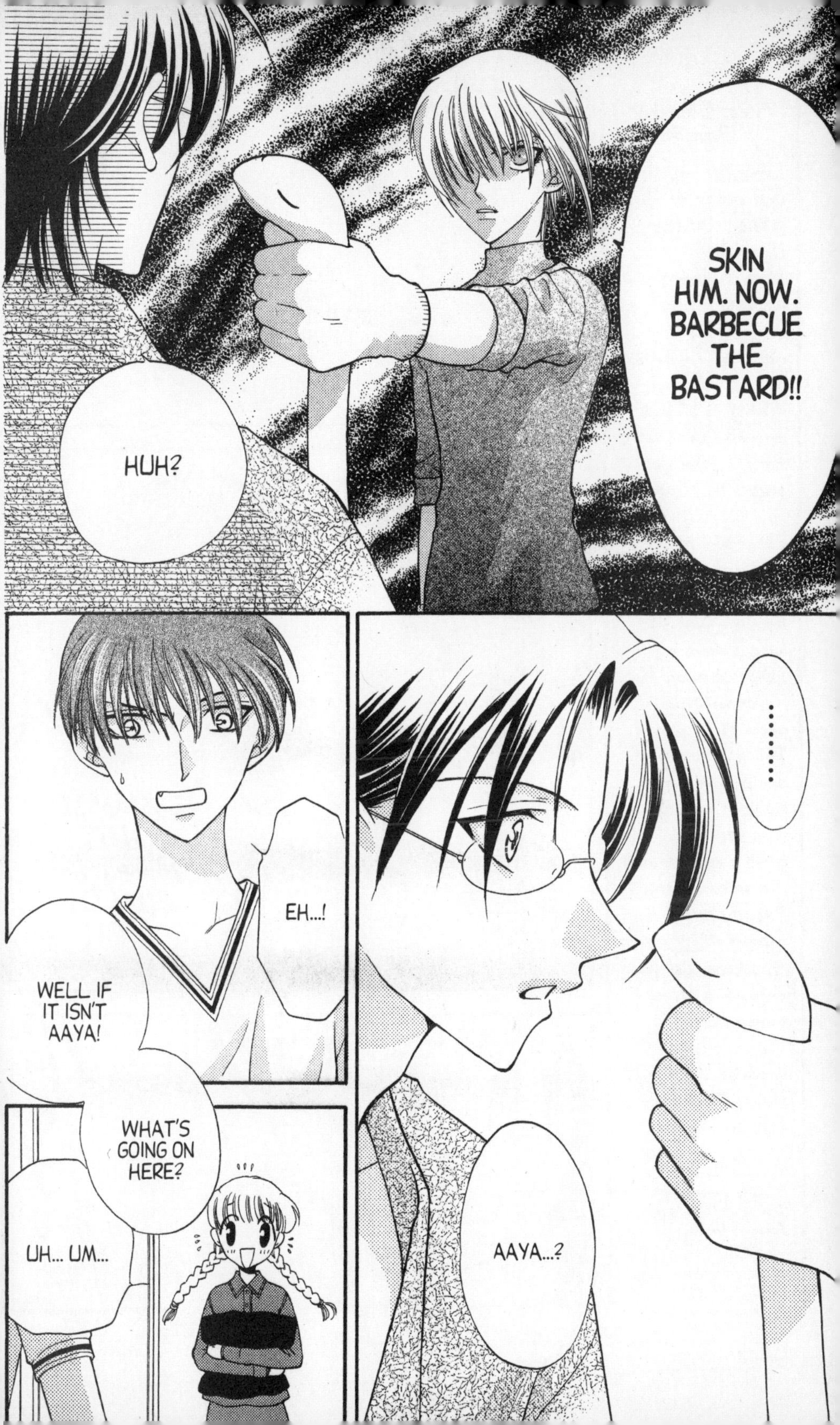
SKIN HIM. NOW. BARBECUE THE BASTARD!!
HUH?
......
AAYA...?
EH...!
WELL IF IT ISN'T AAYA!
WHAT'S GOING ON HERE?
UH... UM...

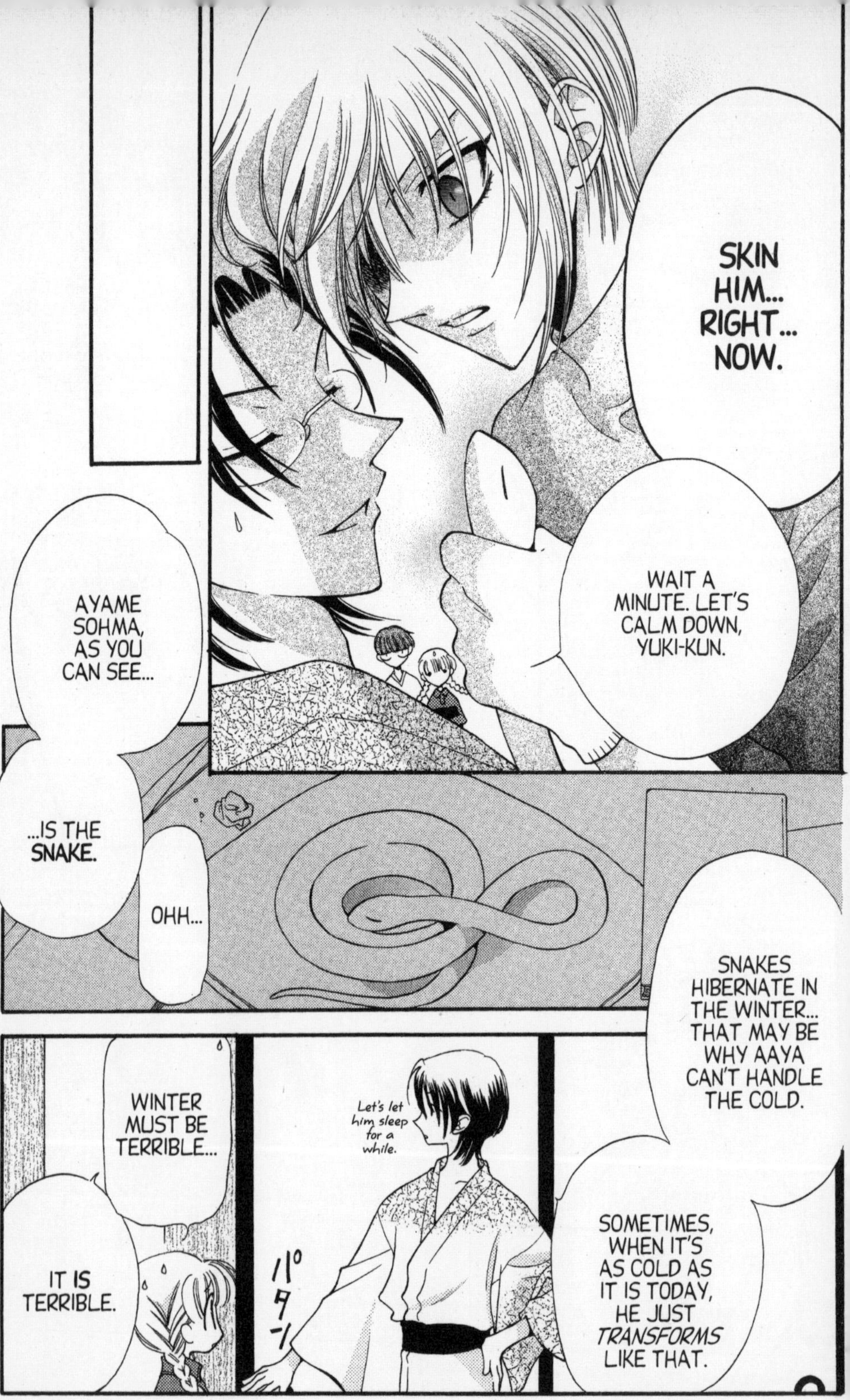
SKIN HIM... RIGHT... NOW.
WAIT A MINUTE. LET'S CALM DOWN, YUKI-KUN.
AYAME SOHMA, AS YOU CAN SEE...
...IS THE SNAKE.
OHH...
SNAKES HIBERNATE IN THE WINTER... THAT MAY BE WHY AAYA CAN'T HANDLE THE COLD.
SOMETIMES, WHEN IT'S AS COLD AS IT IS TODAY, HE JUST TRANSFORMS LIKE THAT.
Let's let him sleep for a while.
パタン
WINTER MUST BE TERRIBLE...
IT IS TERRIBLE.

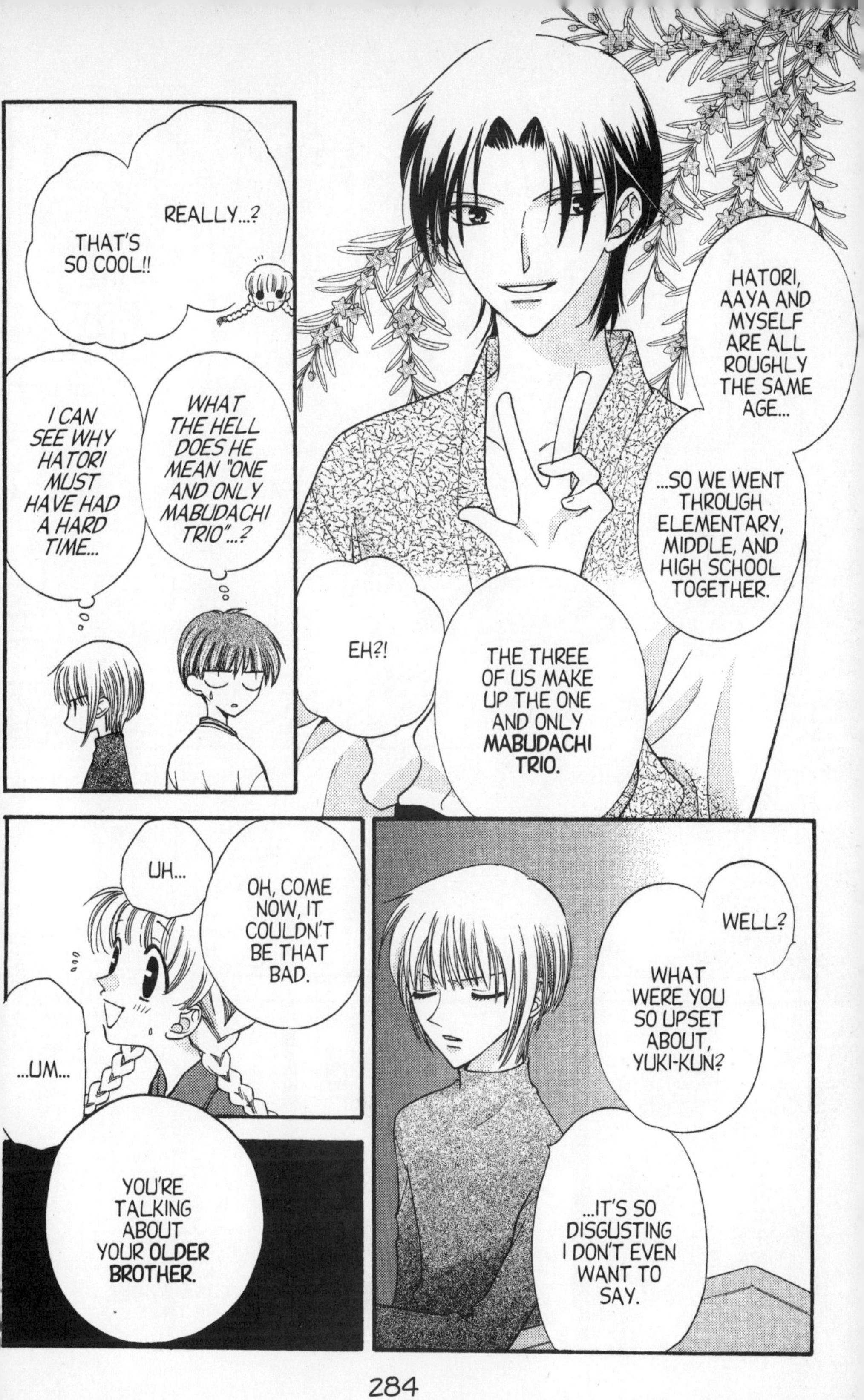
HATORI, AAYA AND MYSELF ARE ALL ROUGHLY THE SAME AGE...
...SO WE WENT THROUGH ELEMENTARY, MIDDLE, AND HIGH SCHOOL TOGETHER.
THE THREE OF US MAKE UP THE ONE AND ONLY **MABUDACHI TRIO.**
EH?!
REALLY...? THAT'S SO COOL!!
WHAT THE HELL DOES HE MEAN "ONE AND ONLY MABUDACHI TRIO"...?
I CAN SEE WHY HATORI MUST HAVE HAD A HARD TIME...
WELL? WHAT WERE YOU SO UPSET ABOUT, YUKI-KUN?
...IT'S SO DISGUSTING I DON'T EVEN WANT TO SAY.
OH, COME NOW, IT COULDN'T BE THAT BAD.
UH...
...UM...
YOU'RE TALKING ABOUT YOUR **OLDER BROTHER.**

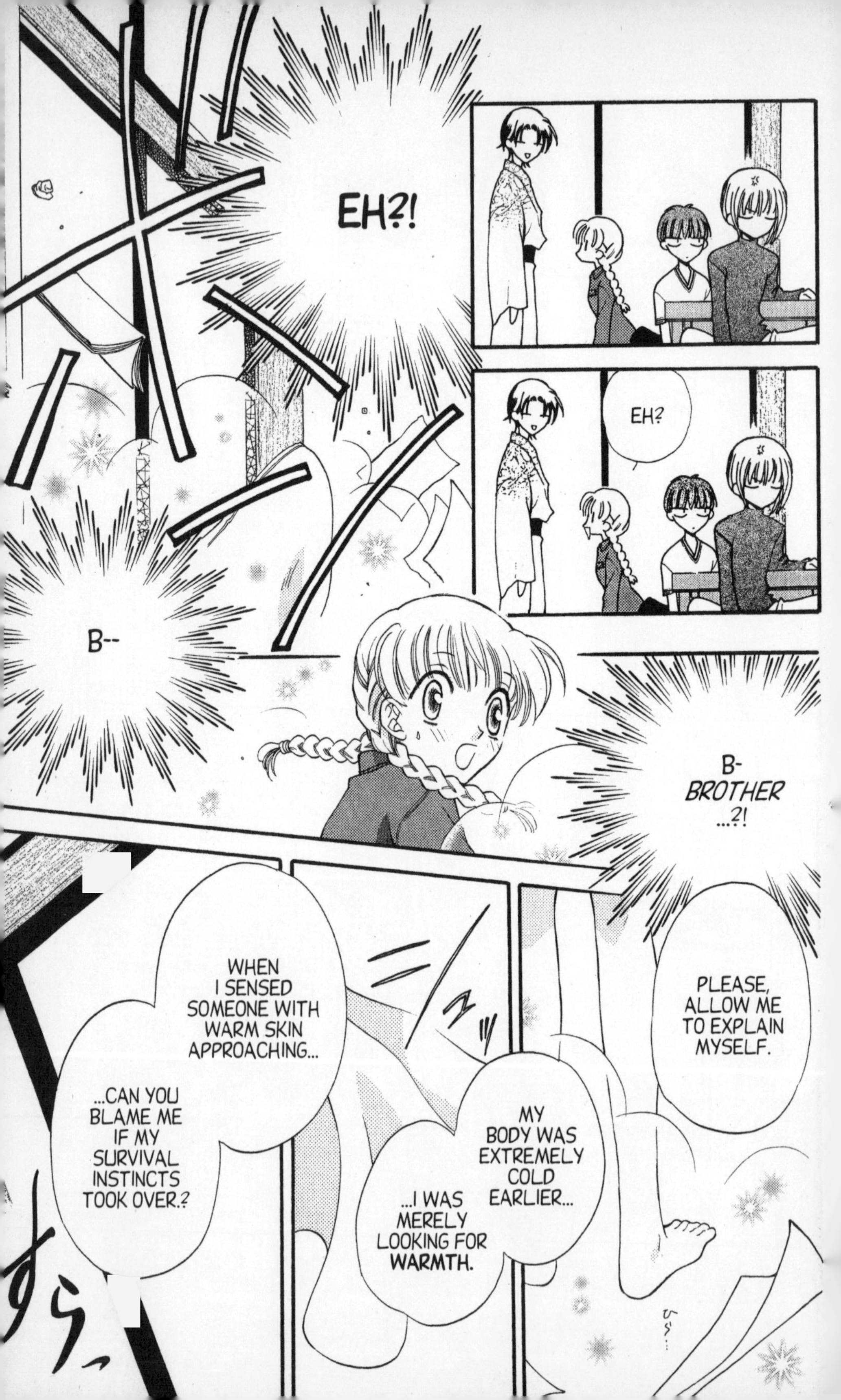
EH?
EH?!
B--
B- BROTHER ...?!
PLEASE, ALLOW ME TO EXPLAIN MYSELF.
MY BODY WAS EXTREMELY COLD EARLIER...
...I WAS MERELY LOOKING FOR WARMTH.
WHEN I SENSED SOMEONE WITH WARM SKIN APPROACHING...
...CAN YOU BLAME ME IF MY SURVIVAL INSTINCTS TOOK OVER?
すらっ

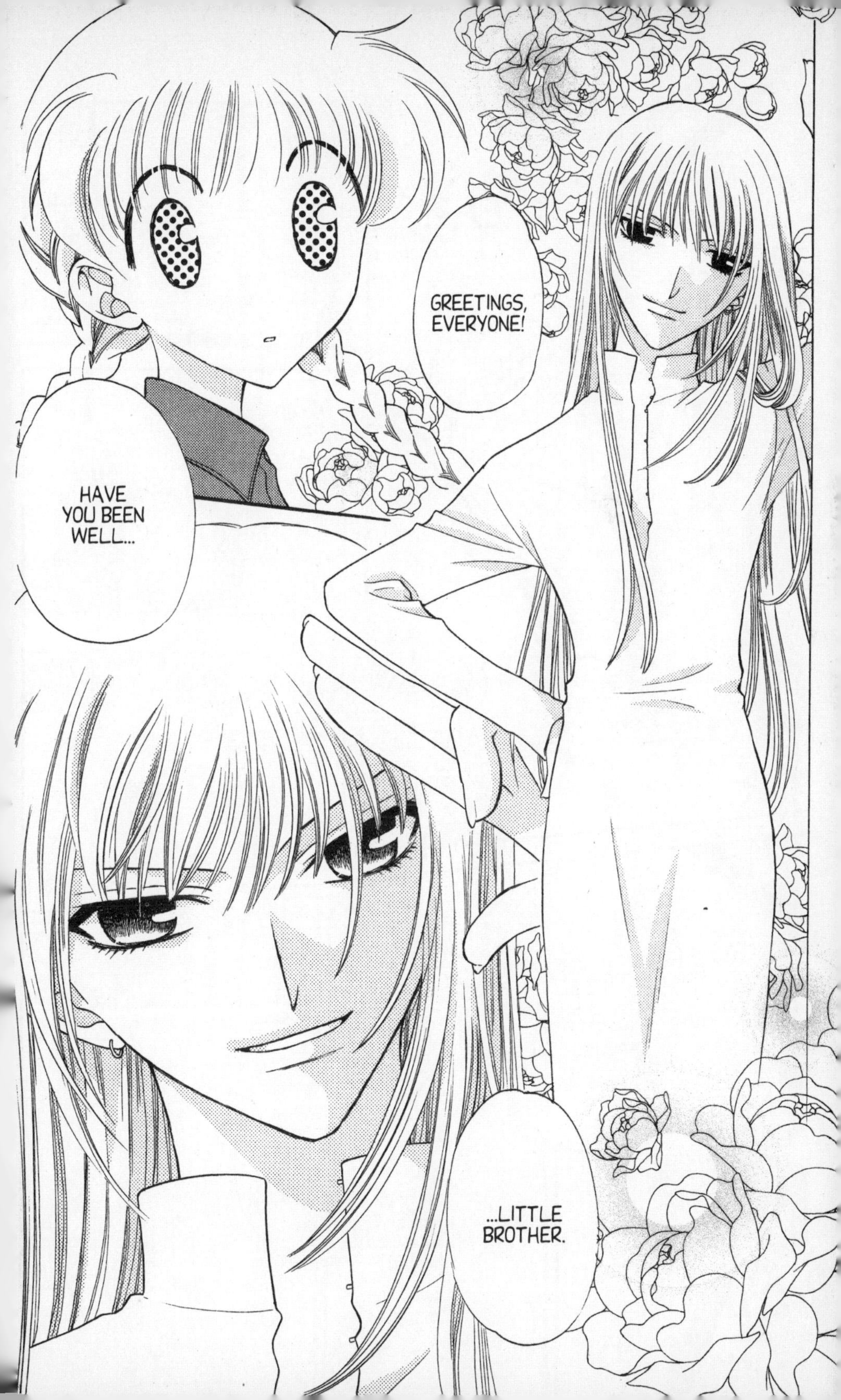
GREETINGS, EVERYONE!
HAVE YOU BEEN WELL...
...LITTLE BROTHER.

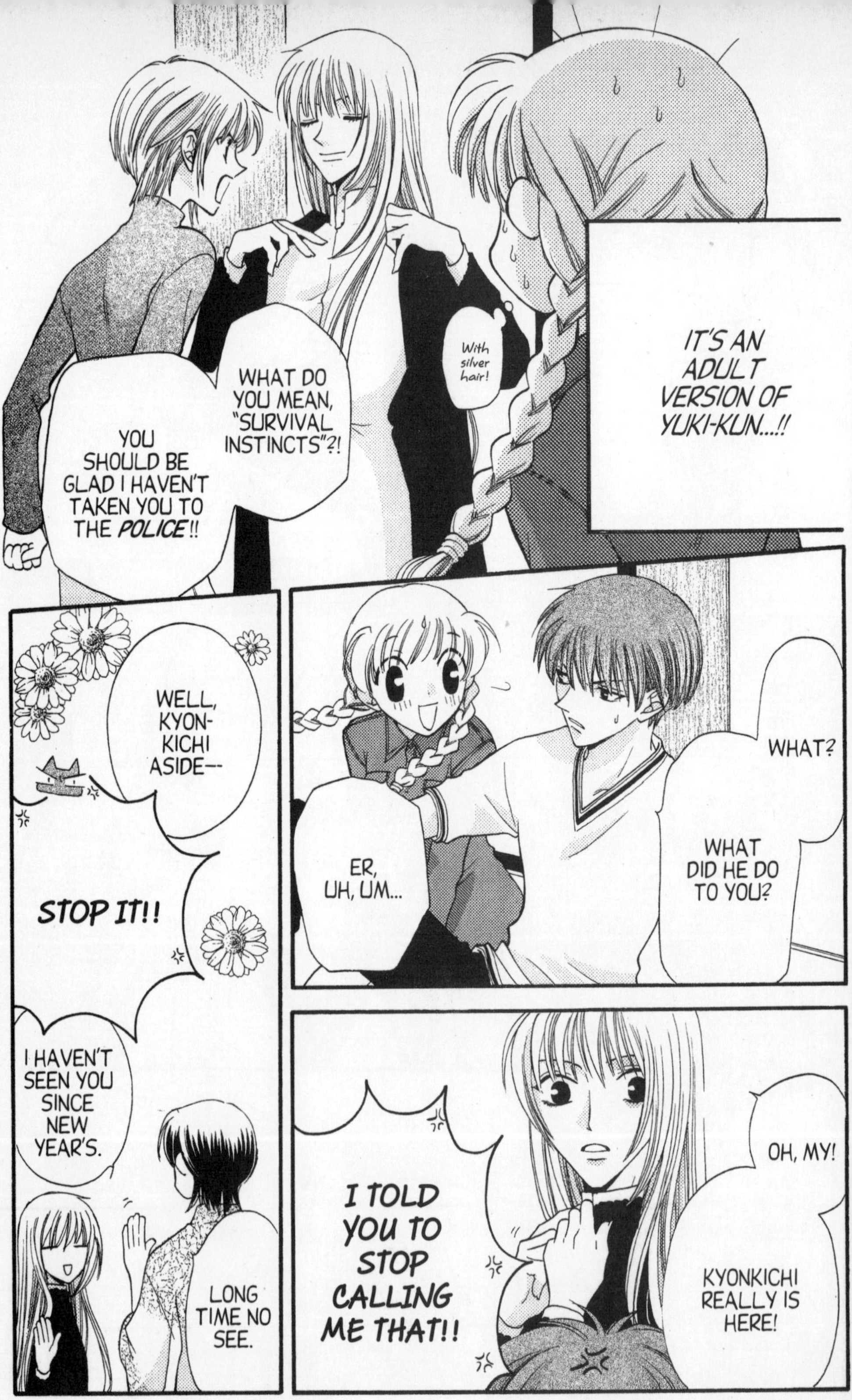

IT'S AN ADULT VERSION OF YUKI-KUN...!!
With silver hair!
WHAT DO YOU MEAN, "SURVIVAL INSTINCTS"?!
YOU SHOULD BE GLAD I HAVEN'T TAKEN YOU TO THE POLICE!!
WHAT?
WHAT DID HE DO TO YOU?
ER, UH, UM...
OH, MY!
KYONKICHI REALLY IS HERE!
I TOLD YOU TO STOP CALLING ME THAT!!
WELL, KYON-KICHI ASIDE--
STOP IT!!
I HAVEN'T SEEN YOU SINCE NEW YEAR'S.
LONG TIME NO SEE.

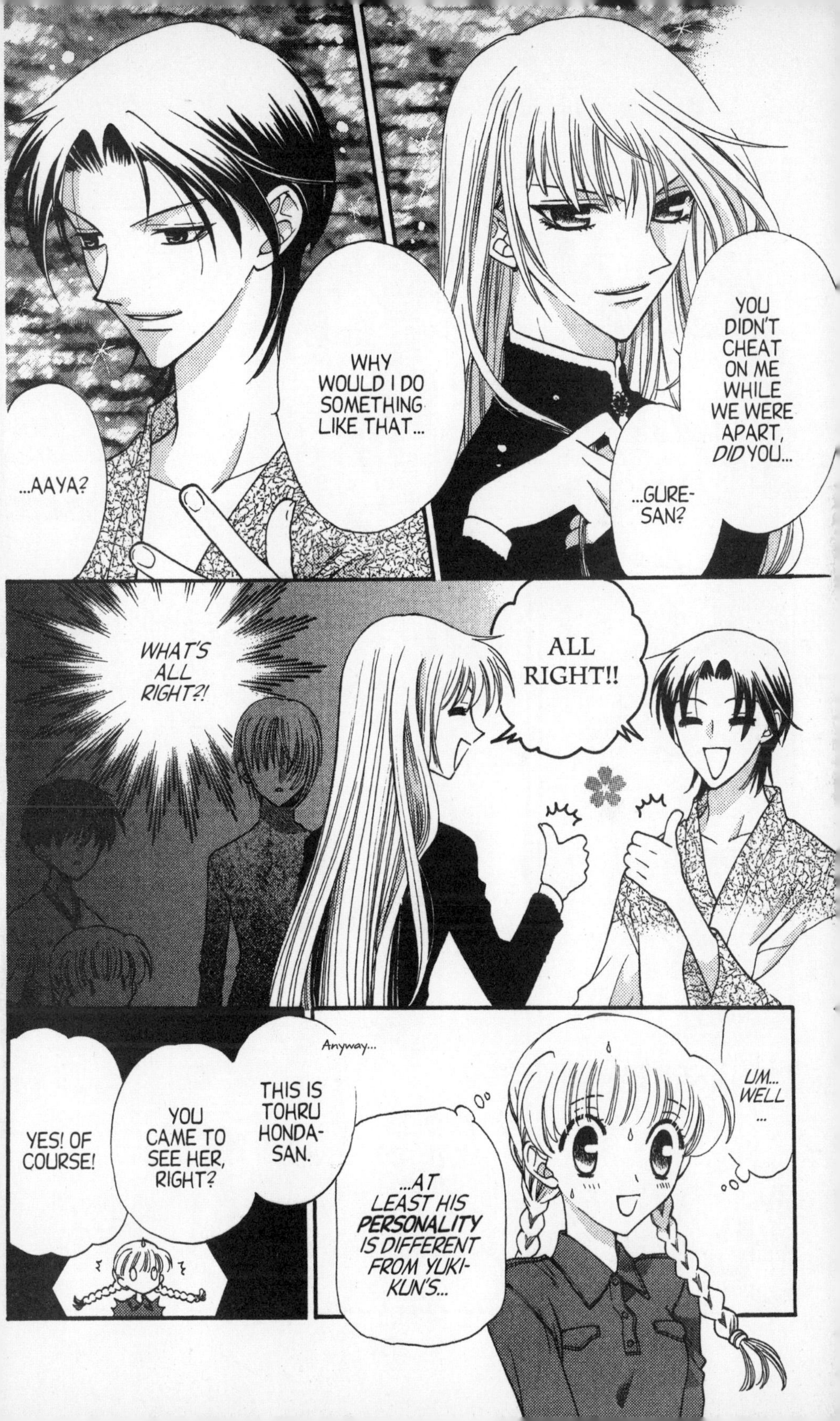
YOU DIDN'T CHEAT ON ME WHILE WE WERE APART, *DID* YOU...
...GURE-SAN?
WHY WOULD I DO SOMETHING LIKE THAT...
...AAYA?
ALL RIGHT!!
WHAT'S ALL RIGHT?!
UM... WELL ...
...AT LEAST HIS ***PERSONALITY*** *IS DIFFERENT FROM YUKI-KUN'S...*
Anyway...
THIS IS TOHRU HONDA-SAN.
YOU CAME TO SEE HER, RIGHT?
YES! OF COURSE!

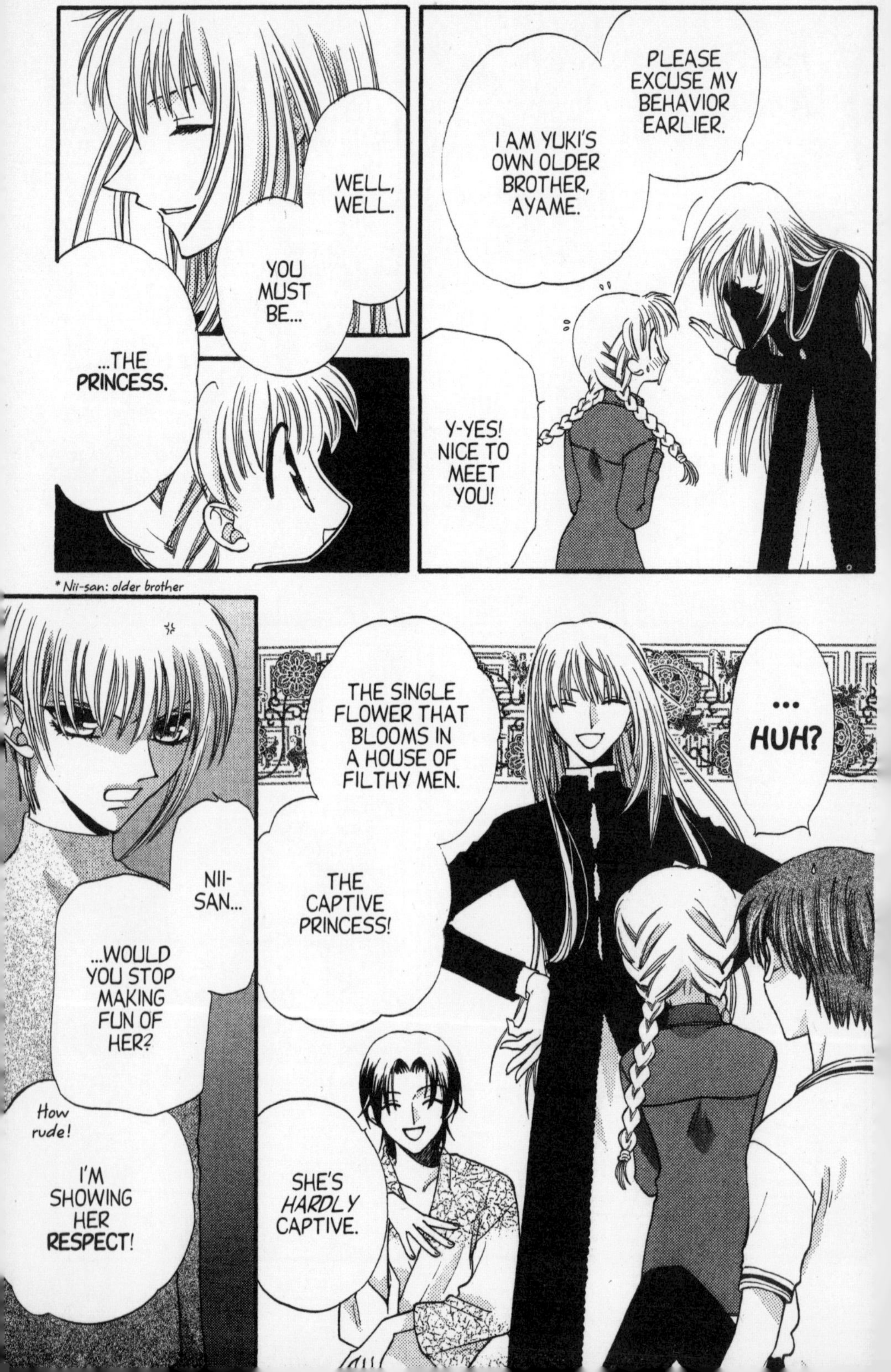
PLEASE EXCUSE MY BEHAVIOR EARLIER.
I AM YUKI'S OWN OLDER BROTHER, AYAME.
Y-YES! NICE TO MEET YOU!
WELL, WELL.
YOU MUST BE...
...THE **PRINCESS.**
... **HUH?**
THE SINGLE FLOWER THAT BLOOMS IN A HOUSE OF FILTHY MEN.
THE CAPTIVE PRINCESS!
SHE'S *HARDLY* CAPTIVE.
NII-SAN...
...WOULD YOU STOP MAKING FUN OF HER?
How rude!
I'M SHOWING HER **RESPECT!**

* Nii-san: older brother

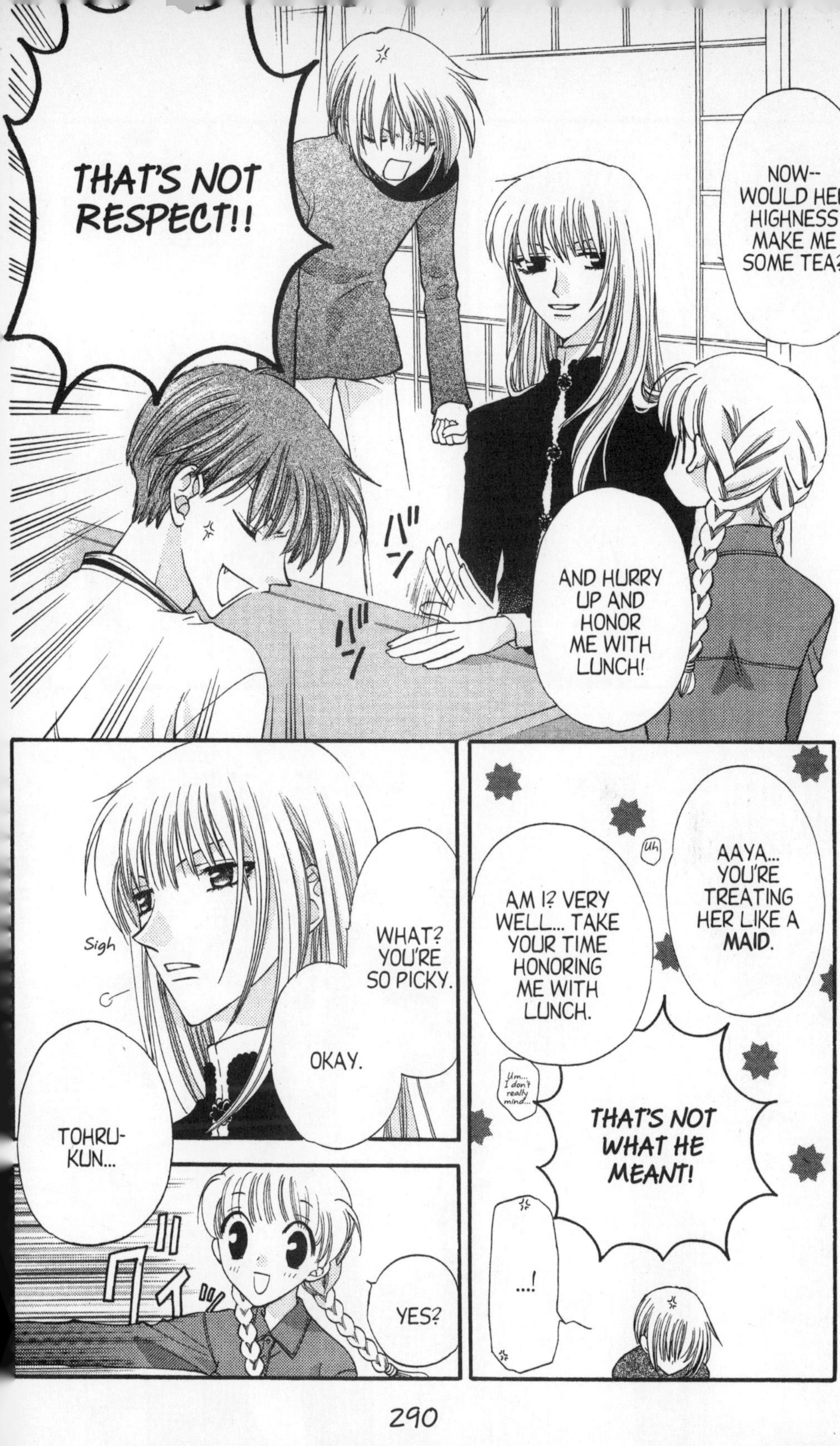
NOW-- WOULD HER HIGHNESS MAKE ME SOME TEA?
AND HURRY UP AND HONOR ME WITH LUNCH!
THAT'S NOT RESPECT!!
バン
バン
Uh
AAYA... YOU'RE TREATING HER LIKE A MAID.
AM I? VERY WELL... TAKE YOUR TIME HONORING ME WITH LUNCH.
Um... I don't really mind...
THAT'S NOT WHAT HE MEANT!
...!
WHAT? YOU'RE SO PICKY.
Sigh
OKAY.
TOHRU-KUN...
YES?

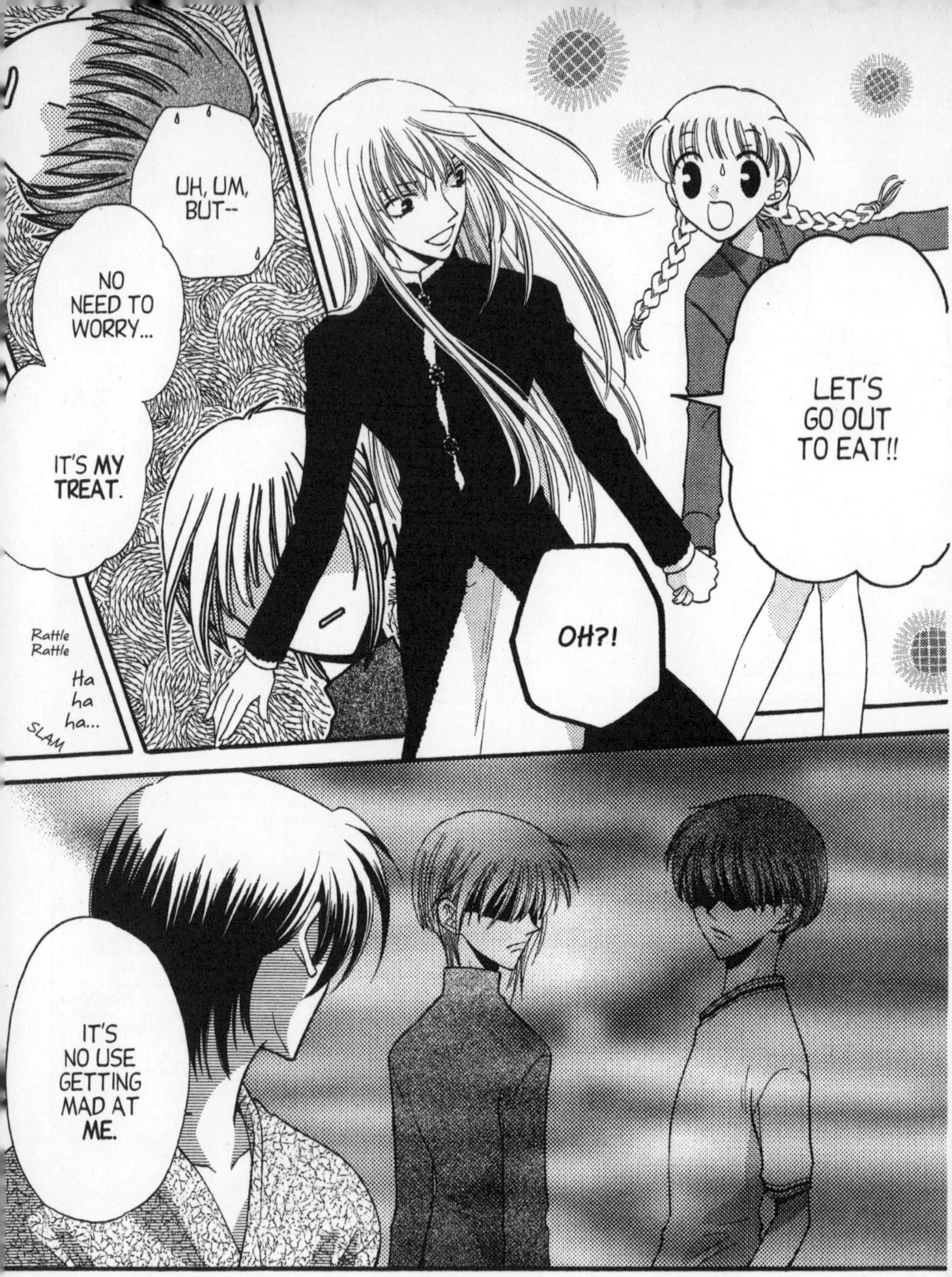

LET'S GO OUT TO EAT!!
OH?!
UH, UM, BUT--
NO NEED TO WORRY...
IT'S MY TREAT.
Rattle Rattle
Ha ha ha...
SLAM
IT'S NO USE GETTING MAD AT ME.

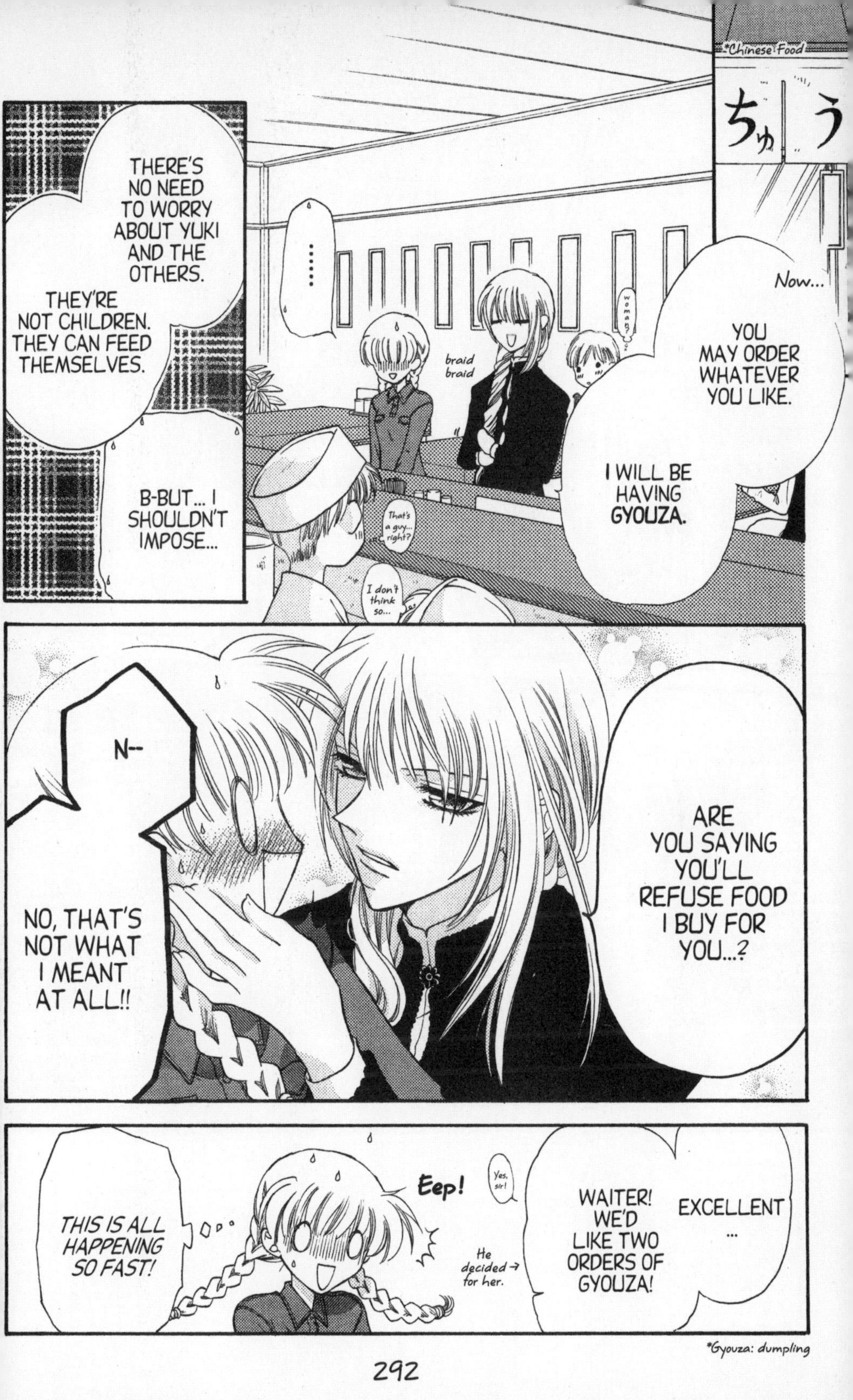
*Chinese Food
ちゅう
Now...
YOU MAY ORDER WHATEVER YOU LIKE.
I WILL BE HAVING GYOUZA.
woman?
......
braid braid
That's a guy... right?
I don't think so...
THERE'S NO NEED TO WORRY ABOUT YUKI AND THE OTHERS.
THEY'RE NOT CHILDREN. THEY CAN FEED THEMSELVES.
B-BUT... I SHOULDN'T IMPOSE...
ARE YOU SAYING YOU'LL REFUSE FOOD I BUY FOR YOU...?
N--
NO, THAT'S NOT WHAT I MEANT AT ALL!!
EXCELLENT ...
WAITER! WE'D LIKE TWO ORDERS OF GYOUZA!
Yes, sir!
He decided for her.
Eep!
THIS IS ALL HAPPENING SO FAST!

*Gyouza: dumpling

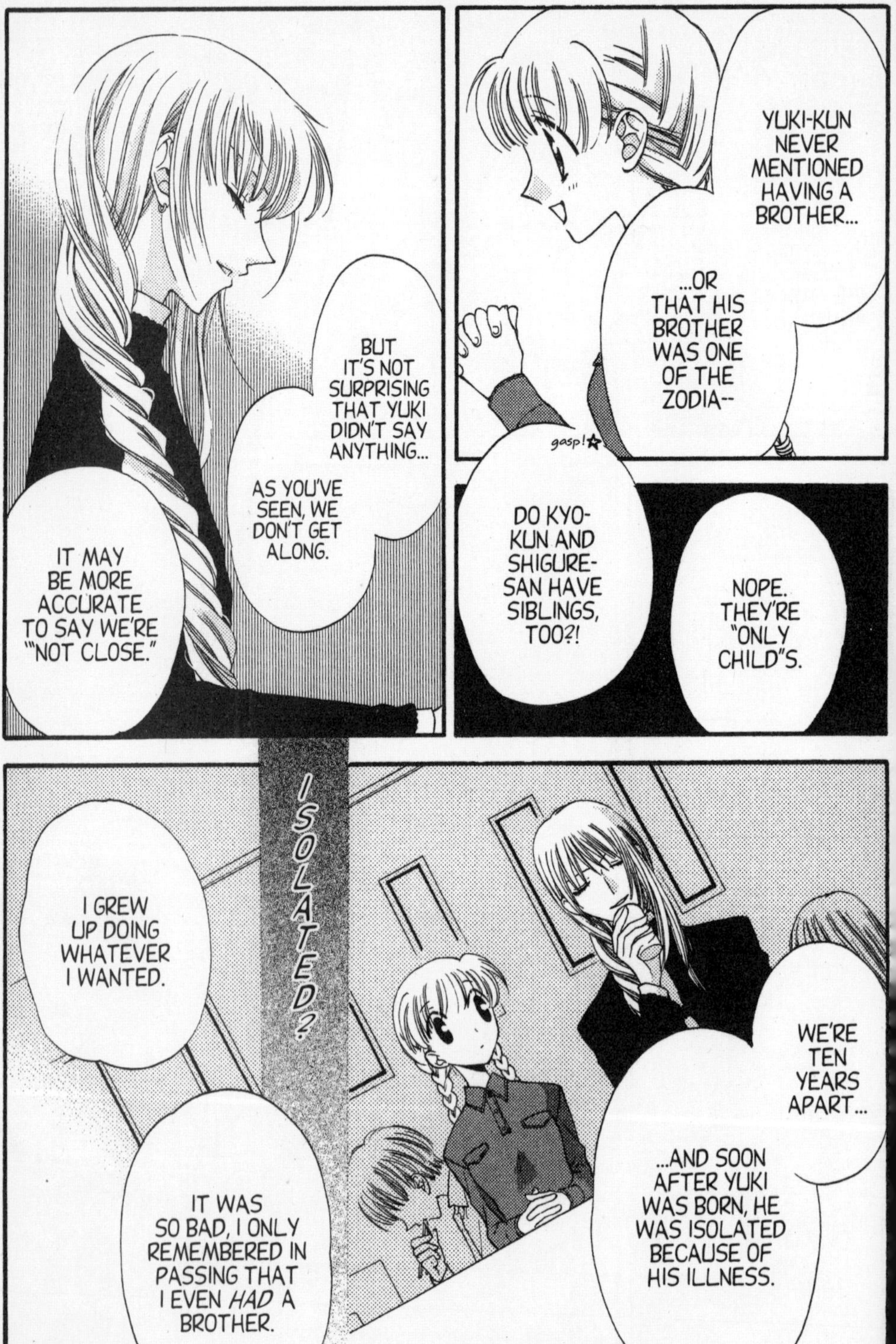
YUKI-KUN NEVER MENTIONED HAVING A BROTHER...
...OR THAT HIS BROTHER WAS ONE OF THE ZODIA--
gasp!
DO KYO-KUN AND SHIGURE-SAN HAVE SIBLINGS, TOO?!
NOPE. THEY'RE "ONLY CHILD"S.
BUT IT'S NOT SURPRISING THAT YUKI DIDN'T SAY ANYTHING...
AS YOU'VE SEEN, WE DON'T GET ALONG.
IT MAY BE MORE ACCURATE TO SAY WE'RE "NOT CLOSE."
WE'RE TEN YEARS APART...
...AND SOON AFTER YUKI WAS BORN, HE WAS ISOLATED BECAUSE OF HIS ILLNESS.
ISOLATED?
I GREW UP DOING WHATEVER I WANTED.
IT WAS SO BAD, I ONLY REMEMBERED IN PASSING THAT I EVEN *HAD* A BROTHER.

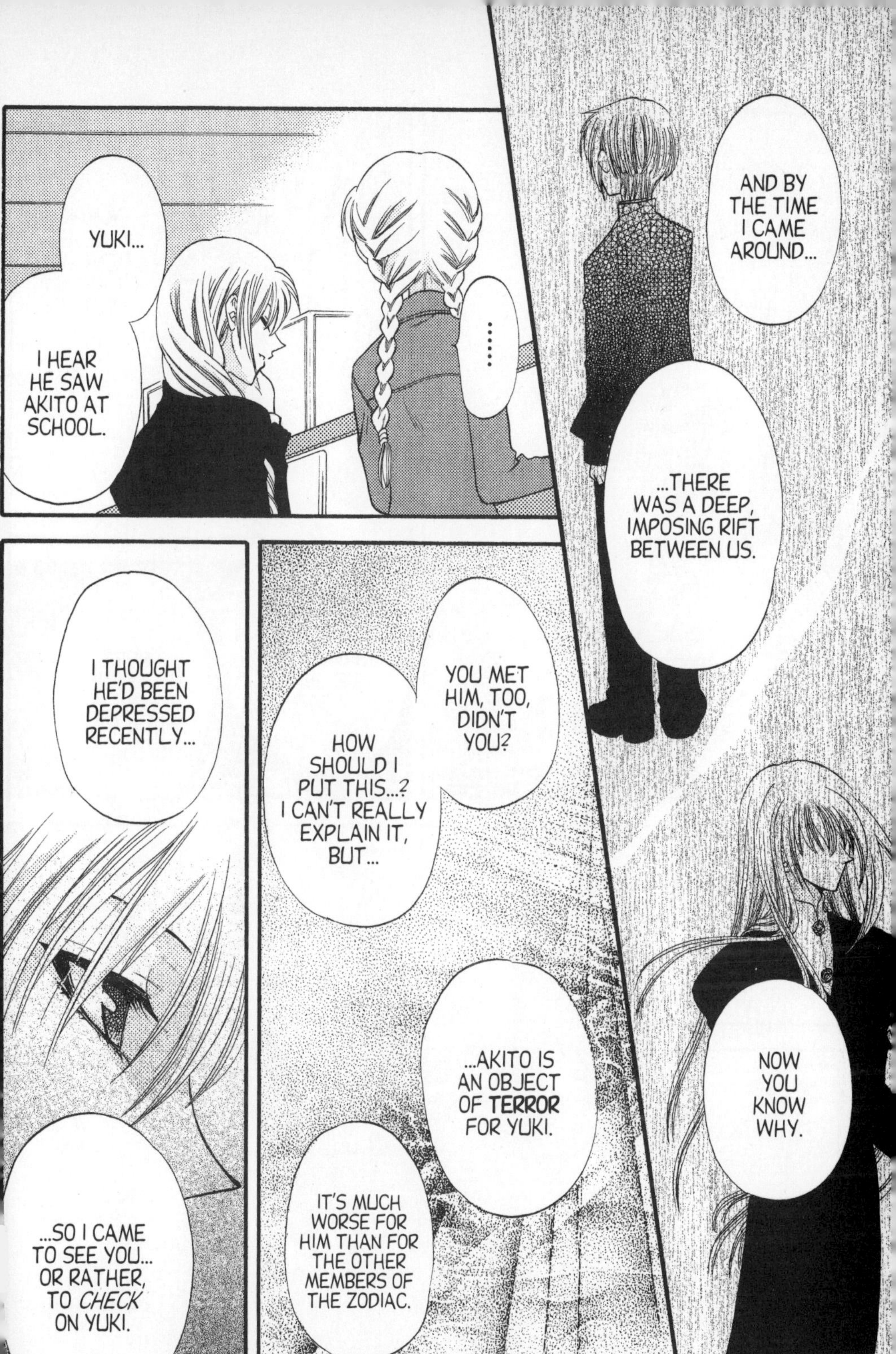
AND BY THE TIME I CAME AROUND...
...THERE WAS A DEEP, IMPOSING RIFT BETWEEN US.
NOW YOU KNOW WHY.
YUKI...
I HEAR HE SAW AKITO AT SCHOOL.
......
YOU MET HIM, TOO, DIDN'T YOU?
HOW SHOULD I PUT THIS...? I CAN'T REALLY EXPLAIN IT, BUT...
...AKITO IS AN OBJECT OF **TERROR** FOR YUKI.
IT'S MUCH WORSE FOR HIM THAN FOR THE OTHER MEMBERS OF THE ZODIAC.
I THOUGHT HE'D BEEN DEPRESSED RECENTLY...
...SO I CAME TO SEE YOU... OR RATHER, TO *CHECK* ON YUKI.

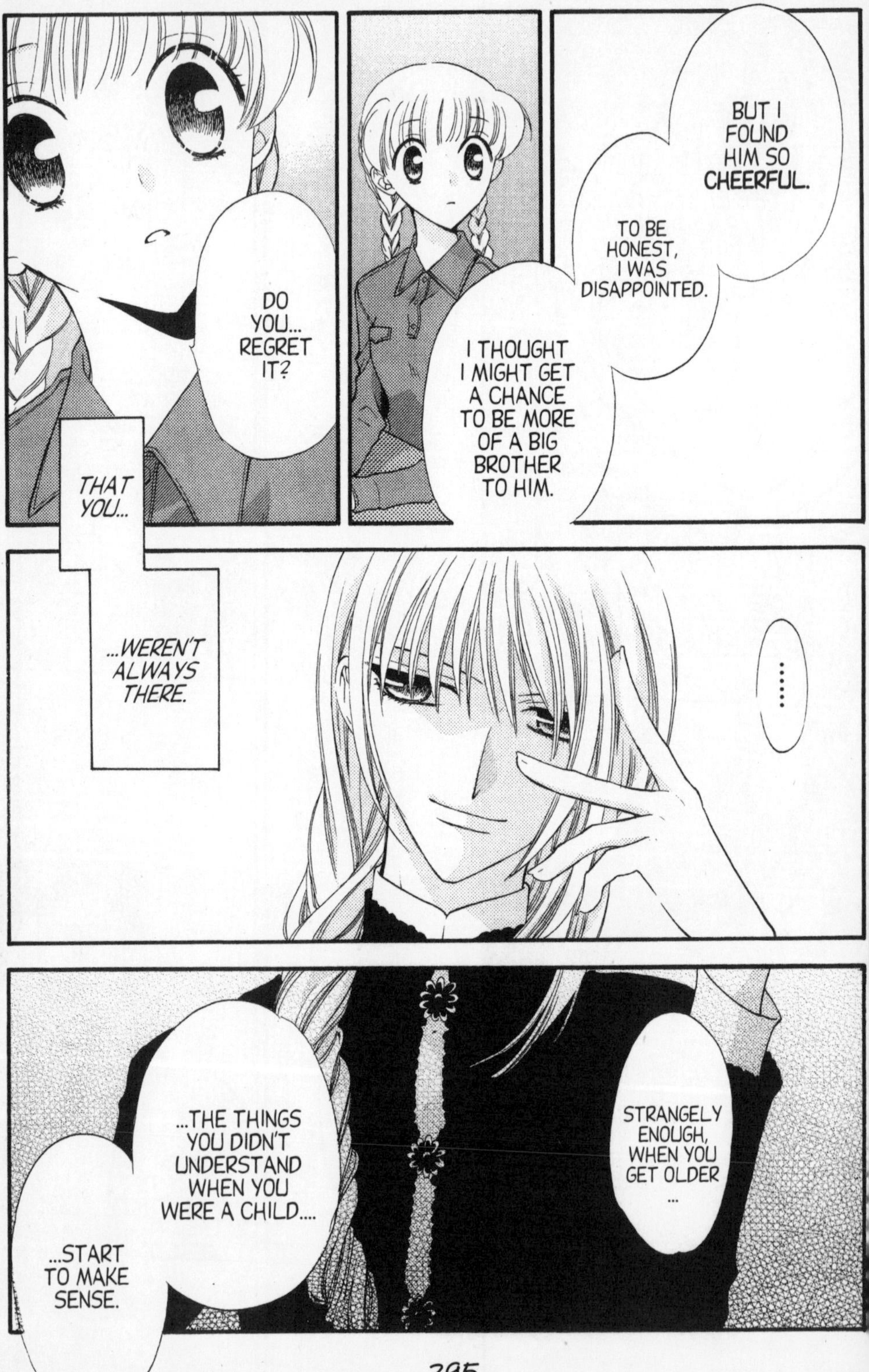
TO BE HONEST, I WAS DISAPPOINTED.
BUT I FOUND HIM SO **CHEERFUL.**
I THOUGHT I MIGHT GET A CHANCE TO BE MORE OF A BIG BROTHER TO HIM.
DO YOU... REGRET IT?
THAT YOU...
...WEREN'T ALWAYS THERE.
......
STRANGELY ENOUGH, WHEN YOU GET OLDER ...
...THE THINGS YOU DIDN'T UNDERSTAND WHEN YOU WERE A CHILD....
...START TO MAKE SENSE.

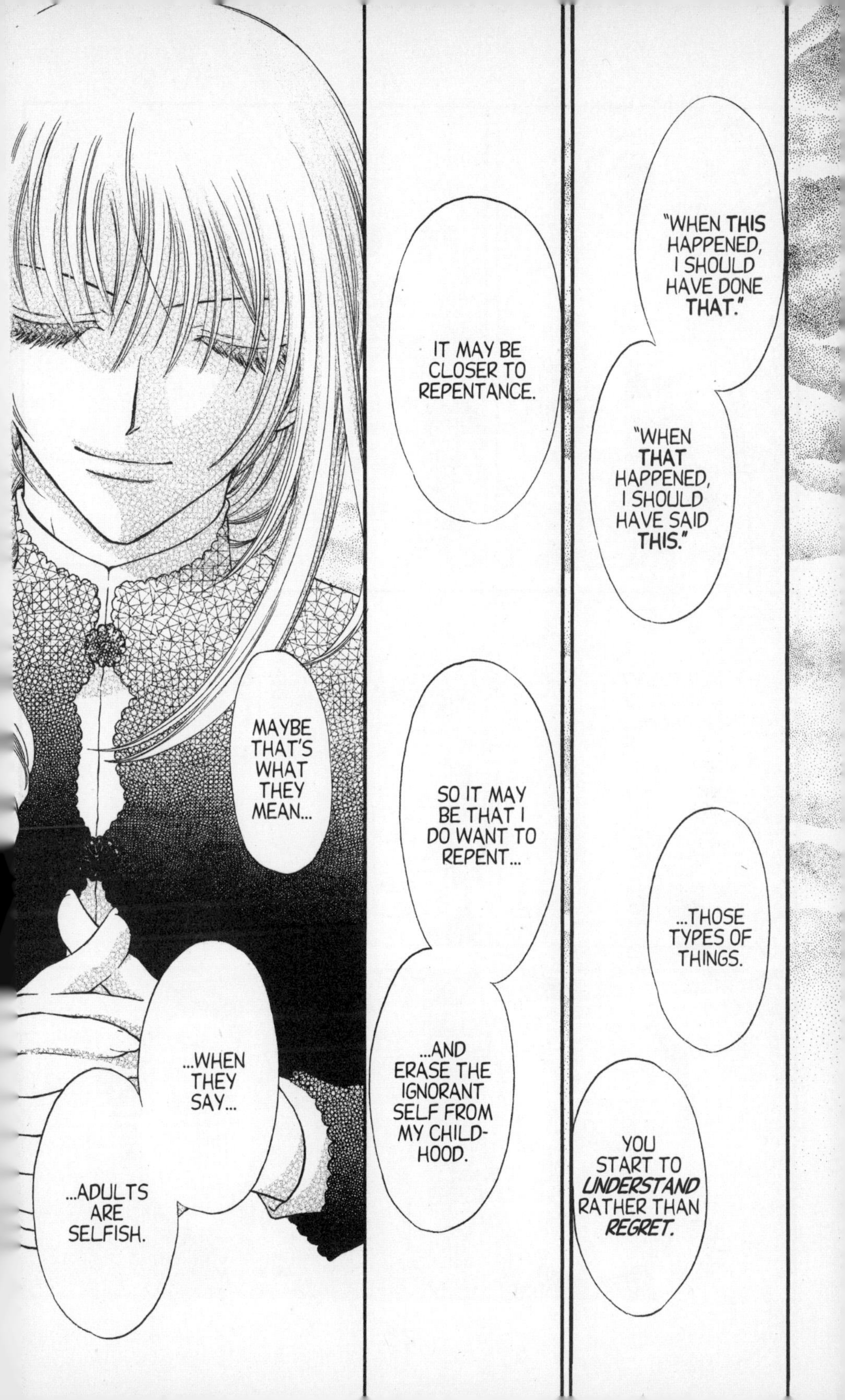
"WHEN THIS HAPPENED, I SHOULD HAVE DONE THAT."
"WHEN THAT HAPPENED, I SHOULD HAVE SAID THIS."
...THOSE TYPES OF THINGS.
YOU START TO *UNDERSTAND* RATHER THAN *REGRET.*
IT MAY BE CLOSER TO REPENTANCE.
SO IT MAY BE THAT I DO WANT TO REPENT...
...AND ERASE THE IGNORANT SELF FROM MY CHILD-HOOD.
MAYBE THAT'S WHAT THEY MEAN...
...WHEN THEY SAY...
...ADULTS ARE SELFISH.

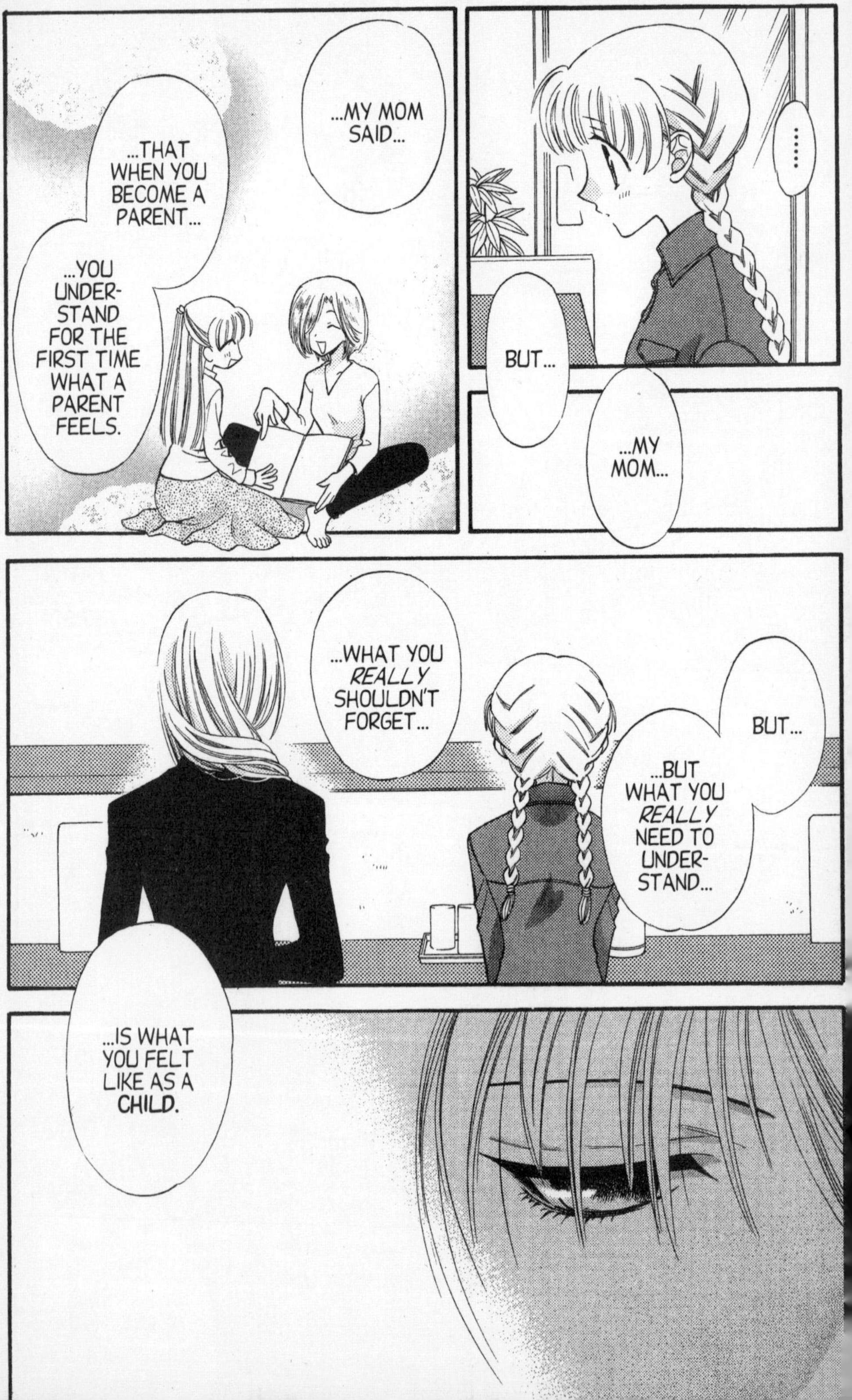
......
BUT...
...MY MOM...
...MY MOM SAID...
...THAT WHEN YOU BECOME A PARENT...
...YOU UNDERSTAND FOR THE FIRST TIME WHAT A PARENT FEELS.
BUT...
...BUT WHAT YOU *REALLY* NEED TO UNDERSTAND...
...WHAT YOU *REALLY* SHOULDN'T FORGET...
...IS WHAT YOU FELT LIKE AS A **CHILD**.

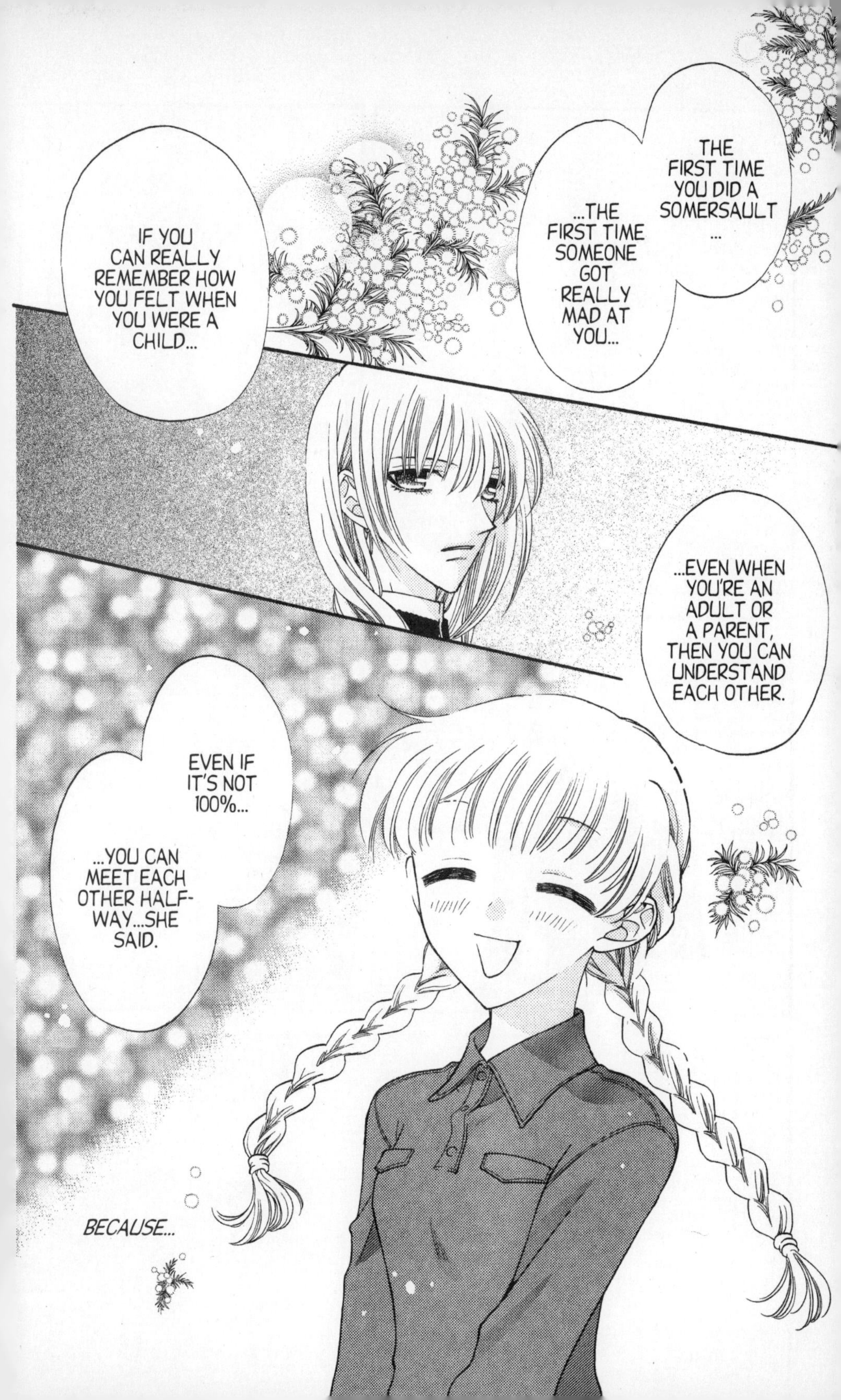
THE FIRST TIME YOU DID A SOMERSAULT ...
...THE FIRST TIME SOMEONE GOT REALLY MAD AT YOU...
IF YOU CAN REALLY REMEMBER HOW YOU FELT WHEN YOU WERE A CHILD...
...EVEN WHEN YOU'RE AN ADULT OR A PARENT, THEN YOU CAN UNDERSTAND EACH OTHER.
EVEN IF IT'S NOT 100%...
...YOU CAN MEET EACH OTHER HALF-WAY...SHE SAID.
BECAUSE...

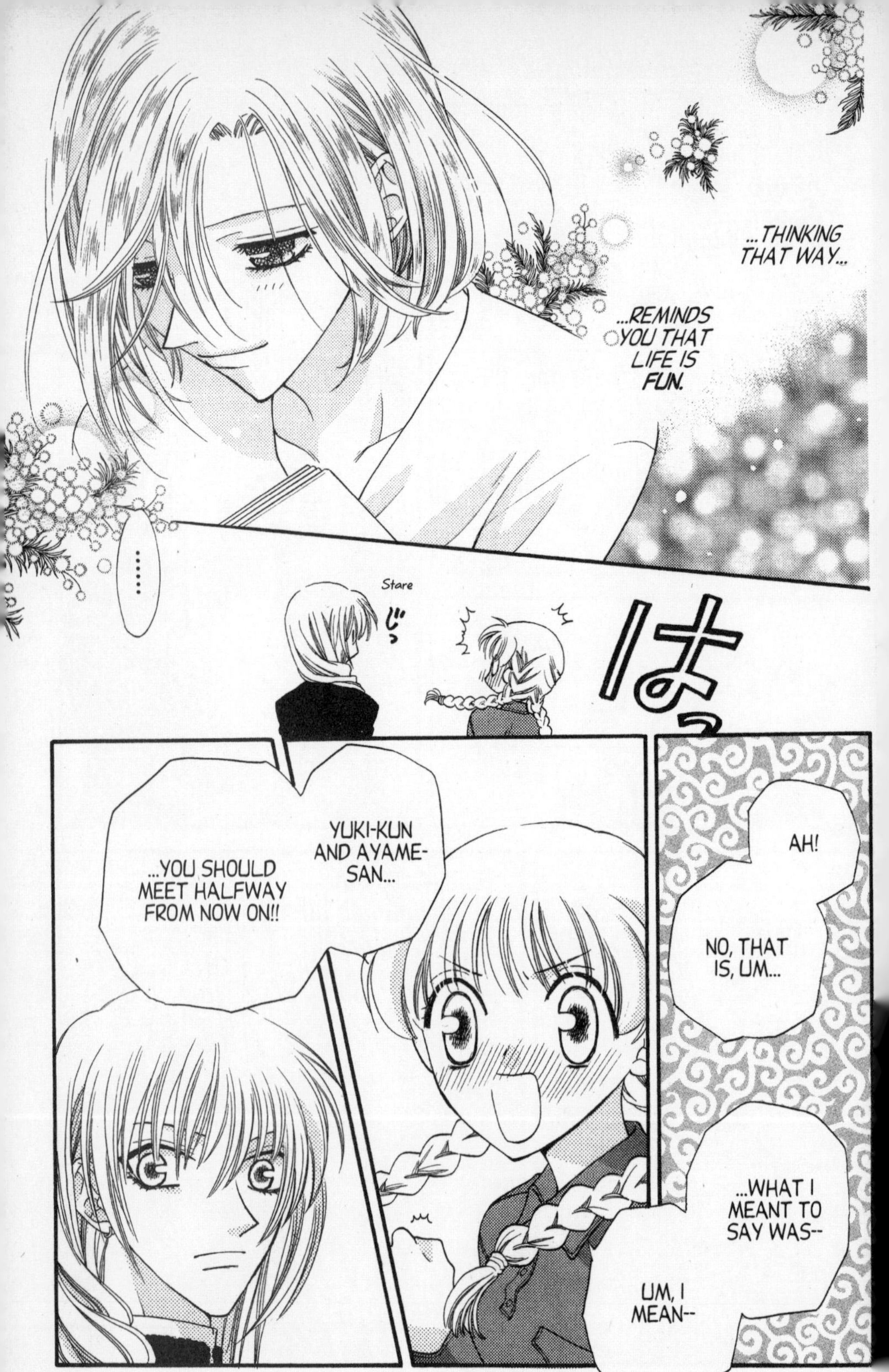
...THINKING THAT WAY...
...REMINDS YOU THAT LIFE IS FUN.
......
は
Stare
じっ
AH!
NO, THAT IS, UM...
...WHAT I MEANT TO SAY WAS--
UM, I MEAN--
YUKI-KUN AND AYAME-SAN...
...YOU SHOULD MEET HALFWAY FROM NOW ON!!

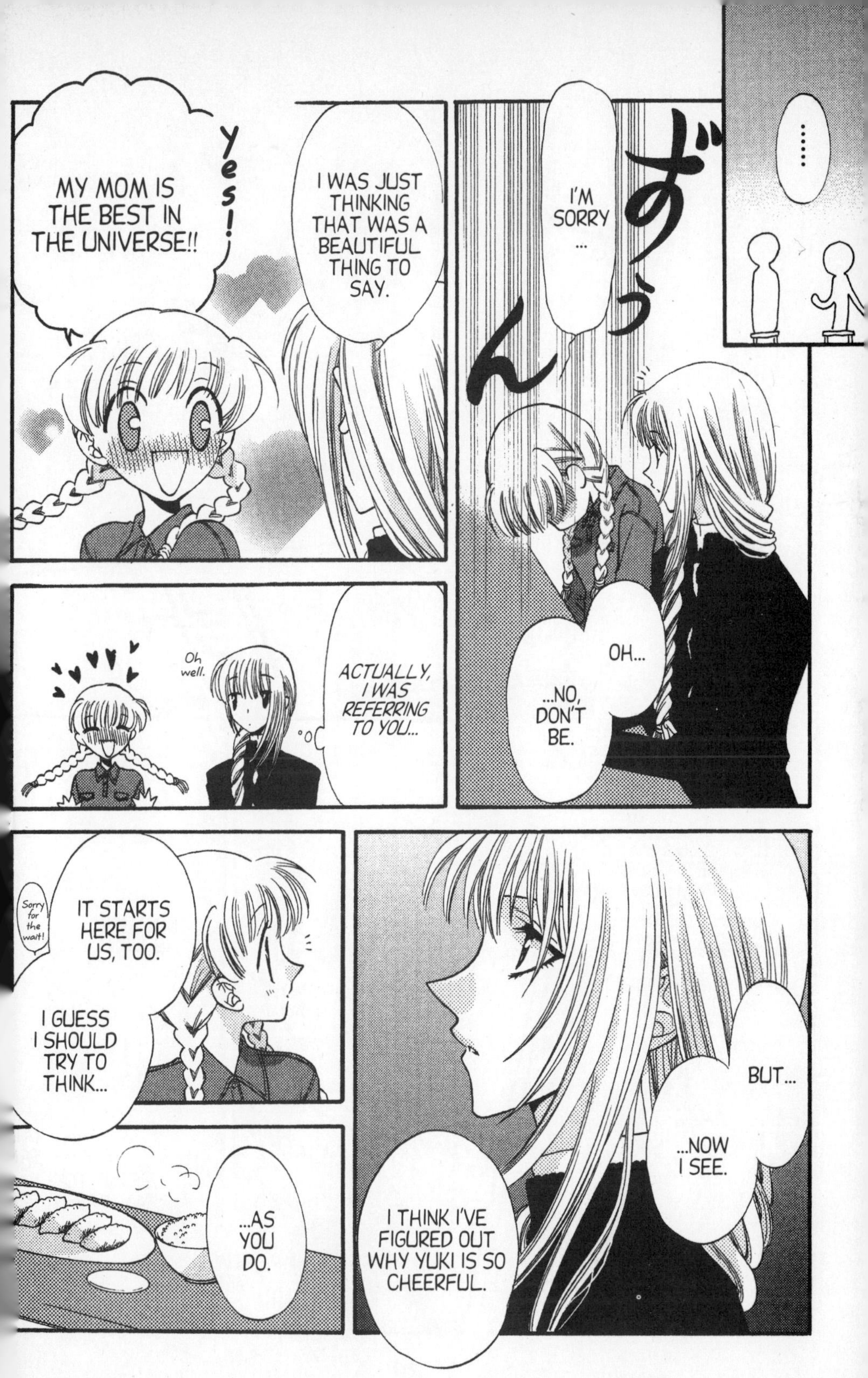
......
ずぅん
I'M SORRY ...
OH...
...NO, DON'T BE.
Yes!
MY MOM IS THE BEST IN THE UNIVERSE!!
I WAS JUST THINKING THAT WAS A BEAUTIFUL THING TO SAY.
ACTUALLY, I WAS REFERRING TO YOU...
Oh well.
BUT...
...NOW I SEE.
I THINK I'VE FIGURED OUT WHY YUKI IS SO CHEERFUL.
IT STARTS HERE FOR US, TOO.
Sorry for the wait!
I GUESS I SHOULD TRY TO THINK...
...AS YOU DO.

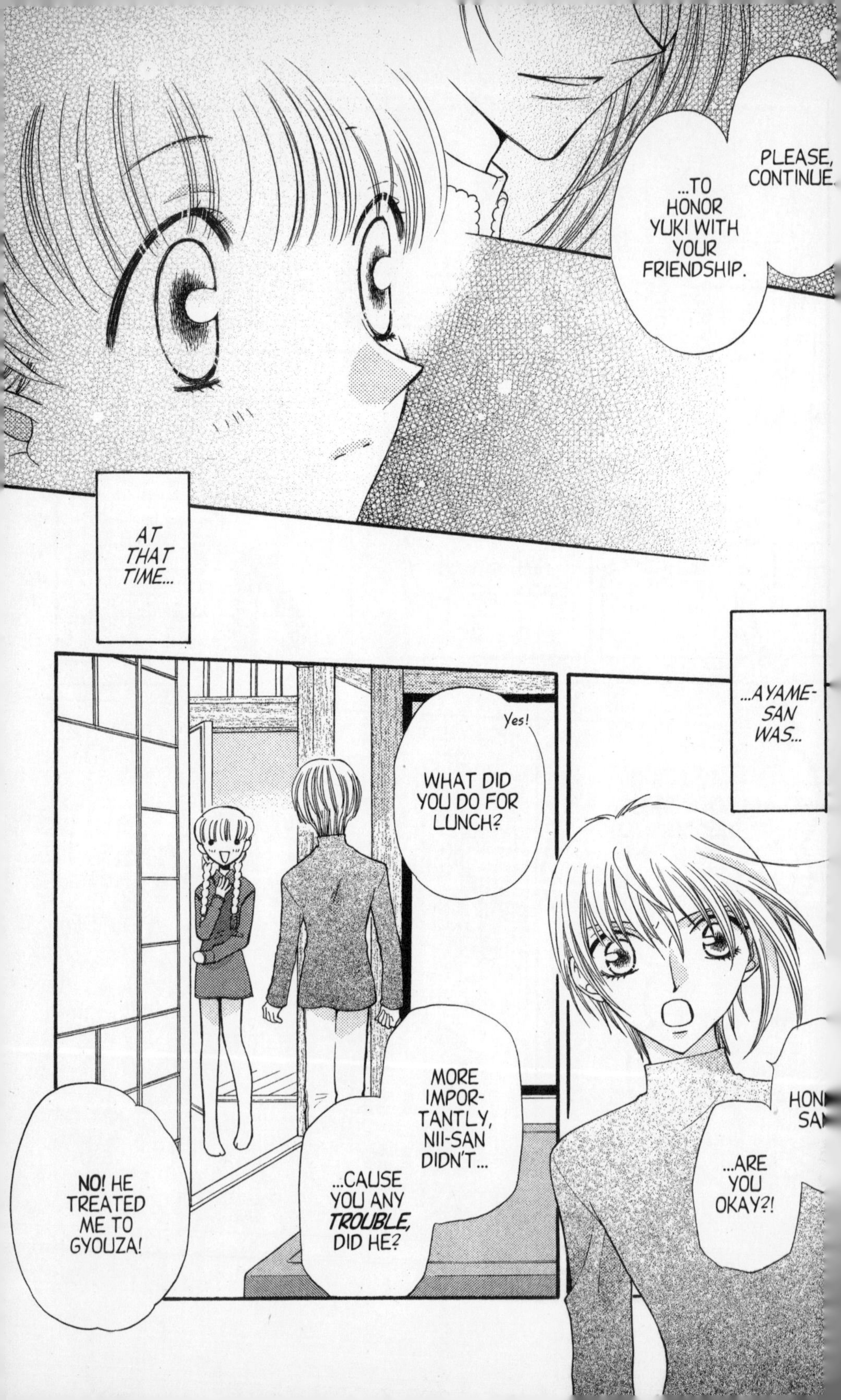

PLEASE, CONTINUE.
...TO HONOR YUKI WITH YOUR FRIENDSHIP.
AT THAT TIME...
...AYAME-SAN WAS...
HON SA
...ARE YOU OKAY?!
Yes!
WHAT DID YOU DO FOR LUNCH?
MORE IMPORTANTLY, NII-SAN DIDN'T...
...CAUSE YOU ANY *TROUBLE,* DID HE?
NO! HE TREATED ME TO GYOUZA!

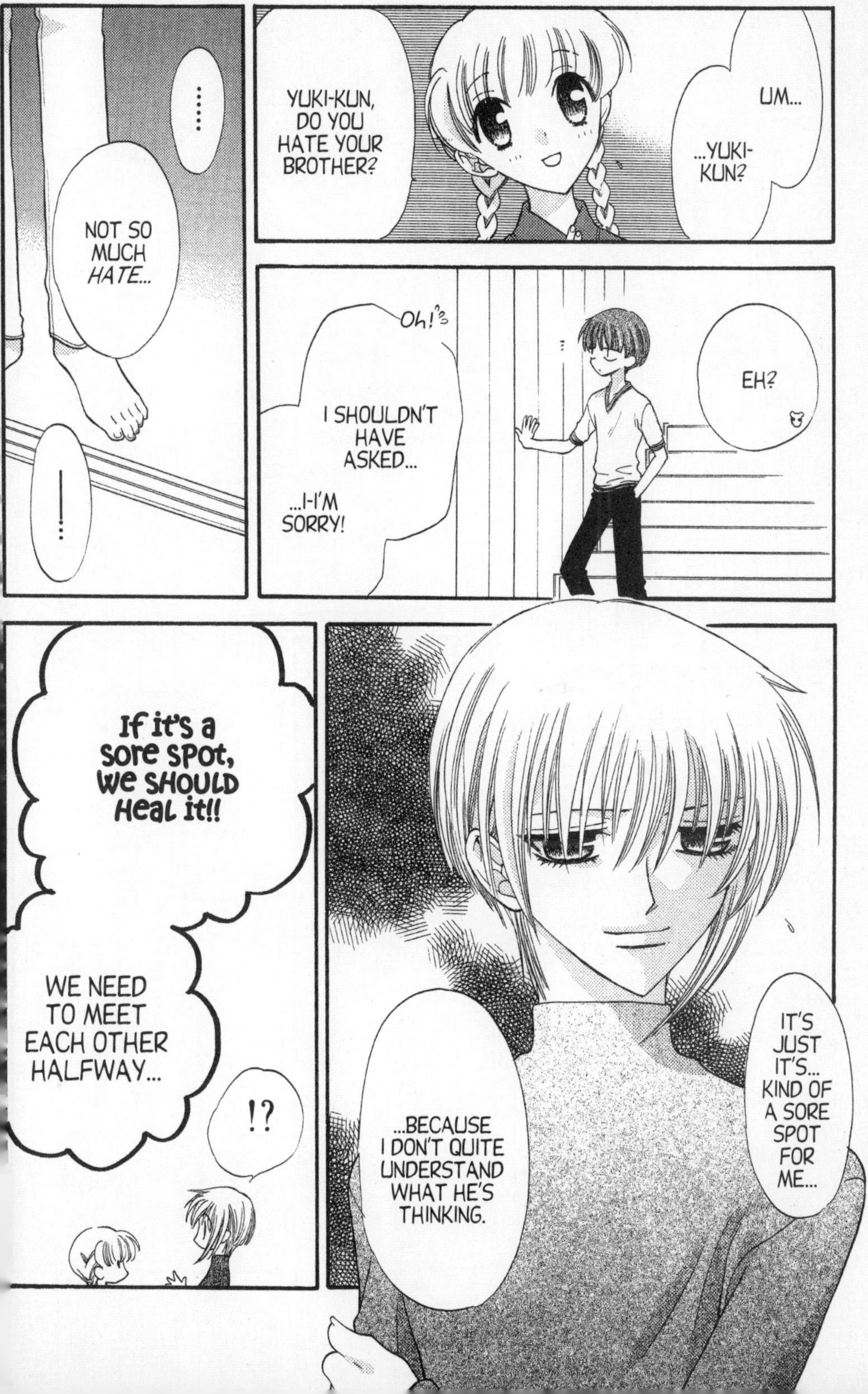
UM...
...YUKI-KUN?
YUKI-KUN, DO YOU HATE YOUR BROTHER?
EH?
Oh!
I SHOULDN'T HAVE ASKED...
...I-I'M SORRY!
......
NOT SO MUCH *HATE*...
...!
IT'S JUST IT'S... KIND OF A SORE SPOT FOR ME...
...BECAUSE I DON'T QUITE UNDERSTAND WHAT HE'S THINKING.
If it's a sore spot, we SHOULD Heal it!!
WE NEED TO MEET EACH OTHER HALFWAY...
!?

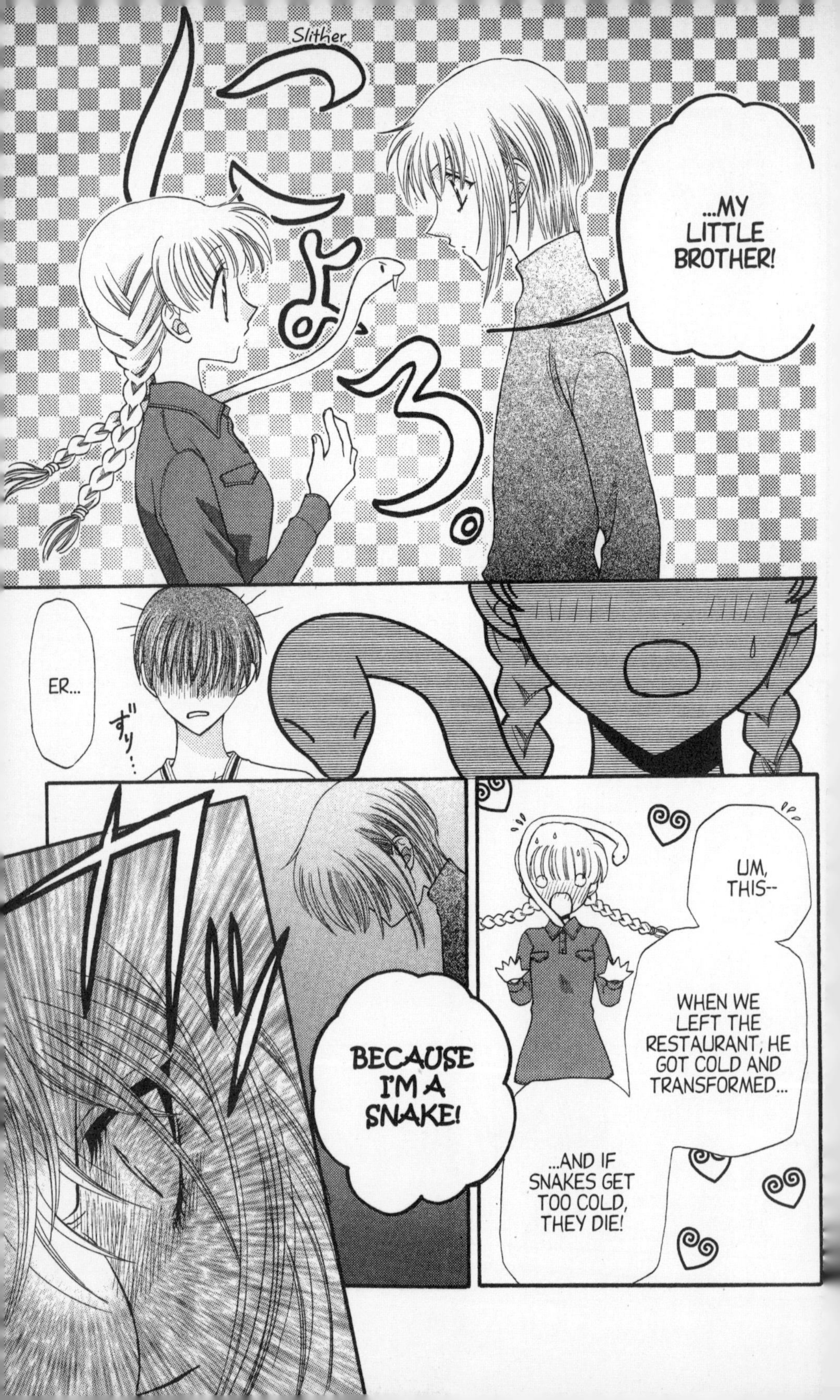
Slither
...MY LITTLE BROTHER!
ER...
ずり...
UM, THIS--
WHEN WE LEFT THE RESTAURANT, HE GOT COLD AND TRANSFORMED...
...AND IF SNAKES GET TOO COLD, THEY DIE!
BECAUSE I'M A SNAKE!

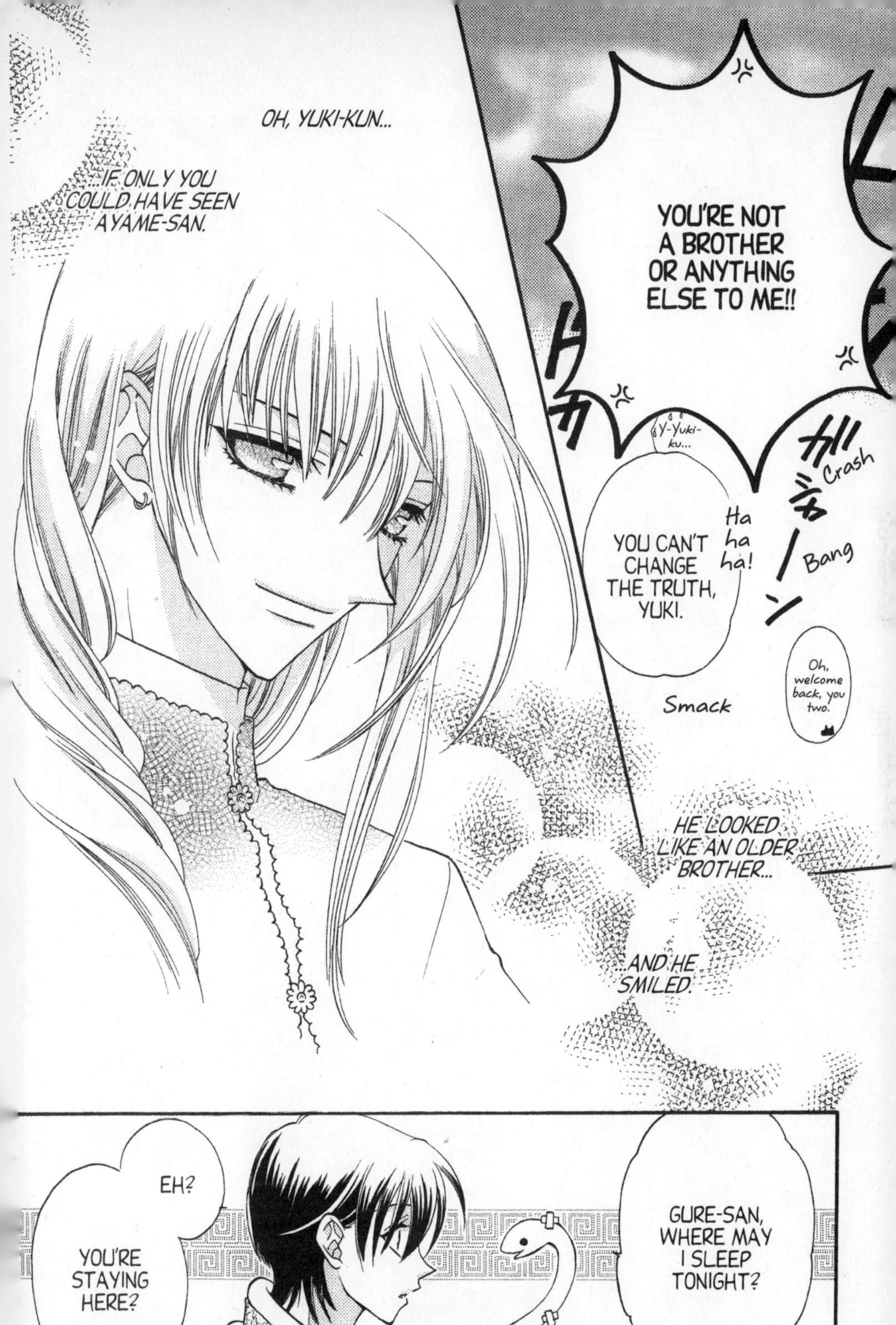
YOU'RE NOT A BROTHER OR ANYTHING ELSE TO ME!!
Y-Yuki-ku...
Crash
Bang
Ha ha ha!
YOU CAN'T CHANGE THE TRUTH, YUKI.
Oh, welcome back, you two.
Smack
OH, YUKI-KUN...
...IF ONLY YOU COULD HAVE SEEN AYAME-SAN.
HE LOOKED LIKE AN OLDER BROTHER...
...AND HE SMILED.
GURE-SAN, WHERE MAY I SLEEP TONIGHT?
EH?
YOU'RE STAYING HERE?

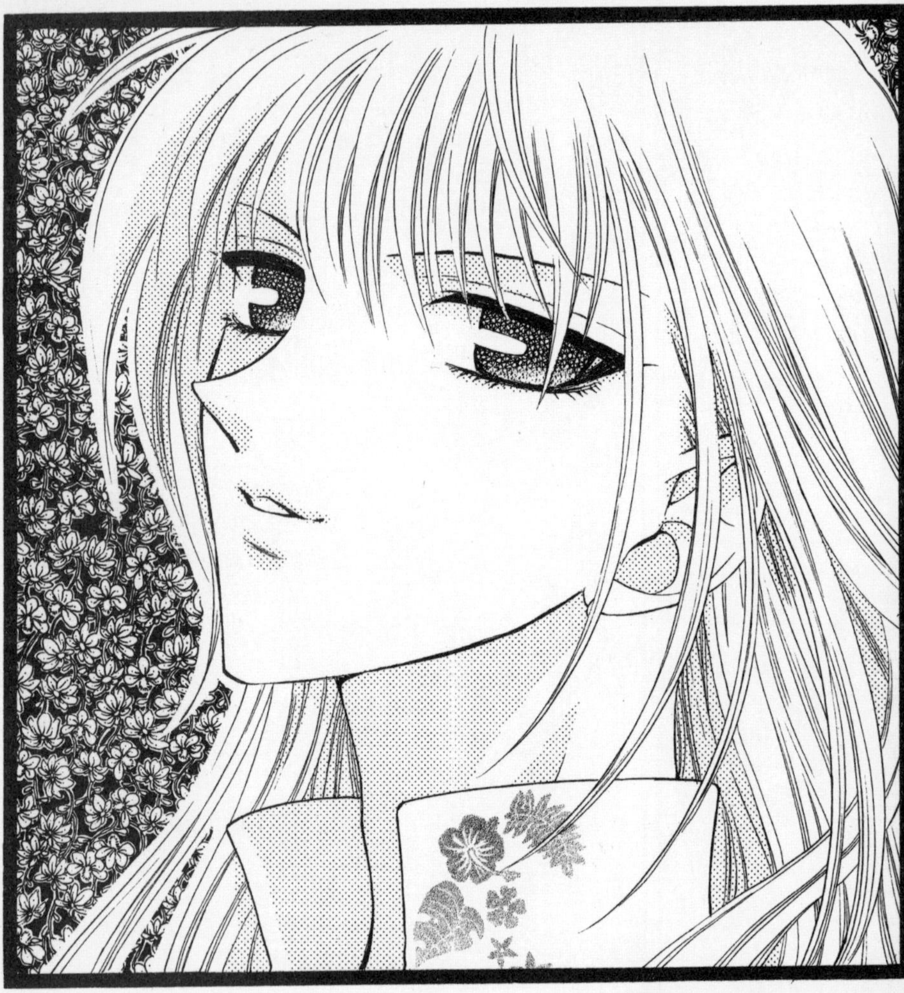

Chapter 22

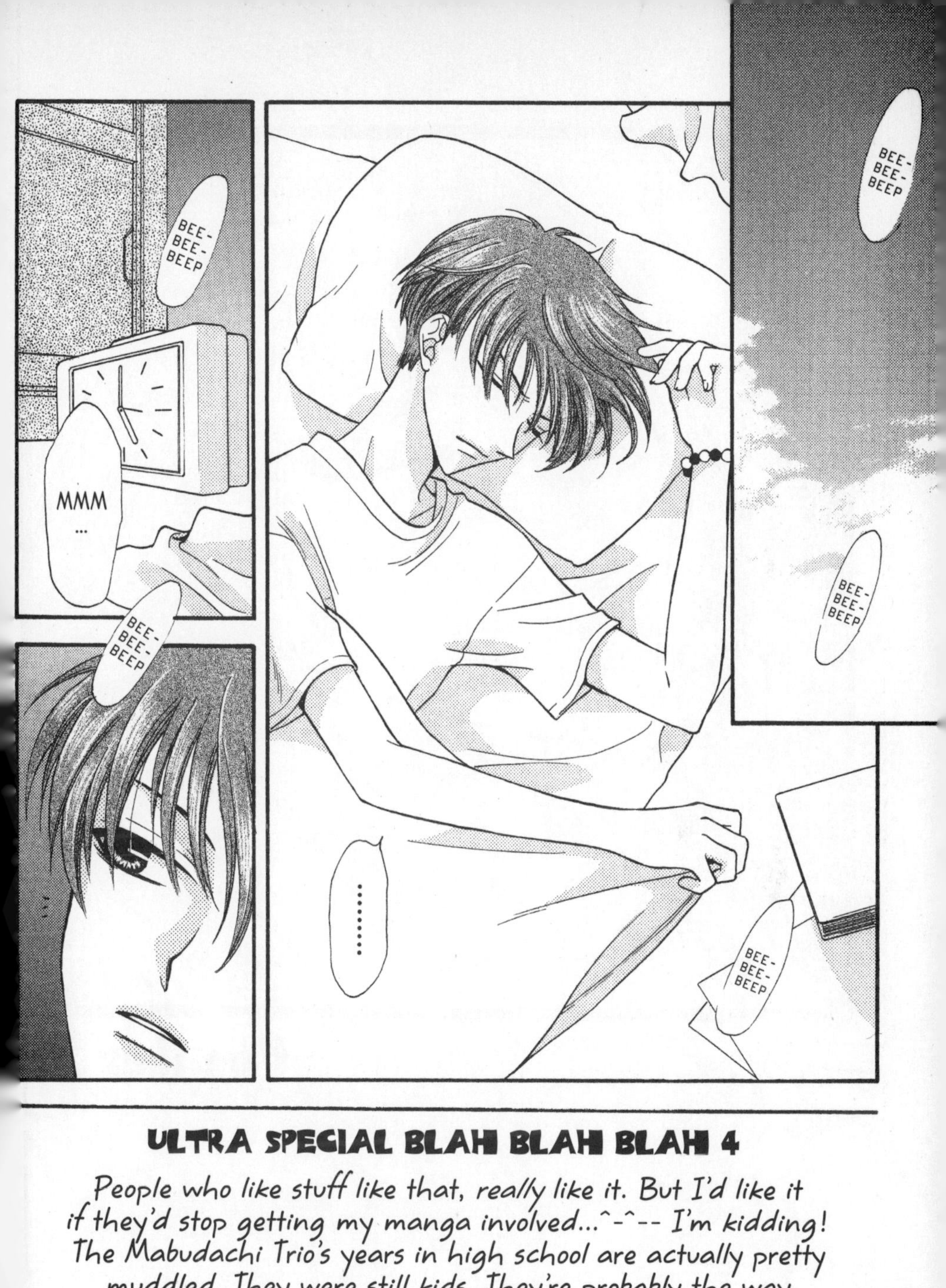
BEE-BEE-BEEP
BEE-BEE-BEEP
BEE-BEE-BEEP
....
BEE-BEE-BEEP
MMM...
BEE-BEE-BEEP

ULTRA SPECIAL BLAH BLAH BLAH 4

People who like stuff like that, really like it. But I'd like it if they'd stop getting my manga involved...^-^-- I'm kidding! The Mabudachi Trio's years in high school are actually pretty muddled. They were still kids. They're probably the way they are now because of their "flower," but it wasn't always fun.

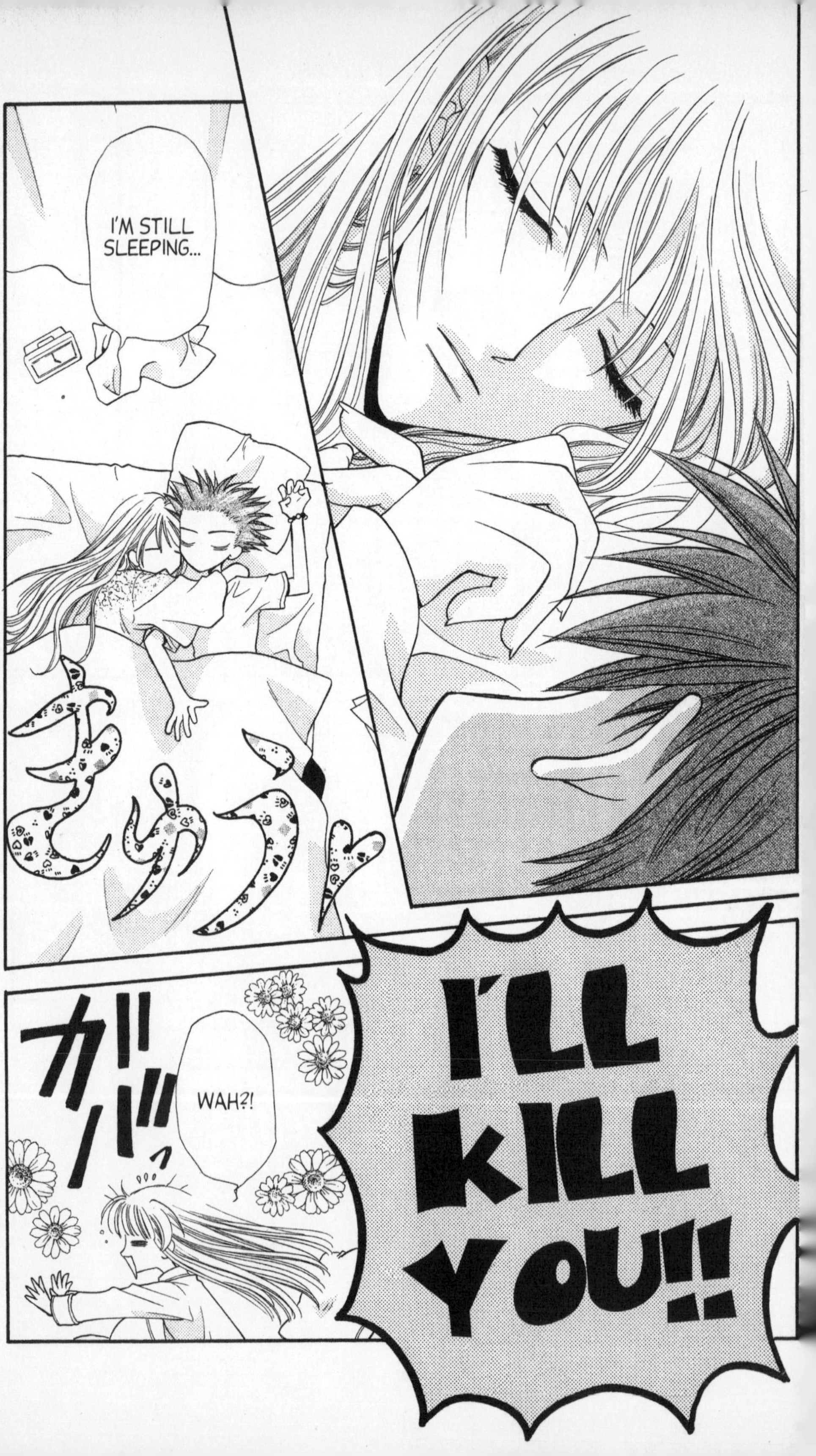
I'M STILL SLEEPING...
ぎゅう
I'LL KILL YOU!!
WAH?!
ガバッ

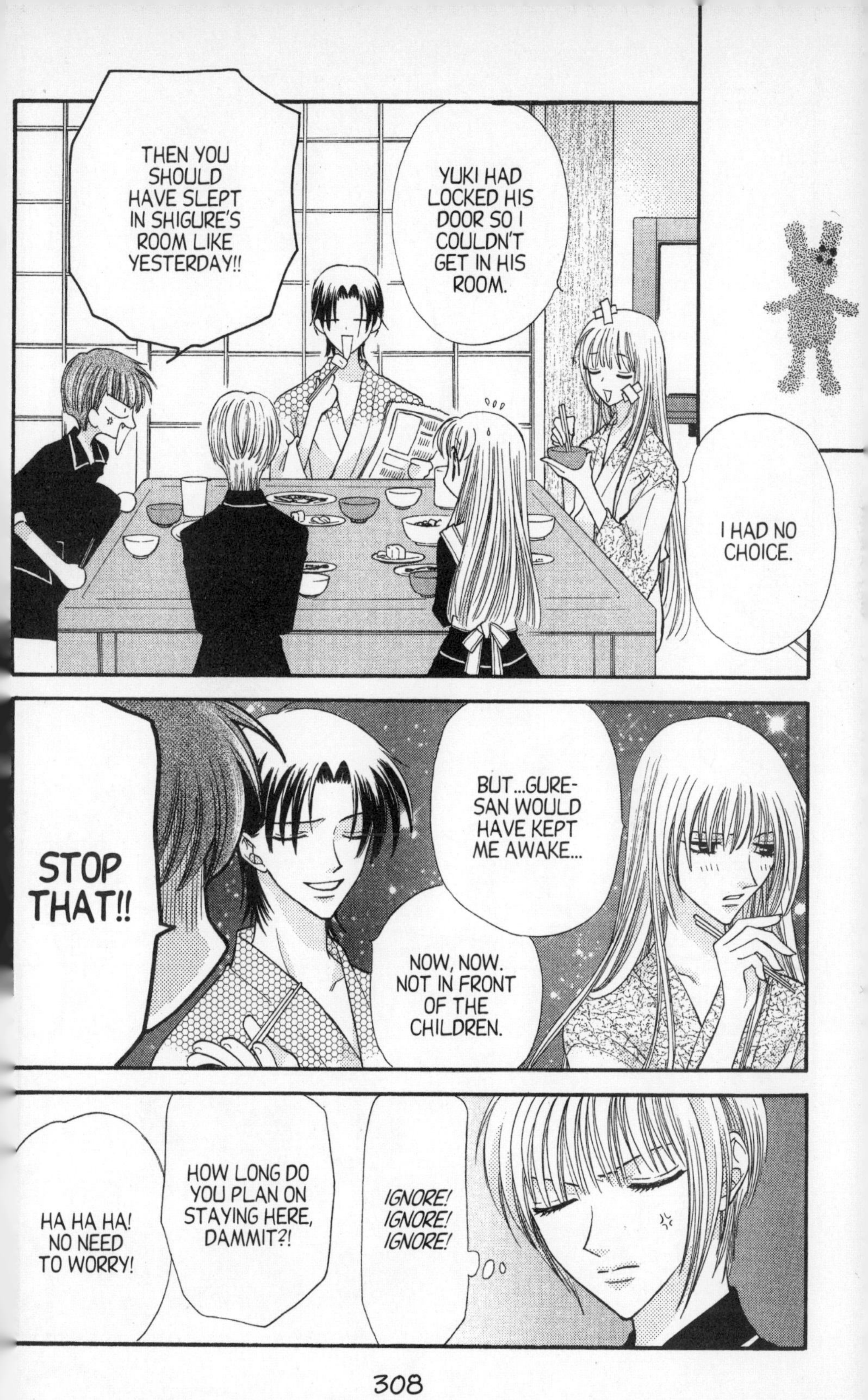
YUKI HAD LOCKED HIS DOOR SO I COULDN'T GET IN HIS ROOM.
THEN YOU SHOULD HAVE SLEPT IN SHIGURE'S ROOM LIKE YESTERDAY!!
I HAD NO CHOICE.
BUT...GURE-SAN WOULD HAVE KEPT ME AWAKE...
NOW, NOW. NOT IN FRONT OF THE CHILDREN.
STOP THAT!!
IGNORE! IGNORE! IGNORE!
HOW LONG DO YOU PLAN ON STAYING HERE, DAMMIT?!
HA HA HA! NO NEED TO WORRY!

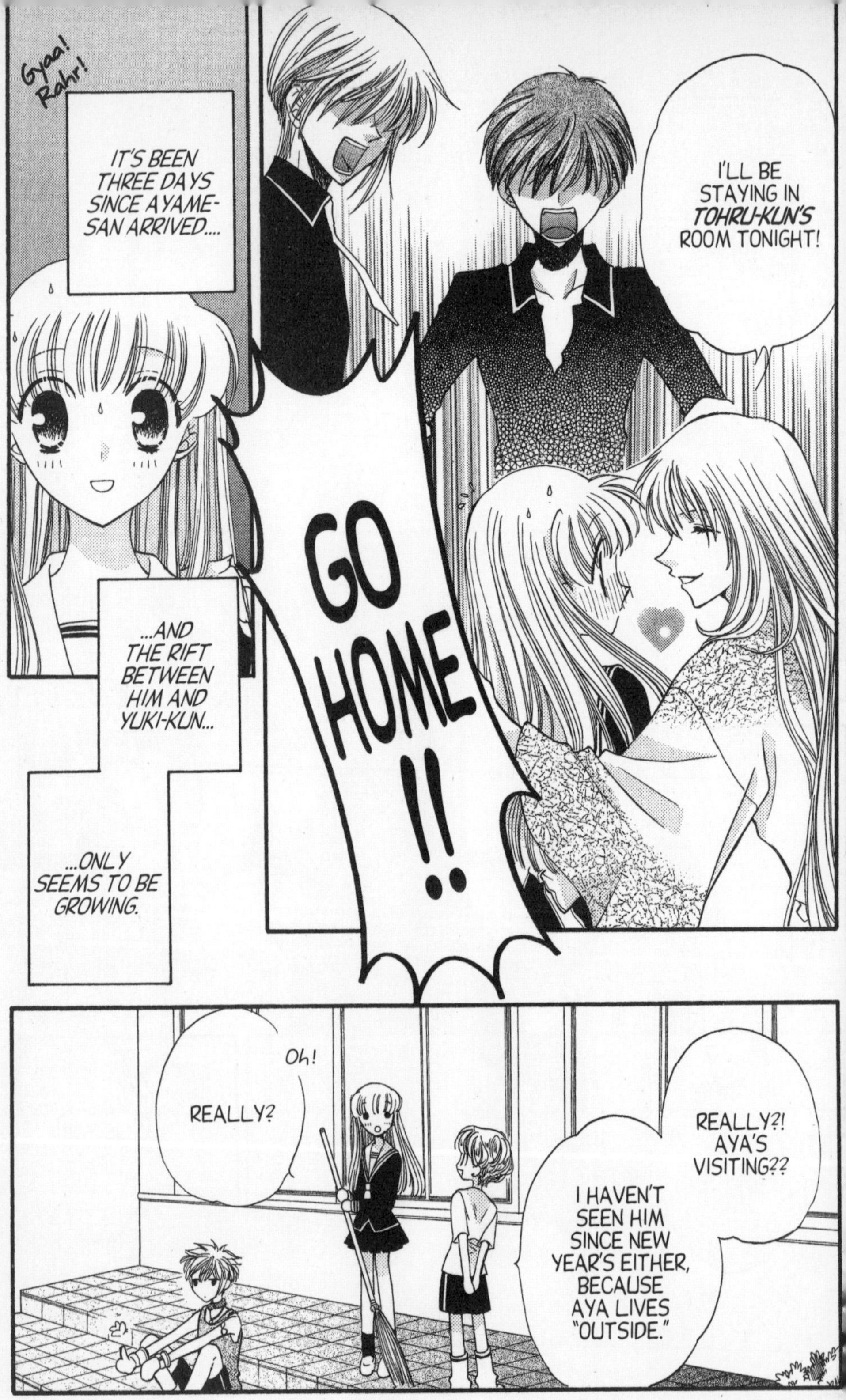
I'LL BE STAYING IN TOHRU-KUN'S ROOM TONIGHT!
GO HOME!!
Gyaa! Rahr!
IT'S BEEN THREE DAYS SINCE AYAME-SAN ARRIVED....
...AND THE RIFT BETWEEN HIM AND YUKI-KUN...
...ONLY SEEMS TO BE GROWING.
REALLY?! AYA'S VISITING??
I HAVEN'T SEEN HIM SINCE NEW YEAR'S EITHER, BECAUSE AYA LIVES "OUTSIDE."
Oh!
REALLY?

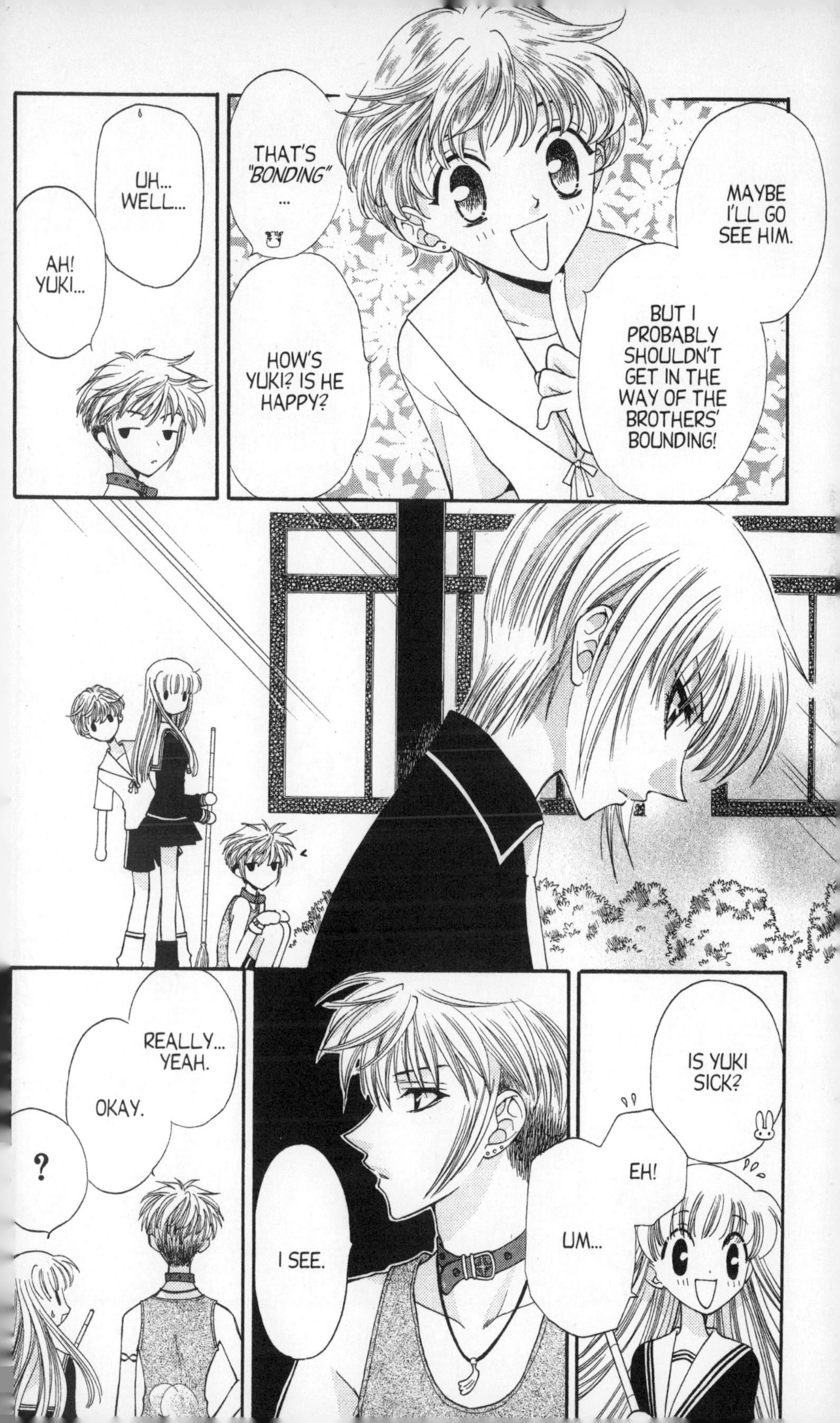
MAYBE I'LL GO SEE HIM.
BUT I PROBABLY SHOULDN'T GET IN THE WAY OF THE BROTHERS' BOUNDING!
THAT'S "BONDING" ...
HOW'S YUKI? IS HE HAPPY?
UH... WELL...
AH! YUKI...
IS YUKI SICK?
EH!
UM...
I SEE.
REALLY... YEAH.
OKAY.
?

Fruits Basket 4 Part 4:

As usual, I'm playing video games. I play so many that I can't list them all. I'm stuck on the last boss in Persona 2....With the Megami Tensei series, I'm the type who, once stopped, takes a while to get back to it. I stopped playing Persona 1 for several months before I finally beat it. I'm also stopped in the middle of "Ore-Shika" (Ed: short for "Ore no Shikabane o Koete Yuke." Not published in the U.S.). It looks like I just can't go on. It's interesting. I wonder why I can't go on...? Actually, I bet I know why--the older I get, the harder it is for me to concentrate. It's scary. I think there are a bunch of other games I'm playing too much. This has nothing to do with it, but my handwriting is really bad.

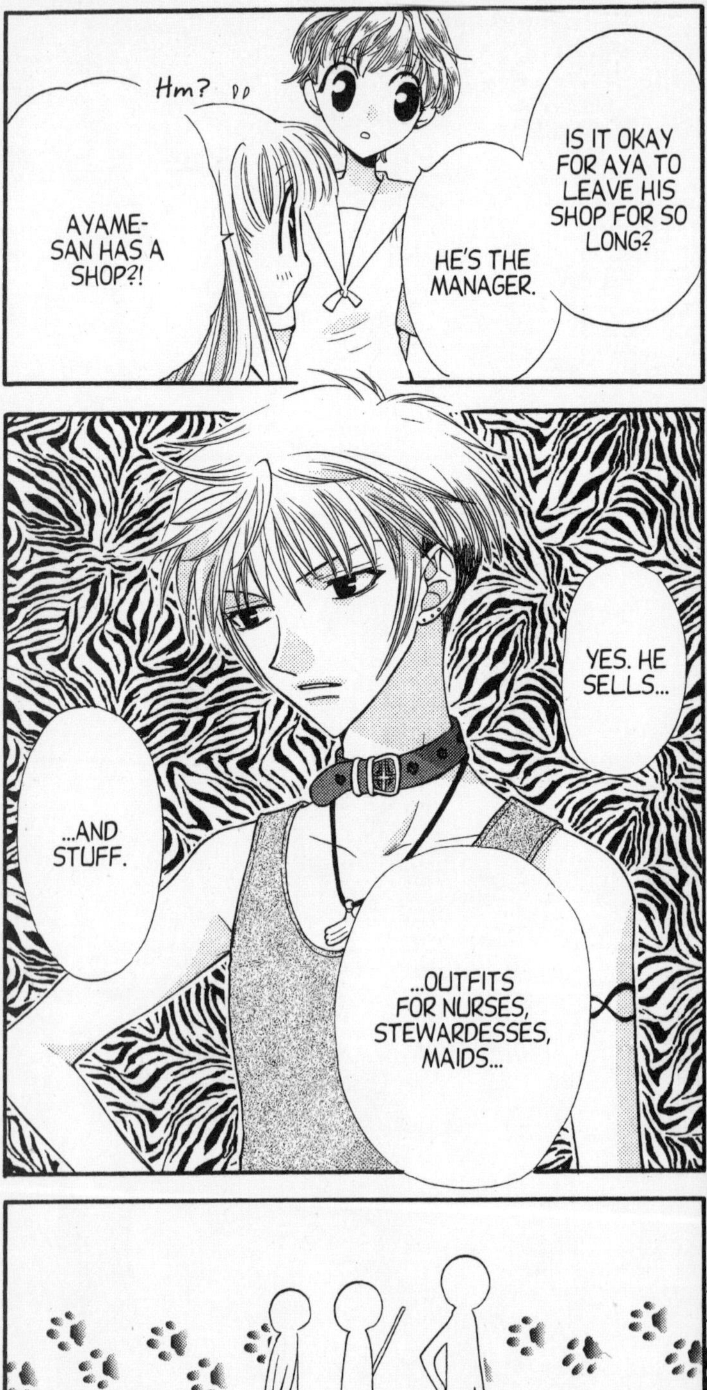
IS IT OKAY FOR AYA TO LEAVE HIS SHOP FOR SO LONG?
HE'S THE MANAGER.
Hm?
AYAME-SAN HAS A SHOP?!
YES. HE SELLS...
...OUTFITS FOR NURSES, STEWARDESSES, MAIDS...
...AND STUFF.

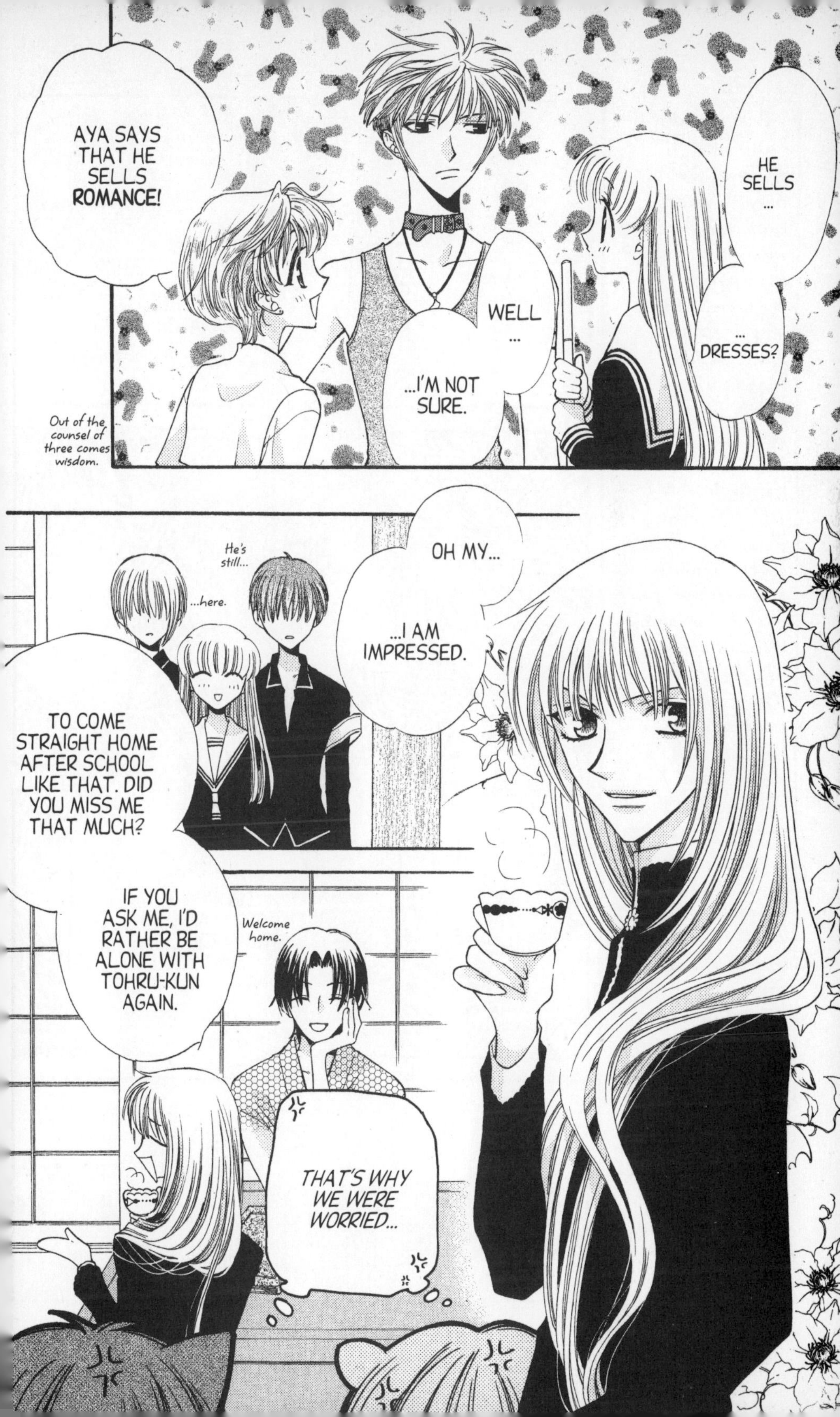
HE SELLS ...
... DRESSES?
WELL ...
...I'M NOT SURE.
AYA SAYS THAT HE SELLS **ROMANCE!**
Out of the counsel of three comes wisdom.
OH MY...
...I AM IMPRESSED.
He's still...
...here.
TO COME STRAIGHT HOME AFTER SCHOOL LIKE THAT. DID YOU MISS ME THAT MUCH?
IF YOU ASK ME, I'D RATHER BE ALONE WITH TOHRU-KUN AGAIN.
Welcome home.
THAT'S WHY WE WERE WORRIED...

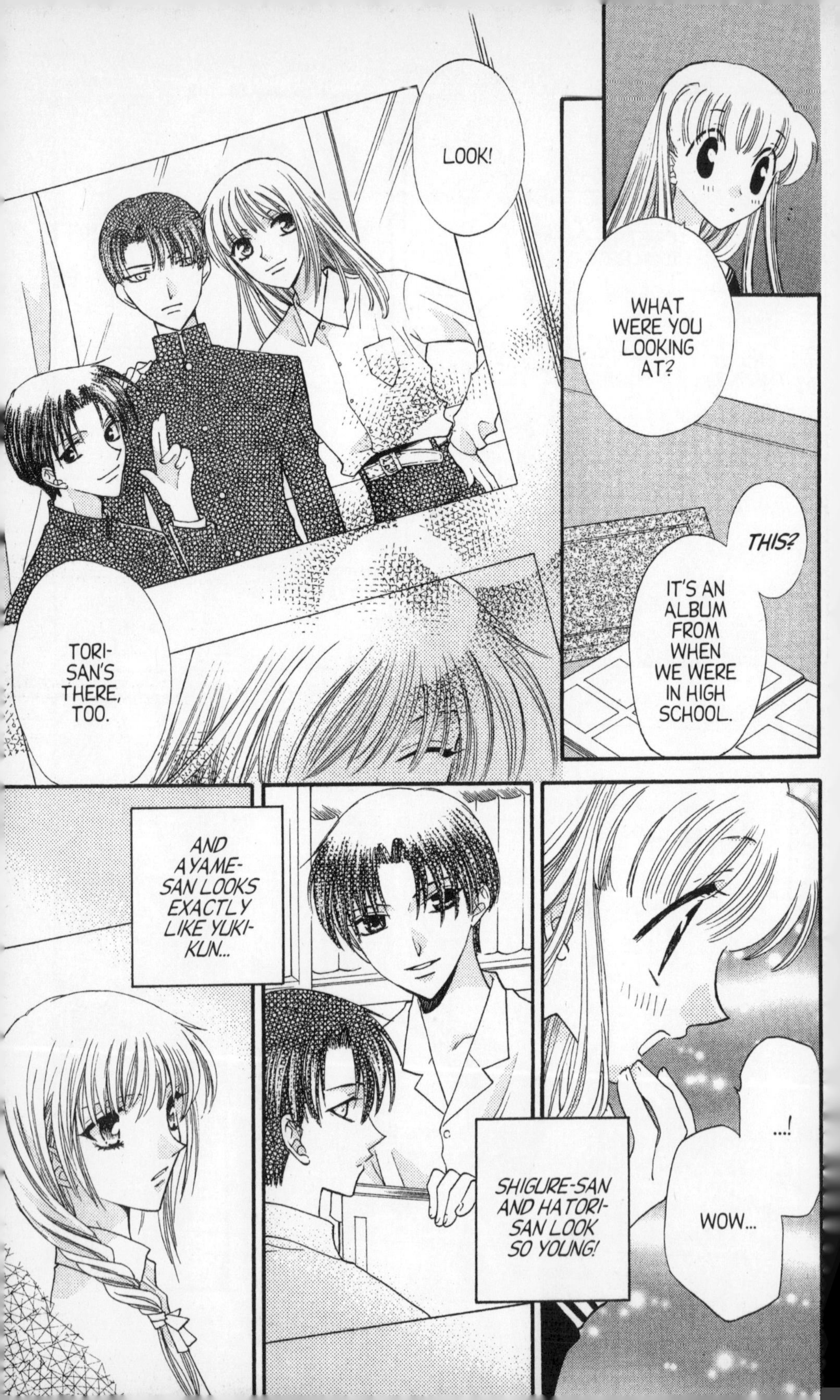
WHAT WERE YOU LOOKING AT?
THIS?
IT'S AN ALBUM FROM WHEN WE WERE IN HIGH SCHOOL.
LOOK!
TORI-SAN'S THERE, TOO.
...!
WOW...
SHIGURE-SAN AND HATORI-SAN LOOK SO YOUNG!
AND AYAME-SAN LOOKS EXACTLY LIKE YUKI-KUN...

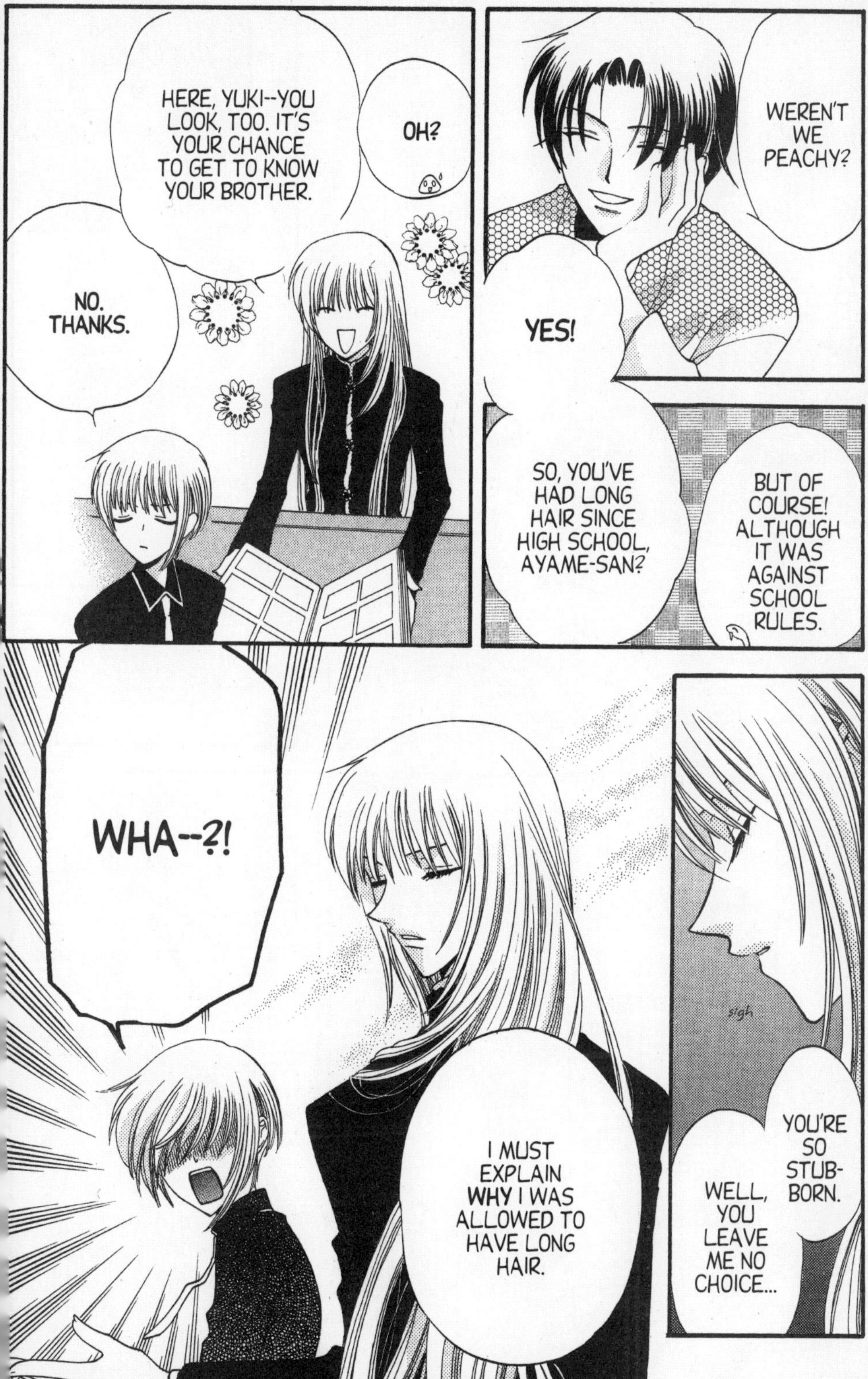
WEREN'T WE PEACHY?
YES!
SO, YOU'VE HAD LONG HAIR SINCE HIGH SCHOOL, AYAME-SAN?
BUT OF COURSE! ALTHOUGH IT WAS AGAINST SCHOOL RULES.
OH?
HERE, YUKI--YOU LOOK, TOO. IT'S YOUR CHANCE TO GET TO KNOW YOUR BROTHER.
NO. THANKS.
sigh
YOU'RE SO STUBBORN.
WELL, YOU LEAVE ME NO CHOICE...
I MUST EXPLAIN WHY I WAS ALLOWED TO HAVE LONG HAIR.
WHA--?!

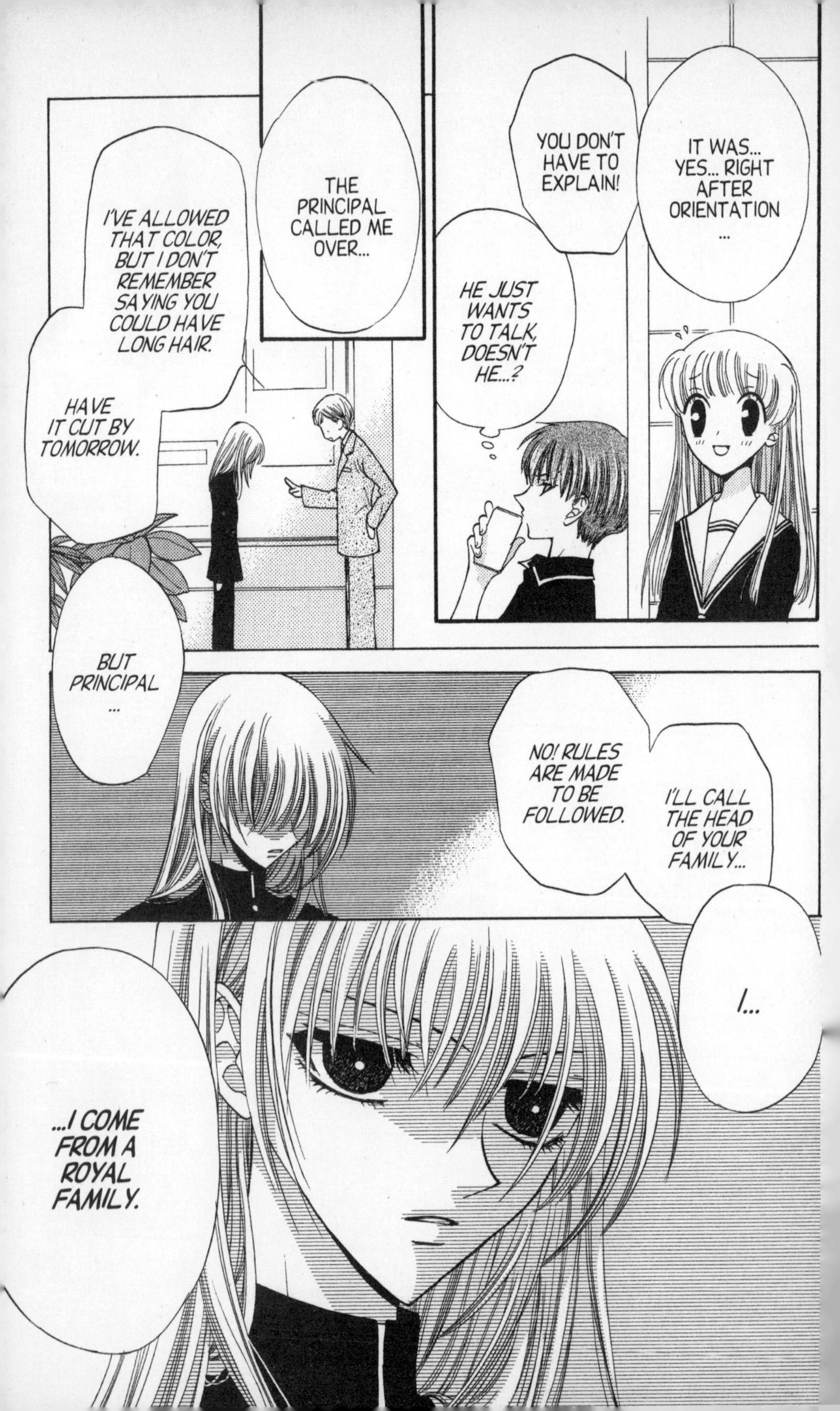
IT WAS... YES... RIGHT AFTER ORIENTATION ...
YOU DON'T HAVE TO EXPLAIN!
HE JUST WANTS TO TALK, DOESN'T HE...?
THE PRINCIPAL CALLED ME OVER...
I'VE ALLOWED THAT COLOR, BUT I DON'T REMEMBER SAYING YOU COULD HAVE LONG HAIR.
HAVE IT CUT BY TOMORROW.
BUT PRINCIPAL ...
NO! RULES ARE MADE TO BE FOLLOWED.
I'LL CALL THE HEAD OF YOUR FAMILY...
I...
...I COME FROM A ROYAL FAMILY.

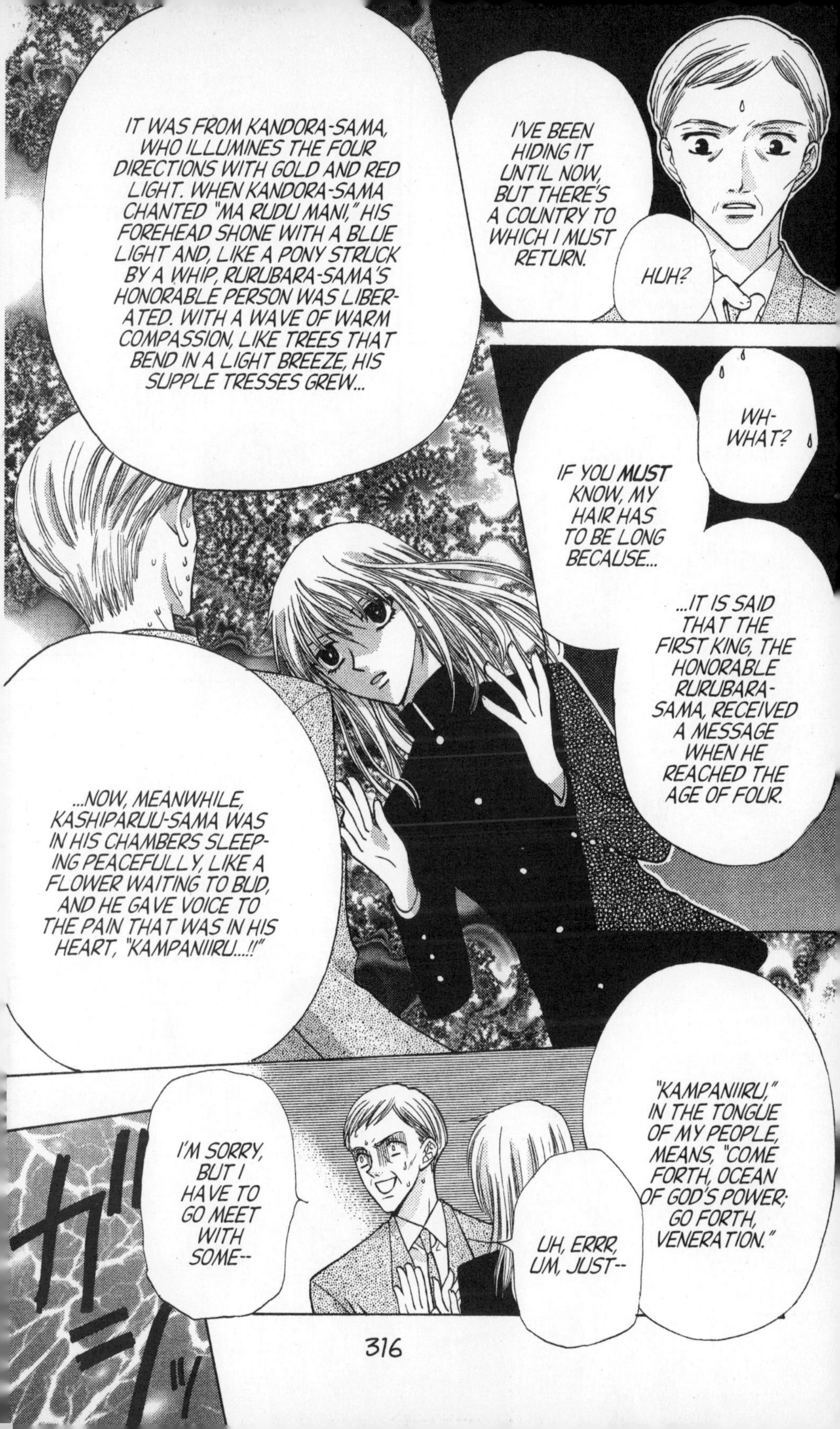

I'VE BEEN HIDING IT UNTIL NOW, BUT THERE'S A COUNTRY TO WHICH I MUST RETURN.
HUH?
WH- WHAT?
IF YOU **MUST** KNOW, MY HAIR HAS TO BE LONG BECAUSE...
...IT IS SAID THAT THE FIRST KING, THE HONORABLE RURUBARA-SAMA, RECEIVED A MESSAGE WHEN HE REACHED THE AGE OF FOUR.
IT WAS FROM KANDORA-SAMA, WHO ILLUMINES THE FOUR DIRECTIONS WITH GOLD AND RED LIGHT. WHEN KANDORA-SAMA CHANTED "MA RUDU MANI," HIS FOREHEAD SHONE WITH A BLUE LIGHT AND, LIKE A PONY STRUCK BY A WHIP, RURUBARA-SAMA'S HONORABLE PERSON WAS LIBER-ATED. WITH A WAVE OF WARM COMPASSION, LIKE TREES THAT BEND IN A LIGHT BREEZE, HIS SUPPLE TRESSES GREW...
...NOW, MEANWHILE, KASHIPARUU-SAMA WAS IN HIS CHAMBERS SLEEP-ING PEACEFULLY, LIKE A FLOWER WAITING TO BUD, AND HE GAVE VOICE TO THE PAIN THAT WAS IN HIS HEART, "KAMPANIIRU...!!"
"KAMPANIIRU," IN THE TONGUE OF MY PEOPLE, MEANS, "COME FORTH, OCEAN OF GOD'S POWER; GO FORTH, VENERATION."
UH, ERRR, UM, JUST--
I'M SORRY, BUT I HAVE TO GO MEET WITH SOME--

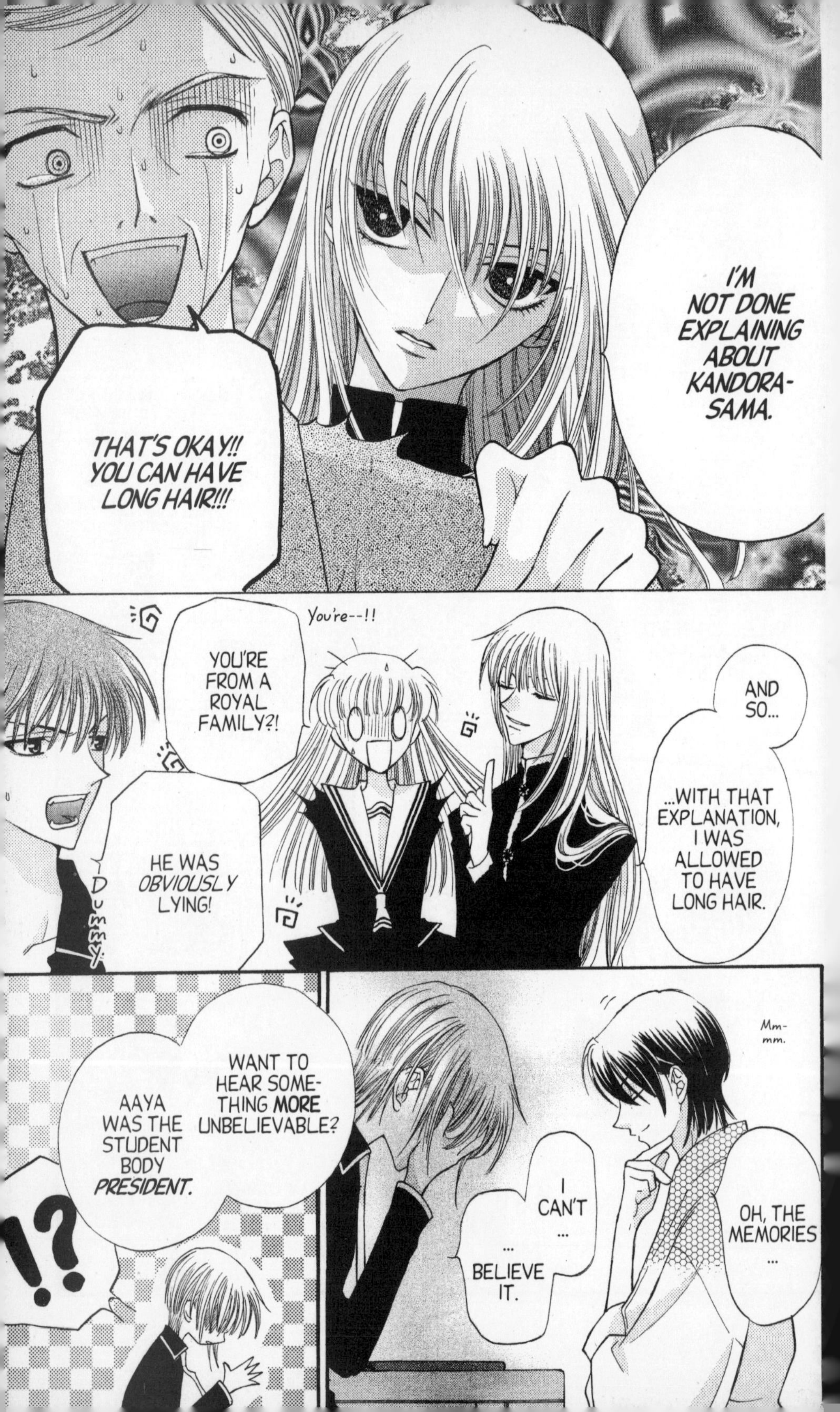
I'M NOT DONE EXPLAINING ABOUT KANDORA-SAMA.
THAT'S OKAY!! YOU CAN HAVE LONG HAIR!!!
AND SO...
...WITH THAT EXPLANATION, I WAS ALLOWED TO HAVE LONG HAIR.
You're--!!
YOU'RE FROM A ROYAL FAMILY?!
HE WAS OBVIOUSLY LYING!
Dummy.
Mm-mm.
OH, THE MEMORIES ...
I CAN'T ... ... BELIEVE IT.
WANT TO HEAR SOMETHING MORE UNBELIEVABLE?
AAYA WAS THE STUDENT BODY PRESIDENT.
!?

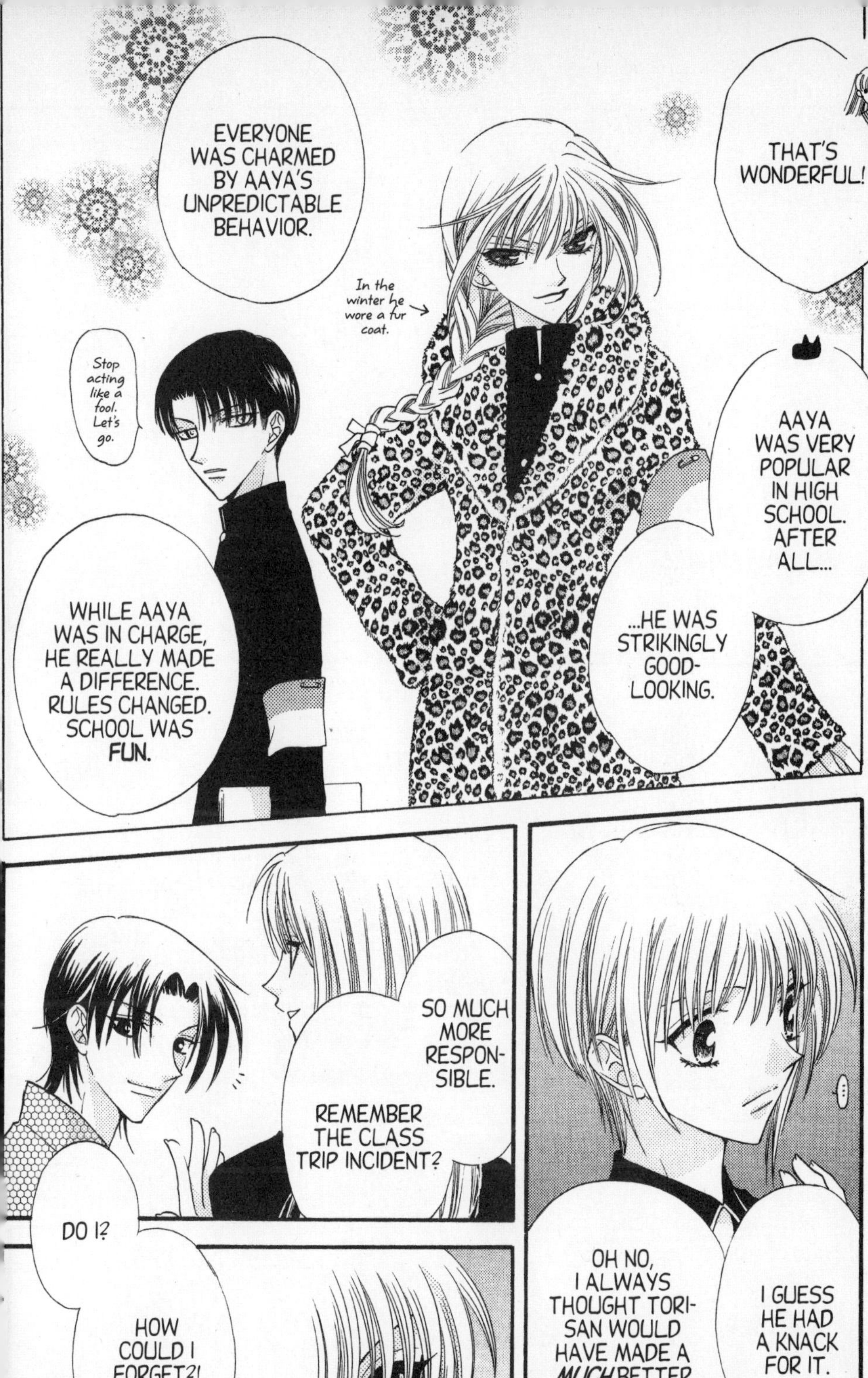
THAT'S WONDERFUL!
EVERYONE WAS CHARMED BY AAYA'S UNPREDICTABLE BEHAVIOR.
In the winter he wore a fur coat.
AAYA WAS VERY POPULAR IN HIGH SCHOOL. AFTER ALL...
...HE WAS STRIKINGLY GOOD-LOOKING.
Stop acting like a fool. Let's go.
WHILE AAYA WAS IN CHARGE, HE REALLY MADE A DIFFERENCE. RULES CHANGED. SCHOOL WAS FUN.
...
I GUESS HE HAD A KNACK FOR IT.
OH NO, I ALWAYS THOUGHT TORI-SAN WOULD HAVE MADE A MUCH BETTER PRESIDENT...
SO MUCH MORE RESPONSIBLE.
REMEMBER THE CLASS TRIP INCIDENT?
DO I?
HOW COULD I FORGET?!

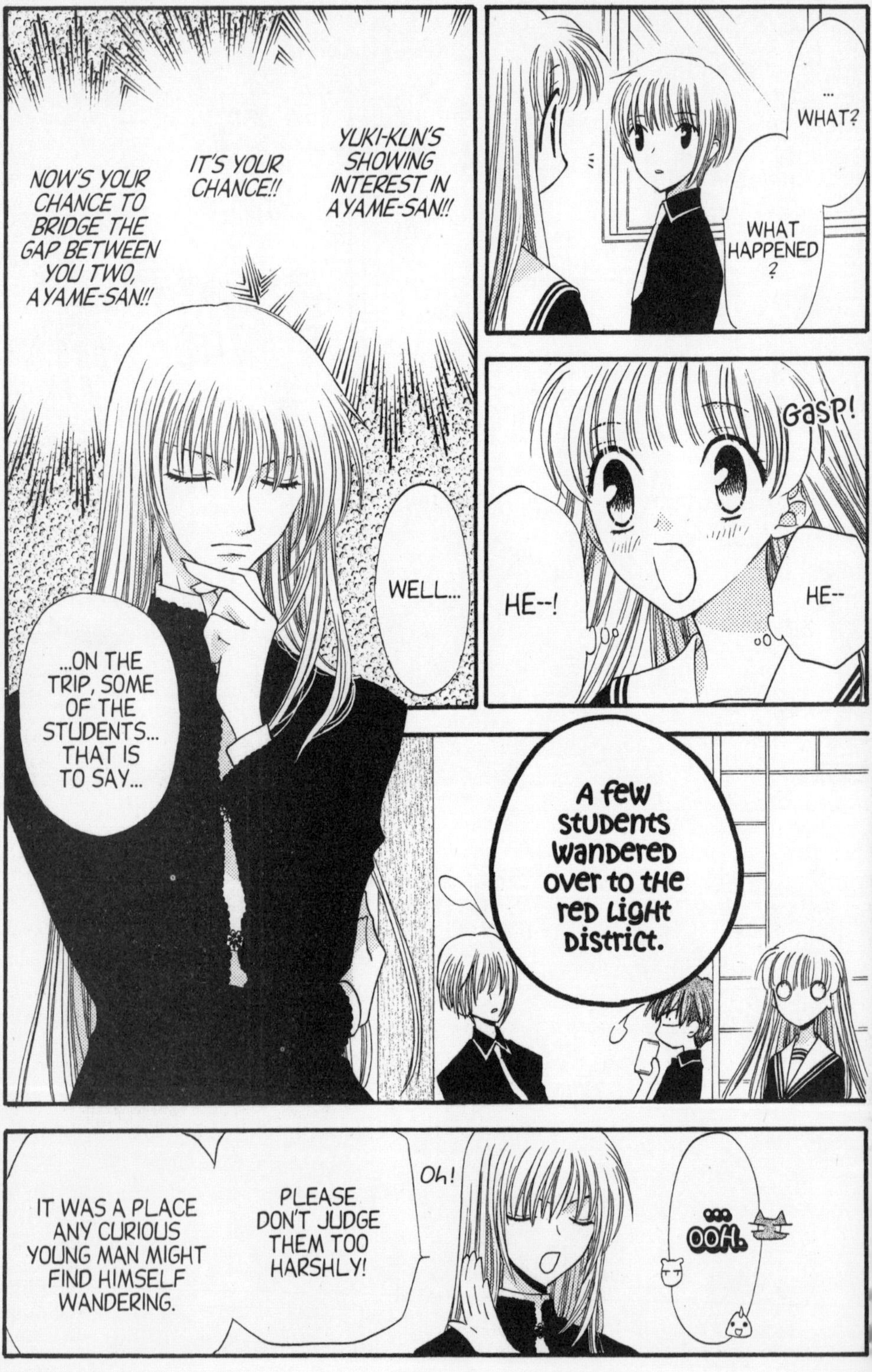
... WHAT?
WHAT HAPPENED?
GASP!
HE--
HE--!
YUKI-KUN'S SHOWING INTEREST IN AYAME-SAN!!
IT'S YOUR CHANCE!!
NOW'S YOUR CHANCE TO BRIDGE THE GAP BETWEEN YOU TWO, AYAME-SAN!!
WELL...
...ON THE TRIP, SOME OF THE STUDENTS... THAT IS TO SAY...
A few students wandered over to the red light district.
...OOH.
Oh!
PLEASE DON'T JUDGE THEM TOO HARSHLY!
IT WAS A PLACE ANY CURIOUS YOUNG MAN MIGHT FIND HIMSELF WANDERING.

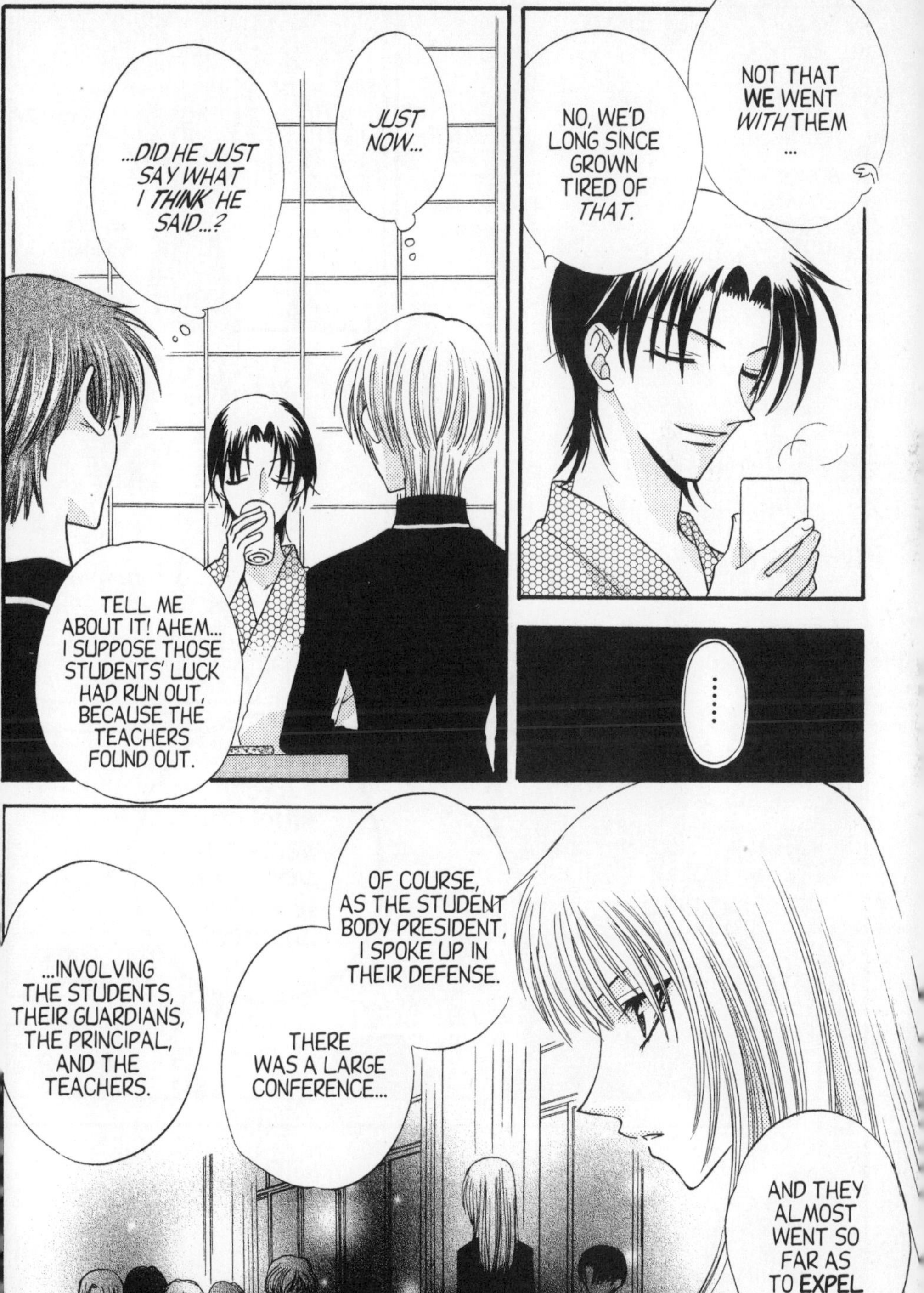
NOT THAT **WE** WENT *WITH* THEM ...
NO, WE'D LONG SINCE GROWN TIRED OF *THAT*.
......
JUST NOW...
...DID HE JUST SAY WHAT I THINK HE SAID...?
TELL ME ABOUT IT! AHEM... I SUPPOSE THOSE STUDENTS' LUCK HAD RUN OUT, BECAUSE THE TEACHERS FOUND OUT.
OF COURSE, AS THE STUDENT BODY PRESIDENT, I SPOKE UP IN THEIR DEFENSE.
THERE WAS A LARGE CONFERENCE...
...INVOLVING THE STUDENTS, THEIR GUARDIANS, THE PRINCIPAL, AND THE TEACHERS.
AND THEY ALMOST WENT SO FAR AS TO **EXPEL** THEM.

THEY SET FOOT IN THE RED LIGHT DISTRICT AS MINORS...NOT A LAUDABLE ACTION.
RULES ARE MADE TO BE FOLLOWED, IT'S SAID. IF THEY ARE NOT, ORDER IS LOST.
HOWEVER, IF ALL SEXUAL DESIRE IS DENIED AS IF IT IS EVIL, WE CANNOT HELP BUT REGRET IT.
BECAUSE HUMANS BEAR THE RE-SPONSIBILITY OF MULTIPLYING AND REPLENISHING THE EARTH.
I BELIEVE THAT SEXUAL DESIRE IS IN PART A DESIRE TO FULFILL THAT OBLIGATION.
PRESI-DENT...
IS THAT SOMETHING TO BE ASHAMED OF? IS IT A SIN?
AYAME-KUN...!
YOU'RE UNUSUALLY SERIOUS TODAY!
Oohh...
SO HE **WAS** JUST PLAYING DUMB ALL THIS TIME...
THEREFORE, HERE AND NOW, I MAKE A PROPOSAL:
TO THE UNDER-AGED YOUTHS WHO CARRY THESE CARNAL DESIRES... TO THOSE WHO HAVE NO PLACE WITHIN OUR VAGUE RULES...
...LET US EXTEND THE **HAND OF SALVATION!!**

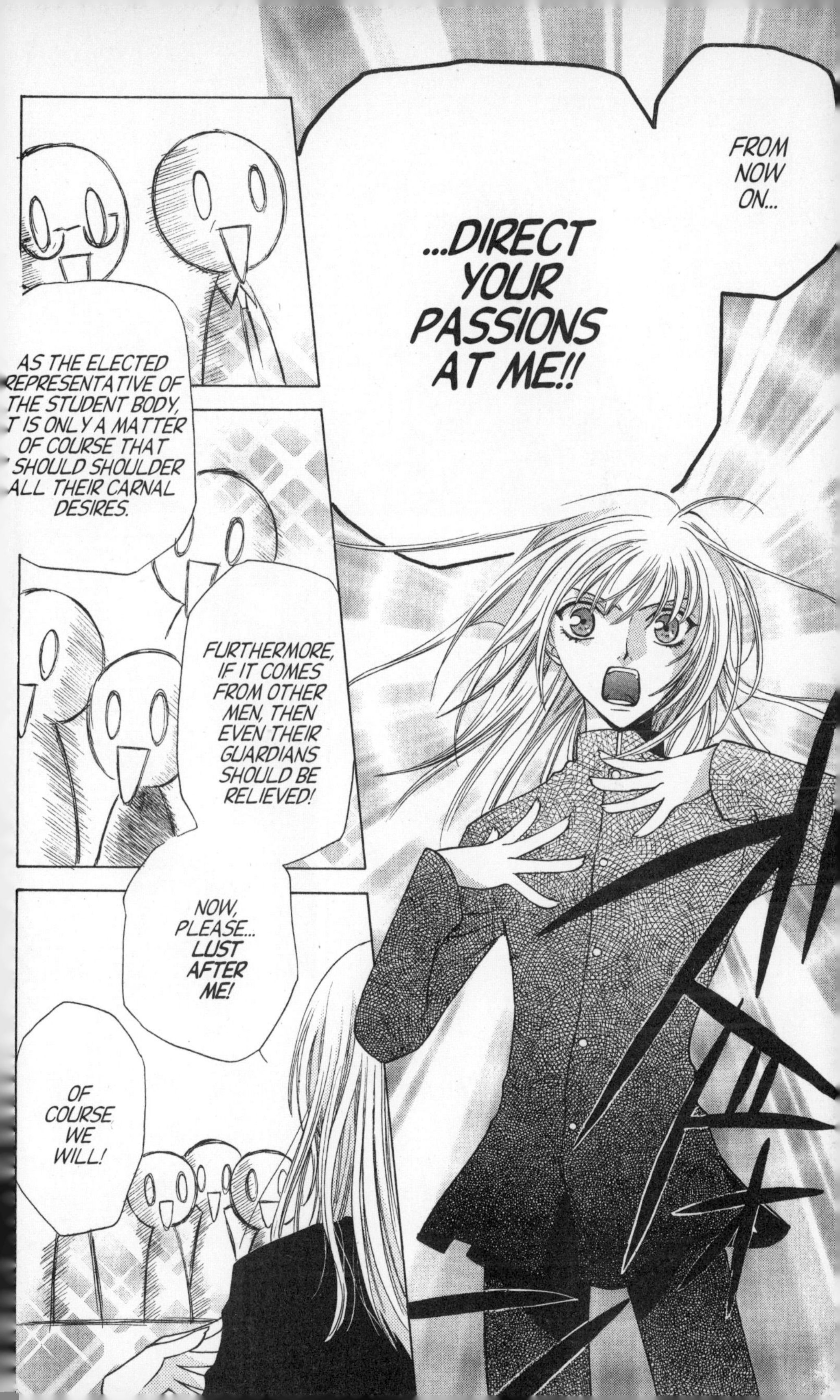
FROM NOW ON...
...DIRECT YOUR PASSIONS AT ME!!
AS THE ELECTED EPRESENTATIVE OF THE STUDENT BODY, T IS ONLY A MATTER OF COURSE THAT SHOULD SHOULDER ALL THEIR CARNAL DESIRES.
FURTHERMORE, IF IT COMES FROM OTHER MEN, THEN EVEN THEIR GUARDIANS SHOULD BE RELIEVED!
NOW, PLEASE... LUST AFTER ME!
OF COURSE WE WILL!

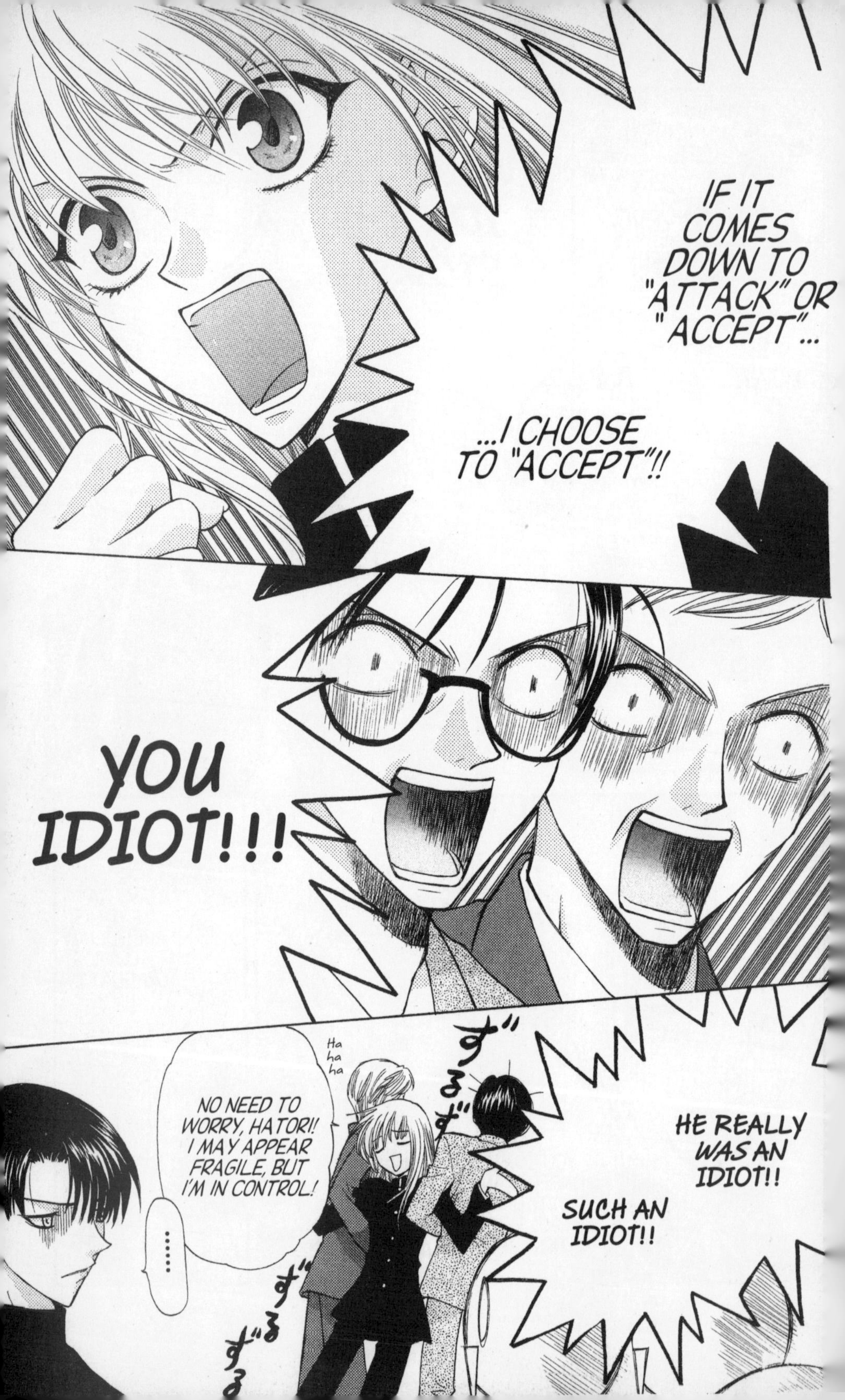
IF IT COMES DOWN TO "ATTACK" OR "ACCEPT"...
...I CHOOSE TO "ACCEPT"!!
YOU IDIOT!!!
HE REALLY WAS AN IDIOT!!
SUCH AN IDIOT!!
ずるずる
Ha ha ha
NO NEED TO WORRY, HATORI! I MAY APPEAR FRAGILE, BUT I'M IN CONTROL!
ずるずる
......

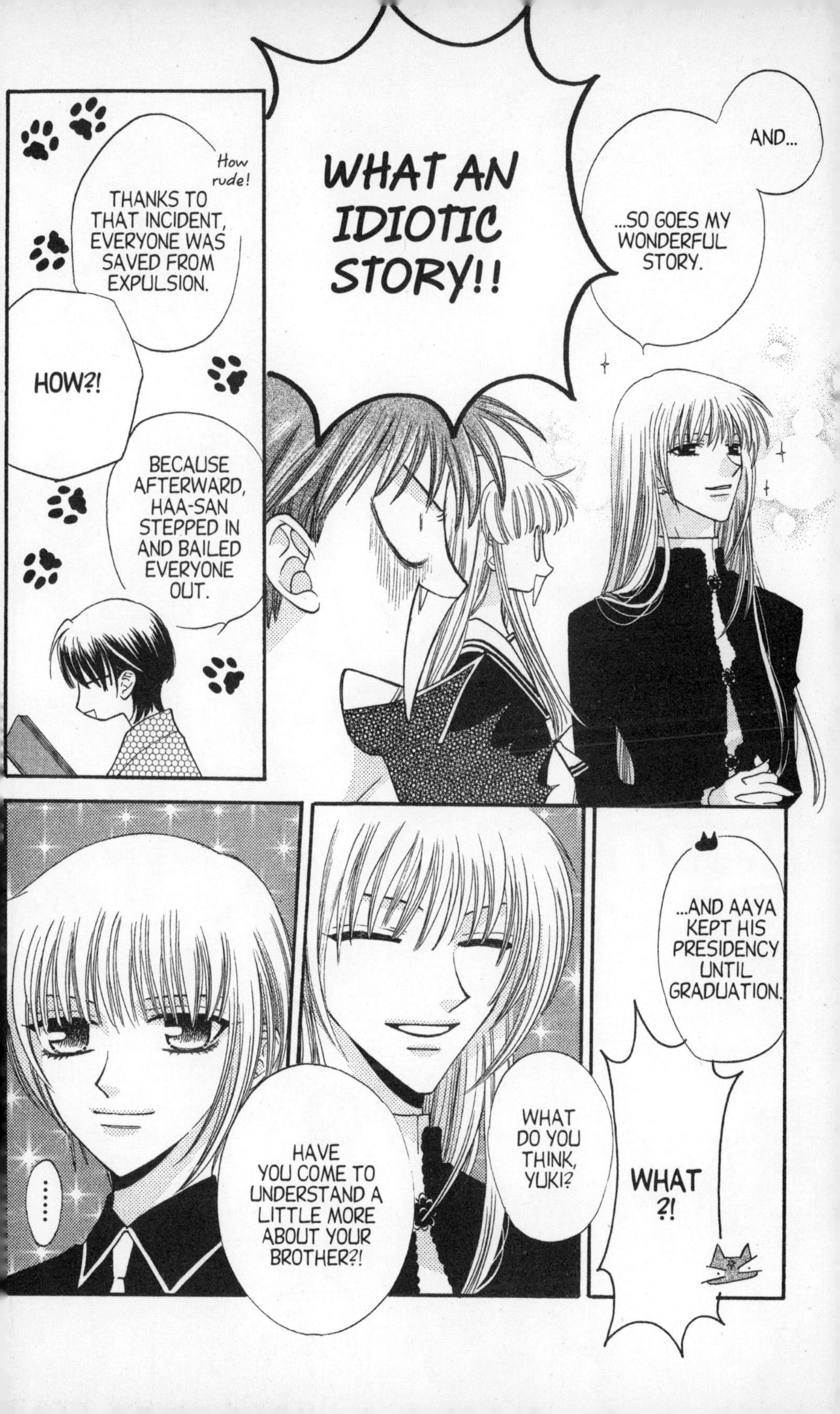
AND...
...SO GOES MY WONDERFUL STORY.
WHAT AN IDIOTIC STORY!!
THANKS TO THAT INCIDENT, EVERYONE WAS SAVED FROM EXPULSION.
How rude!
HOW?!
BECAUSE AFTERWARD, HAA-SAN STEPPED IN AND BAILED EVERYONE OUT.
...AND AAYA KEPT HIS PRESIDENCY UNTIL GRADUATION.
WHAT ?!
WHAT DO YOU THINK, YUKI?
HAVE YOU COME TO UNDERSTAND A LITTLE MORE ABOUT YOUR BROTHER?!
......

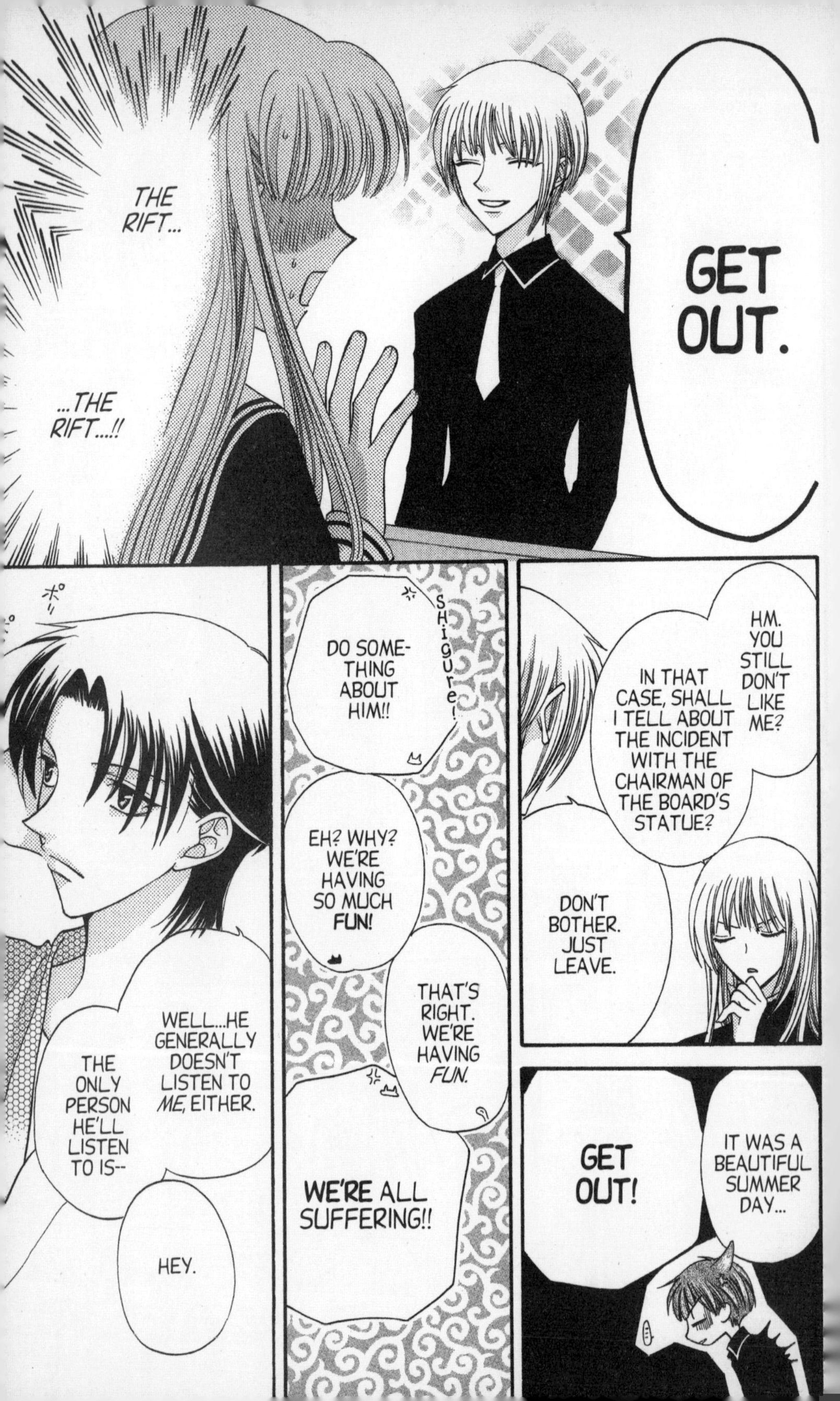

GET OUT.
THE RIFT...
...THE RIFT...!!
HM. YOU STILL DON'T LIKE ME?
IN THAT CASE, SHALL I TELL ABOUT THE INCIDENT WITH THE CHAIRMAN OF THE BOARD'S STATUE?
DON'T BOTHER. JUST LEAVE.
IT WAS A BEAUTIFUL SUMMER DAY...
GET OUT!
Shigure!
DO SOMETHING ABOUT HIM!!
EH? WHY? WE'RE HAVING SO MUCH FUN!
THAT'S RIGHT. WE'RE HAVING FUN.
WE'RE ALL SUFFERING!!
ポ
WELL...HE GENERALLY DOESN'T LISTEN TO ME, EITHER.
THE ONLY PERSON HE'LL LISTEN TO IS--
HEY.

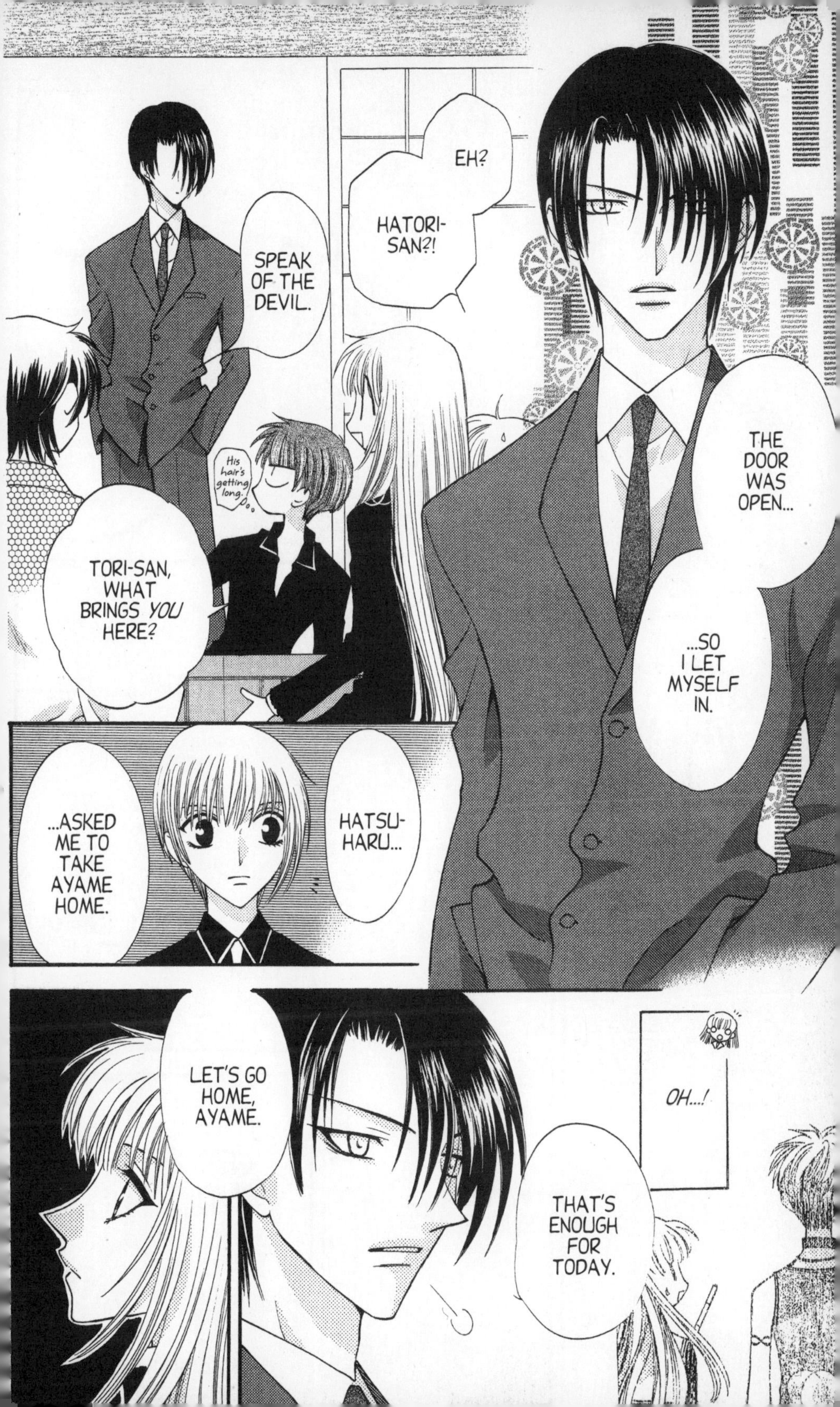
THE DOOR WAS OPEN...
...SO I LET MYSELF IN.
EH?
HATORI-SAN?!
SPEAK OF THE DEVIL.
His hair's getting long.
TORI-SAN, WHAT BRINGS *YOU* HERE?
HATSU-HARU...
...ASKED ME TO TAKE AYAME HOME.
OH...!
THAT'S ENOUGH FOR TODAY.
LET'S GO HOME, AYAME.

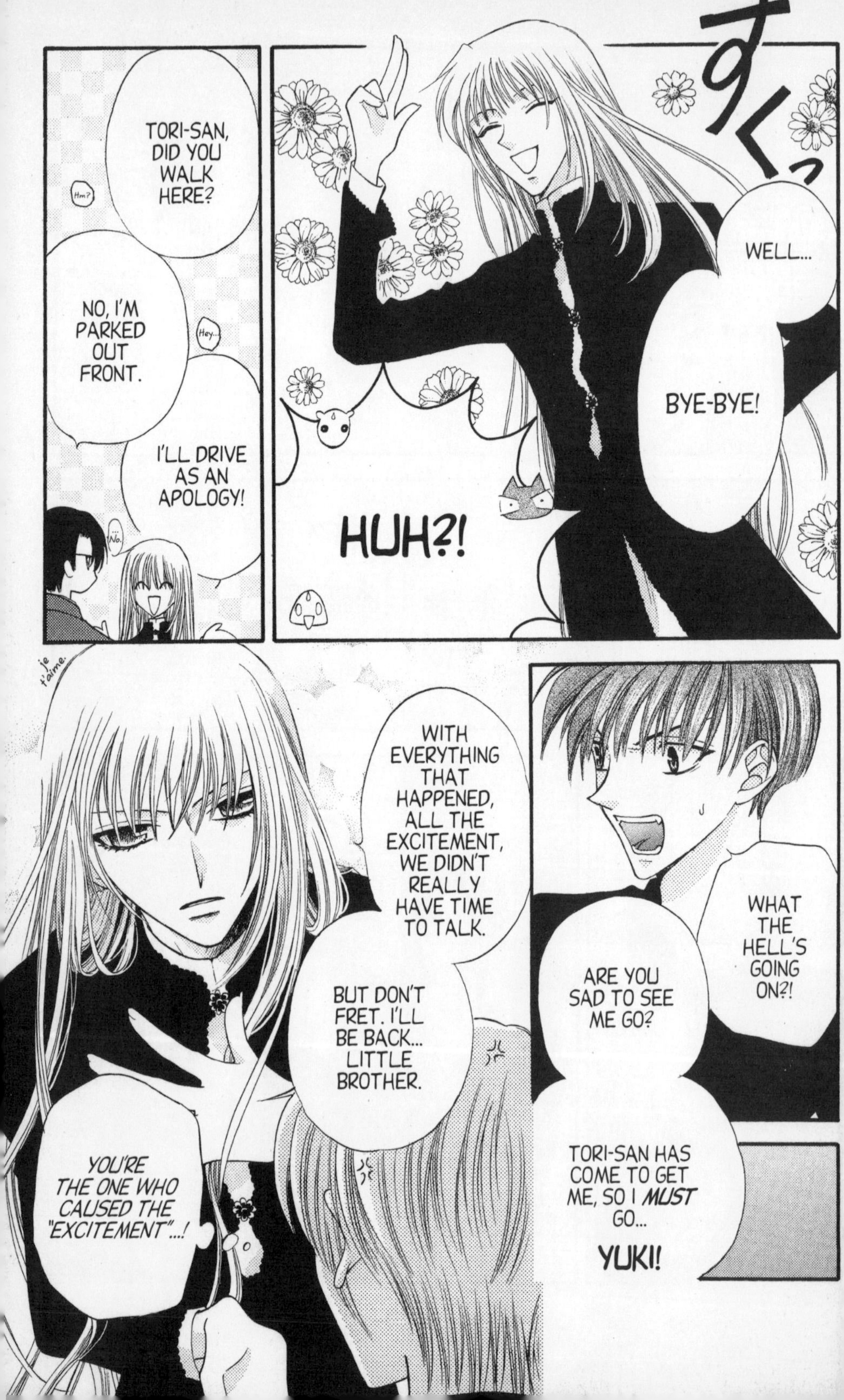
すくっ
WELL...
BYE-BYE!
HUH?!
TORI-SAN, DID YOU WALK HERE?
Hm?
NO, I'M PARKED OUT FRONT.
Hey...
I'LL DRIVE AS AN APOLOGY!
...No.
WHAT THE HELL'S GOING ON?!
ARE YOU SAD TO SEE ME GO?
TORI-SAN HAS COME TO GET ME, SO I *MUST* GO...
YUKI!
je t'aime.
WITH EVERYTHING THAT HAPPENED, ALL THE EXCITEMENT, WE DIDN'T REALLY HAVE TIME TO TALK.
BUT DON'T FRET. I'LL BE BACK... LITTLE BROTHER.
YOU'RE THE ONE WHO CAUSED THE "EXCITEMENT"...!

WELL, TORI-SAN, LET US BE OFF!
GURE-SAN, I'LL SEE YOU AGAIN.
I'LL COME VISIT YOU.
FAREWELL, MY FRIENDS!!
Ha
Ha
Ha!
step
step
step
Slam
WHAT ...
...THE HELL...?
AAYA HAS ONLY EVER LISTENED TO HAA-SAN.
REALLY ?!
I WONDER WHY?
HE LOOKS UP TO HIM.

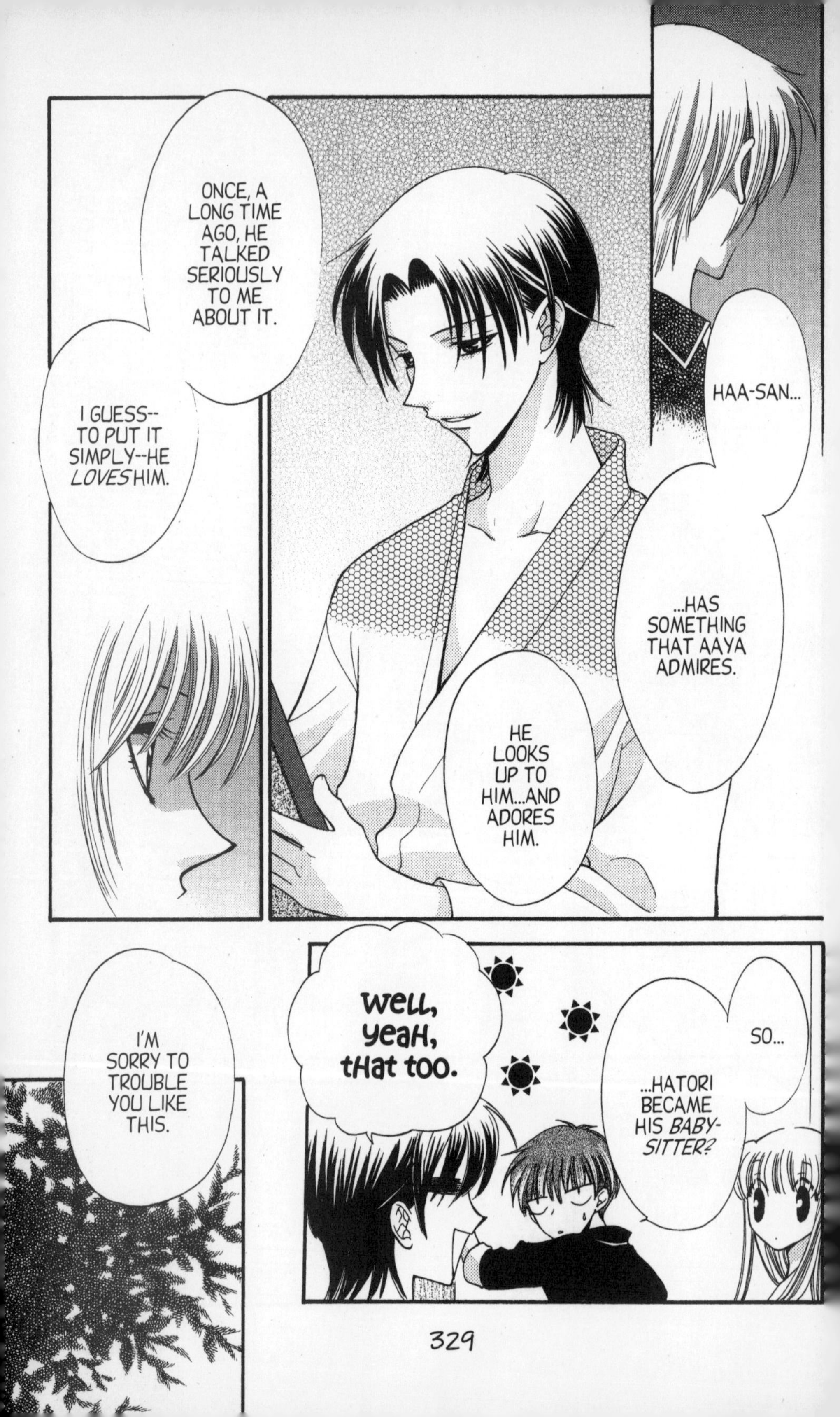
HAA-SAN...
...HAS SOMETHING THAT AAYA ADMIRES.
HE LOOKS UP TO HIM...AND ADORES HIM.
ONCE, A LONG TIME AGO, HE TALKED SERIOUSLY TO ME ABOUT IT.
I GUESS--TO PUT IT SIMPLY--HE *LOVES* HIM.
SO...
...HATORI BECAME HIS *BABY-SITTER?*
Well, yeah, that too.
I'M SORRY TO TROUBLE YOU LIKE THIS.

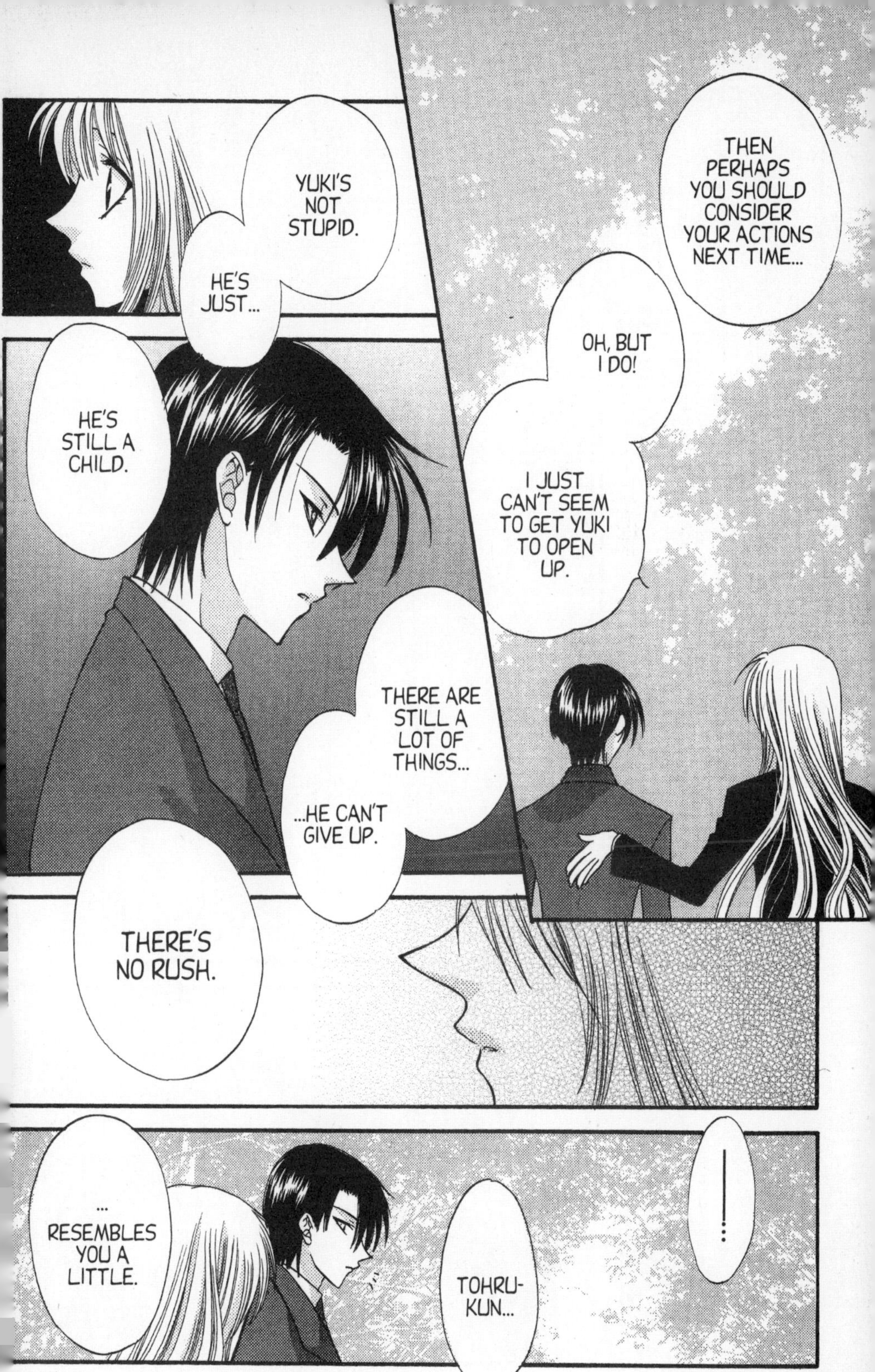

THEN PERHAPS YOU SHOULD CONSIDER YOUR ACTIONS NEXT TIME...
OH, BUT I DO!
I JUST CAN'T SEEM TO GET YUKI TO OPEN UP.
YUKI'S NOT STUPID.
HE'S JUST...
HE'S STILL A CHILD.
THERE ARE STILL A LOT OF THINGS...
...HE CAN'T GIVE UP.
THERE'S NO RUSH.
!
TOHRU-KUN...
... RESEMBLES YOU A LITTLE.

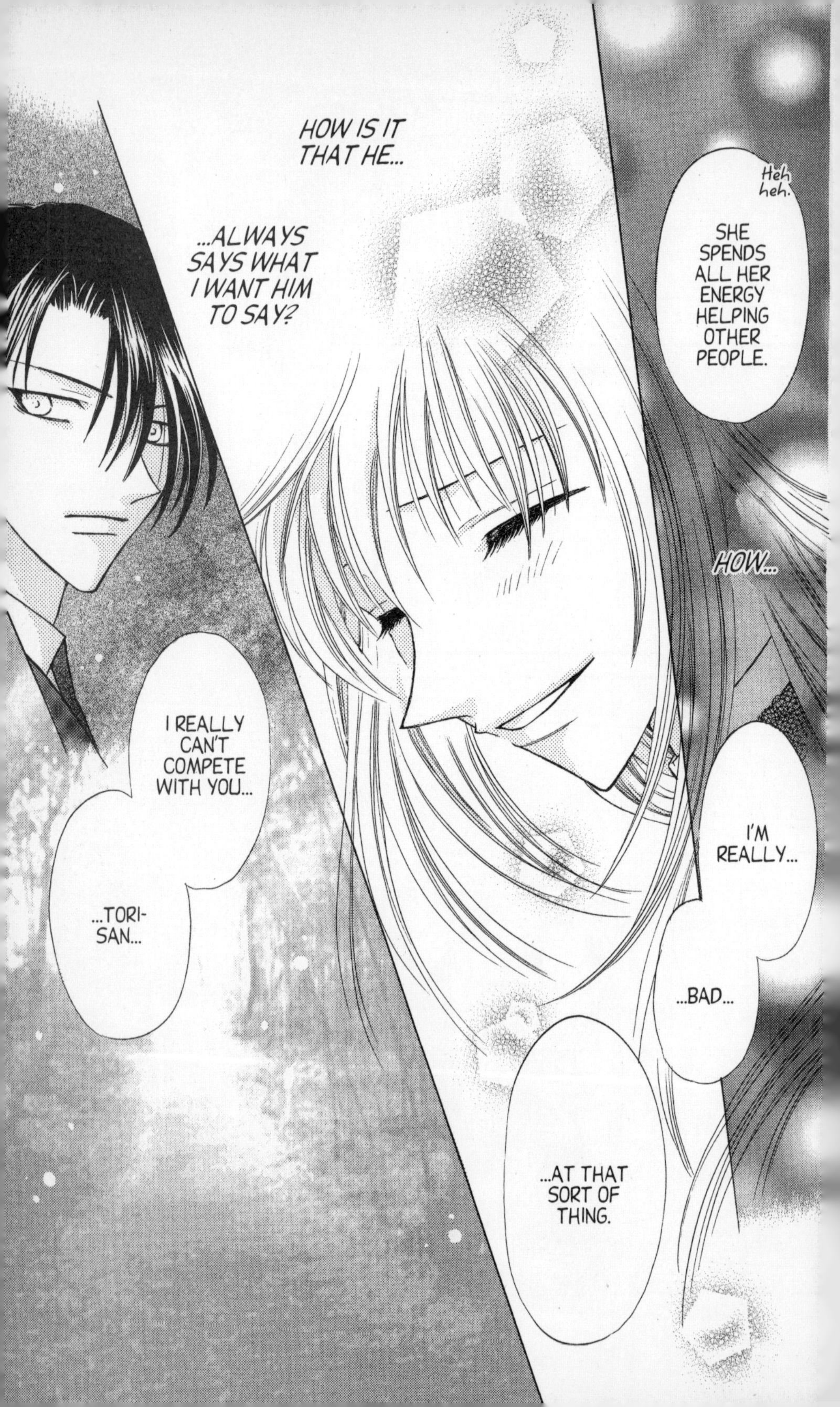
Heh heh.
SHE SPENDS ALL HER ENERGY HELPING OTHER PEOPLE.
HOW...
HOW IS IT THAT HE...
...ALWAYS SAYS WHAT I WANT HIM TO SAY?
I'M REALLY...
...BAD...
...AT THAT SORT OF THING.
I REALLY CAN'T COMPETE WITH YOU...
...TORI-SAN...

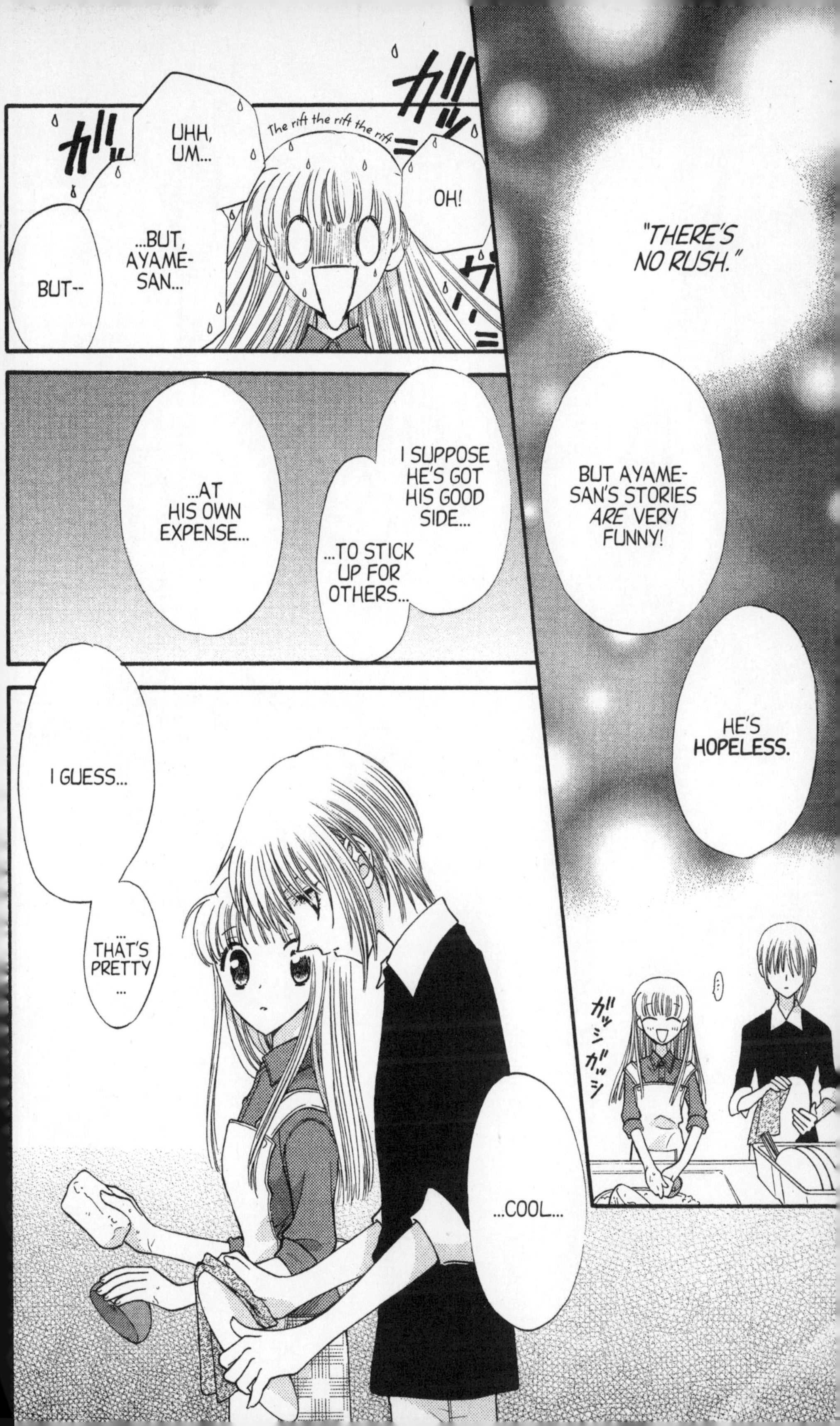
"THERE'S NO RUSH."
BUT AYAME-SAN'S STORIES *ARE* VERY FUNNY!
HE'S **HOPELESS.**
The rift the rift the rift
OH!
UHH, UM...
...BUT, AYAME-SAN...
BUT--
I SUPPOSE HE'S GOT HIS GOOD SIDE...
...TO STICK UP FOR OTHERS...
...AT HIS OWN EXPENSE...
I GUESS...
...THAT'S PRETTY...
...COOL...

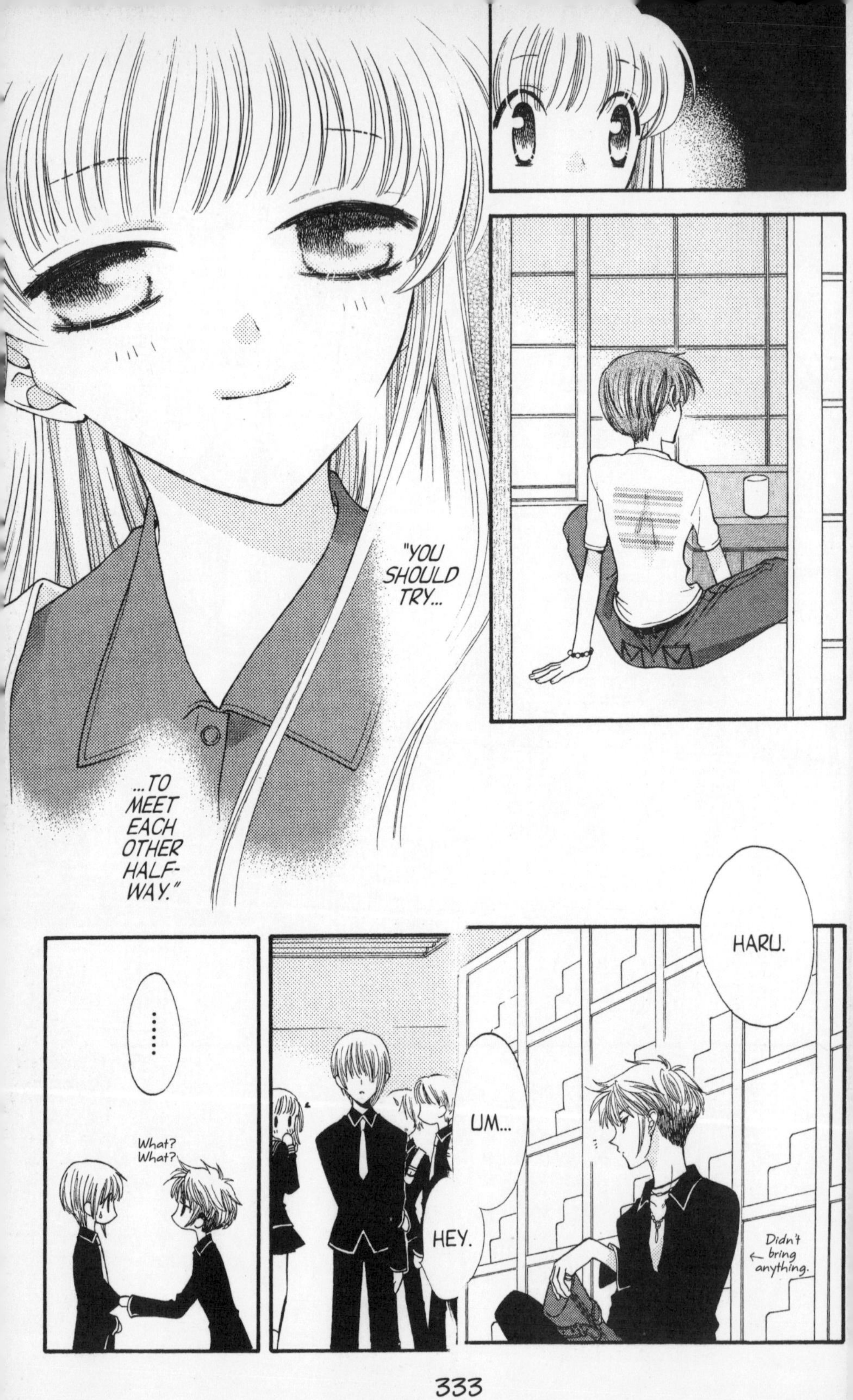
"YOU SHOULD TRY...
...TO MEET EACH OTHER HALF-WAY."
HARU.
UM...
HEY.
Didn't bring anything.
......
What? What?

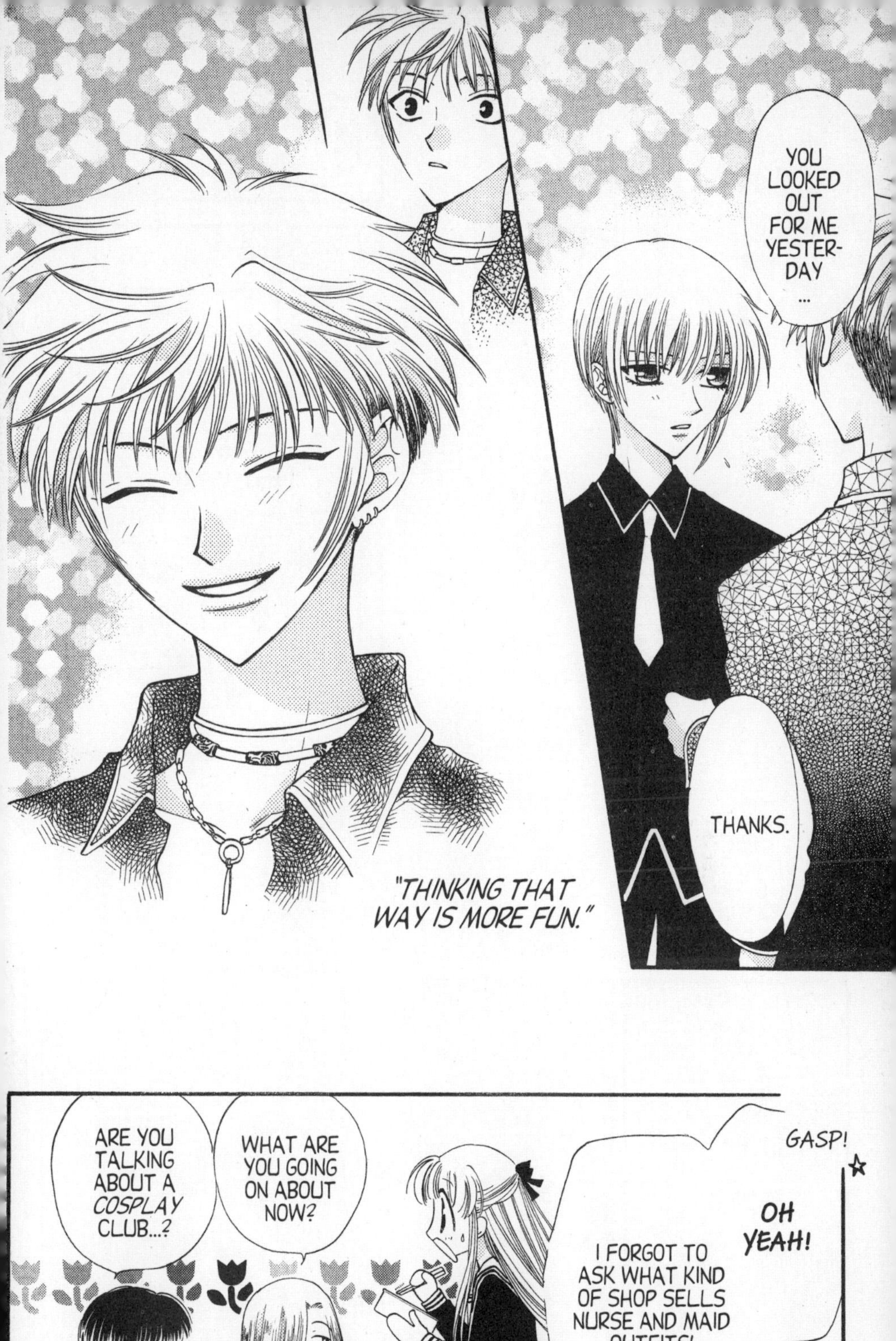
YOU LOOKED OUT FOR ME YESTER-DAY ...
THANKS.
"THINKING THAT WAY IS MORE FUN."
GASP!
OH YEAH!
I FORGOT TO ASK WHAT KIND OF SHOP SELLS NURSE AND MAID OUTFITS!
WHAT ARE YOU GOING ON ABOUT NOW?
ARE YOU TALKING ABOUT A *COSPLAY* CLUB...?

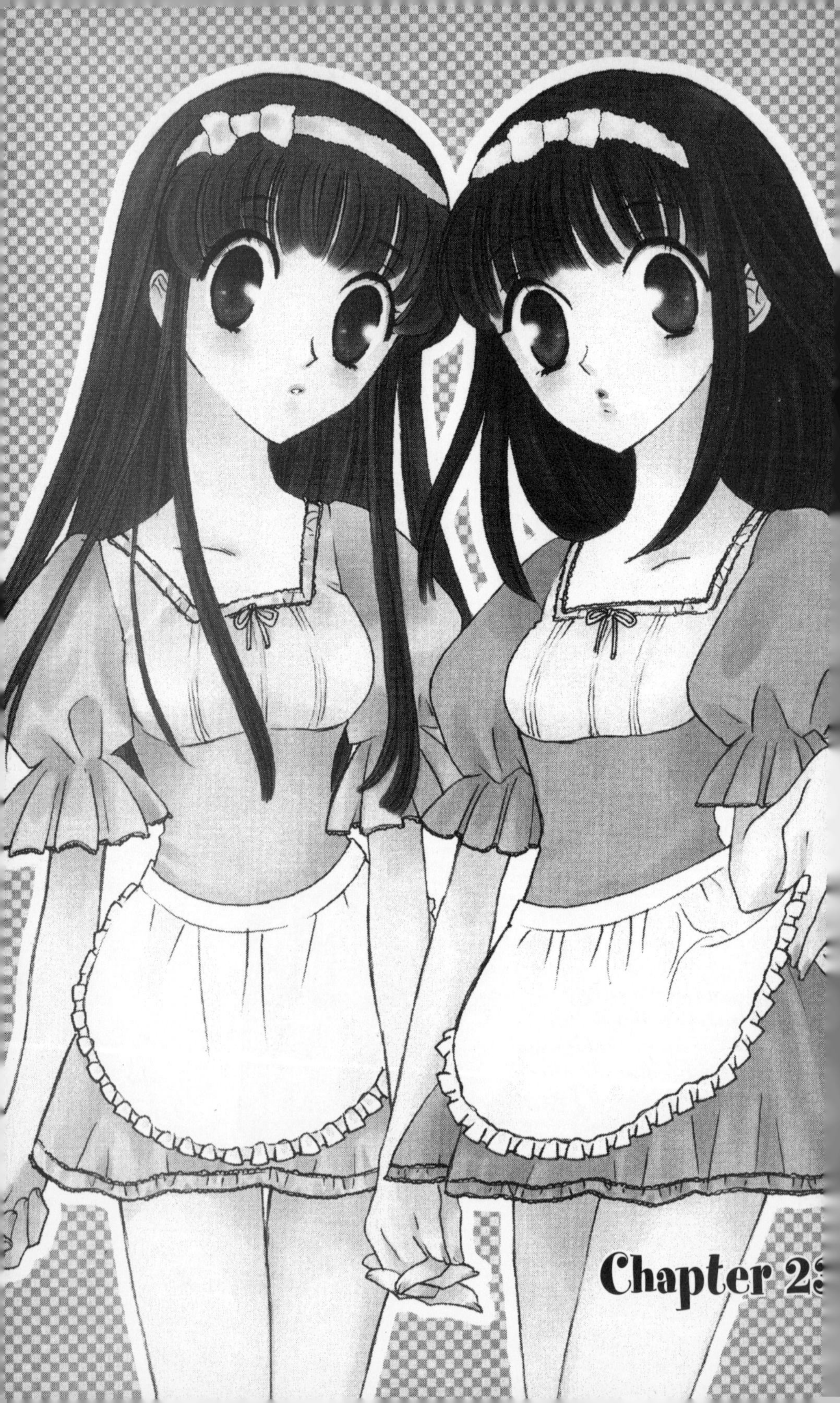
Chapter 23

THANK YOU!

NAN DESU YO, ONCE AGAIN!

Harada-sama, Araki-sama, mother, editor-sama ...and everyone who reads Furuba and supports me!

his has been Natsuki Takaya.

Next is Kagura, a flower. After that will be Momitchi, then Hatori--in the order they appeared in the series (that way, you clearly know their names and faces). I'll keep going through the members of the Zodiac one after another. Of course, even if I haven't gotten to them all, when it's time for Furuba to end, it will end. This is an unpleasant topic, but it can't be avoided.

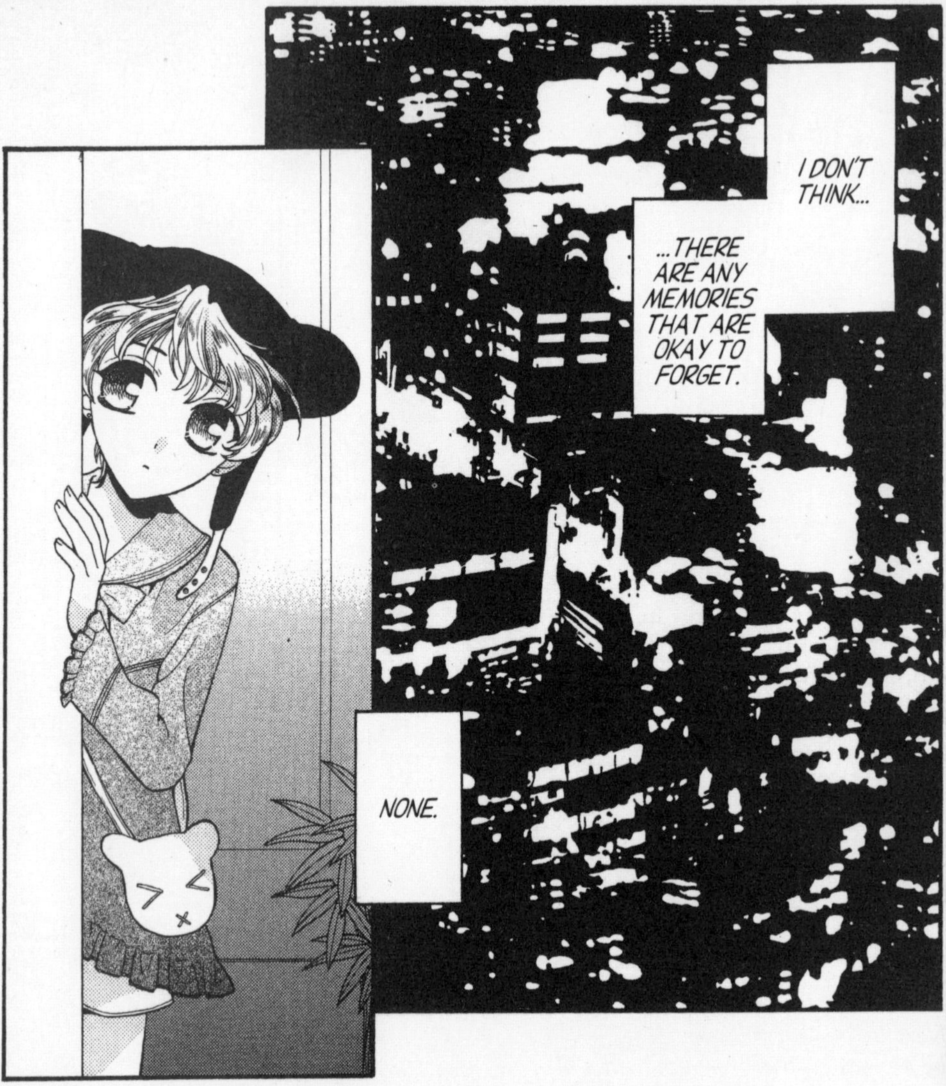
I DON'T THINK...
...THERE ARE ANY MEMORIES THAT ARE OKAY TO FORGET.
NONE.

ULTRA SPECIAL BLAH BLAH BLAH 5

They don't match at all! The chapter title page and the actual contents!! (I have no one to blame but myself.) Whether for good or ill, my mother is a big part of my life, so I can't think of Tohru or Momitchi as strangers. Well, they're not strangers! Each character that I create is an extension of myself. They're closer to me than if they were my children.

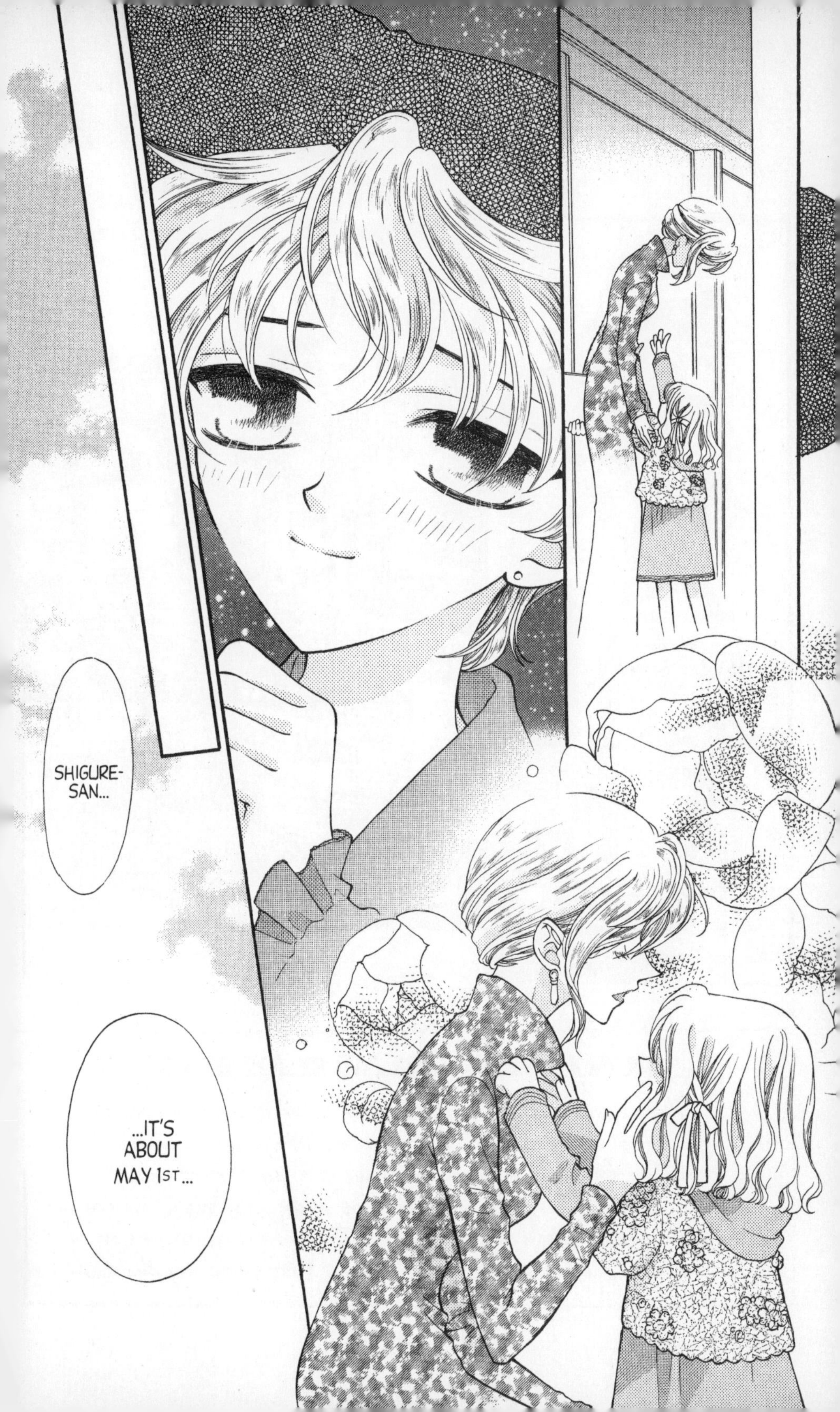
SHIGURE-SAN...
...IT'S ABOUT MAY 1ST...

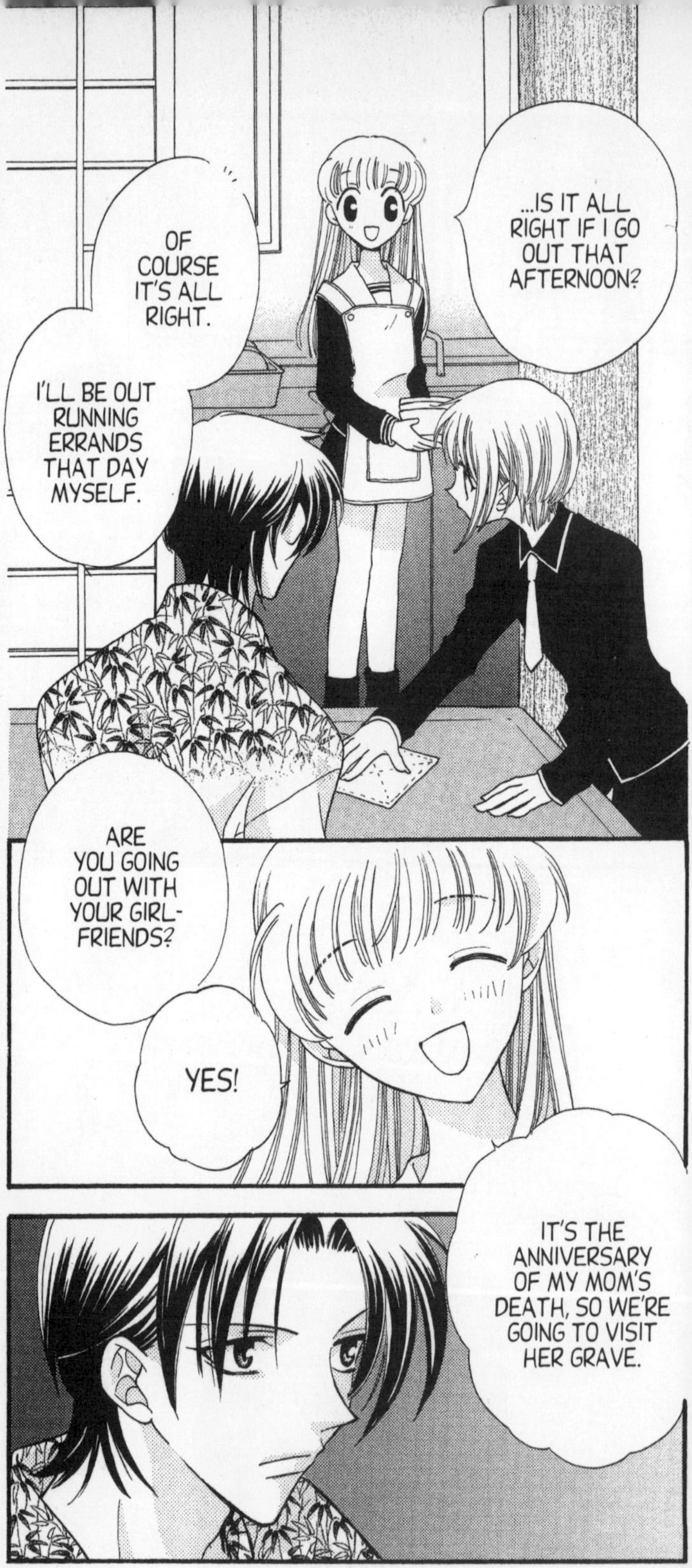
...IS IT ALL RIGHT IF I GO OUT THAT AFTERNOON?
OF COURSE IT'S ALL RIGHT.
I'LL BE OUT RUNNING ERRANDS THAT DAY MYSELF.
ARE YOU GOING OUT WITH YOUR GIRL-FRIENDS?
YES!
IT'S THE ANNIVERSARY OF MY MOM'S DEATH, SO WE'RE GOING TO VISIT HER GRAVE.

Fruits Basket 4 Part 5:

Marlow, from the RPG Kaeru Bibak, is adorable. I haven't seen the ending yet, but I'm really happy that the main character is female. In real life, I don't think I'd get along with Marlow, though. I mean, I think I'm the type of person Marlow hates! I always like the characters that wouldn't like me. Lately, I've been playing Chrono Cross. I wasn't interested before, but I saw the commercial in the game store and I thought, "I have to play it!!" I was caught in their trap. Completely! (ha ha!)

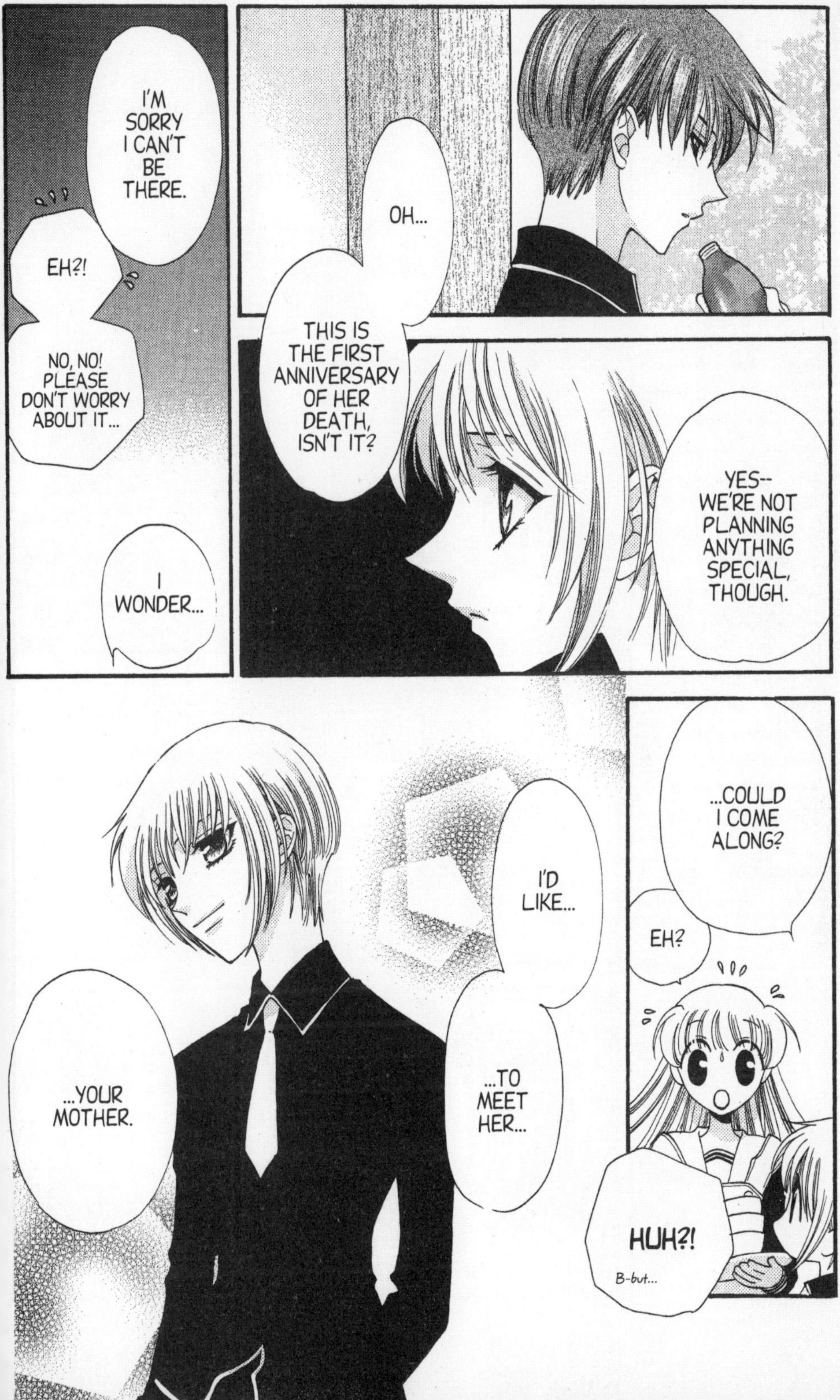
OH...
THIS IS THE FIRST ANNIVERSARY OF HER DEATH, ISN'T IT?
YES-- WE'RE NOT PLANNING ANYTHING SPECIAL, THOUGH.
I'M SORRY I CAN'T BE THERE.
EH?!
NO, NO! PLEASE DON'T WORRY ABOUT IT...
I WONDER...
...COULD I COME ALONG?
EH?
HUH?!
B-but...
I'D LIKE...
...TO MEET HER...
...YOUR MOTHER.

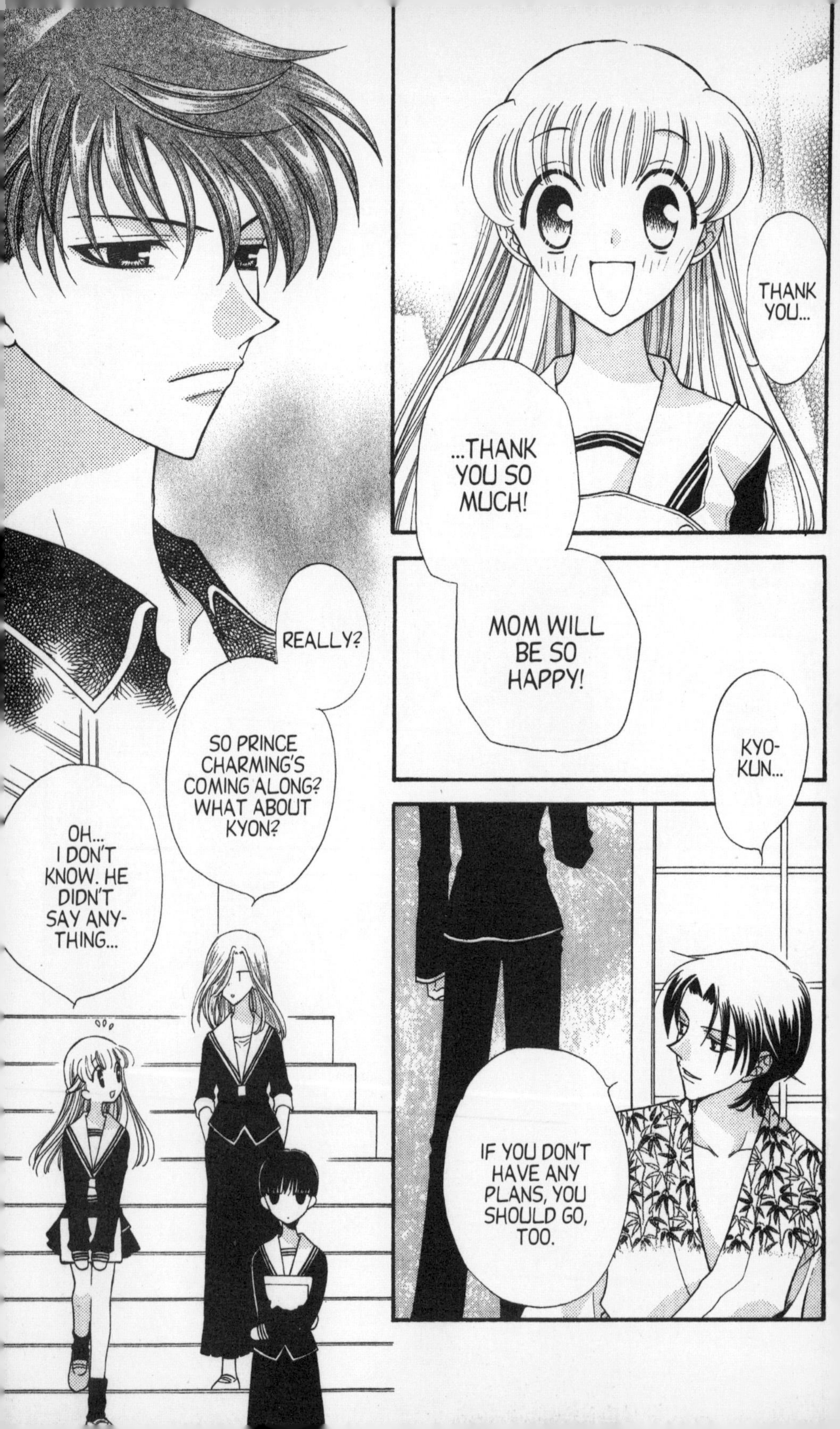
THANK YOU...
...THANK YOU SO MUCH!
MOM WILL BE SO HAPPY!
KYO-KUN...
IF YOU DON'T HAVE ANY PLANS, YOU SHOULD GO, TOO.
REALLY?
SO PRINCE CHARMING'S COMING ALONG? WHAT ABOUT KYON?
OH... I DON'T KNOW. HE DIDN'T SAY ANY-THING...

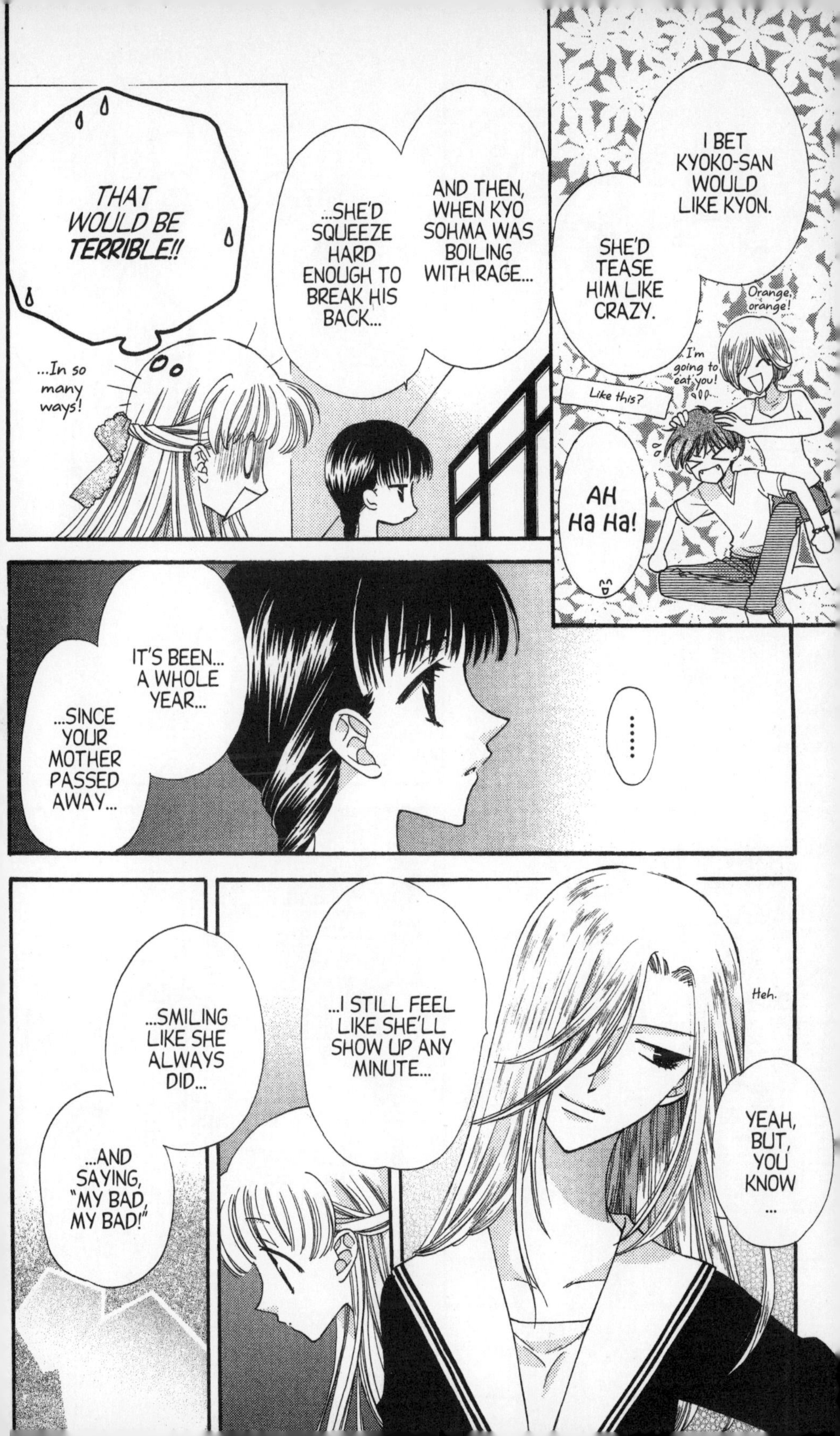
I BET KYOKO-SAN WOULD LIKE KYON.
SHE'D TEASE HIM LIKE CRAZY.
Orange, orange!
I'm going to eat you!
Like this?
AH Ha Ha!
AND THEN, WHEN KYO SOHMA WAS BOILING WITH RAGE...
...SHE'D SQUEEZE HARD ENOUGH TO BREAK HIS BACK...
THAT WOULD BE TERRIBLE!!
...In so many ways!
......
IT'S BEEN... A WHOLE YEAR...
...SINCE YOUR MOTHER PASSED AWAY...
Heh.
YEAH, BUT, YOU KNOW ...
...I STILL FEEL LIKE SHE'LL SHOW UP ANY MINUTE...
...SMILING LIKE SHE ALWAYS DID...
...AND SAYING, "MY BAD, MY BAD!"

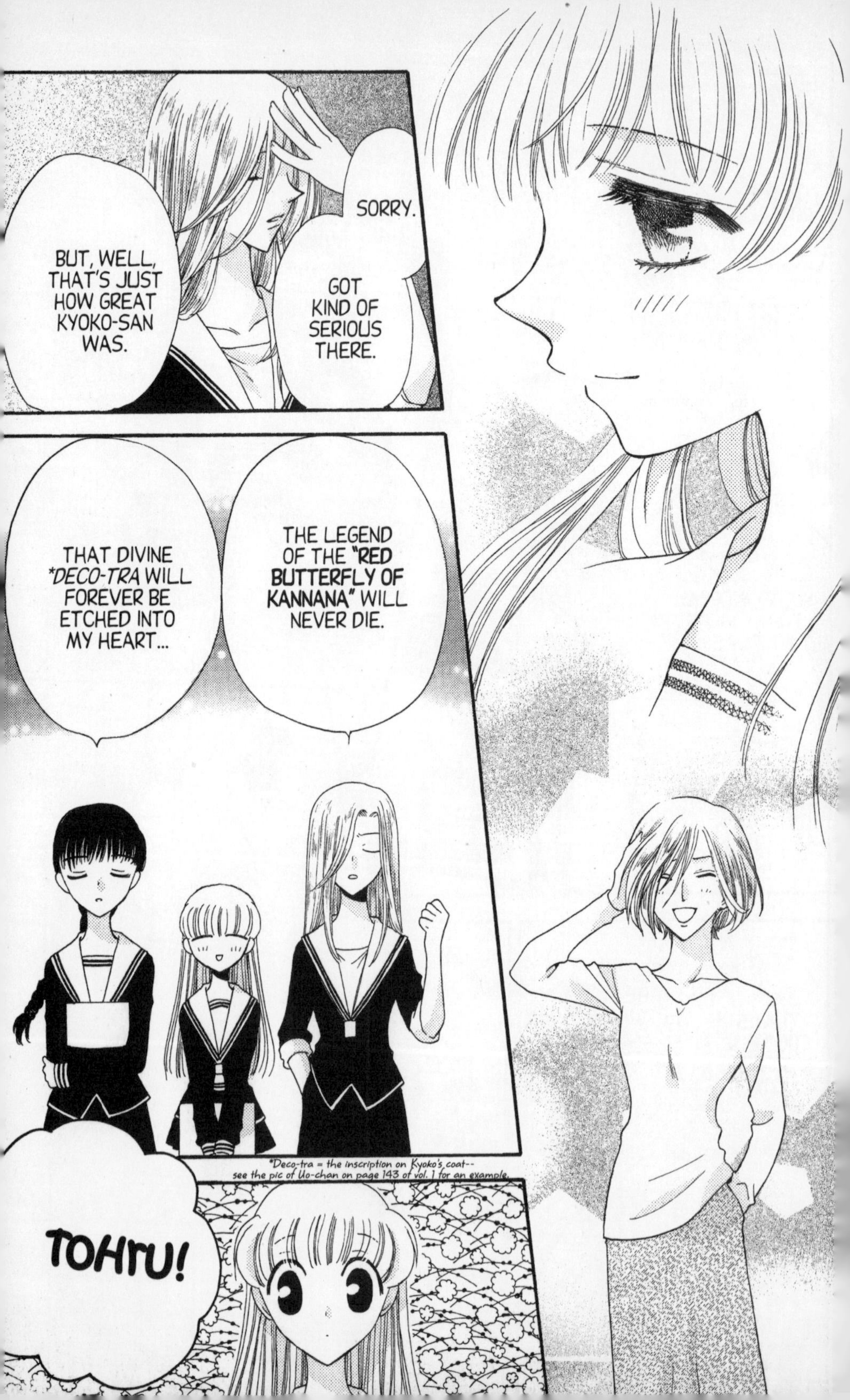
SORRY.
GOT KIND OF SERIOUS THERE.
BUT, WELL, THAT'S JUST HOW GREAT KYOKO-SAN WAS.
THE LEGEND OF THE **"RED BUTTERFLY OF KANNANA"** WILL NEVER DIE.
THAT DIVINE *DECO-TRA WILL FOREVER BE ETCHED INTO MY HEART...
TOHRU!
*Deco-tra = the inscription on Kyoko's coat--see the pic of Uo-chan on page 143 of vol. 1 for an example.

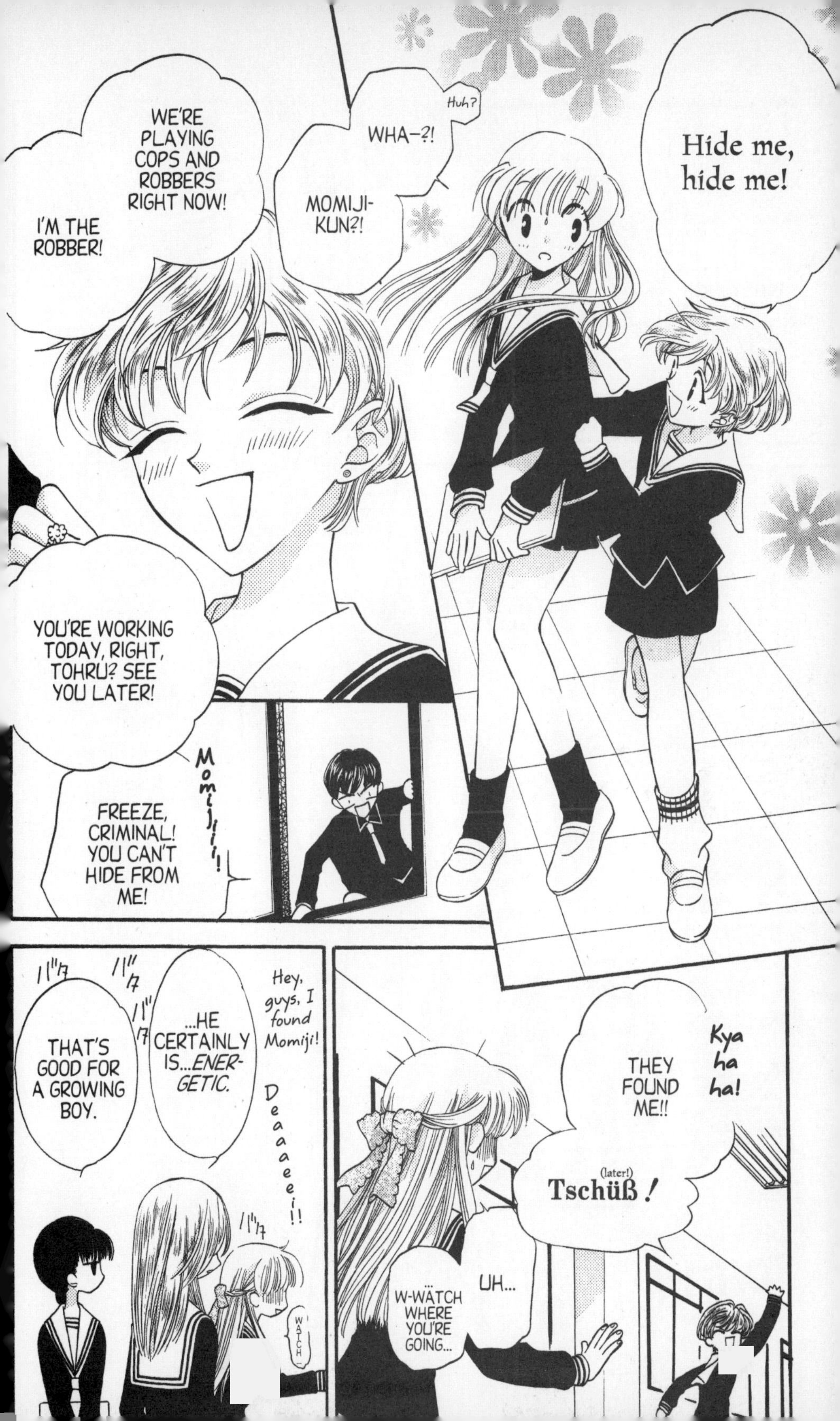
Hide me, hide me!
Huh?
WHA-?!
MOMIJI-KUN?!
WE'RE PLAYING COPS AND ROBBERS RIGHT NOW!
I'M THE ROBBER!
YOU'RE WORKING TODAY, RIGHT, TOHRU? SEE YOU LATER!
Momijiii!
FREEZE, CRIMINAL! YOU CAN'T HIDE FROM ME!
Kya ha ha!
THEY FOUND ME!!
(later!) Tschüß!
UH...
... W-WATCH WHERE YOU'RE GOING...
Hey, guys, I found Momiji!
Deaaaaeei!!
...HE CERTAINLY IS...ENERGETIC.
THAT'S GOOD FOR A GROWING BOY.
WATCH...

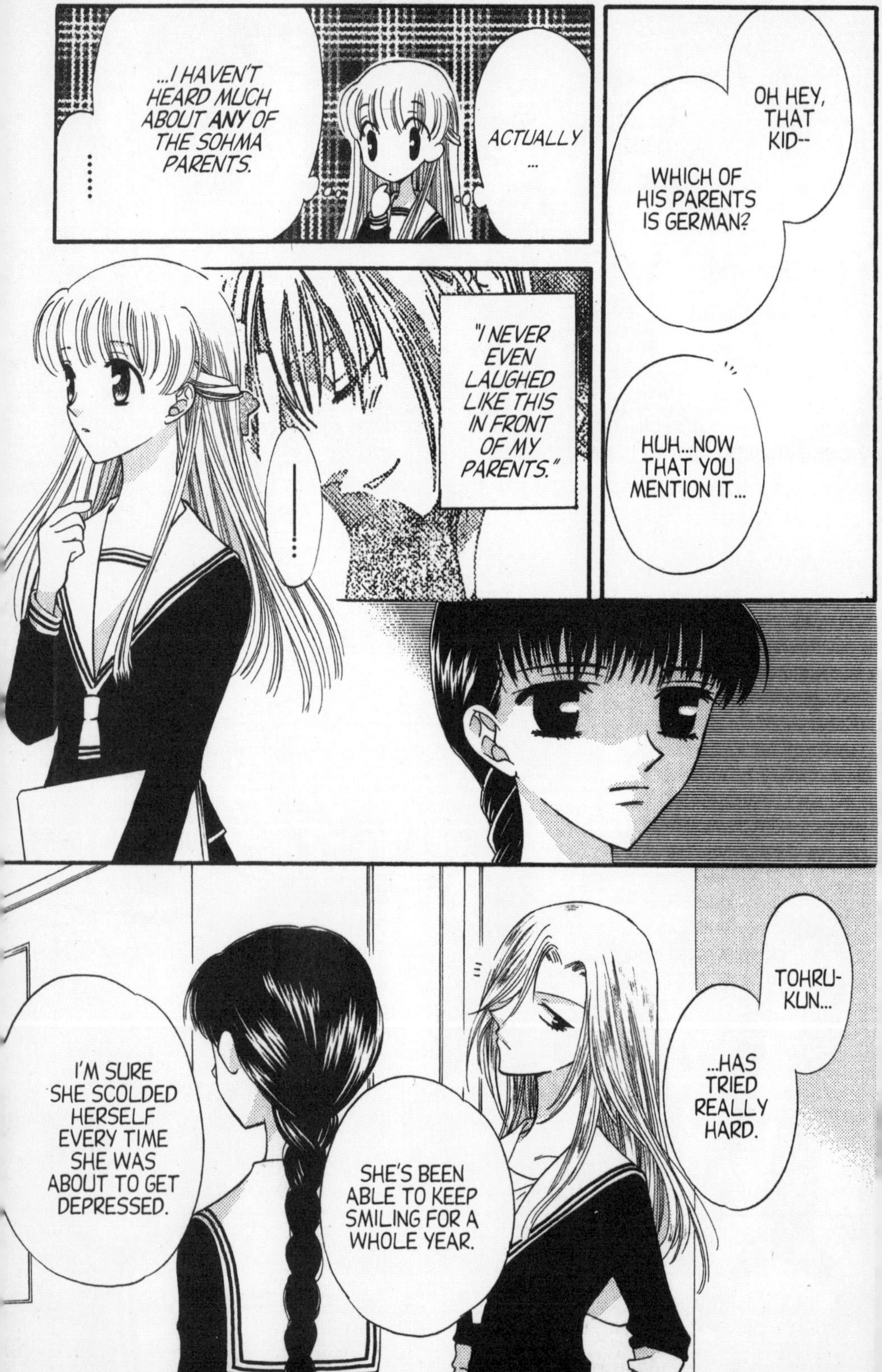
OH HEY, THAT KID--
WHICH OF HIS PARENTS IS GERMAN?
HUH...NOW THAT YOU MENTION IT...
ACTUALLY ...
...I HAVEN'T HEARD MUCH ABOUT ANY OF THE SOHMA PARENTS.
......
"I NEVER EVEN LAUGHED LIKE THIS IN FRONT OF MY PARENTS."
......!
TOHRU-KUN...
...HAS TRIED REALLY HARD.
SHE'S BEEN ABLE TO KEEP SMILING FOR A WHOLE YEAR.
I'M SURE SHE SCOLDED HERSELF EVERY TIME SHE WAS ABOUT TO GET DEPRESSED.

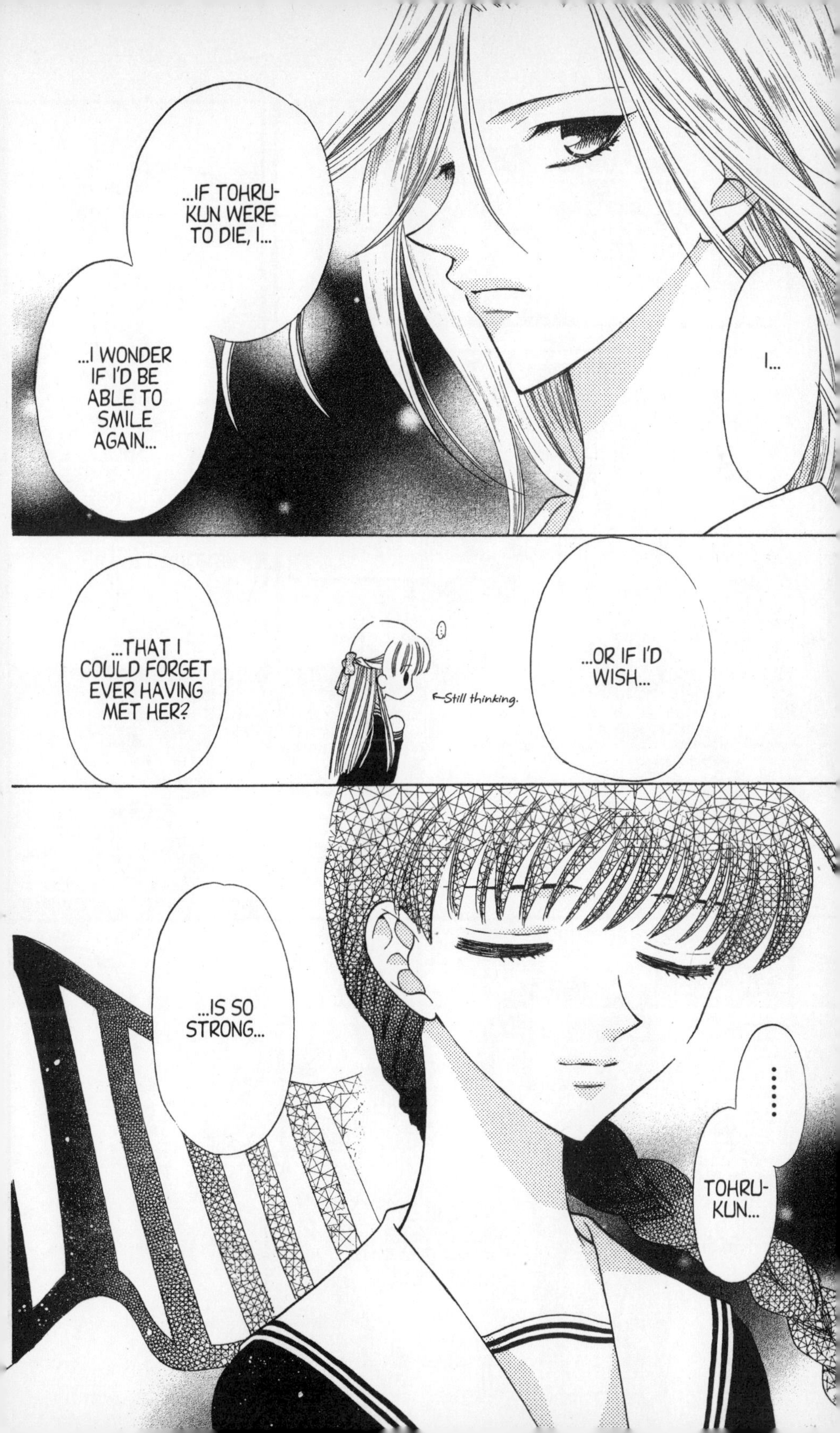
I...
...IF TOHRU-KUN WERE TO DIE, I...
...I WONDER IF I'D BE ABLE TO SMILE AGAIN...
...OR IF I'D WISH...
←Still thinking.
...THAT I COULD FORGET EVER HAVING MET HER?
......
TOHRU-KUN...
...IS SO STRONG...

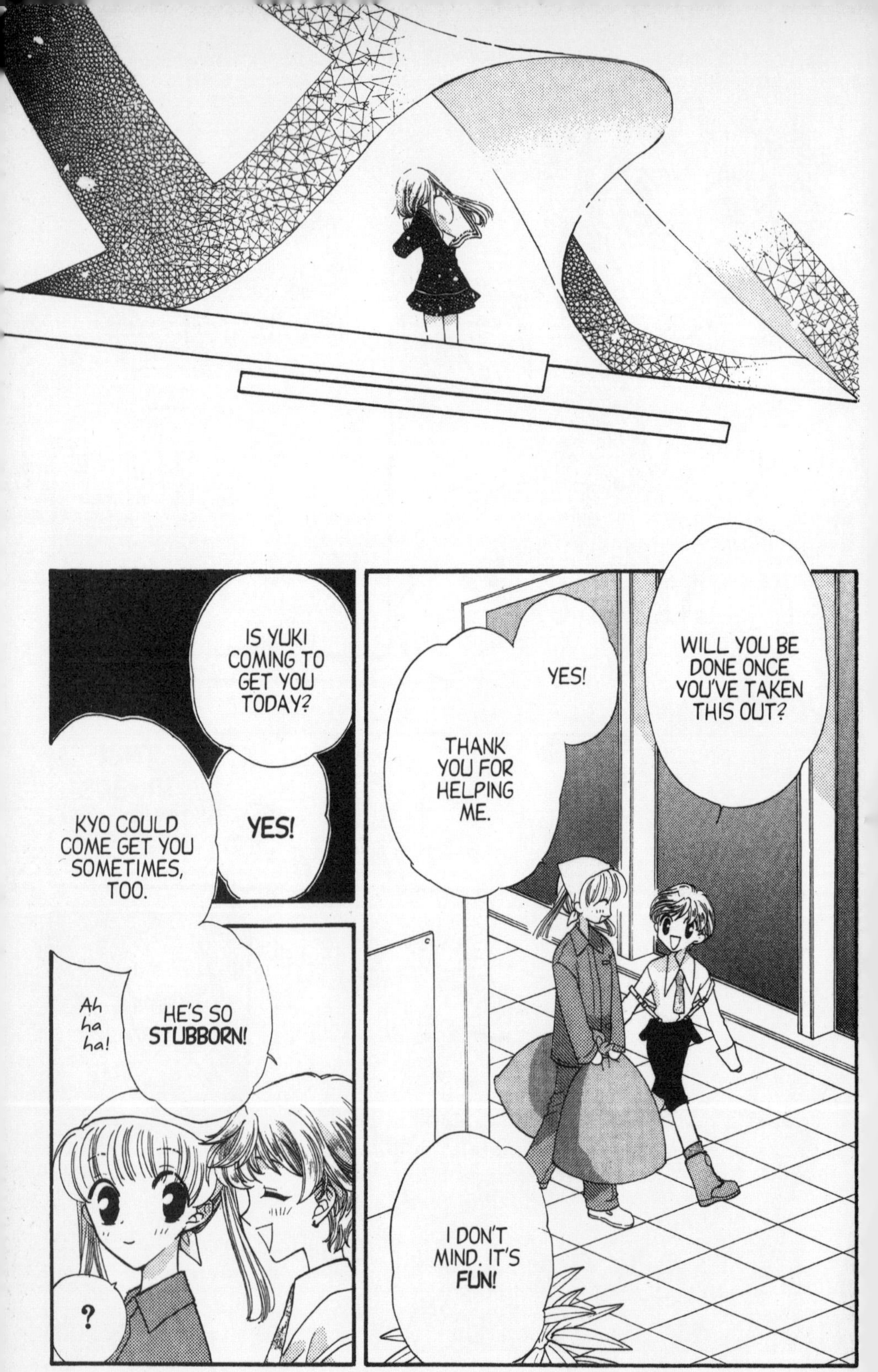
WILL YOU BE DONE ONCE YOU'VE TAKEN THIS OUT?
YES!
THANK YOU FOR HELPING ME.
I DON'T MIND. IT'S **FUN!**
IS YUKI COMING TO GET YOU TODAY?
YES!
KYO COULD COME GET YOU SOMETIMES, TOO.
HE'S SO **STUBBORN!**
Ah ha ha!
?

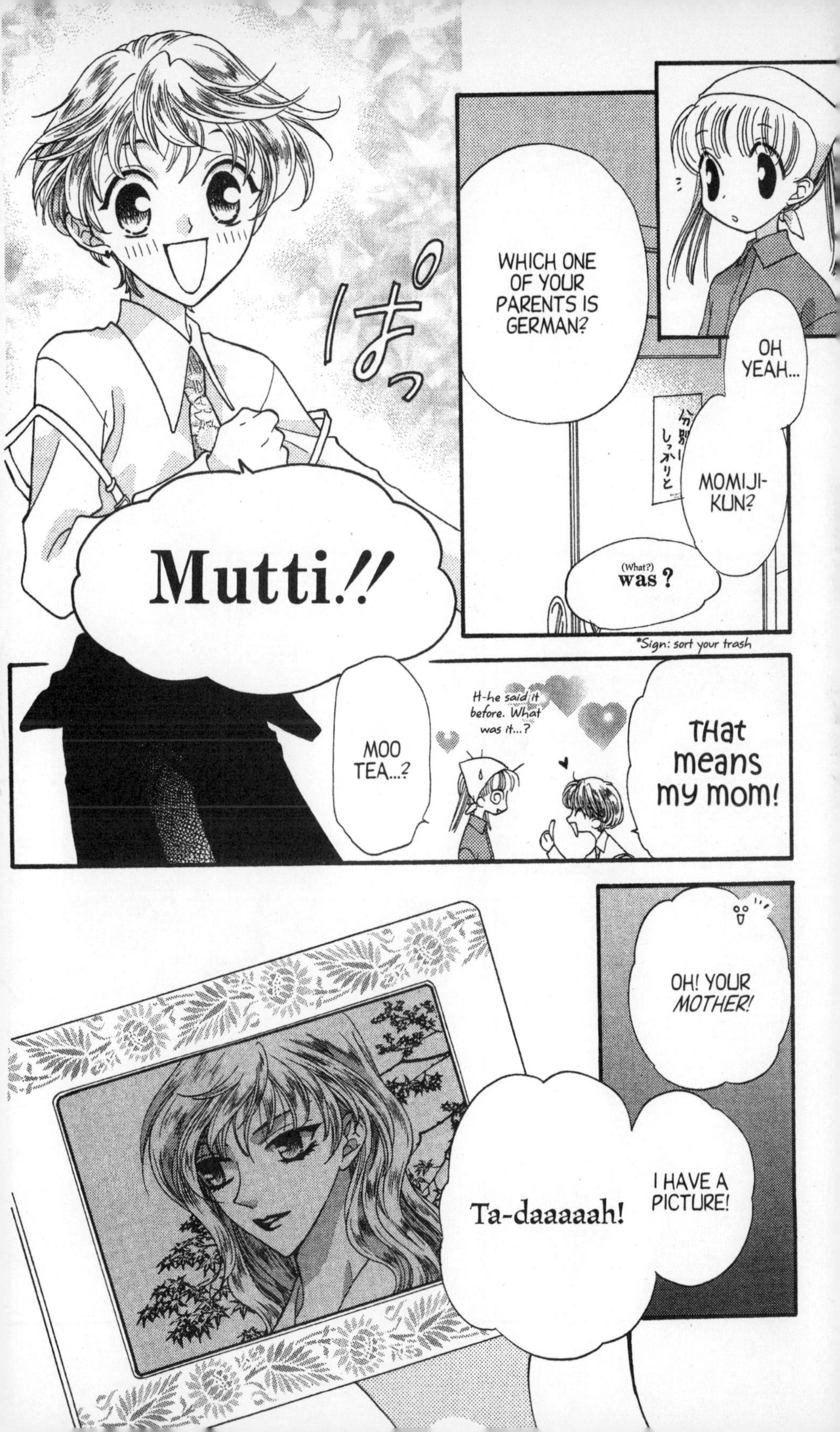
OH YEAH...
MOMIJI-KUN?
WHICH ONE OF YOUR PARENTS IS GERMAN?
(What?) was ?
*Sign: sort your trash
ぱっ
Mutti!!
That means my mom!
H-he said it before. What was it...?
MOO TEA...?
OH! YOUR MOTHER!
I HAVE A PICTURE!
Ta-daaaaah!

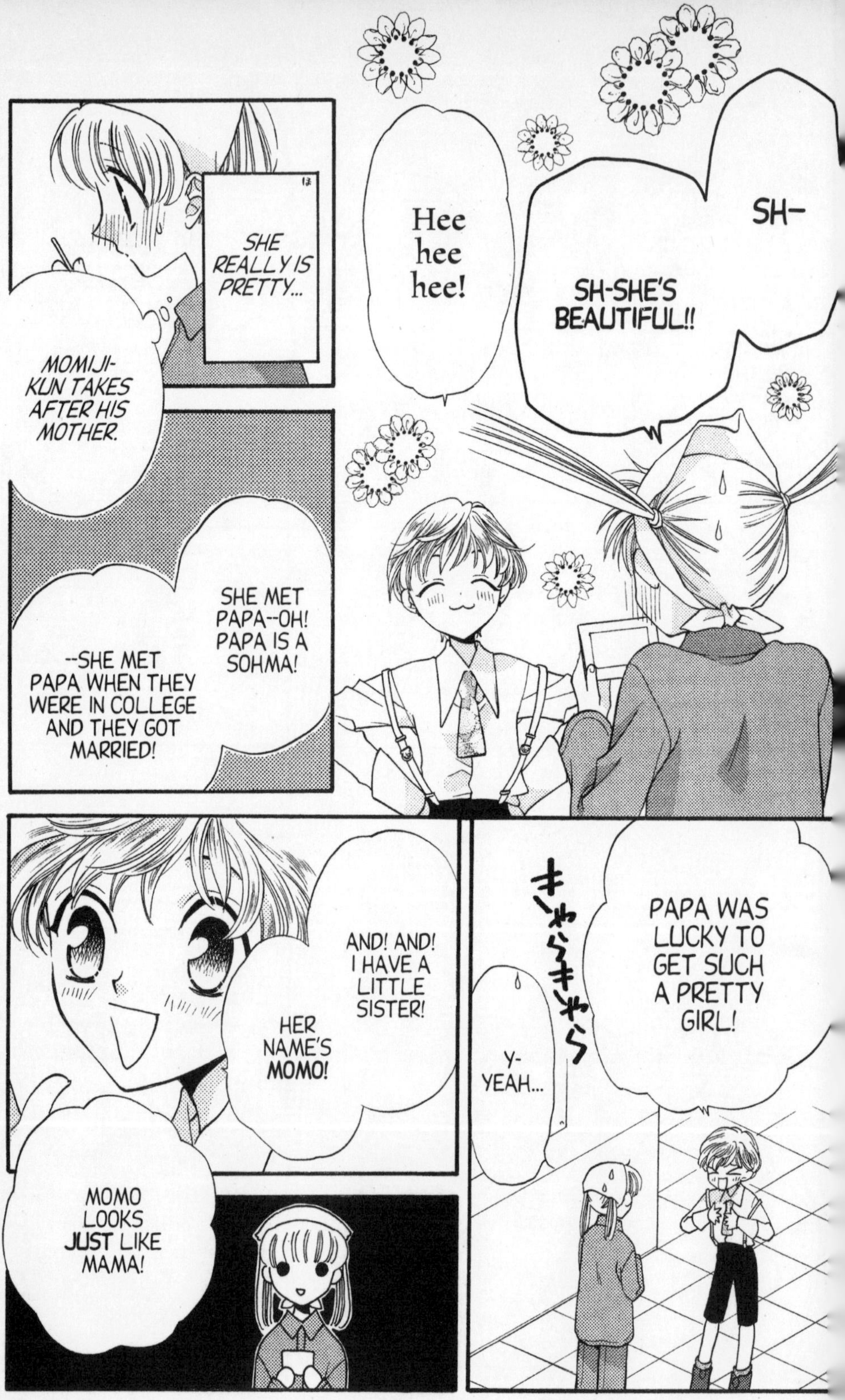
SH-
SH-SHE'S BEAUTIFUL!!
Hee hee hee!
SHE REALLY IS PRETTY...
MOMIJI-KUN TAKES AFTER HIS MOTHER.
SHE MET PAPA--OH! PAPA IS A SOHMA!
--SHE MET PAPA WHEN THEY WERE IN COLLEGE AND THEY GOT MARRIED!
PAPA WAS LUCKY TO GET SUCH A PRETTY GIRL!
きゃらきゃら
Y-YEAH...
AND! AND! I HAVE A LITTLE SISTER!
HER NAME'S MOMO!
MOMO LOOKS JUST LIKE MAMA!

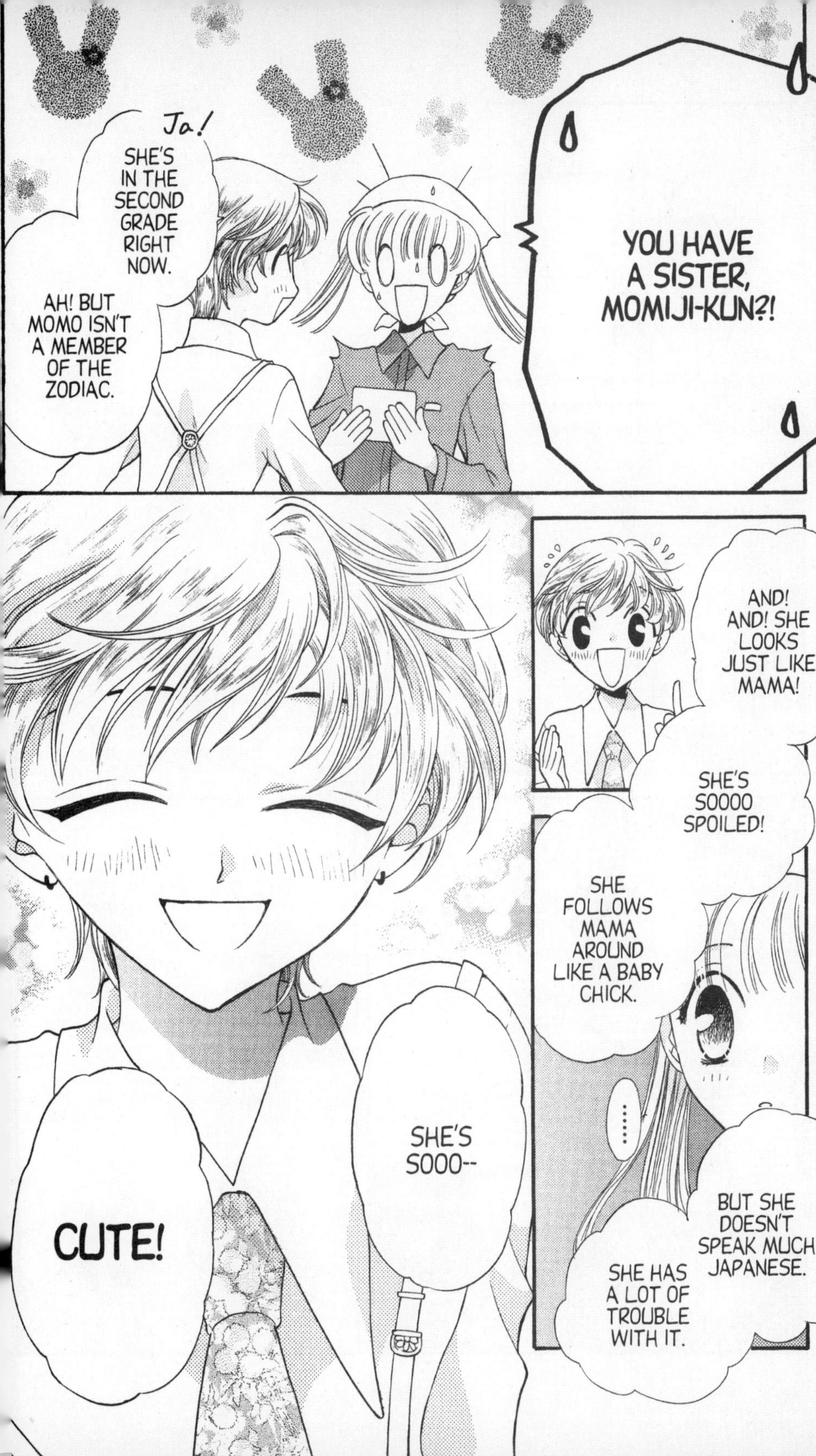
YOU HAVE A SISTER, MOMIJI-KUN?!
Ja! SHE'S IN THE SECOND GRADE RIGHT NOW.
AH! BUT MOMO ISN'T A MEMBER OF THE ZODIAC.
AND! AND! SHE LOOKS JUST LIKE MAMA!
SHE'S SOOOO SPOILED!
SHE FOLLOWS MAMA AROUND LIKE A BABY CHICK.
......
BUT SHE DOESN'T SPEAK MUCH JAPANESE.
SHE HAS A LOT OF TROUBLE WITH IT.
SHE'S SOOO--
CUTE!

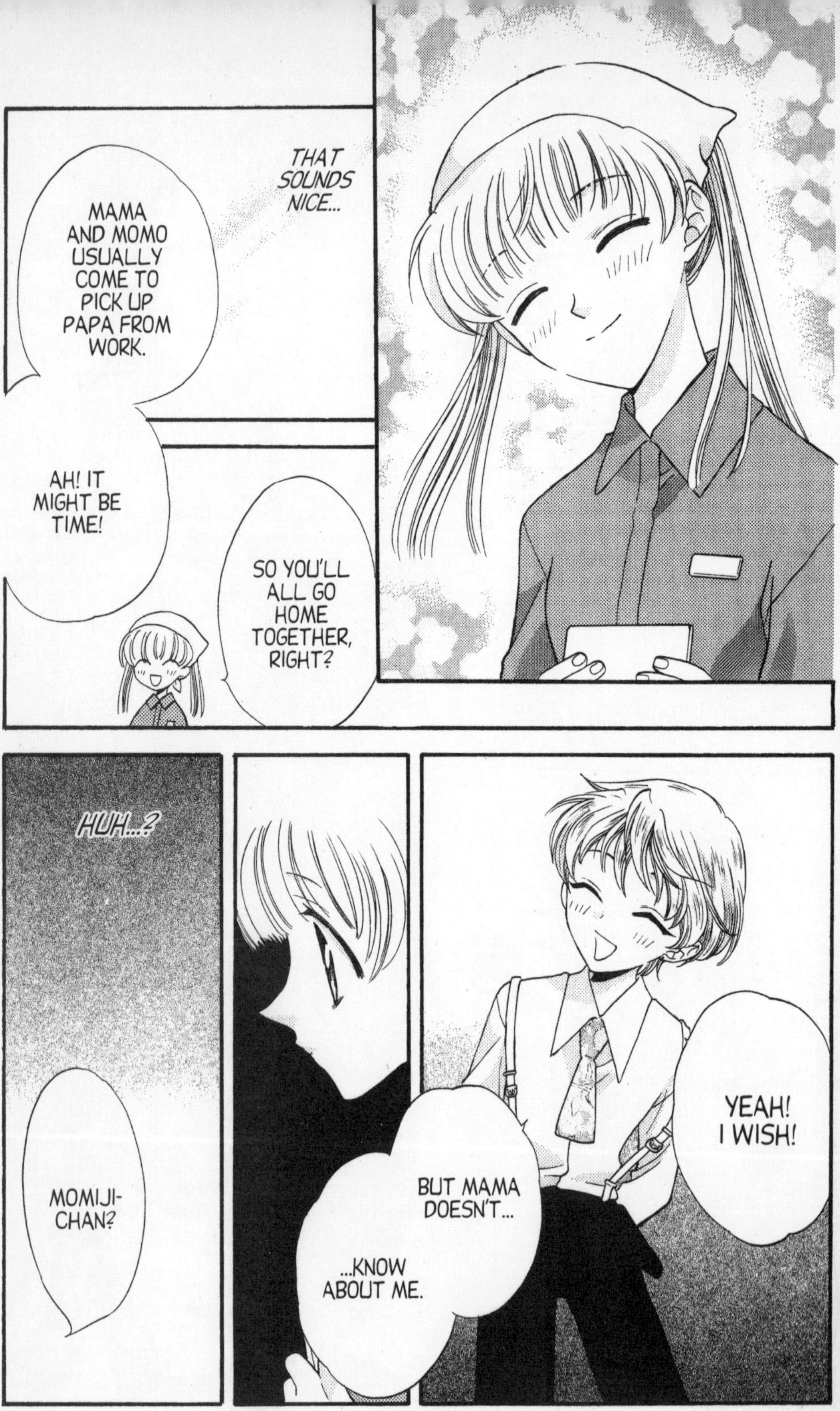
THAT SOUNDS NICE...
MAMA AND MOMO USUALLY COME TO PICK UP PAPA FROM WORK.
AH! IT MIGHT BE TIME!
SO YOU'LL ALL GO HOME TOGETHER, RIGHT?
YEAH! I WISH!
BUT MAMA DOESN'T...
...KNOW ABOUT ME.
HUH...?
MOMIJI-CHAN?

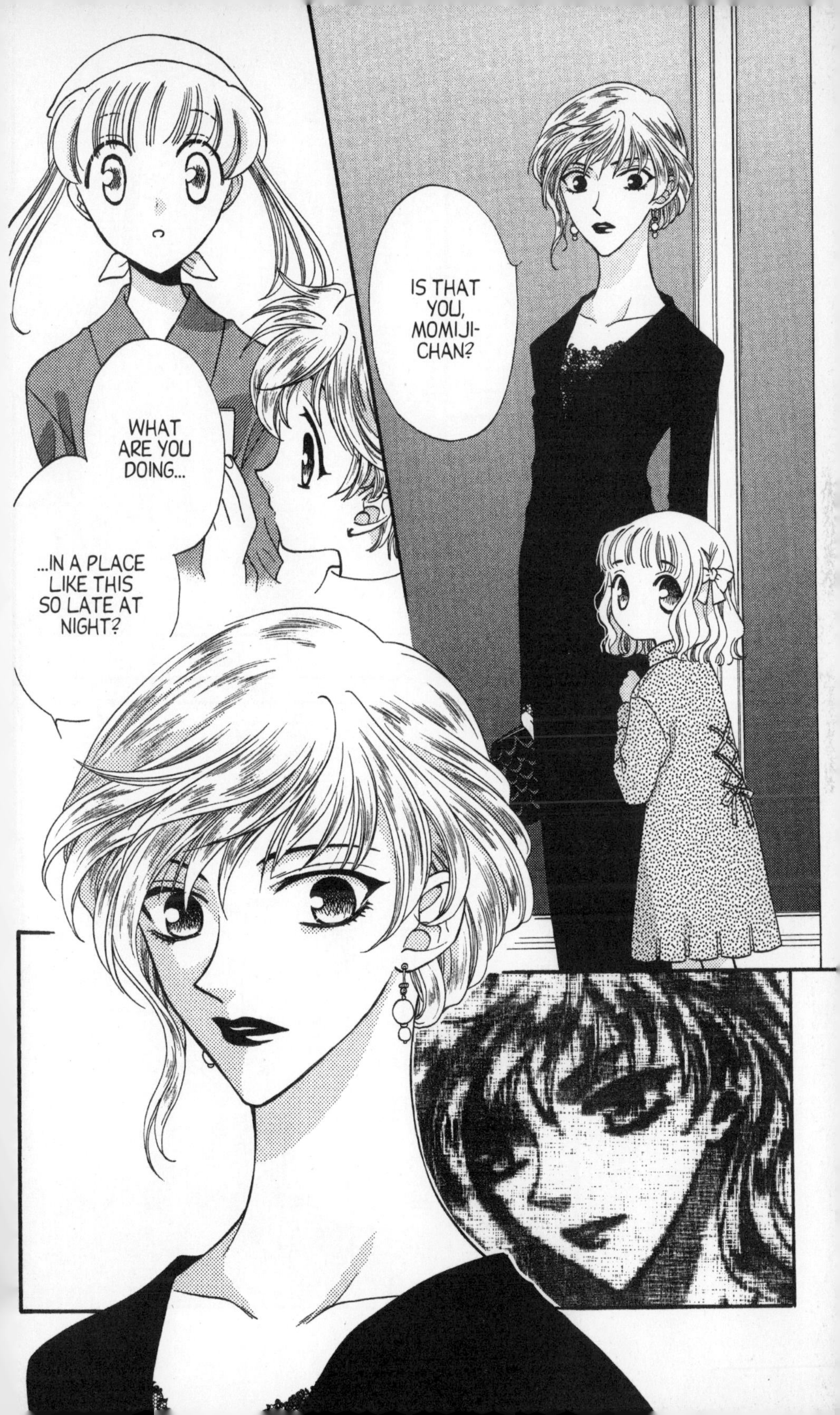
IS THAT YOU, MOMIJI-CHAN?
WHAT ARE YOU DOING...
...IN A PLACE LIKE THIS SO LATE AT NIGHT?

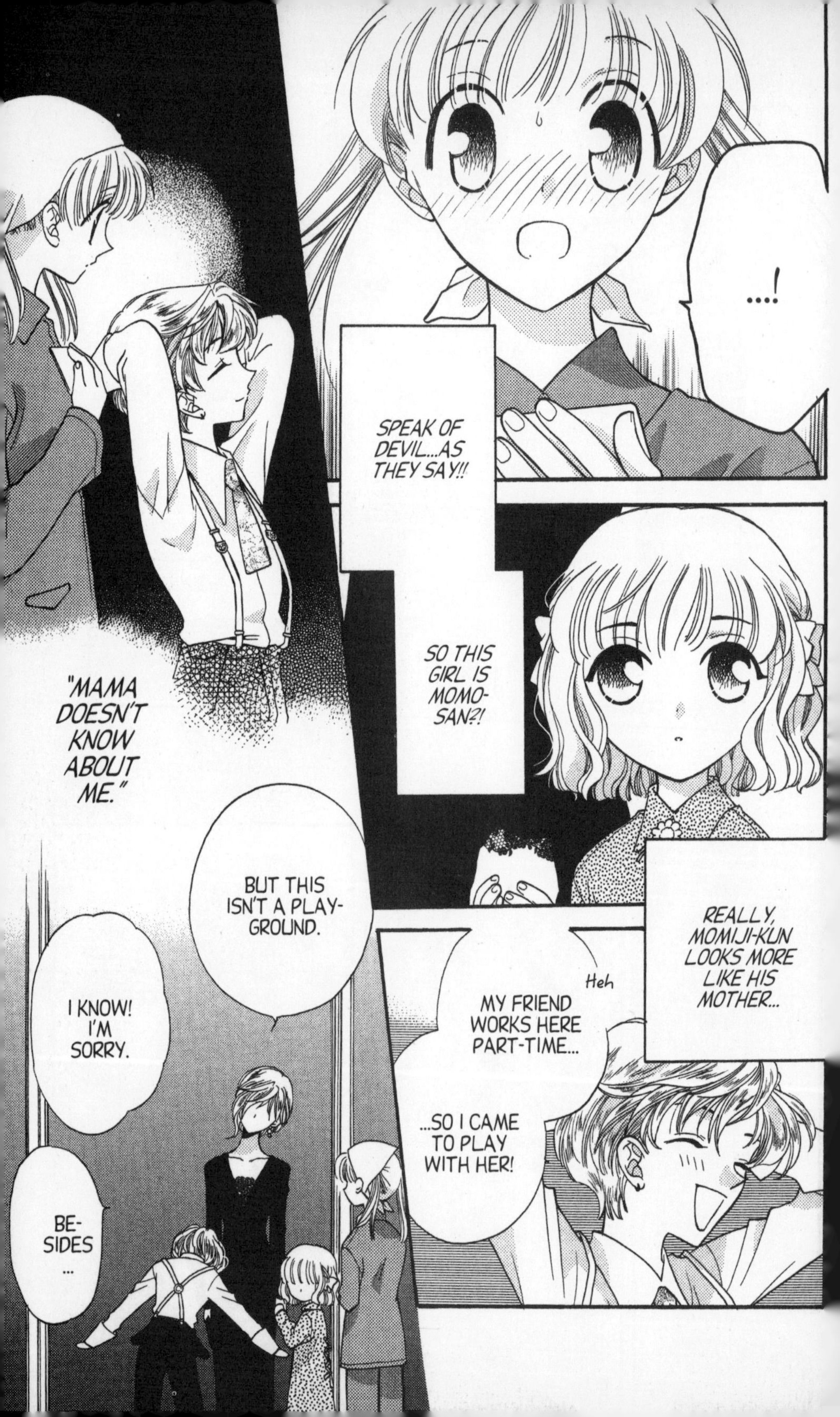

...!
SPEAK OF DEVIL...AS THEY SAY!!
SO THIS GIRL IS MOMO-SAN?!
REALLY, MOMIJI-KUN LOOKS MORE LIKE HIS MOTHER...
Heh
MY FRIEND WORKS HERE PART-TIME...
...SO I CAME TO PLAY WITH HER!
"MAMA DOESN'T KNOW ABOUT ME."
BUT THIS ISN'T A PLAY-GROUND.
I KNOW! I'M SORRY.
BE-SIDES ...

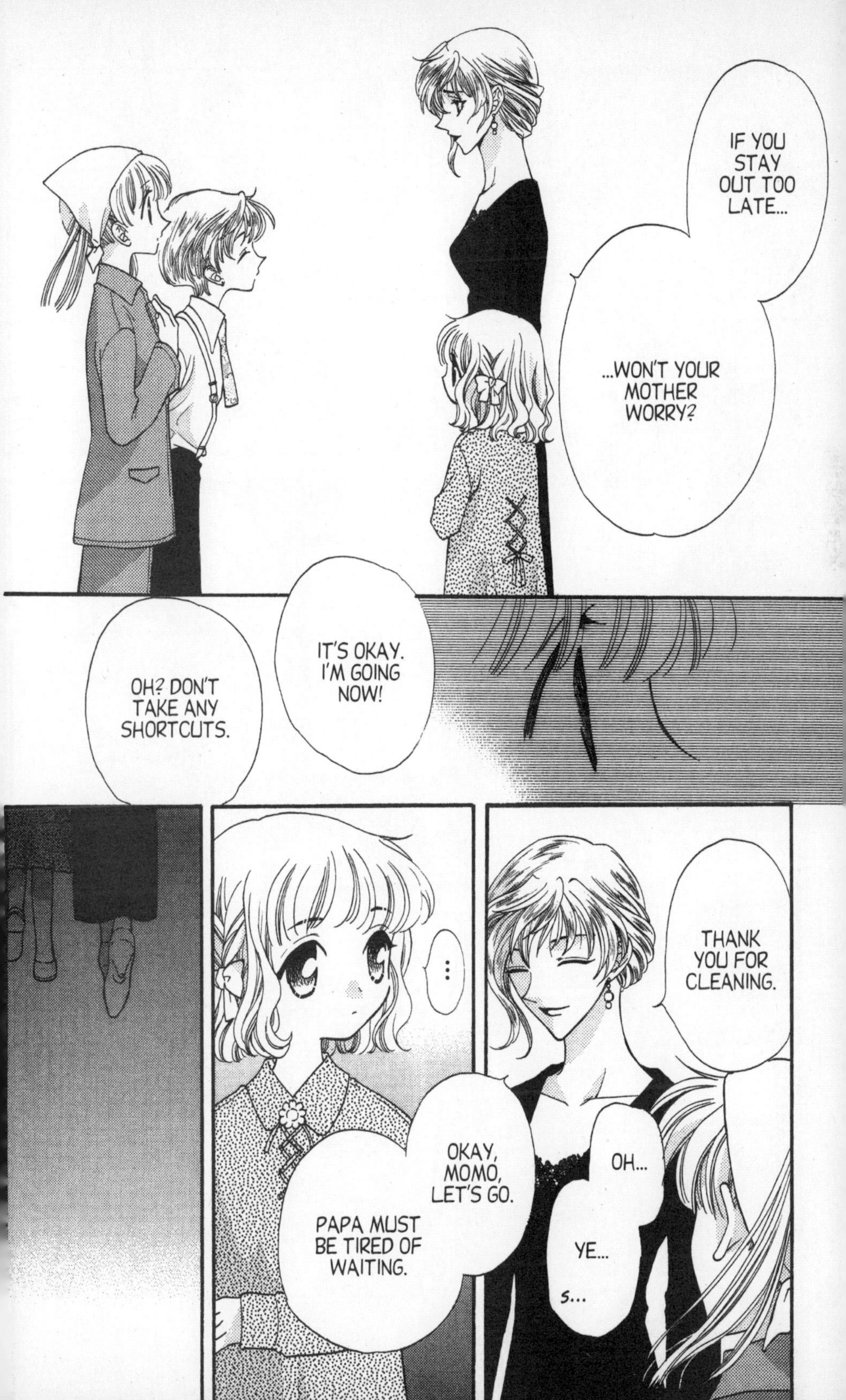
IF YOU STAY OUT TOO LATE...
...WON'T YOUR MOTHER WORRY?
IT'S OKAY. I'M GOING NOW!
OH? DON'T TAKE ANY SHORTCUTS.
THANK YOU FOR CLEANING.
OH...
YE...
S...
OKAY, MOMO, LET'S GO.
PAPA MUST BE TIRED OF WAITING.
...

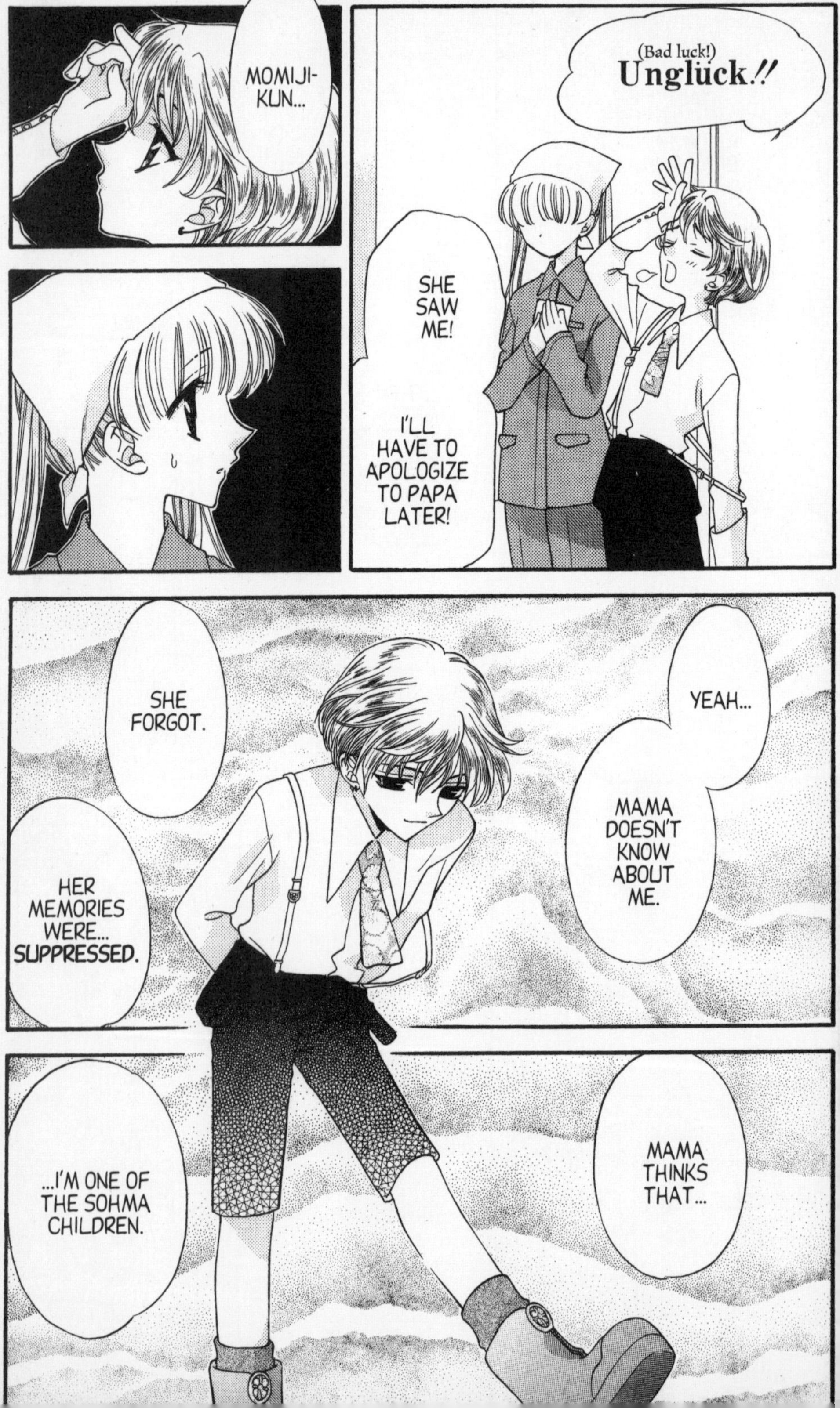
(Bad luck!) Unglück!!
SHE SAW ME!
I'LL HAVE TO APOLOGIZE TO PAPA LATER!
MOMIJI-KUN...
YEAH...
MAMA DOESN'T KNOW ABOUT ME.
SHE FORGOT.
HER MEMORIES WERE... SUPPRESSED.
MAMA THINKS THAT...
...I'M ONE OF THE SOHMA CHILDREN.

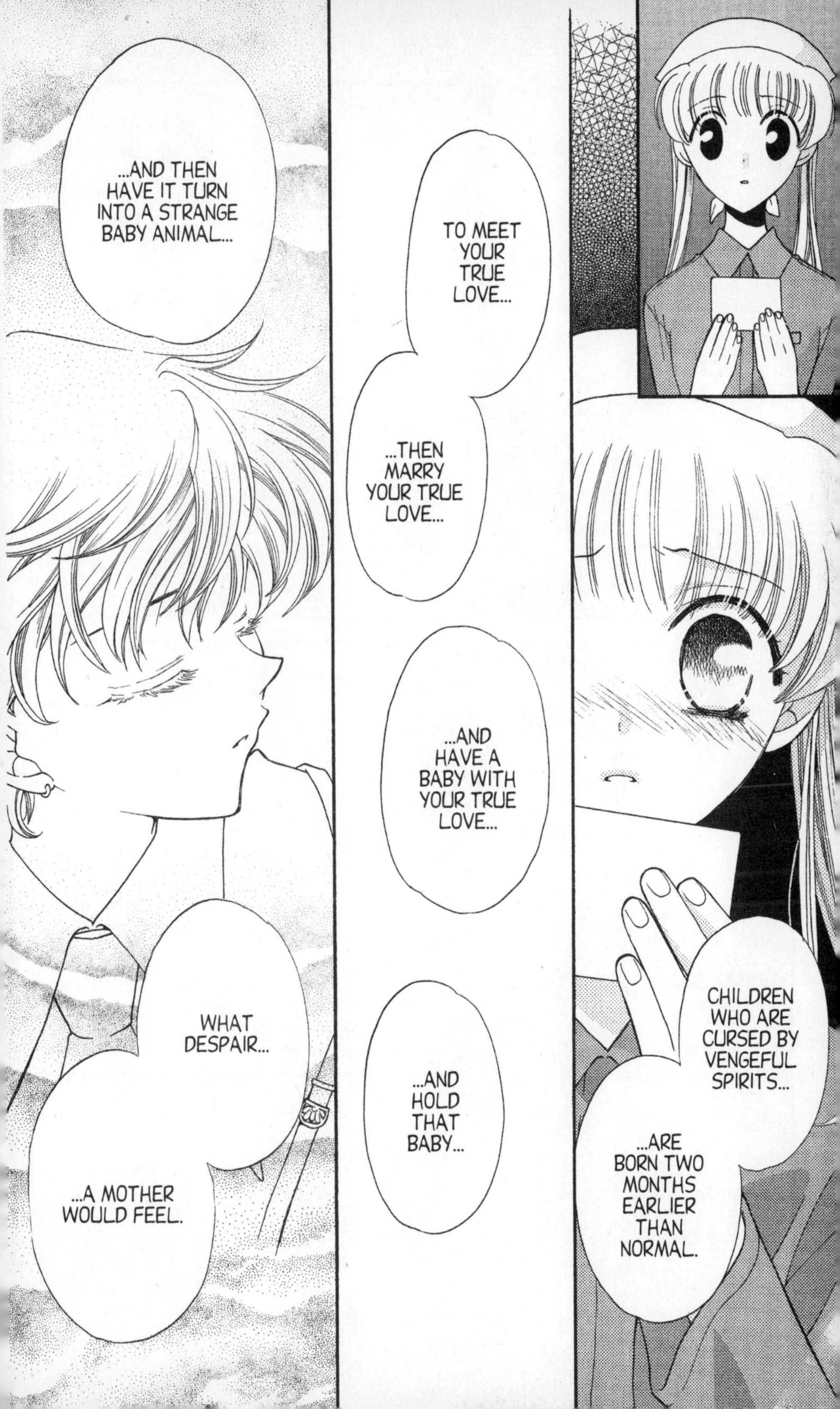
CHILDREN WHO ARE CURSED BY VENGEFUL SPIRITS...
...ARE BORN TWO MONTHS EARLIER THAN NORMAL.
TO MEET YOUR TRUE LOVE...
...THEN MARRY YOUR TRUE LOVE...
...AND HAVE A BABY WITH YOUR TRUE LOVE...
...AND HOLD THAT BABY...
...AND THEN HAVE IT TURN INTO A STRANGE BABY ANIMAL...
WHAT DESPAIR...
...A MOTHER WOULD FEEL.

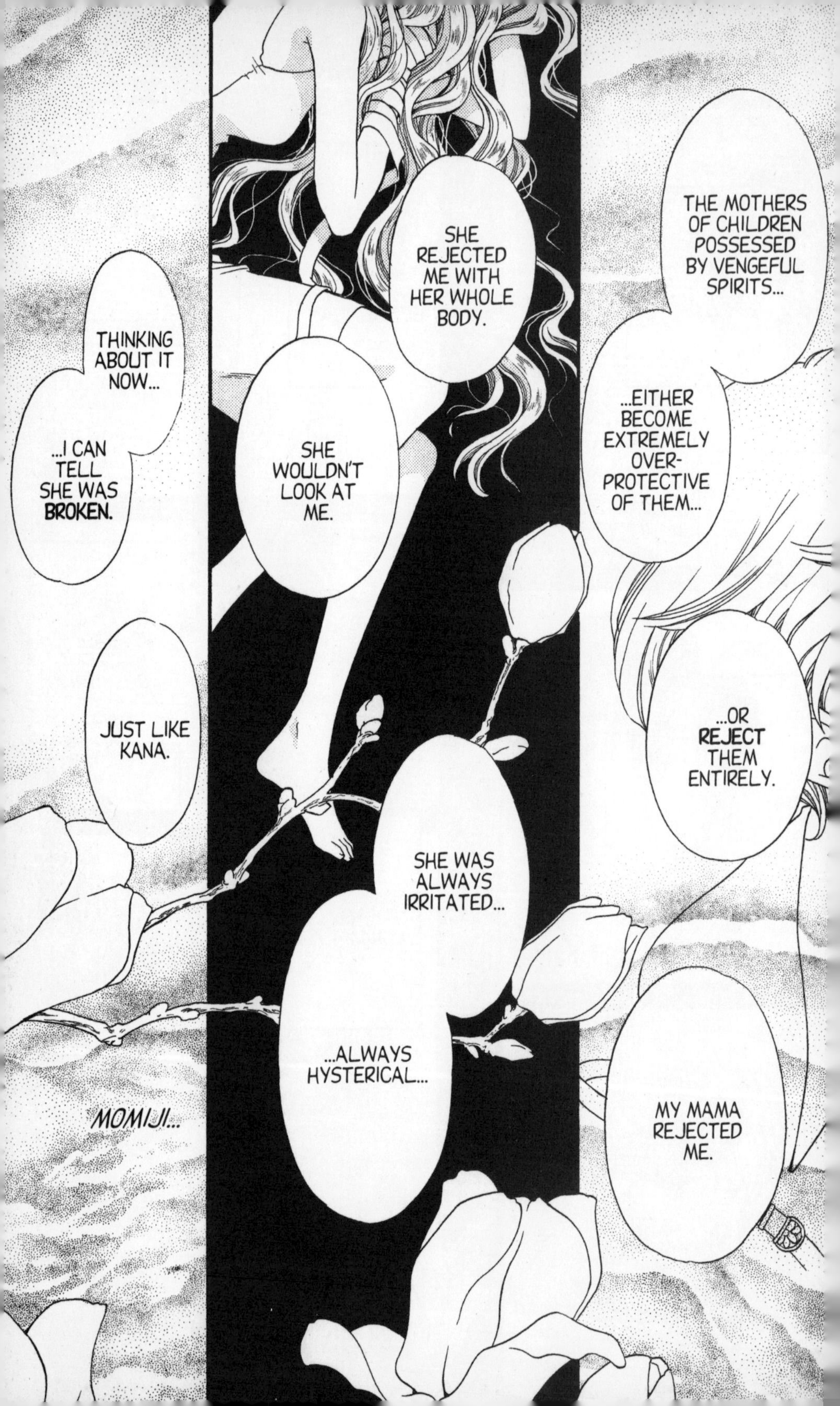
THE MOTHERS OF CHILDREN POSSESSED BY VENGEFUL SPIRITS...
...EITHER BECOME EXTREMELY OVER-PROTECTIVE OF THEM...
...OR **REJECT** THEM ENTIRELY.
MY MAMA REJECTED ME.
SHE REJECTED ME WITH HER WHOLE BODY.
SHE WOULDN'T LOOK AT ME.
SHE WAS ALWAYS IRRITATED...
...ALWAYS HYSTERICAL...
THINKING ABOUT IT NOW...
...I CAN TELL SHE WAS **BROKEN.**
JUST LIKE KANA.
MOMIJI...

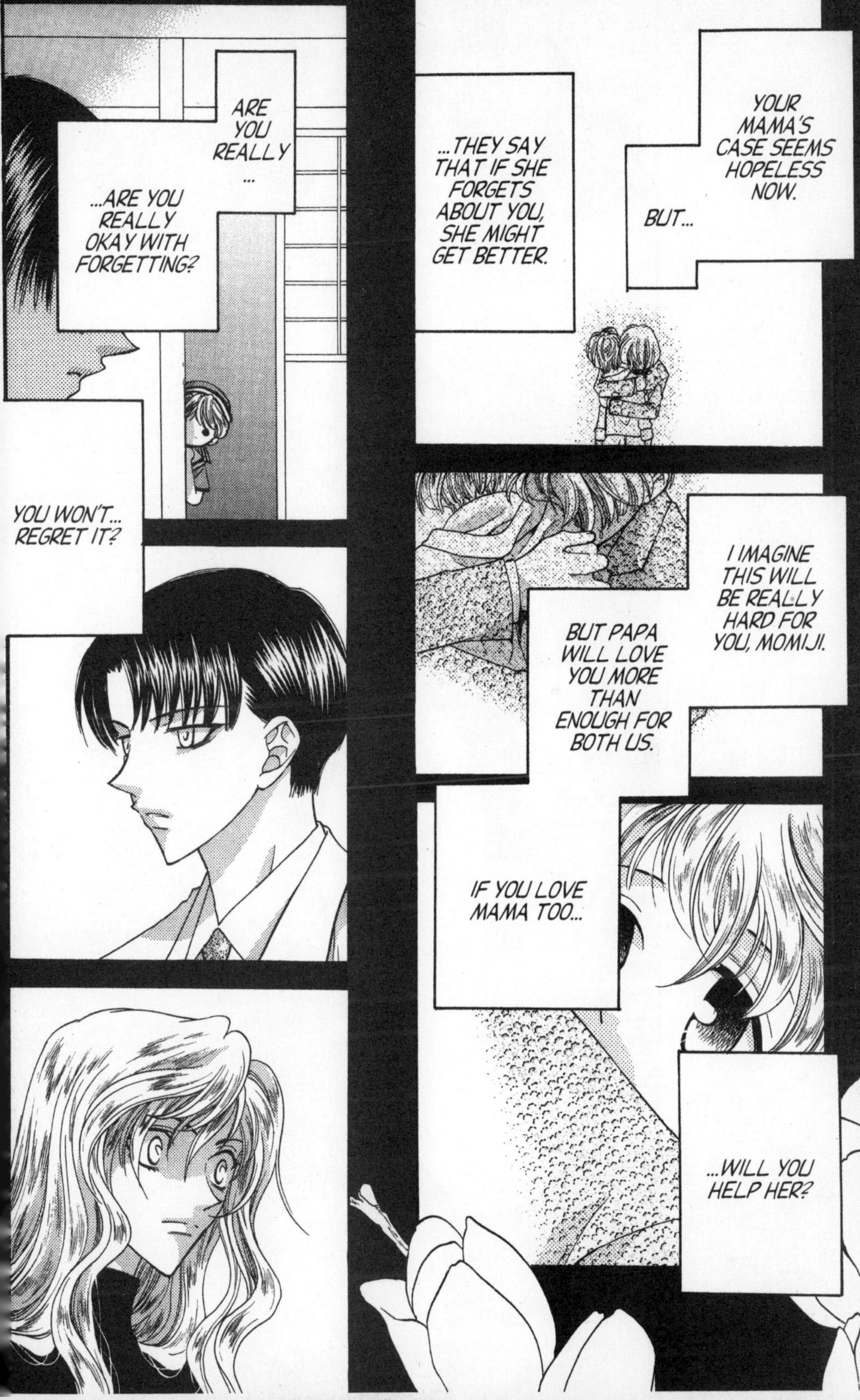
YOUR MAMA'S CASE SEEMS HOPELESS NOW.
BUT...
...THEY SAY THAT IF SHE FORGETS ABOUT YOU, SHE MIGHT GET BETTER.
I IMAGINE THIS WILL BE REALLY HARD FOR YOU, MOMIJI.
BUT PAPA WILL LOVE YOU MORE THAN ENOUGH FOR BOTH US.
IF YOU LOVE MAMA TOO...
...WILL YOU HELP HER?
ARE YOU REALLY ...
...ARE YOU REALLY OKAY WITH FORGETTING?
YOU WON'T... REGRET IT?

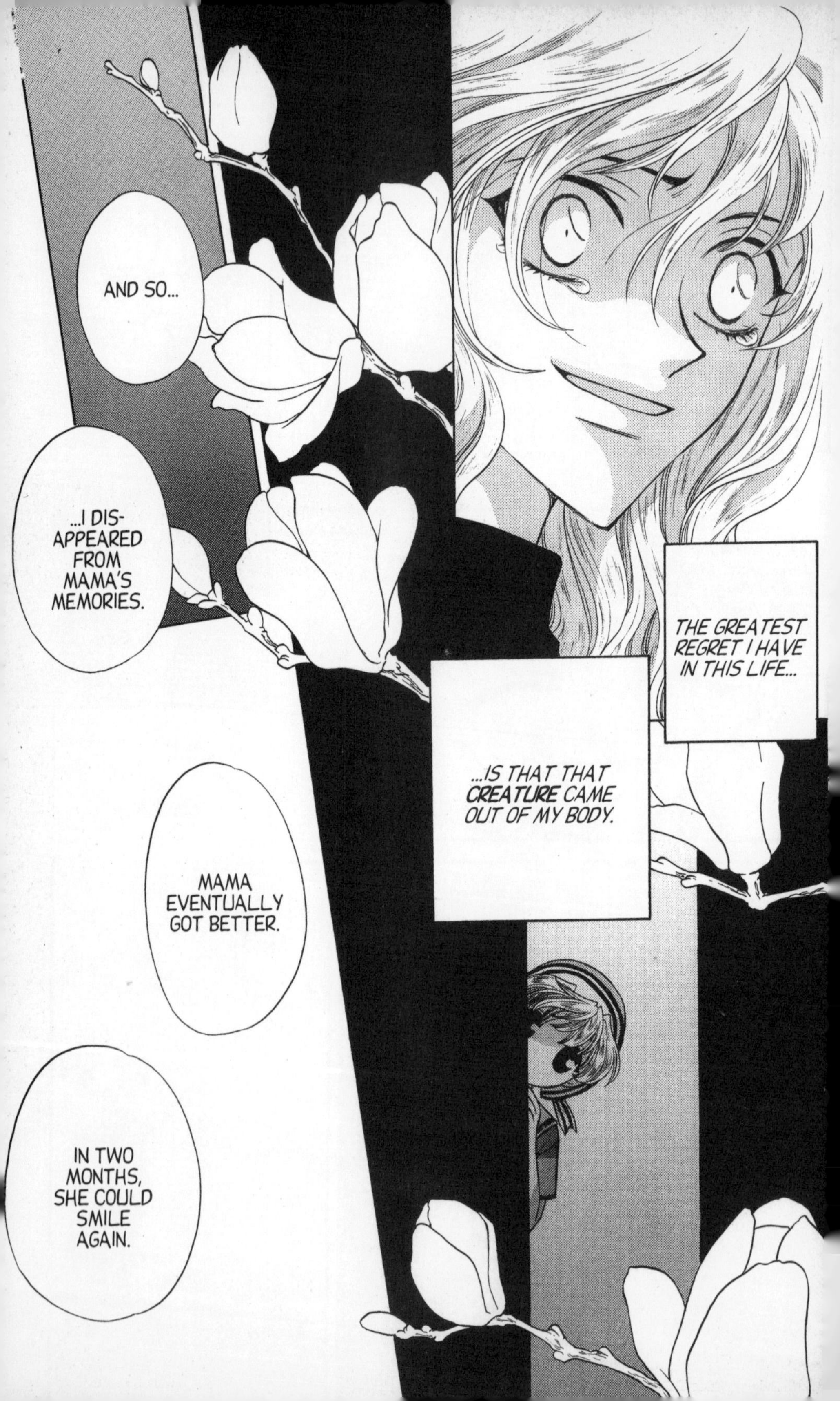
THE GREATEST REGRET I HAVE IN THIS LIFE...
...IS THAT THAT CREATURE CAME OUT OF MY BODY.
AND SO...
...I DIS-APPEARED FROM MAMA'S MEMORIES.
MAMA EVENTUALLY GOT BETTER.
IN TWO MONTHS, SHE COULD SMILE AGAIN.

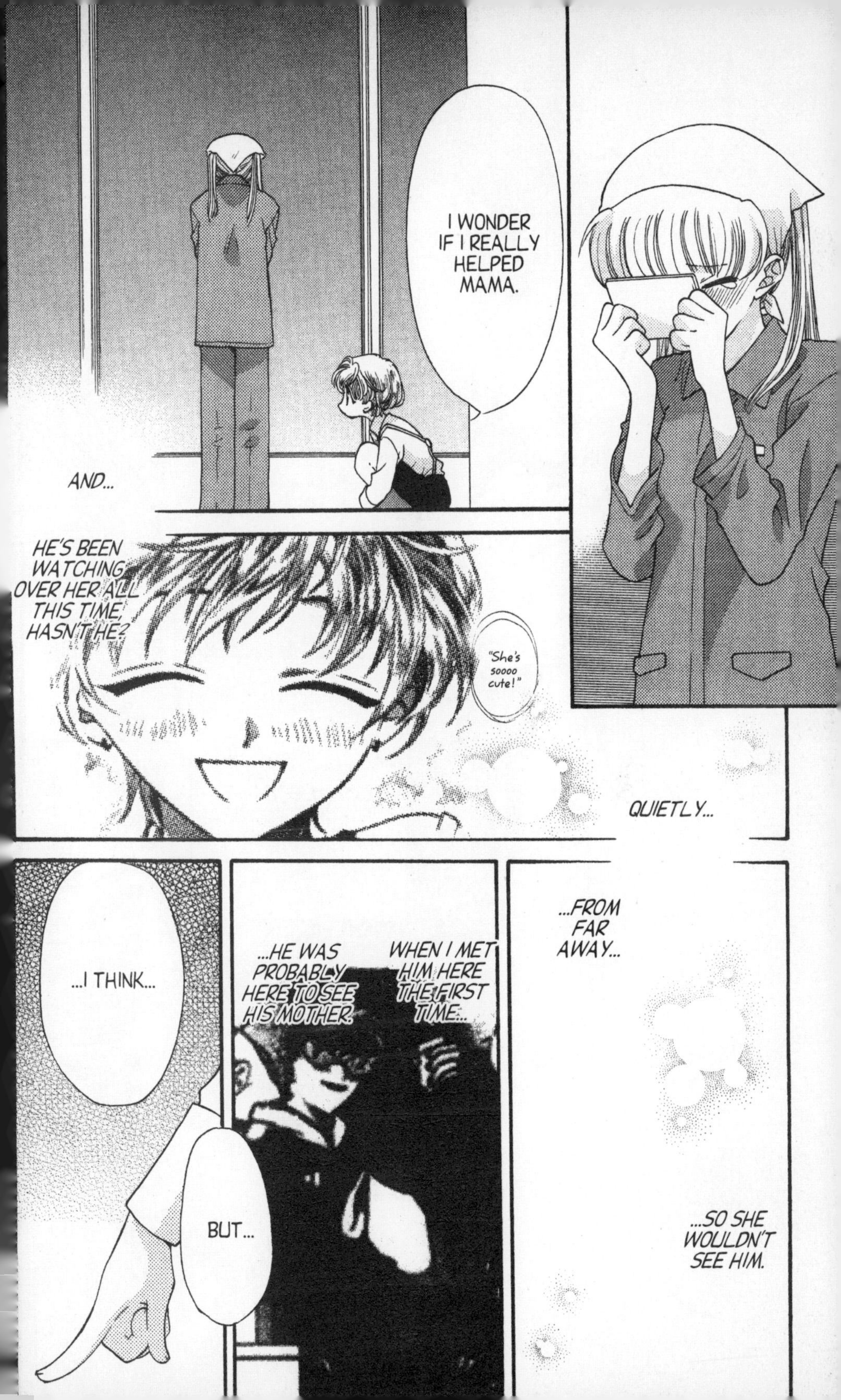
I WONDER IF I REALLY HELPED MAMA.
AND...
"She's soooo cute!"
HE'S BEEN WATCHING OVER HER ALL THIS TIME, HASN'T HE?
QUIETLY...
...FROM FAR AWAY...
...SO SHE WOULDN'T SEE HIM.
WHEN I MET HIM HERE THE FIRST TIME...
...HE WAS PROBABLY HERE TO SEE HIS MOTHER.
...I THINK...
BUT...

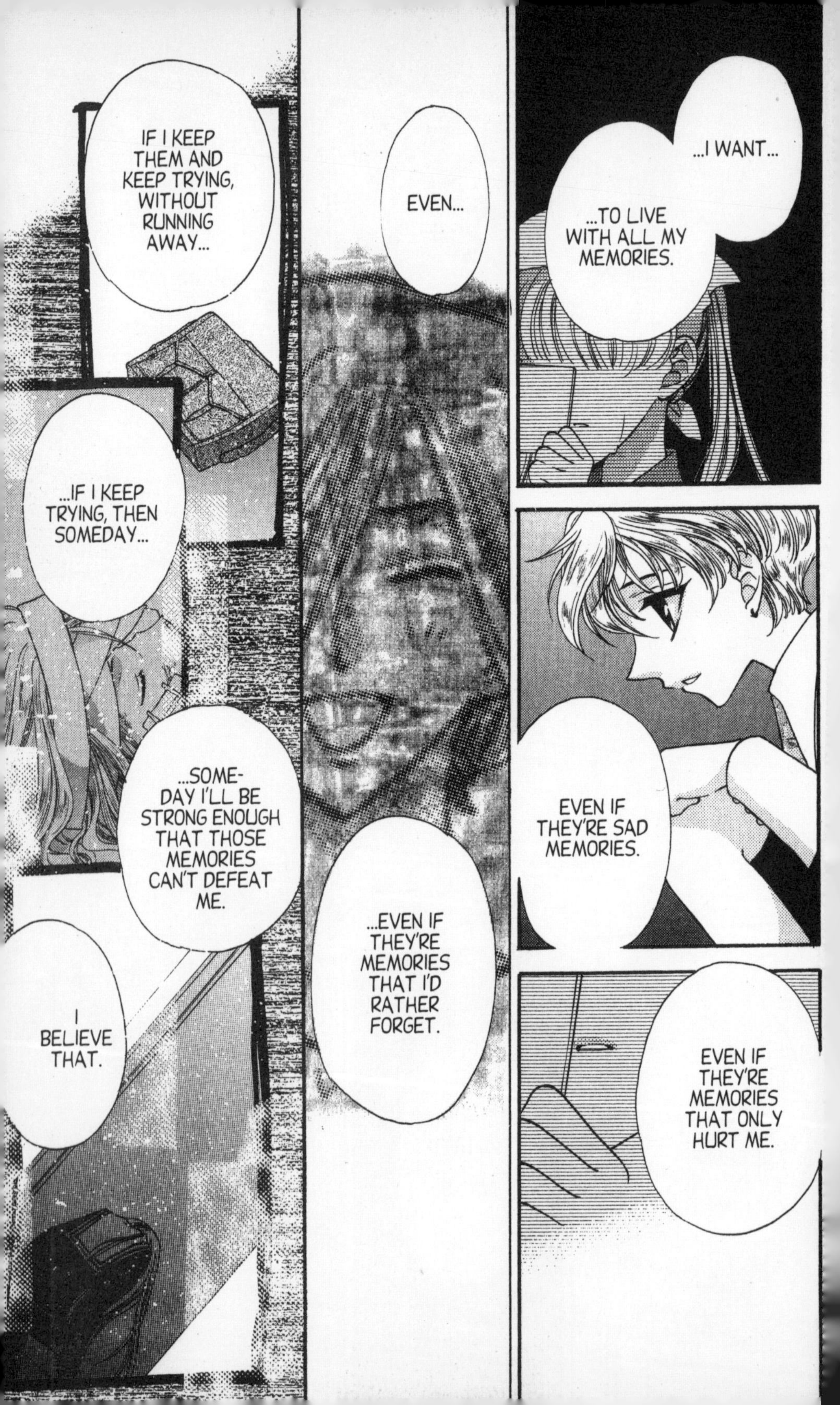
...I WANT...
...TO LIVE WITH ALL MY MEMORIES.
EVEN IF THEY'RE SAD MEMORIES.
EVEN IF THEY'RE MEMORIES THAT ONLY HURT ME.
EVEN...
...EVEN IF THEY'RE MEMORIES THAT I'D RATHER FORGET.
IF I KEEP THEM AND KEEP TRYING, WITHOUT RUNNING AWAY...
...IF I KEEP TRYING, THEN SOMEDAY...
...SOME-DAY I'LL BE STRONG ENOUGH THAT THOSE MEMORIES CAN'T DEFEAT ME.
I BELIEVE THAT.

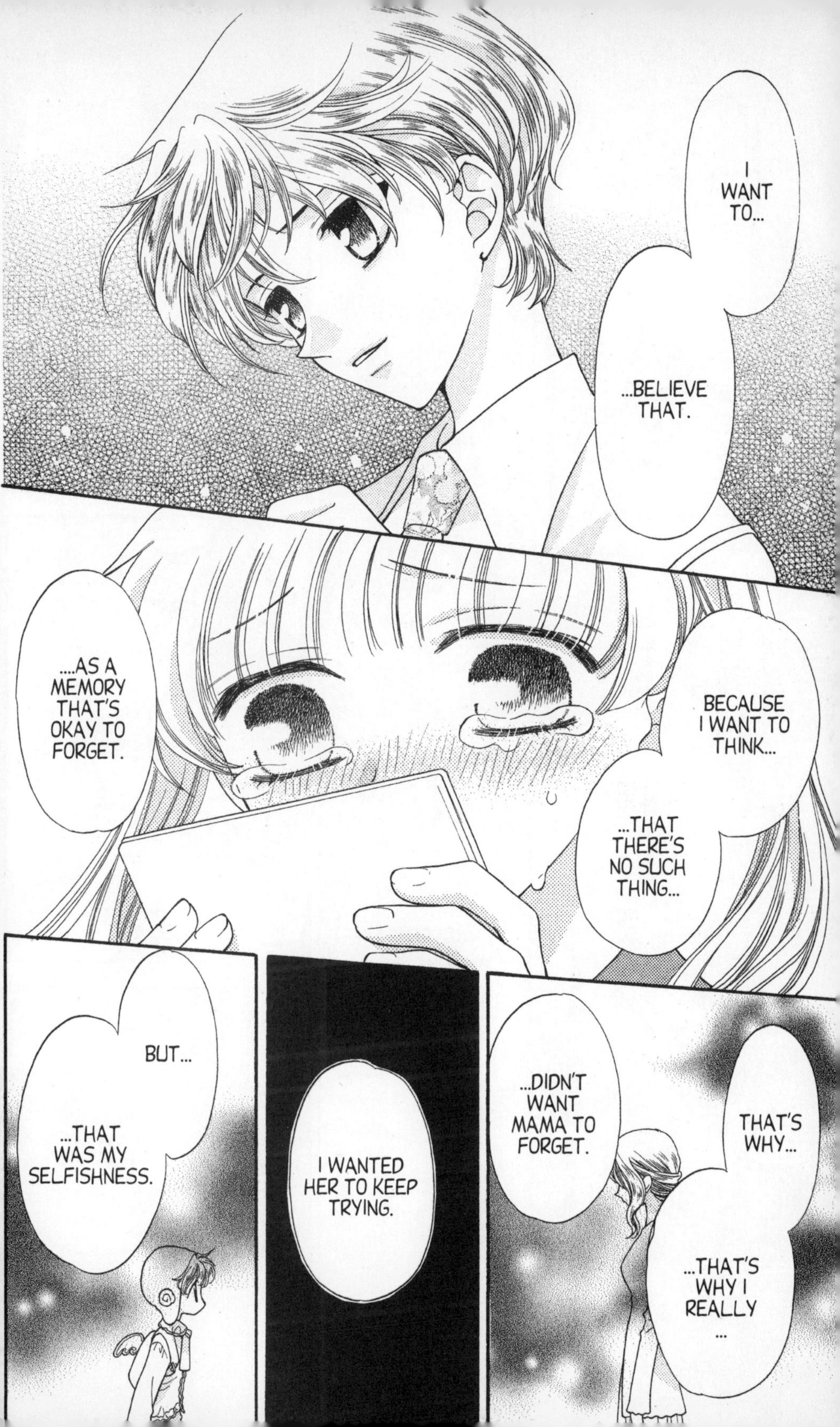
I WANT TO...
...BELIEVE THAT.
BECAUSE I WANT TO THINK...
...THAT THERE'S NO SUCH THING...
....AS A MEMORY THAT'S OKAY TO FORGET.
THAT'S WHY...
...THAT'S WHY I REALLY ...
...DIDN'T WANT MAMA TO FORGET.
I WANTED HER TO KEEP TRYING.
BUT...
...THAT WAS MY SELFISHNESS.

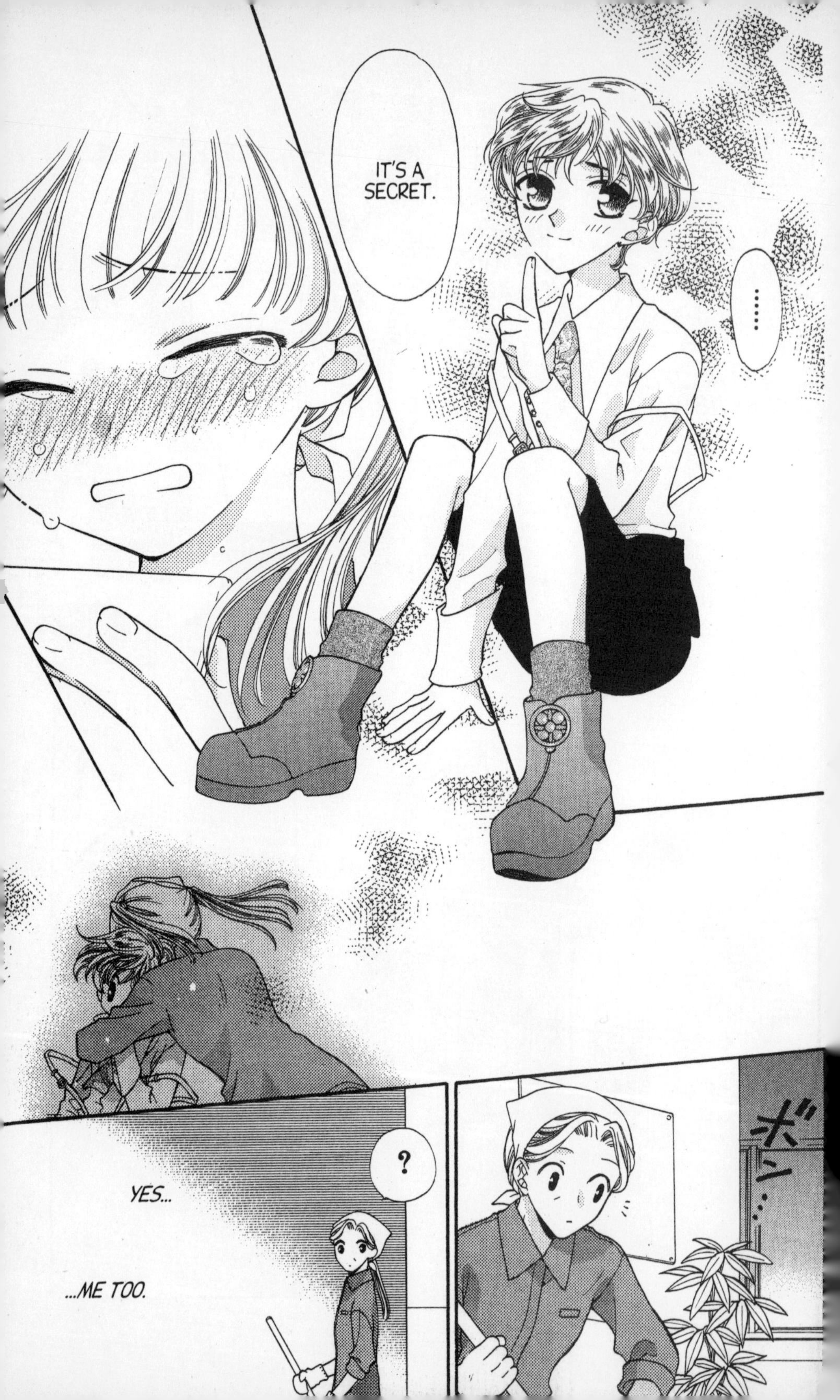

IT'S A SECRET.
......
ボン...
?
YES...
...ME TOO.

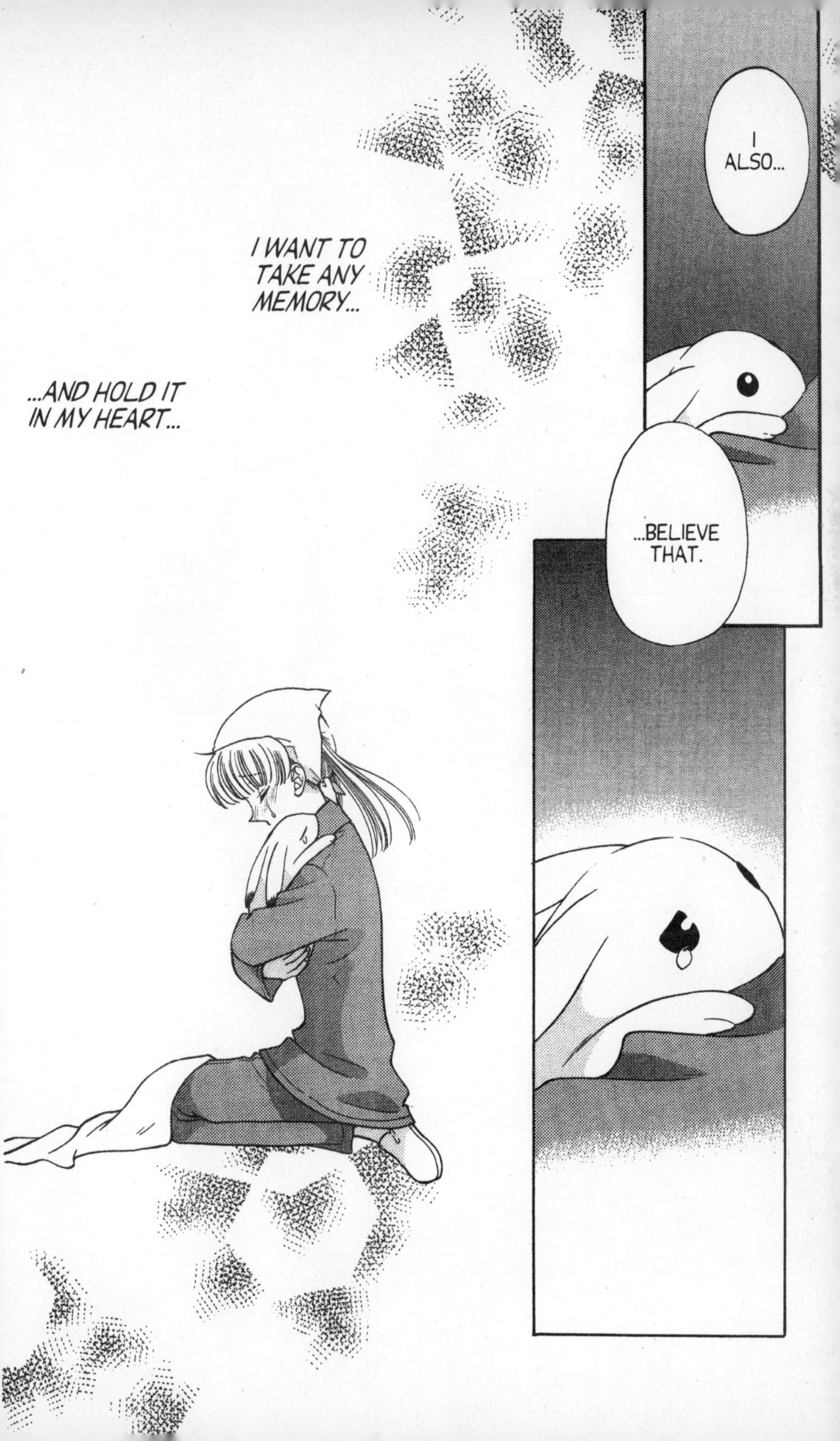
I ALSO...
...BELIEVE THAT.
I WANT TO TAKE ANY MEMORY...
...AND HOLD IT IN MY HEART...

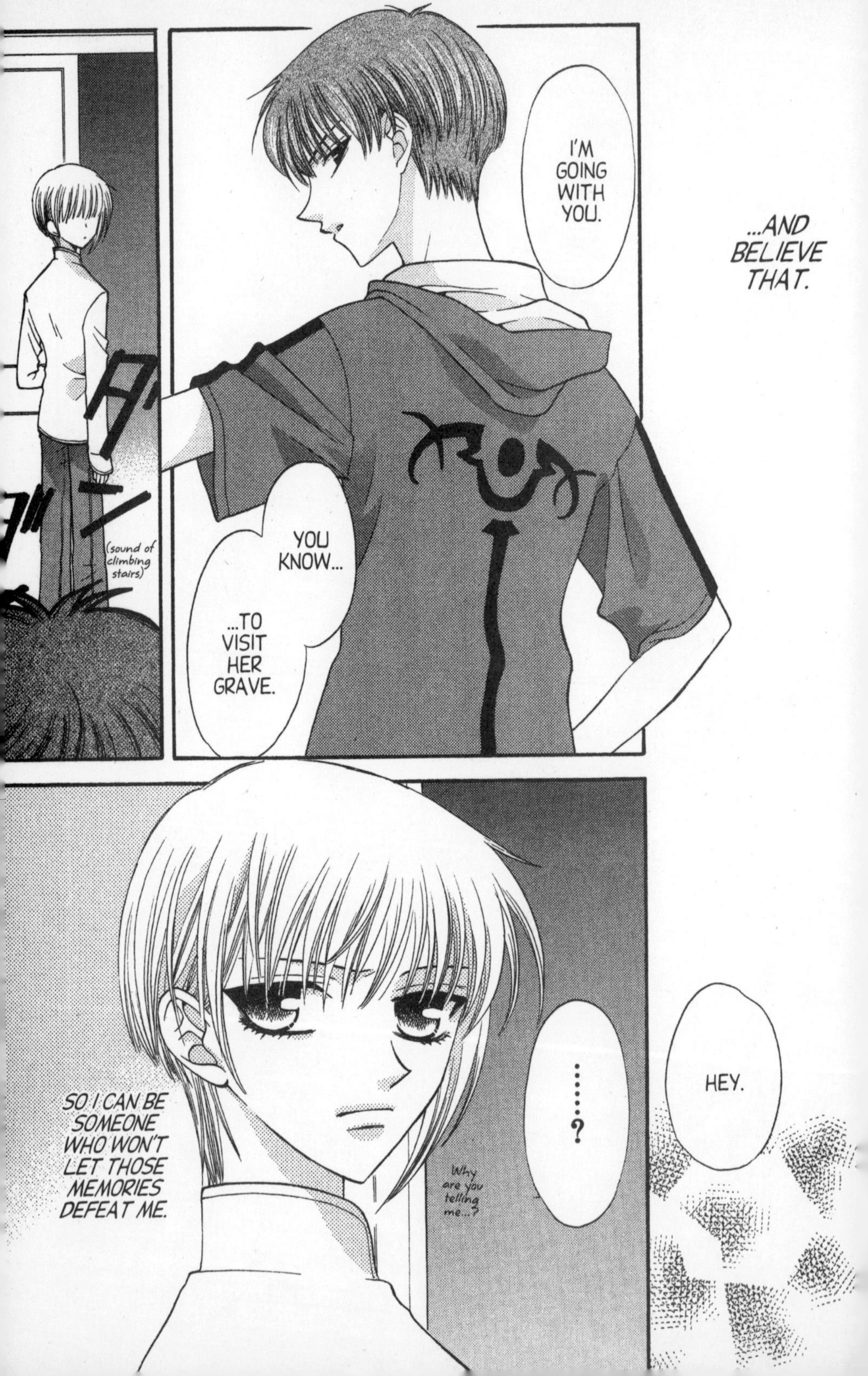
...AND BELIEVE THAT.
I'M GOING WITH YOU.
YOU KNOW...
...TO VISIT HER GRAVE.
(sound of climbing stairs)
HEY.
......?
Why are you telling me...?
SO I CAN BE SOMEONE WHO WON'T LET THOSE MEMORIES DEFEAT ME.

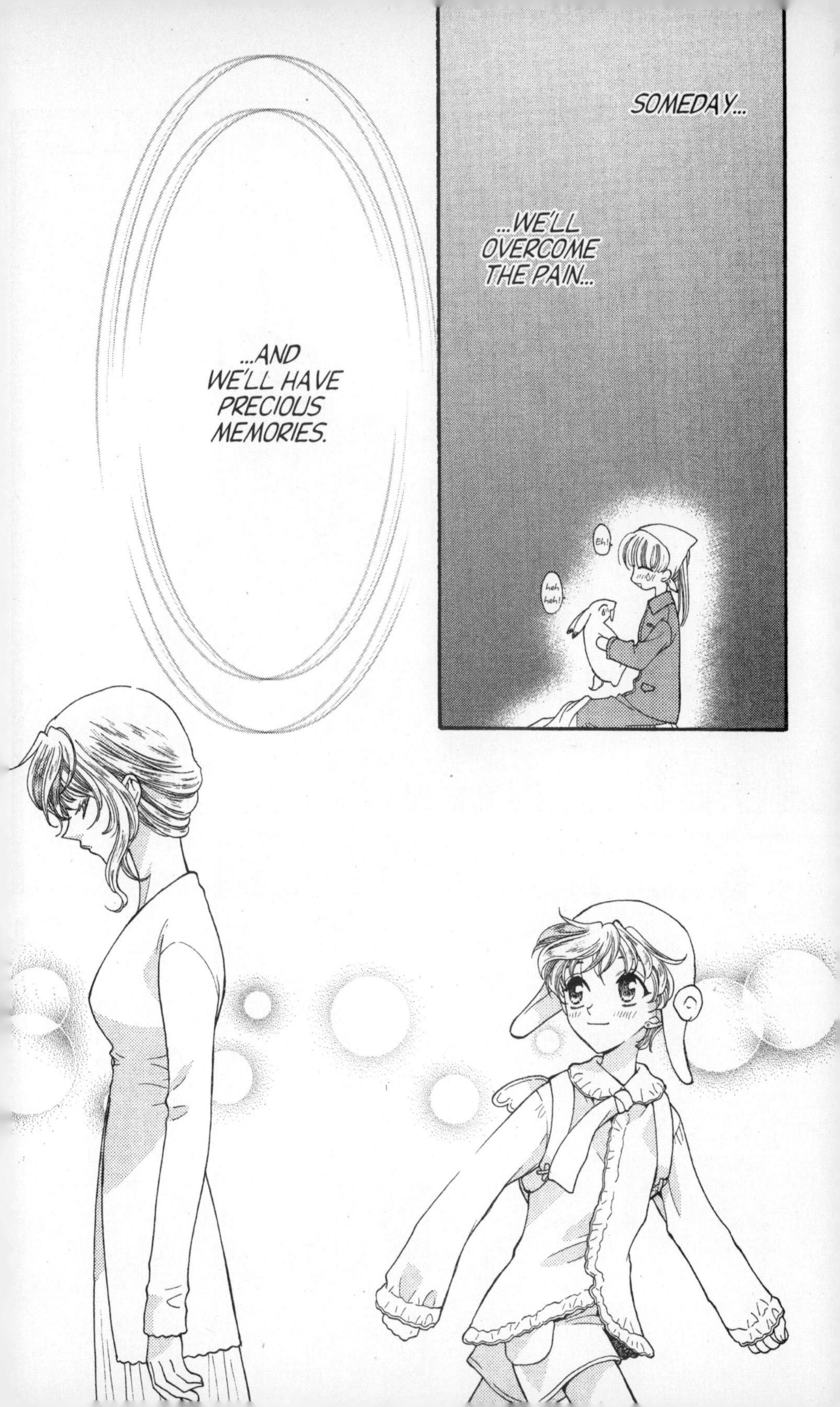
SOMEDAY...
...WE'LL OVERCOME THE PAIN...
Eh!
heh heh!
...AND WE'LL HAVE PRECIOUS MEMORIES.

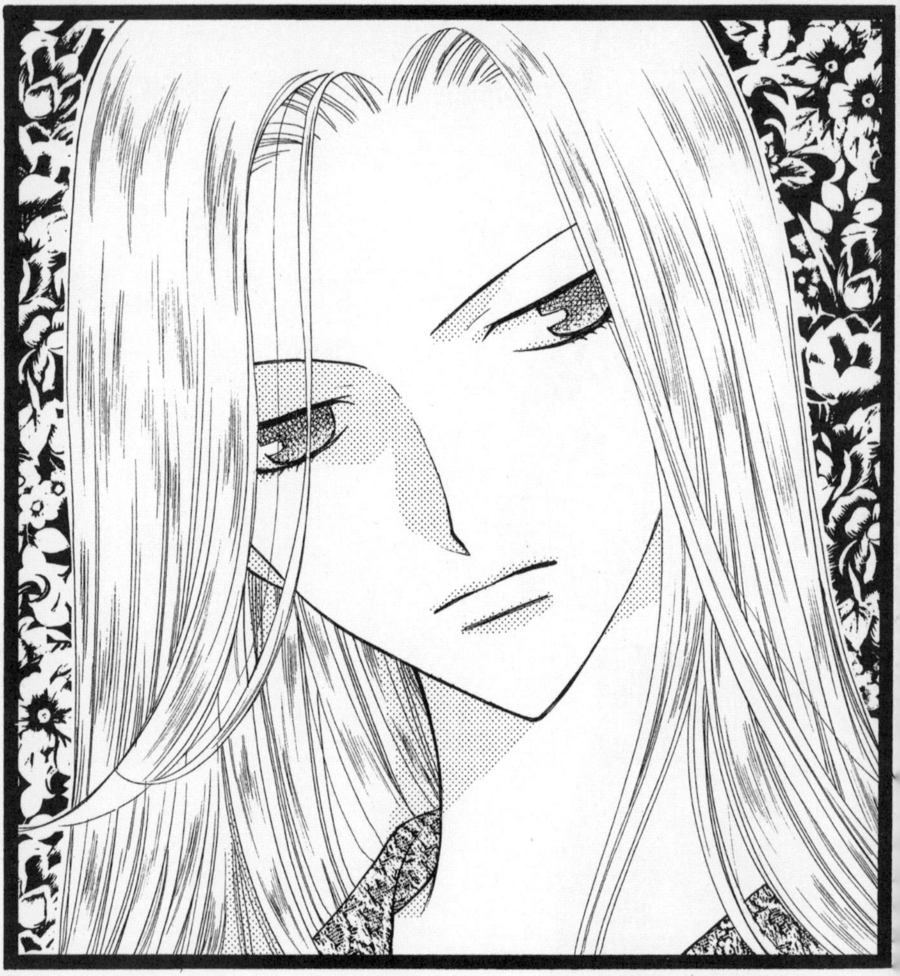

Chapter 24

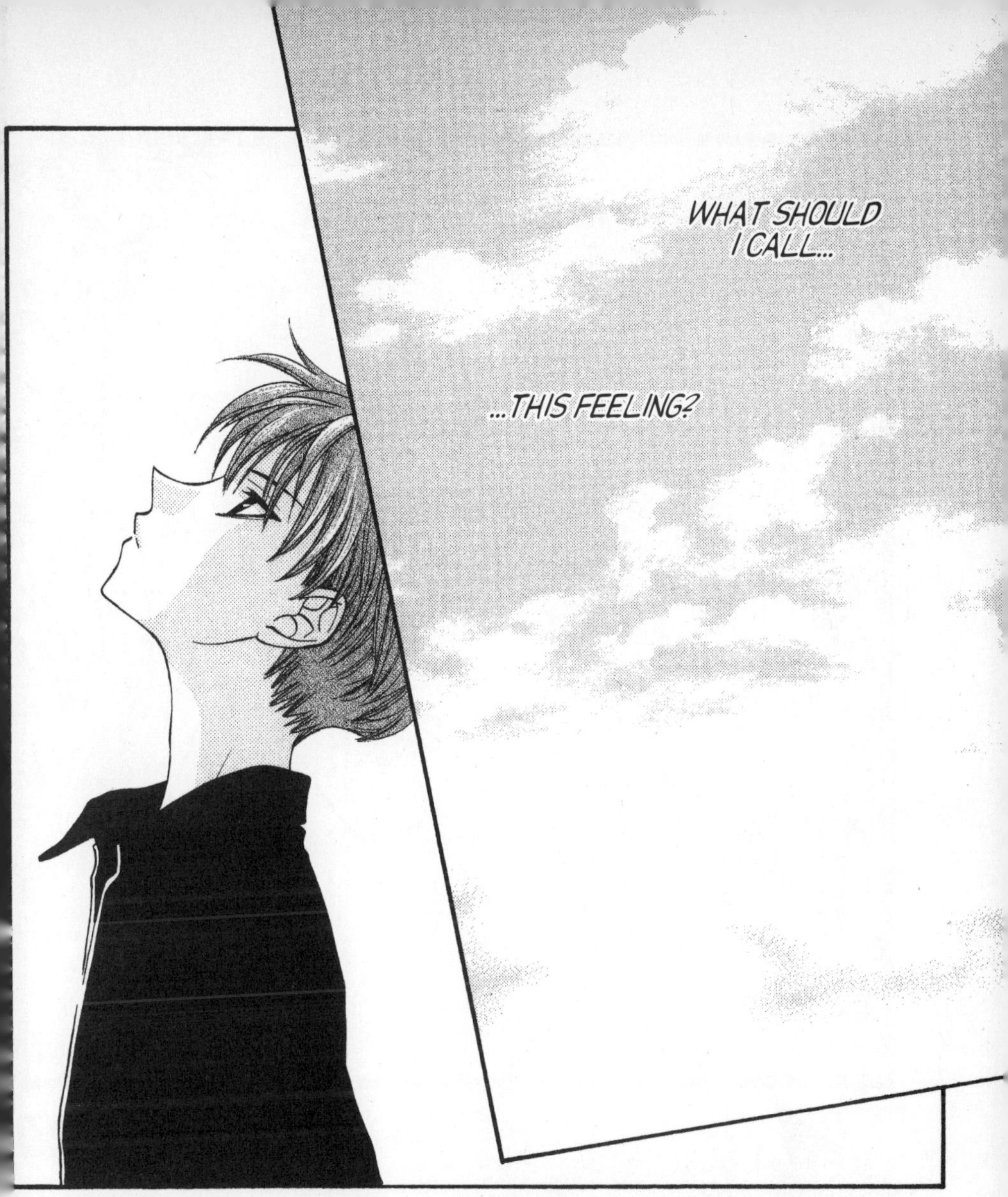
WHAT SHOULD I CALL...
...THIS FEELING?

ULTRA SPECIAL BLAH BLAH BLAH 6

This is where volume 4 ends!! This one's been really talky!! (But once again, I have no one to blame but myself.) But it's okay! (What is?) A lot of people told me they thought they should have kissed. Sorry, but I didn't want them to, and as the author, it's up to me...

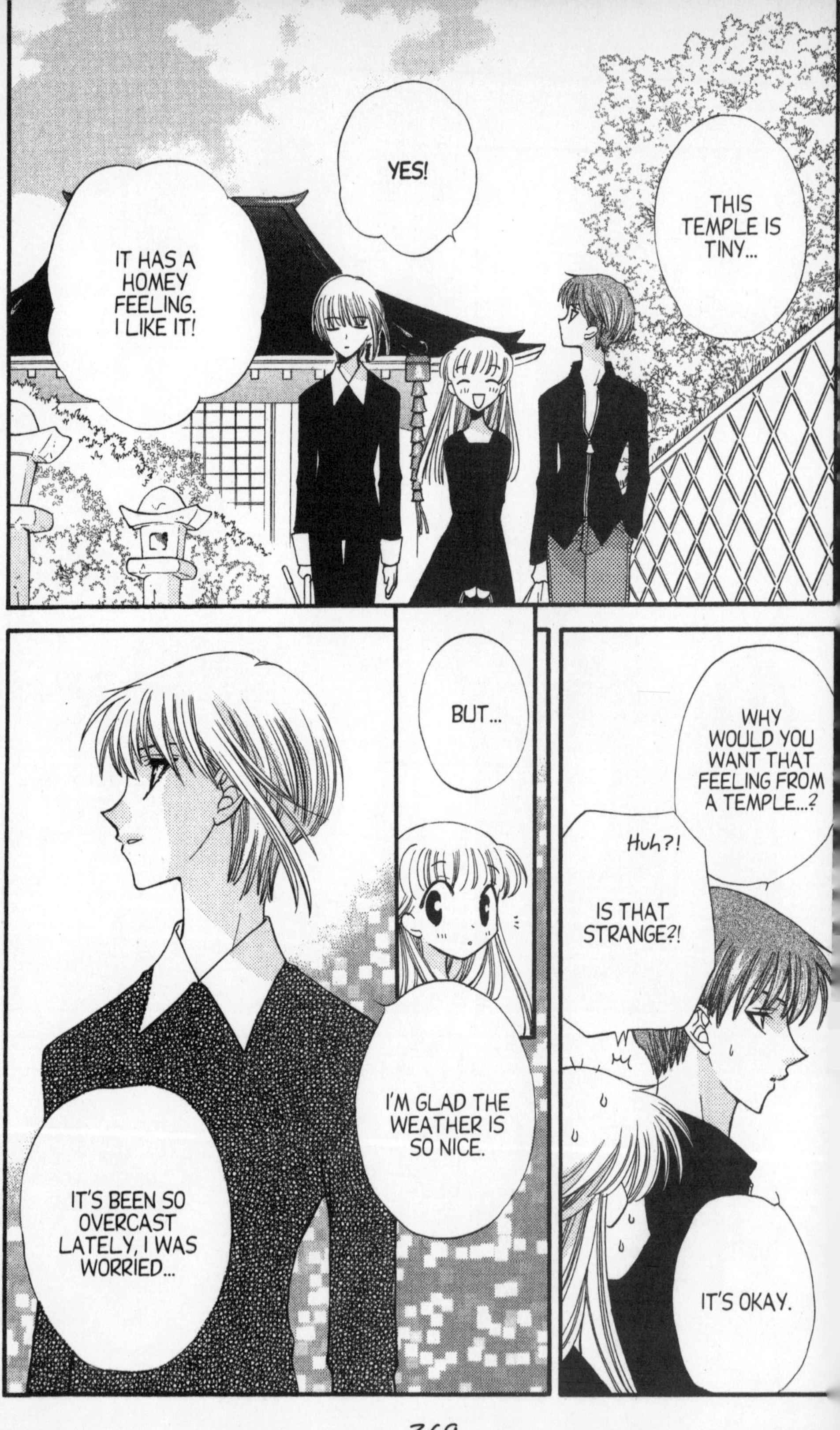
THIS TEMPLE IS TINY...
YES!
IT HAS A HOMEY FEELING. I LIKE IT!
WHY WOULD YOU WANT THAT FEELING FROM A TEMPLE...?
Huh?!
IS THAT STRANGE?!
IT'S OKAY.
BUT...
I'M GLAD THE WEATHER IS SO NICE.
IT'S BEEN SO OVERCAST LATELY, I WAS WORRIED...

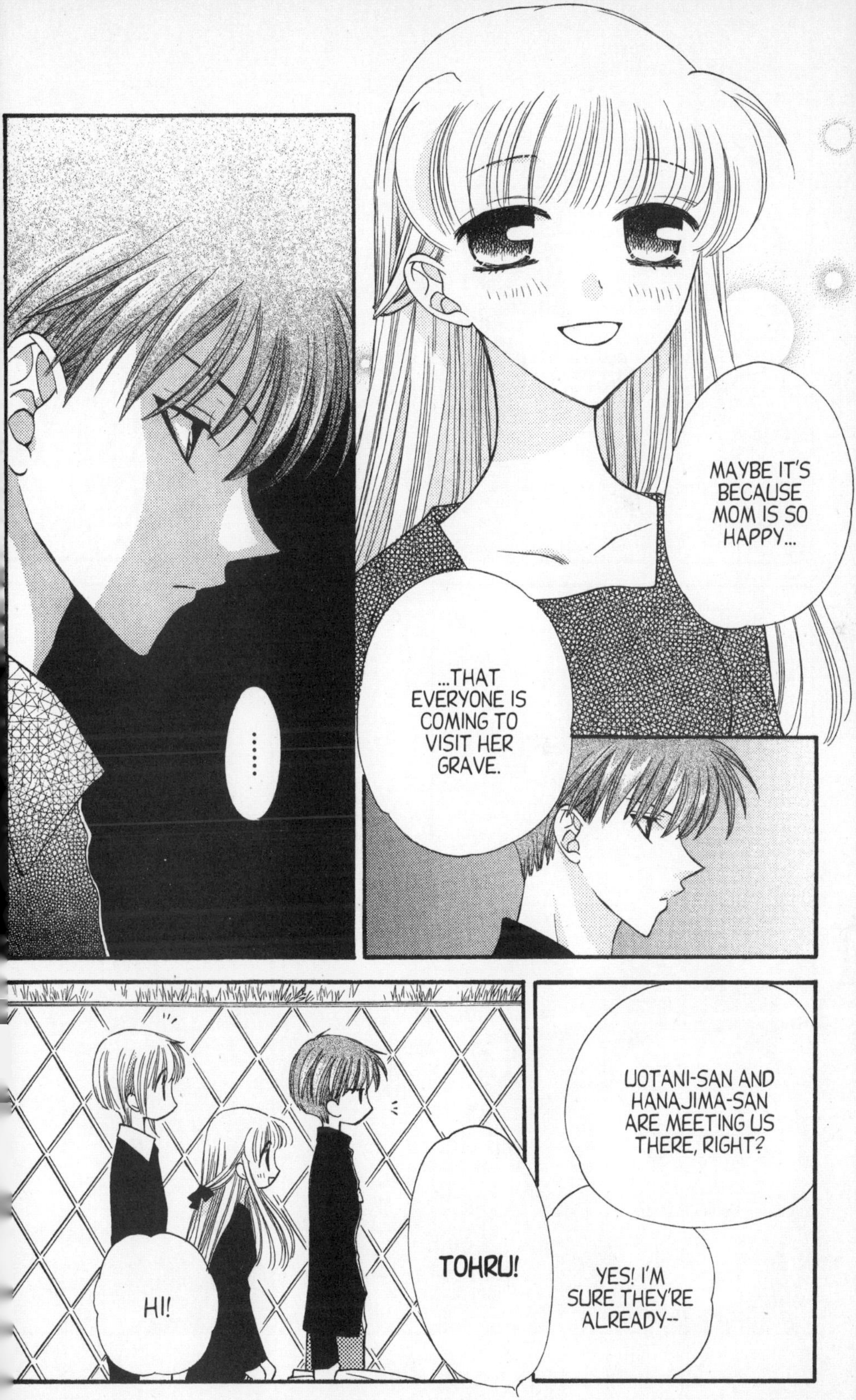
MAYBE IT'S BECAUSE MOM IS SO HAPPY...
...THAT EVERYONE IS COMING TO VISIT HER GRAVE.
......
UOTANI-SAN AND HANAJIMA-SAN ARE MEETING US THERE, RIGHT?
YES! I'M SURE THEY'RE ALREADY--
TOHRU!
HI!

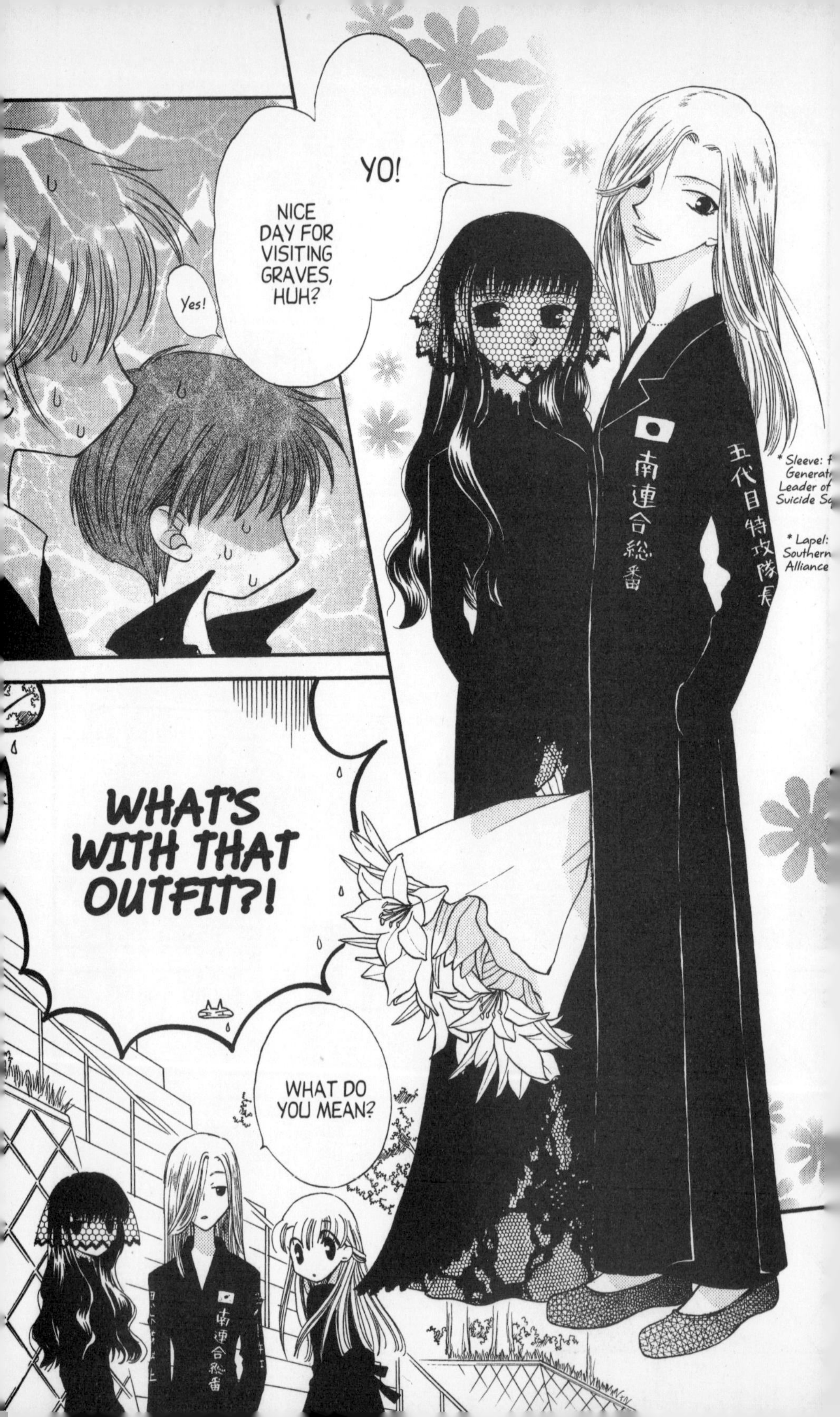

南連合総番
五代目特攻隊長
* Sleeve: F Generat Leader of Suicide Sq
* Lapel: Southern Alliance
YO!
NICE DAY FOR VISITING GRAVES, HUH?
Yes!
WHAT'S WITH THAT OUTFIT?!
WHAT DO YOU MEAN?

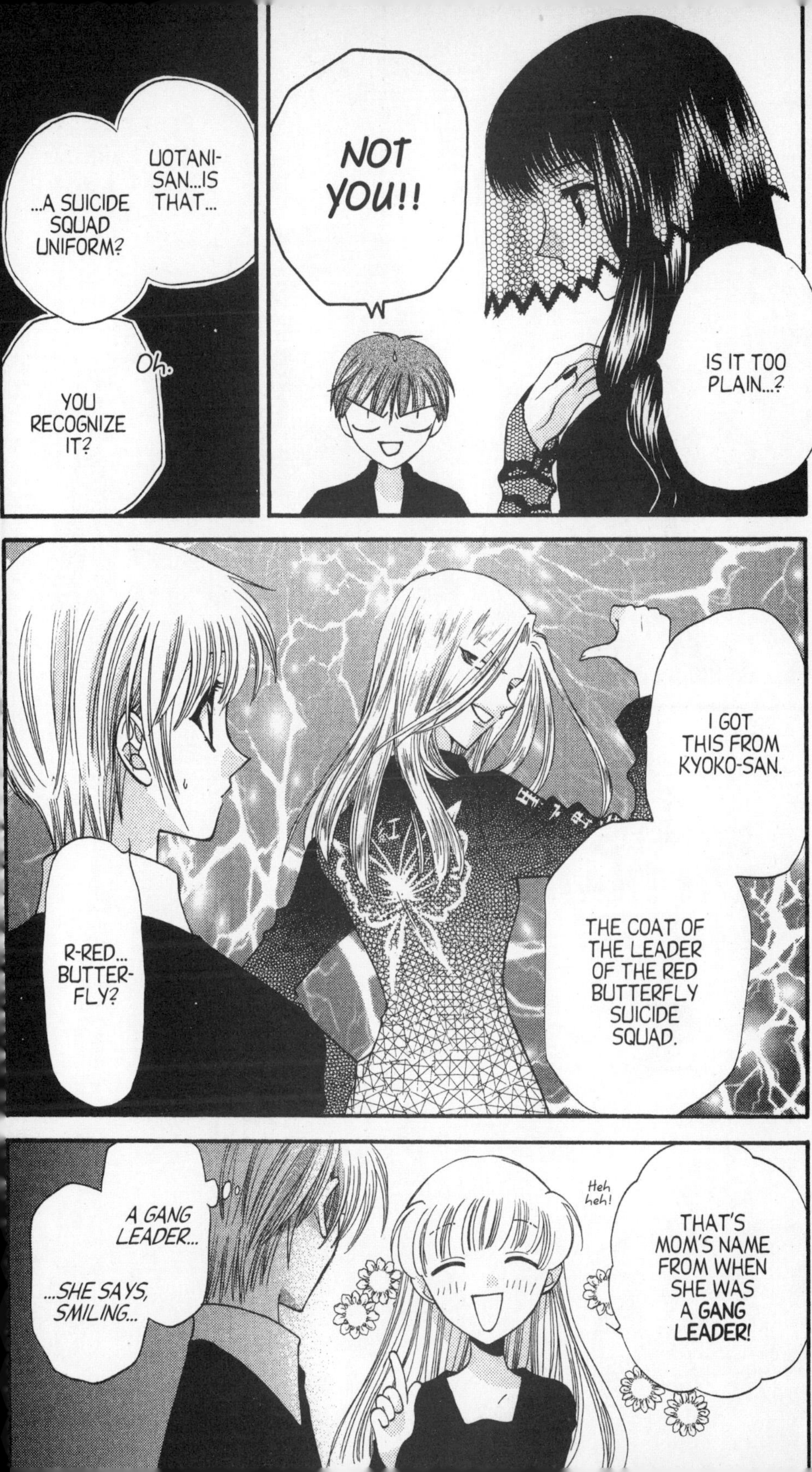
IS IT TOO PLAIN...?
NOT YOU!!
UOTANI-SAN...IS THAT...
...A SUICIDE SQUAD UNIFORM?
Oh.
YOU RECOGNIZE IT?
I GOT THIS FROM KYOKO-SAN.
THE COAT OF THE LEADER OF THE RED BUTTERFLY SUICIDE SQUAD.
R-RED... BUTTER-FLY?
Heh heh!
THAT'S MOM'S NAME FROM WHEN SHE WAS A **GANG LEADER!**
A GANG LEADER...
...SHE SAYS, SMILING...

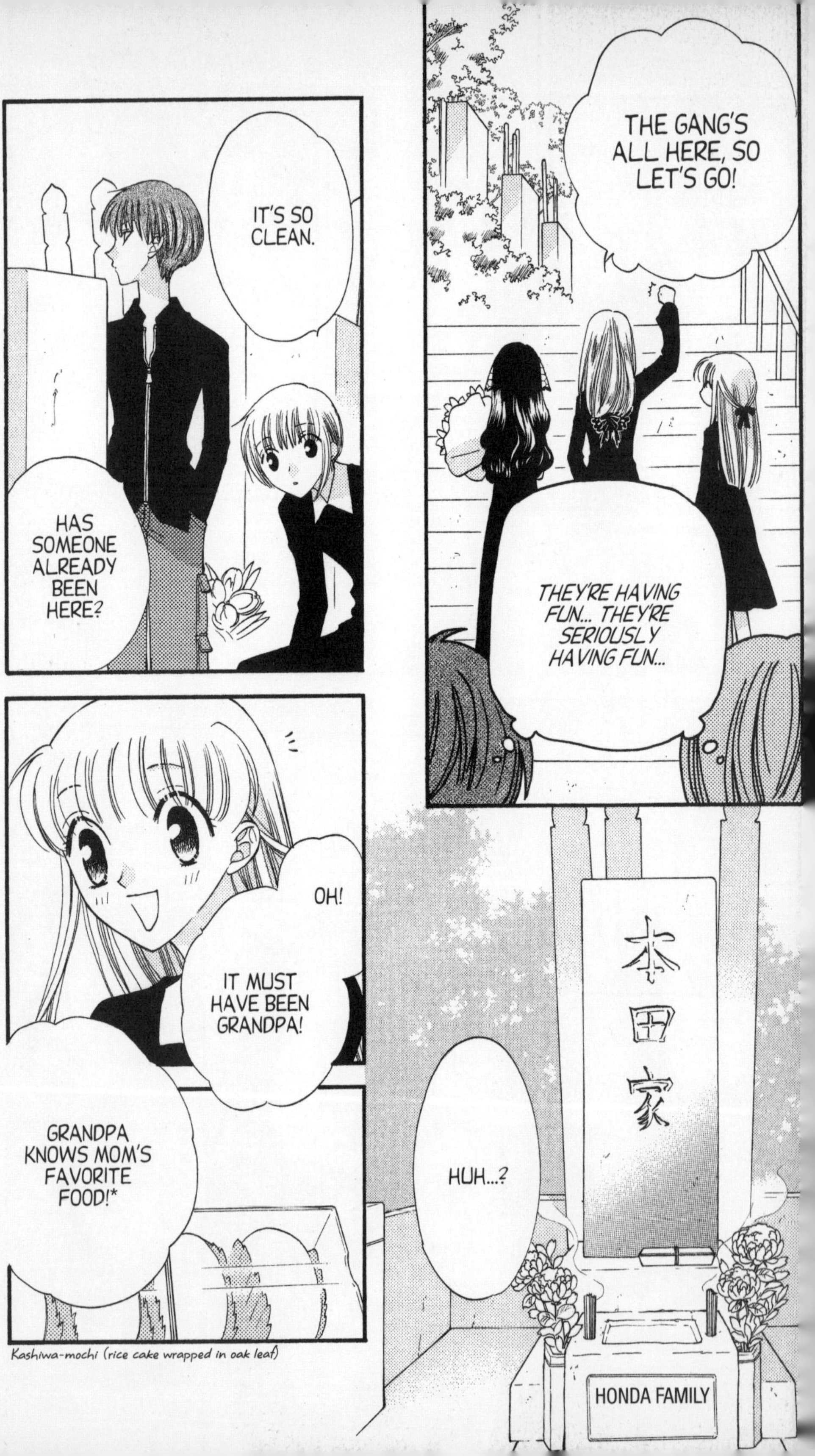
THE GANG'S ALL HERE, SO LET'S GO!
THEY'RE HAVING FUN... THEY'RE SERIOUSLY HAVING FUN...
IT'S SO CLEAN.
HAS SOMEONE ALREADY BEEN HERE?
本田家
HONDA FAMILY
HUH...?
OH!
IT MUST HAVE BEEN GRANDPA!
GRANDPA KNOWS MOM'S FAVORITE FOOD!*

Kashiwa-mochi (rice cake wrapped in oak leaf)

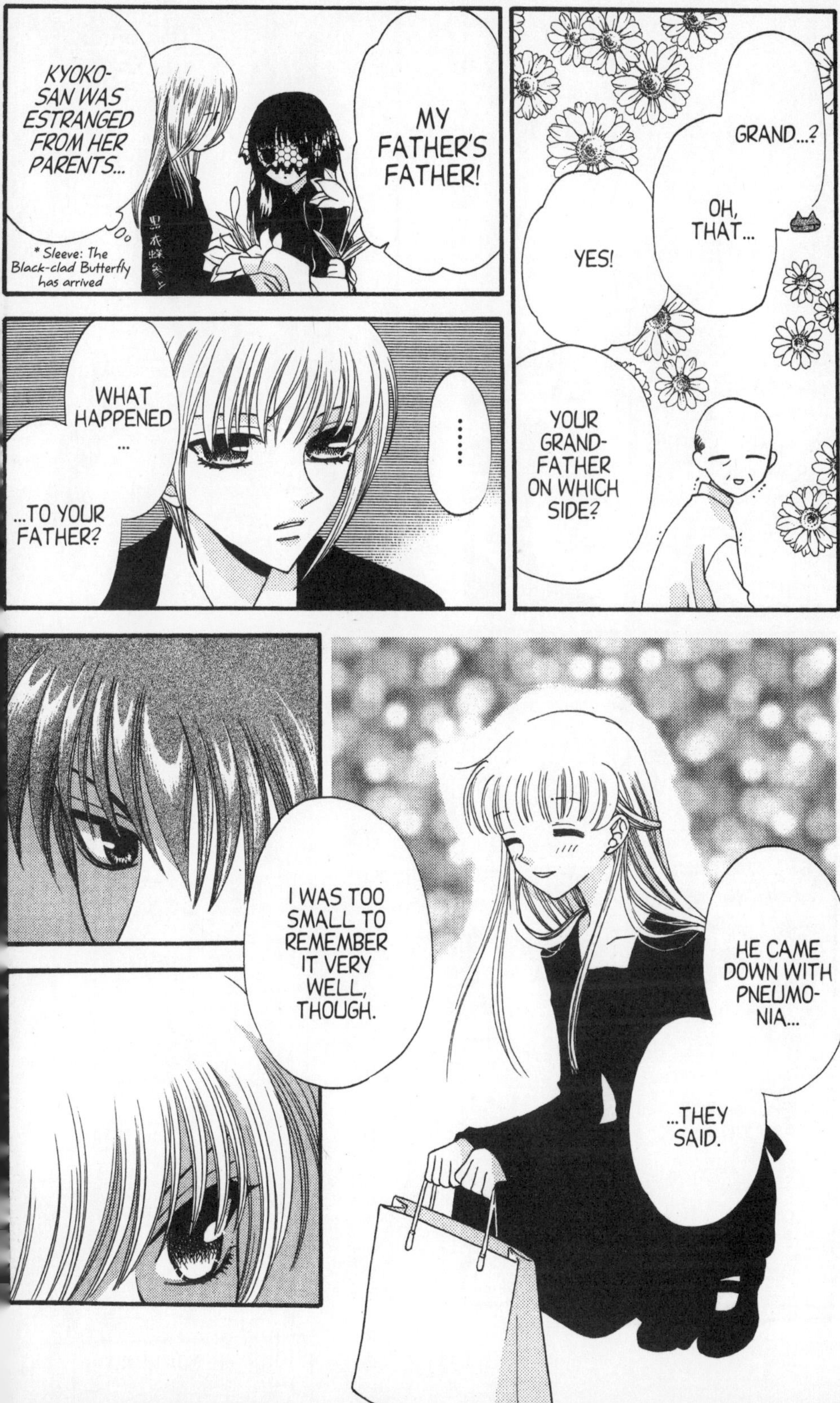
GRAND...?
OH, THAT...
YES!
YOUR GRAND-FATHER ON WHICH SIDE?
MY FATHER'S FATHER!
KYOKO-SAN WAS ESTRANGED FROM HER PARENTS...
* Sleeve: The Black-clad Butterfly has arrived
......
WHAT HAPPENED ...
...TO YOUR FATHER?
HE CAME DOWN WITH PNEUMO-NIA...
...THEY SAID.
I WAS TOO SMALL TO REMEMBER IT VERY WELL, THOUGH.

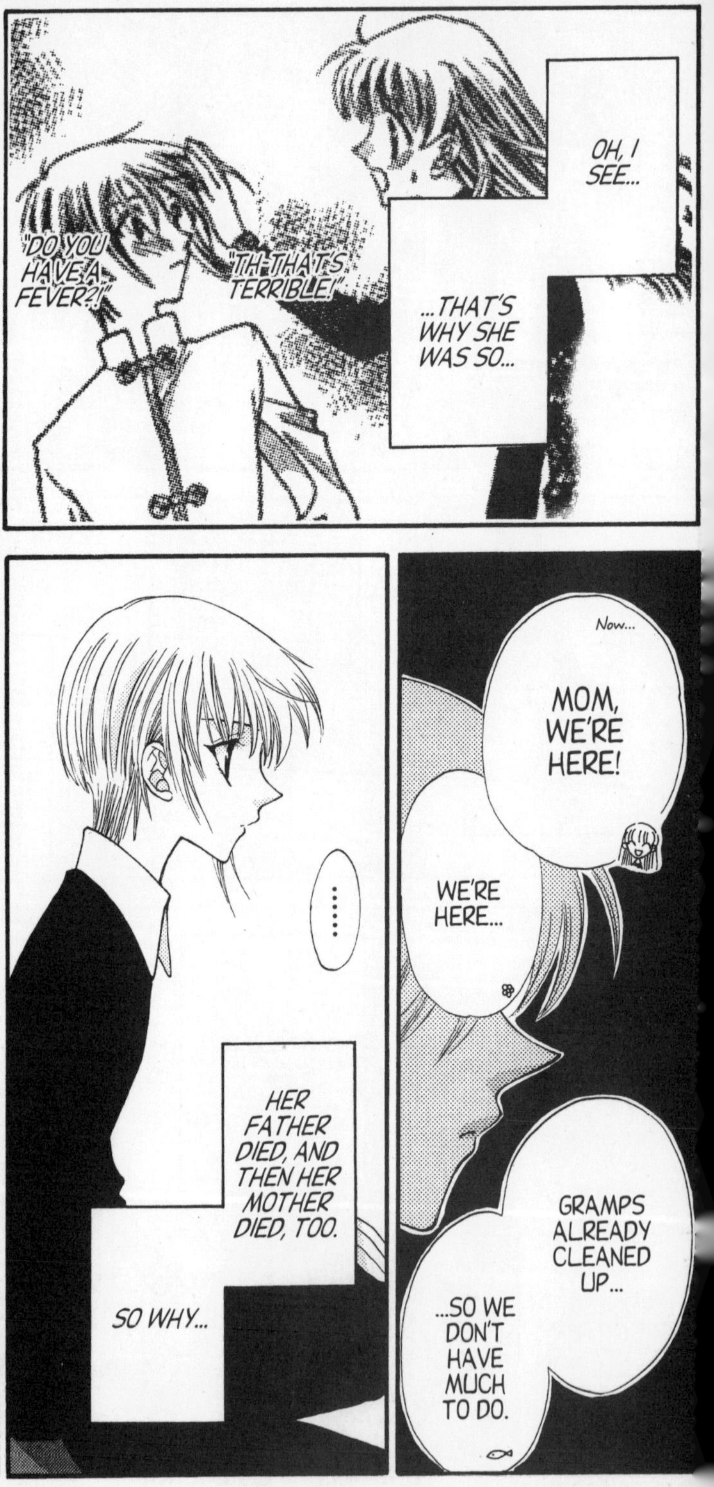
OH, I SEE...
...THAT'S WHY SHE WAS SO...
"TH-THAT'S TERRIBLE!"
"DO YOU HAVE A FEVER?!"
Now...
MOM, WE'RE HERE!
WE'RE HERE...
GRAMPS ALREADY CLEANED UP...
...SO WE DON'T HAVE MUCH TO DO.
......
HER FATHER DIED, AND THEN HER MOTHER DIED, TOO.
SO WHY...

Fruits Basket 4 Part 6:

I started crying when I saw the opening. I thought, "How very, very sad!" And "Oh, poor Serge. I want to protect him." That's proof that I'm totally hooked! He's like Cloud. (But it's worse for Cloud.) Square really does always have good music. I played Chrono Trigger on Su-Fami [Super Nintendo], so the music brought back a lot of memories. Oh, but I cried. It's so sad! I'm also playing Tokimeki Memorial [a popular romance sim]. I'm getting called Takaya-kun. And while I'm doing all this, I'm waiting for Sakura [Taisen] to come out...

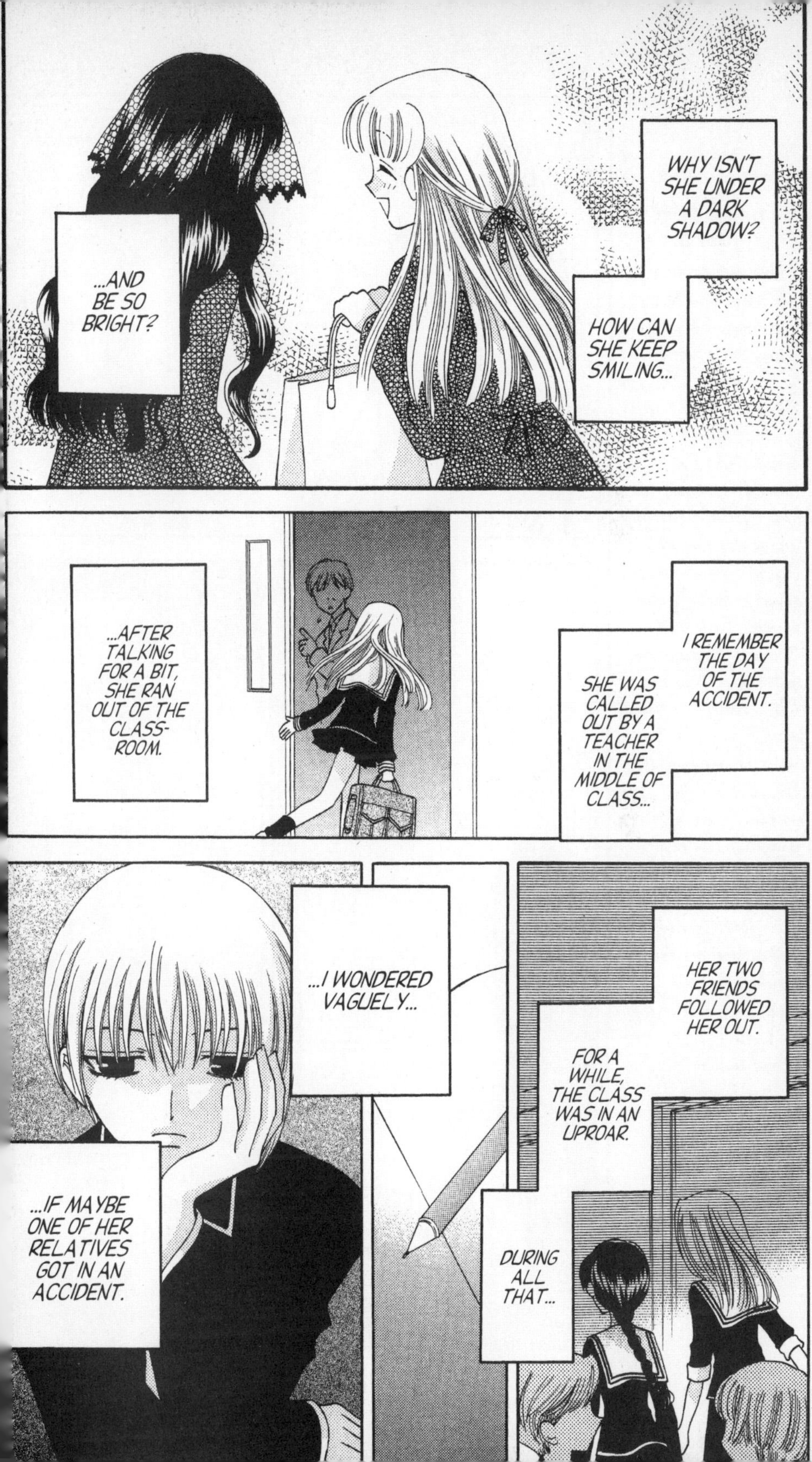
WHY ISN'T SHE UNDER A DARK SHADOW?
HOW CAN SHE KEEP SMILING...
...AND BE SO BRIGHT?
I REMEMBER THE DAY OF THE ACCIDENT.
SHE WAS CALLED OUT BY A TEACHER IN THE MIDDLE OF CLASS...
...AFTER TALKING FOR A BIT, SHE RAN OUT OF THE CLASS-ROOM.
HER TWO FRIENDS FOLLOWED HER OUT.
FOR A WHILE, THE CLASS WAS IN AN UPROAR.
DURING ALL THAT...
...I WONDERED VAGUELY...
...IF MAYBE ONE OF HER RELATIVES GOT IN AN ACCIDENT.

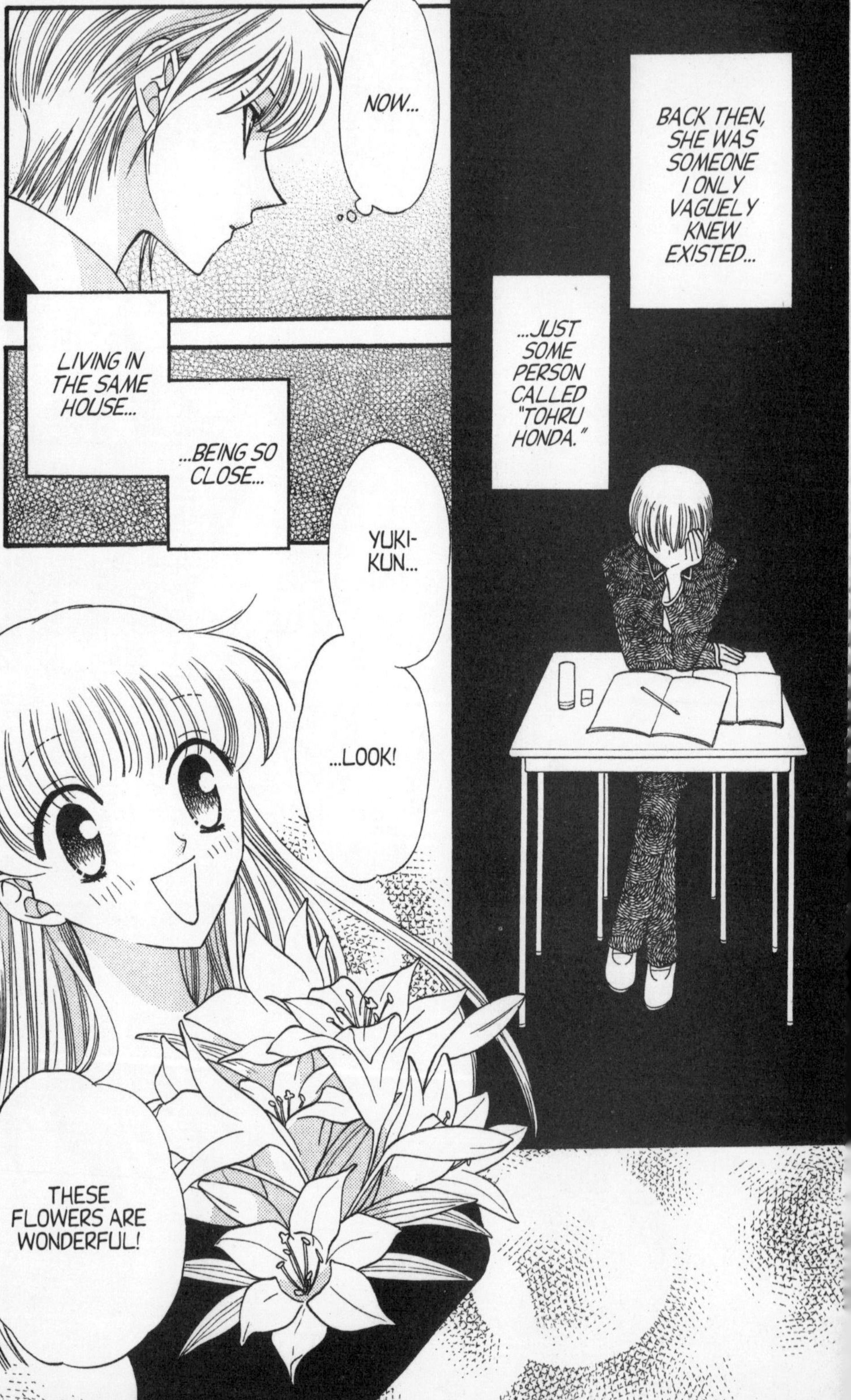
BACK THEN, SHE WAS SOMEONE I ONLY VAGUELY KNEW EXISTED...
...JUST SOME PERSON CALLED "TOHRU HONDA."
NOW...
LIVING IN THE SAME HOUSE...
...BEING SO CLOSE...
YUKI-KUN...
...LOOK!
THESE FLOWERS ARE WONDERFUL!

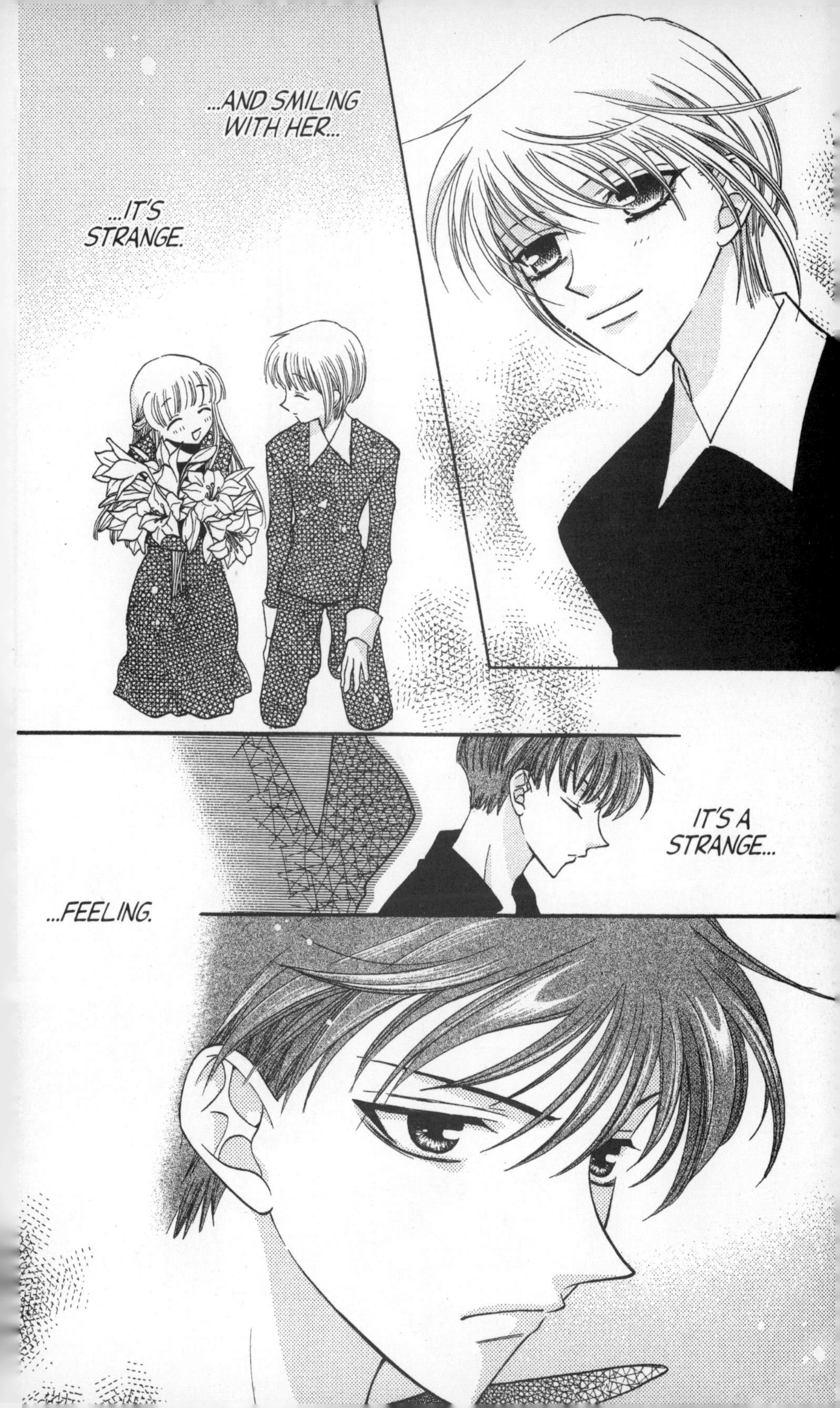
...AND SMILING WITH HER...
...IT'S STRANGE.
IT'S A STRANGE...
...FEELING.

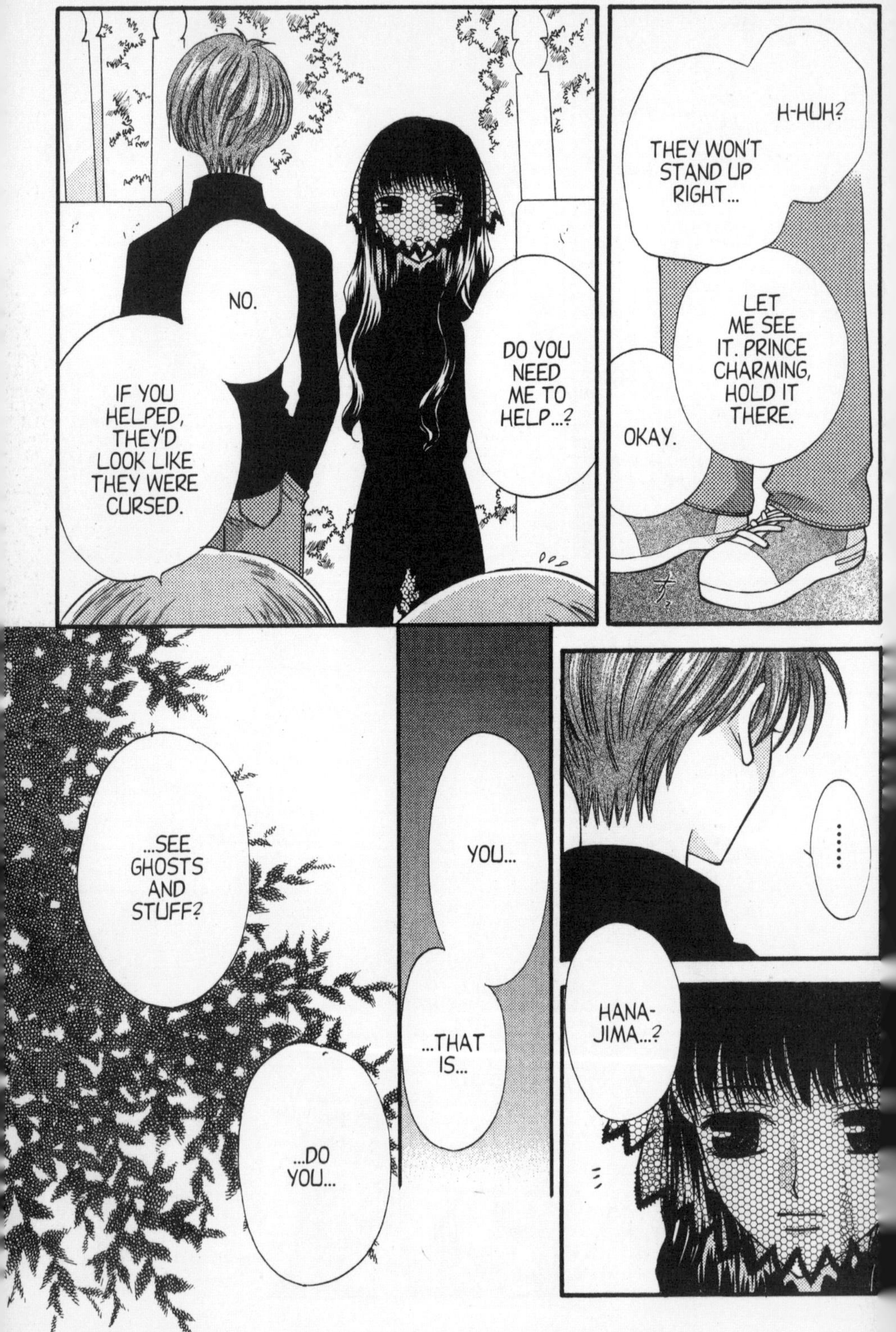
H-HUH?
THEY WON'T STAND UP RIGHT...
LET ME SEE IT. PRINCE CHARMING, HOLD IT THERE.
OKAY.
DO YOU NEED ME TO HELP...?
NO.
IF YOU HELPED, THEY'D LOOK LIKE THEY WERE CURSED.
......
HANA-JIMA...?
YOU...
...THAT IS...
...DO YOU...
...SEE GHOSTS AND STUFF?

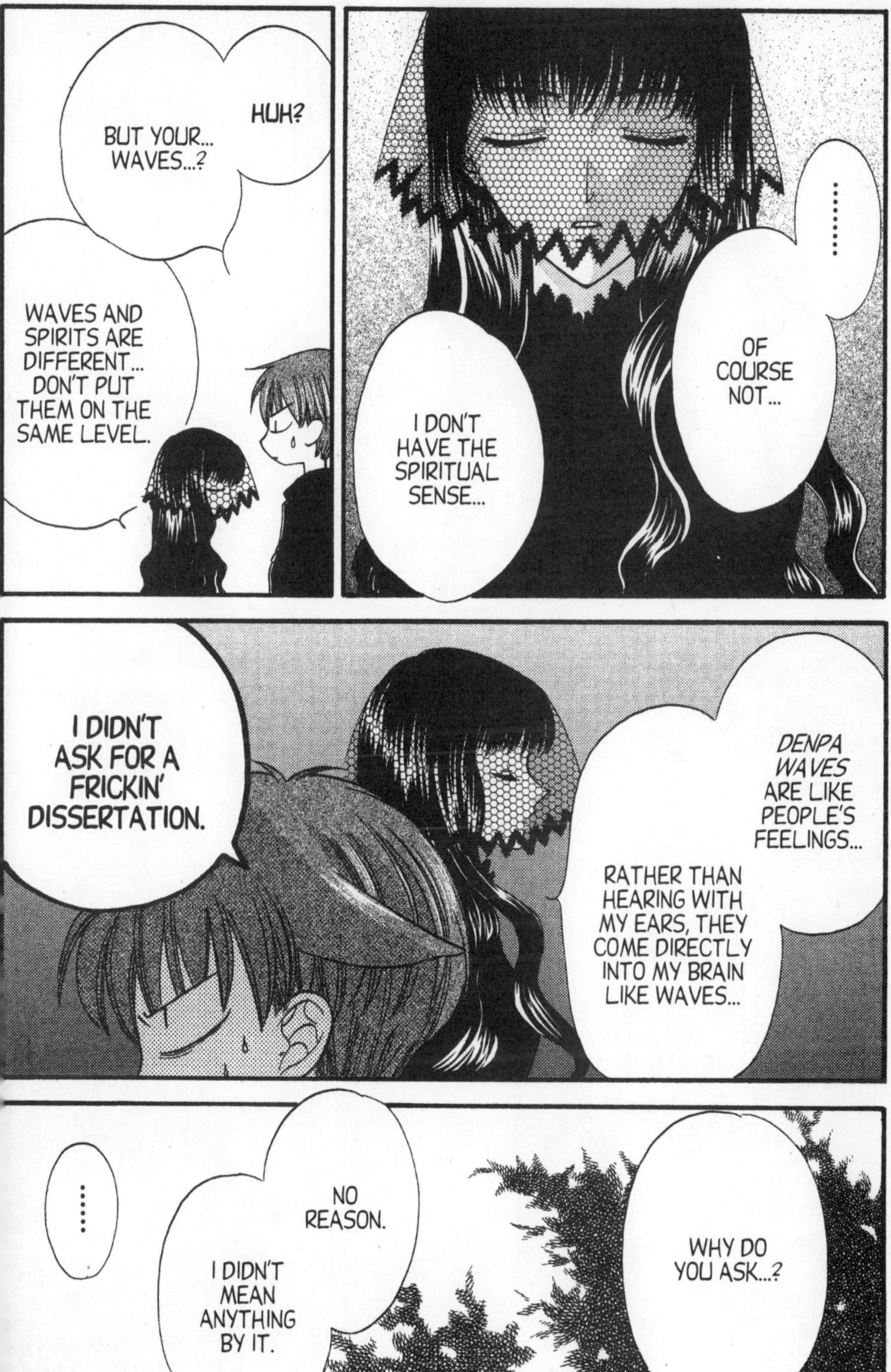
......
OF COURSE NOT...
I DON'T HAVE THE SPIRITUAL SENSE...
HUH?
BUT YOUR... WAVES...?
WAVES AND SPIRITS ARE DIFFERENT... DON'T PUT THEM ON THE SAME LEVEL.
DENPA WAVES ARE LIKE PEOPLE'S FEELINGS...
RATHER THAN HEARING WITH MY EARS, THEY COME DIRECTLY INTO MY BRAIN LIKE WAVES...
I DIDN'T ASK FOR A FRICKIN' DISSERTATION.
WHY DO YOU ASK...?
NO REASON.
I DIDN'T MEAN ANYTHING BY IT.
......

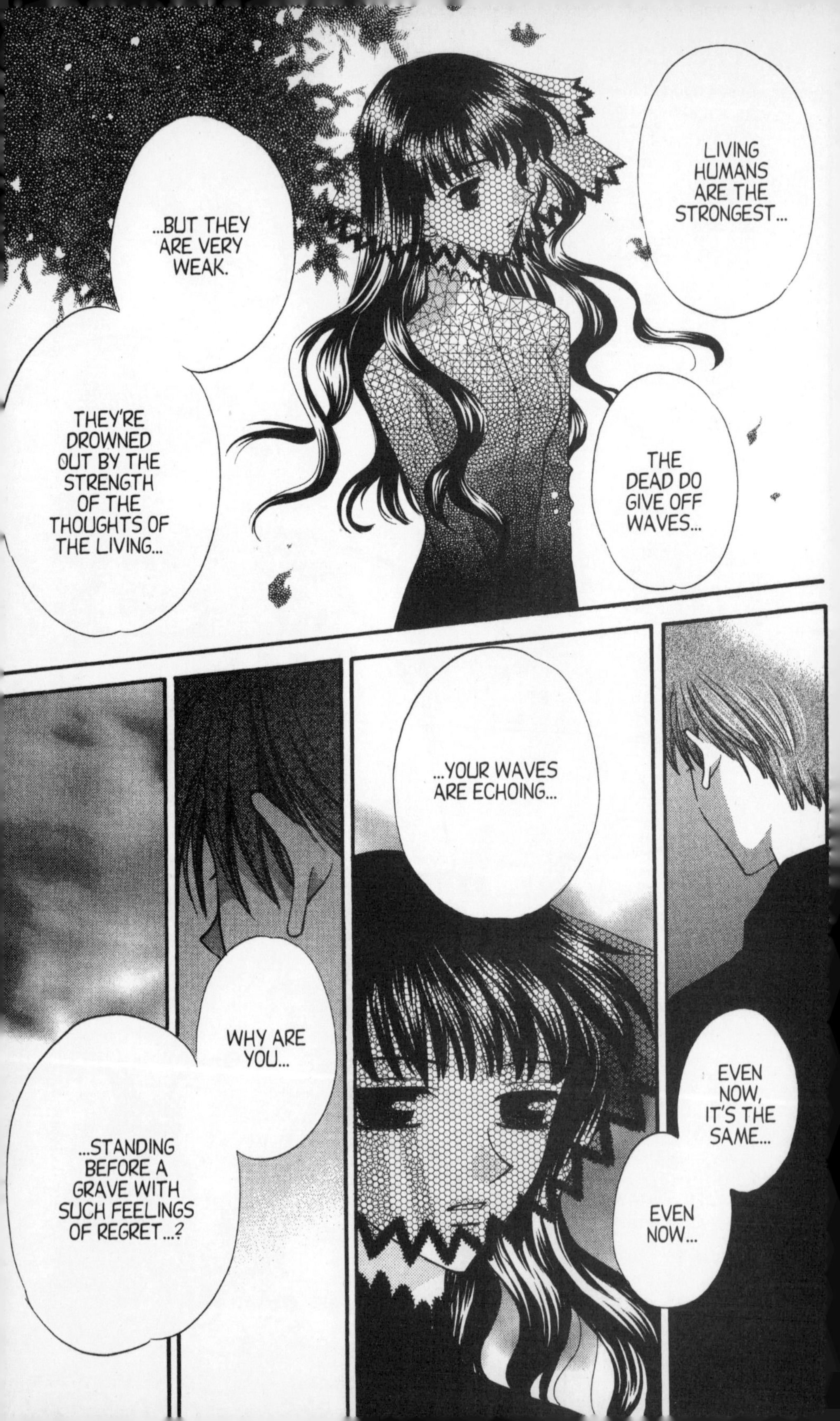
LIVING HUMANS ARE THE STRONGEST...
THE DEAD DO GIVE OFF WAVES...
...BUT THEY ARE VERY WEAK.
THEY'RE DROWNED OUT BY THE STRENGTH OF THE THOUGHTS OF THE LIVING...
...YOUR WAVES ARE ECHOING...
EVEN NOW, IT'S THE SAME...
EVEN NOW...
WHY ARE YOU...
...STANDING BEFORE A GRAVE WITH SUCH FEELINGS OF REGRET...?

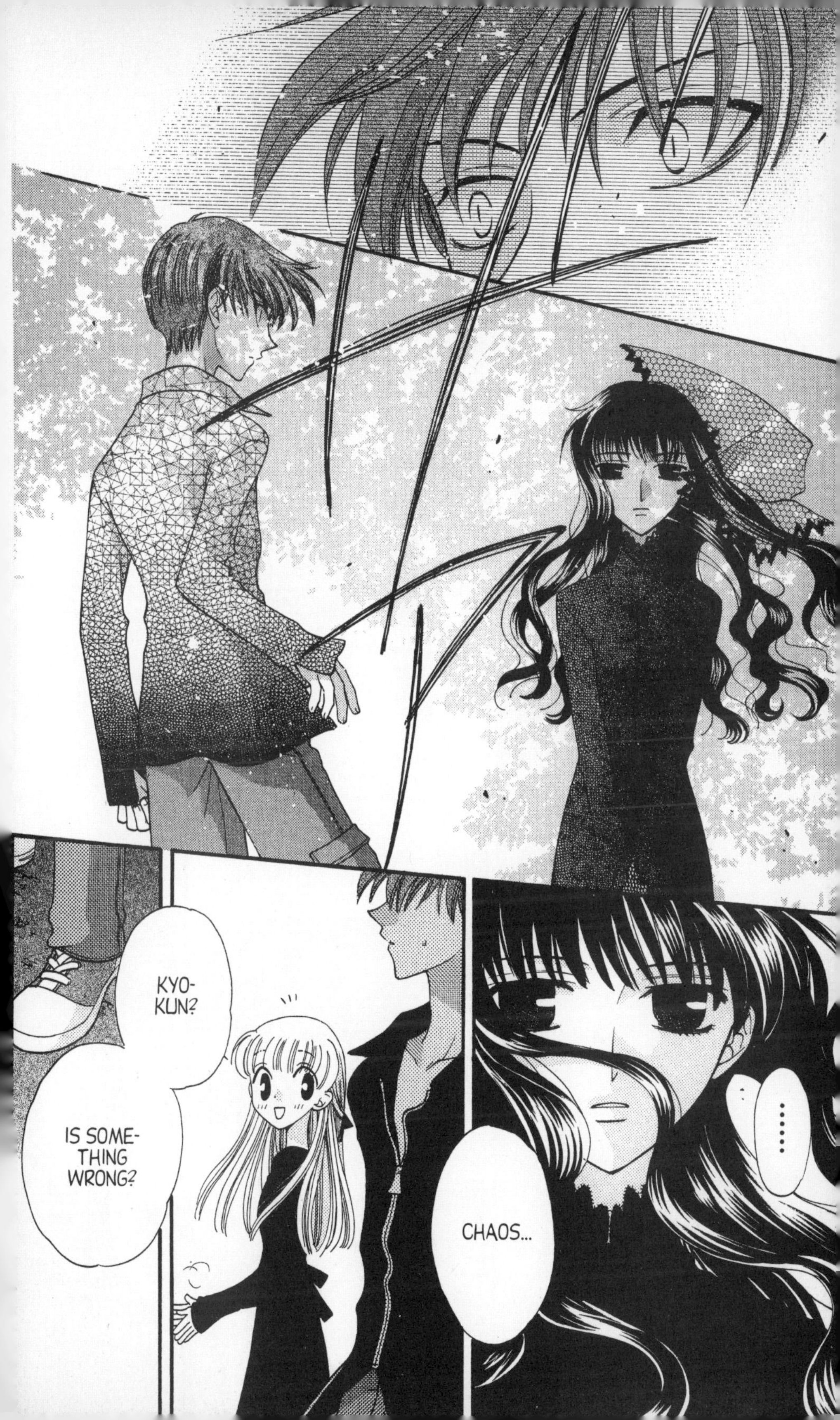
......
CHAOS...
KYO-KUN?
IS SOME-THING WRONG?

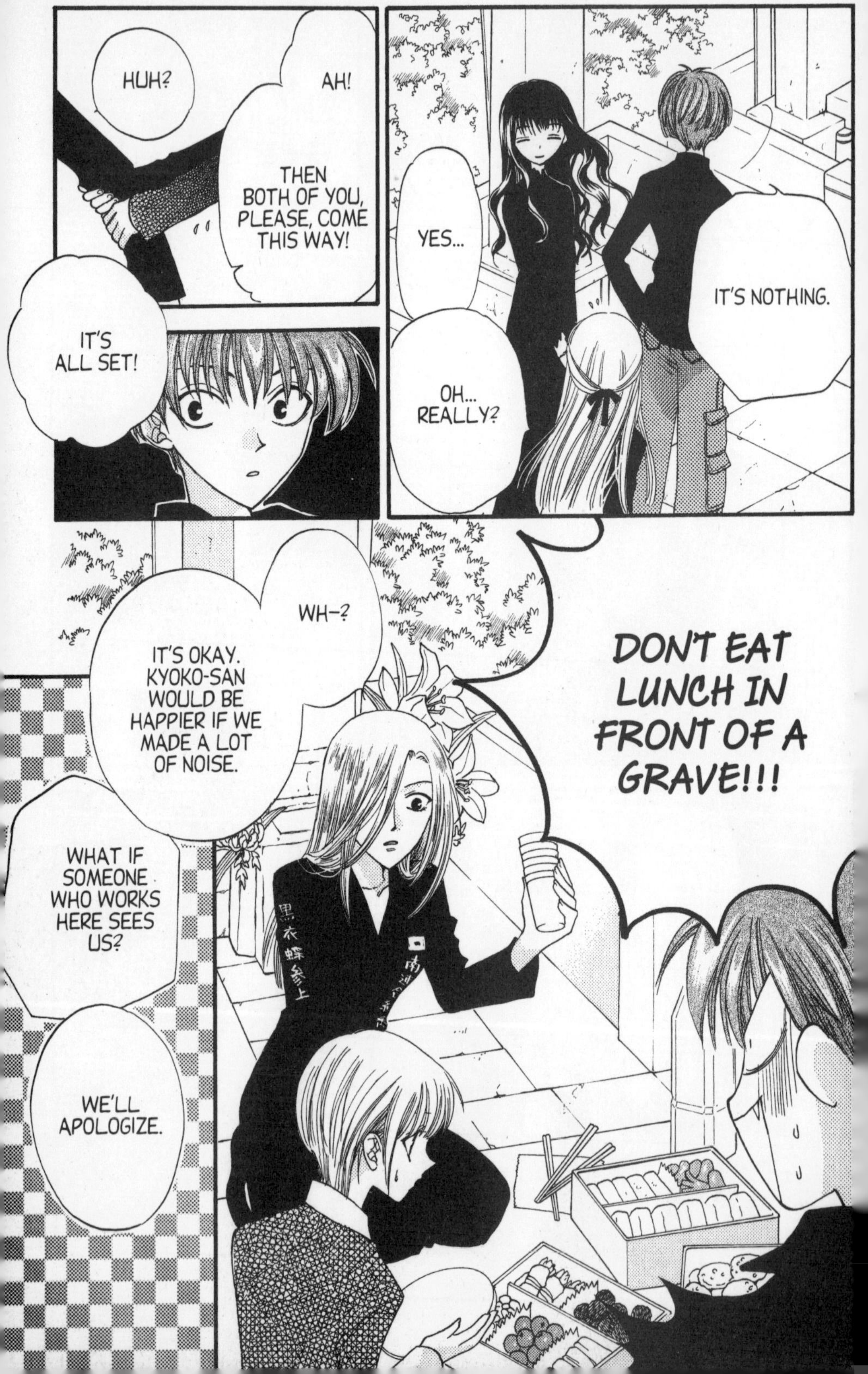
YES...
IT'S NOTHING.
OH... REALLY?
AH!
THEN BOTH OF YOU, PLEASE, COME THIS WAY!
HUH?
IT'S ALL SET!
DON'T EAT LUNCH IN FRONT OF A GRAVE!!!
WH-?
IT'S OKAY. KYOKO-SAN WOULD BE HAPPIER IF WE MADE A LOT OF NOISE.
WHAT IF SOMEONE WHO WORKS HERE SEES US?
WE'LL APOLOGIZE.

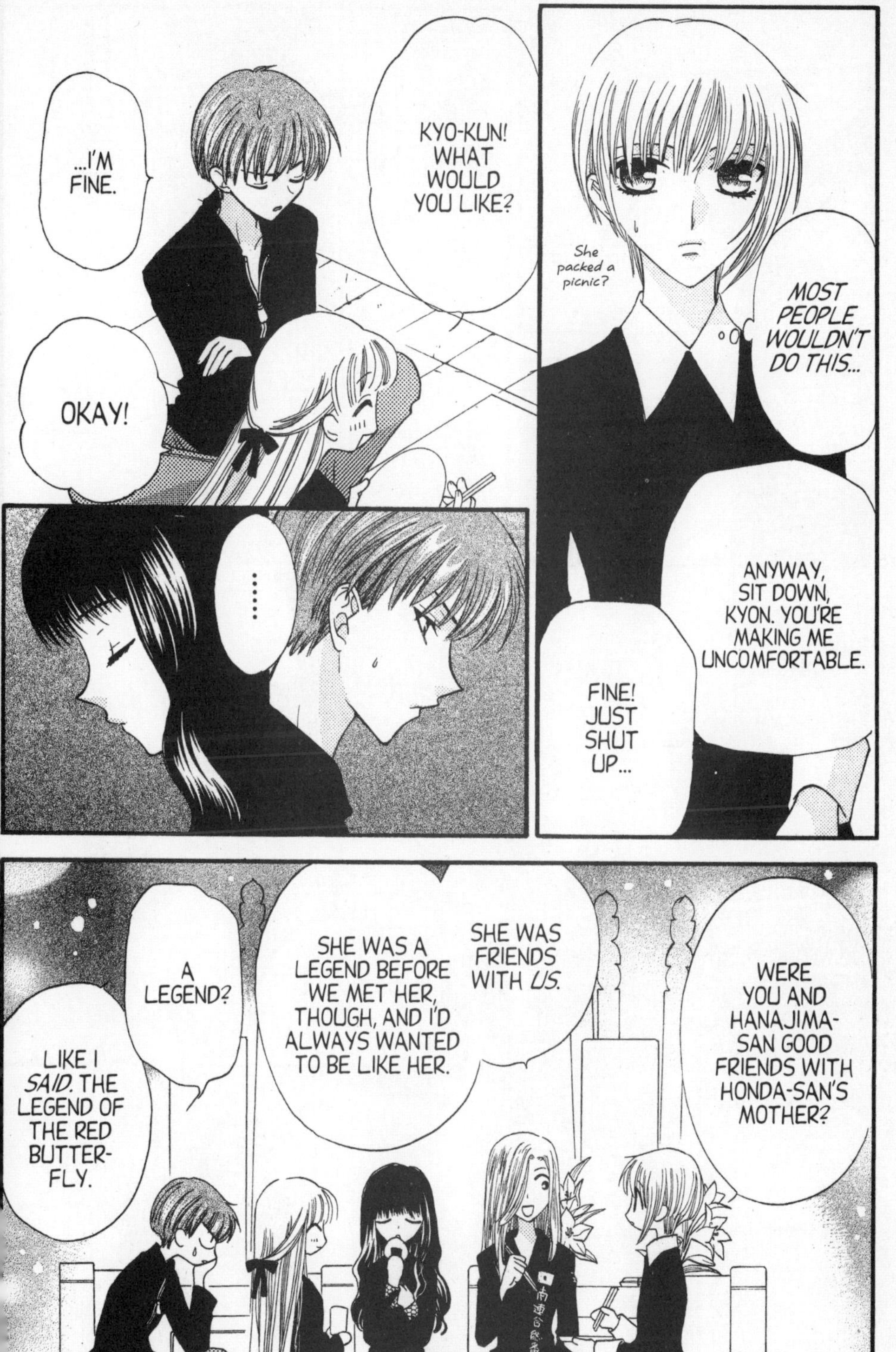
She packed a picnic?
MOST PEOPLE WOULDN'T DO THIS...
ANYWAY, SIT DOWN, KYON. YOU'RE MAKING ME UNCOMFORTABLE.
FINE! JUST SHUT UP...
KYO-KUN! WHAT WOULD YOU LIKE?
...I'M FINE.
OKAY!
......
WERE YOU AND HANAJIMA-SAN GOOD FRIENDS WITH HONDA-SAN'S MOTHER?
SHE WAS FRIENDS WITH *US*.
SHE WAS A LEGEND BEFORE WE MET HER, THOUGH, AND I'D ALWAYS WANTED TO BE LIKE HER.
A LEGEND?
LIKE I *SAID*. THE LEGEND OF THE RED BUTTERFLY.

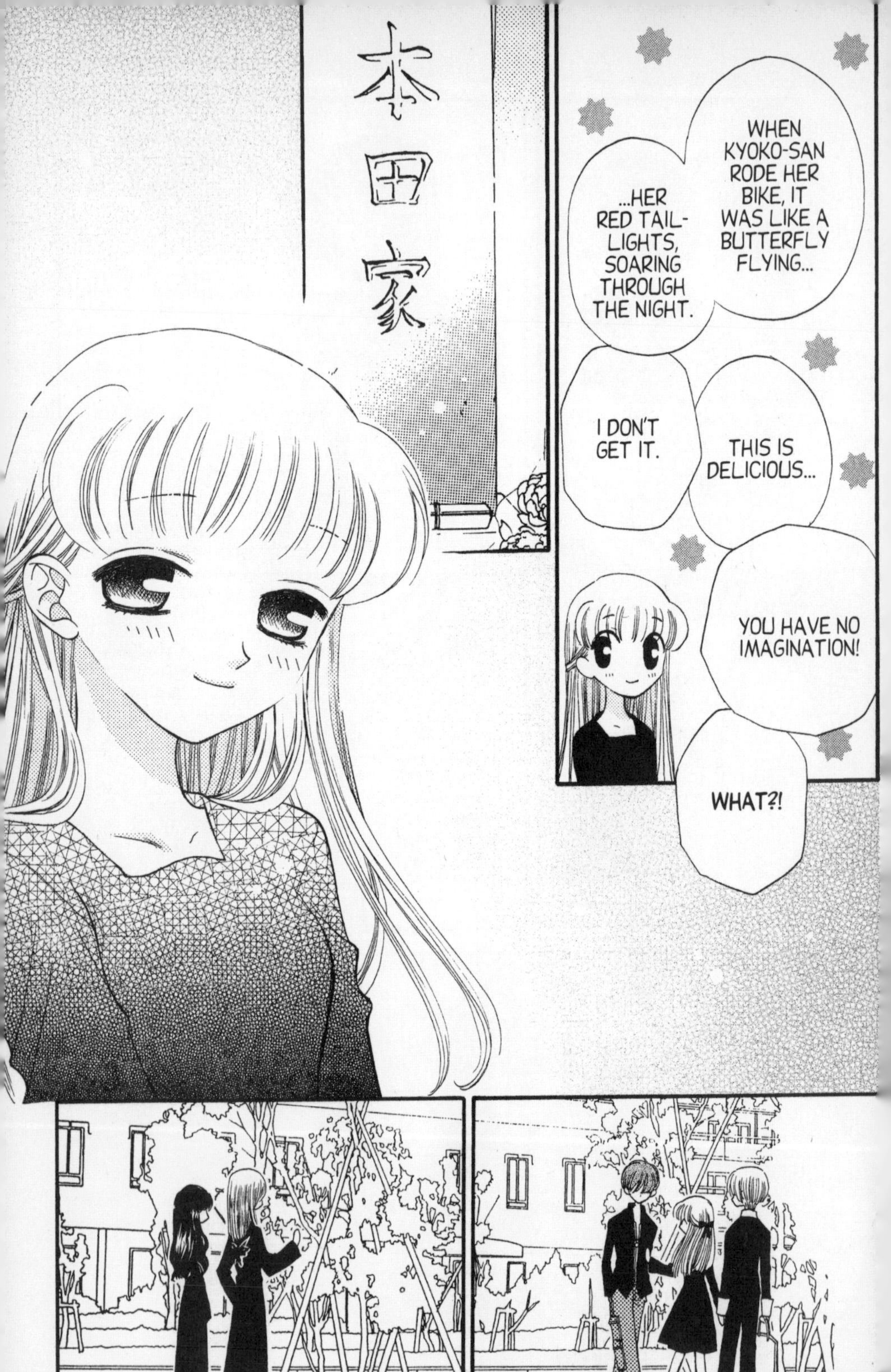
WHEN KYOKO-SAN RODE HER BIKE, IT WAS LIKE A BUTTERFLY FLYING...
...HER RED TAIL-LIGHTS, SOARING THROUGH THE NIGHT.
THIS IS DELICIOUS...
I DON'T GET IT.
YOU HAVE NO IMAGINATION!
WHAT?!
本田家

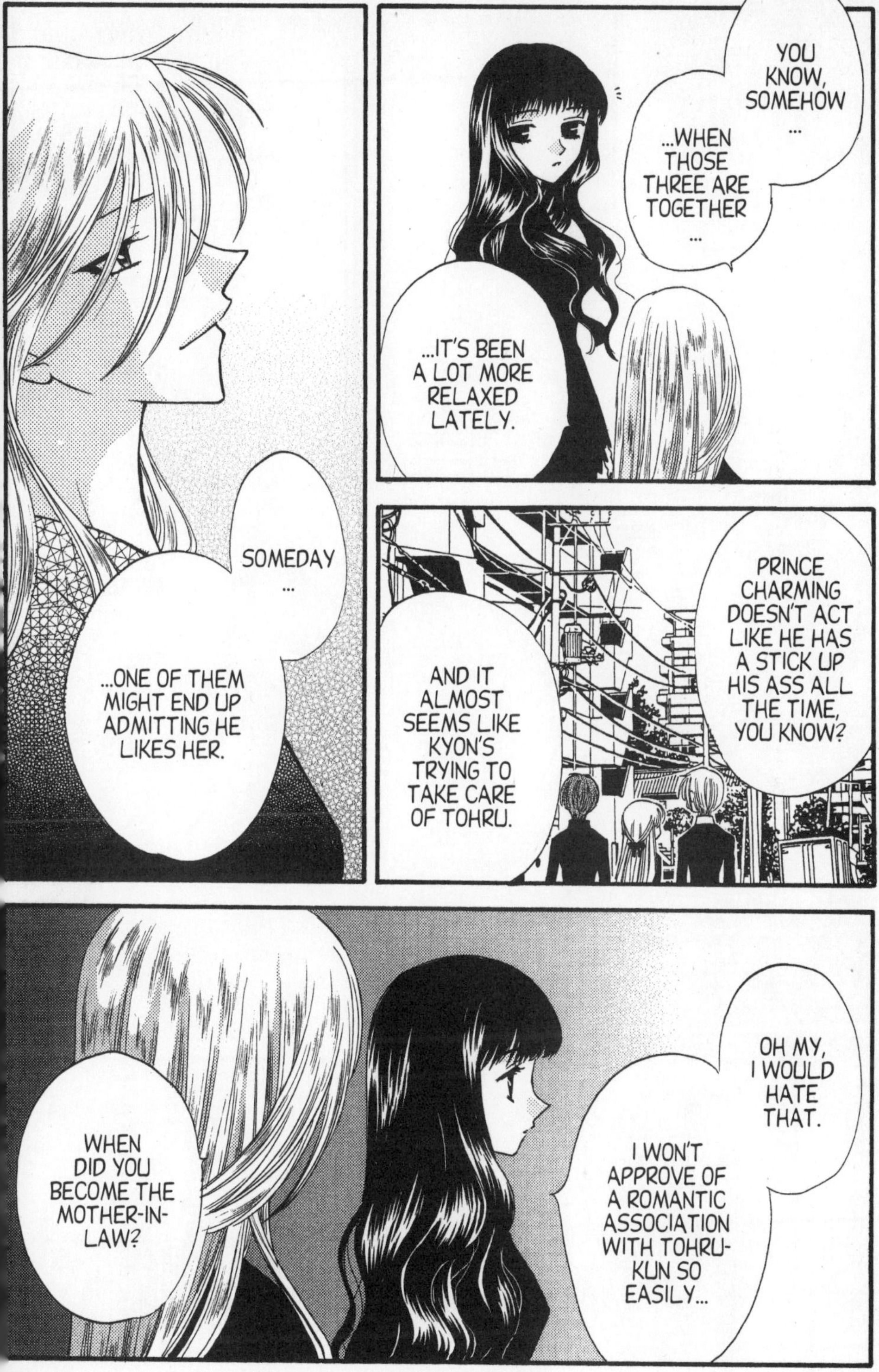
YOU KNOW, SOMEHOW ...
...WHEN THOSE THREE ARE TOGETHER ...
...IT'S BEEN A LOT MORE RELAXED LATELY.
PRINCE CHARMING DOESN'T ACT LIKE HE HAS A STICK UP HIS ASS ALL THE TIME, YOU KNOW?
AND IT ALMOST SEEMS LIKE KYON'S TRYING TO TAKE CARE OF TOHRU.
SOMEDAY ...
...ONE OF THEM MIGHT END UP ADMITTING HE LIKES HER.
OH MY, I WOULD HATE THAT.
I WON'T APPROVE OF A ROMANTIC ASSOCIATION WITH TOHRU-KUN SO EASILY...
WHEN DID YOU BECOME THE MOTHER-IN-LAW?

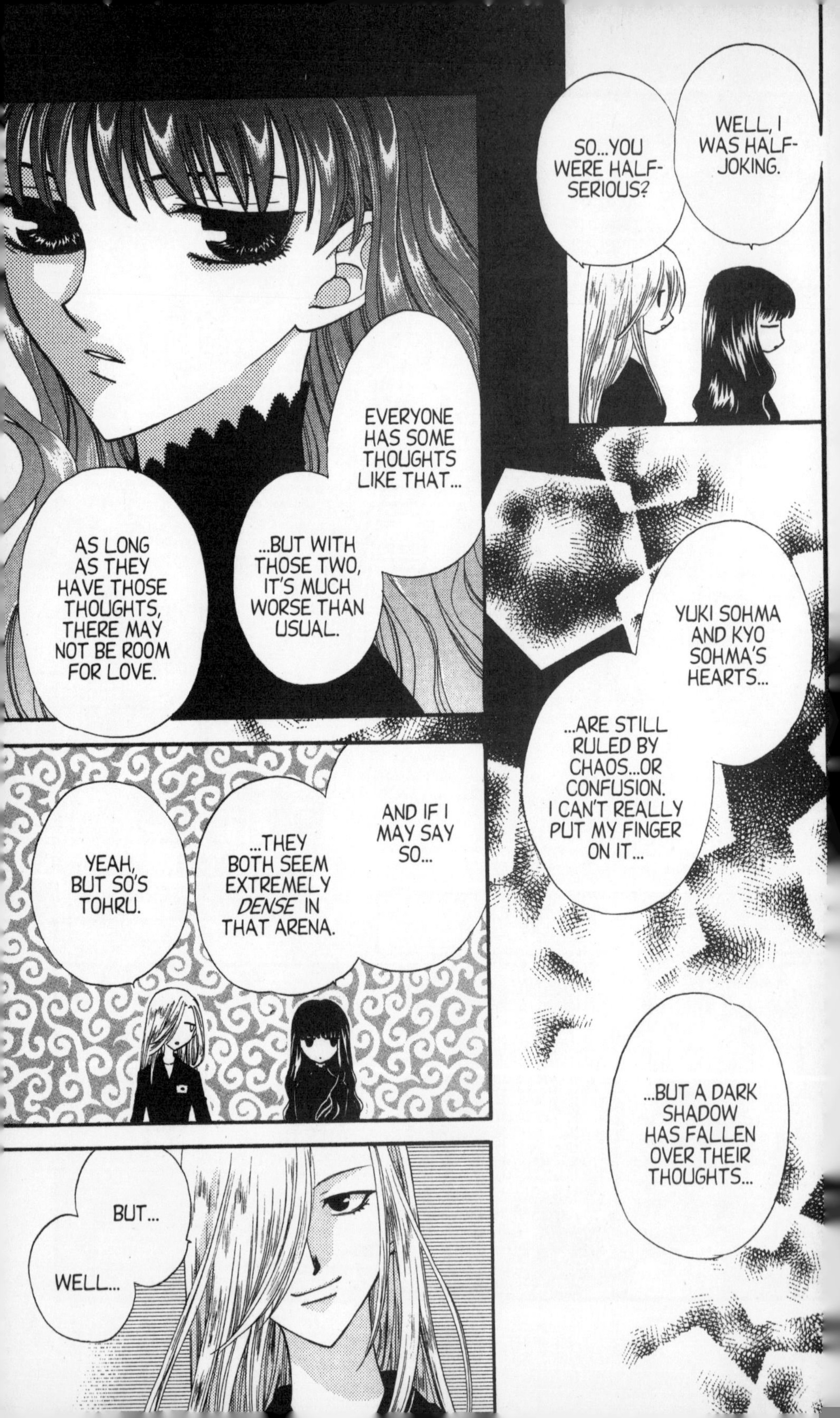
WELL, I WAS HALF-JOKING.
SO...YOU WERE HALF-SERIOUS?
YUKI SOHMA AND KYO SOHMA'S HEARTS...
...ARE STILL RULED BY CHAOS...OR CONFUSION. I CAN'T REALLY PUT MY FINGER ON IT...
...BUT A DARK SHADOW HAS FALLEN OVER THEIR THOUGHTS...
EVERYONE HAS SOME THOUGHTS LIKE THAT...
...BUT WITH THOSE TWO, IT'S MUCH WORSE THAN USUAL.
AS LONG AS THEY HAVE THOSE THOUGHTS, THERE MAY NOT BE ROOM FOR LOVE.
AND IF I MAY SAY SO...
...THEY BOTH SEEM EXTREMELY *DENSE* IN THAT ARENA.
YEAH, BUT SO'S TOHRU.
BUT...
WELL...

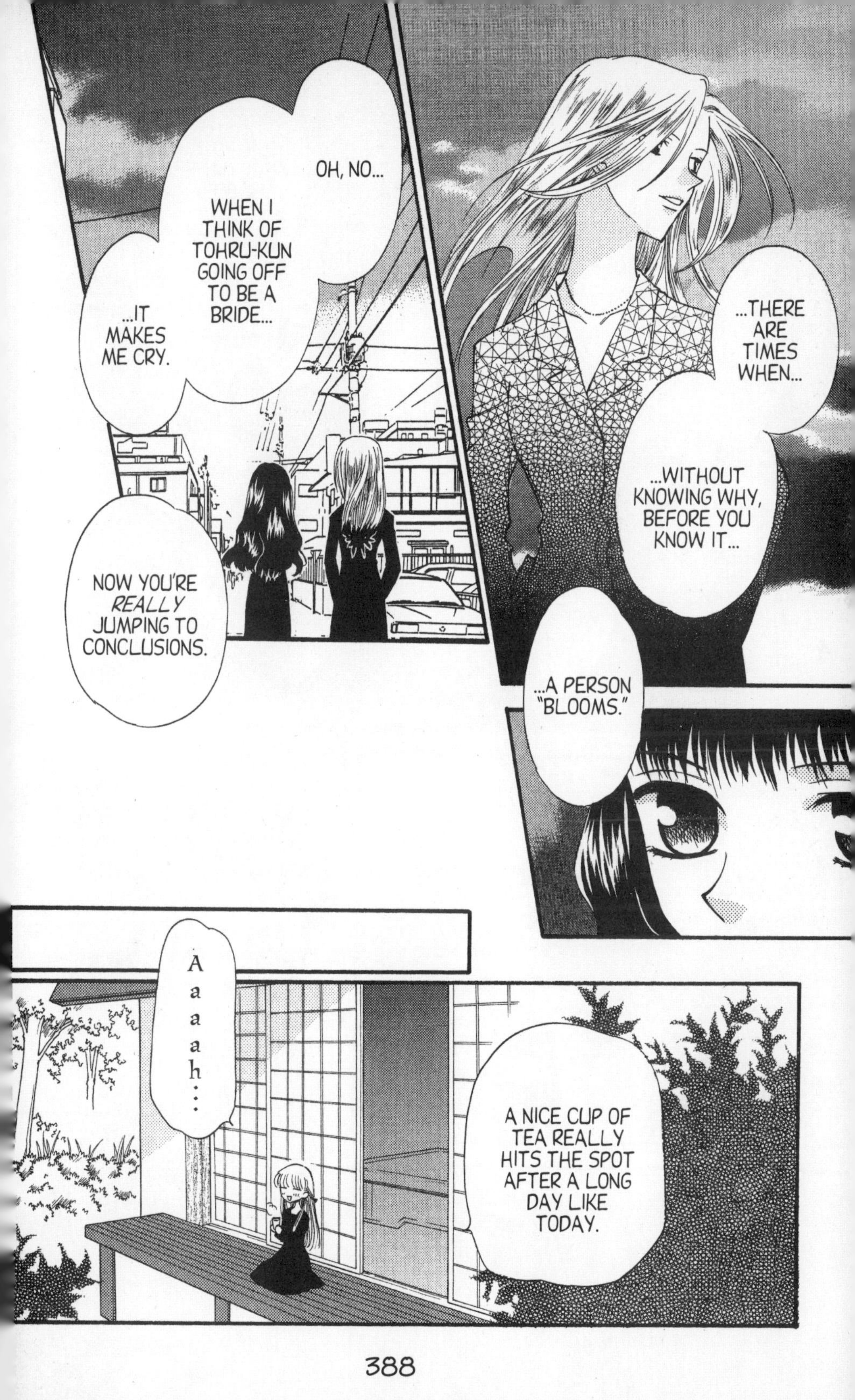
...THERE ARE TIMES WHEN...
...WITHOUT KNOWING WHY, BEFORE YOU KNOW IT...
...A PERSON "BLOOMS."
OH, NO...
WHEN I THINK OF TOHRU-KUN GOING OFF TO BE A BRIDE...
...IT MAKES ME CRY.
NOW YOU'RE *REALLY* JUMPING TO CONCLUSIONS.
Aaaah...
A NICE CUP OF TEA REALLY HITS THE SPOT AFTER A LONG DAY LIKE TODAY.

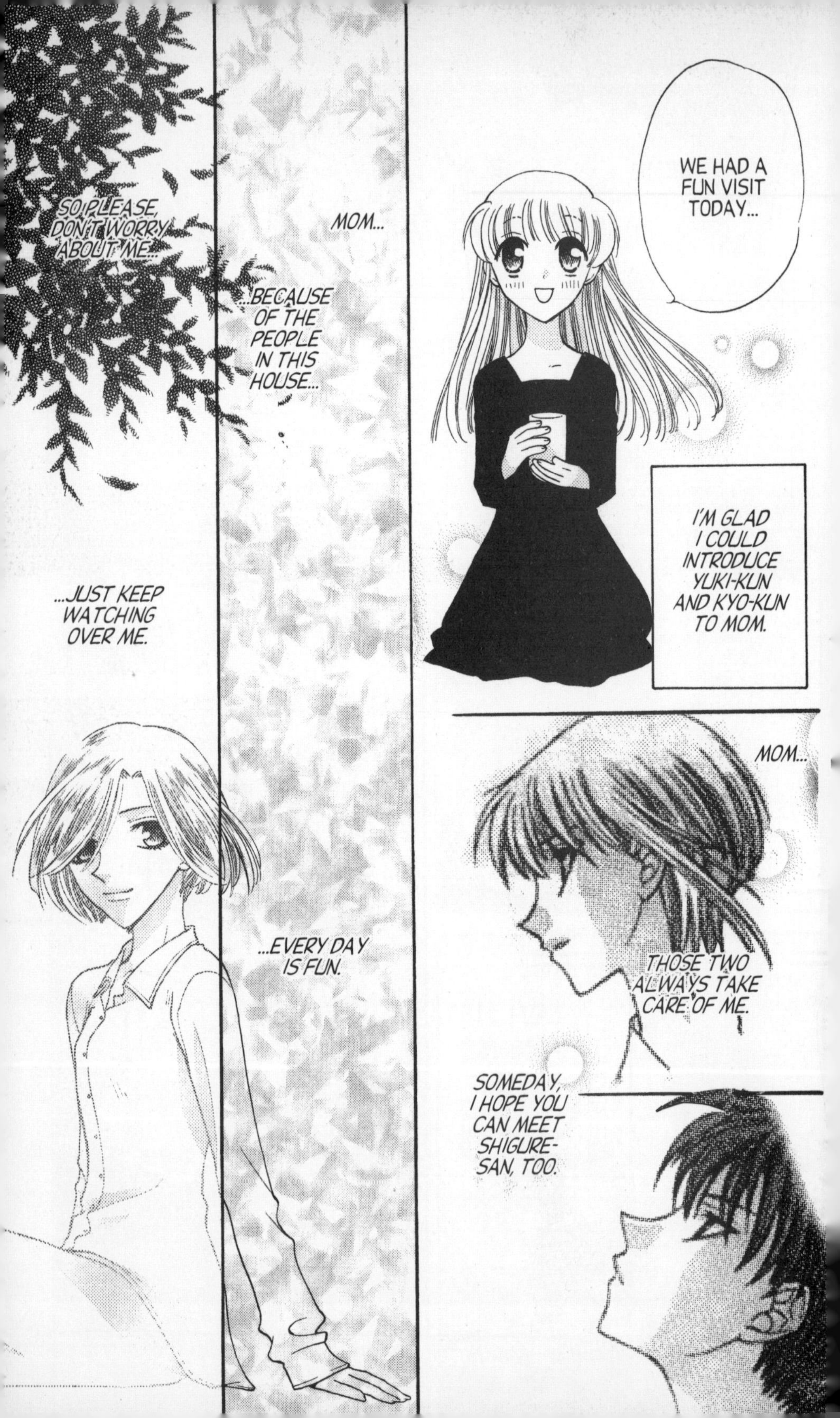
WE HAD A FUN VISIT TODAY...
I'M GLAD I COULD INTRODUCE YUKI-KUN AND KYO-KUN TO MOM.
MOM...
THOSE TWO ALWAYS TAKE CARE OF ME.
SOMEDAY, I HOPE YOU CAN MEET SHIGURE-SAN, TOO.
MOM...
...BECAUSE OF THE PEOPLE IN THIS HOUSE...
...EVERY DAY IS FUN.
SO PLEASE, DON'T WORRY ABOUT ME...
...JUST KEEP WATCHING OVER ME.

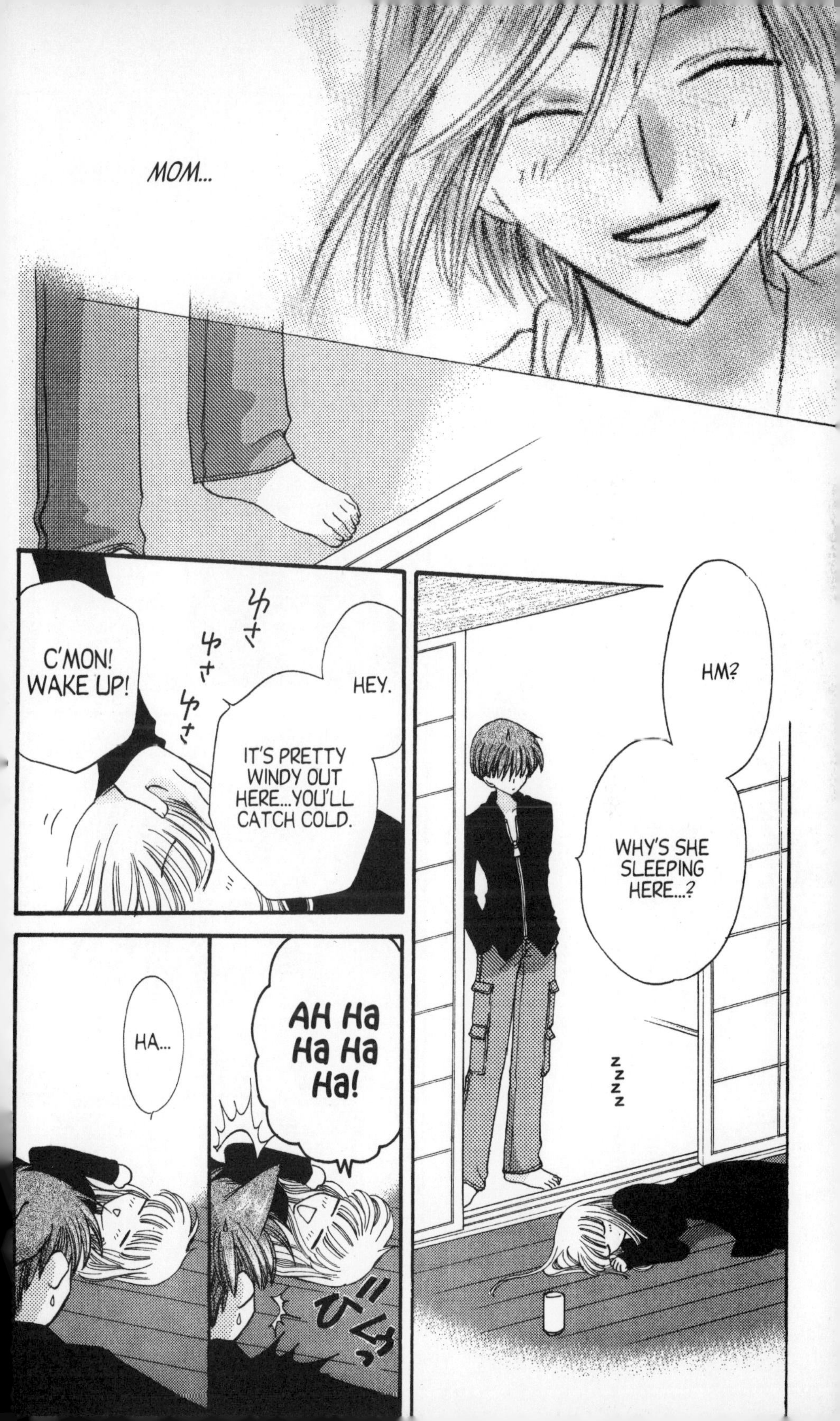
MOM...
HM?
WHY'S SHE SLEEPING HERE...?
ZZZZ
HEY.
IT'S PRETTY WINDY OUT HERE...YOU'LL CATCH COLD.
ゆさゆさゆさ
C'MON! WAKE UP!
AH Ha Ha Ha Ha!
ぴくっ
HA...

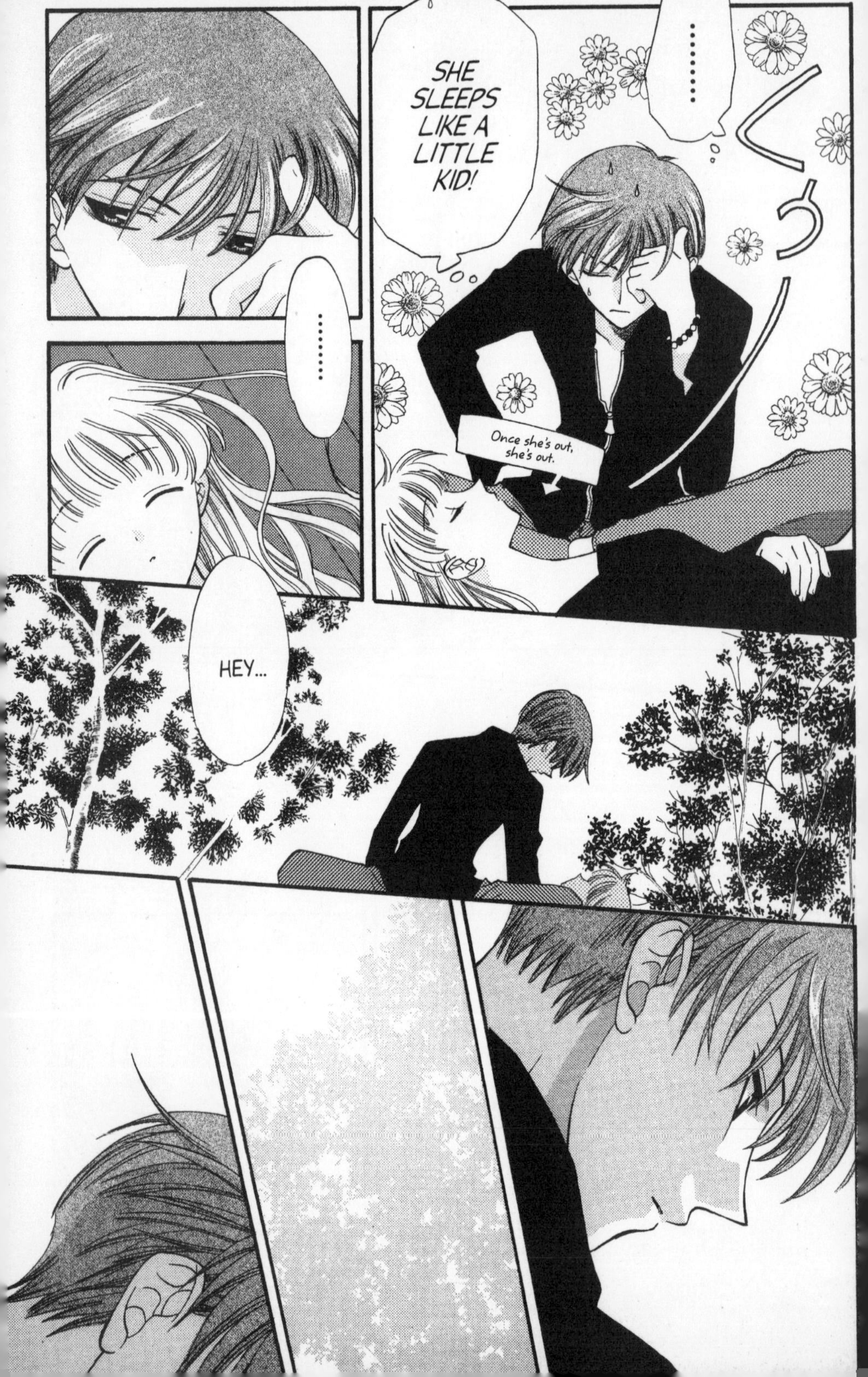
......
SHE SLEEPS LIKE A LITTLE KID!
Once she's out, she's out.
......
HEY...

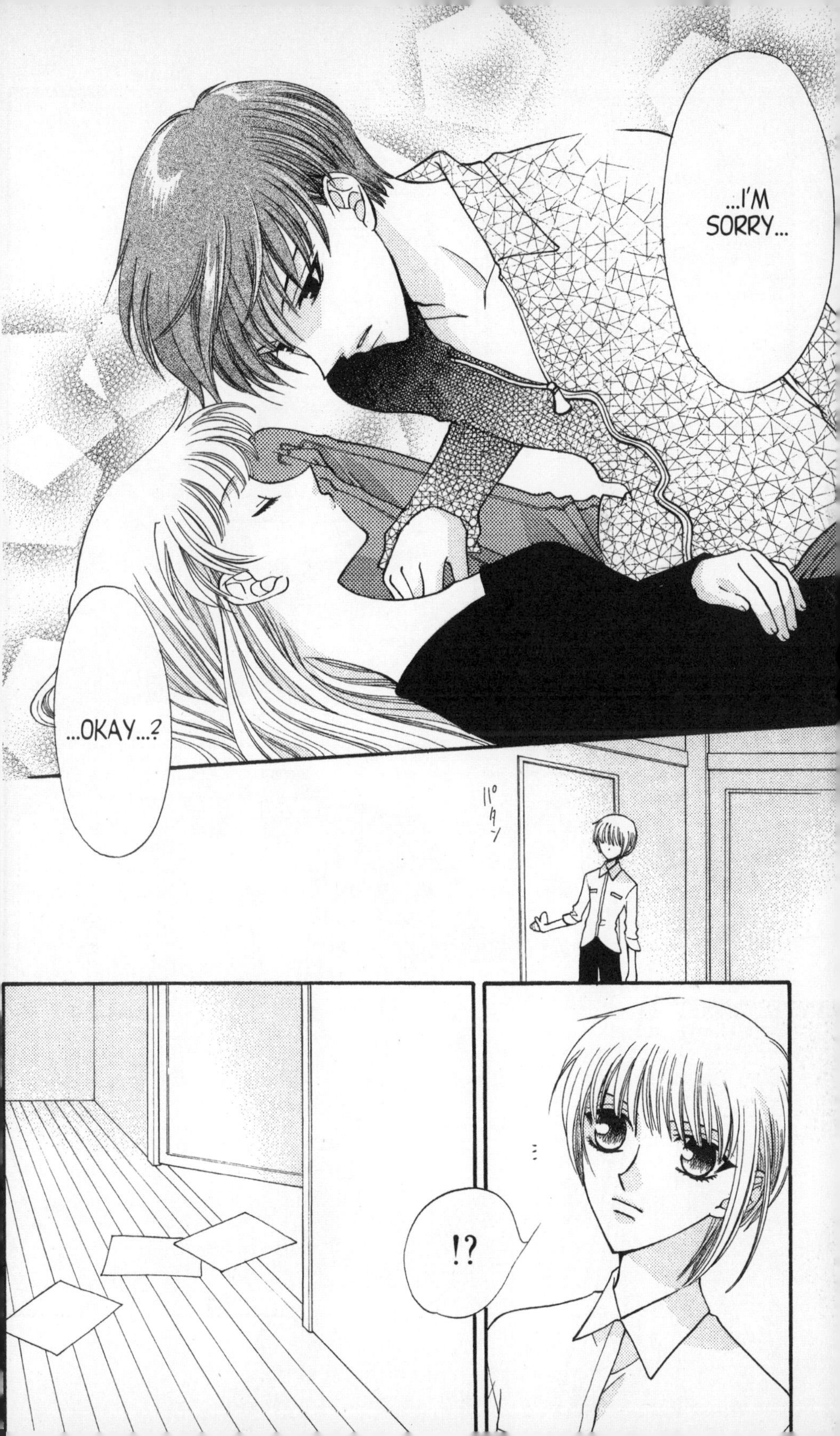
...I'M SORRY...
...OKAY...?
パタン
!?

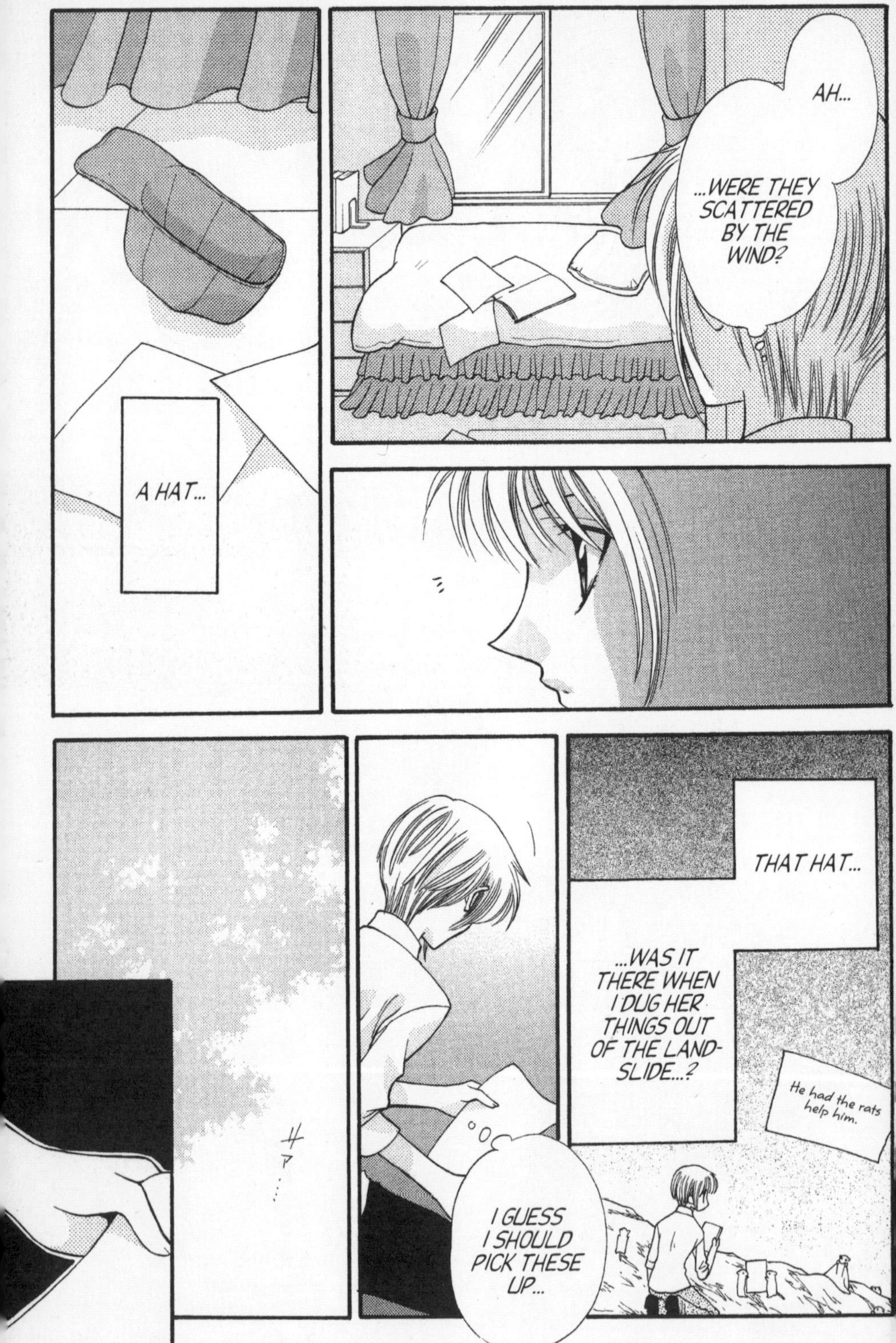
AH...
...WERE THEY SCATTERED BY THE WIND?
A HAT...
THAT HAT...
...WAS IT THERE WHEN I DUG HER THINGS OUT OF THE LAND-SLIDE...?
He had the rats help him.
I GUESS I SHOULD PICK THESE UP...
ハァ...

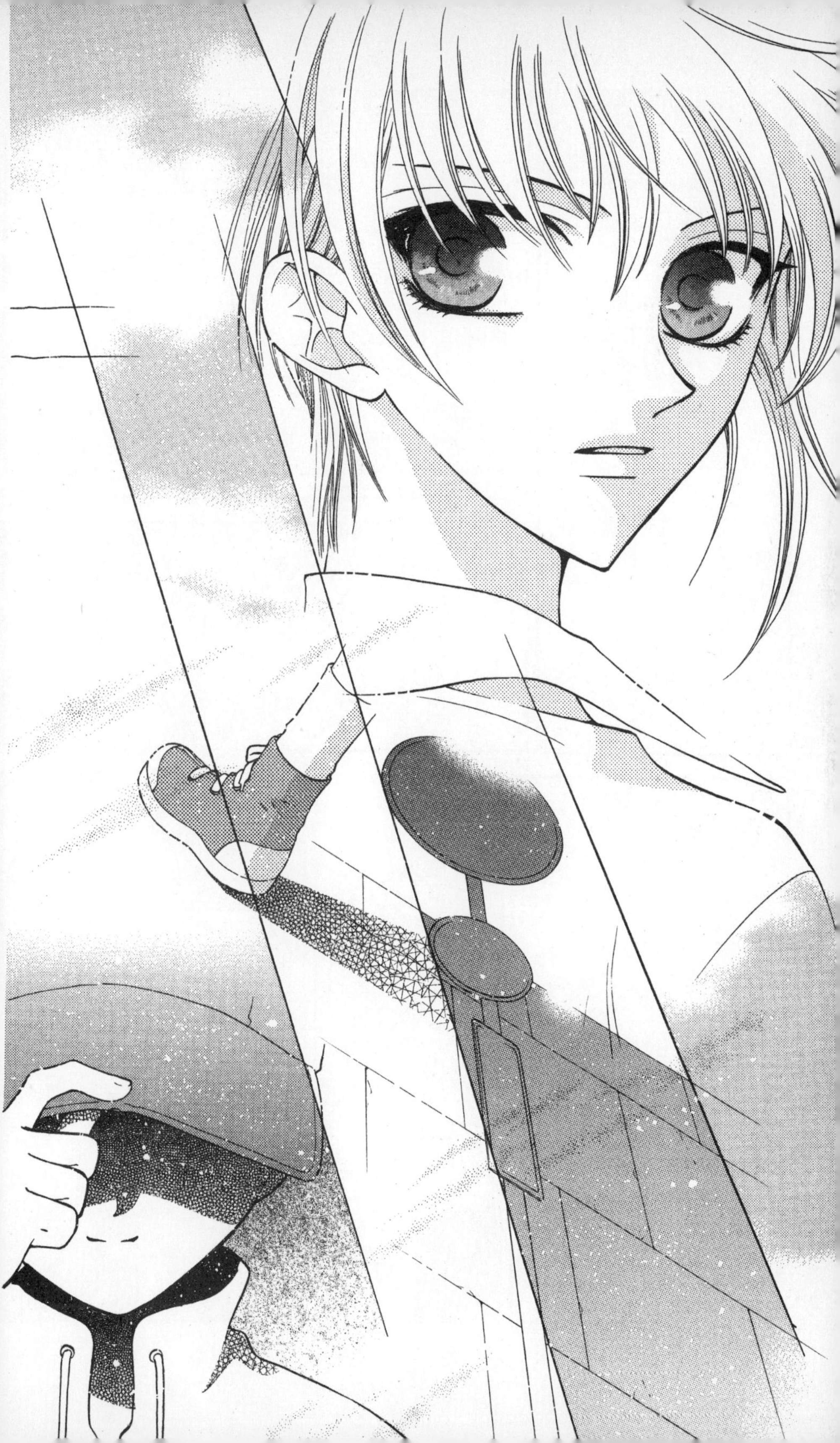

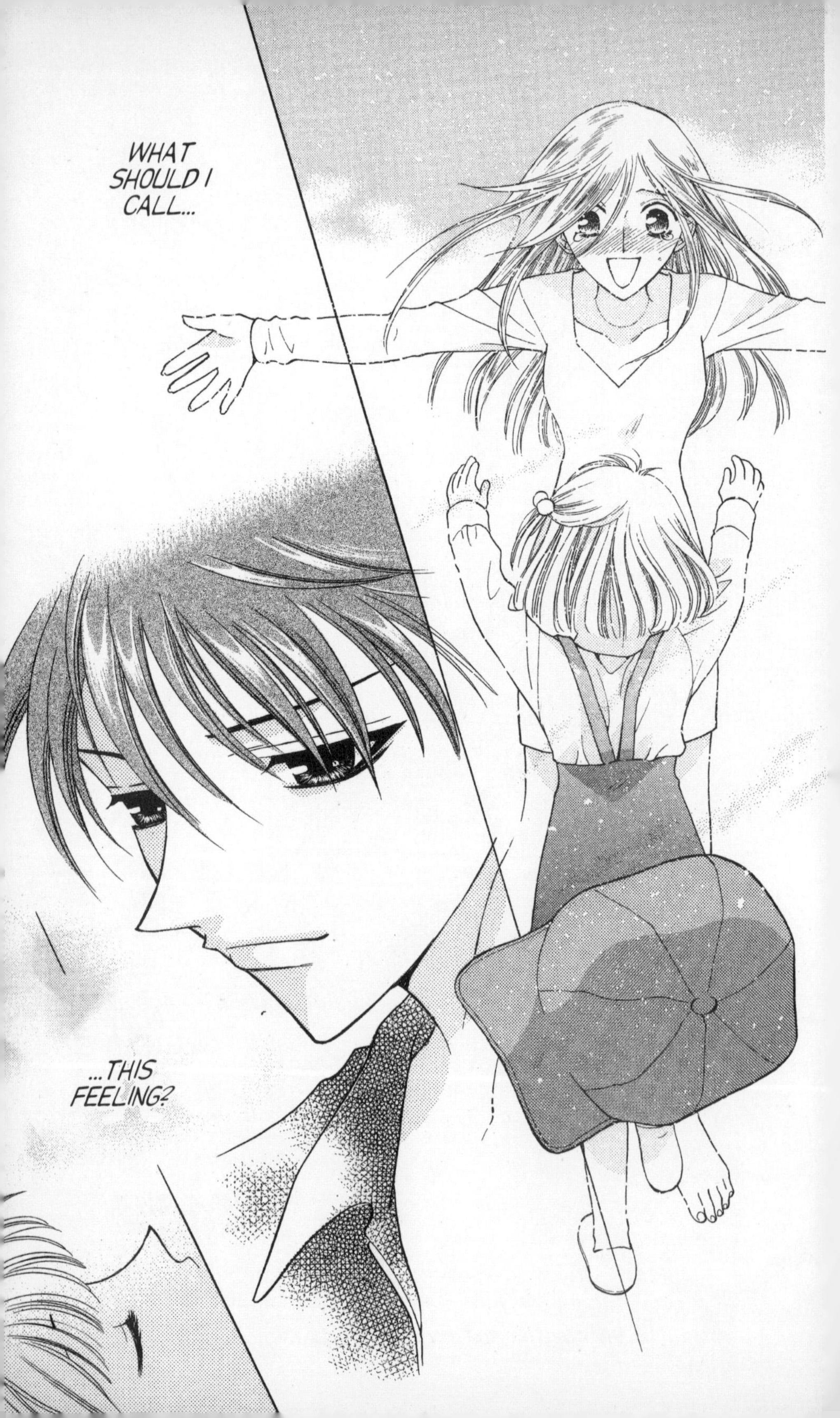
WHAT SHOULD I CALL...
...THIS FEELING?

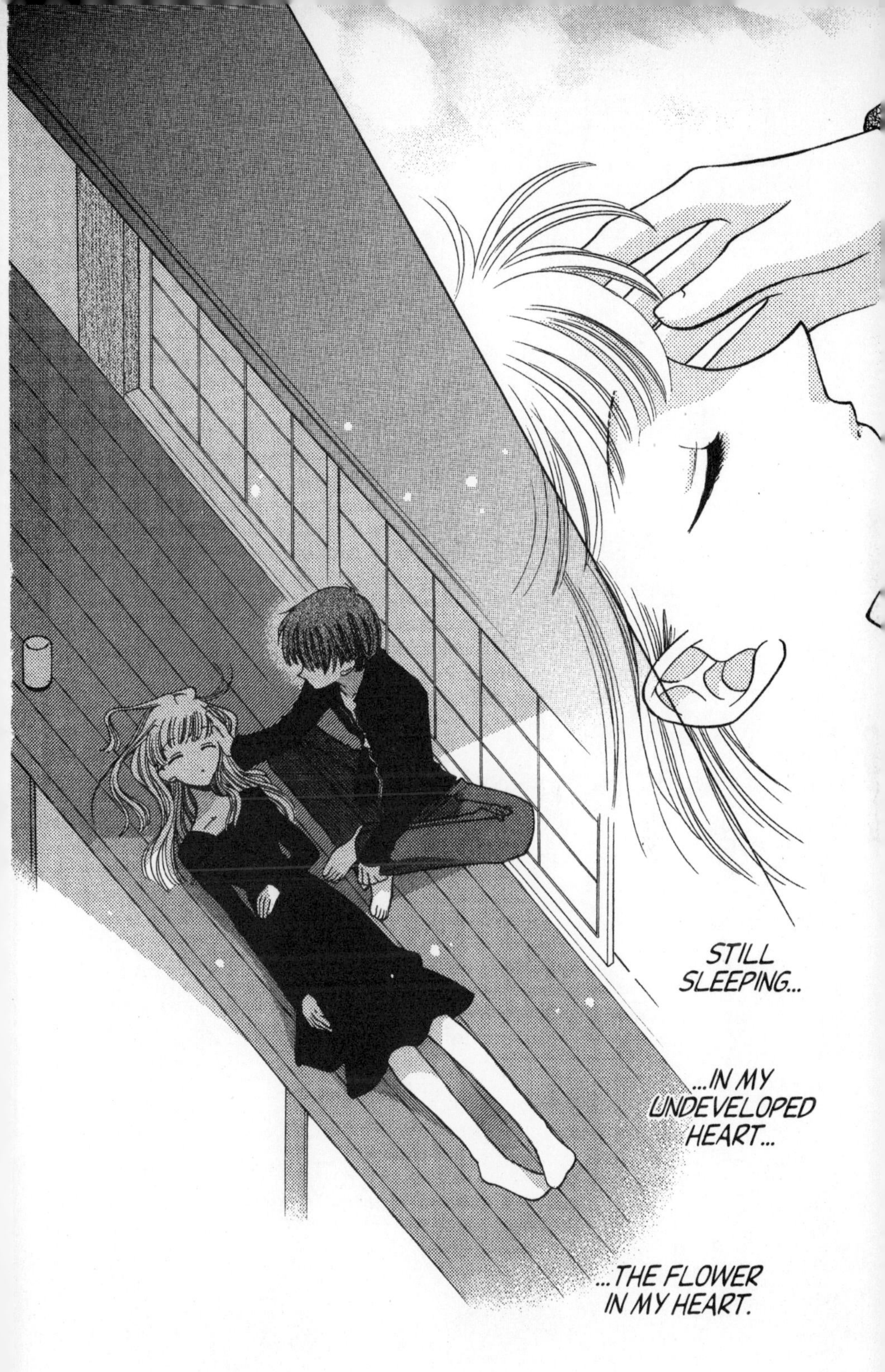
STILL SLEEPING...
...IN MY UNDEVELOPED HEART...
...THE FLOWER IN MY HEART.

To be continued in volume 5...

SHIGURE-SAN, SHIGURE-SAN-- IT'S **TERRIBLE!**

THEY SAY THEY'RE GOING TO MAKE A CD DRAMA ABOUT US!!

AND IT'S GOING TO BE AN ORIGINAL STORY...

...BUT WHAT KIND OF STORY COULD IT POSSIBLY *BE*?!

HA HA HA! WELL, OBVIOUSLY, TOHRU-KUN...

...IT WILL HAVE LOTS...

...of lively, vivacious high school girls.

YOU'RE COMPLETELY WRONG, SHIGURE-SAN!

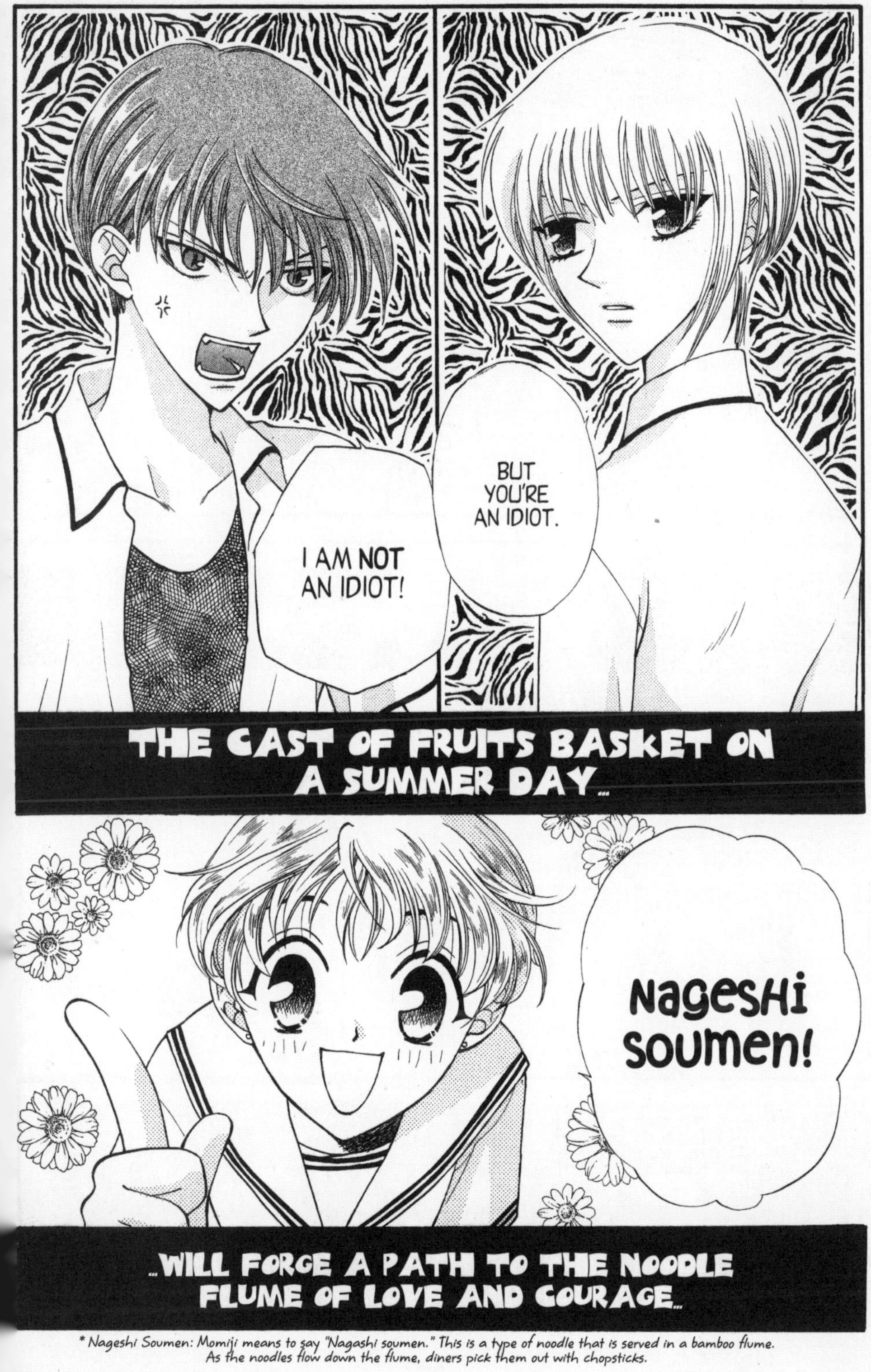
BUT YOU'RE AN IDIOT.
I AM NOT AN IDIOT!
THE CAST OF FRUITS BASKET ON A SUMMER DAY...
NAGESHI SOUMEN!
...WILL FORGE A PATH TO THE NOODLE FLUME OF LOVE AND COURAGE...

* Nageshi Soumen: Momiji means to say "Nagashi soumen." This is a type of noodle that is served in a bamboo flume. As the noodles flow down the flume, diners pick them out with chopsticks.

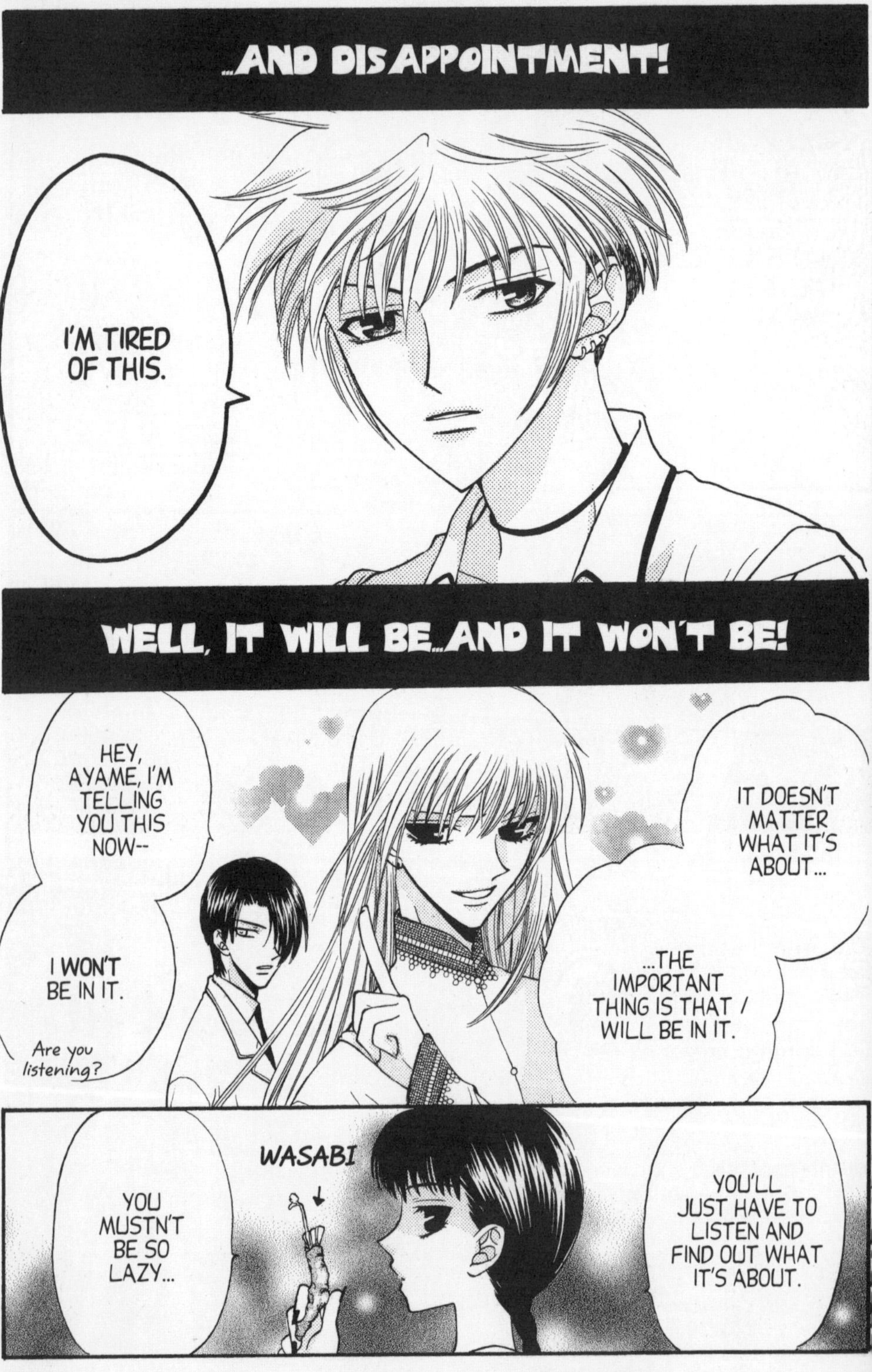
...AND DISAPPOINTMENT!
I'M TIRED OF THIS.
WELL, IT WILL BE...AND IT WON'T BE!
IT DOESN'T MATTER WHAT IT'S ABOUT...
...THE IMPORTANT THING IS THAT I WILL BE IN IT.
HEY, AYAME, I'M TELLING YOU THIS NOW--
I WON'T BE IN IT.
Are you listening?
YOU'LL JUST HAVE TO LISTEN AND FIND OUT WHAT IT'S ABOUT.
WASABI
YOU MUSTN'T BE SO LAZY...

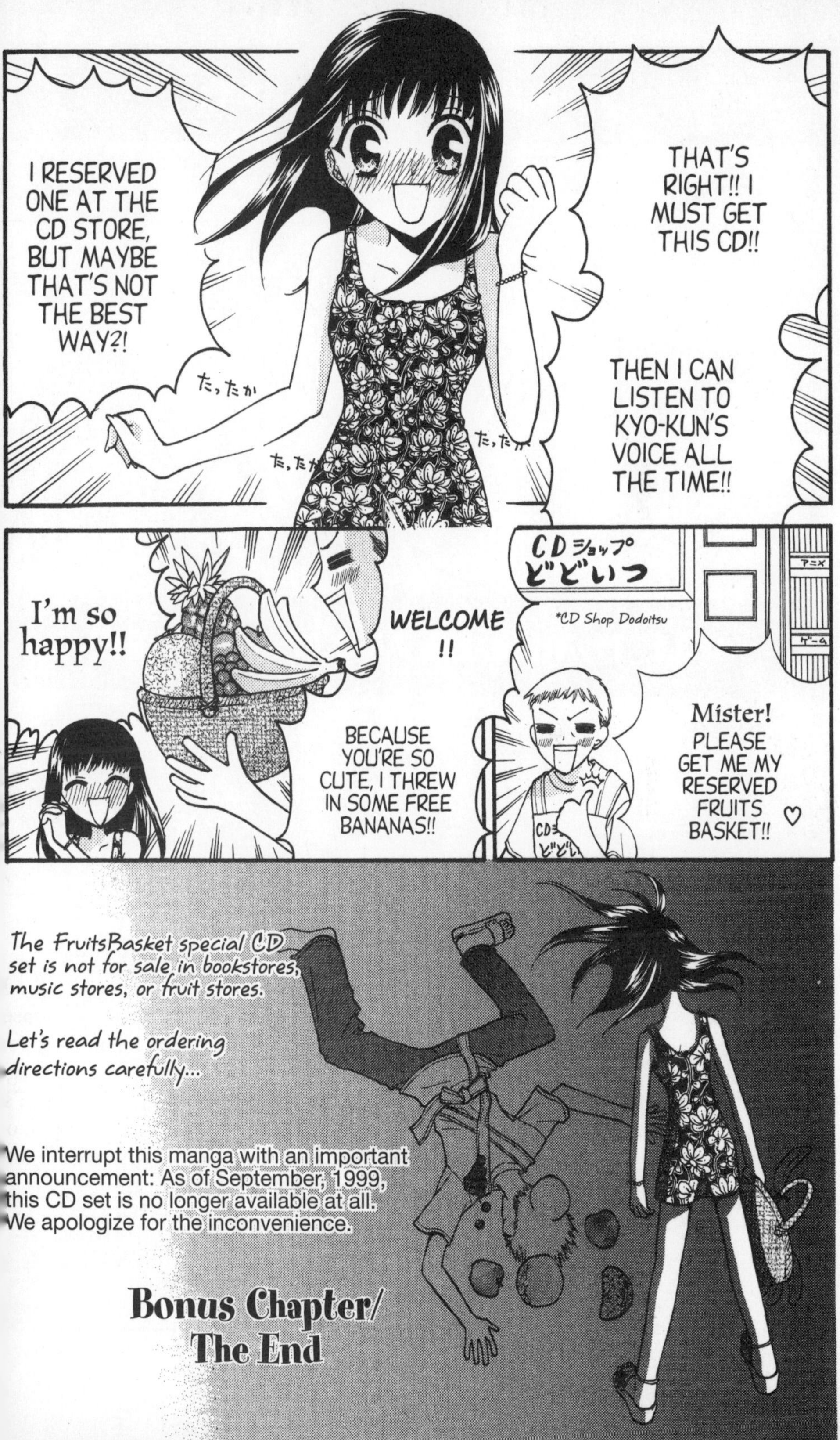
THAT'S RIGHT!! I MUST GET THIS CD!!
I RESERVED ONE AT THE CD STORE, BUT MAYBE THAT'S NOT THE BEST WAY?!
THEN I CAN LISTEN TO KYO-KUN'S VOICE ALL THE TIME!!
たったか
たったか
たったか
CD ショップ どどいつ
*CD Shop Dodoitsu
アニメ
ゲーム
Mister! PLEASE GET ME MY RESERVED FRUITS BASKET!! ♡
CD ショップ どどいつ
WELCOME!!
I'm so happy!!
BECAUSE YOU'RE SO CUTE, I THREW IN SOME FREE BANANAS!!
The FruitsBasket special CD set is not for sale in bookstores, music stores, or fruit stores.
Let's read the ordering directions carefully...
We interrupt this manga with an important announcement: As of September, 1999, this CD set is no longer available at all. We apologize for the inconvenience.
Bonus Chapter/ The End

Next time in...

Fruits Basket
Ultimate Edition

Secrets & Lies...

It's been raining for days on end and Tohru can't help worrying about Kyo's crankiness. On a particularly soggy day at the Sohma household, out of the rain steps Kyo's master! It is time for the Cat to learn the truth!! The drama is almost too much to bear in the 6th volume of the ever-popular Fruits Basket.

Enter the Tiger...

The Sohma household takes to the h for a vacation at their summerhouse However, the peaceful silence is de: ening, as Yuki and Kyo are once ag not on speaking terms. Will Tohru's klutzy kindness get the dueling duo back to their old cat-and-mouse ant once again?

Look for the *Fruits Basket Ultimate Edition* Volume 3 to hit stores in June 2008! Including color art!

Interview with Takaya-sensei
Part 2

bout Takaya-sensei's Hobbies

What kind of music and musical artists do you like?

ately I've been listening to a lot of video game music. Songs, too. I like ematsu-san and Hikaruda-san's music. I like how the video game music rfectly matches the world in the game. That's wonderful, but when I listen the battle music it makes me want to fight, so sometimes I do and that gets e in trouble (ha ha!).

) What movies and TV shows do you like?

ese are old movies but...*Field of Dreams* and *Laputa: Castle in the Sky*. on't watch much TV. Sometimes I think I should watch, but...It just gets in e way, like when I need to be working on my manga.

) You often talk about video games in your freetalks. What type of mes do you like?

retty much like any type of game, but I'm never very good at action ones.

Character sketches for Tsubasa o Motsumono

Character sketches for Geneimusou

12) Do you have a favorite game to recommend?
I like so many that it's hard to name just one. I'd recommend the *Sakura Tais*
series—that's really fun.

13) What do you think makes a good game?
I like it when games do stuff manga can't. Just like how there's stuff you can
only do in manga, there are things you can only do in video games. I think
games where you really feel it's a "game" are best.

14) Are there any game characters you really like?
I really love cute and strong girls with a bit of a dark side. I have more troub
finding male characters I like.

**15) Do you work on your webpage "Chotto Ippuku"(A Short Break) by
yourself?**
Yes, I do it myself. That's why it's never updated…
[editor's note: Her website is no longer active.]

16) What was the hardest part about making a webpage?
Hmm… Well, it was tough when I first started because I had nobody I could
discuss things with. Those were rough times, but now I have a lot of friends
can help me out.

About *Fruits Basket*

17) When and how did you come up with *Fruits Basket*?
I was slowly working on it in my mind as I was finishing up my last series, *Tsubasa wo motsu mono* (*Those with Wings*). But all the final details didn't come together until after "*Boku ga utauto anata ga warau kara*," (*Because When I Sing You Smile*) a one-shot I did before *Furuba* started. I kept thinking there wasn't enough time, but it all came to me inside my head. Tohru just appeared and said "Hello!" The rest came together pretty easily after that.

18) Were there any other title possibilities besides *Fruits Basket*?
There kind of were… Though I'm happy I chose *Fruits Basket*, it's easy to say and remember.

19) Why did you choose the Zodiac animals as a motif?
Basically, I like them a lot and assumed everyone else would, too. Japanese culture is captivating, right?

20) What's the most important thing when creating the plot or doing the rough sketches?
The pacing and dialog, and of course whether it's fun to read. You can't forget what's at the heart of making a reader laugh or cry.

21) In the works you do, the story and tone are often different, but they seem to share an underlying theme. What's your theme?
I'm happy to hear that, thank you very much. As long as I'm creating it, I don't think the underlying theme will ever change. (Actually, if it changed, then there would be no point…) But I don't think the theme needs to be put into *words*. It's something that the reader experiences for themselves. At least, that's my company line, but sometimes I think I'd like to be able to express it in words. (ha ha!)

Read the rest of the interview with Takaya-sensei in Volume 5!

Year of the Dog: Letting the Dogs Out

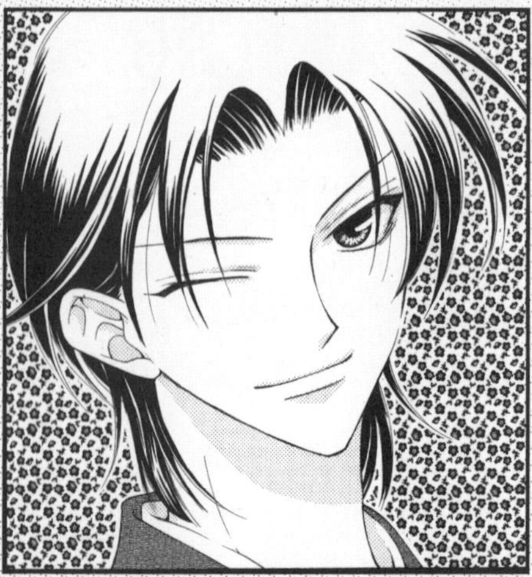

Dog

Years*: 1934, 1946, 1958, 1970, 1982, 1994, 2006, 2018, 2030
Positive Qualities: Honest, faithful, generous, studious, energetic
Negative Qualities: Quiet, cynical, stubborn, eccentric, pessimistic
Suitable Jobs: Writer, teacher, activist, politician, secret agent
Compatible With: Horse, Snake, Monkey, Boar
Must Avoid: Rooster, Ox, Sheep
Ruling Hours: 7 PM to 9 PM
Season: Fall
Ruling Month: October
Sign Direction: West-Northwest
Fixed Element: Metal
Corresponding Western Sign: Libra

Like Shigure, other Dogs are gifted with the ability to see people for who they really are. As, such, Dogs make for excellent advice-givers, as they can so easily see another's shortcomings and quickly point them out in a sensitive, objective and non-hurtful way.

Though Dogs are often cold emotionally and seem distant when in a crowd, they are actually very warm-hearted and love to make friends. Interestingly enough, friendships are often long-lasting, because Dogs always love to listen to others and the friends can never seem to get enough of a Dog's keen advice. Fittingly, a relationship with a Dog is much like the bond between a canine and its master—monogamous and loyal to the end.

Celebrity Dogs:
Alec Baldwin
Kirsten Dunst
Jennifer Lopez
Carrie Anne Moss
Uma Thurman
Snoopy

Possessing the best traits humanity has to offer, Dogs are natural-born leaders and inspire confidence in others. They seldom lose their temper when antagonized, but when they do, it is a surefire way to clear the air around them. These flare-ups can turn hardened rivals into allies as the harsh words being said are never used to air out the other person's dirty laundry or stab them in the back; it is simply a way toward a meeting of minds. Compromise also factors heavily into the Dogs' everyday life and personal dealings with people, as it often leads to much-needed respect and success in their chosen career. Though money is of little value to Dogs, they are never at a loss for finding ways to rake it in when they truly need it.

* Note: If you were born in January or early February, then chances are you are probably the animal of the preceding year. The only way to know for certain is to know on which day Chinese New Year's was held. Example: 1982 actually began on January 25, so anyone born from January 1 to January 24 is actually a Rooster.

Fans Basket

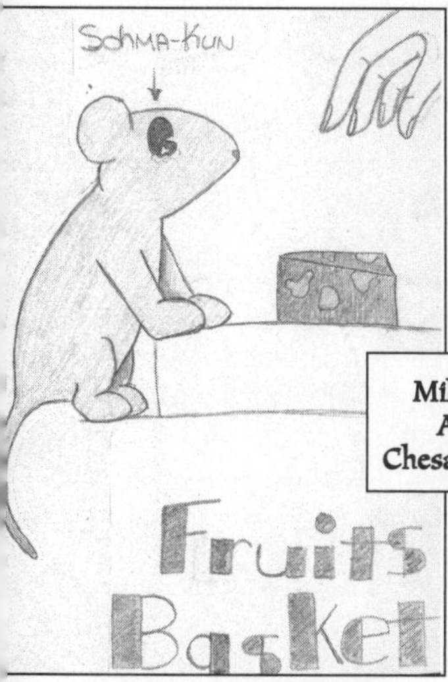
SOHMA-KUN
Fruits Basket

Millicent P.
Age 18
Chesapeake, VA

ur Rat-Yuki is SOOO adorable! only he weren't so freaked out by nfinement in small rooms, I'd love keep him as a pet! (Sorry, Sohma-n...I can't help myself)

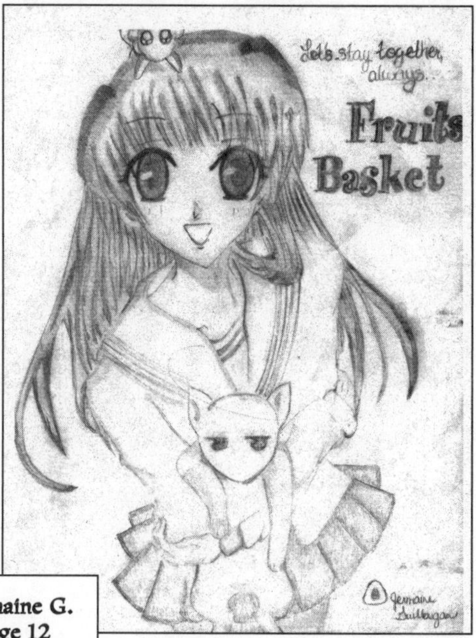
Let's stay together, always...
Fruits Basket

Jermaine G.
Age 12
Sanford, NC

Kawaii desu ne! Cute, isn't it?!

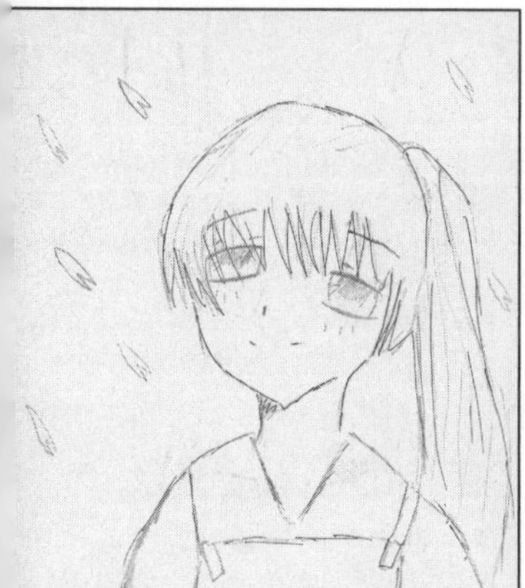

on B.
11
g, MI

Pretty Tohru! I can just imagine her enjoying a nice breeze after a day in the garden...

Rachael J.
Age 15
Clermont, FL

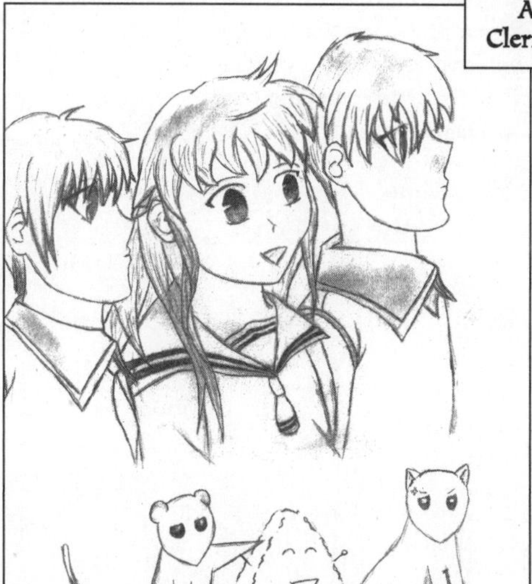

Three students boldly entering their second year... Nice work, Rachael!

Do you want to share your love for *Fruits Basket* with fans around the world? "Fans Basket" is taking submissions of fan art, poetry, cosplay photos, or any other Furuba fun you'd like to share!

How to submit:

1) Send your work via regular mail (NOT e-mail) to:

"Fans Basket"
c/o TOKYOPOP
5900 Wilshire Blvd.
Suite 2000
Los Angeles, CA 90036

2) All work should be in black-and-white and no larger than 8.5" x 11". (And try not to fold it too many times!)

3) Anything you send will not be returned. If you want to keep your original, it's fine to send us a copy.

4) Please include your full name, age, city and state for us to print with your work. If you'd rather us use a pen name, please include that, too.

5) IMPORTANT: If you're under the age of 18, you must have your parent's permission in order for us to print your work. Any submissions without a signed note of parental consent cannot be used.

6) For full details, please check out our website: http://www.tokyopop.com/aboutus/fanart.php

Disclaimer: Anything you send to us becomes the exclusive property of TOKYOPOP Inc. and, as we said before, will not be returned to you. We will have the right to print, reproduce, distribute, or modify the artwork for use in future volumes of Fruits Basket or on the web royalty-free.

Brandon W.
Age 31
Los Angeles, CA

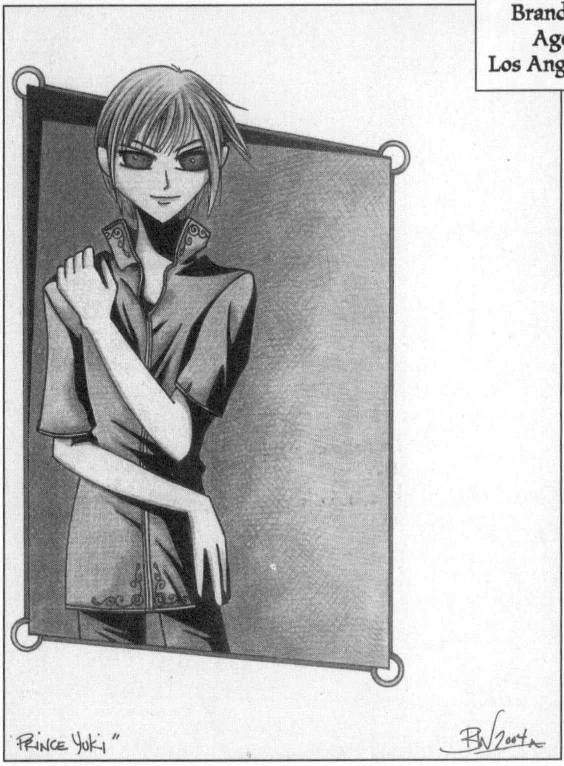
"PRINCE YUKI"
BW 2004

Prince Yuki man of mystery... Very nice. I wish everyc could see th one in color Thanks for sending us your work!

Wendy H.
Age 16
Las Vegas, N

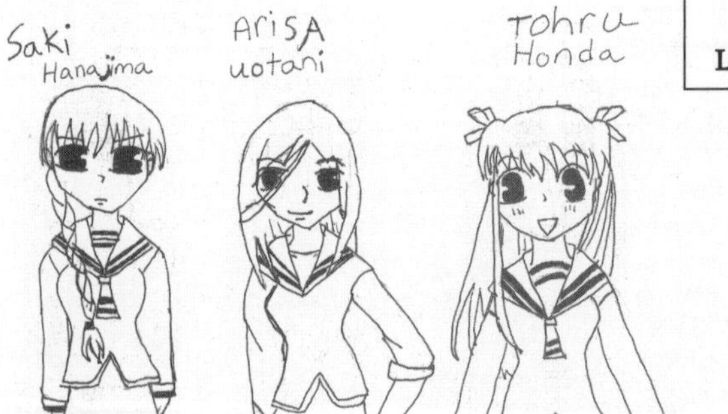
Saki
Hanajima
ArisA
uotani
Tohru
Honda

The three best friends. You did an amazing job of capturing the nuances of everyone's clothing—and this was before we printed Takaya-sensei's fashion notes in volume 3!

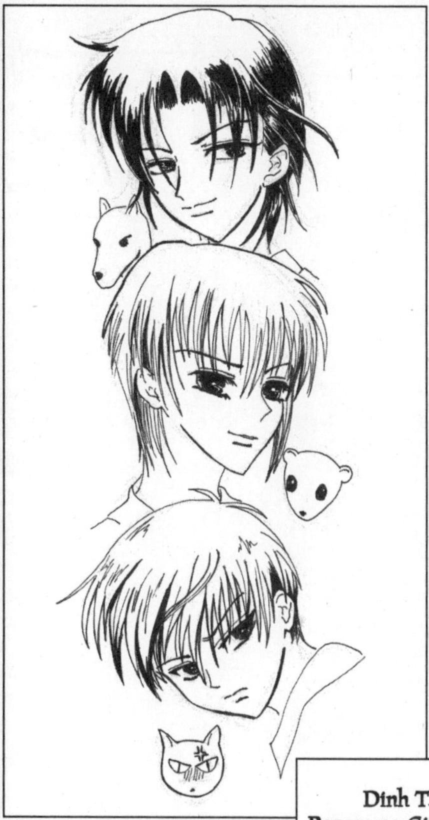

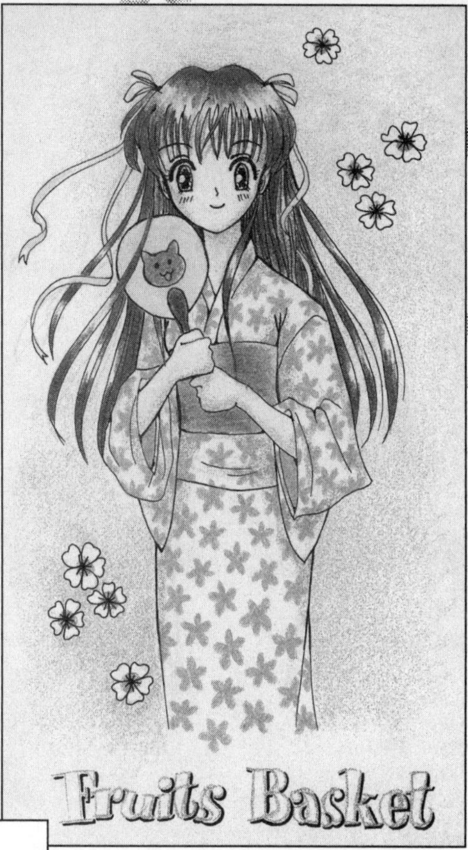
Fruits Basket

Dinh T.
Panorama City, CA

Wow! You're so talented! You capture the spirits of the Fruits Basket characters so well, but your drawings have a style all their own. Very nice! I'm sorry we couldn't print your lovely Tohru picture in color.

Patricia C.
Age 24
San Antonio, TX

I don't think this is what Boys Don't Cry meant when they sang "I Wanna be a Cowboy." Hee hee. That's the most awesome Haru I've ever seen. So cute!

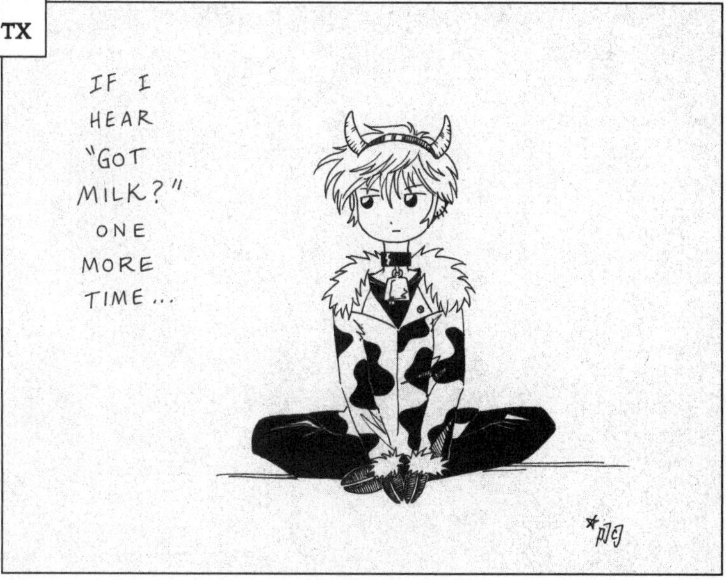
IF I HEAR "GOT MILK?" ONE MORE TIME...

Dear TOKYOPOP,

My name is Jenny and I'm so happy that you guys translate *Fruits Basket*. I totally love this series. I have all the DVDs and manga books 1 and 2. Anyhoo, the reason that I'm writing is I have a question that's been bothering me forever. Why is it that Hatori, the "dragon" sign, turns into a "seahorse"? I've watched the anime over and over and read the manga over and over but still can't figure it out. Also, who are the chicken and horse signs? They weren't in the anime, so I was wondering if the manga will have them. And what sign is Akito? Why is he sick all the time? Can't wait for the answers and for more *Fruits Basket* to come out!

Fellow Anime lover,
Jenny W.
Santa Clarita, CA

Thanks for the kind words, Jenny! You ask a lot of good questions (and not as weird as the ones Takaya-sensei answers back on page 10). I'll see what I can do to help.
1) In Japan, one of the names for a seahorse translates literally to "baby dragon." This is how Hatori refers to himself. Japanese dragons are traditionally associated with the sea, so the bizarre seahorse became associated with the mythical creatures.
2) It's too early to say who the chicken and the horse signs might be, but yes, they do show up in the manga. The anime covers the first 8 volumes of manga, but as of now, the manga is up to 14 volumes in Japan!
3) What's Akito's deal? Well, Takaya-sensei would be really mad if we gave that away. Akito is a deep well of secrets, and he'll continue to be a central part of Fruits Basket until it ends!
To everyone else with burning questions, send them this way and we'll try and answer them.

-Editor

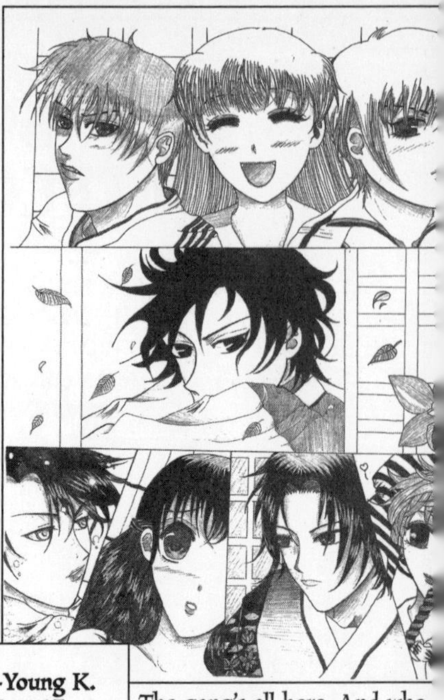

Na-Young K.
Age 15
Sprout Spring, VA

The gang's all here. And who should be at the center of it a dearest Akito... I like the way captured Kagura and Shigure serious side.

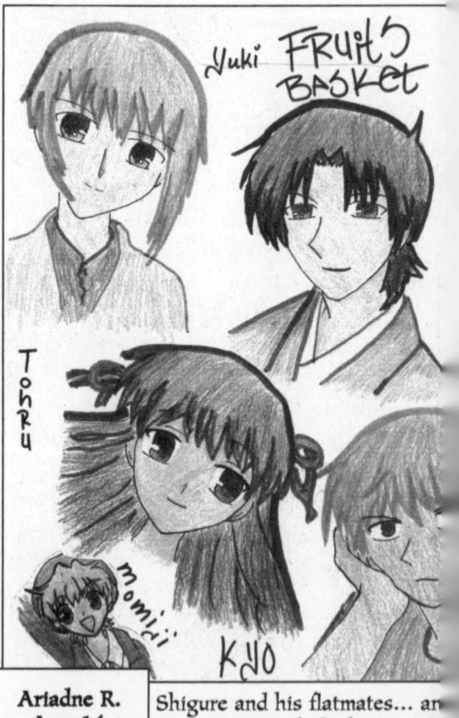
Yuki
FRUITS BASKET
Tohru
momiji
Kyo

Ariadne R.
Age. 14
Daly City, CA

Shigure and his flatmates... ar Momiji, too! Yuki looks especia sweet. Thanks, Ariadne!

SOUND EFFECT INDEX

THE FOLLOWING IS A LIST OF THE SOUND EFFECTS USED IN FRUITS BASKET. EACH SOUND IS LABELED BY PAGE AND PANEL NUMBER, SEPARATED BY A PERIOD. THE FIRST DESCRIPTION IS THE PHONETIC READING OF THE JAPANESE, AND IS FOLLOWED BY THE EQUIVALENT ENGLISH SOUND OR A DESCRIPTION.

3	patan: shut
[illegible]	bon: poof
[illegible]	hira: flutter
[illegible]	shuu: rustle
7	sura: slide
[illegible]	ban x 2: slap
4	guii: grab
2a	ha!: gasp
2b	jii: stare
2	zuun: slump
[illegible]	zuri: slide
.1	don doka gashan: crash bang pow
2	gyuu: squeeze
3	gaba: stumble
5	gashii: grab
5	ban!: slam
[illegible]	zudoon: (fanfare)
3	zuru x 3: drag
5	pori x 2: scratch
1	suku: stand
5	gutari: confused
1	gashi x 2: scrub
2	gashi x 3: scrub
5	bata x 4: pitter patter
.3	pa!: shine
4	bon: poof
3	dan x 2: clack
4	wasa x 3: rub
5	bikuu: twitch
1	kuu: snore
2	patan: shut
6	saa: rustle
1	ta ta ka x 3: dash

16.4	pon: pat
16.5	zuoooo: (creepy aura)
17.3	pekka: perky
19.2	goh: slam
24.1	bah: block
28.3	gyoh: shock
28.5	gah: grab
29.2	bun x 3: shake
31.1	kira x 4: sparkle
32.1	kira x 3: sparkle
33.4	zuru x 3: drag
33.5	patan: shut

キラ
キラ

KIRA KIRA

THE "SOUND" OF SPARKLING, USED FOR LITERAL SPARKLING AND FOR GLAMOR SHOTS. IN SHOUJO MANGA, SPARKLES ARE A COMMON ACCESSORY TO BISHOUNEN--ESPECIALLY WHEN THEY'RE SHOWN DRESSED IN A GIRLS' UNIFORM LIKE YUKI!

33.6	kii: creak
35.2	goh: slam
35.4	pachi: (wake up)
35.5	mukuri: rise
36.1	gakkuu: slump
36.2	kiin koon: (school bells)
75.1	ha!: gasp
75.5	zah: rush
77.1	su: shuffle
77.2	don: ta-da!
77.5	gui: squeeze

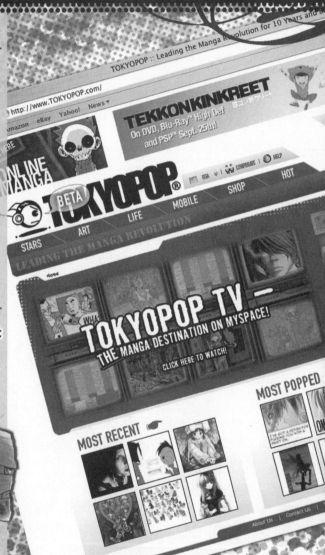
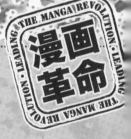

STOP!

This is the back of the book.
You wouldn't want to spoil a great ending!

This book is printed "manga-style," in the authentic Japanese right-to-left format. Since none of the artwork has been flipped or altered, readers get to experience the story just as the creator intended. You've been asking for it, so TOKYOPOP® delivered: authentic, hot-off-the-press, and far more fun!

DIRECTIONS

If this is your first time reading manga-style, here's a quick guide to help you understand how it works.

It's easy... just start in the top right panel and follow the numbers. Have fun, and look for more 100% authentic manga from TOKYOPOP®!